5TH EDITION

THE CHALLENGE OF THIRD WORLD DEVELOPMENT

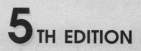

THE CHALLENGE OF THIRD WORLD DEVELOPMENT

HOWARD HANDELMAN
Emeritus Professor, University of Wisconsin-Milwaukee

Upper Saddle River, New Jersey 07458

Library of Congress Cataloging-in-Publication Data

Handelman, Howard
  The challenge of Third World development/Howard Handelman.—5th ed.
     p. cm.
  Includes bibliographical references and index.
  ISBN-13: 978-0-13-605477-1 (alk. paper)
  ISBN-10: 0-13-605477-3 (alk. paper)
  1. Developing countries—Economic conditions.   2. Developing countries—Economic policy.
3. Developing countries—Politics and government.   4. Economic development.   I. Title.

HC59.7.H299 2009
338.9009172'4—dc22

2008009788

Editor: Vikram Mukhija
Editorial Assistant: Elizabeth Daniel
Director of Marketing: Brandy Dawson
Executive Marketing Manager: Ann Stypuloski
Marketing Assistant: Liz Hoens
Production Manager: Kathy Sleys
Creative Director: Jayne Conte
Cover Design: Jon Boylon
Full-Service Project Management/Composition: Shiny Rajesh/Integra Software Services
Printer/Binder: RR Donnelley & Sons, Inc.

Pearson Education Ltd., London
Pearson Education Singapore, Pte. Ltd
Pearson Education Canada, Inc.
Pearson Education–Japan
Pearson Education Australia PTY, Limited

Pearson Education North Asia, Ltd., Hong Kong
Pearson Educación de Mexico, S.A. de C.V.
Pearson Education Malaysia, Pte. Ltd.
Pearson Education Upper Saddle River,
   New Jersey

10 9 8 7 6 5 4 3 2 1
ISBN-13: 978-0-13-605477-1
ISBN-10:   0-13-605477-3

TO ALICE AND MAGGIE

CONTENTS

Chapter 5
Women and Development 136

Chapter 6
Agrarian Reform and the Politics of Rural Change 172

Chapter 9
Soldiers and Politics   250

Chapter 10
The Political Economy of Third World Development   284

PREFACE

While Americans and other Westerners often find the politics of developing areas (Africa, Asia, the Caribbean, Latin America, and the Middle East) difficult to comprehend, events in those regions are an inescapable part of our lives. The recent wars in Iraq and Afghanistan, Islamic fundamentalism and the war on terrorism, genocidal activity in Sudan, rapid economic growth in China and India, and emigration from the developing world are but a few of the events which draw our attention. The purpose of this book is to better understand the dynamics and challenges of political and socioeconomic changes in these developing nations, which account for most of the world's population.

For want of a better term, I refer to the more than 150 disparate, developing nations as the "Third World" (defined in Chapter 1). They include desperately poor countries such as Afghanistan and Ethiopia and rapidly developing industrial powers such as China, South Korea, and Taiwan. Some, like Trinidad and Costa Rica, are stable democracies; others, such as Myanmar and Syria, suffer under highly repressive dictatorships. All of them, however, share at least some of the aspects of political, economic, and social underdevelopment that this book analyzes.

No text is capable of fully examining the political and economic systems of so many highly diverse countries. Instead, we will look for common issues, problems, and potential solutions. We start in Chapter 1 by exploring the nature of political and economic underdevelopment, and then analyze the leading explanatory theories.

The next chapter discusses what has been arguably the most important political change in world politics during the late twentieth and early twenty-first centuries—the wave of democratic transitions that has swept over the developing nations of Africa, Asia, Latin America, and the Middle East (as well as the former Soviet bloc of nations and southern Europe). Because these often still-fragile transitions from authoritarian to democratic government are potentially so important, the chapters that follow contain discussion of how democratization is likely to influence issues such as the level of ethnic conflict, the role of women in the political system, and future economic development.

Chapters 3–5 on religion and politics, cultural pluralism and ethnic conflict, and women and development analyze religious, ethnic, and gender issues that have often divided developing nations, but also provide identities that can be helpful in the processes of political and economic development. Chapters 6 and 7 on rural change and urbanization discuss the specific problems and challenges that many countries face in those two sectors of society. Next, Chapters 8 and 9 on revolutionary change and soldiers and politics consider the records of each of those regime types (such as, revolutionary governments in China and Cuba and military regimes in Brazil and Indonesia) as alternative models of political and economic development. Finally, Chapter 10, dealing with Third World political economies, compares alternative paths to economic development and evaluates the relative effectiveness of each.

It is easy to despair when considering the tremendous obstacles facing most Third World nations and the failures of political leadership that so many of them have endured. Unfortunately, many inhabitants of the First World have suffered from "compassion fatigue" or have become cynical about cooperative efforts with Third World countries. The assaults on the World Trade Center and the Pentagon in 2001 and the subsequent wars (and postwar conflicts) in Afghanistan and Iraq have reinforced many people's perception of the less developed nations (LDCs) as poor beyond redemption, politically unstable, authoritarian, and prone to religious and political fanaticism. Yet the recent burgeoning of democracy, the decline in military rule, and the enormous economic growth that has taken place in parts of Asia all provide new bases for hope. It is incumbent upon the West's next generation of citizens and leaders to renew efforts to understand the challenge of Third World development.

ACKNOWLEDGMENTS

Because of the broad geographic and conceptual scope of any book on Third World politics, I am particularly indebted to others for their kind help and advice.

First, I would like to thank Thomson Wadsworth Press for granting me permission to reproduce a portion of Chapter 1, which is incorporated from *Politics in a Changing World* by Marcus Ethridge and Howard Handelman (copyright 1993 by St. Martin's Press). Thanks also to the many people at Prentice Hall who have worked with me through five editions of this book.

Much of the original research took place during a sabbatical leave from the University of Wisconsin-Milwaukee. I am grateful to my own university for granting me that sabbatical support and to the University of Wisconsin-Madison, whose outstanding libraries, lectures, and other scholarly activities informed me during a wonderful year there.

Finally, my greatest debt is to the scholars who generously agreed to read portions of the manuscript of the first edition and whose insights continue to guide subsequent editions. They include Lourdes Benería (Cornell University), Josef Gugler (University of Connecticut), Stephan Haggard (University of California-San Diego), Kathleen Staudt (University of Texas-El Paso), Mark Tessler (University of Michigan), William Thiesenhusen (University of Wisconsin-Madison), and M. Crawford Young (University of Wisconsin-Madison). Thanks also to Prentice Hall's reviewers: Brian Kessel, Columbia College; Remonda Kleinberg, University of North Carolina at Wilmington; and Andrea Stevenson Sanjian, Bucknell University. The quality of the manuscript benefited enormously from their many insights, suggestions, and corrections. The usual caveat, of course, applies: Any remaining errors of fact or interpretation are my own responsibility.

Howard Handelman
Professor Emeritus
University of Wisconsin-Milwaukee

CHAPTER 1

UNDERSTANDING UNDERDEVELOPMENT

Most Americans focus infrequently on the less developed countries (LDCs) of Africa, Asia, the Caribbean, and Latin America. Media coverage is sporadic and tends to concentrate on tragedies or disturbances of various magnitudes—a tsunami that kills many thousands in Southeast Asia, civil war in Sri Lanka, ethnic conflict in Darfur, and political repression in Syria. To almost any observer, the problems currently plaguing the developing world appear daunting. Warfare, internal violence, and massive human suffering beset the most troubled countries in these regions: insurgency and ethnic violence in Iraq; poverty and revolutionary conflict in Colombia and Nepal; ethnically based massacres in Nigeria and Guatemala; and political repression in Zimbabwe and Myanmar (Burma). Of course, many of those problems exist in industrialized democracies as well, though in a milder form. For example, in recent times both Northern Ireland and the Basque region of Spain have experienced ethnic violence and terrorism. Portions of Washington, D.C. have higher infant mortality rates than does Cuba or Singapore. Nevertheless, it is the scope and persistence of the developing world's political, economic, and social challenges that ultimately draw our attention.

Understanding the nature and causes of underdevelopment is a complex task complicated by theoretical debates between scholars and a profusion of terminology. There is not even agreement on a collective name for the approximately 150 countries that constitute the developing world. At one time, it was common to call these countries *underdeveloped nations*. However, many found this title objectionable, suggesting, as it did, that those countries' political and economic systems were backward. Because of its pejorative connotations and implied inferiority, the adjective *underdeveloped* fell into disfavor. Instead, many political scientists prefer using the term *developing nations (areas)*. Though clearly more positive, this term unfortunately suffers from the opposite problem—excessive optimism.

At various times during the 1970s and 1980s, most African and Latin American countries suffered from political and economic decay, and today many remain trapped on a political or economic treadmill. In the late 1990s, even the previously thriving economies of East Asia were plunged into a crisis from which some countries took years to recover. Finally, countries such as Congo, Haiti, and Nepal still show few signs of forward progress in any dimension. In short, for many years, a number of so-called "developing countries" have shown few signs of political or economic development. Hence, the United Nations and many other international organizations favor the label *less developed countries* (or LDCs), an expression that escapes the normative flaws of its competitors.

The term *Third World countries* (or simply, *the Third World*) is preferred by many social scientists and is the label most frequently employed in this book.[1] It has both the virtue and defect of being somewhat fuzzy. Simply put, Third World countries are the nations of Africa, Asia, the Middle East, Latin America, and the Caribbean that do not belong to the First World—Japan and the Western industrialized democracies that were the first countries to develop advanced industrial economies and liberal democracies. Nor were they part of the now-defunct Second World—the bloc of former communist nations that included the Soviet Union and Eastern Europe.[2]

Thus, Third World is essentially a residual category. Countries fall under its banner not because of any specific quality, but simply because they are not members of either the First or Second World.[3] Like the previously discussed classifications, Third World glosses over the many political and socioeconomic differences among its members, placing all of them under one big tent. Of course, in reality they differ considerably. A few (including Singapore, Taiwan, and Kuwait) are relatively affluent, while many others (such as Afghanistan, Yemen, and Malawi) are desperately poor. Some (Barbados, Costa Rica, and India, for example) are stable democracies. Many others, however, suffer from severe political instability, government repression, or other manifestations of political underdevelopment.

Therefore, like any residual category, the term *Third World* suffers from a degree of imprecision. Its virtue, however, is that unlike *underdeveloped nations* or *developing nations*, it makes no value judgment or predictions. As one author writes, paraphrasing Winston Churchill's comments on democracy, "It is the worst term we have, except for all the others."[4] With some irony, Christopher Clapham has written, "I have chosen to use the term [Third World] because of its meaninglessness. Its alternatives all carry conceptual overtones which are even more misleading, in that they imply positive elements of commonality rather than a simply negative residual category."[5] Taking a less cynical position than Clapham, I maintain in the next section that, despite their many differences, there are enough commonalities among Third World countries to make the category useful and usable. Of course, one may argue that the collapse of Soviet communism has made the term *Third World* rather anachronistic. As there no longer is a Second World (those nations are now called "postcommunist" countries), technically there can be no Third World. Nevertheless, like many political scientists, I continue to use the term in this book (and in the book's title) because I feel that it is conceptually useful and is still comprehensible to many readers.

In order to avoid repetitious usage of the term, throughout this book I alternately use the categories Third World, LDCs, developing countries (nations), and developing world interchangeably.

THIRD WORLD COMMONALITIES: THE NATURE OF UNDERDEVELOPMENT

Despite the substantial differences among them, Third World nations still share a number of common characteristics. All of them suffer from some aspects of political, economic, or social underdevelopment. Although some of East

Asia's newly industrializing countries (NICs)—South Korea, Singapore, and Taiwan—are no longer *economically* underdeveloped, they share a high vulnerability to global economic forces (as evidenced by East Asia's economic crisis in the late 1990s) and continue to suffer from aspects of political underdevelopment. On the other hand, Costa Rica and Botswana are relatively well developed politically and socially, but manifest the problems of economic underdevelopment. In short, while some Third World countries are underdeveloped in all major aspects of modernization, others are far more advanced in some aspects of development than in others. As we shall see, economic, social, and political underdevelopment are closely related to each other, but they are certainly not perfectly correlated.

Economic Underdevelopment

Perhaps the most salient characteristic of most developing countries is their poverty. This is manifested at the national level by some combination of low GDP—Gross Domestic Product—per capita (an indirect measure of per-capita income), unusually unequal distribution of income, poor infrastructure (including communications and transportation), limited use of modern technology, and low consumption of energy.[6] At the individual level, economic underdevelopment connotes widespread poverty, including unemployment, substandard housing, poor health conditions, and inadequate nutrition.

Table 1.1 presents economic data comparing two highly developed countries (United States and Norway); one affluent developing country (Singapore); two middle-income, Latin American countries (Mexico and Brazil); three lower-middle-income, Asian and Middle Eastern nations (China, India, and Egypt); and two impoverished African countries (Ethiopia and Nigeria).[7] The

TABLE 1.1 Measures of Economic Development (by Country)

Country	GDP per capita (PPP) ($)	Annual Economic Growth Rate (1975–2004)	Percent of the Population Living on Less Than $2 a Day	Income Ratio— Richest 20% to Poorest 20% of the Population
United States	39,676	2.0%	—a	8.4
Norway	38,454	2.6	—a	3.9
Singapore	28,077	4.7	—a	9.7
Mexico	9,803	0.9	20.4%	12.8
Brazil	8,195	0.7	21.2	23.7
China	5,896	8.4	46.7	10.7
Egypt	4,129	2.6	43.9	5.1
India	3,139	3.4	79.9	4.9
Nigeria	1,154	0.2	92.4	9.7
Ethiopia	756	−0.2	77.8	4.3

aThe percentage is too small to be counted.

Source: United Nations Development Programme (UNDP), *Human Development Report 2006: Beyond Scarcity-Power Poverty and the Global Water Crisis,* Statistics, http://hdr.undp.org/hdr2006/.

first data column in the table, *GDP per capita* (i.e., *Per-Capita Income*), indicates the dollar value of goods and services produced per person in 2006.[8] The data illustrate both the tremendous gap in living standards between most First and Third World countries and the considerable variation within the developing world. On the one hand, they indicate that the average American earns some *four to five* times as much as an average Mexican or Brazilian. At the same time, however, Mexicans and Brazilians earn about *eight* times more than the average Nigerian. On the other hand, per-capita income in a few developing nations, most notably Singapore and Hong Kong (the latter now shown in the table), nearly equals Britain's, France's, Germany's, and Japan's (also not shown here). Just as per-capita incomes vary considerably between various LDCs so does the rate in which their economies are growing.

The second data column in the table—average, annual economic growth rates—reveals that some economies, particularly in Asia, grew very rapidly from 1975 to 2004.[9] These include India (3.4 percent annual growth), Singapore (4.7 percent), and China, whose economy grew at a phenomenal, average annual rate of 8.4 percent for 30 years.

Ultimately, however, a country's standard of living is determined not only by its per-capita income but also by how equally or unequally that income is distributed. Column 3 in Table 1.1 indicates the percentage of a nation's population living on less than $2 a day, the income level used by the World Bank to identify people who live in "absolute poverty." In Singapore, like the United States and Norway, practically nobody lives at that level. However, in Brazil and Mexico—two of Latin America's most developed and industrialized nations—about 20 percent (one-fifth) of the population does. Moreover, despite their impressive rates of economic growth in the past 30 years, Asia's two economic giants—China and India—still have about 50 (China) to 80 percent (India) of their population mired in absolute poverty. Although rapid economic modernization—especially in China—has benefited many of those country's urban inhabitants, it has so far only slightly improved the lives of rural villagers, who still account for more than two-thirds of each nation's population. Not surprisingly, the two poorest nations in the table, Nigeria and Ethiopia, also have very high poverty rates. Normally, and not surprisingly, poorer countries (such as Egypt) have a greater proportion of their populations living in absolute poverty than do countries with higher per-capita incomes (say, Mexico). Note, however, that Table 1.1 reveals some exceptions to that rule. Nigeria has a higher portion of its population living in absolute poverty (92.4 percent) than does Ethiopia (77.8 percent), even though it has a much higher per-capita income. We can probably safely surmise that the reason for that anomaly is that Ethiopia's per-capita income, though lower than Nigeria's, is more equitably distributed.

Finally, the last column presents a more direct measure of how equally or unequally income is distributed in each country. These figures indicate the ratio of incomes for the richest 20 percent of the population ("the rich") to the incomes of the poorest 20 percent ("the poor"). For example, the 8.4 figure for the United States (Table 1.1) indicates that the richest 20 percent of all Americans earn over eight times as much as do the poorest 20 percent. That is one of the highest levels of inequality within any highly industrialized nation. In Norway, on the other hand, the income ratio is only 3.9 to 1, one of the smallest income gaps in the world.

It is commonly understood that income is more equitably distributed in economically advanced nations than in LDCs (i.e., the gap between rich and poor is smaller). While that is generally true, there are many exceptions. For example, Table 1.1 reveals that the income ratio of the rich to the poor in Ethiopia, Egypt, and India is unexpectedly lower than in the United States.[10] If we turn our focus from individual countries to regions of the developing world (not shown in the table), we find that Latin America has the highest degree of income inequality, as exemplified in Table 1.1 by Mexico and Brazil, the region's two largest countries. Indeed, the enormous income gap between rich and poor in Brazil (23.7 to 1) gives that country and Colombia (another Latin American country) the highest levels of income *inequality* within any sizable economy in the world. In contrast, Asia has the highest degree of income *equality* of any Third World region. In fact, many of the largest Asian nations—including Japan, India, Thailand, Indonesia, Bangladesh, and South Korea—enjoy greater income equality than do most industrialized nations (though economic inequality in China is relatively high and has grown considerably). Sub-Saharan Africa offers a more uneven picture. The gap between rich and poor is relatively small in Ethiopia, Mozambique, Rwanda, and Tanzania (averaging a bit over 5:1). But, at the other end of the spectrum, the African nations of Lesotho, Namibia, and Sierra Leone (not in the table) have the three most unequal income distributions in the world (with the richest 20 percent of the population earning about 50 times as much as the poorest).[11]

Several factors influence a country's income distribution pattern. First, as we have noted, is the *level of industrialization and economic development*. Countries moving into the middle- and upper-middle levels of development generally experience a growing economic gap between classes, as a new class of industrialists, financiers, business owners, and professionals emerges in countries such as Singapore and Brazil.[12] A second important factor is the historical *pattern of land ownership*. Regions or countries that were colonized by the Spanish or Portuguese, such as Latin America and the Philippines, concentrated land ownership in a relatively small number of hands (see Chapter 6). In contrast, most Asian countries historically experienced less concentration of rural property. Third, *government policies* regarding land ownership, taxation, welfare programs, and the like can either reduce or intensify income inequality. Countries with large and open educational systems, agrarian reform programs, and progressive taxation have often reduced income gaps. Generally speaking, communist and former communist countries such as the Czech Republic and Mongolia have some of the world's lowest levels of inequality, but they are closely trailed by several East Asian capitalist success stories, such as Indonesia, Taiwan, and South Korea.[13] In both models—welfare communism and egalitarian capitalism—government policies reduced income disparities. Conversely, since the 1980s, when China moved from a command (communist) economy to a predominantly free-market economy *without* adequate government protections, income inequality has widened considerably.

Social Underdevelopment

Third World poverty tends to correlate with poor social conditions such as high infant mortality and low literacy rates, which, in turn narrow opportunities for human development. If LDCs are to modernize and develop economically, politically, and socially, it is very important that they extend and improve their educational systems. An educated workforce—from farmers and workers who can read instruction manuals to trained professionals—contributes to higher labor productivity. At the same time, improved education also expands mass political participation and facilitates government accountability to the governed. Thus, not surprisingly, political scientists have found that countries with higher literacy rates are more likely to attain and maintain democratic government.[14]

Table 1.2 presents data on several important indicators of social development. It compares two developed nations (the United States and Norway), three Latin American nations (Mexico, Brazil, and Cuba), three Asian countries (China, India, and South Korea), two Middle Eastern nations (Egypt and Saudi Arabia), and two African countries (Ethiopia and Nigeria). The first data column lists each country's Human Development Index (HDI), a composite measure of school enrollment, adult literacy, life expectancy, and per-capita GDP. More than any other social or economic indicator, the HDI is widely considered the best single measure of a nation's living standard. The highest possible HDI score a country may achieve is 1.000 and the lowest is .000. Next to each country's raw HDI score, column 1 lists (in parenthesis) its HDI *ranking* relative to other countries in the world. For example, Norway's HDI score of .965 is the highest in the world, while India's HDI of .611 ranks 126th of all the countries for which we have data. Some developing countries (such as Mexico, Cuba, and, especially, South Korea) have relatively high indices, placing them in the top third of all nations with available scores. In fact, their scores are not far behind those of European nations such as Portugal, Lithuania, and Bulgaria.

TABLE 1.2   Measures of Social Development (by Country)

Country	HDI (Rank)	Infant Mortality (per 1,000 Live Births)	Adult Literacy (%)	Per-Capita GDP Rank minus HDI Rank
United States	.948 (8)	5	99.9	−6
Norway	.965 (1)	4	99.9	3
South Korea	.912 (26)	5	98.0	5
Mexico	.821 (53)	23	91.0	7
Brazil	.792 (69)	32	88.6	−5
Cuba	.826 (50)	6	99.8	43
Saudi Arabia	.777 (76)	21	79.4	−31
China	.768 (81)	26	90.9	9
Egypt	.702 (111)	26	71.4	−2
India	.611 (126)	62	61.0	−9
Nigeria	.448 (159)	101	66.8[a]	−1
Ethiopia	.371 (170)	110	41.5[a]	1

[a]Data were not available for these countries in the UNDP's *Human Development Report 2006* so these figures were drawn from the 2004 Report. Literacy rates have likely improved somewhat since that time.

Source: UNDP, *Human Development Report 2006*, Statistics, http://hdr.undp.org/hdr2006/.

On the other hand, many South Asian and African countries—such as Egypt, India, Nigeria, and Ethiopia—have very low HDI scores.

Columns 2–3 present data for two important individual indicators of a country's standard of living. Infant mortality rates (the proportion of infants that die in the first year after their live birth) reflect the availability of health care, adequate nutrition, and safe drinking water. It also is the most important factor determining average life expectancy. The next column, adult literacy rates, indicates what percentage of the population has access to education. Unlike per-capita income, averages for life expectancy and literacy are not distorted by highly skewed distributions.[15] Table 1.2 indicates that a new-born baby in Nigeria or Ethiopia stands more than 1 in 10 chances of dying before he or she reaches the age of 1 year (the statistics in the table show infant mortality per 1,000 live births). Conversely, the likelihood of such death in Cuba is about 1 in 166 (6 in 1,000). In all, an estimated 12–13 million children under the age of 5 years now die annually in the developing world.[16]

Although economic development usually improves social indicators, government policy determines how large a share of state resources is invested in education, sanitation, and health care—that is to say, the extent to which economic growth stimulates social development. Column 4 compares a country's worldwide ranking for per-capita "real income" (income adjusted for cost of living) with its rank for HDI. For example, South Korea, which ranks 31st in the world in GDP per capita (per-capita income), ranks 26 in HDI, giving it a score in the last column of +5. Any country with a positive score (especially a high positive) is an "overachiever" in the sense that its HDI rank is higher than we might have predicted solely based on GDP ranking. On the other hand, a country whose HDI ranking is lower than its per-capita GDP rank would have a negative score in the fourth column and would be an "underachiever," having scored more poorly on HDI than its per-capita income would predict. This would include Brazil (Table 1.2) with a score of –5 (64th on GDP—69th in HDI). The governments of "overachievers" presumably have a special commitment to education and public health. Conversely, a negative score (for countries in Table 1.2 such as Brazil, India, the United States, and Saudi Arabia) often indicates their failure to fully translate their available economic resources into an improved quality of life. In some cases, it may also be caused by factors somewhat beyond a country's control such as the AIDS epidemic. Cuba's score (+43) makes it the world's greatest "overachiever" (i.e., it has an HDI ranking that is much higher than its per-capita income would predict), while Saudi Arabia (–31) is the greatest "underachiever" in our table. In fact, some of the worst performers on this measure, including Saudi Arabia and other oil-rich nations not shown in the table (United Arab Emirates and Oman), owe their low scores, in part, to their failure to educate adequately their female population because of religious or other cultural barriers (see Chapter 5).

Despite economic declines in Africa and Latin America during the 1980s and early 1990s, and notwithstanding East Asia's economic crisis in the late 1990s, the Third World has enjoyed considerable social development in the past 40–50 years. For example, adult illiteracy is less than half its rate in 1965, falling from 59 to 23 percent. Improved health care and sanitation have helped reduce infant mortality rates by 60 percent. This, in turn, helped raise life expectancy from 53.4 years in 1960 to 64.6 years in 2003.[17] In 1950, people living in economically advanced countries could expect to live 25 years longer than inhabitants of the Third World. By the end of the century, however, that gap had been halved to 12 years. Of course, life expectancy increased in both developed and developing nations, but advances were more dramatic in the latter category. At the same time, the United Nations Development Program (UNDP) estimates that the level of Third World poverty fell faster in the last half of the twentieth century than it had in the previous 500 years.

However, despite these gains, many Third World inhabitants still face a bleak future. Somewhere between 1 and 2 billion people currently live in extreme poverty.[18] Furthermore, in the past decades, AIDS and war have greatly reduced life expectancy in some two dozen African nations.[19] Today, life expectancy in 32 countries worldwide is less than 40 years. Of those, 31 are in Africa, where three nations (Malawi, Niger, and Sierra Leone) have expectancies below 30 years.[20] Had it not been for the AIDS pandemic, health experts estimate that life expectancy in Africa would be about six years higher than it is currently. In all, these statistics indicate both how much progress there has been and how much remains to be done.

Table 1.3 reveals the substantial social and economic differences between Third World *regions*. Latin America, despite relatively slow economic growth since the 1980s (averaging 2.4 percent annually) and several sharp economic downturns, still has the developing world's highest per-capita GDP, life expectancy, and HDI, while trailing East Asia only slightly in adult literacy. East Asia, the world's fastest-growing regional economy since the 1980s (with approximately 7 percent annual growth), ranks close behind Latin America in HDI score and life expectancy and has the developing world's highest literacy rate. In recent decades, economic growth has accelerated dramatically in South Asia (better than 5 percent annually), but the region's social and economic indicators still lag well behind Latin America's and East Asia's, with a particularly low literacy level. Finally, although Sub-Saharan economies have been growing at a 5 percent annual pace since 2003 (after decades of decline), the region's socioeconomic indicators continue to trail the rest of the developing world, most dramatically in life expectancy (Table 1.3).[21]

TABLE 1.3   Indicators of Social and Economic Development (by Region)

Region	GDP per Capita (PPP) ($)	Life Expectancy	Adult Literacy (%)	HDI
Developing Countries	4,775	65	77.0	.679
Arab States	5,680	69	69.7	.680
East Asia and the Pacific	5,872	70	91.7	.760
Latin America and the Caribbean	7,964	72	90.3	.795
South Asia	3,072	63	58.7	.599
Sub-Saharan Africa	1,946	46	61.2	.472

Source: UNESCO Institute for Statistics (September 2006), http://www.uis.unesco.org; The World Bank, *Annual Report 2006*, http://www.worldbank.org/.

While macroeconomic performance has varied considerably from region to region and decade to decade, many countries have made impressive progress in critical areas of public health and education. A number of African countries including Angola, Ethiopia, and Senegal—all of which had shockingly high infant mortality rates in the 1960s (ranging from 173 to 208 infant deaths for each 1,000 live births)—cut those rates roughly in half by the closing years of the twentieth century. Asia's two giants, China and India (with approximately 40 percent of the world's population between them), reduced their infant mortality rates by 76 and 55 percent, respectively, during that same period. Cuba, which already started that era with one of the developing world's lowest infant mortality rates, reduced its rate by a further 79 percent, while Chile's rate fell by 89 percent.[22] Finally, between 1990 and 2005, Bangladesh, Brazil, Egypt, Indonesia, Mexico, and the Philippines all reduced their child mortality rate (the percentage of children dying before the age of 5 years) by 50 percent or more.[23]

During a somewhat longer period (1970–1995), adult illiteracy also dropped impressively across much of the Third World. South Korea and Cuba, which had started those years with low levels of illiteracy (12–13 percent), made notable additional strides as the cut their rates down to 2–4 percent. Meanwhile, Jordan and Kenya, which started with high illiteracy rates in 1960 (53 and 68 percent), also made dramatic progress, reducing their rates of illiteracy by two-thirds or more.[24]

Still, as an aggregate, LDCs continue to lag considerably behind North America, Europe, and Japan. Third World adult literacy rates, life expectancy, and calorie consumption trail those of the industrialized nations by about 20 percent. At the start of the twenty-first century, perhaps 1.4 billion people (about one-third of the developing world's population) lived on incomes of less than $1 per day, 850 million of whom failed to consume the minimum recommended number of calories daily. In addition, 28,000 Third World children under the age of 5 years were still dying every day. Furthermore, *within* the developing world, great gaps persist between urban centers and rural areas. For example, at the end of the 1990s, 72 percent of all city dwellers had access to proper home sanitation (sewage etc.) compared to only 20 percent in the countryside.[25]

Political Underdevelopment

When Western political scientists began to study the Third World systematically, they soon recognized that evaluating political systems in cultural and socioeconomic settings very different from our own was extremely challenging. While many modernization theorists believed that Third World governments should model themselves after Western industrialized democracies, they were also mindful of important differences between the two regions that limited that possibility. Recognizing that most Western European countries did not fully democratize until they were well along the path to industrial development, scholars were often reluctant to criticize the developing world's numerous authoritarian governments. A number of African social scientists added to the debate by arguing that their continent had extensive village- and tribal-based democracies that adequately substituted for competitive elections at the national level. Others feared that, in the ethnically divided countries of Africa and Asia, multiparty systems would inevitably develop along ethnic lines, further contributing to national disintegration.

Conscious of such land mines, some political scientists despaired of defining political development in any meaningful way.[26] Others, however, suggested political standards that seemed relatively free of ideological and cultural biases. Political development, they suggested, involves the creation of specialized and differentiated government institutions that effectively carry out necessary functions, such as collecting tax revenues, defending national borders, maintaining political stability, stimulating economic development, improving the quality of human life, and communicating with the citizenry. In addition, they argued, developed governments must be responsive to a broad segment of society and respect the population's fundamental freedoms and civil rights. Presumably, any government satisfying these standards would enjoy a reasonable level of *legitimacy* (i.e., its own citizens would recognize and accept its right to govern), leading individuals and groups to pursue their political objectives peacefully through established political institutions rather than through violent or illegal channels.

But while analysts agreed that governments should be responsive, representative, and nonrepressive, many of them also believed that a political system could be considered developed even if it was not democratic, at least as that term has been defined in the West. Most accepted definitions of full democracy encompass the following basic components: honest and competitive elections in which opposition parties have a realistic chance of winning; universal or nearly universal adult suffrage; widespread opportunities for political participation; free and open mass media; and government respect for human rights, including minority rights.[27] As we have seen, many political scientists initially felt that it was unrealistic and perhaps culturally biased to expect democracy to quickly flourish in developing countries. Others argued that many developing nations were not ready for democracy. Concerned about the high levels of violence and instability in those political systems, they claimed that the LDCs' first priority had to be political stability, even if that might initially require military rule or other forms of authoritarian government.[28]

More recently, however, troubled by extensive government repression in the developing world and the obvious failures of most authoritarian regimes, political scientists have begun to insist that democracy and some degree of socioeconomic equality must be understood as integral parts of political development.[29] The collapse of communist regimes in the Soviet Union and Eastern Europe reinforced previous criticisms of authoritarian government. Beyond its obvious moral attractions, democracy also has pragmatic appeal. For example, governments whose citizens hold them accountable through competitive elections are more likely to be efficient and honest (although the disappointing records of democratic governments in countries such as Brazil and the Philippines demonstrate that there are no guarantees). Similarly, free and independent forms of mass media also help keep governments accountable. The disintegration of the Soviet bloc and the fall of many dictatorships throughout the Third World in recent decades suggest that authoritarian regimes are often stable in the short run, but fragile in the long term. Thus, there is not necessarily a tradeoff between democracy and political stability, as many had imagined.

In fact, democracies are generally immune to revolutionary insurrection and less susceptible to other forms of mass violence.

Only a restricted, but growing, number of developing countries have fully met the standards of political development and democracy listed above—for example, the Bahamas, Uruguay, and Costa Rica. Others—such as Argentina, India, South Korea, and Taiwan—currently satisfy most of the criteria. Even a cursory review of the developing world, however, reveals that most governments still fall short. At one extreme—in nations such as Somalia and Sierra Leone—warlords have divided control over their country and have so deeply undermined their national governments that political scientists label them "countries without a state." Elsewhere in the Third World, many governments respond disproportionately to the demands of an affluent minority. Self-perpetuating and self-serving elites rule many Middle Eastern and North African nations, while some Sub-Saharan African governments serve the interests of dominant ethnic groups. Political corruption, bureaucratic inefficiency, and police repression are all endemic to much of the developing world.

In the recent past, class-based revolutionary movements erupted in various Asian and Latin American nations, and a number of African countries have been torn apart by ethnic civil wars. Thus, until recently most LDCs were not democratic, stable, or legitimate. In recent decades, however, democracy (and with it, government legitimacy) has advanced in much of the developing world, most notably in Latin America and East Asia (see Chapter 2).[30]

Some Relationships among the Components of Development

It would be logical to assume that political, economic, and social underdevelopment are interrelated. More economically advanced countries can better educate their populations and provide them with superior health care. An educated citizenry, in turn, contributes to further economic growth and participates in politics more responsibly. Responsive and legitimate governments, constrained by competitive elections, are more likely to educate their citizens and to make informed economic decisions. Indeed, these logical intuitions are supported by empirical evidence. Wealthier countries tend to have greater life expectancy, higher literacy rates, and more stable and democratic governments.

However, these correlations are not absolute. For example, a country's literacy and infant mortality rates depend not only on its economic resources but also on government policies in the areas of education, public health, and welfare. Thus, as we saw earlier (Table 1.2), elitist government policies in some countries have contributed to social indicators (HDIs) that are far lower than are those of other nations with comparable economic resources. We noted that this is most apparent in many petroleum-rich states (such as Saudi Arabia and the United Arab Emirates), whom we have labeled "underachievers," but it holds true in countries such as the Dominican Republic and Tunisia as well.[31] On the other hand, governments in Cuba, Uruguay, and Vietnam—with strong commitments to social welfare programs—have generated much higher life expectancy rates and educational levels than their economic resources alone would lead us to predict ("overachievers").

Both economic and social development tend to correlate with political development. Wealthier, more educated countries such as Barbados, Botswana, Costa Rica, and Taiwan tend to have more politically stable, responsive, and democratic governments than poor nations such as Mozambique, Haiti, and Cambodia. Indeed, Third World countries are less likely to become democracies and far less likely to maintain democracy if they have not attained a minimal threshold of socioeconomic development.[32] However, there is no linear relationship between economic and political development. In other words, as countries become more economically developed, there is not necessarily a continuous movement toward, say, greater political stability, democracy, or accountability. To the contrary, Samuel Huntington has observed that while the most affluent countries in the world (e.g., Switzerland, Netherlands, and Canada) are politically stable and the poorest countries (such as Afghanistan, Congo, and Nepal) are generally unstable, countries that are in the mid-stages of economic development often become more unstable as their economies develop.[33] Thus, for example, some of Latin America's most economically advanced countries (Argentina, Brazil, Chile, and Uruguay) experienced internal conflicts and political unrest in the 1960s and 1970s, resulting in the collapse of their democratic governments and the emergence of highly repressive military dictatorships. In 2001–2002, nearly two decades after the restoration of democratic government, Argentina experienced an economic crisis, urban rioting, and political instability that produced five presidents in the space of less than a month. Huntington explained this political instability in mid-level developing nations (i.e., those that are more developed than, say, Nepal, but less developed than New Zealand) by suggesting that as countries modernize, the spread of urbanization, education, and mass media consumption produces an increasingly politically aware and mobilized society whose citizens make greater demands on the government. All too often, however, political institutions, particularly political parties, cannot be strengthened quickly enough to channel and respond to this rising tide of demands. As a result, he maintained, the system becomes overloaded and unstable.

Guillermo O'Donnell posited another theory explaining the rise of extremely repressive dictatorships in South America's more economically advanced nations during the 1960s and 1970s. He suggested that as those countries moved toward a higher stage of industrial growth, they required extensive new investment that they could only secure by attracting foreign capital. Such foreign investment, in turn, would only materialize if the government controlled labor unions and kept down workers' wage demands. In order to achieve those goals, the nations' business leaders and technocrats turned to repressive military rule.[34]

Similarly, some scholars have argued than an authoritarian government might be helpful in the early to middle stages of industrialization in order to control labor unions and workers' wages, thereby increasing company profits and attracting new external investment (see Chapter 10). They point out that the Asian countries that enjoyed the most spectacular economic growth from the 1970s to the mid-1990s—Indonesia, Malaysia, Thailand, Singapore, Taiwan, and South Korea—were all controlled by authoritarian governments during their economic takeoffs. Although these theories have since been challenged, they indicate that the relationships between political, economic, and social development are complex. While the three generally go hand in hand, at least in the long run, they need not progress at the same rate.

THE CAUSES OF UNDERDEVELOPMENT

Our initial discussion suggested that there is some debate concerning the very *definitions* of political and socioeconomic underdevelopment. Social scientists disagree even more intensely over the underlying *causes* of underdevelopment and the most desirable pathways to change. How, for example, do we account for constant military intervention in Pakistani politics, political turmoil in Somalia, government repression in Syria, or a financial crisis in Argentina? Do these problems originate from internal factors such as authoritarian cultural values, weak political parties, or misguided economic planning? Or, did foreign domination—stretching from the colonial era to today's age of multinational corporations (MNCs) and the International Monetary Fund (IMF)—cause many of these difficulties?

Questions about the origins of underdevelopment and the pathways to development elicit very different responses from social scientists. Frequently, their evaluations reflect their personal background, home country, or ideology. Thus, for example, theories that attribute Third World political unrest or economic backwardness to traditional cultural values generally have emanated from the United States. On the other hand, approaches such as dependency theory and world systems theory, which condemn Western exploitation as the root cause of Third World underdevelopment, have been particularly popular among Latin American and African analysts. Similarly, liberal social scientists are drawn to different explanations than are either conservative or Marxist scholars.

For years, two competing paradigms have shaped scholarly analyses of Third World politics and economic change. The first, *modernization theory*, emerged in the early 1960s as American political science's leading interpretation of underdevelopment. The second, *dependency theory*, originated in Latin America and offered a more radical perspective on development, one more popular among Third World scholars generally.[35]

Modernization Theory and the Importance of Cultural Values

During the 1950s and 1960s, as the demise of European colonialism produced a host of newly independent nations in Africa, Asia, and the Middle East, Western social scientists began to study Third World politics and economics more intensively. That interest produced a complex conceptual model of underdevelopment and development known as modernization theory. Its proponents included some of the most prominent figures in comparative politics: Gabriel Almond, James Coleman, Samuel Huntington, Lucian Pye, and David Apter, among others.[36] For a decade or more, modernization theory reigned supreme in the study of political and economic development. Though later challenged, it has continued to influence our understanding of developing nations. While there have been variations and disagreement among modernization theorists, they generally share a number of underlying assumptions and perspectives.

Despite the tremendous array of problems facing the LDCs, modernization theory was initially relatively optimistic about prospects for development.

After all, Western industrialized democracies had also started out as underdeveloped countries. Most Third World nations, the theory argued, could—and should—follow a path of political and economic modernization parallel to the one first traveled by the advanced Western countries. To accomplish this, modernization theorists insisted, developing nations had to acquire modern cultural values and create modern political and economic institutions.

Transforming traditional cultures was seen as the first and, by most accounts, most crucial step in the modernization process. Drawing on the theories of such eminent sociologists as Max Weber and Talcott Parsons, these analysts distinguished between "traditional" and "modern" values.[37] They saw traditional political and economic values as somewhat irrational, or at least unscientific. Conversely modern men and women, they maintained, tend to judge others by universalistic standards (i.e., to hire, vote for, or otherwise evaluate people based on their ability rather than family or ethnic origins); to believe in the possibility and desirability of change; to believe in the value of science and technology; to think about issues outside the sphere of one's family, neighborhood, or village; to believe that average citizens can—and should—try to influence the political system.[38] At its worst, the theory exhibited elements of ethnocentrism and condescension, implying the inferiority of Third World cultures. Thus, one of the founders of Latin American studies in the United States argued:

> There is something in the quality of Latin American . . . culture which has made it difficult . . . to be truly modern. . . . which has made this part of the Western world so prone to excesses of scoundrels, so politically irrational in seeking economic growth, and so ready to reach for gimmicks.[39]

But how can a traditional society make the transition to modernity? How does a culture modernize its values? Modernization theorists identified education, urbanization, and the spread of mass media as the central agents of change. As peasants move to cities, the theory argued, as more children attend schools that teach modern values, and as more citizens access the mass media, cultural modernization will progress. Another critical component, it was suggested, was the diffusion of modern ideas from highly developed nations (especially the West) to the developing world and from city to countryside within the Third World. Foreign aid and institutions such as the Peace Corps could help to speed this process.

Gabriel Almond and G. Bingham Powell, depicting modernization as a rather inexorable force, contended that "the forces of technological change and cultural diffusion are driving political systems in certain directions, which seem discernible and susceptible to analysis in terms of increasing levels of development."[40] Others envisioned modernization as a process of getting developing nations to think and act "more like us" (i.e., the West). "As time goes on," Marion Levy predicted, "they and we will increasingly resemble one another. [The] more highly modernized societies become, the more they resemble one another."[41] Today, as the forces of modernization have spread McDonald's burgers and fries, computer technology, Hollywood movies, rock music, and democratic values around the world, that prophecy may seem accurate.

At the same time, developing nations trying to modernize need to create more specialized and complex political and economic institutions to complement those cultural changes. For example, whereas a tribal culture might have a council of elders that carries out legislative, executive, and judicial activities, a modern society needs separate, specialized institutions for each of those tasks. Modernizing societies also need trained bureaucracies, which base professional advancement on merit rather than personal connections and make decisions according to uniform and consistent standards. Political parties have to channel popular demands and aspirations effectively to government policymakers. Eventually, it was argued, as these cultural and institutional changes progress, a modernizing society can lay the foundation for a more stable, effective, and responsive political system. During the decades after World War II, which featured the Cold War against Soviet Communism, modernization theory became far more than an academic perspective. Its assumptions dominated U.S. foreign policy toward the developing world, including foreign aid distribution, the Peace Corps, and the tactics used during the Vietnam War.[42]

In time, however, many of early modernization theory's assumptions had to be modified. To begin with, it had been too optimistic and too simplistic in its initial view of change. For one thing, its proponents expected developing countries to achieve economic growth, greater equality, democracy, political stability, and greater national autonomy simultaneously and smoothly. As Samuel Huntington noted, the theory erroneously assumed that "all good things go together."[43] In fact, economic growth proved to be no guarantee of democracy, stability, equality, or autonomy. In fact, as we have noted, in nations such as Brazil, Mexico, Singapore, and Taiwan, industrialization and economic development originated and advanced for many years under the direction of authoritarian governments.

Analysts were particularly disturbed to find that the very process of social and economic modernization often ushered in political instability and violence.[44] For example, in some of Latin America's most economically developed nations (Argentina, Brazil, Chile, and Uruguay), industrial growth and greater income inequality unleashed bitter class conflict, causing the collapse of democratic institutions, and the rise of repressive military dictatorships.[45] Elsewhere, in much of Africa, Asia, and the Middle East, the hopes once inspired by decolonization have given way to ethnic conflict, military coups, and political repression.

Thus, the process of development often turned out to be more difficult and unpredictable than originally imagined. Modernization theory's initial optimism gave way to *conflict theory*. Developing nations, this new perspective argued, would have to make hard choices between seemingly irreconcilable development goals. Concerned about growing political turmoil in many developing nations, Samuel Huntington insisted that political stability was crucial, even if maintaining it necessitated authoritarian rule for a time. That is to say, democracy might have to take a back seat to stability, at least temporarily. At the same time, many economists and political scientists argued that the early stages of economic growth required wealth to be concentrated in a small number of hands, so that incipient capitalists could acquire sufficient capital for major investments.

More recently, the experiences of several countries in East Asia and Latin America have produced yet another new perspective. While certainly less naively optimistic than the earliest modernization theories, current analysis is also less pessimistic than conflict theory was. The *reconciliation approach*, offered by contemporary modernization theorists, maintains that, with the right policies, developing nations can simultaneously achieve goals previously thought to be incompatible.[46] Taiwan and South Korea, for example, have shown that it is possible to achieve rapid economic development together with equitable income distribution. Barbados and Costa Rica have managed to achieve democracy and stability simultaneously. Consequently, current research tries to isolate factors such as state policy, historical traditions, and cultural values that may contribute to successful development.

One of the major criticisms of modernization theory, at least as originally formulated, was that it was culturally biased, assuming the superiority of Western values. Explicitly or implicitly it suggested that the western industrialized world was the source of modern (read "good") values and attitudes. Therefore, another modification of the theory addresses its initial view of cultural change. First, it recognized that all modern or modernizing cultures are not identical. Indeed, traditional values, which vary from society to society, may influence the nature of the modern culture that emerges positively or negatively. For example, in East Asian countries, such as Japan and South Korea, traditional Confucian and Shinto beliefs help explain why modern citizens of those countries tend to be less individualistic and more family oriented than are Westerners.

Second, scholars now agree that the differences between traditional and modern cultures are not necessarily as stark or clear-cut as originally thought. For example, even though the United States is a highly modern society, many Americans have retained traditional values such as judging others by the color of their skin. Third, contrary to early modernization theory, it now appears that some traditional values not only are worth keeping but also contribute to political and economic development. For example, students of contemporary Japanese culture and religion have argued that traditional religious values have strengthened that nation's work ethic. Even "magic and miracles," notes one expert on East Asian religions, "are entirely compatible with the 'rationality' of industrial society."[47]

Finally, while modern (Western) values have indeed swept across the Third World, they have not been as universally welcomed as some analysts had expected. In Afghanistan, Iran, Saudi Arabia, and other parts of the Muslim world, for example, many people, including some with advanced educations, have rejected Westernization in favor of either peaceful or violent forms of Islamic fundamentalism. The September 11, 2001, attacks on New York and Washington and the March 2004 train bombings in Madrid, perpetrated by the Al Qaeda terrorist network, were extreme reflections of the distaste that many Muslims feel about Western values and lifestyles. Although terrorists and other extremists represent only a very small fraction of the Muslim world, many other nonviolent Muslims also reject Western culture, which they view as immoral—sullied, for example, by immodest dress, extramarital sex, and pornography.

Dependency Theory

During the 1960s and 1970s, social scientists in Latin America and the United States raised more fundamental objections to modernization theory, insisting that the previously mentioned modifications had failed to correct the theory's fundamental flaws. Under the banner of *dependency theory*, they challenged the modernizationists' most fundamental assumptions. A closely related approach was called World Systems Theory (or, more modestly, the World Systems approach).[48] Like modernization theorists, dependency scholars differ among themselves, but agree on the theory's fundamental premises.

To begin with, *dependentistas* (as dependency theorists are known) rejected the contention that Third World countries can follow the same path to development as Western nations had, if only because the earliest industrialized nations changed the landscape for those that followed them. When Britain became the world's first industrialized nation, it faced no significant competition from other economic powers. Today, however, NICs must compete against well-established industrial giants such as the United States, Japan, and Germany. In addition, argued Brazil's Theotonio Dos Santos, developing countries need to borrow capital and purchase advanced technology from highly developed countries, thereby making themselves dependent on economic forces beyond their borders and beyond their control.[49]

As we have seen, modernization theory views Western influence over the Third World as beneficial, in that it spreads modern values, technology, and institutions. In contrast, dependency theorists maintain that Western colonialism and economic imperialism are precisely what first turned Africa, Asia, and Latin America into providers of cheap food and raw materials for the developed countries. Moreover, they charge, long after the LDCs had achieved political independence, some First World nations have continued to use their economic power to sustain dependent relationships that disadvantage the Third World. For the most part, the production and export of manufactured goods and technology—the most profitable economic activities—along with major control over world finance have remained in the control of the *core*, the *dependentistas* label for the industrialized West (and Japan). Conversely, until recent decades, Third World nations, located in the *periphery*, were largely relegated to the production and export of agricultural goods and raw materials, and were forced to trade for industrial imports on unfavorable terms.[50] That did not mean that the core developed nations controlled every aspect of Third World economic and political development (or misdevelopment), but rather:

> [Dependency is] . . . a historical condition which shapes a certain structure of the world economy such that it favors some countries to the detriment of others and limits the development possibilities of the subordinate economies . . . a situation in which the economy of a certain group of countries is conditioned by the development and expansion of another economy, to which their own is subjected.[51]

Finally, *dependentistas* contend that this *economic* dependence also had brought about the LDCs' *political* dependence on the core. Within the periphery, the argument went, Third World political, military, and economic elites, backed by the might of the United States and other core nations, maintained a political system that benefited the powerful few at the expense of the many. Dependency theorists have noted, for example, how frequently France has militarily intervened in its former African colonies to maintain corrupt and unrepresentative governments with which it is allied. Similarly, for many years the United States has supported friendly, but repressive, regimes in countries such as Cuba (before Castro), Nicaragua, Pakistan, and Saudi Arabia.

As one might expect, many Third World scholars embraced dependency theory enthusiastically, because it maintained that underdevelopment was not the developing world's "fault," but rather the result of foreign domination and exploitation. In time, however, dependency theory even challenged, and often displaced, modernization theory in the United States and Europe as the major scholarly paradigm. As Omar Sánchez has observed, this "marks one of those rare instances in which ideas produced in the Third World come to influence the thinking of scholars in the developed world."[52] Many dependency scholars were Marxists (drawing on his theories of imperialism), but others were not. And, some Marxist writers rejected dependency theory.

However, just as early modernization theory had been overly optimistic about the prospects for simultaneous economic and political development, early dependency theory turned out to be excessively pessimistic about the likelihood of economic and political development. Analysts such as Andre Gunder Frank had warned that Third World nations, consigned to production of non-industrial goods and ruled by unrepresentative elites, were doomed to continued backwardness. Some *dependentistas* believed that radical revolutions were the only solution; others merely prescribed greater economic independence for developing nations; still others offered no solutions.

Yet, despite the bleak prognosis of early dependency theorists, it was clear as early as the mid-1960s that nations such as Brazil and Mexico were undergoing substantial industrialization. In his far more sophisticated version of dependency theory, Brazil's Fernando Henrique Cardoso rejected the contention that all Third World countries were condemned to underdevelopment and precluded from industrial growth.[53] Drawing heavily from the experiences of his own country, Cardoso noted that through the active intervention of the state and the linkage of domestic firms to multinational corporations (MNCs), some developing countries could industrialize and enjoy considerable economic growth. He referred to this process as *associated-dependent development*.

Cardoso radically altered dependency theory by arguing that countries such as Argentina, Brazil, Colombia, and Mexico could experience industrialization and economic growth while remaining dependent on foreign banks and MNCs for loans, investment, and technology. Brazilian industrialization, he noted, had been stimulated largely by a sharp rise in investment from foreign corporations. Still, Cardoso and his colleagues viewed associated-dependent development as tainted in several important ways. MNCs were making critical economic decisions affecting developing countries, outside the developing nation's control. Furthermore, foreign corporations tended to invest in capital-intensive (highly mechanized) production that needed fewer workers than did more traditional, labor-intensive firms. Frequently the new industries produced higher-end products only available to more affluent consumers. Rather than reduce poverty, *dependentistas* maintained, associated-dependent development had widened the income gap. At the same time, Peter Evans and others maintained, an alliance of the MNCs with Latin American economic, political, and military elites helped maintain the power of repressive regimes such as Brazil's military government.

Modernization and Dependency Theory Compared

The dependency approach offered useful corrections to modernization theory. Moreover, it highlighted important influences on Third World societies that the theory had largely neglected—international trade, finance, and investment. In fact, many political scientists now argue that a principal characteristic defining Third World countries is their dependence on the core. Consequently, these scholars still consider relatively wealthy nations such as Saudi Arabia and stable democracies such as Costa Rica to be part of the Third World because their economic and political systems are largely shaped by the developed world.[54]

Regardless of how they view dependency theory, contemporary analysts of underdevelopment now recognize that political and economic modernization requires more than adopting new values or changing domestic political structures (i.e., more than modernization theory had postulated). Dependency theory shifted the focus of research from exclusively internal factors to international economic and political relations. *Dependentistas* also helped redefine the concept of economic development. Whereas early mainstream research on economic development heavily stressed the goal of economic growth, dependency theorists also emphasized the importance of more equitable economic distribution and greater social justice. When rapid economic growth increases the concentration of wealth and income in the hands of a minority, as it frequently does, it offers limited benefits to the poor, or may even worsen their lives. Influenced by dependency theory and other leftist critiques, even establishment pillars such as the World Bank reoriented their focus toward "growth and redistribution."[55]

Despite its contributions, however, dependency theory suffered from serious failings. Just as early modernization theorists overemphasized the *internal* causes of underdevelopment, *dependentistas* erroneously attributed virtually all of the Third World's problems to *external* economic factors. These included international trade, foreign investment and credit, and links between Third World elites and foreign powers.[56] Furthermore many *dependentistas*, particularly the more radical ones who preceded Cardoso's writings, portrayed Third World nations as helpless pawns with no way out of their poverty. As Stephan Haggard charged, "countries are called 'dependent' by virtue of their characteristics and remain so regardless of their action."[57] To be sure, what is striking about much of the dependency literature is its economic determinism and neglect of domestic social or political influences. Its proponents frequently have dismissed Third World governments as agents of the local economic elite who colluded with Western- or Japanese-based MNCs. Consequently, there is a disturbing similarity between many of the dependency-based case studies. The details of Mexican, Nigerian, or Peruvian politics and economic development may differ in these works, but too often *dependentistas*, particularly early proponents, offer identical explanations for their misdevelopment.

Cardoso refined dependency theory by insisting that the types of constraints imposed by core economies on the periphery varied from one developing nation to another. El Salvador may be extremely dependent—economically and politically—on the United States, while Argentina—a larger country more distant from North America—has been better equipped to guide its own course. Furthermore, the effects of external influences emanating from the core are mediated by conditions within each developing country. In other words, he argued, in varying degrees developing nations have options within the limits imposed by their dependency. For example, a country's class structure and the influence of particular classes on government policy influence the level of associated-dependent development it experiences. As he and Enzo Faletto wrote: "We conceive the relationship between external and internal forces . . . as not [being] based on mere external forms of exploitation . . . but [as] rooted in coincidences of interests between local dominant classes and international ones."[58] In other words, decisions made by Third World governments and business leaders *do* matter, and some LDCs have enjoyed notable, if still flawed, economic growth. Combining Cardoso's ideas with elements of modernization theory, Argentine political scientist Guillermo O'Donnell offered a powerful explanation for the rise of authoritarian military governments in the more developed nations of South America.[59] Like Cardoso, he remained pessimistic about the consequences of associated-dependent development.

However, East Asia's "economic miracle" (its remarkable and sustained economic growth) in recent decades—most notably in South Korea, Taiwan, Hong Kong, and Singapore—has confounded dependency theory. These countries have linked themselves very closely to the developed world through trade, credit, investments, and technology transfers. Contrary to what even the more sophisticated dependency scholars had predicted, however, they achieved spectacular economic growth coupled with comparatively equitable income distribution. Countries such as South Korea and Taiwan now have standards of living comparable to Portugal's and Hungary's, along with relatively high income equality. Some *dependentistas* may object that East Asia's severe economic crisis (1997–1998) validated dependency theory, because the region's dependence on foreign investment was largely responsible for the crash. When Thailand was forced to devalue its currency, foreign capital fled the region, sending East Asian stock markets and currencies on a downward spiral. Still, the region's recovery since 1999 suggests that the financial crisis was a temporary setback, though also a signal that the Asian growth model needed some modifications. Moreover, in a further blow to dependency theory, in recent years India, the world's second largest nation, has become one of the world's most dynamic economies by opening its doors to foreign trade and investment. Even Fernando Henrique Cardoso—dependency theory's most renowned exponent during his career as an academic scholar—later embraced foreign investment, trade, and technology in his second career as Brazil's finance minister and then two-term president.

Contemporary Perspectives

Using sophisticated statistical methods, a number of political scientists have tested these alternate theories of underdevelopment and development with recent economic and social data. For example, using regression analysis, they have examined whether there is a correlation between a population's attitude toward science and technology and their country's degree of economic development; that is, do societies with more positive attitudes toward science and technology tend to have higher per-capita incomes? Similarly, is there a relationship between a country's dependence on foreign trade or foreign investment and its HDI?

The results of this research have been mixed. Depending on which set of countries or what time period each scholar examines, his or her answers to such questions may differ. In all, empirical research supports some of modernization theory's hypotheses, but not others. One study found that, in accordance with modernization theory and contrary to dependency theory, the diffusion of technology and communications from highly industrialized nations to developing nations correlates positively with higher HDI scores.[60] On the other hand, exploring the relationship between several modern attitudes and human development, Maria Fernanda Trujillo-Mendoza, found that in 1990 there was a positive correlation, but in 1997 that relationship was not statistically significant (the correlation was not supported sufficiently to draw a conclusion). In all, her analysis indicated that modern values, such as "rational attitudes toward authority . . . [and] openness to ideas . . . do not reflect the underlying differences between developed and developing countries."[61] That is to say, she found no evidence that countries with modern values such as these were more likely to enjoy economic or political development.

But when subjected to empirical testing, dependency theory fared less well than modernization. For example, contrary to the theory's predictions, the developing nations that have experienced the most dramatic improvements in per-capita income and living standards in recent decades—such as Singapore, South Korea, Taiwan, and Chile—tend to be the ones most closely tied to the global economy and its industrialized "core." Conversely, Third World countries that have the lowest levels of foreign investment and foreign trade tend to be the most impoverished. More broadly, there is considerable evidence that developing nations that reduce barriers to free trade, such as tariffs, tend to enjoy faster economic growth than countries that limit international trade.[62]

Similarly, an extensive review of existing research suggests that greater foreign investment also is associated with higher economic growth, in part because technological innovations in foreign-owned corporations are often picked up by local producers. Using cross-national data over a period of years to analyze the effects of several indicators of dependency—including dependence on foreign trade or aid, level of foreign investment, and amount of foreign debt—Brian Farmer found that there was little relationship between these factors and per-capita income, economic growth, income inequality, or HDI. Only one of the measures of dependency that he examined supported dependency theory. Countries that relied heavily on primary exports (agricultural and livestock products, minerals) tended to do more poorly on the various measures of economic and social development.[63] Interestingly, the dependency literature rarely uses comparative data to test its hypotheses. In fact, it often lacks any testable hypotheses that can be confirmed or disproved. Hence, many of its own proponents—including Cardoso—have admitted that dependency is not a theory at all—with predictive powers and clearly defined relationships—but rather an *approach* (a path to greater understanding).

Today, few analysts accept either modernization or dependency theory in their entirety. In their original formulations, both approaches suffered from overgeneralizations that failed to recognize the cultural, political, or economic differences between developing countries. Subsequent theories and approaches, such as *bureaucratic authoritarianism* (which attempted to explain the rise of military dictatorships in some of the Third World's more economically developed nations) or *neoliberal economics* (which offered a set of conservative prescriptions for less developed nations) have avoided global explanations of development and underdevelopment, focusing instead on more specific issues. Indeed, most contemporary analysts reject the very idea of a *single* theory of development.[64] For one thing, the Third World is too diverse and the processes of political and socioeconomic development too complex to be explained by a single theory of change.

This does not mean, however, that the insights offered by dependency and modernization theories have not been useful. Our current understanding of development draws on the strengths of both approaches, while recognizing their limitations. Today, however, most political scientists limit themselves to more manageable and focused issues, such as the function of political parties, the role of government in the economy, or the prerequisites for consolidated democracy.

In fact, the chapters that follow turn from general development theory to specific issues facing LDCs today. Chapter 2 discusses perhaps the most important change in world politics during the past 30–40 years: the spread and legitimization of democratic government. The causes and effects of democratization will be an underlying theme of this text, and most of the succeeding chapters will include some discussion of the effects of democratic change. Chapters 3 through 7 discuss some of the broad social forces that influence contemporary politics in the developing world: the political impact of religion; the nature of ethnic politics and ethnic conflict; the role of women in Third World economic and political development; agrarian reform and rural change; and the political implications of rapid urbanization. Chapters 8 and 9 explore two important types of political regimes—revolutionary and military—that, until recently, were common in much of the Third World. They examine each regime type's approach to the problems of development and discuss the reasons why both types have declined in recent years. Finally, Chapter 10 examines economic development strategies currently employed in much of the Third World.

DISCUSSION QUESTIONS

1. Is democracy an integral part of political development? Why were political scientists initially reluctant to include democracy in their definitions of political development?
2. To what degree does social and economic development contribute to or undermine political development?
3. What have been the main contributions of modernization theory and what have been its greatest weaknesses?
4. What have been the main contributions of dependency theory and what have been its greatest weaknesses?
5. How have both early modernization theory and early dependency theory been modified? Why were those modifications needed?
6. Which theory of underdevelopment—modernization or dependency—has greater empirical support, particularly statistical support? Does such empirical support prove that the opposing theory is weaker?
7. What indicators would you suggest might be useful measures of political development?

NOTES

1. For a discussion of the strengths and many weaknesses of the term, see Allen H. Merriam, "What Does 'Third World' Mean?" in *The Third World: States of Mind and Being*, eds. Jim Norwine and Alfonso Gonzalez (Boston: Unwin Hyman, 1988), 15–22.

2. The term *liberal democracy* indicates that the political system not only supports free and contested elections but also respects civil liberties such as free speech, freedom of the press, and religious freedom. For more on different aspects of democracy, see Chapter 2. Strictly speaking, since the term *Second World* referred to the Communist bloc of nations led by the former Soviet Union, that grouping no longer exists. But, this book uses that label to refer to *former* communist countries in Europe, such as Poland, Hungary, or Romania. This usage is consistent with the original meaning of the term, which indicated that Second World members had been the second group of countries to industrialize (following the Western capitalist nations, the First World).

3. Scholars have disagreed on whether or not to include non-European communist nations such as China, Cuba, and Vietnam in the Third World. I include them in that category because they resemble other developing nations on many dimensions.

4. Merriam, "What Does 'Third World' Mean?" 20.

5. Christopher Clapham, *Third World Politics: An Introduction* (Madison: University of Wisconsin Press, 1985), 2.

6. GDP is a measure similar to Gross National Product (GNP), the indicator often used in the United States, but excludes "net factor income from abroad." Economists and international agencies such as the United Nations generally use GDP, rather than GNP, for comparing the living standards of different countries.

7. Like all statistics, these have their limitations. For example, depending on what statistical methods they use, various institutions (such as the World Bank, IMF, or the UNDP) often publish somewhat different statistics for a particular country's GNP or GDP, or its ranking relative to other nations. Furthermore, national statistics fail to reveal what are sometimes considerable income variations *within* particular nations. Thus, China's coastal region is relatively developed, comparing well with South Korea or Mexico. Its interior, however, is generally quite impoverished, more analogous to rural Pakistan or Bangladesh.

8. While most non-specialists speak of a country's "per-capita *income*" (the average income per person), actual data on income are rarely available. Hence, many data sources instead use the figures in Column 2 ("Real Gross Domestic Product (GDP) per capita converted to Parity Purchasing Power (PPP)") as a surrogate for per-capita income. That is to say, it is a measure of average economic *production* per person (in a given year), which is then statistically controlled to remove the influences of varying price structures and exchange rates in different countries. Thus, PPP adjustments allow a more meaningful comparison of what per-capita incomes in different countries can actually purchase.

9. United Nations Development Programme (UNDP), *Human Development Report 2006*, http://hdr.undp.org/hdr2006/statistics/.

10. Of course, even though the gap between rich and poor is greater in the United States than in India, the poor in India are clearly far worse off because their *absolute* income level and standard of living are far lower than those of their counterparts in the United States. If we think of income distribution as shares of a pie, the poor in India get a larger share (percentage) of the pie, but the Indian economic pie is *far smaller* than the American pie.

11. Income distribution data for countries in Table 1.1 and others mentioned in this paragraph come from the UNDP, *Human Development Report 2006*, http://hdr.undp.org/hdr2006/.

12. Although the early stages of economic development have *usually* produced increased inequality (both in Europe and the developing world), there are important exceptions. For example, Japan, Taiwan, and South Korea (the last two, formerly controlled by Japan) all experienced economic modernization while maintaining a high degree of equality.

13. Robert Wade, *Governing the Market* (Princeton, NJ: Princeton University Press, 1990).

14. Axel Hadenius, *Democracy and Development* (London: Cambridge University Press, 1992).

15. A simple example illustrates the problem with income averages. If one person in a generally poor village makes a million dollars a year, he or she will totally distort the town average, producing a deceivingly high mathematical average (or "mean") income that fails to reflect how the average villager really lives. Consequently, the mode income (the single villager's income that is higher than half his community's and

lower than the other half's) is a more useful measure of village income. However, the same kinds of distortions do not take place with social indicators such as life expectancy, infant mortality, and literacy.

16. *New York Times* (December 28, 2006).

17. That increase occurred between 1960 and 1990 only. Since 1990, the AIDS pandemic in Africa and parts of Asia has actually *reduced* Third World life expectancy slightly from 64.7 to 64.6 years. Currently, life expectancy in Sub-Saharan Africa is only 46.4 years, almost 20 years below the Third World average. The World Bank, DEPweb offers somewhat different estimates, claiming worldwide life expectancy reached 67 in 1998, http://www.worldbank.org/depweb/.

18. Twentieth-century data in this paragraph come from UNDP, *Human Development Report 1997* (New York: Oxford University Press, 1997), 24–26.

19. *United Nations Chronicle*, Online Edition, "AIDS Slashes Life Expectancy in 23 African Countries," http://www.un.org/Pubs/chronicle.

20. Africa Action, "Africa Policy E-Journal," http://www.africaaction.org/docs00/life0006.htm. Data were drawn from the World Health Organization (WHO). Despite Africa's dramatic increase in AIDS treatment during the past five to seven years, the number of new AIDS cases continues to grow, with new cases far outstripping the number of cases being treated. "New AIDS Cases in Africa Outpace Treatment Gains," *New York Times* (June 6, 2007).

21. United Nations Economic Commission for Africa, "Economic Report on Africa 2007," http://www.uneca.org/era2007/.

22. Adapted from data in Chandrika Kaul and Valerie Tomaselli-Moschovitis, eds. *Statistical Handbook on Poverty in the Developing World* (Phoenix, AZ: Oryx Press, 1999), 327–334. Their data were drawn from the World Bank.

23. *New York Times*, "Report on Child Deaths Finds Some Hope in Poorest Nations" (May 8, 2007).

24. UNDP, *Human Development Report 1997*, 4.

25. Ibid. 24–26. Literacy and life expectancy comparisons between the First and Third Worlds are based on the UNDP's 2004 data.

26. Samuel P. Huntington, "The Goals of Development," in *Understanding Political Development*, eds. Myron Weiner and Samuel P. Huntington (Boston: Little, Brown, 1987), 3.

27. Hadenius, *Democracy and Development*; Robert A. Dahl, *Democracy and Its Critics* (New Haven, CT: Yale University Press, 1989); Scott Mainwaring, "Transitions to Democracy and Democratic Consolidation," in *Issues in*

Democratic Consolidation: The New South American Democracies in Comparative Perspective, eds. Scott Mainwaring, Guillermo O'Donnell, and Samuel Valenzuela (Notre Dame, IN: University of Notre Dame Press, 1992), 294–341; Samuel P. Huntington, *The Third Wave: Democratization in the Late Twentieth Century* (Norman: University of Oklahoma Press, 1991).

28. Samuel P. Huntington, *Political Order in Changing Societies* (New Haven, CT: Yale University Press, 1968).

29. Guillermo O'Donnell and Philippe Schmitter, *Transitions from Authoritarian Rule: Tentative Conclusions about Uncertain Democracies* (Baltimore, MD: Johns Hopkins University Press, 1986); Abraham Lowenthal, ed. *Exporting Democracy* (Baltimore, MD: Johns Hopkins University Press, 1991); Dahl, *Democracy and Its Critics*.

30. Huntington, *The Third Wave*.

31. Eighty-six members of the United Nations have been ranked on both economic resources (per-capita GNPs) and socioeconomic indicators of living standards (HDIs). If we subtract each country's HDI rank from its GNP rank, a positive score indicates the country is performing better on social indicators than its economic ranking would predict, whereas a negative score suggests the opposite.

32. Huntington, *The Third Wave*; Mitchell A. Seligson, "Democratization in Latin America: The Current Cycle," in *Authoritarians and Democrats: Regime Transition in Latin America*, eds. James M. Malloy and Mitchell A. Seligson (Pittsburgh, PA: University of Pittsburgh Press, 1987); Hadenius, *Democracy and Development*.

33. Huntington, *Political Order*.

34. Guillermo O'Donnell, *Modernization and Bureaucratic-Authoritarianism: Studies in South American Politics* (Berkeley: University of California Press, 1973).

35. For a useful summary of major theories of development, see Alvin Y. So, *Social Change and Development* (Newbury Park, CA: Sage Publications, 1990); for ongoing contributions in these areas, see Weiner and Huntington, eds., *Understanding Political Development*; Vicky Randall and Robin Theobald, *Political Change and Underdevelopment* (London: Macmillan, 1985).

36. The modernization literature is extensive. The most important works include Huntington, *Political Order*, widely considered the best work in this area; Gabriel Almond and James Coleman, eds. *The Politics of Developing Areas* (Princeton, NJ: Princeton University Press, 1960); Lucian Pye and Sidney Verba, eds., *Political Culture and Political Development* (Princeton, NJ: Princeton University Press,

1965); and Cyril E. Black, ed., *Comparative Modernization: A Reader* (New York: Free Press, 1976). These works, as well as those mentioned below regarding dependency theory, are recommended for advanced undergraduates.

37. Max Weber, *The Protestant Ethic and the Spirit of Capitalism* (New York: Scribner, 1958); Talcott Parsons, *The Social System* (Glencoe, IL: Free Press, 1951).

38. For examples of such arguments, see Parsons, *Social System*; Gabriel Almond and Sidney Verba, *The Civic Culture* (Princeton, NJ: Princeton University Press, 1963); Pye and Verba, *Political Culture*; Alex Inkeles and David Horton Smith, *Becoming Modern: Individual Change in Six Developing Countries* (Cambridge, MA: Harvard University Press, 1974); Daniel Lerner, *The Passing of Traditional Society* (Glencoe, IL: Free Press, 1958); David McClelland, *The Achieving Society* (Princeton, NJ: Van Nostrand, 1961).

39. Kalman H. Silvert, "The Politics of Social and Economic Change in Latin America," quoted in J. Samuel Valenzuela and Arturo Valenzuela, "Modernization and Dependency: Alternative Perspectives in the Study of Latin American Underdevelopment," *Comparative Politics*, vol. 10, no. 4 (July 1978), 542. This article by Valenzuela and Valenzuela is one of the best comparative analyses of these two approaches.

40. Gabriel A. Almond and G. Bingham Powell, *Comparative Politics: A Developmental Approach* (Boston: Little, Brown, 1966), 301.

41. Marion Levy Jr., "Social Patterns (Structures) and Problems of Modernization," in *Readings on Social Change*, eds. Wilbert Moore and Robert Cooke (Upper Saddle River, NJ: Prentice Hall, 1967), 207.

42. Michael E. Latham, *Modernization as Ideology: American Social Science and "Nation Building" in the Kennedy Era* (Chapel Hill: University of North Carolina Press, 2000).

43. Huntington, "The Goals of Development."

44. Huntington, *Political Order*.

45. See Juan Linz and Alfred Stepan, eds., *The Breakdown of Democratic Regimes: Latin America* (Baltimore, MD: Johns Hopkins University Press, 1978); David Collier, ed., *The New Authoritarianism in Latin America* (Princeton, NJ: Princeton University Press, 1979).

46. Huntington, "The Goals of Development."

47. Winston Davis, "Religion and Development: Weber and the East Asian Experience," in *Understanding Political Development*, 258; see also So, *Social Change and Development*, chap. 4.

48. Immanuel Wallerstein, *World-Systems Analysis: An Introduction* (Durham, NC: Duke University Press, 2004). Wallerstein was the principal intellectual father of this approach.

49. Theotonio Dos Santos, "The Structure of Dependence," *American Economic Review*, vol. 60, no. 2 (May 1970), 231–236.

50. Werner Baer, "The Economics of Prebisch and ECLA," in *Latin America: Problems in Economic Development*, ed. C.T. Nisbet (New York: Free Press, 1969). Major early dependency studies include Andre Gunder Frank, *Capitalism and Underdevelopment in Latin America* (New York: Monthly Review Press, 1967); and Paul Baran, *The Political Economy of Growth* (New York: Monthly Review Press, 1957).

51. Theotonio Dos Santos, "The Structure of Dependence," in *Readings in U.S. Imperialism*, eds. K.T. Fann and Donald C. Hodges (Boston: Porter Sargent, 1971), 226.

52. Omar Sánchez, "The Rise and Fall of the Dependency Movement: Does It Inform Underdevelopment Today?" *E.I.A.L. (Estudios Interdisciplinarios de América Latina y el Caribe)*, vol. 14, no. 2 (July–December, 2003), www.tau.ac.il/eial/XIV_2/sanchez.html.

53. The most influential work on this sophisticated version of dependency theory is Fernando Henrique Cardoso and Enzo Faletto, *Dependency and Development in Latin America* (Berkeley: University of California Press, 1979). A more readable work on the same topic is Peter Evans, *Dependent Development: The Alliance of Multinational, State, and Local Capital* (Princeton, NJ: Princeton University Press, 1979).

54. Clapham, *Third World Politics*, 3.

55. Hollis Chenery et al., *Redistribution with Growth* (London: Oxford University Press with the World Bank and the University of Sussex, 1974).

56. Barbara Stallings, "International Influence in Economic Policy," in *The Politics of Economic Adjustment: International Constraints, Distributive Conflicts and the State*, eds. Stephan Haggard and Robert Kaufman (Princeton, NJ: Princeton University Press, 1992).

57. Stephan Haggard, *Pathways from the Periphery: The Politics of Growth in Newly Industrializing Countries*, (Ithaca, NY: Cornell University Press, 1990), 21–22.

58. Cardoso and Faletto, *Dependency and Development*, 26.

59. O'Donnell, *Modernization and Bureaucratic-Authoritarianism*.

60. Richard Labelle, *ICT Policy Formulation and e-Strategy Development* (New Delhi, India: Elsevier and the U.N. Asia-Pacific Development

Information Programme, 2005). A positive correlation means that as one factor (variable) increases or decreases, the other factor varies in the same direction (e.g., more years of education correlates with higher income). A negative correlation means that two factors vary in opposite directions (e.g., as one's education increases, the person's chances of later being imprisoned decreases).

61. Maria Fernanda Trujillo-Mendoza, "The Digital Divide: Exploring the Relation between Core National Computing and National Capacity and Progress in Human Development over the Last Decade." (New Orleans: Tulane University Doctoral Dissertation, 2001), Appendix G-p. 7.

62. Arvind Panagariya, "Think Again: International Trade," *Foreign Policy* (November/December, 2003), 20–28.

63. Brian R. Farmer, *The Question of Dependency and Economic Development* (Lanham, MD: Lexington Books, 1999).

64. See, for example, James Manor, ed., *Rethinking Third World Politics* (New York: Longman, 1991)

CHAPTER 2

DEMOCRATIC CHANGE AND THE CHANGE TO DEMOCRACY

The first decade of the twenty-first century has been difficult for several former dictators and quasi-dictators. The deposed president of Yugoslavia, Slobodan Milosevic, was arrested by Serbian authorities and put on trial at The United Nations International War Crimes Tribunal in The Hague (Netherlands).[1] The father of Serbia's genocidal war against Bosnian Muslims and its attacks on ethnic Albanians in the province of Kosovo, Milosevic became the first head of government since World War II tried on charges of human rights violations before an international court. Augusto Pinochet, Chile's military dictator for 16 years (1973–1989), fought to avoid a human rights trial in Chile after he returned from a humiliating, extended house arrest in England. In 2006 Milosevic died in prison before the conclusion of his marathon trial. Pinochet died later that year while under house arrest and facing numerous human rights charges. Indonesia's long-term dictator, General Suharto, also contemplated possible arrest after he was forced from office by mass demonstrations. Like Pinochet, this once all-powerful leader hid behind a court plea that he was too ill and mentally incapacitated to stand trial. Former Peruvian president Alberto Fujimori—who had imposed authoritarian rule after initially being elected democratically—was recently convicted of abuse of power and is now on trial for murder and kidnapping. In Argentina, Carlos Menem—who, like Fujimori, had been democratically elected but later used his presidential powers to undermine democracy—was indicted for illegal arms sales (though not convicted). Currently, deposed Liberian dictator Charles Taylor awaits trial for war crimes before the International Criminal Court in The Hague, the first former African head of state to face such charges. And, most famously, United States and allied troops ousted Iraqi dictator Saddam Hussein. After months on the run, Saddam was captured and subsequently handed over to the Iraqi authorities.[2] Found guilty of massacring civilians, he was executed in 2006.

These events capped three decades of transitions from authoritarian to democratic government throughout the world. Beginning with a 1974 military revolt that brought down Portugal's fascist dictatorship, numerous authoritarian regimes, particularly in the Third World, fell in the wake of spreading democratic movements. The collapse of Soviet and Eastern European communism was this democratic wave's most renowned manifestation. But in the developing nations, equally dramatic events also merited attention. In early 1990, Nelson Mandela, the world's most revered political prisoner, left his cell in Pollsmoor Prison and was transported triumphantly to South Africa's capital, Pretoria, ending 27 years of incarceration. There, he and other freed Black leaders of his recently legalized political party, the African National Congress, eventually negotiated an end to

White minority rule. President Mandela's triumph accelerated Africa's "second independence"—a wave of political liberalization (easing of repression) that has often culminated in either electoral or liberal democracy.[3]

In Asia, Corazon Aquino succeeded her assassinated husband as the leader of Filipino "people's power"—featuring massive pro-democracy demonstrations staged by students, shopkeepers, professionals, and businesspeople. Her supporters, backed by the Catholic clergy, took to the streets day after day, peacefully challenging government troops. Ultimately, when the nation's dictator, Ferdinand Marcos, tried to deny Ms. Aquino her apparent victory in a hastily called "snap presidential election" (1986), the commander of the armed forces, General Fidel Ramos, along with Defense Minister Juan Ponce Enrile, joined the opposition, forcing Marcos to step down. Soon after, student-led demonstrations against South Korea's military regime (inspired, in part, by events in the Philippines) accelerated that country's transition to democracy. In 1998, "people's power" demonstrations in Indonesia toppled the 30-year dictatorship of President Suharto.

Of course, not all Asian pro-democracy movements have been successful. In China, army tanks crushed student demonstrations in Beijing's Tiananmen Square, putting that county's democracy movement on hold ever since. Most recently (2007), Myanmar's military dictatorship jailed thousands of Buddhist monks and Burmese students who had led large pro-democracy demonstrations. Elsewhere, democratic governments were ousted or failed to take root. For example, in Thailand, where citizen protests established democratic government in 1992, the military returned to power in 2006. And in Kyrgyzstan, although protests in 2005 toppled a 15-year dictatorship, its successor government has resumed the same authoritarian practices. But such setbacks notwithstanding, much of Asia has made substantial progress toward democracy in recent decades.

The most sweeping democratic changes, however, took place in Latin America (1978–1990), affecting almost every country in the region. Whereas all but a handful of countries (Colombia, Costa Rica, and Venezuela) had some type of authoritarian or semi-authoritarian government in the mid-1970s, 25 years later only Cuba and Haiti had failed to establish functioning electoral democracies.[4] Unlike Asia and Africa, Latin America's democratization generally lacked charismatic heroes in the mold of Mandela, Aquino, or Burmese opposition leader and Nobel Peace Prize winner Daw Aung San Suu Kyi. Nor was it typically precipitated by mass demonstrations. Instead, democratic transitions often followed extended negotiations between the outgoing authoritarian government and its opponents, with change coming in stages.

Yet Latin America enjoyed two important advantages over Africa and Asia. First, prior to its wave of military takeovers in the 1960s and 1970s, the region had enjoyed the Third World's strongest democratic tradition, most notably in Chile, Costa Rica, and Uruguay. Furthermore, Latin American countries were among the first LDCs to achieve the levels of literacy and economic development that are generally associated with stable democratic government. Predictably, then, the region's recent democratic wave has been more sweeping and more successful than elsewhere in the developing world, ultimately affecting virtually every country in the hemisphere.

In all, since the 1970s the upsurge of political freedom in the developing world, coupled with the collapse of Soviet and Eastern European communism, has produced history's greatest transition toward democracy. If this progress can be maintained, it promises to influence virtually every aspect of Third World politics discussed in this book.[5]

DEMOCRACY DEFINED

Discussions of democratic transformations have frequently been complicated by disagreements over the meaning of democracy. Currently, most political scientists define democracy procedurally. That is, democracy is characterized by the essential procedures governing the election and behavior of government officials. The least-demanding definition focuses almost exclusively on elections. It simply defines democracy as a political system that holds relatively fair, contested elections on a regular basis, with universal (or almost universal) adult suffrage.[6] We will call countries that meet that minimal standard "electoral democracies." Although this bare-bones definition seems reasonable (after all, most Americans define democracy in terms of free and fair elections), it allows a number of rather questionable governments to be labeled democratic. For example, the current governments in Colombia, Turkey, and Sri Lanka meet this electoral standard, yet they have widely violated human rights while battling armed insurgencies.[7] In all of those countries, government troops frequently massacre villagers and torture prisoners. For much of the past two decades, Guatemala and Bangladesh have also met the standards of electoral democracy, yet both nations' armed forces have regularly intervened in politics, often over-riding decisions made by elected officials.

As the norm of open elections has become more universally accepted in recent decades, the number of electoral democracies worldwide tripled from 1974 to 2005. But many of these governments still manipulate the mass media and violate their citizens' civil liberties. In this chapter, I use the term *semidemocracies* to refer to those electoral democracies whose governments repress civil liberties and otherwise breach the principles of a free society. Alternatively, they may be labeled "partly free." Their elections may be relatively free and fair, but their societies are not. Such semidemocracies currently include Bolivia, Malaysia, Nigeria, and Singapore.

A more stringent definition of democracy demands more than just fair elections. Instead, it defines a "liberal democracy" ("full democracy") as a political system in which most of the country's leading government officials are elected; there is nearly universal suffrage; elections are largely free of fraud and outside manipulation; opposition-party candidates have a real chance of being elected to important national offices; and minority rights as well as general civil liberties are respected, including free speech and a free press (media).[8] All of these conditions help ensure that democratic governments are accountable to their citizens in a way that authoritarian regimes are not.[9] Thus, full (liberal) democracy requires not only freely contested elections but also respect for civil liberties, support for pluralism in civil society, respect for the rule of law, accountability of elected officials, and civilian control over the armed forces.[10] This definition suggests that competitive elections mean little if unelected individuals or groups who are not accountable to the public (such as military officers, organized crime bosses, business elites, or foreign powers) control elected officials from behind the scenes. And, free elections do not bring full democracy if elected officials violate their citizens' civil liberties or arbitrarily arrest opposition leaders.

Finally, some scholars offer an even higher standard for democracy. They argue that any purely procedural definition of democracy, no matter how exacting, is incomplete. Instead, they insist, real democracy requires not only fair elections and proper government procedures (as just outlined) but also fair and just government policy outcomes ("substantive democracy"). For example, substantive democracy requires that citizens have equal access to public schooling and health care regardless of their social class or ethnicity. Consequently, they argue, any procedural democracy—such as India or Brazil—that tolerates gross economic inequalities, ethnic prejudice, or other social injustices is not truly democratic.

These authors make an important point. Procedural democracy alone does not guarantee a just society; it is merely a step in the right direction. But it is a far more important step than its critics acknowledge. Because governments in procedural democracies are accountable to the people, they are less vulnerable to revolution and other forms of civil unrest. They are also extremely unlikely to make war against other democracies (indeed, war between two liberal democracies is virtually unknown). Prodded by a free press and public opinion, they are more responsive to domestic crises such as famines (in fact, there has never been a prolonged famine in any procedural democracy), and the many previously cited exceptions notwithstanding, democracies are usually more respectful of civil liberties.[11]

Mindful of the fact that democratic societies cannot correct all social injustices (the United States, for example, has long tolerated poverty, substantial economic inequality, and racial discrimination), this book defines democracy strictly procedurally. Issues of substantive democracy (eradicating poverty, racism, sexism, and the like) are obviously important, but they are a separate matter.

DEMOCRATIC TRANSITION AND CONSOLIDATION

In the discussion that follows, the term *democratic transition* (or transition to democracy) means the process of moving from an authoritarian to a democratic regime. The transition period begins when an authoritarian government shows the first observable signs of collapsing or of negotiating an exit from power. It ends when the first freely elected government takes office. Thus, for example, in South Africa the democratic transition began in 1990 when the White minority government of President Frederik de Klerk decided to free Nelson Mandela and open negotiations with his African National Congress party. It concluded four years later when Mandela was inaugurated as the first president elected through universal suffrage. Even after their transitions are completed, however, many new democracies remain fragile, with a real possibility that they will falter.

Only when democratic institutions, practices, and values have become deeply ingrained in society can we say that a country has experienced *democratic consolidation*. Consolidation is a process through which democratic norms ("rules of the game") become accepted by all politically influential groups in society—including business, labor, rural landlords, professionals, the church, and the military—and no important political actor contemplates a return to dictatorship. Or, as Juan Linz and Alfred Stepan have put it, democracy is consolidated when it becomes "the only game in town," even in the face of severe economic or political adversity.[12] Consolidation may begin when the democratic transition ends, and it is only complete when democracy is securely entrenched.

Unfortunately, however, not all transitions to democracy are subsequently consolidated. Many countries revert to dictatorship or remain mired in political disorder. For example, between 1958 and 1975, 22 countries that had democratized during the postwar era (1945–1962) slipped back to authoritarianism. Similarly, some of the most recently installed electoral democracies have already collapsed, while democratic values and practices in other countries—such as Guatemala, Indonesia, and Mozambique—are anything but secure.

On the other hand, in successfully consolidated (or reconsolidated) democracies such as Taiwan, Chile, and Uruguay, democratic values predominate. Even previously antidemocratic political parties and groups—including the armed forces, former guerrilla groups, and far-right and far-left political parties—accept democracy as the only game in town. That does not mean that consolidated democracies will never collapse. "Never" is a long time, and in the past, seemingly consolidated Third World democracies such as the Philippines, Chile, Uruguay—and India for a brief period—weakened, and eventually fell to authoritarian forces. However, consolidated democracies are secure for the foreseeable future. They will probably endure unless some deep societal divide (such as class or ethnic conflict) emerges to tear them apart.

AUTHORITARIAN BEGININGS

With the disintegration of Soviet bloc communism and the spread of democracy in the developing world, a growing, worldwide consensus has emerged in favor of democratic government. But that has not always been so. In the decades after World War II, as a host of African, Asian, and Middle Eastern countries achieved independence, many Third World leaders and foreign observers believed that these emerging nations were not ready for democratic government. Others argued that democracy was not even desirable at that stage of their socioeconomic development. To be sure, a number of newly independent countries—particularly former British colonies in the Caribbean, Asia, and Africa—established parliamentary government and other democratic political institutions modeled after their former colonial masters, just as Latin American countries more than a century earlier had patterned their political institutions on the U.S. model. But only in a small number of cases (including India, Costa Rica, Jamaica, and several small, Caribbean-island nations) did democracy take a firm hold.

Since that time, Middle Eastern nations generally have been ruled by monarchs (Saudi Arabia, Kuwait, Morocco, and Jordan), all-powerful single parties (Egypt, Sudan), or personalistic dictators (Iraq under Saddam, Syria). In Sub-Saharan Africa, single-party systems (or dominant-party systems with token opposition) were established in many new nations, including Tanzania, Malawi, and Guinea. Other forms of nondemocratic government included military dictatorships (Nigeria, Liberia, and Ghana) and one-man rule (Uganda, Central African Republic). Democracy fared somewhat better in Asia, but the military frequently sometimes aborted the process (Thailand, South Korea, and Myanmar). Communist revolutionaries toppled corrupt and inept governments in China, Vietnam, Cambodia, and Laos. Latin America, benefiting from greater socioeconomic development and more than a century of self-rule, had by far the most experience with democracy. Indeed, during the 1950s relatively democratic governments predominated in that region. But political intervention by the armed forces persisted, and in the 1960s and early 1970s a new wave of military takeovers swept the region (including Argentina, Brazil, Chile, and Peru), often as a result of political and economic instability. It was not until the 1980s that democracy once again became the norm.

JUSTIFYING AUTHORITARIAN RULE

In the midst of democracy's recent worldwide advance, it seems hard to believe that not long ago, many analysts considered freely elected government and a flourishing civil society unattainable or even undesirable in the developing world. Some modernization theorists believed that the newly emerging African and Asian states were insufficiently developed, economically or socially, to sustain democracy.[13] And dependency theorists declared that democracy was unlikely to emerge in the LDCs because powerful industrialized nations had allied with local political, military, and economic elites to bolster unrepresentative governments.

At the same time, other scholars worried that levels of mass political participation often outstripped governments' capacities to accommodate society's new political demands. Unless Third World political institutions could be strengthened, they warned, political unrest threatened to derail economic and political development.[14] Given the dangers of social disorder, some analysts and Third World leaders justified authoritarian rule as a necessary stopgap. Only after socioeconomic modernization, they argued, could LDCs produce citizens capable of effective political participation. Increased education and literacy were needed to expand society's political understanding and develop effective political participation. Until recently, countries were very unlikely to establish stable, democratic government unless they had risen above the lower ranks of poverty (as expressed by per-capita income) and had reached a literacy rate of at least 50 percent.[15] To be sure, recently a small number of countries have achieved liberal democracy without having reached that level (including Mali, with only 20 percent literacy, Benin, and Senegal), but they are few and far between. In addition to raising literacy, modernization also enlarges the size of the middle class and the organized (unionized) working class, both of whom are essential for a more stable and inclusive democracy.[16]

But, this left a troubling question. If socioeconomic modernization was necessary to establish democracy, how could a country modernize its economy under a democratic government? Some answered that it could not and that only a strong and stable authoritarian government—such as General Augusto Pinochet's dictatorship in Chile or South Korea's various military governments—could jump-start modernization, economic growth, and industrialization. Only authoritarian rule, it was argued, could control labor strife and limit wages so that more capital would be available for investment. Furthermore, a strong-armed government could contain other forms of social unrest in order to create a safe climate for foreign or domestic investment. In East Asia in particular, where several authoritarian regimes presided over spectacular economic growth, their supporters insisted that dictatorial governments could better impose rational, long-term development plans than could democratic regimes. Thus, for example, former President Lee Kuan Yew, the father of Singapore's semi-authoritarian political system and its enormously successful economic development, stated, "I believe what a [developing] country needs to develop is discipline more than democracy. . . . [D]emocracy leads to indiscipline and disorderly conduct, which are inimical to development."[17]

Only later, when the country was "ready," would dictatorships give way to democracy.[18] Other scholars pointed to yet another alleged obstacle to democratic government in the developing world. They argued that many LDCs were held back by authoritarian traditional values, deep ethnic divisions, and the absence of a democratic political culture. Consequently, democracy would have to be preceded by the modernization of social values.[19]

Not long ago, many Third World leaders insisted that, not only would it be difficult to establish democracy in their country, but democratization would not even be desirable at that stage of social and economic development. In Africa, they often created single-party systems, banning or restricting opposition political parties. Foreign and domestic analysts often defended party dictatorships, claiming that ethnic tensions in much of that continent made competitive elections too risky because candidates would further polarize the nation by appealing to particular ethnic groups (see Chapter 4). Other leaders of emerging nations were influenced by Marxist-Leninist ideology, more popular at that time than it is today. They maintained that poverty, tribalism, and dependency at home were so severe that an all-powerful state, led by a "vanguard party" (i.e., one that knows what is in the best interests of the masses), was needed to lead the country forward. By 1964, roughly two-thirds of the independent African countries had become "one-party states."[20] Later, as many of these governments failed miserably, military dictators took their place, claiming that civilian rulers were too corrupt or too weak to govern effectively (Chapter 9). In the Middle East, similar justifications were used to defend one-party or military rule. More recently, Islamic fundamentalist governments in Iran, Sudan, and Afghanistan also have prohibited or restricted political opposition groups.

By contrast, many Latin American nations had enjoyed democratic or semi-democratic governments in the 1950s and 1960s. But, the 1970s and 1980s witnessed the rise of military dictatorships in most of the region. The new leaders justified their rule by pointing to perceived leftist threats and the need to reinvigorate the economy. Meanwhile, authoritarian rulers in East Asian nations such as South Korea, Taiwan, and Singapore clung to power long after their countries had surpassed the thresholds of economic and social modernization normally associated with democratic transitions. The political leaders of these countries insisted that their dictatorships were necessary to ward off external threats (from North Korea, China, or Indonesia) or that their own society's Confucian culture viewed political opposition groups as disruptive to social harmony.

Thus, in the mid-1970s only about 39 of the world's nations were functioning democracies. Virtually all of them were industrialized, economically prosperous countries in North America, Europe, and Australia-New Zealand. Indeed, from the 1960s into the early 1970s, democracy seemed to be in retreat in the LDCs, as countries such as Argentina, Chile, Nigeria, and the Philippines succumbed to dictatorships. Thus, Larry Diamond observes:

> The mid-to-late 1970s seemed a low-water mark for democracy and the empirical trends were reified by intellectual fashions dismissing democracy as an artifice, a cultural construct of the West, or a "luxury" that poor states could not afford.[21]

THE THIRD WAVE AND ITS EFFECT ON THE THIRD WORLD

Since that time, however, developing countries have played a notable role in history's most sweeping transition from authoritarianism to democracy (or partial democracy). Writing shortly before the 1991 dissolution of the Soviet Union, Samuel Huntington counted 29 countries throughout the world that had democratized in the previous 15 years alone. Of these, 20 were LDCs.[22] Although some of the countries on that list had questionable democratic credentials (Romania, Peru, and Pakistan, for example) and others subsequently slid back to authoritarian rule, there can be no denying that the worldwide trend toward democracy since the mid-1970s has been palpable.

Huntington noted that the recent surge of democracy is actually the third such wave that the modern world has experienced since the early 1800s. In each case, democratic political forces and intellectual trends in key countries had a contagious impact on other nations. However, the first two waves were followed by periods of backsliding in which some countries reverted to authoritarian rule. As we have noted, that backsliding has already happened in some Third Wave nations.[23] The first democratic wave (1828–1926), by far the longest, began under the influence of the American and French Revolutions (as well as the Industrial Revolution) and was ended in part by the great economic depression of the 1920s. Democratization during that wave was largely confined to Europe and to former British colonies with primarily European populations (the United States, Canada, New Zealand, and Australia). The second, much shorter, wave (1943–1962) was precipitated by the struggle against fascism during World War II and the subsequent collapse of European colonialism in Africa, Asia, and the Middle East. In this period, democratic governments emerged in a number of LDCs, though most of these only met the standards of electoral democracy (competitive elections).

It is the recent Third Wave (starting in 1974 and winding down or ending by the early twenty-first century) that most draws our attention here because of its pervasive and seemingly lasting reverberations in the Third World. Of course, third-wave transitions were most dramatic in the former Soviet Union and its Eastern European allies, which brought the Cold War to an end. Pictures of young Germans breaking off pieces of the Berlin Wall and of Boris Yeltsin facing down a military coup in the Soviet Union were among the most powerful political images of the late twentieth century. But in developing nations as diverse as South Africa, Mali, the Philippines, South Korea, Argentina, and

Brazil, years of authoritarian or semi-authoritarian rule ended in the 1970s and 1980s as well. This wave of democratization continued into the start of the twenty-first century, with some notable setbacks in countries such as Pakistan and Sudan.

For more than 30 years, the most widely used and respected measurements of democracy have been published annually by Freedom House, a nongovernmental research and advocacy group.[24] Each year a panel of experts evaluates the world's nations in terms of the two dimensions of democracy: first, the level of political rights (including the degrees of electoral competition and citizen participation); and, second, the quality of civil liberties (such as free speech) and the strength of the rule of law. Based on their evaluations, countries are rated as Free, Partly Free, or Not Free.[25] As Table 2.1 indicates, in 1972, less than one-third of the world's 145 countries (29 percent) enjoyed fully democratic government and nearly one-half (46.2 percent) were not free. Since then, the Third Wave of democracy has swept over Latin America and other parts of the developing world, with the number of full democracies increasing each decade. Some of the most extensive and dramatic advances, however, came from the mid-1980s to the mid-1990s. These included the fall of communism in the Soviet bloc and the overthrow of decades-long dictatorships in Chile and the Philippines. During the most recent decade covered by Table 2.1 (1996–2006), the rate of democratization slowed a bit, but several important transitions took place in countries such as Indonesia, Mexico, and Nigeria (all three are now partly free). By 2006, the proportion of free countries in the world had risen to 47 percent of all nations, while the number of countries rated "not free" had declined to 23 percent, almost a perfect reversal of the ratio in 1972.

Of course, that is the percentage of free countries in the entire world, including the highly developed nations of Europe, North America, and Oceana. So, the percentage of free nations in the developing nations alone is obviously lower (see Table 2.2 for a breakdown of Third World regions). However, the recent *pace* of democratic change has been faster in the developing world than anywhere else.

In 1998, student-led demonstrations in Indonesia, the world's fourth most populous nation (and the world's largest Muslim country), toppled its long-standing military dictatorship and opened the way for the nation's first democratic elections since independence. One year later relatively free elections

TABLE 2.1   The Global Growth of Democracy: 1972–2006

Year	Percent of Free Countries	Percent of Partly Free Countries	Percent of Countries Not Free	Number of Countries in the World
1972	29.0	24.8	46.2	145
1985	33.5	33.5	32.9	167
1996	41.0[a]	31.0	28.0	191
2006	47.0[a]	30.0	23.0	193

[a]Freedom House rounded out data for these years to the nearest percentage point.

Sources: Larry Diamond, "Is the Third Wave Over?" *Journal of Democracy*, vol. 7, no. 3 (July 1996), 20–37; Freedom House, *Freedom in the World 2007*, http://www.freedomhouse.org.

TABLE 2.2   Democracy by Region (2006)

Region	Free Countries (percent)	Partly Free Countries (percent)	Countries Not Free (percent)
Latin America and the Caribbean[a]	70	27	3
Asia and the Pacific	41	31	28
Sub-Saharan Africa	23	46	31
The Middle East and North Africa	6	33	61

[a]The Freedom House data were adjusted to remove Canada and the United States (developed countries) from the Freedom House category called "The Americas."

Source: Freedom House, *Freedom in the World 2007*, http://www.freedomhouse.org.

in Nigeria, Africa's most populous country, brought an end to its long-standing military regime.[26] In 2007 that administration handed power to another elected government, the first time this had happened since Nigeria's independence in 1960. And, at the start of the twenty-first century, Vicente Fox was elected president of Mexico (Latin America's second most populous nation), ending the 71-year reign of the PRI, the world's longest-ruling political party.[27] Most recently (2006), mass protests forced Nepal's king to relinquish his emergency powers and recognize parliamentary sovereignty.

Table 2.2 reveals substantial differences in the extent of democratic government within major regions of the Third World. Latin American and Caribbean nations are the most likely to be free, while the Middle East and North Africa lag far behind, with Sub-Saharan Africa somewhere in between. But even in Sub-Saharan Africa, between 1988 and 1994, Freedom House evaluations suggested that the number of electoral democracies rose from only 3 to 18.[28] Using a less stringent definition of democracy, Michael Bratton and Nicolas van de Walle calculated that 5 of 47 Sub-Saharan states were electoral democracies in 1988, with that the number rising to 21 by 1994.[29] And, in 2006, Freedom House classified over two-thirds (69 percent) of that region's governments as either Free or Partly Free. Worldwide there has been substantial progress in every region except the Middle East and North Africa (Table 2.2).[30]

INTERNATIONAL CAUSES AND CONSEQUENCES OF THE THIRD WAVE

Obviously, widespread political change of this magnitude is inspired and influenced by broad currents that transcend the politics of any particular nation. A number of factors contributed to the recent democratic transitions. For one thing, the economic crises that devastated so many developing nations in the 1980s revealed that their authoritarian regimes were no more effective and no less corrupt than the elected governments that they had contemptuously swept aside years before (indeed, they were frequently less efficient and more dishonest). Furthermore, because dictatorships lack the legitimacy that free elections bestow on democratic governments, their support depends much more heavily on satisfactory job performance. So when authoritarian governments in countries such as Argentina, Nigeria, and Peru dragged their country into war, economic decay, or rampant corruption, their support rapidly eroded. In Africa, the gross mismanagement and dishonesty of both military and single-party regimes caused their already-poor economies to implode, as the continent's per-capita GNP declined by some 2 percent annually throughout the 1980s. Within Latin America, the economic record of military rulers was relatively strong in Chile and for a period of time in Brazil, but military regimes fared poorly elsewhere. In time, almost all of the region's authoritarian governments were undermined by the 1980s' foreign debt crisis.

By contrast, many East Asian dictatorships (most notably in South Korea, Taiwan, Indonesia, and Singapore) enjoyed spectacular economic success from the 1960s through the late 1990s. However, rather than generate wider support for those governments, rapid economic growth and modernization often generated a burgeoning middle class possessing democratic aspirations and the political skills to pursue them. As the number of informed citizens grew, many of them resented government repression, state corruption, and the absence of opportunities for meaningful political participation.

Throughout the world, no sooner had democratic upheavals occurred in one nation than they then spread quickly to neighboring countries. In Eastern Europe, Poland's Solidarity movement inspired democratic challenges in Hungary, East Germany, and Czechoslovakia. They, in turn, prompted protests in Bulgaria, Albania, and Romania. Students in South Korea watched television news stories covering antigovernment demonstrations in the Philippines and took the lessons of "people's power" to heart.

As the democratic tidal wave swept forward, some authoritarian leaders began to get the message. Generals in Ecuador and Paraguay watched neighboring military dictatorships fall and decided to abdicate while the going was still good. After more than 40 years of political domination by the mainland Chinese minority and authoritarian rule by the Kuomintang Party, Taiwan's government opened up the political system to authentic electoral competition and political freedom. In Africa, a number of single-party states liberalized their political systems, allowing greater freedom and political space for opposition groups, while a smaller, but growing, number transformed themselves into liberal democracies (including Benin, Cape Verde, Ghana, Mali, and São Tomé & Príncipe).

As we noted earlier, the demise of Soviet and Eastern European communism exposed more clearly the deficiencies of their ideology and behavior. As Marxism-Leninism was discredited, even among many of its once-fervent adherents, democracy assumed greater worldwide legitimacy. The end of the Cold War also permitted the United States to be more consistent in its advocacy of political freedom. That is to say, the United States now had no reason to coddle allied Third World dictators whose friendship it had previously cultivated in the struggle against Soviet communism. For example, the United States had supported corrupt and repressive dictators in Zaire, Iran, and the Philippines, because they were considered necessary allies in the Cold War. With the collapse of the Soviet bloc, there was less reason to stand by such regimes. There remain, however, notable exceptions as the United States maintains close ties to several repressive regimes, including strategically important Pakistan and several oil-rich countries, most notably Saudi Arabia.

To be sure, the United States and Western Europe had already been more actively championing Third World democratic reform in the years preceding the fall of Soviet communism. The Reagan administration, for example, reversed its initial support for Chile's military dictatorship and allowed America's reform-minded ambassador to that country to work closely with the democratic opposition. But the end of the Cold War permitted Washington to pursue its democratic agenda more aggressively. In the Caribbean—where the United States once supported such notorious dictators as Fulgencio Batista (Cuba), Rafael Trujillo (Dominican Republic), and "Papa Doc" Duvalier (Haiti)—President Bill Clinton threatened U.S. military intervention in Haiti unless its generals allowed the country's elected president, Jean Bertrand Aristide, to return to office.[31]

THE PREREQUISITES OF DEMOCRACY IN INDIVIDUAL COUNTRIES

Although international developments served as catalysts, providing developing countries with incentives and opportunities to democratize, not all developing nations reacted to those forces in the same way. Today (more than 30 years after the start of the Third Wave), some LDCs—such as North Korea, Myanmar, and Saudi Arabia—remain mired in dictatorship, with no openings in the political system to date. Others—such as El Salvador, Mozambique, and Thailand—are either in some stage of democratic transition or have alternated between authoritarianism and weak democracy. Finally, some fortunate countries (including Chile, Costa Rica, Botswana, South Africa, South Korea, and Taiwan) seem to have consolidated their democracies.[32]

What accounts for these differences? What determines whether a particular country embarks on the road toward democracy, whether it completes that voyage successfully, and whether it eventually consolidates democratic values, practices, and institutions? For example, how do we know whether democracy will take root and survive in Brazil, Indonesia, or Madagascar? Finally, why has democracy advanced further in some regions, such as Latin America, than in other regions such as the Middle East?

As with most fundamental questions about politics, there are no simple answers. Scholars have debated these issues for decades and have identified a number of historical, structural, and cultural variables that help account for democracy's presence in, say, India and Uruguay, and its absence in countries such as Syria or Laos. But experts still disagree about the relative importance of those variables. In the discussion that follows, we examine a number of factors that have been widely identified as prerequisites for democracy.

Social and Economic Modernization

Over 40 years ago, Seymour Martin Lipset observed that democracy was far more prevalent in industrialized countries such as the United States and Sweden than in poorer nations—a finding congruent with modernization theory (Chapter 1).[33] Subsequent political science research has largely supported that claim. The reasoning behind this relationship was that

> industrialization leads to increases in wealth, education, communication and equality; these developments are associated with a more moderate lower and upper class and a larger middle class, which is by nature moderate; and this in turn increases the probability of stable democratic forms of politics.[34]

Over the years, statistical analysis has identified more precisely the particular aspects of modernization that promote democracy. Philips Cutright determined that when other factors are held constant, there is a strong correlation between the extent of a country's mass communications and its degree of democracy, stronger even than the correlation between economic development and democracy.[35] A free and active mass media and opportunities for citizens to exchange ideas, he reasoned, promote a free society. Years later, Axel Hadenius, examining the influence of dozens of independent variables, found that democracy correlates most strongly with higher levels of literacy and education.[36] An educated population, it appears, is more likely to follow politics and to participate in that process. It is also more capable of defending its own interests. Thus, one hopeful sign for the future of democracy in the LDCs is the substantial growth of literacy in recent decades. For example, since 1965 adult illiteracy in the developing world has fallen by more than half, with the rate currently at about 20 percent.[37] As we have noted, countries whose populations are over half literate are far more likely to sustain democracy than those that fall below that mark. Similarly, Mitchell Seligson has found an income threshold for sustaining democracy. Although that dollar amount has risen over the years (because of inflation), the per-capita income threshold at which democracy becomes likely is currently about $2,500.[38]

That does not mean that countries inevitably become more democratic as their economies develop. In fact, there is evidence that middle-income countries are frequently less stable and more prone to dictatorship.[39] For example, in the 1960s and 1970s, although some of South America's most industrialized countries (Argentina, Brazil, Chile, and Uruguay) were ranked as upper-middle-income nations by the World Bank, their democratic governments fell to military dictatorships. These exceptions are quite important, but the long-term global evidence still shows a correlation between economic development and democracy. While poor countries may be as likely as richer ones to make the transition to democracy, they are less likely to *sustain* democratic government. In recent decades, for example, East Asia's rapid economic growth, higher literacy, and expanding middle classes promoted democratic transitions in South Korea, Thailand, and Taiwan (though Thai democracy was suspended, at least temporarily, in 2006). In Latin America, where levels of modernization are relatively high by Third World standards, democracy has been spreading since the close of the 1970s. Conversely, Africa, which is home to most of the world's poorest nations, has had less democratic success.

However, as the Third Wave of democracy has spread to further reaches of the developing world, the correlation between economic development and democracy has weakened somewhat. In fact, a growing number of very poor countries has overcome the odds and established some level of liberal democracy.

As of 2004, there were 38 countries with per-capita incomes of $3,500 or less that Freedom House rated as "free" (liberal democracies), 15 of which had incomes of $1,500 or less.[40]

Class Structure

Some scholars maintain that it is not economic growth per se that induces and sustains democracy but rather the way in which that growth affects a country's social structure. Specifically, they reason, economic development supports stable democracy only if it induces appropriate changes in the country's class structure.

Since the time of Aristotle, political theorists have linked democracy and political stability to the presence of a large and vibrant middle class. The middle class, they suggest, tends to be politically moderate and serves as a bridge between the upper and lower classes. Its members also have the political and organizational skills necessary to create political parties and other important democratic institutions. So, in those countries where economic growth fails to create a politically independent and influential middle class, modernization does not necessarily buttress democracy and may even weaken it. In fact, the political independence and influence of the emerging middle classes have varied between regions of the world, depending on the historical period in which they industrialized. For example, industrialization and urbanization produced a larger, more powerful, and more independent middle class in Northern Europe than it did one century later in Latin America. In the latter case, wealth and income were more concentrated and the middle class correspondingly weaker and more dependent. Predictably, democracy did not take hold as readily in Latin America as it had in Northern Europe.

Barrington Moore Jr. in his widely acclaimed study of economic and political change, *The Social Origins of Dictatorship and Democracy*, identified three discrete paths to modernization, each shaped by the relative power of the state and the strength of the major social classes. In one path, typified by nineteenth- and early-twentieth-century Germany, modernization was led by a strong state allied with powerful and antidemocratic agricultural land owners and a bourgeoisie (business class) that was dependent on the state. In Germany and subsequently in Third World countries with similar political configurations, that combination ultimately resulted in the rise of fascism (or other far-right authoritarian regimes). A second path to modernization, found in countries such as China, was characterized by a highly centralized state, a repressive land-owning class, a weak bourgeoisie, and a large and eventually rebellious peasantry. The end result of that alignment was a communist revolution fought by the peasantry.

Finally, Moore's third path, identified most closely with Britain, featured a weaker state and a strong bourgeoisie at odds with the rural land-owning elite. Only this alignment of forces, distinguished by the bourgeoisie's powerful and independent political role, has led to liberal democracy. "No [strong and independent] bourgeoisie," Moore noted, "no democracy."[41] Similarly, in developing nations today, a vibrant middle class, including an influential business class (bourgeoisie), has been a critical ingredient in the establishment and consolidation of democracy. It should come as no surprise, then, that in countries as diverse as Chile, Indonesia, the Philippines, and South Korea, middle-class citizens, including university students (often the children of the bourgeoisie), have been on the front lines in recent struggles for democracy. During the 1992 pro-democracy street demonstrations that brought down Thailand's military government, student leaders were observed using their cell phones to coordinate the protests—a far cry from Southeast Asia's peasant revolutions decades earlier.

Very poor countries, such as Afghanistan, Haiti, Kenya, and Nepal, whose middle classes are small and dependent on the state or on rural landlords, are far less likely to attain or maintain democracy. But it is also important to remember that even though a strong middle class and bourgeoisie are necessary for democracy, those sectors are not always democratically oriented. For example, in pre-Nazi (Weimar) Germany and in Argentina and Chile during the 1970s, as the middle class felt threatened by social unrest from below, many of its members came to support fascist or other right-wing extremist dictatorships.

More recently, Rueschemeyer, Huber Stephens, and Stephens have focused attention on the importance of organized labor in building democracy. They argue that while the bourgeoisie and the middle class generally fostered democracy in Western Europe, Latin America, and the Caribbean, those groups usually favored a restricted form of democracy that enhanced their own political strength (vis-à-vis the upper class and the state) but also limited the political influence of the lower class. Consequently, countries have only achieved comprehensive democracy when, in addition to a large bourgeoisie, they also had a politically potent working class organized into labor unions that pushed for broader political representation and increased social justice.[42]

In summary, democracy tends to flourish best where economic modernization produces a politically influential and independent bourgeoisie/middle class and where labor unions effectively defend the interests of the working class. When any of those classes are small, weak, or politically dependent on authoritarian elements in society such as powerful rural land owners, democratic development is less likely.

Political Culture

In the final analysis, however, neither a country's level of socioeconomic development nor its class structure can fully explain whether or not it has been able to democratize. For example, during the early decades of the twentieth century, Argentina was one of the most affluent nations on earth (far wealthier than Italy or Japan), with substantial middle and working classes. Yet the country failed to develop into a liberal democracy. Instead, it embarked on a half-century of recurring coups and military dictatorships. More recently, Singapore, South Korea, and Taiwan retained authoritarian governments for many years after those countries had reached the normal social and economic thresholds for democracy.[43] Also, Middle Eastern petroleum states such as Kuwait and Saudi Arabia have made little progress toward democracy despite their considerable economic wealth. On the other hand, India sustained democracy for decades despite its extensive poverty and very low literacy rate until recently. And, several African nations have become democratic in recent years despite literacy rates well below 50 percent. The same holds true for a growing, though still small, number of low-income countries.

Aside from its level of economic development and its class structure, a nation's democratic potential is also influenced by its political culture—that is, its cultural beliefs, norms, and values relating to politics. A country's constitution may call for contested elections, a free press, and the separation of powers, but unless the people, especially elites and political activists, value these objectives, constitutional protections are unlikely to have great weight. Some of the most important values needed to sustain democracy include a widespread conviction that one's vote and other forms of individual political participation are important and potentially productive; tolerance of dissenting political opinions and beliefs, even when those views are very unpopular; accepting the outcome of free and fair elections as definitive, regardless of who wins; viewing politics as a process that requires compromise; and, commitment to democracy as the best form of government, regardless of how well or poorly a particular democratic administration performs. Obviously in no country will every citizen subscribe to all of these values or beliefs, but democracy normally is only sustainable if a large portion of the population supports them.

The recent wave of successful democratic transitions has renewed interest in how a country's political culture affects its capacity to consolidate democracy. Survey research allows us to measure more precisely the nature of a society's political beliefs. For example, polls conducted after the collapse of the Soviet Union revealed that Russia had yet to develop a broadly based democratic political culture. Only one in eight Russians expressed confidence in the new postcommunist administration. A substantial minority, distressed by Russia's economic decline, yearned for the security and stability of the communist era, and many respondents cared little for protecting civil liberties and minority rights. For example, almost one in three favored the death penalty for homosexuals and for prostitutes.[44] That intolerance has faded since then, but there is still widespread prejudice against groups such as Russians of central Asian origin. Moreover, the country's political elite has manifested little spirit of compromise. One cause for optimism, however, is that younger Russians are more likely to endorse democratic values than older citizens are.

Robert Dahl, a leading democratic theorist, observes that all political systems eventually confront a major crisis such as the Maoist insurgency in Nepal or ethnic violence in Nigeria. At those times, political leaders in unconsolidated democracies are often tempted to seek authoritarian solutions such as limiting civil liberties or imposing martial law.[45] If, however, a broad segment of the population (including portions of the political and economic elites) shares democratic values—that is, if a democratic political culture has taken root in society—democracy can survive the crisis intact. Dahl stresses two particularly important democratic values: first, the armed forces and police must willingly submit to the control of democratically elected civilian authorities; second, government and society must tolerate and legally protect dissident political beliefs.

The first value (civilian control of the military) is taken for granted in industrialized democracies, but not in countries such as Guatemala, Bangladesh, and Turkey, where the armed forces often have exercised veto power over the policy decisions of elected officials. Even in a relatively consolidated democracy such as contemporary Chile, the military has insisted on substantial autonomy. Dahl's second cultural standard (tolerance of dissent) also presents a challenge to many developing countries where even freely elected governments sometimes silence critics and muzzle opposition leaders. The crucial question, then, says Dahl, is: "How can robust democratic cultures be created in countries where they previously have been largely absent?"[46] He responds that there is no easy answer; developing a democratic culture is a gradual process in which socioeconomic modernization and political development need to reinforce each other.

Sometimes external actors may promote or even impose a democratic political culture on another country, as U.S. occupation forces did in Japan after World War II. Many African and Asian countries were first introduced to modern politics by the colonial powers that controlled them. Analysis of developing countries reveals that one of the factors most closely associated with democratic government today is having once been a British colony.[47] Of course, not all former British colonies are democracies; in fact, until recently most of those in Africa have not been. However, in general, countries that experienced British colonial rule were significantly more likely to maintain democracy after independence than were those nations previously colonized by France, Belgium, the Netherlands, Spain, or Portugal. This pattern suggests that Britain more successfully inculcated its colonies with democratic values than did other European powers. However, external intervention has had a mixed record of success. And, today, many analysts question whether the current U.S. intercession in Afghanistan and Iraq will contribute to the emergence of a democratic culture in those two nations.

It seems obvious that a country's political culture influences its political system in some manner. For example, communities with high levels of mutual tolerance and citizens who actively follow politics are more hospitable to democracy than are less tolerant or less knowledgeable societies. But how fixed in a nation's psyche are such values? Is there something inherently more democratic or more authoritarian about Norwegian, French, or Chinese cultures? Are some religions or philosophies, such as Christianity, more conducive to democracy than, say, Confucionism? Here scholars disagree strongly. Cultural stereotypes are inherently controversial and often prejudiced. But is it not possible that objective analysis might show that countries with certain religions or cultural traditions are more likely to support democratic values, while others are more prone to authoritarianism? In fact, the data clearly show that predominantly Christian nations, particularly Protestant ones, are more likely to be democratic than are countries with other dominant religions, even when other causal factors (such as economic development or literacy) are held constant. For example, Protestant countries are more likely to be democracies than are countries with other religions, even when economic differences are controlled. "Protestantism is said to foster individual responsibility and is thereby also more skeptical and less fundamentalist in character."[48]

More recently, observers have noted democracy's poor record of accomplishment in Islamic countries, especially in the Middle East. Some maintain that Islamic beliefs do not readily support democratic institutions because they fail to separate religion and politics (i.e., church and state). Similarly, when impressive economic growth and increased educational levels during the 1970s and early 1980s failed to bring democracy, at least initially, to China, Singapore, South Korea, and Taiwan, some experts concluded that cultural constraints must have been overriding the positive influences of economic modernization. They argued that Confucian culture promotes rigidly hierarchical societies and encourages excessive obedience to authority, values that are antithetical to democracy.[49]

Not surprisingly, cultural explanations such as these are highly controversial. They are very difficult to prove and often smack of prejudice and ethnocentrism. Thus, Catholics may feel uneasy with theories that contrast the traditional strength of democracy in the United States, Canada, and the English-speaking Caribbean with Latin America's authoritarian tradition and conclude that Catholic values offer less support for democracy than Protestant norms.[50] Similarly, most Muslims and Confucians reject theories that depict their religions as authoritarian. But do the facts support these hypotheses, however unpleasant some people may find them?

Although Protestant nations are more likely to be democratic than are countries with other religions, and even though democracy surely has not fared well in most Islamic nations, it is difficult to ascertain how much these disparities reflect contrasting religious values rather than myriad other historical, economic, and cultural factors that are not easily controlled. We know that several Islamic nations—including Turkey, Lebanon, Malaysia, and, most recently, Indonesia—have achieved a degree of democracy. Moreover, Alfred Stepan and Graeme Robertson have demonstrated that, while Arab countries, even wealthier ones, have rarely achieved democracy, *non-Arab* Muslim nations are at least as likely to be democracies as a matched sample of non-Muslim countries with comparable levels of economic and social development.[51] Finally, if Islamic and Catholic cultures inherently promoted nondemocratic values, one would expect that American Catholics would be less democratically inclined than their Protestant counterparts are. Similarly, we would predict that Bosnian Moslems would be less committed to democracy than Bosnian Serbs (Christians) and Indian Moslems would be less democratic than Hindus. But there is no evidence to support any of those predictions.

Furthermore, even if it were true that certain religions are more likely to predispose their adherents toward democracy or toward authoritarianism, there is so much variation within most world religions (e.g., Unitarian and Southern Baptist branches of Christianity, or Shi'a, Sunni, and Sufi sectors of Islam), each with its own political subculture, that it is misleading to suggest that there is a uniform Protestant, Muslim, or Buddhist political culture.

Finally, religious and political cultures are capable of change and do not permanently mire a country or region in a particular value system. For example, during World War II, the Japanese and German political cultures were considered militarily bellicose and authoritarian. Today, however, these countries are highly consolidated democracies whose citizens are far less inclined to support armed interventions (such as in Iraq) than Americans are. Similarly, not long ago, many analysts viewed Confucian values as obstacles to East Asian democratization. However, despite such pessimism, Confucianism has apparently not impeded South Korea's and Taiwan's democratic transitions. The fact that Catholic societies were less hospitable to democracy in the past did not mean that they remained so in the closing decades of the twentieth century. Indeed, from Portugal and Spain to Chile, Brazil, and Uruguay, democracy has recently taken root in Catholic nations that not long ago were depicted as culturally authoritarian. Moreover, in recent decades the Church hierarchy itself has been a pivotal voice for democratic change in Catholic countries such as Poland, the Philippines, Chile, and Brazil.[52]

In short, political cultures appear to be more malleable than previously recognized. As Larry Diamond notes, often "democratic culture is as much the product as the cause of effectively functioning democracy."[53] Just as democratic values support democratic consolidation, sustained democratic *behavior* helps inculcate democratic values. Therefore, while some new democracies may initially lack a healthy democratic political culture, the longer they continue democratic practices, the better are their chances of absorbing democratic values. Indeed, if a country can sustain democracy for two decades, it is relatively unlikely to ever fall. For example, Robert Dahl's examination of 52 countries in which democracy had collapsed identified only two (Chile and Uruguay) that had enjoyed democracy for more than 20 years prior to that collapse.[54] And even those two exceptions have since more successfully reinstituted democracy than have neighboring countries such as Bolivia and Peru, which lack comparable democratic traditions. The Czech Republic has enjoyed a similar advantage over its Eastern European neighbors.

HOW DO DEMOCRACIES PERFORM?
PUBLIC POLICY COMPARED

To be sure, some of the benefits of democracy are obvious: protection of civil liberties and government subject to the consent of the governed, to name but a few. Nonetheless, over the years scholars have debated whether democratic governments also better provide for the economic and social welfare of their citizens. As we noted earlier, during the closing decades of the twentieth century, many governments, international agencies, journalists, and scholars maintained that certain dictatorships—in countries such as Chile, China, Indonesia, Singapore, South Korea, and Taiwan—had imposed the efficiency and discipline necessary to generate rapid economic growth.[55] The dramatic economic growth these authoritarian regimes produced was often compared to the less impressive performance of democratic governments in India and Uruguay.

But, the passage of time and a more complete examination of over 100 LDCs dispel such claims. Generally, proponents of authoritarian rule in the service of economic development base their argument on the accomplishments of a few impressive cases. But for every authoritarian star economic performer— including China, South Korea, Singapore, and Taiwan—there were far more authoritarian regimes with disastrous economic records—such as Myanmar, Tajikistan, and Zimbabwe. In fact, "between 1960 and 2000, 95 percent of the world's worst economic performances . . . were overseen by nondemocratic governments."[56] Furthermore, prior to its market-oriented reforms begun in the late 1980s, China's communist leadership had a much more erratic record of economic growth. Chile's rate of growth was generally strong under its military dictatorship, but growth improved when the country restored democracy. Finally, during the past two decades, the once-stagnant economy of India—the world's largest democracy—has become one of the most dynamic in the world.

Analyzing annual economic growth data from more than 150 countries between 1960 and 2001, Halperin, Siegle, and Weinstein compared the performance of nations classified as democracies with those of autocracies (dictatorships). They found that in every one of the more than 40 years studied, the democratic nations as a group grew faster than the autocracies. Furthermore, "citizens of democracies live longer, healthier lives, on average, than those in autocracies [with comparable per capita incomes]."[57] To be sure, when they examined only the world's poorest nations, they observed no difference in the economic growth rate of democracies versus dictatorship. Still, even among the poorest countries, economic growth was less volatile in democracies than in autocracies (less subject to sharp ups and downs). Similarly, Dani Roderik used regression analysis to examine data for more than 80 countries over a period of 24 years (1970–1994). He found that there was no appreciable difference between the long-term economic growth rates of democracies and authoritarian governments. But, democracies outperformed authoritarian regimes on several other important economic indicators. Their economies were less volatile, more predictable, paid better wages to workers, and could "handle adverse shocks [like the Asian financial crisis or severe jumps in oil prices] much better."[58] Finally, another recent study comparing democracies with nondemocracies found that democratic countries spent more on public education, had higher school enrollments, higher literacy rates, and greater public access to health care services.[59]

In theory, democratically elected government officials should be less corrupt than officials in authoritarian regimes because they are held accountable in the next election. But in countries that have simultaneously switched from command economies to capitalism, in nations that have enormous sources of natural resource wealth (such as oil revenues) linked to the government, and in countries with a historical tradition of corruption, democratization may not improve government honesty and may actually make things worse. Thus, for example, Russia's transition to capitalism and the enormous quantities of petroleum previously controlled by the state opened up a floodgate of corruption. In Cambodia, the communist regime has been replaced by a government of competing "mafias."

Nigeria has both extensive petroleum reserves and a tradition of deep government corruption. The military governments that had ruled the country for 16 years were enormously dishonest, even by Third World standards, and turned their leaders into billionaires. But, the 1999 transition to democracy brought little improvement. The Nigerian government is still considered one of the most corrupt in the world. Governors of the country's 36 states "get a check each month that represents their state's cut of Nigeria's booming oil fortune, and have almost no one to answer to for how they spend that money."[60] Small wonder that some governors, when faced with serious electoral opposition in their bids for reelection, have threatened the lives of their opponents and, in some cases, had them eliminated.

DEMOCRATIC CONSOLIDATION

It is important to keep in mind that while the breadth of democratic transitions in the developing world has been impressive, political change can occur in both directions. Countries that have achieved electoral or liberal democracy have seen their new governments fail, followed by a return to authoritarian rule. In 1994, a military coup in Gambia ended 28 years of democratic government. Recent examples of renewed authoritarianism include Pakistan, Bangladesh, and Thailand. Between 1980 and 2000, democracy collapsed in 26 countries, though a number of those (such as Ecuador and Turkey) subsequently resumed being free or partly free.[61] What makes democracy endure or falter? Which of the Third World's new democracies have the qualities needed to consolidate democracy? To answer that question, Adam Przeworski and his associates analyzed data for 135 countries during a period of 40 years.[62] Democracy, they found, is most fragile in poor countries (with per-capita incomes of less than $1,000), and it becomes more stable as national income rises. "Above $6,000 [per-capita income], democracies are impregnable and can be expected to live forever; no democratic system has ever fallen in a country where per-capita income exceeds $6,055 (Argentina's level in 1976)."[63] Several factors explain why richer democracies are more likely to last. For one thing, they normally have a crucial foundation for democratic government—high educational levels.[64] For another, class conflict over the distribution of economic rewards is typically less intense in more affluent societies.

Contrary to what many political scientists had believed, Przeworski et al. also found the faster a nation's economy grows, the more likely it is to sustain democracy. Conversely, democracy is less likely to survive in countries suffering economic decline, high inflation rates, or other forms of economic crisis. However, important as domestic economic factors are, the authors discovered that international political conditions exert a more powerful influence on democratic survivability. Specifically, the more prevalent and fashionable democratic government becomes worldwide, the more likely any particular Third World country is to sustain democracy, regardless of its per-capita income, literacy rate, or economic growth rate. In other words, as many scholars had suspected, democracy is contagious. Other analysts have noted that developing and maintaining effective political institutions—including representative and responsible political parties, a broad array of interest groups, a representative and influential legislature, a strong but controlled executive branch, an honest and independent judicial system—are absolutely critical for maintaining stable and effective democracy. Too often Third World judicial systems lack independence from the executive branch, lack adequate legal training, and are excessively corrupt. Consolidating democracies must strengthen their judiciary systems, so that they can stand up to power-hungry presidents or prime ministers and so that court decisions are respected by the electorate. A related problem in many new and reestablished democracies is executive-branch dominance over the national legislature. In Latin America, Russia, and elsewhere, democratically elected presidents have sometimes interpreted their electoral victories to mean that the voters had effectively delegated absolute authority to them. For example, although elected democratically, Presidents Carlos Menem (Argentina) and Alberto Fujimori (Peru) ran roughshod over their nation's congress and court system upon assuming office. That is perhaps one reason that Juan Linz and Arturo Valenzuela have found that democracy is more likely to collapse in presidential systems than in countries with parliamentary forms of government.[65]

Improving the Quality of Democracy

Some three decades after the start of the Third Wave, its reach has become far broader than the previous two waves, and, equally importantly, to date there has been no extensive backlash. To be sure, a number of new democracies have collapsed. But, there has been no "reverse wave," no widespread reversion to authoritarianism comparable to what followed the first and second waves. The fact that democracy has been accepted so widely as the best form of government, is cause for satisfaction. At the same time, however, in many Third World countries (and former communist nations), democratic governments have failed to meet the needs of their citizens. While free and fair elections, improved civil liberties, and civilian control over the military are all important achievements, too often democratic rule has not lived up to mass expectations. As a consequence, many political scientists have turned their attention from the consolidation of democracy (making it last) to improving the *quality* of democracy. In recent times, public opinion surveys in both advanced industrial democracies and Third World democracies have indicated that citizens are generally becoming more distrustful of government and suspicious of political parties and politicians. Frequently they consider government officials corrupt and self-serving. The search for higher quality democratic government, then, has two important objectives: first it is a moral imperative (fair, effective, and honest government is obviously desirable); second, more effective and honest democratic government normally increases support for democracy and, thereby, increases democracy's longevity. Larry Diamond and Leonardo Morlino argue that the quality of democracy can be envisioned in terms of seven dimensions, which, in turn can be grouped into three broad categories:[66]

1. *Procedural Dimensions:* The procedures used to elect government officials and the procedures that the state uses to govern must be honest, fair, and equitable. These procedures can be divided into five categories:
   A. Participation: All adult citizens must have the right to vote as well as to participate in the political system in other ways. Powerful groups should not intimidate the poor or ethnic minorities from participating. A politically aware citizenry should not allow apathy to restrict their own participation.
   B. Competition: There should be free and fair elections between competing political parties, and the incumbent party should not have any built-in advantage in gaining access to state funds or to the media. The electoral system should not give certain parties automatic advantages.
   C. Accountability: While a democratic electoral system must guarantee that government officials are fairly elected, it is also important that officials be held accountable for their actions between elections. Vertical accountability refers to procedures that allow citizens or independent groups to challenge or criticize a government official's behavior. Horizontal accountability refers to the ability of one government body to check the power of another branch, such as the Supreme Court overruling a decision by the president or the parliament removing a prime minister.
   D. The Rule of Law: The legal system must apply equally to all citizens and all laws must be publicly known and clear. The judiciary must be neutral and independent.

2. *Substantive Dimensions:* Beyond adhering to proper procedures, quality democracies must pursue policies that advance:
   A. Respect for Civil Liberties and the Pursuit of Freedom: This includes respect for individual liberty, security and privacy, freedom of information, expression, and religion, and due process.
   B. Reductions in Political, Economic, and Social Inequalities: In order to attain political equality, where there is substantial social and economic inequality, government needs to reduce income gaps. Scholars such as Terry Karl and Dietrich Rucschemeyer argue political equality, and democracy are not feasible in the face of glaring income inequality in Latin America and parts of Africa.[67] Different analysts, however, will disagree on how much equality is desirable or acceptable.
3. *Result Dimensions:* This final category includes only a single dimension—Responsiveness. A democratically responsive government is one in which "the democratic process induces the government to form and implement policies that the people want."[68] In order to achieve that there needs to be a stable political party system, with parties that offer coherent and distinguishable programs.

CONCLUSION

Too frequently, democratic transitions have produced unfulfilled economic aspirations, corrupt government, and widespread dissatisfaction with government institutions. Naturally, this has made many Third World citizens cynical about the *performance* of democratic regimes, even though most of them maintain an abstract belief in democracy as a form of government. In 2004 the United Nations Development Program commissioned a survey of 18,643 citizens in 18 Latin American countries. Although Latin America is the Third World region that has made the most far-reaching progress toward democracy, the study uncovered growing disillusionment regarding its ability to remedy poverty and economic stagnation. Thus, "while a broad majority (64 percent) of those interviewed said they agreed that democracy is the only system capable of achieving development, about half (52 percent) admitted they would not mind if an authoritarian regime came to power as long as it could solve their financial problems."[69] Indeed, 55 percent of all respondents said that they would favor a dictator over a democratically elected leader if that improved their economic conditions.[70] The latest survey by Latinobarómetro (2006) demonstrated a modest increase in support for the concept of democracy. Thus, 74 percent of the 18,000 respondents agreed that "democracy may have its problems but it is the best form of government," up from 64 percent three years earlier. At the same time, however, their evaluation of the specific performance of their own democratic governments was far more negative. In 2005 and 2006 surveys, respondents were asked "Would you say that [your country] is governed for the benefit of a few powerful groups or is it governed for the good of all?" Some 70 percent chose "for the benefit of a few powerful groups" while only about 25 percent chose "for the good of all." Similarly, most Latin Americans had low opinions of fundamental democratic institutions such as their political parties or the national congress.[71]

Afrobarometer's survey of 18 Sub-Saharan African nations in 2005–2006 revealed that, despite the checked history of elections in that continent, citizens had a surprisingly positive view of elections in their own country. Two-thirds (66 percent) believed that their most recent national election was either completely or largely free and fair. Most Africans (62 percent) continued to agree that "democracy [as an ideal] is preferable to any other kind of government." But, like Latin Americans, they had become disillusioned with the performance of their new democratic governments. For example, even though 46 percent of the population believed that elections worked well or very well at ensuring that their parliament reflects the views of the voters, almost as many (40 percent) disagreed. Moreover, only one-third felt that their parliamentary representatives listen to what their constituents have to say, while fully two-thirds felt that they never or only sometimes listened.[72] Most troubling, the number of respondents who were satisfied with democracy as it is practiced in their country declined from 58 percent in 2000 to 45 percent in 2005–2006.[73]

To date, it appears that even the large number of Third World inhabitants who have been dissatisfied with their democratic government's performance have tacitly accepted Winston Churchill's conclusion that "democracy is the worst form of government except for all the others that have been tried . . ." But, without some improvement in social conditions during the coming years, democratic governments may no longer be able to command the support of the poor. In Latin America, where income inequality is higher than in any region of the world, the gap between "haves" and "have nots" has generally widened since its transition to democracy. Similarly, income inequality has soared in post-communist Eastern Europe and the former Soviet Union. From Colombia to the Philippines and from Pakistan to Peru, the poor suffer from highly unequal land and income distribution, pervasive poverty, rising crime rates, inadequate public health service, and corrupt police and judicial systems. Until such injustices are addressed, democracy will remain incomplete and precarious.

DISCUSSION QUESTIONS

1. Discuss the differences between electoral democracy, liberal democracy, and substantive democracy. Which definition seems most useful to you?
2. What is the Third Wave of democracy, and what accounts for its emergence?
3. Which social classes have historically been most supportive of democracy, and which have been most antagonistic? What kind of class structure is most likely to support democratic consolidation?
4. What is the evidence that some religions are more supportive of democracy than others? What are the strengths and weaknesses of the argument that there is a link between a country's religion and its potential for democracy?
5. What is the relationship between social and economic development, on the one hand, and democracy, on the other?
6. Some analysts have argued that authoritarian governments are better able to manage the early stages of economic development. Others have insisted that democratic governments have better records of economic development. What are the arguments and the evidence on each side?
7. Compare the performances and policy commitments of democratic versus authoritarian governments as they relate to economic growth, education, and health care.

NOTES

1. Serbia was the most powerful of six republics that constituted the Yugoslav federation. Other republics included Bosnia-Herzegovina, Croatia, Macedonia, and Slovenia. In 2003, after those four republics seceded from Yugoslavia, the remaining two republics formed the Federation of Serbia and Montenegro. Four years later, Montenegro's citizens voted to secede from that union and its two republics became independent states.

2. Saddam Hussein did not use his family ("last") name, which was al-Majd. Saddam was his given ("first") name and Hussein was his father's given name. While some news sources call him Hussein as a shortened version, he is normally referred to in the media and in scholarly accounts as Saddam or Saddam Hussein, but not Hussein.

3. Richard Joseph, "Africa: The Rebirth of Political Freedom," in *The Global Resurgence of Democracy*, eds. Larry Diamond and Marc F. Plattner (Baltimore, MD: The Johns Hopkins University Press, 1993), 307–320. The terms "electoral democracy" and "liberal democracy" are discussed in greater detail later in this chapter. Briefly, electoral democracies are governments that have free and fair elections. However, a number of those governments have weak records in the areas of civil rights and individual liberties and are, thus, not fully democratic. Liberal democracies are political systems that have both competitive elections and civil liberties.

4. As noted in footnote 3 and later in this chapter, "electoral democracies" elect their political leaders democratically, but do not have the level of civil liberties and freedoms found in "liberal democracies." For example, contemporary Latin American electoral democracies in Colombia, Guatemala, and Venezuela permit or author serious human rights violations.

5. By definition, consolidation of democracy reduces military rule. It also lowers the likelihood of revolutionary movements. Greater democracy also should eventually contribute to better conditions for women, the urban poor, and peasants, though those effects are not necessarily immediately apparent.

6. For example, Samuel P. Huntington, *The Third Wave: Democratization in the Late Twentieth Century* (Norman: University of Oklahoma Press, 1991).

7. Colombia is one of Latin America's more enduring electoral democracies, but its government is also perhaps the region's worst human rights violator. See *New York Times* (April 26, 1994). Sri Lanka's civil war seemed to be nearing

an end not long ago but peace negotiations broke down and hostilities have resumed.

8. Of course, in all democracies some high-ranking office holders are appointed. In the United States these include the justices of the Supreme Court and members of the cabinet. But these people are appointed by a popularly elected official (the president) and are subject to confirmation by the Congress. Note that, if the standard of near-universal suffrage were applied, the United States would not be considered a democracy prior to the 1960s because large numbers of southern Blacks were barred from voting. In the nineteenth and early twentieth centuries, of course, women also could not vote.

9. There has been a long, ongoing debate over what conditions, and how many of those conditions, a country must meet in order to be called a democracy. The definition offered here represents the current consensus and is drawn from the following sources: Philippe C. Schmitter and Terry Lynn Karl, "What Democracy Is and Is Not," *Journal of Democracy*, vol. 2, no. 2 (Summer 1991), 75–88; Scott Mainwaring, "Transitions to Democracy and Democratic Consolidation," in *Issues in Democratic Consolidation: The New South American Democracies in Comparative Perspective*, eds. Scott Mainwaring, Guillermo O'Donnell, and Samuel Valenzuela (Notre Dame, IN: University of Notre Dame Press, 1992), 297–298; Robert A. Dahl, *Polyarchy: Participation and Opposition* (New Haven, CT: Yale University Press, 1971); Robert A. Dahl, *Democracy and Its Critics* (New Haven, CT: Yale University Press, 1989); Huntington, *The Third Wave*.

10. Civil society is essentially the array of societal organizations—churches, unions, business groups, farmers' organizations, women's groups, and the like—that may influence the political system, but operate independently (i.e., they are free of government control). Frequently, authoritarian governments weaken civil society, so that it does not generate a challenge to their rule. Consequently, rebuilding and strengthening civil society are essential tasks for establishing and consolidating democratic government.

11. Huntington, *The Third Wave*, 28–30.

12. Juan Linz and Alfred Stepan, "Toward Consolidated Democracies," in *Consolidating the Third Wave Democracies*, eds. Larry Diamond, Marc F. Plattner, Yun-han Chu, and Hung-mao Tien (Baltimore, MD: The Johns Hopkins University Press, 1997), 15.

13. Seymour Martin Lipset, *Political Man: The Social Basis of Politics*, expanded and updated

(Baltimore, MD: The Johns Hopkins University Press, 1980). For a review of such research see Dietrich Rueschemeyer, Evelyne Huber Stephens, and John D. Stephens, *Capitalist Development and Democracy* (Chicago: University of Chicago Press, 1992), chap. 2.

14. Samuel P. Huntington, *Political Order in Changing Societies* (New Haven, CT: Yale University Press, 1968).

15. Mitchell A. Seligson, "Democratization in Latin America: The Current Cycle" in *Authoritarians and Democrats: Regime Transition in Latin America*, eds. James M. Malloy and Mitchell A. Seligson (Pittsburgh, PA: University of Pittsburgh Press, 1987), 7–9. Since the time that Seligson did his research, the mid-1980s, literacy rates have risen sharply and few countries now have rates below 50 percent.

16. It is generally agreed that the emergence of the middle class and business class (bourgeoisie) in Western Europe was associated with the growth of modern democracy. See, for example, Barrington Moore Jr., *The Social Origins of Dictatorship and Democracy* (Boston: Beacon Press, 1966). More recently, political scientists such as Rueschemeyer, Huber Stephens, and Stephens, *Capitalist Development*, have emphasized the contributions of organized labor.

17. Quoted in Morton H. Halperin, Joseph T. Siegle, and Michael M. Weinstein, *The Democracy Advantage* (New York: Routledge and the Council on Foreign Relations, 2005), 25.

18. Of course, even defenders of authoritarian governments had to concede that most dictatorships are not efficient modernizers. Far from it! The developing world has had more than its share of corrupt dictators (Mobutu in Zaire, Somoza in Nicaragua, Marcos in the Philippines) who have stolen millions, run their country's economy into the ground, and wrecked the nation's infrastructure and educational system. What these scholars did claim, however, was that *efficient* dictatorships such as Taiwan's or Singapore's offered the best hope for modernization. Communists saw revolutionary dictatorships, such as Cuba or China, as necessary for greater social equality, improved literacy, better health care systems, and related indicators of modernization.

19. For example, Glen Caudill Dealy, *The Latin Americans, Spirit and Ethos* (Boulder, CO: Westview Press, 1992). The ground-breaking major study of political culture was Gabriel A. Almond and Sidney Verba, *The Civic Culture: Political Attitudes and Democracy in Five Nations* (Boston: Little, Brown and Company, 1965), which examined political culture in the United States, Britain, Germany, Italy, and Mexico.

20. "Introduction," in *Women in African Parliaments*, eds. Gretchen Bauer and Hannah E. Britton (Boulder: CO: Lynne Rienner Publishers, 2006), 10.

21. Larry Diamond, "Introduction: In Search of Consolidation," in *Consolidating the Third Wave Democracies*, xv. While Diamond suggests there were 39 democracies, Samuel Huntington counted only 30 at that time. Part of the reason for Huntington's lower total is that he excluded from his research any country with a population below 1 million.

22. Huntington, *The Third Wave*, 271.

23. Huntington's *The Third Wave* refers to these setbacks as a "reverse wave." It appears that the reversal following the Third Wave will be much smaller than the first and second reverse waves.

24. Because Freedom House receives funding from the U.S. government and recent members of its board of directors have included several prominent neoconservatives such as Donald Rumsfeld and Paul Wolfowitz, some critics have accused the organization of having a conservative and pro-American bias. However, its founders included Eleanor Roosevelt and its board has also included prominent liberals and civil rights leaders. During the Cold War, it tended to evaluate communist regimes more harshly than repressive but pro-American dictatorships. But it has also criticized right-wing dictatorships in countries such as Chile (under General Pinochet) and in current American allies such as Saudi Arabia.

25. The panel of experts rates each country's level of political rights and civil liberties on a scale of 1 (most free) to 7 (least free). Countries which had an average score of 1.0–2.5 for these two factors were categorized as "Free." Those with average ratings of 3.0–5.0 were ranked as "Partly Free." And those countries with ratings of 5.5–7.0 were labeled "Not Free."

26. International observers agreed that the election was deeply flawed by fraud and that the winner, Umaru Yar'Adua, had certainly not honestly attained the landslide victory with which he had been credited. But, it is likely that he still would have won an honest vote count.

27. I have not included the 2003 ouster of Iraqi dictator Saddam Hussein in this chronology of democratic transitions because his regime was toppled by foreign intervention, rather than by internal forces. Moreover, while the level of violence has diminished since the 2007 American troop surge, as of this writing (2008) there has been very little political progress and limited democracy.

28. Larry Diamond, *Prospects for Democratic Development in Africa* (Stanford, CA: Hoover

Institution Press, 1997), Appendix; Adrian Karatnycky, "The 1999 Freedom House Survey: A Century of Progress," *Journal of Democracy*, vol. 11 (January 2000), 187–200.

29. Michael Bratton and Nicolas van de Walle, *Democratic Experiments in Africa: Regime Transitions in Comparative Perspective* (New York: Cambridge University Press, 1997), 120.

30. *Freedom in the World 2007*, http://www.freedomhouseorg/uploads/press_release/fiw 07_charts.pdf. If this page no longer exists, go to freedomhouse.org and follow the links. See endnote 25 for an explanation of Freedom House's scoring.

31. Ironically, years later, following an uprising against Haiti's Aristide, the Bush administration helped force him from power. For a broader discussion of international influences favoring democratization, see Laurence Whitehead, ed., *The International Dimensions of Democratization: Europe and the Americas* (New York: Oxford University Press, 1996); Abraham F. Lowenthal, ed., *Exporting Democracy: The United States and Latin America* (Baltimore, MD: The Johns Hopkins University Press, 1991).

32. Determining whether or not democracy has been consolidated (i.e., has become "the only game in town") in any particular country is a judgment call over which experts may disagree. Only the test of time ultimately reveals whether a democratic government has endured.

33. Seymour Martin Lipset, *Political Man*, 1st ed. (Garden City, NY: Anchor Books, 1960).

34. Rueschemeyer, Huber Stephens, and Stephens, *Capitalist Development and Democracy*, 14.

35. Philips Cutright, "National Political Development: Measurement and Analysis," *American Sociological Review*, vol. 28, no. 2 (April 1963), 253–264.

36. Axel Hadenius, *Democracy and Development* (New York: Cambridge University Press, 1992).

37. United Nations Development Programme, *Human Development Report, 2004*, Table 1: Human Development Indicators, http://hdr.undp.org// reports/global/2004; UNESCO Institute for Statistics, September 2006 report, http://www.uis.unesco.org/ev.php?URL_ID=5204&URL_DO= DO_TOPIC&URL_SECTION=201.

38. Seligson, "Democratization in Latin America: The Current Cycle."

39. Huntington, *Political Order in Changing Societies*. On the rise of repressive authoritarian regimes in Latin America's most industrialized nations, see Guillermo O'Donnell, *Modernization and Bureaucratic Authoritarianism* (Berkeley, CA: Institute of International Studies, 1973).

40. Adrian Karatnycky, "National Income and Liberty," *Journal of Democracy*, vol. 15 (January 2004), 82–93. As literacy rates have climbed sharply in poorer Third World nations, the gap in literacy between relatively higher-income LDCs and much poorer ones has narrowed. Thus, today even very poor countries generally exceed Seligson's threshold of 50 percent literacy.

41. Barrington Moore, *The Social Origins*, 418.

42. Rueschemeyer, Huber Stephens, and Stephens, *Capitalist Development and Democracy*.

43. South Korea and Taiwan have subsequently democratized, but Singapore still has not.

44. Stephen White, "Russia's Experiment with Democracy," *Current History*, vol. 91 (October 1992), 313.

45. Even in a deeply consolidated democracy such as the United States, many critics charge that the threat of terrorism has promoted troubling infringements on this country's civil liberties. These include the Homeland Security Act and subsequent implementation following the 9/11 Al Qaeda attacks.

46. Robert Dahl, "Development and Democratic Culture," in *Consolidating the Third Wave Democracies*, 34.

47. Kenneth A. Bollen and Robert Jackman, "Economic and Non-economic Determinants of Political Democracy in the 1960s," in *Research in Political Sociology*, ed. R. G. Braungart (Greenwich, CT: JAI Press, 1985).

48. Hadenius, *Democracy and Development*, 118–119.

49. Samuel P. Huntington, "Will More Countries Be Democratic?" *Political Science Quarterly*, vol. 99 (1984), 193–218; Huntington, *The Clash of Civilizations and the Remaking of World Order* (New York: Simon & Schuster, 1996).

50. For an argument along those lines, see Dealy, *The Latin Americans*.

51. Alfred Stepan with Graeme B. Robertson, "An 'Arab' More than 'Muslim' Electoral Gap," *Journal of Democracy*, vol. 14, no. 3 (July 2003), 30–44.

52. Daniel Philpott, "The Catholic Wave," *Journal of Democracy*, vol. 15, no. 2 (April 2004), 32.

53. Larry Diamond, "Three Paradoxes of Democracy," in *The Global Resurgence of Democracy*, 104.

54. Robert A. Dahl, "The Newer Democracies: From the Time of Triumph to the Time of Troubles," in *After Authoritarianism: Democracy or Disorder?* ed. Daniel N. Nelson (Westport, CT: Greenwood Press, 1995), 7.

55. See, for example, M. G. Quibria, *Growth and Poverty: Lessons from the Asian Economic Miracle*

(Asian Development Bank, Working Paper No. 33, 2002); more broadly, Huntington's *Political Order* argues that countries in the early stages of development often need authoritarian government.

56. Halperin, Siegle, and Weinstein, *The Democracy Advantage*, p. 13.

57. Ibid., p. 35. See also, pp. 29–43. Data were collected from the Polity IV project, an inter-university project which collects a wide range of data on all the world's nations with populations exceeding 500,000. Polity ranks each country on a scale of 1 to 10 based on its degree of democracy.

58. Deni Roderik, *Democracy and Economic Performance* (Cambridge, MA: Unpublished Paper, Harvard University, December 14, 1997), 2. See also, pp. 7–10.

59. Iñias Macías-Aymar, "Does Income Inequality Limit Democratic Quality?" in *An Unequal Democracy?* eds. Carlo Benetti and Fernando Carillo-Flórez (Washington: Inter-American Development Bank, 2005), 84–85.

60. *New York Times*, "Money and Violence Hobble Democracy in Nigeria" (November 24, 2006).

61. Halperin, Siegle, and Weinstein, *The Democracy Advantage*, 71.

62. Adam Przeworski et al., "What Makes Democracies Endure?" in *Consolidating Third Wave Democracies*, ed., 295–311.

63. Ibid., 297. All dollar figures are in constant dollars, meaning that they are adjusted for inflation, so that a per-capita income of $1,000 in 1960 and 1990 is actually equivalent.

64. In other words, countries that are more economically advanced have higher literacy and education rates, and countries with higher literacy rates are more likely to be democratic. There are several petroleum-producing countries in the Middle East (such as Saudi Arabia and the United Arab Emirates) which, though wealthy, do not have exceptionally high literacy rates. None of those are democracies.

65. Juan Linz and Arturo Valenzuela, eds. *The Failure of Presidential Democracy* (Baltimore, MD: The Johns Hopkins University Press, 1994).

66. The ideas in this section are based on Larry Diamond and Leonardo Morlino, *Assessing the Quality of Democracy* (Baltimore, MD: The Johns Hopkins University Press, 2005), a collection of writings by leading scholars in the field. My major adaptation from Diamond and Morlino's introduction was to combine vertical and horizontal accountability into one category.

67. Terry Lynn Karl, "Economic Inequality and Democratic Instability," *Journal of Democracy*, vol. 11 (January 2000), 149–156; Dietrich Rueschemeyer, "Addressing Inequality," in *Assessing the Quality* ed.

68. G. Bingham Powell Jr., "The Chain of Responsiveness," in *Assessing the Quality*, 62.

69. Inter-American Development Bank News, "*Democracy and Wallets*" (April 1, 2004), http://www.iadb.org/news/articledetail.cfm?Language=EN&artid=2019&artType=WS.

70. *New York Times* (April 22, 2004 and June 24, 2004).

71. Corporación Latinobarómetro, *Latinobarómetro Report 2006: Online Data Bank*, http://www.latinobarometro.org/uploads/media/Latinobar_metro_Report_2006.pdf.

72. "Citizens and the State: New Results from Afrobarometer Round 3" (Afrobarometer, Working Paper Number 61, 2006), www.afrobarometer.org/papers/AfropaperNo61.pdf.

73. "Afrobarometer Media Briefing" (May 24, 2006) and "Afrobarometer Briefing Paper No. 40" (November, 2006), http://www.afrobarometer.org/papers/AfrobriefNo40.

CHAPTER 3

RELIGION AND POLITICS

A death knell for traditional religion was sounded in the 1960s, not by an opponent of religion but by one of America's preeminent Protestant theologians, Harvey Cox. He was not predicting the demise of religion per se, but rather the end of its traditional form, including its historic role in politics and other areas of public life. Cox's influential book, *The Secular City*, coincided with the observations and predictions of social scientists at that time. And while religion obviously remained a pervasive force in the Third World, secularization of society seemed inevitable there as well.

In Latin America the Catholic Church no longer exercised nearly as much control over education or reproductive rights as it once did. Following independence, the government of India tried to ameliorate the injustices of the caste system, a cornerstone of Hindu religious practice. And in the Middle East, modernizing regimes in Egypt, Syria, and Turkey created more secular political systems. Accordingly, one leading authority, Donald Eugene Smith, observed, "Political development includes, as one of its basic processes, the secularization of politics, the progressive exclusion of religion from the political system."[1]

Generally speaking, early modernization theorists viewed religion as an impediment to political and economic development, while dependency theorists deemed it so unimportant as to warrant only an occasional footnote in their writings (see Chapter 1). Since the time Cox and Smith chronicled its decline, however, religion has been an unexpectedly resilient political force that has withstood the onslaughts of modernization. In some instances, such as prerevolutionary Iran, rapid and destabilizing modernization has even stimulated a militant religious backlash. As David Little has observed, "Modernization was supposed to mean the gradual decline and eventual disappearance of religion from public life, but, as we know, that hasn't happened. Religion is very much alive as a part of politics."[2] In fact, since the 1970s much of the Third World has experienced a religious resurgence, which has intensified the role of religion in the political arena.[3] In the Middle East, "ironically, the technological tools of modernization have often served to reinforce traditional belief and practice as religious leaders who initially opposed modernization now use radio, television, audio- and videotapes to preach and disseminate."[4]

Nowhere is the change more apparent than in the Middle East and parts of Africa and Asia, where a resurgence of Islamic fundamentalism (or *Islamism*, the term preferred by many scholars), along with an intensification of sectarian violence between Sunni and Shi'a, has had a dramatic political impact on Afghanistan, Algeria, Iran, Iraq, Lebanon, Egypt, Pakistan, Somalia, Saudi Arabia, and Sudan. The 1979 seizure of American hostages in Iran, subsequent hostage-taking in Lebanon, the assassination of Egyptian President Anwar Sadat, the attack on a U.S. air force barracks in Saudi Arabia, the bombing of two U.S. embassies in East Africa, recurring suicide bombings in Iraq, and, above all, the 9/11 attack on the World Trade Center and the Pentagon all have focused Western attention on "religion and politics." Subsequent Islamist terrorist attacks on mass transit in Madrid and London along with the civil war between Shi'ites and Arab Sunnis in Iraq have reinforced that focus. In fact, since the end of the Cold War, radical (militant) Islamic fundamentalism has supplanted Soviet communism as the greatest perceived threat to Western security. Well before the first Gulf War, a Gallup Poll survey revealed that 37 percent of British respondents expected a war in the 1990s between Muslims and Christians.[5] The U.S. overthrow of Afghanistan's Taliban government, the Taliban's recent resurgence, the Iraqi quagmire, and ongoing Al Qaeda-linked terrorism have fortified that perspective. While Western anxieties are sometimes based on prejudice and misunderstanding, the discussion of Islamic and Hindu fundamentalism that follows later indicates reason for concern.

THE MEETING OF CHURCH AND STATE

Many preconceptions about religion and politics are based on serious misunderstandings, both of our own government and of political systems elsewhere. Americans generally accept a constitutional separation between church and state as the normal state of affairs (though some may wish to blur that line). That formal barrier, however, does not exist in many industrialized democracies and LDCs. Moreover, even in the United States, religious organizations and beliefs continue to influence political behavior. Black Baptist churches, for example, were in the forefront of the American civil rights movement. Since the 1980s, the so-called "Christian right" has been an influential force within the Republican Party. In recent decades, conflicts over issues such as school prayer and abortion have led one expert to observe that "far from rendering religion largely irrelevant to politics the structure of [American] government may actually encourage a high degree of interaction."[6] Most Western European nations, though more secular in many ways than the United States (and less church-going), have not built walls between religion and politics. In Britain, for example, the Anglican Church (or Church of England) is the official state religion. Italy's Catholic Church was closely linked to the Christian Democratic Party, once that nation's dominant political party.[7]

Religion is even more firmly embedded in many Third World cultures, and its impact on politics is correspondingly more pronounced. Indeed, religion is so central to traditional values that we often identify national or regional cultures by their predominant religion: Buddhist culture in Thailand, Confucian culture in China and Korea, Hindu culture in much of India and Nepal, and Islamic culture in North Africa and the Middle East.[8]

The blending of religion and politics is most apparent in theocratic states (political systems dominated by religious leaders and institutions) such as Iran where, since that nation's 1979 Islamic revolution, public policy has been governed by the Shi'a clergy. Similarly, Afghanistan's Taliban government made national politics an extension of religion. But it is also significant in Islamist (Islamic fundamentalist) states like Sudan, and in American allies such as

Pakistan and Saudi Arabia. In Latin American countries such as Brazil and Nicaragua, the theology of liberation, espoused by radical Catholics, motivated priests and nuns to organize the poor against economic and political injustices. And in India, the Bharatiya Janata Party (BJP), which led the country's governing coalition from 1998 to 2004, carries the torch of Hindu fundamentalism.

GREAT RELIGIONS OF THE THIRD WORLD

Four of the world's "great religions" are predominant in the Third World. Catholicism, the only major religion to have penetrated extensively into both industrialized democracies and the developing world, is preeminent in the Philippines and Latin America and also represents significant portions of the population in a number of Sub-Saharan African countries.[9] Hinduism is the dominant religion only in India and neighboring Nepal. However, there are also Hindu populations exceeding 1 million persons in nearby Bangladesh, Indonesia, Sri Lanka, Pakistan, and Malaysia, as well as significant immigrant communities in South Africa and English-speaking Caribbean nations such as Trinidad-Tobago. Buddhism is a major religion in East Asia, Southeast Asia, and parts of South Asia. Finally, Islam, the world's second largest religion, predominates across a broad span of Asia, the Middle East, and Africa, from Indonesia in the east through Pakistan and Bangladesh in the Indian subcontinent to the former Soviet republics of Central Asia, into the Middle East, and North Africa. It also represents about half the population of Malaysia and Nigeria, as well as substantial minorities in countries as far-flung as the Philippines, Tanzania, and Trinidad-Tobago.[10]

To be sure, not everyone in the developing world belongs to one of these major religions. Protestantism is the leading religion in the English-speaking islands of the Caribbean and represents important minorities in a number of other LDCs. Confucianism (perhaps more a philosophy and way of life than a religion) still influences Chinese society, even after its revolution, as well as Japan, South Korea, and Taiwan. Christian Orthodox minorities are significant in Lebanon and Egypt, while many Africans believe in local traditional religions. The impact of these religions on politics, however, is more limited. Consequently, this chapter limits its analysis to the four global religions mentioned earlier, with particular emphasis on Islam and Catholicism.

None of the Third World's major religions is monolithic, though the Catholic Church, with its doctrine of papal infallibility and its hierarchical structure, comes closest. Buddhism has two major schools, each basing its doctrines on certain ancient texts. Theravada ("Way of Elders" or Southern) Buddhism, practiced in Myanmar, Sri Lanka (Ceylon), Thailand, Laos, Cambodia, and parts of Vietnam, is an older form of Buddhism. Mahayana ("Great Vehicle" or Northern), a later, politically more liberal, form of Buddhism emerged in China, Japan, Korea, most of Vietnam, and Tibet.[11] In some religions, most notably Buddhism, doctrinal differences have not provoked political conflict or violence, but in others, particularly Islam, conflict has often been intense and violent.

The most important division within Islam is between its major branches, Sunnism and Shi'ism. The split between them, dating to the decades following the death of the Prophet Muhammad (570–632 A.D.), centered on the issues of "who should succeed him and the nature of the successor's [spiritual and political] role[s]".[12] Today, the Shi'ites have a more hierarchical clergy than the Sunnis, and they revere their most prominent politico-religious leaders, particularly the Imam (the Guide), who must be a direct descendant of the Prophet Muhammad and his son-in-law, Ali. As one scholar notes, "Shi'ism makes a cult of death and martyrdom," including "pilgrimages to the tombs of the Imams and their descendants."[13] Religious practices of the two branches also differ somewhat. To be sure, the two communities live in peace in some countries, and there are frequently intermarriages, even in nations such as Iraq. Moreover, the similarities in their beliefs far outweigh the differences. Yet, many Sunnis do not consider the Shi'a authentic Muslims, and many Shi'a resent Sunni political domination. Differences between each group's political power and social status often exacerbate these tensions. In the chapter that follows this one (The Politics of Cultural Pluralism and Ethnic Conflict), we will examine political conflicts in Iraq and Lebanon linked to these discrepancies.

Today, 85–90 percent of the world's 1–1.5 billion Muslims are Sunni, while Shi'ites account for about 10–15 percent (there is also a small Sufi branch). Shi'ism is the dominant faith only in Iran and the small nations of Azerbaijan, Oman, and Bahrain. But Shi'ites also constitute over half of Iraq's population, a plurality in Lebanon, and significant minorities (15–35 percent) in Yemen, Pakistan, Syria, Kuwait, Afghanistan, and Saudi Arabia. Countries such as Iraq, Lebanon, and Syria, with significant Sunni and Shi'a populations, have experienced sharp political and cultural tensions between the two.[14] In countries in which each group represents a sizable segment of the population, Sunnis have almost always enjoyed greater political power and social status, even when they were in the minority. Consequently, Shi'ites see themselves as "champions of the downtrodden," and glorify suffering and self-flagellation.

Other religions that lack such formal divisions may still include groups with competing theological or ideological outlooks. For example, even though they are united by a single church hierarchy, Latin American Catholics span the ideological spectrum from the ultra-conservative members of Opus Dei to leftist believers in liberation theology. In the name of God and anticommunism, some Latin American Catholics have supported fascist movements, rightist death squads, and repressive military regimes. Conversely, in the name of God and social justice, other Catholic priests and nuns have supported the Sandinista revolution in Nicaragua, fought with Marxist guerrillas in Colombia, and organized the poor in the slums of Brazil and Peru.

RELIGION, MODERNITY, AND SECULARIZATION

We have already observed that social and economic modernization does not necessarily reduce religious observance, at least not in the short run. What about the reverse side of that relationship? That is, what is the impact of religion on modernity? Here again, early analysts felt they were incompatible. "It is widely, and correctly, assumed," said Donald Smith, "that religion is in general an obstacle to modernization."[15] In the realm of politics, this interpretation suggested that the intrusion of religious institutions into government impedes the development of a modern state. Others associated traditional Catholic, Islamic, and Hindu beliefs with authoritarian values.

Subsequently, political scientists have developed a more nuanced understanding. Religious institutions may inhibit development in some respects, while encouraging it in others. For example, all of the great religions have legitimized the state's authority at some point in history. As nations modernize their political systems, religious authorities or groups may oppose important aspects of change (Hindu and Islamic fundamentalists, for example), or they may offer explicit or tacit support (Islamic leaders in Indonesia and the Catholic clergy in Chile). No longer facilely dismissing organized religion's contributions to development, many scholars now credit Confucianism with facilitating East Asia's rapid modernization in the second half of the twentieth century.[16] Specifically, they credit the Confucian work ethic and its spirit of cooperation.

Depending on their theology and structure, individual religions may either bolster or impede government development initiatives. Different religions emphasize distinctive values; thus, states wishing to create welfare programs based on communal responsibility (i.e., programs tied to ethnic communities) often receive strong support from Islamic leaders or the Catholic Church. At the same time, modernizing political leaders who emphasize individual rights and responsibilities find those values warmly received by Buddhist monks. Ultimately, then, organized religions can strengthen the modern nation-state by bestowing legitimacy and by disseminating the government's political message. Should religious leaders oppose the state, however, they can often delegitimize the political system.[17]

The argument that political modernization requires secularization has two components, one empirical and the other normative. The *empirical* component notes that as Western societies modernized (i.e., became more literate, urban, institutionally organized, and industrialized), their political systems almost invariably became more secular. In effect, Western societies experienced a specialization of functions. Increasingly, the state has controlled politics, while the church has overseen religion, and each has refrained from interfering in the other's realm. Political scientists anticipated that as the Third World modernized, it would experience the same division of responsibilities. The related *normative* assumption holds that secularization is not only a common trend, but it is also desirable because it increases religious freedom, reduces the likelihood of state persecution of religious minorities, and permits the state to make more rational decisions free of religious bias.

We have already indicated the weakness of the first assumption. To be sure, modernization has induced political secularization in many developing countries, such as Turkey and Mexico. But elsewhere it has not altered church-state relations; in fact, it frequently has precipitated a religious backlash when pursued too rapidly. Saudi Arabia, India, and Iran illustrate three possible governmental approaches to managing the forces of modernization. In the most cautious approach, the Saudi royal family has introduced far-reaching socioeconomic changes but has carefully controlled the style of modernization in order to preserve a very traditional Islamic culture and maintain the close links between Islam and the state. India represents an intermediate case, where the modernization of politics and constitutional secularization were widely accepted (at least until recently). Religious factors do affect the Indian government in some respects; thus, Hindus and Muslims are governed by distinct legal codes in areas such as family law. And while the prime minister's post has always been held by a Hindu (the majority religion), the largely ceremonial presidency has been reserved for a Muslim. Iran represents one of the most dramatic examples of religious backlash against modernization and a relinking of church and state. As we will see, the Shah (emperor) imposed rapid Western-style socioeconomic development (including "unveiling" women), which destabilized society and helped precipitate a radical Islamic revival.

At an individual level, many people in Africa, Asia, and the Middle East have defied the notion that more educated and professionally trained citizens will be less religiously orthodox. For example, Hindu and Islamic fundamentalist activists in India, Afghanistan, and Egypt are frequently professionals, not poor uneducated peasants.[18] Most of the terrorists who attacked the Pentagon and World Trade Center in 2001 were relatively well educated and middle class. And, the terrorists who failed in their 2007 attempt to bomb downtown London and the Glasgow, Scotland airport terminal were all health workers, mostly doctors. Nor are traditional religious values and modern technology necessarily incompatible. Evaluations of the church-state relationship need to be more complex than early development theory had assumed. Clearly, some religious influences contradict accepted norms of modernity, as when they induce political leaders to violate the rights of religious minorities (or majorities). Iran's Islamic government, for example, has persecuted members of the Baha'i faith.[19] In Guatemala, the government of General Efraín Rios Montt, a right-wing Evangelical, converted Catholic peasants to Protestantism at virtual gunpoint. Similarly, religiously inspired restrictions on women (common in Islamist societies) are clearly antithetical to modernization.

Can one infer from such cases, however, that there need always be a strict wall between politics and religion or between clerics and politicians? The same people who lamented the political activities of Catholic priests in Nicaragua and Brazil, the protest marches by Buddhist monks in Sri Lanka, or the Islamist (fundamentalist) government in Afghanistan may have cheered political involvement by Dr. Martin Luther King Jr. or the Reverend Jerry Falwell in the United States.

Ultimately, most people's normative evaluations of religion's role in politics are influenced by whether that religious activity furthers the goals and policies the observers believe in. Perhaps this is as it should be. The recent histories of Iran and Tibet illustrate this point well. Iran has been a theocracy (a religiously driven political system) since its 1979 revolution, just as Tibet had been prior to its absorption by China in the 1950s. Each has had a political system "in which the political structures are clearly subordinate to the ecclesiastical establishment."[20] Yet the world has judged them quite differently.

Under the leadership of its Islamic mullahs (clerics), Iran became an international outcast because of its repression of civil liberties, persecution of religious minorities, support for international terrorism, and its nuclear energy enrichment program. Until the late 1950s, Buddhist clerics also dominated Tibetan politics.[21] Viewed as divine by his people, the Dalai Lama had been the country's secular and spiritual leader. Buddhist monks held key posts in the government bureaucracy. Because of Tibetan Buddhism's record of pacifism and tolerance, however, theocratic rule aroused no foreign indignation. On the contrary, the world was appalled when China occupied Tibet and secularized the state. Since that time the Dalai Lama's long struggle to free his people has won him worldwide admiration and the Nobel Peace Prize. All of this suggests that the issue of separation of church and state may be less important than the way in which "the church" uses its political influence when it holds power.

STRUCTURAL AND THEOLOGICAL BASES OF CHURCH–STATE RELATIONS

The extents to which religions influence political attitudes and behavior and the degree of political involvement by organized religions vary considerably from place to place. Just as the separation of church and state in Western Europe has historically been more pronounced in predominantly Protestant nations (e.g., Denmark and Britain) than in Catholic ones (such as Italy and Spain), the political impact of the Third World's four major religions also differs. Two factors help define a particular religion's political involvement: its theological position regarding the relationship between temporal and spiritual matters; and the extent and strength of its hierarchical structure. The second factor refers to how well organized and centrally controlled a religion is.

Donald Smith distinguishes two different types of religio-political systems: the *organic* and the *church*. In the organic system, there is a weak or non-existent religious hierarchy. Hence the clergy is insufficiently organized as an institution to influence or challenge the country's political leaders, although their religious beliefs may still influence politics. Examples of organic systems include Hinduism and Sunni Islam in most cultures. Church religio-political systems, on the other hand, have a well-organized ecclesiastical structure that frequently exercises considerable political influence. These churches include Catholicism, Shi'a Islam, and Buddhism in some countries, such as Tibet and Myanmar. These normally have more official links between church and state, which may result in either greater religious challenges to the state (Brazil) or state domination of the church (Iran).[22]

Islam

From its inception in seventh-century Arabia, Islam has been a "religio-political movement in which religion was integral to state and society."[23] That remains particularly true in Shi'a communities. More than any other world religion, traditional Islam normally recognized no borderline between religion and politics. On the one hand, the Islamic faith and its clergy legitimized the state. At the same time, however, the political leadership recognized the supremacy of Islamic law, the Shariah (path of God). Thus, prior to the intrusion of colonialism, many Muslims assumed that they lived in an Islamic state. Because religious Muslims believe that God wants them to live in a community governed in accordance with the Koran (or Quran)—Islam's sacred scripture perceived as the word of God—the concept of separating church and state is alien to their culture. This does not mean that historically Islamic culture and theology were inhospitable to other religions. Perhaps because it accepted Jewish and Christian scriptures and drew from both of those religions since its inception, Islam was historically tolerant of other faiths. From the eight to the eleventh centuries, for example, the large Jewish community in Muslim-controlled Spain enjoyed greater freedom and influence than in most of Christian Europe.[24] But even then, ultimate political authority remained Muslim.

The bond between religion and politics remains strong in most Muslim societies today, though there is considerable variation. John Esposito distinguishes three types of Islamic regimes: the *secular state*, the *Islamic state*, and the *Muslim state*.[25] Since its formation in the early years of the past century, Turkey has been the most notable secular state in the Islamic world. Starting in the 1920s, Mustafa Kemal Ataturk (the father of modern Turkey) ousted the sultan of the Ottoman Empire, abolished the basis of the sultan's religious authority, emancipated women, closed down Muslim seminaries, and westernized Turkish society in many ways. Today, Turkey's constitution still mandates compulsory state-supervised "instruction in religious culture . . . in the curricula of primary and secondary schools."[26] But, this mandate was not designed to strengthen Islam, but rather to establish state control over Muslim religious instruction and over Islamic institutions. In the words of one leading Middle-East scholar, "the state [under Ataturk and his early successors] aimed to end the power of organized Islam and break its hold on the minds and hearts of the Turkish people."[27] Moreover, the constitution offers Islam no special status in society and guarantees "freedom of . . . religious belief."

At the other end of the spectrum, Islamic states base their governing philosophies on the Koran and Islamic law. Afghanistan (under the Taliban), Iran, and Saudi Arabia are among the best-known examples, but Sudan, Pakistan, and Libya also fall in this category. These regimes can be quite distinct from each other. Whereas Iran subscribes to Shi'a Islam, the other countries in this group are primarily Sunni. Islamic regimes in Afghanistan (before U.S. intervention), Libya, Iran, and Sudan have pursued militantly anti-Western foreign policies and supported international terrorism. On the other hand, Saudi Arabia is quite conservative and closely allied to the West (though it has often tried to appease Al Qaeda and other extremist groups for strategic reasons). Thus, the term Islamic state (like the concept of fundamentalism) must be applied carefully to avoid artificial categorization that hides more than it reveals.

Finally, Muslim states, such as Egypt and Morocco, occupy an intermediate position on church–state relations and the role of religion. Unlike secular states, they identify Islam as the official religion and require the head of state to be Muslim. However, the impact of religion on politics is far more limited than in Islamic states. For example, unlike Iran, Egypt's political leaders are not clerics, and some have not even been Muslims. For example, former Foreign Minister Boutros Boutros-Ghali, who later served as secretary general of the United Nations, is a Christian. So too is Iraq's Tariq Aziz, who served as Saddam Hussein's Deputy Prime Minister and Foreign Minister.

Catholicism

More than any other major religion, Catholicism has a well-defined and hierarchical ecclesiastical structure that enables it to have a considerable impact on the political system. At the Church's apex is the Pope, whose authority is unchallenged and whose pronouncements on matters of faith and morals are believed to be infallible. Consequently, papal declarations can carry considerable political weight. For example, many of the twentieth-century, Catholic reform movements in Latin America can be traced to Pope Leo XIII's 1891 encyclical, Rerum Novarum, which included an indictment of early capitalism's exploitation of the working class. Within each country, the Church hierarchy is headed by bishops, who often have tremendous political influence in Latin America and in other Catholic countries such as the Philippines.

Like Islam in the Middle East, Catholicism once was the state religion in many Latin American countries. For example, in Colombia as recently as 1953, government treaties with the Vatican gave the Church special authority in areas such as education.[28] Over the years, however, most Latin American nations either ceased having an official state religion or have rendered that link unimportant. Still, Church doctrine has generally supported the established political regime and helped legitimize it. "The ruling powers," said one encyclical, "are invested with a sacredness more than human. . . . Obedience is not the servitude of man to man, but submission to the will of God."[29]

That does not mean, however, that the Church has always supported the government. There have been periodic clashes between the two, most notably when the state challenged Church authority in areas such as education and, more recently, when it violated human rights. Thus in the Philippines, Church support of Corazón Aquino's political reform movement helped topple the dictatorship of Ferdinand Marcos. Similarly, Catholic authorities opposed conservative military dictatorships in Brazil and Chile during the 1970s and 1980s. At the same time, Church relationships with Marxist regimes in Cuba and Nicaragua were often tense, though relations with Castro's government improved after the Pope's visit to Cuba.[30] And, in the 1980s, Salvadorian Archbishop Oscar Romero spoke out forcefully against the regime's human-rights violations. He was subsequently assassinated by a military "death squad."

Hinduism and Buddhism

Asia's organic religions, Hinduism and Buddhism, usually have been less directly involved in politics than Catholicism and Islam have. To be sure, India's BJP, led by Hindu fundamentalists, has recently governed that country. But the party has no linkage to the Hindu "clergy," and its ranks include a small number of non-Hindus. Of course, Hinduism's cultural and philosophical values, most notably the caste system, have affected Indian and Nepalese politics profoundly. For example, the king of Nepal was considered until recently an incarnation of the god Vishnu.[31] But the religion is so diverse—composed as it is of local religious groups, cults, and sects loosely tied together by a common set of beliefs—that there is no centralized political influence. Moreover, although there are gurus, holy men, temple priests, and even a priestly caste (Brahmans, though most of them no longer choose to be priests), there is no ecclesiastical organization comparable to, say, the Catholic priesthood.

Buddhism grew out of the Hindu religion in the sixth century B.C., emerging from the teachings of a Nepalese prince, Siddhartha Gautama, who later came to be known as the Buddha (Enlightened One). Though greatly influenced by Hinduism, Buddhism rejects one of its basic tenets, the caste system.

Indeed, as Buddhism spread through Asia, one of its great appeals was its egalitarian outlook. In recent decades, many of India's untouchables have left Hinduism for Buddhism, a religion far more hospitable to them.[32] Buddhism differs from Hinduism in that it has an organized ecclesiastical organization, namely the sangha (the monastic orders). In some countries, such as Myanmar, each sangha has its own leader, providing a hierarchical structure. Still, when compared to the Roman Catholic Church or the mullahs of Shi'ite Islam, Buddhism's religious structure is much less centralized and, thus, less able to impact the political system.

To be sure, Buddhist and Hindu groups sometimes have strongly influenced their nation's politics. In the 1960s, for example, protests led by South Vietnamese Buddhist monks helped topple three successive government leaders in a short period of time.[33] Monks have led major protests against government violations of human rights in Tibet and Thailand as well. On the other hand, Myanmar's military regime brutally crushed prodemocracy demonstrations led by monks in 2007, arresting hundreds of them. In India, Hindu extremists have carried out periodic massacres of that country's Muslim community. But, these have been the exceptions, not the norm.

In addition to having less-hierarchically organized ecclesiastical orders, Eastern religions are less theologically inclined to political involvement than are Catholicism and Islam. Their otherworldly philosophy places less emphasis on such temporal matters as politics; hence, the remainder of this chapter focuses on the political impact of Islam and Catholicism in the Third World, with some discussion of Hindu fundamentalism as well.

RELIGIOUS FUNDAMENTALISM: ISLAM AND HINDUISM

No expression of religious influence on Third World politics has attracted more attention or inspired more fear and loathing than Islamic fundamentalism. In the 1980s and early 1990s, highly influential Washington columnists such as Morton Zuckerman (*U.S. News and World Report*) and Charles Krauthammer (*New Republic*) warned of Islamic "religious Stalinism" and a fanatical international movement orchestrated from Iran.[34] Nor are such concerns limited to Westerners. They are frequently expressed by the leaders of moderate Muslim nations who find themselves under siege from militant Islamists. Thus, for example, Tunisia's President, Zine el-Abidine Ben Ali, cautioned about a "fundamentalist international" financed by Iran and Sudan.[35]

The horrific September 11, 2001 attacks on the World Trade Center and the Pentagon confirmed the world's worst nightmares about Islamic fundamentalist terrorism. However, experts on Islam insist that it is unfair to blame a major world religion that has over 1 billion adherents for the actions of a small minority. President George W. Bush and other leading U.S. government officials went out of their way to make that very point in the days after the attack. Some people have noted that blaming the Islamic religion for Osama bin Laden's actions would be as misguided as holding Christianity responsible for violent actions taken in its name. For example David Koresh, head of a religious cult called the Branch Davidians, claimed to be acting in the name of Christianity when he included underage girls in his large harem and when he later led the group into battle with U.S. federal agents, resulting in the death of most of the group. More recently, a number of "pro-life" extremists have bombed abortion clinics and assassinated doctors who perform those procedures.

Others point out that not even all Islamists (fundamentalist Muslims) support violence. Indeed, many scholars reject the very term fundamentalism to describe current militant revivals. The word, they charge, may falsely imply the existence of a unified threat to the West and, in the case of Islam, it lumps together groups and regimes that have little in common, such as conservative Saudi Arabia and radical Libya. Instead, these analysts prefer such terms as revivalism or militancy or Islamist movements rather than Islamic fundamentalism. One author observes "that the term 'Islamic Fundamentalism' . . . possesses Christian roots and carries considerable emotional baggage that makes it offensive to many Muslims."[36] Still, a number of leading authorities accept and even use the label fundamentalism in their writings.[37] Fred Halliday notes that "there are some problems with applying the term fundamentalist to Muslim movements, but with the necessary caveats it can legitimately be so used."[38] In this chapter, I will use the term fundamentalism because of its common usage in contemporary political discourse. On occasion, however, I employ the terms revivalism (referring to its desire to revive the true faith) or Islamism to refer to Islamic fundamentalism, while the term Islamists refers to believers in Islamism.

Semantic questions aside, experts such as John Esposito and Fred Halliday warn that whatever labels they use, Western writers too often distort and exaggerate the nature of the "Islamic threat."[39] Many of those critics also seem unaware of the long tradition of liberal theology within Islam, which has advocated religious tolerance, progress for women, and democratic values.[40]

> At the very core of this supposed [Islamic] challenge or conflict lie confusions: the mere fact of peoples being "Islamic" . . . [has been confused] with that of their adhering to beliefs and policies that are . . . "Islamist" or "fundamentalist." It has been assumed . . . that most Muslims seek to impose a political program supposedly derived from their religion. The fact that most Muslims are not supporters of Islamist movements is obscured.[41]

Clearly, instances of Islamist terrorism in Israel, Western Europe, the United States, and other parts of the world (including the September 11 attacks) indicates that though it may be wrong—as Esposito and Halliday insist—to speak of an "Islamic threat," it is reasonable to speak of an "Islamist threat." Hopefully, this chapter's discussion of Islamic (as well as Hindu) fundamentalism conveys that distinction. Thus, when this text discuss Islamic and Hindu revivalism at some length, two caveats should be kept in mind: most Muslims and Hindus are not fundamentalists, and not all fundamentalists are repressive at home or violent abroad.

Defining and Explaining Fundamentalism

> Fundamentalism is the . . . effort to define the fundamentals of a religious system and adhere to them. One of the cardinal tenets of Islamic fundamentalism is to protect the purity of Islamic precepts from the adulteration of speculative exercises.

> Related to [Islamic] fundamentalism is . . . revival or resurgence, a renewed interest in Islam. Behind all this is a drive to purify Islam in order to release all its vital force.[42]

The precise meaning of fundamentalism varies somewhat from religion to religion.[43] But its adherents do share certain points of view across religious lines. To begin with, they all wish to preserve their religion's traditional worldview and resist the efforts of religious liberals to reform it. They also want to revive the role of religion in private and public life, including politics, lifestyle, and dress.

In the developing world, fundamentalism often appeals particularly to people who are disgusted by the inequalities and injustices in their country's political-economic system. This disgust reflects popular revulsion against local political and economic elites, against pervasive corruption, and against repression. In Lebanon the radical Hezbollah grew out of Shi'a resentment against the economically powerful Christian community, as well as anger against Israel and the West. In India, the BJP attracted some of its support from voters embittered by government corruption (though also from people of higher castes who were unhappy with their loss of privileges). And in Algeria, Egypt, and the Sudan, militant fundamentalists expanded their support as a result of government repression directed against them.[44]

Radical fundamentalists also tend to be nationalistic or chauvinistic, rejecting "outside" influences that they feel challenge or pollute their culture and their true faith. Islamists view Western culture as particularly insidious, perceived as featuring immodest dress as well as scandalous films and music that promote promiscuity and drugs. But they reject Western values for another reason as well. For years, government leaders, such as the Shah of Iran and Egypt's President Anwar Sadat, promoted Western-style modernization as the route to national development. After decades of failed development in the Middle East, North Africa, and other parts of the Third World, however, many of their citizens feel deceived and consequently look elsewhere for answers to their problems.

Fundamentalists: Radical and Conservative

Any analysis of revivalism must distinguish between radical and conservative fundamentalists. Radicals, inspired by a "sacred rage," feel that they are conducting a "holy war" against forces that threaten to corrupt their fundamental religious values.[45] As a Hezbollah manifesto declared, "We have risen to liberate our country, to drive the imperialists and the invaders out of it, and to take our fate in our own hands."[46] Islamic *mujahideen* ("holy warriors") in Afghanistan first waged *jihad* (holy war) against the country's Marxist government and the occupying Soviet troops who supported it.[47] Iran's Ayatollah Khomeini and Al Qaeda's Osama bin Laden both declared jihads against the United States ("the great Satan"). Elsewhere, battles have been waged against domestic enemies as well. Having been denied an almost certain electoral victory in 1992, when the military canceled parliamentary elections, Algeria's fundamentalist movement, the Islamic Salvation Front (FIS), attacked the nation's armed forces, the police, secular politicians, and foreigners.[48] Soon, more violent militant organizations, most notably the Armed Islamic Group (GIA), launched a war of terrorist attacks against Algerian civilians, often mixing banditry with religious warfare. From 1992 through early 2001, the GIA the armed forces, and government-supported civilian militias massacred more than 100,000 Algerians between them. In India, Hindu fundamentalists have periodically directed their rage against the country's Muslim minority. (For a more detailed discussion of the massive communal violence between Hindus and Muslims in the post independence period, see Chapter 4.) Elsewhere in recent years, Muslim extremists have killed innocent civilians in New York City, London, Madrid, Tel Aviv, and Baghdad.

Such radical militancy contrasts with the views and behavior of nonviolent fundamentalists, such as Hasidic Jews or Saudi princes, who do not see themselves in such a battle. To be sure, leaders of various nonviolent fundamentalist groups also wish to shield their flocks from unwanted outside influences, but they do not view believers in other religions or nonfundamentalist members of their own faith as enemies.[49]

In recent years, radical Islamic fundamentalists have been a major political force in Middle Eastern and North African countries such as Algeria, Lebanon, and Sudan as well as Afghanistan and Pakistan. Afghanistan's Taliban regime was surely the world's most rigidly fundamentalist. For example, it prohibited girls and women from attending school or working outside the home. Similarly, the Ministry for the Prevention of Vice and Promotion of Virtue banned television, sports events, dancing, and secular music. The prohibition on female employment meant that the country's estimated 50,000 widows (the legacy of years of war) and their dependants—numbering several hundred thousand—were denied any legal means of support.[50] The Taliban government also sheltered Osama bin Laden and his Al Qaeda terrorist group. Until the 1990s and the emergence of Al Qaeda's onto the world scene, however, radical Islamic fundamentalism's greatest international impact came from the Iranian revolution, which served as a beacon for other Islamist movements in various parts of the Muslim world.

"Sacred Rage and the Iranian Revolution": Radical Islamism as a Reaction to Western-Style Modernization

The origins of the Iranian revolution can be traced to the early decades of the twentieth century, with the Muslim clergy's resistance to a government program of secular modernization imposed by the royal family.[51] Military, political, and economic intervention by a series of foreign powers—Czarist Russia, Britain, and the United States—turned the country into "a virtual protectorate" and made the ruling Shahs (emperors) appear to be tools of the great powers.[52] Consequently, years later resentment against foreign domination became an important component of the Islamic revolution.

Starting with the reign of Shah Reza Pahlavi (1925–1941), the imperial government antagonized the Shi'a mullahs (clergy) with a series of modernizing reforms that included unveiling women, mandatory Western dress, and transferring control over various economic, educational, and political resources from the clergy to the state.[53] The Shah's son, Mohammed Reza Pahlavi, ruled from 1941 to 1979 as a close ally of the United States. His so-called "White Revolution" of the 1960s and 1970s expanded women's rights, extended general literacy, and promoted a land reform program that included the transfer of land from Islamic institutions to the peasants.

As a result of these programs, land was redistributed to some three million peasants, educational levels rose substantially, and oil wealth doubled the size of the middle class.[54] By 1976, Iran had the developing world's highest GNP per capita. On the other hand, the large gap between rich and poor widened, widespread government corruption alienated the population, and suspected political opposition was brutality suppressed by the Shah's dreaded secret police, the Savak. Because of his close ties to the U.S. government (including the CIA), many Iranians saw the Shah as a tool of American neocolonialism. At the same time, the Islamic clergy and other devout Muslims objected to the secularization of society and the intrusion of Western values and customs. As tension between the government and the mullahs intensified, a revered religious leader, the Ayatollah Ruhollah Khomeini, emerged as one of the Shah's leading critics.[55] When Khomeini was briefly imprisoned in 1964, riots erupted in several Iranian cities, culminating in an army massacre of up to 10,000 demonstrators.[56] Khomeini was sent into exile for nearly 15 years. The effect was to turn him into a martyr in a culture that greatly admires martyrdom, thereby greatly enhancing his influence over the masses. In January 1979, with much of Iran's urban population involved in strikes and demonstrations against the regime, the Shah went into exile. Khomeini returned home to a frenzied welcome shortly thereafter.

Three interrelated developments set the tone for the Islamic revolution. First was the merger of the country's religious and political leadership. The new "Islamic republic," declared the Grand Ayatollah, is "the government of God."[57] While nonclerical figures have since held many important government posts, including most of the seats in the parliament, ultimate power has resided in the hands of the Guardian Council (a body dominated by hard-line Islamist clerics), which has the power to overrule both the parliament and the president and can ban prospective candidates for office.[58]

The second important development was the revival of traditional Islamic observances. Women now must be veiled in public and are strongly encouraged to wear the chador, the shapeless shroud that conceals all parts of the body.[59] Highly intrusive Revolutionary Guards have penetrated all aspects of Iranian life, policing possible violations of "correct" Islamic behavior. In the first years of the Revolution (into the early 1990s) the Guards joined with neighborhood vigilante committees to arrest or harass Iranians who violated the clerics' highly conservative Islamic standards. During the 1980s, in the Shi'a tradition of martyrdom, many thousands of young volunteers died in a holy war against Iraq. Assuring their families that it was a privilege to die for the faith, the Ayatollah Khomeini proclaimed, "We should sacrifice all our loved ones for the sake of Islam. If we are killed, we have performed our duty."[60]

Finally, Iran's radical revivalism embraced an aggressive foreign policy that supported kindred Islamist groups abroad—such as Lebanon's Hezbollah—and was intensely antagonistic toward countries that its leaders consider enemies of Islam—especially, Israel and the Western powers. Prior to the revolution, Khomeini had declared, "America is worse than Britain! Britain is worse than

America! The Soviet Union is worse than both of them! They are all worse and more unclean than each other!"[61] The regime's hostility toward the outside world was best illustrated by two events.

First, on November 4, 1979, revolutionary students seized the U.S. embassy in Tehran, taking diplomats and embassy staff hostage in an extraordinary breach of diplomatic protocol and international law.[62] It was not until 444 days later that the last of the 52 hostages were released. For five nights a week, for over 14 months, ABC television covered developments in a show whose name reflected worldwide sentiment—"America Held Hostage." That embassy seizure, Iran's later support for Middle Eastern terrorist groups, and, most recently, its clandestine nuclear program, have made it an international pariah.

In 1980, Iraqi President Saddam Hussein sent troops into Iran following a number of border disputes. Saddam was probably also motivated by Iranian support for Iraq's repressed Shi'a population, and by his desire to lead the Gulf region. Once the conflict began, "both sides . . . portrayed the war as a noble crusade: Iraq saw the conflict as a historic defense of Arab sovereignty . . . against the marauding Persians [Iranians]; Iran depicted it as a holy war against the [Iraqi] infidels."[63] Before the war finally ground to a halt eight years later, with no victor, it had inflicted grave damage to the Iranian economy and cost a combined total of some 1 million lives. Following the U.S. overthrow of Saddam Hussein's regime in 2003, Iraq's formerly repressed Shi'a majority asserted its new political power. Ironically, Iranian influence in Iraq grew substantially because of the religious bonds between the two Shi'a communities. Indeed many leading Shi'a clergy from Iraq had found refuge in Iran after escaping Saddam's persecution.

After Khomeini's death in 1989, the Islamic revolution moderated somewhat. The Revolutionary Guard relaxed its grip on daily life; fewer women wore the chador; students openly violated Muslim orthodoxy; in the secrecy of their homes, middle-class Iranians at private social gatherings danced to Western music while women shed their head coverings.[64] Mohammad Khatami, twice elected president of the country (1997–2005) with particular support from young voters and women, moderated the country's confrontational foreign policy and tried to introduce a number of democratic reforms. But, although his supporters achieved a parliamentary majority, the Guardian Council blocked the most far-reaching attempts at political liberalization. In 2005, Iranian voters, disillusioned with the reformist faction's inability to bring about significant change, elected a hard-line conservative president, Mahmood Ahmadinejad. His government has since clashed with the West over Iran's nucleur energy program and other issues. At the same time, religious conservatives have cracked down on the press and rolled back many of the personal freedoms gained under Khatami.[65]

Al Qaeda and Militant Islamism

Since the 9/11 attacks on New York and Washington, international attention on Islamic fundamentalism has focused on the Al Qaeda terrorist network. Although government intelligence agencies, the media, and scholars have revealed a great deal about that organization (and its leader, Osama bin Laden), many aspects of its objectives, religious beliefs, organization, and behavior remain unclear or misunderstood. Because of Al Qaeda's secretive nature and its links to a religious tradition little understood in the West, a number of analysts have waged heated debates about its nature.[66] Much of that controversy—particularly as it relates to the war on terrorism—lies outside the scope of this chapter. Instead, this section focuses on the origin of the terrorist network, its relationship to Islamic religious beliefs, and its level of support within the Muslim world.

Defeating the Soviet Infidels in Afghanistan (1979–1989) Although officially founded in 1988, Al Qaeda's roots trace back to 1979, the year of the Iranian Islamic Revolution and the Soviet invasion of Afghanistan. The victory of the Iranian mullahs heartened Islamic fundamentalists elsewhere, anxious to challenge Western-style modernization and to oust their national leaders whom they perceived as corrupt and insufficiently devout. Subsequently Al Qaeda appears to have established various links with Iran, but tensions between Shi'a (Iran) and Sunnis (Al Qaeda) have created difficulties for their relationship.

A more powerful influence on bin Laden and his associates was the Soviet Union's occupation of Afghanistan, aimed at shoring up that country's unpopular communist regime.[67] When Afghan mujahideen (guerrilla "holy warriors") resisted the Soviet occupation, they were joined by a growing number of foreign volunteers drawn primarily from the Middle East. Among the earliest arrivals was Osama bin Laden, the Saudi-born son of a self-made, construction tycoon. Under the influence of Dr. Abdullah Azzam, his Palestinian mentor at that time, bin Laden used his enormous wealth, international contacts, and magnetic personality to recruit large numbers of foreign volunteers. Ironically, because they were fighting the Soviet army, the mujahideen also received weapons and encouragement from their future enemies, Saudi Arabia and the United States (as well as Pakistan).

In 1984, Azzam and bin Laden established the Afghan Service Bureau (MAK),—later the foundation of Al Qaeda—which

> played a decisive role in the anti-Soviet resistance. . . . In addition to recruiting, indoctrinating, and training thousands of Arab and [other] Muslim youths from countries ranging from the U.S. to the Philippines, MAK distributed $200 million of [the] Middle Eastern, . . . American, and British, aid destined for the Afghan jihad. Osama also channeled substantial resources of his own to the cause, a gesture that resonated with his fighters [and raised] his own credibility.[68]

Eventually, foreign mujahideen (primarily Saudis, Egyptians, Yemenis, and Algerians) numbered between 25,000 and 50,000 fighters who helped their more than 200,000 Afghan counterparts force the Soviet withdrawal from Afghanistan in 1989.[69] One year earlier, bin Laden, Abdullah Azzam, and Ayman Muhammad al-Zawahiri (an Egyptian physician and terrorist leader) had created Al Qaeda, built largely out of MAK and two smaller Egyptian, Islamist terrorist organizations. Soon after, Azzam and his two sons were killed by a bomb in Pakistan, Al Qaeda's base at the time. Bin Laden then assumed undisputed leadership of the organization, with al-Zawahiri as his chief ideologist.[70]

Fighting Another Super Power: The United States With the Soviets vanquished in Afghanistan and many of the "Arab Afghans" (as the Middle-Eastern volunteers were known) returning home, bin Laden and al-Zawahiri looked for new worlds to conquer. They embraced a target that widened their original objective of defending Islamic nations against conquest by infidels (those who do not believe in Islam). In this expanded jihad, they vowed to topple religiously "derelict" Islamic regimes in countries such as Egypt and Indonesia and to support the struggles of Muslims against non-Islamic governments in countries or regions such as the Philippines, Chechnya (Russia), and Kashmir (India). In addition, the mujahideens' underdog victory over the Soviets in Afghanistan convinced Al Qaeda's leaders that they were capable of defeating the world's remaining superpower, the United States.

A number of factors spurred Al Qaeda's hostility toward the United States. First was American support for Israel, a nation reviled in the Arab world for its control of Jerusalem (holy to the Muslims) and for its occupation of the Palestinian homeland. Second, they blamed the United States for propping up corrupt and despotic, allied regimes in Muslim nations such as Egypt and Iraq—regimes that many Islamists considered to be heretical. Third, like most Islamic fundamentalists, Al Qaeda despised the West's secular values and its perceived decadence.

Iraq's invasion of Kuwait and the ensuing Gulf War was a major turning point for Al Qaeda. Following the Iraqi invasion, bin Laden offered troops to Saudi Arabia's King Fahd—a close friend of bin Laden's father and a major supporter of the mujahideen in Afghanistan—to protect the kingdom and its Muslim holy sites against Saddam Hussein's military (Saddam was a secular leader whom bin Laden despised). When the king refused the offer and turned, instead, to the United States for protection, bin Laden was outraged. His rage intensified after the war when U.S. troops remained in Saudi Arabia in proximity to the Moslem sacred cities of Mecca and Medina. "The presence of infidels on Arabian sacred soil was too much for . . . bin Laden to bear."[71] By 1994, his relationship with his former supporter, the Saudi government, had deteriorated to the point where the Saudis revoked his citizenship.[72]

From 1989 to 1991, as Al Qaeda's relations with the Pakistani government also deteriorated, bin Laden took some 1,000 of his most radical and battle-trained supporters to Sudan, an African Muslim nation bordering on Egypt and several other primarily Islamic nations. Now Al Qaeda's operations were moving much closer to the Middle East, the primary concern of most mujahideen. Sudan's fundamentalist regime welcomed them and the financial resources that bin Laden brought. The dispatch of 25,000 American troops into nearby, strife-torn Somalia ("Operation Restore Hope"), trying to establish order and begin famine relief (1992–1993), reinforced bin Laden's determination to protect Muslim nations such as this against Western intervention.[73] Three years later, when U.S. pressure forced Sudan to expel Al Qaeda, bin Laden moved his forces back to Afghanistan. There they were protected by their allies, the Taliban government, until the United States ousted that regime in 2001 in reaction to the 9/11 attack.

Western intelligence agencies had been slow to realize that Al Qaeda existed. And even today experts differ sharply regarding the extent of its involvement in high-profile terrorist strikes and the degree of top-down control the Al Qaeda's leaders exerts over its tactical operations. There is general agreement, however, that bin Laden and Al Qaeda were directly or indirectly responsible for the following terrorist acts: the 1993 truck-bombing of the World Trade Center in New York; the attack on the American military barracks in Saudi Arabia (1996); the nearly simultaneous bombing of the U.S. embassies in Tanzania and Kenya, which killed 258 people and wounded more than 5,000 (1998); the attack on the naval ship, USS Cole in the port of Aden (2000); the 9/11 assault on the World Trade Center and the Pentagon, which killed some 3,000 people, and, most likely, an intended attack on the White House or the Capitol by a fourth hijacked plane that crashed in Pennsylvania (2001); the bloody bombing of a nightclub in Bali (Indonesia) (2002); the bombing of commuter trains in Madrid (2004); subway and bus bombings in London (2005); and a major share of the early suicide bombings in Iraq.

Still, many experts do not see it as a centrally controlled, tightly knit unit whose every move is controlled by bin Laden and al-Zawahiri. Rather, they argue that it is a loosely linked network of organizations, many of which operate independently as "terrorist entrepreneurs" who come to Al Qaeda (the name means "the base" or "base of operation") for financial or logistical support. In the words of one observer:

> Although bin Laden and his partners . . . create[d] a structure . . . that attracted new recruits and forged links among preexisting Islamic militant groups, they never created a coherent terrorist network. . . . Instead, Al Qaeda functioned like a venture capital firm—providing funding, contacts, and expert advice to many different militant groups and individuals from all over the Islamic world.[74]

The destruction of Al Qaeda's home base following the allied invasion of Afghanistan and the death or capture of many of its leaders since 2001 have contributed to further decentralization. Consequently, "some analysts have suggested that the word Al Qaeda is now used to refer to a variety of groups connected by little more than shared aims, ideals and methods." The most deadly terrorist attacks in Europe since 9/11—London and Madrid—were carried out by young, European-born Muslims inspired by Al Qaeda, but acting independently. In the eyes of many analysts, such as Britain's International Institute of Strategic Studies, this decentralization has made it even more elusive, "more insidious [than] and just as dangerous" as it was at the time of 9/11.[75]

Support for bin Laden Despite Al Qaeda's unbending theology and brutal attacks on civilians (often including Muslims, as in Iraq), opinion polls suggest that the organization and Osama bin Laden enjoy considerable support in the Islamic world. In fact, the mass media have described the popularity of Osama T-shirts in countries such as Jordan and Indonesia and have noted the many newborns named after him in Pakistan and other Islamic nations. To be sure, a Gallup opinion poll of nine Muslim countries, conducted one year after 9/11, found that, in eight of the nine a majority of respondents condemned the attack.[76] Yet, a Pew Center survey (in 2004) revealed that almost two-thirds of all Pakistanis (65 percent) and approximately half the populations of Jordan (55 percent) and Morocco (45 percent) viewed bin Laden favorably.[77]

It seems hard to reconcile widespread condemnation of the 9/11 attack and substantial support for bin Laden. But the Gallup survey revealed that in five of the nine Islamic countries a majority of respondents did not believe that Al Qaeda or any other Arab group was really behind the September 11 events.

Instead, many claimed that the American or Israeli governments had staged the attack in order to pin the blame on Al Qaeda and the Taliban government. Moreover, most Muslims—89 percent of Indonesians, 80 percent of Pakistanis, and 69 percent of Kuwaitis—believed that the U.S. invasion of Afghanistan in the wake of 9/11 was "morally unjustifiable."[78] Probing the viewpoint of Muslims on the use of terrorism, the Pew survey found that 86 percent of all Jordanians, 74 percent of Moroccans, and 47 percent of Pakistanis felt that suicide attacks on Israelis (including those that kill civilians) were justifiable.[79]

Those attitudes persist even though many leading Islamic clerics and scholars insist that the killing of innocent civilians is not moral or compatible with Islamic values. How well, then, do bin Laden's words and deeds correspond to traditional Islamic beliefs? Sohai H. Hashmi, a student of Islamic thought, suggests that there are two relevant questions to be asked here: first, "under what circumstances or for what ends is war justified?"—a question also much debated in the Western, Christo-Judaic concept of "just war." Second, "once war has begun, how may fighting be properly conducted?"[80] In this case, what means are acceptable to achieve legitimate jihadist goals?

In two important Al Qaeda policy statements (issued in 1996 and 1998), bin Laden and his associates declared a holy war against "the Zionist-Crusader alliance and their collaborators"—that is, Israel, the Jews, Christians, and Muslim states such as Saudi Arabia, Egypt, Morocco, and Jordan that have ties to the United States. The use of the term Crusaders to refer to Westerners was meant to evoke historical Islamic resentment against the Christian Crusades and contemporary opposition to the presence of American troops in Saudi Arabia, Islam's sacred soil. The 1996 declaration also expressed bitterness over Israel's occupation of Jerusalem. Hashmi argues that the stated goal of Al Qaeda's attacks on the West—protecting the Muslim world against the threat of U.S. and Israeli imperialism—is consistent with the long-established Islamic tradition of "defensive jihad" and, therefore, resonates with many mainstream Muslims and clerics. "By declaring that it is willing to take on the world's greatest power in order to redress widely felt injustices [in Saudi Arabia, Israel, and elsewhere]," wrote Hashmi, "Al Qaeda garners the support of many ordinary Muslims."[81] Other scholars also have noted that in mainstream Islamic doctrine, "Muslims are enjoined to take up arms against their oppressors, be they local despots or foreign occupiers. Jihad is one of the fundamental duties of a Muslim."[82]

But, Hashmi and others argue that where bin Laden and Al Qaeda clearly fail to adhere to Islamic standards of morality is in the means they have adopted to achieve their goals—a willingness to kill innocent civilians including women, children, and elderly men. Bin Laden has justified the killing of civilians by claiming that it is merely reciprocity for what the West has done to the Muslims. Thus, in an October 21, 2001, interview with the Arabic television network, al-Jazeera, he stated, "We will do as they do. If they kill our women and our innocent people, we will kill their women and their innocent people until they stop." But Hashmi draws on Koranic verse, the Prophet Muhammad, and "the vast majority of 'ulama [orthodox Islamic scholars] who have condemned his terrorism" to insist that "the jihad tradition relaxes restrictions on the weapons or methods of warfare in the face of military necessity, but never the principle that civilians are not to be directly targeted." These experts "cite well-known sayings of Prophet Mohammad that forbid killing the enemy's women and children or burning down their vegetation—what are today known as scorched earth tactics."[83]

Still, despite mainstream Islamic theological objections to its use, terrorism will continue to attract considerable support within the Muslim world as long as its practitioners are a leading voice against corrupt and repressive Middle-Eastern regimes, against American and Israeli military power, and against the perceived "sinful" aspects of Western culture.

Turkey and Moderate Fundamentalism (Islamism)

Before ending our discussion of Islamic fundamentalists, we should understand that Islamist political movements and parties are not all ultra-traditionalist, anti-modernization, or anti-Western. Recent political developments in Turkey offer an excellent example. Soon after the founding of the Turkish Republic in 1923, its leader, Mustafa Kemal Ataturk, abolished the Ottoman Empire's link between church and state and introduced a series of secular reforms. Women were emancipated (up to a point), while the the government westernized the alphabet, clothing, and the nation's legal code. In stark contrast with Saudi Arabia, Iran, and other orthodox Islamic countries, which require women to cover their hair, Turkey banned women from wearing headscarves in public high schools, universities, or any government building (the ban is often referred to as "unveiling women" although even religious Muslim women in Turkey generally do not wear veils). These changes, designed to modernize and westernize the country, are still supported by most of the urban middle class and are guaranteed by the politically powerful military, which considers itself to be the guardian of the nation's secular tradition. On the other hand, many devout Turks, especially within the rural population and the urban poor, resent aspects of secularization. For example, the law unveiling women creates a dilemma for any observant, young woman wishing to teach, work in the judicial system, work in the government bureaucracy (a major employer), or merely attend university. She must choose between uncovering her head, in violation of her religious principles, or abandoning her educational and career aspirations.

From the 1950s through the 1980s, as the Turkish regime became less autocratic, the state relaxed its control over religiously based political groups. As a result, the first Islamist political party was founded in 1970. Since that time, various Islamist parties have been organized by a newly emerging, fundamentalist sector of the middle class. At the same time, Turkey's economic modernization has brought millions of religious villagers into the country's major cities, where most have settled in teeming urban slums. Influenced by the surge of revivalism elsewhere in the Muslim world and by the challenges of urban life, these migrants have been the backbone of the fundamentalist resurgence that has challenged the nation's secular tradition. Not surprisingly, the growing Islamist movement alarmed Turkey's secular establishment and much of the nation's urban, middle class. During the last decades of the twentieth century, a series of Islamist parties were created. One after another, they were banned by the courts or banished by the armed forces, only to reorganize subsequently under a new name—the National Order Party, followed by the National

Salvation Party, the Welfare Party, the Virtue Party, and, currently, the Justice and Development Party (known as the AK). In 1996, the Welfare Party briefly headed a multiparty (coalition) government, but was ousted by the military and banned as a party less than 18 months later. Sobered by that experience, more moderate Islamist leaders, with a more moderate party platform, established the AK in 2001. Led by Recep Tayyip Erdogan, who had earned a reputation for honesty and efficiency while serving as Mayor of Istanbul, the party swept to power in the 2002 national election, winning only one-third of the popular votes (still the most of any single party), but two-thirds of the seats in parliament. Interestingly, opinion surveys indicated that fewer than half of the AK's followers supported the party out of religious conviction. A greater number of voters favored it because of its record of honest and efficient government in a country plagued by corrupt and ineffective politicians.[84]

Since taking office, the AK government has presided over unprecedented economic growth, widened civil liberties, supported close ties to Europe and the United States, and worked hard to secure eventual Turkish admission to the European Union. As further evidence of its moderation, the government has maintained Turkey's longstanding economic and military ties to Israel. Both President Bush and former British Prime Minister Tony Blair have cited Erdogan's government as proof that Islamic beliefs and democracy can be compatible. Earlier in his career, when serving as mayor of Istanbul, Erdogan used city funds to help renovate Christian churches and Jewish synagogues, as well as Mosques. And he has indicated his respect for other faiths by declaring that "a person who is a genuine believer would not harm the community no matter what his religion is."[85] Finally, most Western scholars agree that the Erdogan government has modernized the country more effectively than previous administrations had.

Yet, despite its strong performance in office and its moderation to date, the AK has failed to earn the trust of Turkey's secular establishment—government bureaucrats, professionals, and, especially, the military. Their worries are based less on what the Erdogan government has done, than on what its leaders have said in the past and what secularists fear the party may do in the future if it gains sufficient power. In other words, many secular Turks believe that the current government's restraint may be no more than a tactical smokescreen. These suspicions are understandable. While the AK's leaders now express moderate positions, they held more radical Islamist views a decade ago when they were activists in the AK's predecessor, the Welfare Party. But, even if Erdogan's moderation is sincere, his opponents fear that he may be succeeded by more militant Islamists in his party. To be sure, AK officials elected at the local level have sometimes violated Turkey's secular tradition by distributing religious literature in the public schools and by allowing religious study groups to meet in them. Many secular Turks, though themselves Muslims, fear that this is only the opening wedge toward a broader Islamist push in the future. While the Erdogan administration has not interjected its religious beliefs into government policy, more strident Islamists have often been appointed to midlevel posts in government.[86]

Still, most objective observers of Turkish politics feel that the AK leadership has truly moderated its position, either out of pragmatism or conviction. To be sure, the Erdogan government has sometimes been guilty of human rights' violations. Most significantly, it has continued its predecessor's repression of the Kurds (an important minority group, many of whom favor self-rule) and has periodically arrested journalists for "anti-Turkish" writings. The fact is, however, Turkey has a history of human rights violations that long preceded the current Islamist government. In fact, the AK's human rights record is superior to those of its secular predecessors. Amnesty International's [AI] 2005 report lamented Turkey's continuing human rights violations, but also noted that "the [Erdogan] government introduced further legal and other reforms with the aim of bringing Turkish law into line with international standards." Specifically, it observed that "international law was given precedence over domestic legislation. All references to the death penalty were removed from the Constitution and the Penal Code."[87] Subsequent AI reports have shown less progress than it had hoped for.

Symbolic issues, such as the country's restrictions on headscarves, have evoked emotional reactions. Indeed, headscarves have been the major lightening-rod in recent Turkish politics.[88] As we have seen, even though more than half of all Turkish women surveyed say they wear them—either for religious reasons or in deference to tradition—Turkish law prohibits teachers, professors, and students (in universities and public high schools) from wearing them in the classroom. Hundreds of university students have been expelled and some 300 school teachers have been fired for refusing to unveil.[89] Not surprisingly, many international human rights groups, such as Human Rights Watch, have condemned the ban. Earlier attempts by the AK government to end the headscarf regulations were beaten back by the president, the military, and the secular political parties. Indeed, because she wears a headscarf, Prime Minister Erdogan's wife could not attend state dinners hosted by former President Ahmet Necdet Sezer (2000–2007), a firm secularist who prohibited women from wearing scarves anywhere in the presidential palace. In fact, Prime Minister Erdogan did not take his wife to any official functions for that very reason.

Tensions between secular and Islamist Turks came to a head in 2007, when President Sezer's term drew to an end. Prime Minister Erdogan asked parliament, which selects the Turkish president, to elect his Foreign Minister and close ally, Abdullah Gul. Fearing that turning over the presidency to the AK, which already controlled parliament and the Prime Minister's office, would allow the Islamists to impose some hidden agenda, hundreds of thousands of secular, mostly middle-class, Turks took to the streets, with one anti-Gul rally drawing as many as a million participants in Istanbul. Many outside observers, however, believe that the protests had more to do with contrasting lifestyles and middle-class snobbery toward the AK's many lower-class supporters.[90] Ironically, Gul himself is a former economics professor with a Ph.D. in that field and two years of graduate study in Britain. With the armed forces indicating that they might oust Prime Minister Erdogan and his cabinet—just as they had removed the first elected Islamist government a decade earlier—the country's constitutional court annulled Gul's election on procedural grounds. Thus, the subsequent (2007) parliamentary election became a national referendum on the presidential crisis. The AK's smashing victory (described below) strengthened its bargaining position.

While these events threatened Turkey's political stability, the conflict largely reflected secular fears rather than the AK's behavior in office. As we have noted, the Erdogan government had pursued a very moderate course. In fact, some of their proposals—most notably, giving observant female students the right to wear headscarves in school—are accepted practice in countries such as the United States and Canada (though not in France),. Ironically, while serving as Turkey's Foreign Minister, Abdullah Gul, had carried out a pro-Western foreign policy, featuring vigorous efforts to join the European Union. To strengthen those efforts, the AK implemented a number of measures improving civil liberties and bringing the country more in line with Western European standards. In the 2007 parliamentary election, the AK raised its share of the national vote from 34 percent in the previous election to 47 percent, a clear indication that its moderate policies and strong economic record had won over many previously skeptical voters. Shortly thereafter, parliament again selected Gul as President, a decision that the military and the courts accepted this time.

Radical Hindu Fundamentalism

Compared to its Muslim counterparts, Hindu fundamentalism has received scant attention in the West for several reasons: Hinduism is largely confined to one country (India); the leading fundamentalist political party (the Bharatiya Janata Party or BJP) has only emerged from political obscurity to national leadership since the 1980s; and the party has not been particularly anti-Western.[91] To be sure, the party is divided into several factions. Hardliners are militantly chauvinistic and hostile toward India's Muslim minority. India's largest religious minority, Muslims comprise only 13–14 percent of the total population (Hindus make up some 80 percent). Even so, with a population of 150 million people, they constitute the second largest Muslim community in the world (after Indonesia). Many observers blame BJP hardliners for the Hindu mob destruction of the famed Babri Mosque in 1992 , the 1995 anti-Muslim riots that killed 3,000 people, and other acts of religious violence . On the other hand, the party moderates and pragmatists who headed the national government for six years (1998–2004) recognize that they cannot hope to govern the country without the parliamentary support of allied secular parties. Consequently, they have presented a brand of Hindu nationalism that stresses broad Indian cultural themes. Moreover, despite virulent anti-Muslim factions in the party, the BJP's national leaders have tried, in recent years, to attract Muslim voters.

Still, the roots of Hindu revivalism lie in India's communal politics, that is, the tensions between the Hindu majority community, the Muslim minority, and the smaller Sikh population (about 2 percent of the population) (see Chapter 4). During the 1980s, militant Hinduism grew rapidly, partly as a response to the surge of Islamic revivalism in Pakistan and the Middle East. In fact, Muslim, Sikh, and Hindu fundamentalists have all fed on their mutual hostility. Another factor that has troubled many Hindus and increased their militancy is the conversion of large numbers of untouchables and lower-caste Hindus to Buddhism or Islam. In the eyes of many middle- and higher-caste Hindus, these conversions threaten the caste system, a linchpin of the religion. The BJP and other Hindu nationalist groups also gained considerable support among voters disgusted with corruption within the secular parties, including the Congress Party (though once in office the BJP had its own corruption scandals). The party's strength is rooted in northern India's Hindi-speaking heartland, but extends throughout the country, particularly within the urban middle class.

Because Hinduism, unlike Islam, lacks a formal church structure and is therefore less hierarchical and centrally controlled, its fundamentalist beliefs are less clearly spelled out. Nationalism and religious chauvinism are important elements, specifically the movement's demand that India cease supporting multiculturalism and, instead, define itself as a Hindu nation. Sometimes fundamentalist spokespersons endorse traditional religious practices shunned or prohibited by modern Indian society. For example, some party leaders have defended sati, the brutal traditional practice of widows throwing themselves on their husband's funeral pyre and dying in the flames.

In the absence of a centralized church or clergy, revivalist leadership has been divided between various interest groups and parties, not all of whom share the same views. Furthermore, some groups (including the BJP itself) have changed their policies sharply over time. Two of the most militant groups, the Vishwa Hindu Parishad (VHP) and Shiv Sena, have openly encouraged attacks on Muslim mosques and neighborhoods, most notably in the Hindu strongholds of Uttar Pradesh, Madhya Pradesh, and Bihar states. In its worst manifestations, such violence has threatened national stability.

The majority of India's Hindus rejected fundamentalist political parties for many years. The BJP and its predecessor party, the Bharatiya Jana Sangh (BJS), were shunned by the country's secular parties and excluded from national and state coalition governments. From the mid-1980s until 2004, however, the party's electoral support climbed as voters grew disenchanted with the mainstream secular parties, particularly the once-dominant Congress Party. A 1992 BJP rally in New Delhi calling for limits on Islamic rights attracted 1 million demonstrators. In its nationalistic platform, the BJP called for development of nuclear weapons (India has since developed them), limits on foreign investment, greater economic self-sufficiency, and reduced imports. Party leaders also opposed birth-control programs and at times expressed the belief that it was not necessary for peasants and other poor Indians to be literate.[92] After moderating its platform and denouncing communal violence, however, the BJP emerged as the largest party following the 1996 national election. It subsequently headed a stable coalition government from 1998 to 2004. Faced with the need to maintain the support of their secular coalition partners, the party's pragmatic leadership generally avoided anti-Muslim positions or other forms of extremism. At the same time, however, many local and state leaders, such as the recently re-elected Chief Minister of the state of Gujarat, continue to espouse extremist views.

Under BJP Prime Minister Atal Behari Vajpayee, India—like Pakistan, its Muslim neighbor and longtime antagonist—developed nuclear weapons, a fulfillment of the party's program. At times their decade-old conflict over Kashmir (a region bordering Pakistan that is ruled by India, but populated primarily by Muslims) seemed to bring these two nuclear antagonists perilously close to the brink of war. When a December 2001 suicide attack on India's parliament by Kashmiri Islamic militants, allegedly based in neighboring Pakistan, killed 12 people, relations between the two nations took a particularly hostile turn. However, in 2003 Pakistani President Pervez Musharraf, under pressure from the United States and threatened by Islamic extremists in his own country, pledged to contain Kashmiri guerrilla attacks on India. In a startling turn of events, the two longtime antagonists conducted a dramatic series of confidence-building diplomatic measures and public relations gestures (including a cricket match between the two nations). With surprisingly strong public support in both their countries, they began a historic rapprochement. That peace offensive continued after the BJP was voted out of office in 2004 because of discontent over its economic policies. Thus, just as former President Richard Nixon, known for his hard-line anticommunist views, opened the door for relations with Communist China, Vajpayee's Hindu nationalist party may have opened the door for an accommodation with Pakistan. Still, differences between the two countries regarding Kashmir remain unresolved and militant, fundamentalist groups (Muslim and Hindu) in both countries continue to oppose any compromise settlement.

THE PROGRESSIVE CATHOLIC CHURCH

At roughly the same time that many Muslims and Hindus were becoming more conservative and traditional, important sectors of Latin America's Catholic Church were embarking on a progressive path. From the time of Spanish colonialism through the first half of the twentieth century, the Church had supported the political and economic status quo, thereby legitimizing Latin America's elite-based governments. In a region marked by a high concentration of land and wealth, the Church was a major land owner until late in the nineteenth century. Alienated by the anticlerical positions of European and Latin American liberals, the Catholic hierarchy allied with conservative political parties and factions.

In the decades after World War II, however, many Catholic clergy, particularly at the parish level, began to abandon the Church's erstwhile conservatism. That process accelerated in the 1960s, when Pope John XXIII moved the "Church universal" in a more liberal direction, placing greater emphasis on social concerns. "The Second Vatican Council [convened by Pope John between 1962 and 1965] moved international Catholicism from a generally conservative and even authoritarian position to one that supported democracy, human rights, and social justice."[93] Catholics were encouraged to address pressing social issues and to enter into political dialogue with liberals and leftists.

In 1968, the Latin American Bishops Conference (CELAM) met in Medellín, Colombia, to apply the lessons of Vatican II to their own region. Challenging the status quo, their ideas reflected the influences of the reformist theologians of the so-called "progressive church" (those who followed the reformist orientation of Vatican II).[94] The themes of dependency and the liberation of Latin America's poor echoed through many of CELAM's pronouncements. The clergy, said the bishops, must heed the "deafening cry . . . from the throats of millions asking their pastors for a liberation that reaches them from nowhere else." To do so, the Church must "effectively give preference to the poorest and the most needy sectors." In short, an institution historically allied with the region's power elite was now to be the Church of the poor.[95]

The CELAM conference must be understood in the broader context of political change that was shaking Latin America at the time. In 1959, the triumph of the Cuban revolution spotlighted the poverty and oppression afflicting much of Latin America. The far-reaching educational, health, and land reforms being carried out in Cuba impressed and radicalized many Catholics. Three years before CELAM, Colombian priest Camilo Torres had left the priesthood to join a guerrilla movement. He was soon killed by counterinsurgency forces, but became a hero to leftists throughout Latin America.[96] Few other priests or nuns joined the armed struggle. Many, however, accepted elements of Marxist political and economic analysis, identified with the plight of their poor parishioners, and helped organize and politicize peasants and slum dwellers.

Though always a minority within the Church, leftist clergy had an important influence in Central America during the 1970s and 1980s, most notably in Nicaragua, El Salvador, and Guatemala.[97] Many Nicaraguan priests and nuns supported the Marxist-leaning Sandinista revolution in the 1970s. When the Sandinistas came to power, Maryknoll priest Miguel D'Escoto was named foreign minister, Jesuit priest Xavier Gorostiaga was appointed head of national planning, Father Ernesto Cardenal served as minister of culture, and his brother, Father Fernando Cardenal, became director of the national adult literacy campaign and then minister of education. No government in Latin America has had nearly the number of priests in its cabinet as Nicaragua's revolutionary government did.

For most of Latin America, however, the 1970s and 1980s were not years of revolution. Instead, much of the region came under the control of right-wing military dictatorships. Reacting to a perceived radical threat, repressive military regimes replaced civilian democracies in Argentina, Brazil, Chile, and Uruguay. At the same time, armed-forces rule continued in much of Central America and the central Andes, where democratic traditions had never been strong. Ironically, right-wing repression spurred the growth of the progressive church more than the Cuban or Nicaraguan revolutions had.

Not surprisingly, radical clergy and laity were outspoken in their criticism of the military regimes and, consequently, suffered severe reprisals. Dozens of priests and nuns were murdered and many more persecuted in countries such as Brazil, El Salvador, and Guatemala. In El Salvador, for example, a far-right death squad called the White Warriors distributed handbills reading, "Be a Patriot, Kill a Priest."[98] But such repression only radicalized many moderate Catholics. "When committed Catholics were imprisoned, tortured, and even killed, bishops in a significant number of cases then denounced the state, setting off a spiral of greater repression against the Church, followed by new Church denunciations of authoritarianism."[99]

In Chile, Brazil, El Salvador, and Peru, the Church became a leading critic of government human-rights violations.[100] The most celebrated example was El Salvador's Archbishop Oscar Romero, the nation's highest-ranking cleric, who had begun his tenure as a conservative.[101] Increasingly appalled by the military's widespread human-rights abuses, he gradually moved to the left. In 1980, Romero wrote President Carter asking him to terminate U.S. military aid to the ruling junta until human-rights violations had ended. Subsequently, he broadcast a sermon calling on Salvadorian soldiers to disobey orders to kill innocent civilians. "No soldier is obliged to obey an order against God's law," he declared. "In the name of God and in the name of this suffering people, I implore you, I beg you, I order you—stop the repression."[102] The following day

Archbishop Romero was assassinated as he said a requiem mass, killed by a death squad linked to the armed forces.

Like Romero, Latin America's progressive clergy have far more commonly been reformers rather than radicals. At times their political rhetoric and analysis may find some common ground with the Left. For example, they share the Marxists' indignation over the plight of the poor, and many of them identify dependency and U.S. domination as root causes of Latin American underdevelopment. But almost all have rejected revolutionary violence and the Leninist state as solutions. Reform, not revolution, was also the proscription of CELAM's bishops when they suggested progressive Catholic theology as an alternative to both capitalism and Marxism.

A number of the bishops' pronouncements originated with a radical Peruvian priest, Gustavo Gutiérrez, the father of liberation theology. In the succeeding decades, writings by Gutiérrez and other liberation theologians greatly influenced the progressive church in Latin America and other parts of the world. Liberation theology calls on Catholic laity and clergy to become politically active and to direct that activity toward the emancipation of the poor. Drawing on Marxist analysis, Gutiérrez accepted the notion of class struggle, but his form of struggle was nonviolent. The poor, liberation theologians argued, should organize themselves into Christian (Ecclesial) Base Communities (CEBs) where they can raise their social and political consciousness. In that way, they can recognize the need to transform society through their own mobilization.[103] CEBs spread through much of Latin America, most notably to Brazil, Chile, Peru, and Central America. While the number of communities and even their precise definition are subject to debate, a CEB is essentially "any group that meets on a regular basis to deepen its members' knowledge of the gospel, stimulate reflection and action on community needs . . . and evangelize."[104] In part, the Church created CEBs as a response to the serious shortage of priests in Latin America, particularly among the poor.

Typically composed of 10–40 people, these Base Communities are primarily located in poor urban neighborhoods and, to a lesser degree, in rural villages. Estimates of how many have existed in Latin America vary widely, but one calculation placed the number at their peak in the 1980s at perhaps 200,000, with a total membership of several million people. Perhaps 40 percent of all communities were in Brazil, home of the world's largest Catholic population.[105] Most CEB members probably are not politically active and join for strictly religious purposes.[106] Still, many communities were the foundations for popular protests against oppression, most notably in Central America but also in Brazil, Chile, and Peru.[107] In other cases, CEBs helped raise political awareness and sharpen political skills among the poor.

Since the early 1980s, the influence of Latin America's progressive church has diminished considerably.[108] One cause, ironically, has been the region's transition from military dictatorships to democracy. Absent massive human-rights violations and open assaults against the poor, Catholic clergy have generally been less motivated to enter the political arena. Furthermore, without a common foe, moderate and radical priests no longer have a common cause. Finally, many political activists who had used the Church as a protective "umbrella" during the military dictatorships (since those regimes were less likely to persecute Church-affiliated radical groups) are now able to participate in politics through other political organizations.[109]

Perhaps more importantly, since the 1980s the Vatican has been unsympathetic to any type of political activism among priests and nuns, particularly when related to the CEBs and liberation theology. "Rome has called liberation theologians such as Leonardo Boff and Gustavo Gutiérrez to account, if not to recant."[110] As progressive bishops and archbishops such as Brazil's Don Helder Camara have died or retired, they have been replaced by more conservative clerics.[111] The Vatican's conservatism and its distaste for Liberation Theology since the 1970s will undoubtedly continue under Pope Benedict XVI. Indeed, in his previous capacity as Cardinal Joseph Ratzinger, Benedict authored some of the Vatican's strongest criticisms of the progressive church. Though liberation theology and the progressive church have lost much of their momentum, they were critical forces in the political mobilization of Latin America's poor. Moreover, many of today's activists in left-of-center political parties, such as Brazil's governing Workers' Party (PT), emerged from the Catholic left.[112]

RELIGION AND POLITICS IN THE DEVELOPING WORLD: LOOKING TO THE FUTURE

The hold of religion on the human heart and spirit, and its consequent impact on the political process, has been frequently misunderstood by Western scholars. As we have seen, the initial error of both modernization and dependency theorists was to undervalue the significance of religion. Several factors account for the unanticipated resurgence of fundamentalism and other forms of religiously based politics in recent decades. In many countries, rapid modernization has left people psychologically adrift, searching for their cultural identity. The breakdown of village life and the erosion of traditional customs and values often create an emotional void not filled by the material rewards of modern life. In the Middle East, the indignities of colonialism and neocolonialism, resentment against Israel and the West, and dismay over decades of failed development since independence have all contributed to the region's religious revival.[113] However, contrary to many Western stereotypes, the appeal of Islamic fundamentalism is by no means limited to poor and uneducated Muslims who are relatively unfamiliar with modern ideas and lifestyles. For example, most of the 9/11 terrorists had university educations and had lived outside the Muslim world. A biographical study of 173 jailed Islamist terrorists—from nearly a dozen countries—found that the majority were middle or upper class, most had received secular educations in primary and secondary schools, nearly two-thirds had at least some college or university education, and more than 40 percent were professionals (including physicians, architects, teachers, and preachers).[114] Most recently (2007), when British intelligence units averted terrorist car-bomb attacks in London and Glasgow, most of the arrested conspirators were doctors practicing in the United Kingdom. Lastly, many jihadists operating in Europe (such as the London mass transit bombers) have been young men, raised in the West, who felt like outcasts, isolated from both European lifestyles and their own culture.

Turning to Latin America, the progressive church offered a shield against political repression and a voice for the poor. As vastly different as they are,

Islamic revivalism and the progressive Catholic Church have a few similarities. For example, both were grounded in revulsion over poverty and over government repression and corruption. Thus, the resurgence of Third World religion often was linked to a yearning for social and political justice, even if its vision of justice is unpalatable to those outside the movement. Other religious movements, not discussed in this chapter, have different worldviews. For example, the most rapidly growing religious movement in Latin America is Evangelical Christianity, particularly Pentecostalism. The number of Pentecostals and Charismatics in the region has exploded from under 13 million in 1970 to nearly 160 million today (28 percent of Latin America's population)[115] Unlike progressive Catholics, these converts generally are politically conservative and pursue different lifestyles.

Having previously underestimated the impact of religion on Third World politics, analysts now risk overstating its importance. To begin with, the political weight of the movements that have attracted the most attention—Islamic and Hindu radical fundamentalism and progressive Catholicism—must be put into perspective. Influential as they have been, they are not representative of the religions from which they have sprung. This point requires particular emphasis in relation to Islam, because a militant minority has left many Westerners with an extremely negative image of the entire Muslim world. They consider Islam to be backward and intolerant when, actually, like all religions, it encompasses a range of outlooks, some reactionary, and some progressive.[116] For example, the media sometimes suggest that all Muslim women are repressed and confined, yet there are many Islamic feminists and professional women in countries such as Egypt, Lebanon, and Malaysia. It is worth remembering that four Muslim nations—Bangladesh, Indonesia, Pakistan, and Turkey—have had female prime ministers or presidents, something the United States has yet to achieve. Similarly, contrary to stereotype, some Muslim countries, including fundamentalist Saudi Arabia, are on good terms with the West. Lastly, when fundamentalist parties (Muslim or Hindu) have assumed power, no matter their original intentions, their behavior in office was often moderated by their need for parliamentary coalition partners, their desire to appeal to a wide range of voters in future elections, and the dangers of offending powerful secular forces, such as the Turkish military.

Finally, when evaluating the current religious revival, we cannot assume that current trends will continue long into the future. History reveals that "religious resurgence is a cyclical phenomenon."[117] Consequently, Jeff Haynes argues that, "there is no reason to doubt that the current wave of religion-oriented political ideas and movements will in time give way . . . to [a] partial resurrection of secular ideologies."[118] For the foreseeable future, however, religion will continue to be an important force in the politics of many developing nations. Nowhere is this more dramatically evidenced than in terrorist groups such as Al Qaeda.

CONCLUSION: RELIGION AND DEMOCRACY

The relationship between institutionalized religions and democracy has been complex and varied. Traditionally, the leaders of influential religions have tended to ally with their country's political and economic elites, becoming a pillar of the status quo. Jeffrey Haynes's explanation of why most local Christian religious leaders, from the 1960s through the 1980s, failed to speak out against Africa's authoritarian rulers applies equally well to other religions in the Third World:

> Church and state developed mutually supportive relationships . . . [Frequently] it was in . . . the interests of both Church and state for there to be social and political stability, even if required authoritarian rule to achieve it.[119]

Speaking out against a dictator, at the very least would cut off government financial support for the church and, at worst, would subject the clergy and perhaps their parishioners to persecution. Sometimes, Church leaders actually held official positions in the ruling regime. In Rwanda, for example, for many years the Catholic archbishop of Kigali (the nation's capital and primary city) was a member of the central committee of the country's only legal party. The 32-year dictator of Zaire (now the Congo), President Mobutu Sese Seko, gave Cardinal Malula a mansion to live in and subsequently gave a Mercedes to every Catholic and Protestant bishop in the country.[120] While there were also some prominent clergymen who demanded social justice and criticized government repression and corruption (e.g., Catholic Archbishop Frances of Liberia), it was not until the 1990s that the Church became a prominent voice for democracy.

In Latin America and southern Europe, the Catholic Church hierarchy also supported authoritarian regimes. Historically, Latin American churches had close links with the landholding elite (and were themselves major landowners). Frequently, Europe's Catholic Church also supported right-wing, antidemocratic parties and movements. But, as we have seen, many organized religions became more progressive in the closing decades of the twentieth century, supporting democratization and greater social and economic justice. Indeed, Samuel Huntington credits the Latin American Catholic Church as being a leading force for democratic change during the Third Wave. The Church and its leader, Cardinal Jaime Sin, also lent critical support to Corazon Aquino's "People Power" movement, which brought democracy to the Philippines. In South Korea, social movements led by several Protestant churches as well the smaller Catholic Church also played an important role in that country's transition to democracy.[121]

Looking beyond these cases, two important questions come to mind regarding the relationship between religion and democracy. First, does liberal democracy require the separation of the church from a secular political system? Second, are the cultural values of some religions more supportive than others of democracy?

In his classic work, *Democracy in America*, the French author Alexis de Tocqueville suggested that a linchpin of democracy in the United States was the separation of church and state.

> I learned with surprise that [the clergy] filled no public appointments . . . [and] I found that most of its members seemed to retire from their own accord from the exercise of power, and that they made it the pride of their profession to abstain from politics. . . . They saw that they must renounce their religious influence if they were to strive for political power.[122]

Today, many analysts still believe that maintaining the pluralist values and the tolerance underlying democracy requires limiting the influence of religion on politics. But others reject the notion that democracy can only exist under a strict separation of church and state. In their recent book, *Religion and Democracy*, David Marquand and Ronald Nettler insist:

> Even in the absence of a . . . bargain keeping church and state apart, religion and democracy can coexist. Communities of faith do not necessarily imperil the foundations of pluralist democracy by seeking to pursue essentially religious agendas through political action.[123]

But, they add, there is a necessary restriction if this intermingling of religious political action and democracy is to work. "A degree of mutual tolerance, or at least of mutual self-restraint, is indispensable. Religious groups have to accept the right of other religious groups—and . . . the right of the non-religious— to abide by their own values."[124] Many countries and religions uphold that tolerance, but in some fundamentalist religions—Islamic or otherwise—it is absent.

Our second question—whether certain religious cultures are more supportive than others of democratic values—has been the subject of intense debate. Various empirical studies have shown that Protestant countries are significantly more likely to be democratic than are Catholic or Muslim nations.[125] In contrast, Islamic nations have had a rather poor democracy record, leading some scholars to conclude that Islam has authoritarian underpinnings. For example, in the mid-1990s, Turkish sociologist Serif Mardin suggested that the values of democracy may be tied to broader Western cultural values, values the Islamic world does not accept.[126]

One problem with such arguments is that, while they may have an element of truth, they fail to take into account differences within religions. Not all religious Catholics or priests, for example, have the same political values. Militant Islamic fundamentalist cultures that have flourished in Afghanistan and Sudan are surely unacceptable environments for democracy. Yet, most analysts agree that Islamic values can be quite compatible with democracy in a more moderate Muslim setting such as Indonesia or Malaysia.[127] Indonesia, the largest Muslim country in the world, encompasses a range of Muslim believers, ranging from Islamists (a small portion of whom are active in terrorist groups) through very progressive clerics and laity. Traditionally, Indonesians have practiced a more moderate form of Islam than is normally found in Middle Eastern or North African countries. The streets of its cities feature many unaccompanied women on motor scooters, and women have been free to choose whether or not they wished to wear the *jilbab* (the Islamic headscarf), though that has begun to change somewhat in recent years. Perhaps the country's most influential Muslim cleric in the years leading to the country's democratic transition (in 1998) was Abdurrahman Wahid, then head of Indonesia's largest Muslim organization, the Nahdlatul Ulama (NU). While religiously conservative, the NU preached tolerance toward Indonesia's Christian and Hindu minorities and was an important actor in the campaign against the long-standing dictator, Suharto.[128] In Indonesia's first democratic presidential election (1999), Wahid was chosen by parliament to lead the country. In office, he continued to support the values of tolerance so essential to democracy. Criticizing the frequent grass-roots violence against Indonesia's Christian minority, he insisted that Christians were equal to Muslims in the eyes of God. Moreover, in a rather dramatic departure from most Islamic heads of state, he publicly and enthusiastically supported Zionism and took one of his first presidential visits to Israel.[129]

Another important factor limiting generalizations about the compatibility of particular religions with democracy is that, like most institutions and value systems, religions change over time. At one time, there was solid empirical evidence that Protestant countries were more likely to sustain democracy and economic growth, while Catholic and Confucian nations were less supportive. Today neither relationship (political or economic) seems to hold. Confucian East Asia and Catholic Southern Europe both enjoyed rapid economic growth in the second half of the twentieth century, faster growth than in many Protestant countries. And more recently, as democracy has spread to various Catholic and Confucian nations (including Spain, Portugal, Poland, Brazil, Mexico, Taiwan, and South Korea), the suggested linkage between religions and democratic norms has become more questionable. That doesn't mean that some religions are not more tolerant or more authoritarian than others. Rather, it does mean that we need to avoid sweeping generalizations and consider differences within religions and changes over time.

DISCUSSION QUESTIONS

1. Discuss the various types of relationships that exist between church and state under the world's major religions—Catholicism, Protestantism, Islam, and Hinduism.
2. What factors caused the growth of the progressive church in Latin America, and what is distinct about its followers' beliefs? Why has the progressive church lost much of its influence in recent times?
3. Discuss why the Buddhist and Hindu religions have usually been less actively involved in national politics than Islam or Catholicism. How has that changed in India in recent years?
4. What factors have led to the resurgence of Islamic fundamentalism (or revivalism) in Afghanistan, Iran, and other parts of the Muslim world? Why do you think so many people in that part of the world admire Osama bin Laden?
5. Discuss the debate over *jihad* (holy war) in the Muslim religion and how Al Qaeda's vision of *jihad* differs from that of mainstream Muslim clerics.
6. Do recent political events in Turkey suggest that there are Islamist governments that are friendly to the West and acceptable to the West? What is unique about Turkey that may make its experience difficult to repeat elsewhere in the Muslim world? Why do secular Turks still distrust the country's Islamist political leaders?

NOTES

1. Donald Eugene Smith, ed., *Religion and Modernization* (New Haven, CT: Yale University Press, 1974), 4.

2. Quoted in Timothy D. Sisk, *Islam and Democracy* (Washington, DC: United States Institute of Peace, 1992), 3.

3. Emile Sahliyeh, ed., *Religious Resurgence and Politics in the Contemporary World* (Albany, NY: SUNY Press, 1990), 1–16.

4. John L. Esposito, *Islam and Politics*, 4th ed. (Syracuse, NY: Syracuse University Press, 1998), 311. Of course, since that time, groups

like Al Qaeda have added the Internet to that list.

5. Jeff Haynes, *Religion in Third World Politics* (Boulder, CO: Lynne Rienner Publishers, 1994), 3.

6. Kenneth D. Wald, "Social Change and Political Response: The Silent Religious Cleavage in North America," in *Politics and Religion in the Modern World*, ed. George Moyser (New York: Routledge and Kegan Paul, 1991), 240.

7. The Christian Democratic Party was the dominant party in Italian politics for decades but was devastated in the early 1990s by scandal. It has since changed its name to the Italian Popular Party.

8. One of the most influential and controversial books using the framework of clashing, religiously based cultures is Samuel P. Huntington, *The Clash of Civilizations and the Remaking of World Order* (New York: Simon & Schuster, 1996); see also Bernard Lewis, "The Roots of Muslim Rage," *Atlantic Monthly* 226, no. 3 (September 1990). Leonard Binder, a leading specialist on the Middle East, is critical of such terminology, arguing, for example, that Islam is only one part of Middle Eastern culture; see *Islamic Liberalism* (Chicago: University of Chicago Press, 1988), 80–81.

9. Of course, Catholicism is the dominant religion in a number of European nations and is the largest single denomination in the United States. The discussion in this chapter, however, is limited to the Third World.

10. For data on the size and percentage of the Islamic populations in the nations of the world, see John L. Esposito, ed., *Islam in Asia* (New York: Oxford University Press, 1987), 262–263. While the absolute size of Muslim populations has obviously changed since Esposito's book was published, there has been little change in the Islamic *percentage* of those national populations.

11. Donald Eugene Smith, *Religion and Political Development* (Boston: Little, Brown, 1970), 40.

12. Latif Abul-Husn, *The Lebanese Conflict: Looking Inward* (Boulder, CO: Lynne Rienner Publishers, 1998), 35; see also Robin Wright, *Sacred Rage: The Crusade of Modern Islam* (London: Andre Deutsch, 1986), 63; William Montgomery Watt, *Islamic Fundamentalism and Modernity* (London: Routledge and Kegan Paul, 1988), 125–131; Dilip Hiro, *Holy Wars: The Rise of Islamic Fundamentalism* (New York: Routledge and Kegan Paul, 1989), 5–26.

13. Yann Richard, *Shi'ite Islam: Polity, Ideology, and Creed* (Oxford UK and Cambridge USA: Blackwell, 1995), 7 and 11; see also, Heinz Halm, *Shi'ism*, 2nd ed. (Edinburgh, Scotland: University of Edinburgh Press, 2004).

14. Akbar S. Ahmed, *Discovering Islam* (New York: Routledge and Kegan Paul, 1988), 55–61; Saleem Qureshi, "The Politics of the Shia Minority in Pakistan," in *Religious and Ethnic Minority Politics in South Asia*, eds. Dhirendra Vajpey and Yogendra K. Malik (New Delhi, India: Monhar, 1989), 109. Adherents.Com http://www.adherents.com/.

15. Smith, *Religion and Political Development*, xi.

16. For a discussion of the strengths and weaknesses of such arguments, see Winston Davis, "Religion and Development: Weber and the East Asian Experience," in *Understanding Political Development*, eds. Myron Weiner and Samuel Huntington (Boston: Little, Brown, 1987), 221–280.

17. Terrance G. Carroll, "Secularization and States of Modernity," *World Politics* 36, no. 3 (April 1984): 362–382.

18. For discussions of religion as a positive force for development, see Jeffrey Haynes, *Religion and Development* (London: Palgrave Macmillan, 2007); John L. Esposito, *Islamic Revivalism* (Washington, DC: American Institute of Islamic Affairs, American University, 1985), 5–6; Eden Naby, "The Changing Role of Islam as a Unifying Force in Afghanistan," in *The State, Religion, and Ethnic Politics*, eds. Ali Banuazizi and Myron Weiner (Syracuse, NY: Syracuse University Press, 1986), 137; Yogendra K. Malik and V. B. Singh, *Hindu Nationalism in India* (Boulder, CO: Westview Press, 1994), 53, 206.

19. John L. Esposito, *Islam and Politics*, 2nd ed. (Syracuse, NY: Syracuse University Press, 1987), 231.

20. Smith, *Religion and Political Development*, 70.

21. H. E. Richardson, *Tibet and Its History* (London: Oxford University Press, 1962).

22. Smith, *Religion and Political Development*, 57–84.

23. Esposito, *Islam and Politics*, 2nd ed., 1.

24. Contemporary hostilities between Jews and Muslims in the Middle East, as well as Islamic fundamentalist hostility toward the West, are relatively recent phenomena that are not rooted in Islam's core beliefs.

25. John L. Esposito, *The Islamic Threat: Myth or Reality?* (New York: Oxford University Press, 1992), 78–79.

26. Article 24 of the Turkish Constitution (as amended October 17, 2001). http://www.tbmm.gov.tr/anayasa/constitution.htm.

27. Bernard Lewis, *The Emergence of Modern Turkey* (London: Oxford University Press, 1976), 416, quoted in Yesim Arat, *Rethinking Islam and Liberal Democracy: Islamist Women in Turkish Politics* (Albany: SUNY Press, 2005), 4.

28. Donald Eugene Smith, *Religion, Politics and Social Change in the Third World* (New York: Free Press, 1971), 12–22.

29. Smith, *Religion and Political Development*, 54.

30. While Nicaragua's leading prelate, the Archbishop of Managua, broke bitterly with the nation's Marist-oriented Sandinista government, many parish priests and nuns supported the revolutionary regime and several priests served in the first Sandinista cabinet.

31. Ibid., 34–39, 57; Haynes, *Religion in Third World Politics*, 146. In 2006, after a period of mass demonstrations against his rule, the king had to cede his political power to parliament. Subsequently, the picture of Vishnu on the new national banknotes (currency) was replaced by the image of Buddha.

32. Janet A. Contursi, "Militant Hindus and Buddhist Dalits: Hegemony and Resistance in an Indian Slum," *American Ethnologist* 16, no. 3 (August 1989), 441–457.

33. Donald Eugene Smith, "The Limits of Religious Resurgence," in *Religious Resurgence and Politics*, 36–39.

34. Morton Zuckerman, "Beware of Religious Stalinists," *U.S. News and World Report* (March 22, 1993), 80; Charles Krauthammer, "Iran: Orchestrator of Disorder," *Washington Post* (January 1, 1993), A19. Both articles are also cited in the 1993 preface to the paperback edition of Esposito, *The Islamic Threat*.

35. Esposito, *The Islamic Threat*, vii.

36. Joseph S. Szyliowicz, "Religion, Politics and Democracy in Turkey," in *The Secular and the Sacred*, ed. William Safran (London: Frank Cass, 2003), 190; for similar objections to the use of the term Islamic fundamentalism, see Esposito, *The Islamic Threat*, 7–24; Shireen T. Hunter, ed., *The Politics of Islamic Revivalism* (Bloomington: Indiana University Press, 1988); Esposito, *Islamic Revivalism*; Sisk, *Islam and Democracy*, 2–7, 73, fn. 1, 2.

37. Among the many examples are Watt, *Islamic Fundamentalism and Modernity* and Hiro, *Holy Wars*.

38. Fred Halliday, *Islam and the Myth of Confrontation: Religion and Politics in the Middle East* (London: I. B. Tauris Publishers, 1996), 233, fn. 1.

39. Esposito, *The Islamic Threat*; Akbar S. Ahmed, *Discovering Islam* (New York: Routledge and Kegan Paul, 1988); Esposito, *Political Islam: Revolution, Radicalism or Reform* (Boulder, CO: Lynne Rienner Publishers, 1997); Halliday, *Islam and the Myth of Confrontation*.

40. Charles Kurzman, ed., *Liberal Islam: A Source Book* (New York: Oxford University Press, 1998).

41. Halliday, *Islam and the Myth*, 107.

42. Hiro, *Holy Wars*, 1–2.

43. Watt, *Islamic Fundamentalism and Modernity*, 2.

44. Peter Woodward, "Sudan: Islamic Radicals in Power," in *Political Islam*.

45. Wright, *Sacred Rage*.

46. Robin Wright, "Lebanon," in *The Politics of Islamic Revivalism*, 66.

47. Naby, "The Changing Role of Islam," 124–154; Paul Overby, *Holy Blood: An Inside View of the Afghan War* (Westport, CT: Praeger, 1993).

48. For a discussion of the origins of the FIS and the nature of Algeria's violence since 1992, see Claire Spencer, "The Roots and Future of Islamism in Algeria," in *Islamic Fundamentalism*, eds. Abdel Salam Sidahmed and Anoushiravan Ehteshami (Boulder, CO: Westview Press, 1996), 93–109; also Esposito, *Islam and Politics*, 4th ed., 302–307.

49. To be sure, some "ultra-orthodox" Israeli Jews are radical fundamentalists who have carried out violent attacks against Muslims and secular Jews. The most notorious examples were the attack by an ultra-orthodox Jewish gunman against Arab worshipers in a Hebron mosque and the assassination of Israeli Prime Minister Izhak Rabin by a Jewish fundamentalist who objected to Rabin's efforts to achieve peace with the Palestinian Liberation Organization (PLO). But these are exceptions.

50. Brian R. Farmer, *Understanding Radical Islam* (New York: Peter Lang, 2007), 115.

51. Useful sources on the background of the revolution include Robin Wright, *In the Name of God: The Khomeini Decade* (New York: Simon & Schuster, 1989); Hiro, *Holy Wars*, chap. 6.

52. Hiro, *Holy Wars*, 151.

53. Ibid., 151–153; See also Shireen T. Hunter, *Iran after Khomeini* (New York: Praeger, 1992), 11–12. Hunter argues that the shahs also antagonized Iranian Muslims by emphasizing the country's (pre-Islamic) Persian heritage at the expense of its Islamic (Arabic) heritage.

54. Cheryl Bernard and Zalmay Khalilzad, *The Government of God: Iran's Islamic Republic* (New York: Columbia University Press, 1984), 12–13.

55. The title of Ayatollah is bestowed on the highest and most respected Shi'ite religious authorities and interpreters of Islamic law. Khomeini eventually attained the title of Grand Ayatollah, the highest rank in the Shi'a clergy. There are only about 20 Grand Ayatollahs worldwide. M. M. Salehi, *Insurgency through Culture and Religion: The Islamic Revolution of Iran* (New York: Praeger, 1988), 54.

56. Hiro, *Holy Wars*, 160.

57. Wright, *In the Name of God*, 65.

58. Ibid., 180–181.

59. But women are less repressed than in some of the Gulf states. For example, women may hold jobs in most fields, may run for political office (including parliament), and may drive automobiles—opportunities denied women in Saudi Arabia and under Afghanistan's Taliban government. And in some areas women have made important gains. Unlike the Taliban government, which barred females from attending school (at any level), Iran's Islamic government doubled the female literacy rate from 36 to 72 percent in its first two decades.

60. Wright, *In the Name of God*, 87.

61. Quoted in Bernard and Khalilzad, *The Government of God*, 151–152.

62. Wright's *In the Name of God* offers one of the better accounts of the hostage situation, but there are many others.

63. Gary Sick, "Trial by Error: Reflections on the Iran-Iraq War," in *Iran's Revolution*, ed. R. K. Ramazani (Bloomington: Indiana University Press, 1990), 105.

64. Wright, *In the Name of God*, 191; Hunter, *Iran after Khomeini*, 32–41. Hunter had a more cautious view regarding possible moderation of the revolution and her doubts so far seem to have been well-founded.

65. Nikki R. Keddie, *Modern Iran: Roots and Results of Revolution* (New Haven, CT: Yale University Press, 2006), 263–346 offers an excellent analysis of developments since the death of Khomeini; see also, Ali Gheissari and Vali Nasr, *Democracy in Iran: History and the Quests for Liberty* (New York: Oxford University Press, 2006).

66. A number of articles and books on Al Qaeda seek to debunk alleged myths about it. See, for example: Jason Burke, "Think Again: Al Qaeda," *Foreign Policy* (May/June 2004) reprinted in wysiwyg://2http://www.foreignpolicy.com/story, and Rohan Gunaratna, *Inside Al Qaeda: Global Network of Terror* (New York: Columbia University Press, 2002).

67. On the Soviet war in Afghanistan, see Steve Coll, *Ghost Wars: The Secret History of the CIA, Afghanistan, and bin Laden, from the Soviet Invasion to September 10, 2001* (New York: Penguin Press, 2004); Artem Borovik, *The Hidden War: A Russian Journalist's Account of the Soviet War in Afghanistan* (New York: Atlantic Monthly Press, 1990); Henry S. Bradsher, *Afghanistan and the Soviet Union* (Durham, NC: Duke University Press, 1983).

68. Gunaratna, *Inside Al Qaeda*, 18–19.

69. Peter L. Bergen, *Inside the Secret World of Osama bin Laden* (London: Weidenfeld & Sicolson, 2001), 59–60.

70. Azzim and bin Laden had clashed over bin Laden's intention to use terrorism against Muslim governments such as Egypt's or Saudi Arabia's. Therefore, many analysts believe that Osama either ordered his former mentor's assassination or, at least, condoned it. Bin Laden, for his part, never acknowledged their falling out.

71. Marc Sageman, *Understanding Terror Networks* (Philadelphia: University of Pennsylvania Press, 2004), 38.

72. Ibid., 35. There is evidence, however, that the Saudi regime continued to accommodate Al Qaeda until 2004. A lawsuit filed by relatives of 9/11 victims charged that members of the Saudi royal family paid the network $300 million in "protection money" during the 1990s (see London's *Sunday Times*, August 25, 2002) and others have alleged that some members of the royal family funneled additional money to bin Laden through fictitious charities.

73. In December 1992, during the final weeks of his administration, President George H.W. Bush ordered U.S. troops into Somalia as civil war and lawlessness were destroying that nation and spreading famine (with perhaps 300,000 dead). Despite their success in restoring humanitarian food relief, the troops were repeatedly engaged by armed Somali militias and were resented by many civilians. When an American helicopter was shot down in October 1993, 18 soldiers were killed and several of their bodies were dragged through the streets of Mogadishu, the Somali capital. Under pressure from American public opinion and the U.S. Congress, President Bill Clinton then withdrew U.S. forces from that country. These events were popularized in a 2001 Hollywood film entitled *Black Hawk Down*. Al Qaeda allegedly provided training for some of the Somalis who attacked the American troops.

74. Jason Burke, "Think Again: Al Qaeda."

75. Both quotes are from a May 16, 2003, BBC report; see http://newsvote.bbc.co.uk/mpapps; in a March 21, 2004, interview with Australian television, Dr. Rohan Gunaratna, head of terrorism research at Singapore's Institute of Defense and Strategic Studies and a leading authority on Al Qaeda, also maintained that, despite the capture or demise of many of its top leaders, the organization "has grown significantly in the past two years . . . [by infecting] local groups with its ideology. . . ." See http:/seven.com.au/sundayssunrise/politics_040321_gunaratna.

76. http://www.publicagenda.org/specials/terrorism, cited in Jeff Haynes, "Al-Qaeda: Ideology and Action" (Uppsala, Sweden: Paper

prepared for the EPCR Joint Sections of Workshops, April 2004), 2.

77. The Pew Research Center for the People and the Press, "A Year After the Iraq War: Mistrust of America in Europe Even Higher, Muslims' Anger Persists" (March 16, 2004), 1. http://people-press.org/reports.

78. Haynes, "Al-Qaeda," 2.

79. Pew Research Center, "A Year After," 1.

80. Sohail H. Hashmi, "9/11 and the Jihad Tradition," in *Terror, Culture, Politics: 9/11 Reconsidered*, eds. Daniel J. Sherman and Terry Nardin (Bloomington: Indiana University Press, 2005).

81. Ibid.

82. "Analysis: Interpreting Islam," *BBC* (Friday, 9 July, 2004), http://news.bbc.co.uk/1/h/world/middle_east/3880151.stm. This does not mean that most Muslims specifically endorse a holy war against Israel and the West. It merely means that Al Qaeda's call for jihad is broadly consistent with mainstream Muslim theology.

83. Ibid.

84. Szyliowicz, "Religion, Politics and Democracy in Turkey."

85. Metin Heper, "The Justice and Development Party: Toward a Reconciliation of Islam and Democracy in Turkey?" (Tel Aviv University: The Annual Georges A. Kaller Lecture, 2003), 6.

86. *New York Times*, "A Secular Turkish City Feels Islam's Pulse Beating Stronger, Causing Divisions," (June 1, 2007) and "Turkish Army Threatens as Presidential Vote Derails," (April 28, 2007).

87. *Amnesty International Report 2005*, Turkey, http://web.amnesty.org/report2005/tur-summary-eng.

88. For a clear and balanced discussion of the arguments on both sides of this debate, see Yesim Arat, *Rethinking Islam and Liberal Democracy*, 23–27.

89. Human Rights Watch, *Combating Restrictions on Headscarves* http://www.hrw.org/reports/2000/turkey2/Turk009–05.htm.

90. *New York Times* (April 30, 2007). Even in their worst nightmares, few serious critics believe that the AK would impose an Islamist lifestyle remotely similar to Iran's or Afghanistan's under the Taliban. That type of hard-line fundamentalist belief scarcely exists in Turkey. What many do fear, however, is that a powerful AK government would be subtly less tolerant of the secular lifestyle.

91. This section draws heavily on Gail Omvelt, "Hinduism, Social Inequality and the State," in *Religion and Political Conflict in South Asia*, ed.

Douglas Allen (Westport, CT: Greenwood Press, 1992), 17–36. See also Ian Talbot, "Politics and Religion in Contemporary India," in *Politics and Religion in the Modern World*, 135–161; and Malik and Singh, *Hindu Nationalism in India*.

92. *New York Times*, February 26, 1993.

93. Paul Sigmund, *Liberation Theology at the Crossroads* (New York: Oxford University Press, 1990), 19; David Lehmann, *Democracy and Development in Latin America* (Cambridge, England: Polity Press, 1990), 108–110.

94. Scott Mainwaring and Alexander Wilde, eds. *The Progressive Church in Latin America* (Notre Dame, IN: University of Notre Dame Press, 1989).

95. Sigmund, *Liberation Theology at the Crossroads*, 29–30.

96. Father Camilo Torres, *Revolutionary Writings* (New York: Harper & Row, 1962).

97. Philip Berryman, *Stillborn Hope: Religion, Politics and Revolution in Central America* (Maryknoll, NY: Orbis Books, 1991); Margaret E. Crahan, "Religion and Politics in Revolutionary Nicaragua," in *The Progressive Church*.

98. Jennifer Pearce, "Politics and Religion in Central America: A Case Study of El Salvador," in *Politics and Religion in the Modern World*, 234.

99. Mainwaring and Wilde, *The Progressive Church*, 13.

100. Scott Mainwaring, *The Catholic Church and Politics in Brazil* (Stanford, CA: Stanford University Press, 1986); Brian H. Smith, *The Church and Politics in Chile* (Princeton, NJ: Princeton University Press, 1982).

101. Philip Berryman, "El Salvador: From Evangelization to Insurrection," in *Religion and Political Conflict in Latin America*, ed. Daniel H. Levine (Chapel Hill: University of North Carolina Press, 1986), 58–78.

102. Ibid., 114.

103. Sigmund, *Liberation Theology at the Crossroads*, 28–39. These communities also are called Ecclesial Base Communities or Base Christian Communities.

104. W. E. Hewitt, *Base Christian Communities and Social Change in Brazil* (Lincoln: University of Nebraska Press, 1991), 6.

105. Hewitt, *Base Christian Communities*; Thomas C. Bruneau, "Brazil: The Catholic Church and Basic Christian Communities," in *Religion and Political Conflict in Latin America*, 106–123.

106. John Burdick, "The Progressive Catholic Church in Latin America," in *Latin American Research Review* 24, no. 1 (1994), 184–198; Hewitt, *Base Christian Communities*.

107. Daniel H. Levine and Scott Mainwaring, "Religion and Popular Protest in Latin America," in *Power and Popular Protest: Latin American Social Movements*, ed. Susan Eckstein (Berkeley: University of California Press, 1988).

108. Burdick, "The Progressive Catholic Church."

109. Thomas C. Bruneau, "The Role and Response of the Catholic Church in the Redemocratization of Brazil," in *The Politics of Religion and Social Change*, eds. Anson Shupe and Jeffrey K. Hadden (New York: Paragon House, 1986), 95–98.

110. Mainwaring and Wilde, *The Progressive Church*, 30.

111. Lehmann, *Democracy and Development*, 144–145.

112. José Ivo Fullman, "Progressive Catholicism and Left-Wing Politics in Brazil," in *The Church at the Grassroots in Latin America: Perspectives on Thirty Years of Activism*, eds. John Burdick and W.E. Hewitt (Westport, CT: Praeger, 2000), 53–68.

113. Mark Tessler and Jamal Sanad, "Women and Religion in Modern Islamic Society: The Case of Kuwait," in *Religious Resurgence*, 209.

114. Sageman, *Understanding Terror Networks*, 74–78.

115. *The Pew Forum on Religion and Public Life: Surveys* (July 7, 2007), http://pewforum.org/surveys/pentecostal/latinamerica/.

116. For a collection of writings by progressive Islamic scholars and political figures, see *Liberal Islam*.

117. Smith, "The Limits of Religious Resurgence," 34.

118. Haynes, *Religion in Third World Politics*, 155.

119. Jeff Haynes, "Religion and Democratization in Africa," in *Religion, Democracy and Democratization*, ed. John Anderson (New York: Routledge, 2006), 68.

120. Ibid., 69.

121. Tung-Jen Cheng and Deborah A. Brown, eds., *Religious Organizations and Democratization: Case Studies from Contemporary Asia* (Armonk,

NY: M.E. Sharpe, 2006). See especially the chapters on the Philippines and South Korea.

122. Alexis de Tocqueville, *Democracy in America*, ed. Alan Ryan (London: Everyman's Library, 1994), 309–312.

123. David Marquand and Ronald L. Nettler, "Forward," in *Religion and Democracy*, eds. David Marquand and Ronald L. Nettler (Oxford, England: Blackwell Publishers, 2000), 2–3.

124. Ibid., 3.

125. Axel Hadenius, *Democracy and Development* (New York: Cambridge University Press, 1992).

126. Serif Mardin, "Civil Society and Islam," in *Civil Society: Theory, History, Comparison*, ed. John A. Hall (Cambridge, England: Polity Press, 1995); for a similar perspective, see Chris Hann, "Introduction: Political Society and Civil Anthropology," in *Civil Society: Challenging Western Models*, eds. Chris Hann and Elizabeth Dunn (London: Routledge, 1996), 1–26.

127. Robert W. Hefner, *Civil Islam: Muslims and Democratization in Indonesia* (Princeton, NJ: Princeton University Press, 2000).

128. Chang and Brown, eds., *Religious Organizations and Democratization*, 223–230; see also, Robert W. Hefner, "Muslim Democrats and Islamist Violence in Post-Soeharto Indonesia," in *Remaking Muslim Politics: Pluralism, Contestation, Democratization* ed. Robert W. Hefner (Princeton, NJ: Princeton University Press, 2006), 273–301.

129. In 2001, parliament removed Wahid from office based on his incompetence as president and possible corruption. I am not arguing that Wahid was a perfect democrat. When faced with impeachment, he acted questionably on a number of occasions. Nor am I suggesting that all Indonesian Muslim leaders were as tolerant as he was. I am merely noting that Wahid, despite his obvious faults as president, represented a brand of Islam that is quite compatible with democracy. Despite the enormous economic and ethnic problems facing Indonesia's new government, democracy (at least electoral democracy) stands a good chance of surviving.

CHAPTER 4

THE POLITICS OF CULTURAL PLURALISM AND ETHNIC CONFLICT

In the early years of the twenty-first century, like the early decades of the twentieth, much of the Third World suffered from ethnic, racial, and religious tensions periodically punctuated by outbreaks of brutality and carnage. Progress in one area was often followed by deterioration in another. For example, in 2005, the Sudanese government (led by Arab Muslims) signed a peace accord with the Sudan People's Liberation Movement/Army (SPLM/A)—a secessionist movement in the country's south, representing that region's predominantly Black (Christian and animist) population. The treaty, granting the south considerable autonomy (self-rule within Sudan), ended a 21-year civil war that had left about 2 million people dead, mostly southerners killed or starved by the government. Soon after ending that conflict, however, the Sudanese government intensified its "ethnic cleansing" in the western region of Darfur, where government-supported Arab militias (called Janjaweed) killed many thousands of Muslim Blacks from the Fur, Masalit, and Saghawa tribes. The Janjaweed "raped women and destroyed villages, food stocks, and other [essential] supplies" and drove 1 million people into refugee camps, where they have often been victimized once again.[1]

Such conflicts are not new. Nearly a century earlier (1915–1916), in the midst of World War I, Turkey's government massacred perhaps 1.5 million Armenians within that country's borders.[2] Thirty years after that, as Britain relinquished power over India, it divided that "jewel in the [imperial] crown," into two nations—largely Hindu India and overwhelmingly Muslim Pakistan. The religious communities in each country then savagely turned on each other, with a resulting death toll of approximately 1 million. More recently, Hutus in the African nation of Rwanda massacred some 800,000 of their Tutsi countrymen, while in the former country of Yugoslavia, Serbian militias initiated "ethnic cleansing" of their Muslim and Croat neighbors, killing and raping untold thousands. During the twentieth century, religious conflicts (India and Lebanon), tribal animosities (Nigeria and Rwanda), racial prejudice (South Africa), and other forms of ethnic rancor frequently produced violent confrontations, civil wars, and genocidal activity. Continuing ethnic tensions in the early years of the twenty-first century seem to confirm Mahabun ul Haq's prediction—that wars between "peoples" (ethnic, religious, or cultural groups) will continue to far outnumber wars between nation-states.

> Classic accounts of modernization, particularly those influenced by Marx, predicted that the old basis for divisions, such as tribe and religion, would be swept aside. As hundreds of millions of people poured from rural to urban areas worldwide, during the nineteenth and twentieth centuries, it was expected that new alliances would be formed, based on social class in particular.[3]

But, significant as class conflict has been, no cleavage has more sharply, and oftentimes violently, polarized nations in modern times than ethnicity. "Cultural pluralism [i.e., ethnic diversity]," notes Crawford Young, "is a quintessentially modern phenomenon." It has been closely linked to the growth of the middle class and the emergence of politicians who articulated nationalist or other ethnic aspirations while mobilizing workers and peasants behind that ideal.[4]

To be sure, ethnic minorities have been victimized by violence for hundreds of years. One needs only look to the nineteenth-century frontier wars between White settlers and Native Americans in the United States and Chile to identify just two examples. Furthermore, contrary to common perception, the level of ethnic protests and rebellions within states actually diminished slightly since the early 1990s, after having grown steadily for the previous 50 years.[5] Alarmist warnings notwithstanding, the world has not been crumbling into a maze of small ethnically based states.[6]

Still, as we begin a new century, the level of ethnically based *internal* conflict remains far higher than in the decades prior to the 1990s, in marked contrast to the dramatic decline in wars *between* nations in the same period. Indeed, over the past 50 years, the most frequent settings for violent conflict have not been wars between sovereign states, but rather internal strife tied to cultural, tribal, religious, or other ethnic animosities.[7] According to one recent estimate, "nearly two-thirds of all [the world's] armed conflicts [at that time] included an ethnic component. [Indeed], ethnic conflicts [were] four times more likely than interstate wars."[8] Another study claimed that 80 percent of "major conflicts" in the 1990s had an ethnic element.[9] Any listing of the world's most brutal wars in the past few decades would include ethnically based internal confrontations in Bosnia, Serbia (Kosovo), Rwanda, the Congo (formerly Zaire), Ethiopia, Sudan, Lebanon, and Indonesia (East Timor).[10] Perhaps 20 million people have died in ethnic violence since World War II.[11] Most recently, the collapse of Soviet and Eastern European communism released a torrent of pent-up ethnic hatreds in Azerbaijan, Armenia, Chechnya, Georgia, the former Yugoslavia, and other parts of Central and Eastern Europe. Particularly since the end of the Cold War, the world's attention has focused increasingly on ethnic clashes. Moreover, some experts predict that poor, densely populated countries, including several in Africa, will experience increased ethnic conflict over scarce resources (such as farm or grazing land) in the coming decades.[12]

Warfare between Serbs, Croats, Bosnian Muslims, and Kosovars in the former Yugoslavia, separatist movements by French-speaking Québécois, racially based riots in Los Angeles, Basque terrorism in Spain, and Protestant–Catholic clashes in Northern Ireland all have demonstrated clearly that interethnic friction and violence can also erupt in Western democracies and in former communist countries. But ethnic conflict has been particularly widespread and cruel in Africa, Asia, and other regions of the Third World—in part because LDCs tend to have more ethnically diverse populations, and in part because their political systems often lack the institutions or experience needed to resolve these tensions peacefully. A recent exhaustive study determined that there are approximately 275 "minorities at risk" (i.e., ethnic groups facing actual or potential repression) throughout the world, with a total population exceeding 1 billion (about one-sixth of the world's populations) scattered in 116 countries. Approximately 85 percent of that population at risk lives in the LDCs. Although Asia has the highest *absolute* population of ethnic minorities, Sub-Saharan Africa has the highest *proportion* of its population at risk (about 36 percent), followed by North Africa and the Middle East (26 percent).[13]

The intensification of ethnic, racial, and cultural hostilities during the twentieth century undercut several assumptions of modernization theory; it also contradicted an influential social psychology theory known as the "contact hypothesis." That hypothesis predicted that as people of different races, religions, and ethnicities came into greater contact with each other, they would better understand the other groups' common human qualities, causing prejudice to decline.[14] Although there is evidence to support the contact hypothesis at the *individual* level (i.e., as individuals of different races or religions come to know each other better, their prejudices *often* diminish), increased interaction between different ethnic *groups*, occasioned by factors such as urban migration, frequently *intensifies* hostilities. This is particularly true when the political and economic systems are biased in favor of one ethnic group or if ethnic leaders play on their followers' prejudices to advance their own political agendas.

This chapter focuses on the most protracted and intense ethnic group conflicts in the developing world. In doing so, it runs the risk of conveying the mistaken notion that all LDCs are aflame with violent ethnic clashes. In truth, most ethnic tensions do not lead to systematic violence and many developing nations have been largely free of such conflict. Ethnic warfare is more pronounced in the Indian subcontinent, the Middle East, Southeast Asia, and portions of Africa and is less common in Latin America and the Far East. A number of developing countries—Uruguay and Korea, for example—are fairly ethnically homogeneous, eliminating the possibility of such conflict. Others have developed a relatively stable, if not necessarily just, relationship between ethnicities—Venezuela, Ghana, and Taiwan. A number of Latin American countries are multiracial, and have varying degrees of racial discrimination and tension. But rarely do those conflicts become violent. So, although this chapter focuses on the difficult and violent cases in order to illustrate the obstacles that ethnic conflicts may present to political and economic development, it does not imply that most LDCs are riddled with ethnic tensions and violence.

DEFINING ETHNICITY

Although it is difficult to define ethnicity precisely, certain common qualities set ethnic groups apart. Most analysts agree that ethnic identity is usually a *social construction*—a way that certain groups have come to view themselves as distinct from others over time—rather than an inherent or primordial characteristic. Each ethnicity "share[s] a distinctive and enduring collective identity based on a belief in a common descent and on shared experiences and cultural traits."[15] While they frequently have some basis in fact, these identities and histories are usually created or embellished, by entrepreneurial politicians, intellectuals, and journalists who gain some advantage by "playing the ethnic card." The real or imagined common history, tradition, and values not only unite the group, but distinguish it from proximate ethnicities, sometimes giving rise to ethnic conflict.[16] Thus, J. E. Brown's cynical definition of a "nation" can be applied to ethnic identities generally: "A group of people united by a common error about their ancestry and a common dislike of their neighbors."[17] In times of great uncertainty or crisis, intellectuals and politicians are likely to create historical myths that give their ethnic group a sense of security in the face of perceived external challenges. In the words of Vesna Pesic, a Serbian peace activist, ethnic conflict is caused by the "fear of the future, lived through the past."[18]

Pakistanis and Indians in Uganda, Chinese in Malaysia, Hmong in Laos, and indigenous people (Indians) in Peru may form their own political organizations, business groups, or social clubs. However, ethnic groups are usually not socially homogeneous or politically united. Frequently, class, ideology, or religion divides them. For example, Sri Lanka's Tamil-speaking minority is divided between those who have lived in the country for centuries and those brought from India to work on plantations in the nineteenth century, with each group holding somewhat different political views. These two subgroups are, in turn, divided by caste. Indian Muslims and Nigerian Ibos are internally divided by class. South Koreans may be Buddhist or Christian (or both). Still, the factors that bind an ethnic group are more powerful than elements that divide it. Thus, Ibo peasants normally identify more closely with businesspeople from their own tribe than they do with fellow peasants from the Hausa or Yoruba communities. Indeed, Cynthia Enloe notes that "of all the groups that men [or women] attach themselves to, ethnic groups seem the most encompassing and enduring."[19]

Some ethnic classifications were initially imposed by outsiders. In the Belgian Congo, White colonial administrators, missionaries, explorers, and anthropologists erroneously lumped together people of the upper Congo region into a nonexistent tribe (or ethnicity) called the Bangala. After a number of decades, the "myth of the Bangala" took on a life of its own, as migrants from the upper Congo settling in the city of Kinshasa joined together under the ethnic banner that had been imposed on them by the Belgians.[20] Similarly, the classification of "Coloured" (written here with its South African and British spelling), once used to denote racially mixed or Asian South Africans, was an artificial construct established by the White regime. And although few Mexicans feel much in common with Cubans, Ecuadorians, or Nicaraguans when they live in their home countries, all of these nationalities become an ethnic group called "Latinos" or "Hispanics" after they immigrate to the United States and are viewed as a homogeneous mass by their "Anglo" neighbors. Once individuals begin to accept the group label imposed on them, however, even externally created ethnic classifications become politically relevant.[21]

Ethnic groups may have their own social clubs, soccer teams, schools, or cemeteries. For an insecure Peruvian Indian recently arrived in Lima from her rural village, or the Hausa migrant seeking a job in Lagos, ethnically based social clubs are invaluable for finding employment, housing, and friendships in an otherwise cold and inhospitable city. In the threatening environment associated with modernization and social change, "fear, anxiety, and insecurity at the individual level can be reduced within the womb of the ethnic collectivity."[22] At the same time, however, ethnic consciousness normally creates barriers between groups. People may frown upon interreligious or interracial marriages, for example. Inevitably, when two or more ethnic groups live near or amongst one another, there will be some tension or apprehension. But the way in which society handles these relationships varies considerably from place to place. Countries such as Canada, Malaysia, and Trinidad-Tobago have managed ethnic divisions relatively amicably and peacefully. More frequently, however, ethnic divisions lead to ethnic tensions or even conflict. In multiethnic countries such as India, Angola, Indonesia, and the United States, common consciousness and culture unite certain religions, castes, tribes, or races, while generating distrust toward other ethnicities.

ETHNIC AND STATE BOUNDARIES

If the world were composed of relatively homogenous countries such as Uruguay, South Korea, or Iceland, ethnically based wars might continue between nation-states, but there would be no ethnic tensions or strife within individual countries. In other words, the underlying cause of most internal ethnic conflict is that boundaries for *nations* (distinct cultural-linguistic groups such as Serbs, Russians, or Kurds) and other ethnicities frequently fail to coincide with boundaries for *states* (self-governing countries).[23] Thus, for example, if Serbia's Kosovo province had not been home to a substantial ethnic-Albanian community, that region would have avoided a bloody secessionist war. In the Middle East, 25–30 million Kurds have their own language, customs, and traditions, but not their own state. Consequently, they have struggled for decades to carve out the state of Kurdistan from the four countries in which they primarily reside. Similarly, Sikh militants in the Indian state of Punjab have demanded the creation of a Sikh nation-state. When minority (or, on occasion, majority) groups feel that they have been denied their fair share of political and economic influence, they will frequently mobilize and demand their rights.

A recent study of 191 independent countries throughout the world revealed that 82 percent contain two or more ethnic groups.[24] Furthermore, earlier research indicated that no single ethnic group accounts for even half of the total population in 30 percent of the world's countries.[25] This pattern is most striking in Sub-Saharan Africa, where virtually every country is composed of several ethnic (tribal) groups.[26] For example, it is estimated that Nigeria, the most populous Black African state, has more than 200 linguistic groups.[27]

Many Africans attribute their continent's legacy of tribal conflict to the European colonizers who divided the region into administrative units little connected with ethnic identities. In some cases, antagonistic groups were thrown together into a single colony, while elsewhere individual tribes were split between two future countries. In Africa, Asia, and the Middle East, many colonial powers exacerbated ethnic tensions by favoring certain groups over others, and by using "divide and conquer" strategies to control the local population. Yet colonialism must be seen as but one of many factors contributing to ethnic discord. Given the enormous number of tribal groups in Africa, even if the European powers had shown greater ethnic sensibility, many multiethnic nations would have inevitably developed. The only alternative would have been the creation of hundreds of tiny states, which would not have been economically viable.

Ironically, the *breakdown* of European colonialism also led to a number of extremely unhappy ethnic marriages. When the Portuguese withdrew from the small Southeast Asian colony of East Timor in 1975, neighboring Indonesia annexed it against the local population's will. In its efforts to crush the organized Timorese opposition, the Indonesian military killed approximately 150,000 people (about 25 percent of the population), mostly through policies that resulted in mass starvation and disease. After the Timorese was finally allowed to vote for independence in 1999, local militias tied to the Indonesian military slaughtered thousands more.[28] Elsewhere, following years of Italian colonial rule and a brief British occupation, the East African colony of Eritrea was forcibly merged with Ethiopia in the early 1950s. The Eritrean people (who have different religions and cultures than the Ethiopians) generally resented the Ethiopian takeover and soon embarked on a long struggle for independence.[29] Three decades of civil war resulted in the deaths of hundreds of thousands. Ultimately, the Ethiopian army fell to rebel forces from the provinces of Eritrea and Tigray.[30] The collapse of the Ethiopian military dictatorship in 1991 allowed Eritrea to finally achieve independence, though the two countries fought a bloody border war in 1998–2000 and are still on a war footing.

TYPES OF ETHNIC-CULTURAL DIVISIONS

In order to better grasp the range of ethnic tensions that currently pervade much of the developing world, I will first classify all types of ethnicities into a set of somewhat overlapping categories: nationality, tribe, race, and religion.[31]

Nationality

In ethnic analysis the term *nation* takes on a specialized meaning distinct from its more common usage designating a sovereign country (as in the *United Nations*). It refers, instead, to a population with its own language, cultural traditions, historical aspirations, and, often, its own geographical home. Frequently, nationhood is associated with the belief that "the interests and values of this nation take priority over all other interests and values."[32] Unlike other types of ethnic groups, many nationalities claim sovereignty over a specific geographic area. But, as we have seen, these proposed *national* boundaries frequently do not coincide with those of *sovereign states* (independent countries). For example, Russia, India, Spain, and Sri Lanka are all sovereign states that encompass several distinct *nationalities* (cultural identities). In each case, members of at least one of those nationalities—Chechens (Russia), Kashmiris (India), Basques (Spain), and Tamils (Sri Lanka)—have waged long struggles for independence. On the other hand, the Chinese are a nationality that, through migration, has spilled over to several East Asian countries and to other parts of the world. The Kurds also reside in several countries—including Turkey, Iraq, Iran, Syria, and, to a far lesser extent, the former Soviet Union. Unlike the Chinese, however, they are a nation without a state of their own.

As with many types of ethnicity, the political significance of national identity is related to highly subjective factors. Nationality becomes politically important only when members *believe* themselves to have a common history and destiny that both unites them and distinguishes them from other ethnicities in their country. The most critical basis for national identification is the preservation of a distinct spoken language. Because French Canadians, Turkish Kurds, and Malaysian Chinese have maintained their "mother tongues," their national identities remain politically salient.[33] Chinese speakers in Southeast Asia have maintained their own cultural and political organizations and feel strong emotional ties to China. Quebec's government, when in the hands of the separatist Parti Québécois, has supported autonomy or even independence for the primarily French-speaking province. On the other hand, because most immigrants to such countries as the United States, Canada, and Australia fully assimilate into their new language and culture, dropping their language of origin after one or two generations, their original national identity loses much of its political and social significance.

The appeal of militant ethnic nationalism tends to vary over time as the result of changing political and economic conditions. Despite its distinct language and culture, Spain's Basque population had begun to assimilate into Spanish society in the nineteenth century. However, since the 1970s two factors caused an upsurge in nationalist demands for self-rule (including bombings and assassinations). The first was Spain's transition to democracy following the death of the country's long-time dictator, Francisco Franco. That raised Basque hopes for greater autonomy and permitted nonviolent nationalist parties to campaign openly. The second was a decline in the region's industrial economy.[34]

In their more limited manifestations, nationalist movements simply seek to preserve the group's cultural identity and promote its economic and political interests. For example, neither the large Lebanese community in Brazil nor the Irish in Liverpool nor East Indians in Guyana have entertained visions of self-governance. On the other hand, nationalist movements become more provocative when they seek to create a separate nation-state of their own. Such separatist movements can arise when an ethnic minority is concentrated in a particular region of the country and represents a majority of the population in that area. Those conditions exist in Sri Lanka (formerly Ceylon until 1972), off the coast of India, where the Tamil-speaking population is most heavily concentrated in the country's northern and eastern provinces, particularly the Jaffna Peninsula region in the far north.[35] Even before the intrusion of Dutch, Portuguese, and British colonizers, the Tamils kept themselves apart from other ethnicities inhabiting Ceylon. The British conquest and colonization of the entire island (from 1815 until independence) produced a nationalist reaction among the majority Sinhalese (Sinhala-speaking) population, which, in turn, provoked friction between them and the Tamil minority.

Since Sri Lanka's independence in 1948, political power has been concentrated in the hands of the Sinhalese (about three-fourths of the country's population). As in most nationality-based ethnic clashes, language issues were at the heart of the conflict. Eight years after independence, Sinhala replaced English as the country's official language, giving the Sinhalese population a significant advantage in securing government jobs. As one Tamil political leader put it, "Not until 1956 did we really believe that we were second-class citizens. Until then all we engaged in were preventive measures, which we thought would hold."[36] From that point forward, however, the battle for Tamil self-rule intensified. Conversely, when Tamil acquired equal legal status in 1978, many Sinhalese, particularly those wanting government jobs, felt victimized. Religious differences between the largely Hindu Tamils and the predominantly Buddhist Sinhalese augment their language and cultural divisions.

As early as 1949, Tamil leaders (representing almost one-fifth of the country's population) demanded a federal system that would grant Tamil regions substantial autonomy (a degree of self-rule within the Sri Lankan state).[37] Sinhalese nationalists, in turn, tried to impose their language on the entire nation. Even though they were far more numerous than the Tamils, the Sinhalese suffered from a "minority complex," feeling threatened by the 50 million Tamils living on the nearby Indian mainland. In 1958, Sinhalese mobs attacked Tamils in various parts of the country, and in 1964, the Sri Lankan government signed an agreement with India calling for the eventual return to India of 525,000 Tamils whose families had migrated from India.[38] Faced with such threats, Tamil nationalism became increasingly strident and violent. Early calls for autonomy were superseded by demands for secession and the creation of a sovereign Tamil state. By the early 1980s, the most powerful force in the country's predominantly Tamil areas was the Liberation Tigers of Tamil Eelam (better known simply as the Tamil Tigers, or LTTE), a secessionist force engaged in guerrilla warfare and terrorism.[39]

In 1987, following a major national government offensive against the LTTE, India (concerned about possible demands for autonomy from its own Tamil minority) intervened militarily in Sri Lanka. The resulting Indo-Lanka Peace Accord called for a multiethnic, multilingual Sri Lankan state with increased regional autonomy for the Tamil areas. Though signed by the Indian and Sri Lankan governments and supported by much of the Tamil population, the accord was rejected by many Sinhalese, particularly the ultra-nationalist National Liberation Front (JVP). From 1987 to 1989, the JVP launched its own campaign of strikes, boycotts, and terrorism, resulting in thousands of deaths. A brutal government campaign eventually crushed the JVP, but the war against the Tamil Tigers continued. Although many Tamils welcomed the Indo-Lanka accord, the Tigers rejected it as inadequate. Instead, they expanded their bloody guerrilla war, first against the Indian 60,000-man occupation force and then, after the 1990 withdrawal of foreign troops, against the Sri Lankan government and moderate Tamils.[40]

The LTTE allegedly has raised more than $60 million annually by smuggling illegal immigrants and drugs into Europe and the United States and has received millions more in donations from Tamil supporters living abroad. The Tigers are responsible for the 1993 assassination of Sri Lankan President Ranasinghe Premadasa, the 1999 suicide bombing that wounded another national president, a June 2000 bombing that killed 23 people, including the Industry Minister, and more than 200 other suicide bombings. Human rights groups have condemned the Tigers for using young girls as suicide bombers, who are more likely to get past police and army checkpoints with bombs strapped to their bodies. As of mid-2000, an estimated 62,000 people had been killed in the civil war, out of a total population of 21 million people. A cease-fire signed in 2002 restored relative peace to that devastated country for several years. But subsequent Norwegian efforts to broker a peace treaty stalled, impeded by divisions among Tamil factions and by distrust on both sides. By late 2005, the truce had broken down. In the next 18 months, the renewed fighting and suicide bombing took some 5,000 additional lives.[41]

Tribe

The very use of the category *"tribe,"* especially when applied to African cultures, is fairly controversial. Many anthropologists and political scientists find it arbitrary and unhelpful. They note that when cultural anthropologists first worked in Africa and South Asia, often they assumed that the social characteristics of the small groups of people they were studying could automatically be extended to larger units they called a *tribe.*[42] (See my earlier discussion of the Congo's "myth of the Bangala.") Critics also point out that the term "tribe" is sometimes used to describe African ethnic groups as large as the 15 million Yoruba (in Nigeria), a population that elsewhere in the world would be called a *nationality.* Hence, many scholars prefer to use the terms *ethnicity* or *ethno-linguistic groups.* This text, however, still refers to tribal groups because that term is familiar to most readers and has long been used by some scholars of ethnic politics and by numerous political leaders in Africa and Asia. For example, in describing the problems of his own country, former Ugandan President Milton Obote lamented "the pull of the tribal force."[43] This chapter uses *tribe* to describe subnational groups that share a collective identity and language and believe themselves to hold a common lineage. The term is most often used regarding Africa and, to a lesser extent, Asia. In India, Vietnam, Burma, and other parts of Asia, tribe refers to nonliterate hill peoples, such as the Laotian Hmong, who live traditional lifestyles in relative isolation from modern society. The term has also been used, of course, in discussions of North American Indians as well as the lowland (Amazonian) Indians of South America. In none of these cases do we use the term pejoratively.

Recent survey data from 12 African nations indicate that tribal (or sociolinguistic) identifications tend to be the major determinant of support for political parties, though other variables—such as age, urban versus rural origin, and education—also play a role and sometimes reduce (though not eliminate) the influence of tribe.[44] Moreover, intertribal conflict has frequently sparked violence in Sub-Saharan Africa, affecting more than half the countries in that region at one time or another. Nigeria, Ethiopia, Rwanda, Burundi, Uganda, Sudan, the Congo, and Ivory Coast, among others, have been torn apart by civil wars that were partially or primarily ethnically based. In Liberia, Angola, and Mozambique, conflicts begun about other issues were aggravated by tribal divisions. From the time of its independence, Nigeria experienced antagonism between the Muslims in the North and the peoples of the South and East. With 50 percent of the country's population, the Hausa-Fulani and other northern tribes were a dominant political force, resented by southerners and easterners such as the Ibo, who considered them backward.[45] Northerners, in turn, feared the influence of the more modern and commercially successful Ibo people who prevailed in the East. Each of the three major ethnic groups (Hausa-Fulani, Ibo, and Yoruba) prevailed in one region of the country, casting a shadow over smaller tribes in their area. Each major tribe, in turn, feared domination by the others.[46]

Two military coups in 1966 intensified friction between officers of differing ethnic backgrounds and sparked violence against the many Ibos who had migrated to the North. As many as 30,000 Ibos may have been killed. In fear of their lives, 1–2 million more fled from northern Nigeria to their homeland. In May 1967, Colonel Chukwuemeka Ojukwu, an Ibo military leader, declared that Eastern Nigeria was withdrawing from the country to become the independent nation of Biafra. Backed by the Organization of African Unity (OAU), the Nigerian national government was determined to prevent Biafra's secession.[47] Despite its initial military success, Biafra eventually suffered from the antipathy that many smaller eastern tribes felt toward the Ibos. A number of those tribes sided with the federal army. In the end, the armed forces surrounded Biafra and tightened their grip. Up to 1 million Ibo civilians died (largely of starvation) in a pattern of war-induced famine that later became tragically familiar in other parts of Africa. On the other hand, when Biafra finally did surrender in early 1970, the Nigerian military government was disciplined, refraining from acts of vengeance. Since that time, the Ibos have been relatively successfully reintegrated into Nigerian society, but intertribal tensions and periodic religious violence persist.[48]

Unfortunately, the Nigerian conflict was but one of earliest of the ethnically based civil wars that were to plague the African continent over the next 40 years. Some of the most intense and prolonged tribal conflicts took place in the former Belgian colonies of Burundi and Rwanda in the Great Lakes region of Eastern Africa. Burundi's ruling Tutsi minority has crushed a series of uprisings by the majority Hutus (about 85 percent of the population), since they gained power in the early 1970s, massacring perhaps 100,000 people in 1972 alone.[49] In 1993, when a Tutsi soldier assassinated Melchior Ndadaye, a Hutu who was the country's first freely elected president, new bloodshed erupted. One year later, in the neighboring country of Rwanda, the Hutu president's death in a plane crash set off an orgy of violence. A government-directed massacre led by Hutu extremists was directed at the minority Tutsis and, to a lesser extent, moderate Hutus. During the next 100 days, local Hutu militia and allied villagers beat or hacked to death approximately 750,000 Tutsis and 50,000 Hutus.[50] Eventually, a well-trained Tutsi revolutionary army, supported by neighboring Uganda, gained control of the country and jailed thousands of Hutus. Hundreds of thousands more fled to nearby Congo, where many of them starved to death or were massacred by the anti-Hutu regime of then-President Laurent Kabila.

In other conflicts, such as the Angolan and Mozambican civil wars (which had both ideological and ethnic origins), major powers supported one side or the other, thereby intensifying the war and adding to the bloodshed. Cold War superpowers often armed one of the sides or interceded through surrogates. For example, acting in consort with the Soviet Union, Cuba provided military assistance to the leftist governments of Ethiopia, Angola, and Mozambique. The United States armed UNITA, the Angolan rebel force, while the South African military supported Mozambique's RENAMO guerrillas. Belgium and France armed the Rwandan regime prior to its genocidal attacks on the Tutsi population. In each of those countries, hundreds of thousands perished from warfare or starvation. Although the end of the Cold War has reduced such inflammatory, super-power intervention, the recent brutal wars in the Congo, Liberia, Sierra Leone, and Ivory Coast indicate that tribally based violence will undoubtedly continue in the region for some time. Since the late 1990s, Rwanda, Uganda, Zimbabwe, and Angola all have intervened in the ethnically related civil war in the Congo.

In other cases, corrupt dictators launched campaigns against tribal minorities in order to curry favor with other ethnic groups and thereby deflect protest against their own governments. For example, Daniel Arap Moi, Kenya's long-standing strongman (1978–2002), attached the Kikuyu tribe, and Congolese President Laurent Kabila (1997–2001) massacred his country's Hutu minority for the same reason.

Race

Race is normally the most visible ethnic division within society. That is to say, although it may be difficult to pinpoint people's religion or tribe from their appearance, physical differences between Blacks, Whites, and East Asians are usually rather apparent. Yet, in some instances racial distinctions can be more subtle and elusive. The Aymara-speaking woman in La Paz, Bolivia, who wears a bowler hat and a distinctive native skirt, is obviously indigenous (an Indian). Yet her Spanish-speaking son, wearing a suit and teaching at a nearby high school, is considered a Mestizo (a person of mixed Indian and White heritage). African Americans or South African "Coloureds" of mixed racial origin are some-times physically indistinguishable from Whites. Unlike other ethnic divisions, racial divisions are frequently not linked to language or cultural differences.

We have noted that cultural identity involves a common set of values and customs and a shared sense of history and destiny. Of course, people of the same race living in a particular country may not experience that sense of community. Serbs, Croats, Bosnian Muslims, and ethnic Albanians in the quasi-independent, Serbian province of Kosovo are all Whites; both Lebanese Muslims and Christians are Arabs; and Ethiopia's Amharic majority as well as the Eritreans and Tigrayans are all Blacks. Yet despite their common racial backgrounds, these groups most assuredly do not share a common cultural bond. Because the populations of each of those countries are the same race, that could not be an ethnic marker. Only when people live in *multiracial* settings do individual racial groups use their race to define themselves and distinguish themselves from "others." Indeed, Crawford Young indicates that "there was no common sense of being 'African', 'European', or 'Indian', prior to the creation of multiracial communities by the population movements of the imperial age."[51] Slavery and other manifestations of Western imperialism in the Third World produced a wide range of negative racial stereotypes about Asians, Africans, and (North and South) American Indians. The subsequent migration of Asians to the plantations of East Africa and the Caribbean created further racial cleavages.

South Africa presented the most notorious example of racially based political conflict. From its colonization by the British until its 1994 transition to majority rule, the country was ruled by a White minority constituting only 15 percent of the population. In the years following World War II, political power shifted from English-speaking Whites to the more conservative Afrikaners, descendants of Dutch and French Protestant settlers.[52] Meanwhile, Blacks, the majority population, were denied fundamental legal and economic rights, including the right to vote or hold political office.

Until renounced by President F. W. de Klerk's administration (the last White minority government), the legal centerpiece of South African racial policy was *apartheid* (separateness). That system rigidly segregated employment, public facilities, housing, marriage and more, envisioning a day when most Blacks lived in eight allegedly self-ruling "homelands." In fact, these homelands, consisting of desolate rural territories, could not possibly support the country's Black population. Moreover, because important sectors of the South African economy, most notably its mines, were dependent on Black labor, the geographical segregation envisioned by apartheid was implausible even from the perspective of the White business community. Meanwhile, the millions of Blacks who lived outside the homelands were denied the right to own land and lacked fundamental civil liberties.

Apartheid was based on a four-fold racial classification that defied international standards and often fell victim to its own logical contradictions. *Blacks*, who constitute 70–75 percent of the national population, were by far the largest racial group and were subjected to the greatest level of legal discrimination. *Coloureds*—people of mixed race—totaled about 10 percent of the population, primarily concentrated in Cape Town and Cape Province. Asians (mostly Indians and Pakistanis) represent about 3 percent of the nation. Both Coloureds and Asians enjoyed a higher socioeconomic status and greater legal and political rights than Blacks, but still ranked considerably below Whites. Finally, *Whites* (some 15 percent) maintained virtually all political and economic power.

The Constitutional Act of 1983 established a three-house Parliament—representing Whites, Coloureds, and Asians, but not the Black majority. This was part of a broader government strategy aimed at driving a wedge between Coloureds and Blacks. In truth, the Coloured and Asian parliamentary houses had no meaningful powers.

Despite international disapproval, South Africa's minority government seemed determined to maintain apartheid forever. By the 1980s, however, cracks began to develop in the country's segregation policies, as many middle-class Coloureds and Asians moved into "Whites only" neighborhoods by subletting from Whites. Again, in its efforts to divide the many middle-class Coloureds and Asians from the mostly impoverished Blacks, the government often ignored such violations, while simultaneously brutally repressing Black civil rights demonstrations emerging in the townships.

In time, South Africa came under intense domestic and international pressure to end apartheid and White domination. The country became an international pariah—particularly after several massacres of peaceful Black protestors—subject to diplomatic and cultural isolation, including a United Nations boycott restricting trade, travel, and investment. South African athletes could not compete in the Olympics or other international sporting events. Though slow to take effect, economic sanctions, particularly restrictions on investment, eventually impaired the country's economic growth. Growing protest and unrest in the Black townships, coupled with international isolation and a worldwide trend toward democracy, compounded the pressures for change.[53] Finally, a growing number of powerful voices within the White economic, legal, and intellectual elites pressed the government for racial reform.

By the start of the 1990s, then, President de Klerk's government, recognizing that apartheid was no longer viable, rescinded a number of segregation laws. It also legalized the African National Congress (ANC), the leading Black opposition group, along with two more radical organizations, after decades of banishment. The ANC's legendary leader, Nelson Mandela, the world's most celebrated political prisoner, was released from jail (after 27 years of imprisonment) along with hundreds of other political prisoners. These changes, coupled with the ANC's suspension of its armed struggle, opened the door to a new constitution enfranchising the Black majority and ending White minority rule.

In December 1991, the Convention for a Democratic South Africa (CODESA) brought together the government, the ANC, the Zulu-based Inkatha Freedom Party, and 16 smaller groups for discussions of the new political order. Public opinion among Whites was mixed but most acknowledged that Apartheid could no longer continue and supported the peace process. Indeed, Nelson Mandela expressed amazement at the hundreds of Whites who lined the road to cheer him when he was released from prison. In a 1992 national referendum called by de Klerk, nearly 70 percent of all White voters endorsed negotiations with the ANC and other Black groups. The following year the government and the ANC agreed to the election of a constitutional assembly that would create a new political system with equal rights for all South Africans. Universal suffrage ensured a Black majority in the assembly, but Whites were guaranteed special minority protection until 1999. In May 1994 the ANC parliamentary majority elected Nelson Mandela president of the new South Africa.

A decade later, the road to multiracial democracy remains difficult. Blacks have discovered that although majority rule has engendered greater social justice and human dignity, many of them remain mired in poverty. To be sure, government housing programs have benefited numerous urban slum dwellers and the Black middle class has mushroomed. On the other hand, with most farm land still owned by Whites and limited funds available for schools and clinics in the countryside, the Black rural population remains impoverished. Due to high unemployment, soaring crime rates, and one of the world's highest incidences of AIDS, the urban poor also continue to struggle. The governments of President Mandela and his successor, Thabo Mbeki, have pursued moderate economic policies to reassure the White business community. These policies have brought economic growth but have been slow to alleviate poverty. The ANC remains popular and still dominates all national elections. Over time, however, if Black living conditions do not improve and if there is not a sizable redistribution of economic resources, the ANC's Black constituency may demand more radical policies. An indication of that sentiment was the recent ANC party vote ousting Mbeki as party president, replacing him with a more populist leader, Jacob Zuma, who thus became the overwhelming favorite to succeed Mbeki as the next national president in 2009. The country's soaring crime rate, a reflection of widespread poverty and pervasive inequality, could also turn into wider political violence.

Religion

Because it involves deeply felt values, religion has frequently been the source of bitter communal strife (i.e., conflict between ethnic communities of any type). In Chapter 3, we examined the influence of religious *beliefs* on political attitudes and behavior, particularly those of fundamentalists and others favoring close links between church and state. We saw that a group's religious orientation often shapes its political beliefs, including its ideas of a citizen's political rights and obligations as well as its understanding of the country's constitutional and legal systems. In countries with multiple religions, for example, the state must create inheritance and family laws that are acceptable to religious communities with dissimilar views on these issues. Consequently, Israel has different codes of family law applying to Jews, Muslims, and Christians. The same is true in India for Hindus, Muslims, and Sikhs.[54]

In this chapter, on the other hand, we look at a related but distinct aspect of religion, namely the degree to which coreligionists identify strongly with each other and try to enhance their political and economic power relative to other religious groups. In other words, we are concerned here, not with the constitutional and legal ramifications of religion (considered in Chapter 3), but with the potential tension or even conflict *between* religious groups (defined here as ethnic communities) living in the same country. Such discord may pit one religion against another or, particularly in the case of Islam, may involve conflict between two branches of the same religion. Two factors influence the likelihood of tensions between religious groups: first, the extent to which one religious community feels dominated by another; and, second, the degree to which any religion regards their religion as the one true faith and that alternate theologies are unacceptable. Thus, Catholics and Protestants coexist rather harmoniously in the United States and Germany because neither of these conditions applies. On the other hand, in Northern Ireland, where Catholics have resented the Protestants' political and economic power and Protestants have feared that the Catholic majority may prevail over them, paramilitary groups representing both sides engaged in a bloody, 30-year armed struggle.

In 1992, thousands of Hindu fundamentalists destroyed a sixteenth-century Muslim mosque in the northern Indian town of Ayodhya. Like many such clashes, the incident grew out of centuries-old beliefs and hostilities.[55] Many Hindus believe this to be the spot where the god Ram had been born thousands of years ago. To the Bharatiya Janata Party (BJP), the leading Hindu political party, and to the more militant World Hindu Council, the mosque was a symbol of Islamic domination during the 300 years of Mogul rule prior to the British colonial era. The Indian courts had been debating its status for some six years. Within days of the 1992 assault, rioting in northern and central India left about 2,000 dead. Ten years later (2002), Hindu mobs in the village of Ahmedabad murdered over 1,000 Muslims, raping women, burning some alive, and occasionally cutting fetuses out of pregnant women.[56] In neighboring Islamic countries, Pakistani crowds attacked Hindu temples while Bangladeshis assaulted Hindu-owned shops and burned Air India offices.

Ironically, some of the worst Hindu–Muslim bloodshed in 1992 took place in Bombay, India's financial and cultural center and one of the country's most modern and least sectarian cities. An extremist Hindu group, Shiv Sena, with 30,000 armed members in that city, was responsible for much of the violence. Since that time, not only have city authorities failed to prosecute Shiv Sena's leader, but he has been protected by the Bombay police.

In fact, India and Pakistan were born of communal violence, and neither has been free of it since. Although both countries had been part of a single British colony, when negotiations for independence advanced in the late 1940s, the Muslim League insisted on the creation of a separate Muslim state. Using language that classically defines an ethnic group, League leader Mohammed Ali Jinnah declared: "We are a nation with our own distinctive culture and civilization, language and literature . . . customs . . . history and tradition."[57] In 1946, as independence approached, political conflict between the Muslim League and the leading voice of Indian independence, the Congress Party (a nonreligious party led largely by secular Hindus), touched off communal violence between Hindus and Muslims that left thousands dead. Finally, the British reluctantly divided their most important colony into two countries: India, with roughly 300 million Hindus and 40 million Muslims at that time; and Pakistan, with approximately 60 million Muslims and 20 million Hindus. No sooner had independence been declared (August 15, 1947), when horrendous religious massacres took place in both countries. Whole villages were destroyed, 12 million refugees of both faiths fled across the border in either direction, more than 75,000 women were abducted and raped, and up to 1 million people were killed in one of the twentieth century's worst ethnic conflagrations.[58] Two decades later, Pakistan split in two as geography, language, and cultural differences divided the Muslim population. With support from India, the country's Bengali-speaking eastern region broke away from the dominant, primarily Urdu-speaking, west to form the country of Bangladesh.

Today, Muslim separatists in the Indian state of Kashmir are waging guerrilla warfare aimed either at Kashmiri independence or unification with Pakistan. In 2001 Muslim fundamentalists attacked the Indian parliament, once again bringing India and Pakistan (both now nuclear powers) to the brink of war. Since early 2004, the two countries have engaged in a series of peace talks and confidence-building measures, as both countries have made an impressive effort to step back from the brink of conflict. But basic differences over Kashmir keep that region potentially volatile.

Other religious conflicts in India also have extracted a heavy toll. In the economically dynamic state of Punjab (where members of the Sikh religion constitute 55 to 60 percent of the population), Sikh militants demand the creation of their own country, to be called Khalistan ("the land of the pure").[59] Sikh terrorism, including random murders of Hindu civilians, along with police and military brutality against the Sikhs created an ever-rising cycle of violence. In 1984, government troops attacked the holiest Sikh temple, the Golden Temple of Amritsar, which had been seized by the militant Sikh leader Sant Jarnail Singh Bhindranwale and several hundred of his followers. In a three-day battle on the temple grounds, more than 100 people, including Bhindranwale, were killed along with hundreds of civilians nearby. Soon afterwards, there was a small rebellion by Sikh soldiers dismayed over the army's assault on the temple, the first armed forces mutiny since Indian independence. Then, on October 31, months after the attack on the Golden Temple, two Sikh members of Prime Minister Gandhi's personal bodyguard assassinated her.[60] Lashing out after the assassination, roaming Hindu mobs killed thousands of innocent Sikh civilians. The battle for an independent Khalistan continued for years. Despite attempts at reconciliation by Indira's successor—her son Rajiv Gandhi—government repression and Sikh terrorism continued unabated. But, by the mid-1990s, following 20,000 deaths on both sides, the Indian military had contained the separatist movement and Sikh separatism seemed on the wane.

From the 1970s through the 1980s, Lebanon was also a battlefield for warring religious factions. Today the danger of renewed violence again looms large. Among the 17 religious communities represented in the Lebanese political system, the most important have been Maronite Catholics, Shi'a Muslims, Sunni Muslims, and Druze (a religion that combines Muslim and other religious beliefs).[61] Despite its religious heterogeneity, for its first 30 years after independence (1943) the country was considered "the Switzerland of the Middle East"—a bastion of peace and economic prosperity in the midst of a troubled region. During that time the dominant Maronite and Sunni communities coexisted under the terms of a political power-sharing arrangement dating back to the 1920s, when Lebanon had limited home rule, and reinforced in 1943.

But power sharing and the peace it had brought broke down in the 1970s as the Muslim population, particularly the Shi'a community, perceived that the terms of the old agreement no longer reflected the relative sizes of the major religious groups. Muslims, with between 55 and 70 percent of the population (depending on whose estimate one believed), had long been allocated only 50 percent of the nation's bureaucratic and political posts. Religious, economic, and political differences also caused conflict between Shi'a and Sunni Muslims. Despite having a larger population than the Sunnis, Shi'as had less political power, fewer allocated seats in parliament, and a lower standard of living than either the Sunnis or the Christians. Lebanon's two most powerful political offices—president and prime minister—were reserved, respectively, for a Maronite Christian and a Sunni.[62]

External intervention further aggravated the ethnic tensions. The influx of many Palestinian refugees (fleeing Jordan), including armed PLO militia, radicalized Lebanon's political arena. Many impoverished Shi'as were drawn to the Palestinians' revolutionary rhetoric. On the other hand, Christian leaders were concerned that PLO attacks against Israel were provoking retaliatory raids into Lebanon. Christian militias, who feared the threat to their power posed by both the Shi'a and the Palestinians, entered a military alliance with Israel. At the same time, Syria, wishing to expand its power in the Middle East and create a buffer zone between itself and Israel, occupied much of Lebanon and manipulated various factions.[63] By 1975 Lebanon's national government had become an ineffectual, hollow shell, as power shifted to a range of communal warlords. Confrontations between the army and civilian protestors, along with clashes between Palestinian guerrillas and Christian militias, engulfed Lebanon in a civil war that lasted more than 15 years and took more than 150,000 lives. The country's religious conflict had elements of a class struggle as well, pitting the more prosperous Christian community against Shi'as, who saw themselves as the oppressed poor. Foreign forces, in the form of the Palestinian militia, occupying Israeli forces in the South, and Syrian military domination in much of the rest of the country, all added to the bloodshed.

As Lebanese cities lay in ruins and Palestinian, Israeli, and Syrian forces threatened to destroy the nation's sovereignty, the Arab League (representing the region's Arab governments) helped negotiate a treaty between the warring factions. The Taif Accord, signed in late 1989, raised the percentage of Muslims in various government posts and established the basis for a "national pact" between the warring factions.[64] During the next 15 years, the Lebanese rebuilt their economy and maintained a fragile peace between religious factions, although Syrian troops and intelligence units continued their occupation and often dictated policy to the Lebanese government.

But even before the 1989 agreement was signed, there were further confrontations between the Sunnis and Shi'ites. In the early 1980s, Shi'a clergy founded Hezbollah (the "Party of God"), a combination political party, social-services provider, and armed militia. Its goals included driving Israeli forces out of southern Lebanon (and, ultimately, destroying the state of Israel), promoting Shi'a fundamentalism with close ties to Iran (the party's leading financial backer and arms supplier), and asserting Shi'a political power, not only in Lebanon, but in the Middle East generally. The United States, Britain, Canada, and Israel all have included Hezbollah in their list of terrorist organizations. But, the party gained widespread popularity within the Shi'a and Palestinian communities when it helped drive Israeli forces out of Lebanon's south (ending an 18-year occupation) and subsequently launched mortar and terrorist attacks on that country. Furthermore, it set up a parallel system of schools, health clinics, and other services that have operated far more effectively than the government's social services and have better served the Shi'a poor.

In 2006, after Hezbollah fighters crossed into Israel and captured two soldiers, Israeli troops invaded Lebanon and carried out saturation bombings of urban Hezbollah strongholds. Large portions of the country's southern cities were destroyed, about 1,150 Lebanese and 150 Israelis were killed, and the country's rebuilt economy once again lay in ruins. While many Christians and Sunnis blamed Hezbollah for foolishly provoking Israel, the movement's support intensified within the large Shi'a community as Hezbollah outperformed the Lebanese government in supplying emergency housing and services to the 400,000 civilians who had been forced from their homes during the 34-day war. By launching several thousand rockets (supplied by Syria and Iran) into northern Israel during the war, Hezbollah also enhanced its military reputation. Following the war, it led massive popular demonstrations (largely Shi'ite) against the government.

Elsewhere in the Middle East, bloody conflict between Sunnis and Shi'ites has, of course, been particularly newsworthy during the current war in Iraq. But, like many of the Third World's ethnic clashes, its origins can be traced back to an earlier period. When Iraq received full independence in 1932, the outgoing British rulers transferred power to the Sunni Arab elite. For the next 70 years the relatively small Arab Sunni community (about 15 percent of the total population) dominated both the Arab Shi'a majority (about 60 percent), and the Kurdish minority (20 percent). Although most Kurds are also Sunnis, they are not on good terms with the Arab Sunnis. In fact when the U.S. media and other analysts refer to the Sunni community in Iraq, they mean only the Arab Sunnis, not Kurdish Sunnis. Upon taking full power, Saddam Hussein intensified persecution of the Shi'a, particularly after Iraq's defeat in the 1991 Gulf War. Believing that President George H. W. Bush's call to the Iraqi people to overthrow Saddam after that war meant that the United States would support such an uprising, the

Shi'a heartland in southern Iraq, like the Kurds in the Northeast, rose up against the dictator. When U.S. assistance failed to materialize, both revolts were crushed. Towns across the south were razed and tens of thousands of Shi'a were massacred, whether or not they had participated in the uprising. In the years that followed, Saddam limited delivery of food and other basic services to the south. As a consequence, thousands of Shi'ites migrated to the country's Sunni-dominated, central region. In greater Baghdad, neighborhoods such as Sadr City became home to huge Shi'ite enclaves, bringing them into closer contact with the Sunnis.[65]

Given Saddam's relentless persecution of the Shi'as, it was not surprising that they rejoiced in his overthrow. Indeed, when the United States first invaded Iraq, the Shi'ites most respected religious leader, the grand ayatollah Ali al-Husayni Sistani, instructed his followers not to resist the American forces. But, contrary to the expectations of Pentagon planners, this did not mean that Sistani or the Shi'a masses allied with the United States. Once Sunni political domination was terminated—symbolized by the American program of "debathification," a purge of former members of Saddam's ruling (mostly Sunni) Ba'ath party from government posts—Sistani opposed several important elements of U.S. policy. For example, the American occupation authorities initially favored institutional arrangements that would have given each of the three ethnic communities substantial veto power over critical government decisions so as to allay the Sunni and Kurdish minorities' fear of being dominated by the newly empowered Shi'a majority.[66] Similarly, the United States hoped to delay national elections until ethnic tensions had eased. Sistani and other Shi'ite leaders blocked both proposals, arguing that America's own democratic principles mandated that elections be held quickly and that they be based on the principle of "one man, one vote" and majority rule (i.e., no vetoes for minorities).

Despite his differences with the U.S. high command, however, Sistani favored peaceful negotiation with the occupation authorities. On the other hand, the Sunni community, unaccustomed to being out of power, was increasingly hostile toward American and allied occupation forces, while opposing Shi'a political aspirations. Indeed, most Sunnis saw the American debathification of the Iraqi miliary's and security police's officers corps as a de facto program of "de-Sunnification" of the government. Meanwhile, Shi'ites eagerly anticipated the dawn of a new Shi'a-dominated state. Adding to long-standing theological differences between the two religious communities, the Shi'a deeply resented the persecution they had suffered at the hands of the Sunni-dominated, Saddam government. The Sunnis, for their part, viewed the Shi'as as agents of the Iranian government and its religious leaders. Iraq and Iran are among the few nations in the Middle East with majority Shia populations. But, they were separated by language (most Iranians speak Farsi) and by each country's long-term aspirations for leadership in the Gulf region. As we noted in the previous chapter, during the 1980s the two had fought a brutal war. The fact that many of Iraq's leading Shi'a clerics had lived in exile in Iran while fleeing Saddam's persecution added to the Sunni leadership's fears. Indeed, the grand ayatollah Sistani himself was born and raised in Iran and still speaks Arabic with a thick Persian accent. But, most of all, the Sunnis were afraid of losing political power to the Shi'as whom they had so long dominated and often mistreated.

Within a year of Saddam's fall, Sunni extremists were using their most lethal weapons—roadside bombs and suicide bombings directed aginst police stations, markets, bus stations, religious shrines, and other crowded sites in Shi'a neighborhoods. Initially, foreigners carried out many of the suicide bombings, especially Saudis, Syrians, and Jordanians. In time, however, native Iraquis committed most terrorist acts. Their reach has been horrifying to the American troops and to Shi'ite civilians. In April 2007 a suicide bomber penetrated the supposedly impregnable security of the parliament building in the American-controlled Green Zone, the most fortified area in Iraq. Although only one member of parliament was killed, the attack sent a psychologically powerful message that no place in Iraq was safe from terrorism. From the start of the Sunni insurgency in 2003 through April 2007, there were more than 350 confirmed suicide bombings, killing thousands of Iraquis and many American soldiers. While other terrorist groups also have used suicide bombers in countries such as Lebanon, Sri Lanka, and Israel, never have such attacks reached Iraq's level. Of the bombers who have been identified posthumously, all have been Sunnis and almost all suicide attacks were directed at Shi'ites or foreigners. Bombs are delivered in cars, trucks, or, occasionally, on foot.

In May 2007, a leading American authority on these bombings noted, "Since our invasion, suicide terrorism has been essentially doubling in Iraq every year."[67] In fact, suicide bombings have become so frequent that the mere rumor of a bomber can caused mass panic. For example, on August 31, 2005, 1 million Shi'a pilgrims converged on a holy shrine in Baghdad, their line stretching for miles. In the morning, a mortar attack on the worshippers killed 16 people. Later in that same day a rumor spread in the massive crowd that a suicide bomber was in their midst. Panic produced a stampede in which more than one thousand people died—trampled or drowned in the nearby river while trying to escape the carnage.

The 2007 surge in the number of U.S. troops reduced the level of violence during the second half of that year. At the same time, there have been important Sunni militia defections. Sunni military and terrorist organizations fall into two broad categories: first, religously inspired groups (*jihadists*), often led by foreigners with ties to al Qaeda; and, second, secular groups, led by Iraqis linked to the Ba'thist resistance. Of late, tensions between the two have been mounting. In 2007, some of the Sunni militias that had earlier battled U.S. troops, formed alliances of convenience with the Americans in order to battle the jihadists. American arms and training seemingly have improved those militias ability to fight al Qaeda, but they also risk helping Sunni extremists in the event of future religious conflict. To date attempts to reconcile differences between the three ethnic communities within the parliament and other high levels of government have gone nowhere and it remains to be seen whether the presurge level of ethnic violence will resume once the United States begins to reduce its troop commitment.

Ayatollah Sistani remains the most respected Shi'a clergyman in matters of theological and legal interpretation. But the Sunni terrorists' repeated attacks have caused many Shi'ites to reject his admonitions against violence and civil war. Consequently, a young cleric named Muqtada al-Sadr has emerged as the face of Shi'a militancy. In contrast to the aging Sistani, a relative moderate who rarely appears in public and issues most of his pronouncements through his aides, Al-Sadr has a more charismatic personality. A fiery nationalist, he has demanded an immediate withdrawal of American troops from Iraq. Al-Sadr's support is most pronounced in Baghdad's huge Shi'a enclave, Sadr City—named after his father, a grand ayatollah who had been executed by the Saddam government—and, to a lesser extent, in Basra, Iraq's second largest city and the largest Shi'a stronghold. He and his followers have acted on two fronts: first, they formed a militia of several thousand men, called the Mahdi Army. Since 2004 the militia has occasionally battled American troops. But its primary role has been to react to Sunni assaults on Shi'a neighborhoods, retaliating with kidnapping, torture, and execution of suspected Sunni militants. It has also provided medical and other services to Shi'a neighborhoods in the wake of Sunni bombings. Second, like Lebanon's Hezbollah, al-Sadr's faction has also created a political party that won several legislative seats in the 2005 national election. Though the party's support is limited to perhaps 15 percent of the Shi'a community—mostly among the poor and the young—its parliamentary seats give al-Sadr some leverage since the governing coalition needs its votes. At about the time of the U.S. troop surge, al-Sadr gave his militias the order to stand down. Again, it is uncertain how long this will last and some break-away units have resumed their attacks.

The other major Shi'a militia is the Badr Brigade, the military wing of the Supreme Islamic Iraqi Council (SIIC), known prior to May 2007 as the Supreme Council for the Islamic Revolution in Iraq (SCIRI). The first Council was formed in 1982 and helped lead the Shi'a resistance to Saddam Hussein. Currently, its political party has one of the largest delegations in parliament. Though tied closely to Iran, SIIC has steered a relatively moderate course—more militant than Sistani but less militant than al-Sadr—while fashioning a reasonable working relationship with the U.S military. As the Shi'ite government coalition's largest party, it wields considerable political influence. Furthermore, members of the Badr Brigade control important segments of the Iraqi government's security forces, where their history of reprisals against the Sunnis has included torture and extra-judicial killings. In its Basra stronghold, many observers see the corrupt SIIC-led city government as a "theocracy mixed with thuggery."[68] In 2006, the Badr Brigade and al-Sadr's Mahdi Army clashed on a number of occasions in a power struggle for control of the Shi'a community and its financial resources. Thus, like the Sunnis, Shi'a paramilitary groups are not united. Still, Iraq's most extensive and most brutal conflict continues to pit all Shi'ite and Sunni factions against each other, with Sunni suicide bombers taking the greatest toll. Here again, the surge seems to have reduced that level of violence somewhat.

DEPENDENCE, MODERNIZATION, AND ETHNIC CONFLICT

Western analysts once assumed that improved education and communications in the Third World would break down ethnic conflicts. Because of their country's experience as a "melting pot" for immigrant groups, Americans in particular have supposed that socioeconomic modernization enhances ethnic integration and harmony.[69] Yet in Africa and Asia, early modernization has frequently politicized and intensified ethnic antagonisms. In fact, Crawford Young observes that "cultural pluralism [and ethnic strife] as a political phenomenon" was not significant in traditional societies but, rather, emerged "from such social processes as urbanization, the revolution in communications and spread of modern education."[70] Early modernization theorists, who were quite optimistic regarding the positive effects of literacy, urbanization, and modern values, clearly underestimated the extent to which these factors might mobilize differing ethnic groups and set them against each other. Dependency theorists, on the other hand, provided a rather superficial analysis of ethnic issues, tending to blame conflicts on colonialism or neocolonialism (the industrialized "core's" post-independence economic of the LDCs).

During the era of European colonialism, ethnic divisions in Africa and Asia were often kept in check by the struggle for independence, which encouraged a common front against the colonial regime. "The transcendent obligation of resistance to the colonizer . . . largely obscure[d] the vitality of ethnicity as a basis of social solidarity."[71] After independence, however, previously submerged ethnic rivalries frequently rose to the surface.[72] In the new political order, religious, racial, tribal, and nationality groups competed for such state resources as roads, schools, medical clinics, irrigation projects, and civil service jobs. Subsequently, rural-to-urban migration has brought previously isolated ethnic groups into proximity with each other for the first time. Furthermore, urbanization, rising educational levels, and the spread of mass communications have politicized previously nonparticipating sectors of the population. Because many of these newly mobilized citizens identify primarily with their own caste, religion, nationality, or tribe, their recently acquired political awareness often brings them into conflict with other ethnicities. The spread of higher education, rather than generating greater harmony, frequently produces a class of ethnically chauvinistic professionals and intellectuals, who become the ideologists of ethnic hostility. In time, as these ethnic groups come to know each other or as ethnic identities take on more conciliatory forms, ethnic conflicts may diminish. For now, however, ethnic conflict remains a potent and possibly growing phenomenon in the Third World.

LEVELS OF INTERETHNIC CONFLICT

Although most countries are ethnically heterogeneous, there are wide variations in how different ethnicities relate to each other. In some cases, different races or religions interact fairly amicably; in others, deep resentments inspire the most horrifying atrocities. Having examined the various types of ethnic communities, we will now consider the *nature* and *intensity* of relations *between* them. In theory, these relationships can be measured by the frequency of interethnic friendships and marriages, by the degree to which political parties, trade unions, and other civic organizations are ethnically based, and by the extent to which ethnic divisions are reinforced by other social cleavages such as class. In any particular country, relations between ethnic communities may range from relative harmony (Brazil) to systematic violence (Sudan).

Relative Harmony

As we have seen, modernization often intensifies ethnic antagonisms in the short run, but usually ameliorates them in the longer term. Consequently, affluent democracies are more likely than LDCs to enjoy amicable ethnic relations. In Switzerland, for example, German-, French-, and Italian-speaking citizens have lived together peacefully for centuries. That is particularly impressive because linguistic barriers within a country are usually the most difficult ethnic divisions to overcome.[73] The United States and Canada also enjoy relative ethnic harmony, having successfully assimilated a large assortment of immigrant groups. In North Dakota or Saskatchewan, for example, few people are concerned when a person of Ukrainian-Orthodox or German-Catholic origin marries a Lutheran of Norwegian ancestry. Despite considerable progress in recent decades, race relations in the United States constitute the one dramatic exception to the pattern of ethnic harmony.

Relative ethnic harmony is less common in developing countries. However, in Brazil and the island nations of the Caribbean, relations between Blacks and Whites are generally more harmonious than in the United States. For instance, interracial dating and marriages are quite common, particularly among lower-income groups. Still, that harmony is relative, because even those countries have maintained a clear social hierarchy between races. Although there are many middle-class Black Dominicans, Brazilians, and Panamanians, most Blacks remain mired in the lower class, and virtually none make it to the highest ranks of the political and economic order.

In short, even the countries classified as harmonious are only categorized that way relative to other, more sharply divided societies. They continue to have some glaring examples of ethnic discrimination and tension. In Cuba, despite a long history of interracial marriage and more recent government efforts to promote equality, Blacks have yet to attain their share of leadership positions in government or the Communist Party. Among average Cubans, one can still hear occasional racial slurs in private conversations.[74] And Canada, in many ways a more successful melting pot than the United States, has not resolved the vexing problem of French separatism in Quebec. But such tensions are the exception, and conflict is rarely violent, though there are some obvious exceptions such as the past African-American urban riots in Los Angeles and elsewhere.

Uneasy Balance

In LDCs such as Trinidad-Tobago and Malaysia, relations between the principal ethnic groups are more strained than in the previous category of relative harmony. Although still generally peaceful, interethnic relations are in an *uneasy balance*, in which different groups predominate in specific areas of society. For example, in Malaysia the Muslim Malay majority dominates the political system, including parliament and the government bureaucracy, while the Chinese minority dominates the private sector. Race riots in 1969 led to the Malaysian government to introduce a "New Economic Policy" designed, in part, to redistribute more of the country's wealth to the Malays. Fearful of Chinese domination, the Malays have benefited from a system of ethnic preferences in education and the civil service.[75] Today the two communities continue to maintain their distance, and some analysts see signs of slowly growing ethnic antagonisms. Still, even during the stress created by the 1990s economic crisis, ethnic relations remained peaceful.

The Caribbean nation of Trinidad and Tobago offers another example of uneasy balance. During the second half of the nineteenth century, British colonial authorities encouraged the migration of indentured plantation workers from India who joined the Black majority and the small White elite. Contrary to the common Caribbean practice of extensive racial mixing, there was less interracial marriage between Blacks and East Indians, at least until the twentieth century.[76] Each currently constitutes about 40 percent of the population, with the remaining 20 percent made up of Chinese, Whites, Arabs, mixed races, and others. Although there has been little overt hostility between the two dominant groups, there was also limited interaction between them, and, over time each group developed a number of negative stereotypes about the other.[77] Following Trinidadian independence in 1962, ethnic frictions increased as Blacks and East Indians competed for state resources. Most of the important political, civil service, military, and police positions since that time have been held by Blacks, who predominate within the urban middle and working classes. Whites continue to predominate in the upper ranks of the business community. Traditionally, most East Indians have been either small to medium-sized businesspeople (with significant collective economic power) or poor farmers and farm workers.

Trinidadian politics do not feature the same overt ethnic appeals that characterize many LDCs, but most of its political parties and unions principally represent one race. During the first parliamentary elections after independence, each of the major parties each received 80–90 percent of its votes from one ethnic group. For 24 years (1962 to 1986) the People's National Movement (PNM), the party that dominated the independence movement, headed the national government. While drawing votes from various races, the PNM's leadership and voter base have been primarily Black. For more than two decades the opposition was led by various Indian-dominated parties, including the Democratic Labour Party (DLP) and the United Labour Front (ULF). Major labor unions also tended to be either chiefly Black or East Indian.[78] Only in 1986 did the newly formed National Alliance for Reconstruction (NAR) finally dislodge the PNM from power by forging the first electoral alliance between East Indians and Blacks.[79] Since 1991 the government has alternated between the PNM and the United National Congress (the UNC, a break-away from the NAR).

Black and Indian political and labor leaders have cooperated periodically and in 1995 a party representing both races elected Trinidad's first prime minister of East Indian origin. At the same time, however, the two communities continue to maintain their social, political, and economic distance. In 1990, a radical Black Muslim movement, the Jamaat al Muslimeen, briefly captured the parliament building and held the prime minister and members of parliament hostage for six days while many poor Blacks rioted in the nation's capital. Jamaat's manifestos reflected the antagonism that many Black Trinidadians feel toward East Indians, but their violent behavior was an aberration in the nation's racial relations.

Enforced Hierarchy (Ethnic Dominance)

One important factor permitting ethnic balance in countries such as Malaysia and Trinidad-Tobago has been the division of political and economic power between the different ethnicities. Typically, one ethnicity predominates in the political arena and the other is more influential in the economy. But, in *enforced hierarchies* both forms of power are concentrated in the hands of the ruling ethnic group. South African apartheid represented the most blatant example of such a relationship. Through the 1980s, Whites dominated both the private sector and the state, including the courts, police, and armed forces. Blacks were denied the most basic rights.

Latin American nations with large Indian populations—including Guatemala, Bolivia, Ecuador, and Peru—have a less overt, but still significant, form of hierarchy. Historically, almost all Indians in those countries have been poor peasants at the bottom of the social and political ladder. Even today, despite important recent gains in Indian rights, most positions of political and economic influence remain in the hands of Whites or Mestizos. At the same time, however, unlike the United States, racial classifications in Latin America tend to be culturally rather than biologically defined. Consequently, they are more flexible and open up opportunities for at least some people of color. If a young Indian villager moves to the city, adopts western dress, and speaks Spanish, he or she becomes a Mestizo (or *Cholo*). And in the rural highlands of Ecuador and Peru, many peasant communities that spoke Quechua a generation ago have switched to Spanish and changed to western clothing in a process called *mestizaje* (becoming Mestizo). Consequently, over the years the percentage of the population considered Mestizos (usually a more prestigious ranking than Indian) has increased, with a corresponding decline in the proportion identified as indigenous (Indian). This, more flexible, cultural definition has obvious advantages, but an important disadvantage as well. Although it facilitates upward social mobility, unfortunately Indians have only been able to enjoy that mobility by abandoning their own culture.[80]

Since the 1980s, however, Indians have begun to assert their cultural rights and political influence in several South American countries through grass-roots political movements and through the election of indigenous government officials, sometimes at the highest levels. In Bolivia, where 60 percent of the population is indigenous, new Indian social movements organized mass protests against the government's free-market (neoliberal) economic policies. Those protests brought down the nation's president and subsequently led to the 2006 election of Evo Morales, the country's first indigenous president. Morales has placed several indigenous leaders in his cabinet and introduced laws to protect the rights of the country's Indian majority. In Ecuador, a national Indian federation (CONAIE) joined the military in a 2000 coup that briefly installed a three-person ruling junta (including the president of the federation). Founded in 1996, Pachakutik ("Awakening"), an Indian political party growing out of CONAIE, has held as many as five of that country's 22 provincial governorships and 10 percent of Congress.[81] Peru elected a president of Indian descent in 2001 and another candidate of indigenous origin won the first round of the 2006 election, but lost in the run-off. Finally, in the Mexican state of Chiapas, a group known as the Zapatistas staged a 1994 peasant rebellion in behalf of Indian rights. Though it never had a chance to seize national power (nor did it intend to), the group received a remarkable amount of national support from Mexicans of all ethnicities and social classes.

In all of these cases of enforced hierarchy, racial and class distinctions are closely intertwined. Those higher up the social ladder tend to be lighter skinned; those at the lower ranks of society are generally darker. One study of more than 80 members of the Ecuadorian industrial and commercial elite revealed only a single business leader who admitted having any Indian ancestors, though undoubtedly some of the others also did as well.[82] In Brazil, being Black is generally associated with being poor. Indeed, many people of color who rise to the middle or upper-middle class cease being considered Black. Although upward mobility through the class-race hierarchy is possible, it remains difficult. Racial prejudice shapes social relationships and creates barriers to equality. Moreover, most Indian families in the Andes and Blacks in Brazil and the Caribbean are too poor to provide their children with the education needed for upward social and economic mobility into the elite. Brazil prides itself in being a racial melting pot and in many ways it is. For example, there are numerous social and cultural bonds between Blacks, Mulattos, and Whites, including many cross-racial marriages (at least within the lower class). Yet, the most recent national census documented what almost all Brazilians already knew—people of color have less education and far lower incomes than Whites. Though Blacks and Mulattos constitute about 40 percent of the Brazilian population, they made up only 2–3 percent of university students. Furthermore, they are nearly twice as likely as Whites to earn below the official minimum wage. To rectify this situation, the current administration of President Lula da Silva has created affirmative action quotas that set aside university positions and government jobs for people of color. But, the program has received a negative reaction from the White middle and upper classes, which may weaken its implementation.[83]

Unlike South Africa's old apartheid system, Latin America's racial hierarchy is informal and not included in the legal system. And, unlike South Africa, it usually has not been enforced through police repression. Still, during nearly 40 years of revolutionary upheaval and intense government oppression, the Guatemalan armed forces viewed rural Indian communities as breeding grounds for Marxist guerrillas. Consequently, successive military regimes massacred tens of thousands of Indian peasants in a policy bordering on genocide. Fortunately, since the 1990s a peace treaty with the guerrillas has curtailed such violence.[84] During the 1980s and 1990s, Indian villagers in Peru were victimized by both the brutality of the Maoist guerrilla insurgency (Shining Path) and the military's indiscriminate anti-insurgency methods. Although Shining Path organizers focused on class struggle rather than racial divisions, much of their support came from Indian peasants resentful of the White-Mestizo power structure.[85]

Systematic Violence

In the worst-case scenario, deep ethnic resentments have sometimes turned into mass violence or even civil war. As we have seen, in a number of Third World countries as well as in some European nations, *systematic violence* has resulted in thousands or hundreds of thousands of deaths and huge numbers of displaced refugees, and rape victims. This has happened in countries such as Bosnia, Chechnya, Lebanon, India, Bangladesh, Ethiopia, Nigeria, Rwanda, and Sudan, among others. Often, as with enforced hierarchies, violence develops when ethnic divisions are reinforced by class antagonisms. Muslim antipathy toward Lebanon's Christian community has been fueled by Christian economic superiority.[86] Similarly, in Nigeria, many Islamic northerners resent the economic success of the Christian Ibos.

Ethnic bloodshed sometimes occurs when one ethnicity seizes political power and then takes retribution for real or imagined past indignities. Thus, when General Idi Amin seized power in Uganda, he ordered the slaughter of Langi and Acholi soldiers who were identified with the regime of ousted President Milton Obote. Following the overthrow of the communist government in Afghanistan in 1992, the country faced disintegration as Tajiks, Hazars, and Uzbeks challenged the long-standing political dominance of the Pashtun (Pathan) population.

OUTCOMES AND RESOLUTIONS

Whether ethnic antagonisms arise from competition over government resources, resentments over the division of political power and economic assets, or an ethnic community's demands for greater autonomy, there are a number of possible results. Although some outcomes are peaceful, others may spawn intense violence. While some resolutions are successful, others do not endure. In seeking a peaceful and lasting resolution, government and ethnic leaders are constrained by the history and intensity of their ethnic cleavages, by the degree of previous ethnic cooperation, and by the country's political culture. Nonetheless, within these constraints, the creativity and statecraft of national leaders and outside mediators can contribute to successful solutions. Of course, political elites may seek reasonable, negotiated solutions or they may choose to play on ethnic tensions for their own advantage. For example, the unexpectedly peaceful dismantling of White minority rule in South Africa was made possible by the leadership and spirit of compromise demonstrated by national President F. W. de Klerk and, especially, ANC leader Nelson Mandela. Conversely, the government of Sudan and some rebel groups have shown little interest to date in resolving the humanitarian crisis in Darfur.

Unfortunately, all too often self-serving, chauvinistic political leaders make a bad situation worse.[87] For example, although Bosnian Serbs and Muslims had enjoyed relatively amicable relationships for many years, after the breakup of Yugoslavia extremist leaders such as then Serb President Slobodan Miloscvic promoted ethnic hatred and mass murder in order to build their own political power base. In the end, Milosevic (who died in prison while on trial before an international tribunal for crimes against humanity) brought both Bosnia and Serbia to ruin.[88] Similarly the appalling 1994 massacres in Rwanda were orchestrated from above. Government officials induced Hutu villagers to attack their Tutsi neighbors with whom they had been living peacefully for many years.

When more responsible elites are willing to resolve intense ethnic conflicts through negotiations, they may arrive at one of several types of resolutions. In the next section, we examine those possible outcomes and also look at several options that have been attempted when negotiations failed. Although the alternatives presented here are not exhaustive, they cover a wide range of Third World experiences.

Power Sharing: Federalism and Consociationalism

Power-sharing arrangements are designed to create stability by constitutionally dividing political power among major ethnic groups. These settlements generally follow protracted negotiations and constitutional debate. If power sharing is introduced into the constitution at the time of independence, it may head off ethnic conflict before it gets started. Unfortunately, however, such arrangements often break down.

Federalism, the primary form of power sharing, is "a system of government [that] emanates from the desire of people to form a union without necessarily losing their various identities."[89] It may involve the creation of autonomous or semi-autonomous regions, each of which is governed by a particular ethnicity.[90] For example, prior to its collapse, Yugoslavia consisted of six autonomous republics mostly governed by individual nationalities, including Serbs, Croats, and Slovenes. The constitution mandated power sharing between the various republics at the national level. But, that compromise began to unravel in the 1970s following the death of Marshal Joseph Broz Tito, the country's long-term strong man. It collapsed completely in the early 1990s when the Communist Party lost its grip on several republics. The Soviet Union represented another federalist effort that lasted for nearly 70 years but also disintegrated with the demise of Communist Party rule. Unlike Yugoslavia, however, Soviet federalism was largely a fraud, because Moscow exercised firm control over the ethnically based republics, and Russians (roughly half of the total Soviet population) completely controlled the political apparatus.

Industrialized democracies have had greater success with ethnically based federalism. Each of Switzerland's 22 cantons is dominated by one of the country's three major language groups, with German-, French-, and Italian-speaking cantons coexisting harmoniously. Canada's federalism, though not based on ethnic divisions, has allowed the primarily French-speaking province of Quebec a substantial amount of autonomy regarding language and other cultural matters. Although the country's constitutional arrangement has not satisfied Québécois nationalists, it has accommodated many of their demands and, at least until now, has induced the province's voters to reject independence.

In the developing world, power sharing has been less successful. Following independence, Nigeria tried to accommodate its ethnic divisions through federalism. As we have seen, the country's north was dominated by the Hausa and Fulani, the east by the Ibos, and the west, to a lesser extent, by the Yoruba. That union came apart when the Ibos tried to secede. Although the Biafran war took a terrible toll, a new federal solution has subsequently taken hold since the secession failed. On the other hand, Pakistani federalism failed to overcome the antipathy between the country's more powerful western region (populated largely by Urdu speakers) and the Bengali-speaking east. In 1971, relations between the two regions broke down completely, resulting in the massacre of 500,000 Bengalis by western Pakistani troops.[91] When India went to war with Pakistan, the eastern region was able to secede and form the new nation of Bangladesh. Federalist arrangements also failed to prevent the breakup of Ethiopia because the central government did not adequately respect those arrangements.[92]

Consociationalism offers another potential solution to ethnic conflict. Like federalism, however, it has had a mixed record. Consociational democracy in plural (multiethnic) societies entails a careful division of political power designed to protect the rights of all participants.[93] It involves the following components:

1. The leaders of all important ethnic groups must form a ruling coalition at the national level.
2. Each group has veto power over government policy, or at least over policies that affect them.
3. Government funds and public employment, such as the civil service, are divided between ethnicities, with each receiving a number of posts roughly proportional to its population.
4. Each ethnic group is afforded a high degree of autonomy over its own affairs and over the region it populates.[94]

Thus, consociational democracy consciously rejects pure majority rule. Instead, it seeks to create a framework for stability and peace by guaranteeing minorities a share of political power—sometimes veto power—to protect them against the majority. It has been tried in several developing nations, including Cyprus (where it failed) and Malaysia (where it has generally succeeded). Perhaps the most widely known effort has been in Lebanon. From independence in 1943 until civil war erupted in 1975, Lebanon's government positions and political authority were divided proportionally between the nation's various Muslim and Christian communities. As we saw, the system eventually broke down, in part because formulas for the proportional division of government posts were not adjusted to reflect the higher rate of population growth over the years among Shi'ites and other Muslims. After 15 years of fighting that left that once-admired Middle Eastern country shattered, Lebanon's civil war came to an end in 1990. The settlement restored consociational rule with a division of government positions that more accurately reflected the Muslim share of the population. Yet, recent confrontations between the national government and Hezbollah, the militant Shi'a militia and political party, demonstrate that ethnic tensions continue.

Arend Lijphart argues that the very success of consociational systems in reducing ethnic conflict often causes such systems to wither away. For example, after World War II, the European nations of the Netherlands, Austria, Belgium, and Switzerland all designed consociational democracies to manage internal ethnic divisions. Beginning in the late 1950s, however, as ethnic tensions diminished—partly as the result of consociationalism—they reduced consociational arrangements. But, a degree of mutual trust and cooperation between the leaders of contending ethnic groups is the key to effective consociational arrangements. Sadly, trust is difficult to establish in times of ethnic hostility and becomes ever more problematic after that hostility has erupted into bloodshed. Iraq's current consociational arrangements involve the division of leadership posts (including prime minister, president, and speaker of the parliament) between the three major ethnic groups and the use of parliamentary election rules that indirectly guarantee a bloc of seats for the Kurds and Sunnis. But, in the total absence of trust between the three blocs, the parliament has been stalemated.

Lijphart maintains that power-sharing arrangements are most likely to succeed under two circumstances: first, when no single ethnic group constitutes a majority of the country's population; and, second, when the socioeconomic gap between the ethnic groups is not large.[95] Neither of these conditions holds in Iraq or Lebanon. But there are no certain formulas for success or, for that matter, for failure. Malaysia meets neither of these two standards (its Malay population constitutes a majority, and its Chinese minority is far more affluent), yet it has succeeded reasonably well with power sharing. Other countries with more auspicious conditions have failed.

Secession

When power sharing or other forms of compromise do not succeed, disgruntled ethnic minorities may attempt to secede (withdraw) from the country in order to form their own nation or join their ethnic brothers and sisters in a neighboring state. As one author put it, "Secession, like divorce, is an ultimate act of alienation."[96] It offers a potential way out of a "failed marriage" between ethnic groups within a nation-state. Unfortunately, however, like divorce, secessionist movements frequently provoke bitterness and hostility.[97]

Ralph Premdas indicates that these movements have several characteristics:

1. An ethnic group—defined by factors such as language, religion, culture, or race—claims the right of self-determination. That is to say, secession involves not just greater autonomy from the central government, but rather full independence. Disenchanted ethnic groups often begin by seeking only limited self-rule. But, if their more modest objectives are denied, they often escalate to a demand for full independence.
2. The ethnic community has a defined territorial base that it claims as its homeland.
3. There is almost always some organized struggle.[98]

Given the large number of ethnically divided LDCs, we should not be surprised to find many secessionist movements in the Third World. Central governments, faced with such breakaway efforts, almost always try to repress them because they are unwilling to part with some of their country's territory or resources, just as President Abraham Lincoln was unwilling to part with the Confederate states in the lead-up to the American Civil War. This chapter previously examined secessionist movements by Tamils in Sri Lanka, Ibos in Nigeria, Eritreans in Ethiopia, and Sikhs in northern India. To that list we might add, among others, Christian and other non-Muslim Blacks in southern Sudan, Karens in Myanmar, Moros in the Philippines, and Muslims in Kashmir (India).

Following the Gulf War, the world briefly focused its attention on Saddam Hussein's persecution of Iraq's Kurdish population. A decade later, Kurdish militia supported American-led coalition forces in the war to topple Saddam. But the Kurdish secessionist movement preceded Saddam's government and transcended Iraq's borders. Separatist efforts date to the collapse of the Ottoman Empire at the close of World War I. Residing in a mountainous region that they call Kurdistan, perhaps as many as 30 million Kurds live in adjacent regions of Turkey (home to about half of the region's Kurds), Iraq, and Iran, with a smaller community in Syria.[99] Over the year, the Kurds have often been persecuted in all of those countries, and today they still have little prospect of attaining the independent Kurdistan that so many of them desire (though they have achieved regional self-rule in northeastern Iraq).[100]

Although many aggrieved Third World nationalities would like to secede, few have accomplished that goal. The Bangladeshi withdrawal from Pakistan is one of the few "successful" Third World cases, but it was only achieved at a great cost in human lives. Moreover, it could not have happened without India's military intervention. Eritrea attained independence from Ethiopia in 1993 after decades of struggle. But, more often than not, the most that secessionist movements can hope to attain is greater autonomy and government recognition of their group's rights.

Noting the spread of secessionist conflicts in the 1970s and 1980s and the disintegration of the Soviet Union, Yugoslavia, and Czechoslovakia in the 1990s, many analysts predicted that Eastern Europe and portions of the developing world would see the disintegration of an ever-growing number of nation-states. Many voiced alarm over the violence and disorder that this prospect suggested. For example, a widely cited book by noted sociologist and former U.S. Senator, Patrick Moynahan, predicted that the number of independent states in the world would increase from about 200 to 300 by the middle of the twenty-first century.[101] But, in fact, the number of secessionist wars has actually declined significantly since the start of the 1990s. From 1991 to 1999, 16 such wars were settled and 11 others were confined by cease-fires or continuing negotiations. Particularly in Africa, successful peace negotiations in one country have apparently encouraged parallel efforts in other nations. Thus, as this century began, only 18 secessionist wars continued worldwide, fewer than at any time since 1970.[102]

Outside Intervention

Because ethnic conflicts sometimes produces a considerable loss of lives and other horrors—particularly when a conflict pits a government against a minority group—outside actors may face a moral and practical dilema. On the one hand, they may feel morally compelled to somehow intervene on behalf of the victimized minority. Such intervention can span the gamit from simply agreeing to take in refugees all the way to armed intervention aimed at puting a stop to the bloodshed. At the same time, however, leaders of outside nations may be constrained from intervening by international law (concerning national sovereignty), international power allignments, lack of sufficient resources, or fear of alienating their own citizens. Even the nonaggressive act of offering refuge to the victims of ethnic strife and persecution may seem too costly, too risky, or too unpalatable to the home country's population. For example, during the 1930s, as many Jews tried to flee the Nazis, Western democracies limited the number of refugees they would accept, fearing that a flood of refugees would upset public opinion at home. In recent times, the outside world stood by as millions died in ethnic massacres in such countries as Bosnia, the Congo, Rwanda, and Sudan.[103] Looking at the world's prolonged inaction regarding the Serbs' and Croats' bloody "ethnic cleansing" in Bosnia, military strategist Edward Luttwak asked, "If the Bosnian Muslims had been needle-nosed dolphins, would the world have allowed the Croats and Serbs to slaughter them by the tens of thousands?"[104] His blunt question raises important ethical and pragmatic questions about the world's obligations and limitations in such situations.

Unless outside forces are invited in by a country's own government (as when Sri Lanka asked India's armed forces to quell its civil war), external intervention would violate the principle of national sovereignty. But, very rarely do governments invite outside intervention because it is often the national government itself that has perpetrated, encouraged, or at least condoned the ethnic violence. Normally, then, external interference raises a number of difficult issues. At what point, if any, do other nations or international organizations (such as the United Nations, NATO, or the African Union) have the right to violate a country's sovereignty in order to save innocent lives? For example, should the United Nations or the West have sent troops into Rwanda or the Congo, with or without the permission of their governments, in order to stop the massacres of hundreds of thousands? Does the community of nations currently have any legal and moral obligations to protect the people of Darfur from genocide, even if that violates Sudanese sovereignty? Many westerners would answer affirmatively. But if those interventions are justified, wouldn't the same moral principles have given United Nations the authority to send troops into Birmingham, Alabama, and rural Mississippi in the 1960s in order to protect the lives of Blacks who were being terrorized by the Ku Klux Klan and the local police? Who is to decide in which situations outside intervention is legitimate?

Of course, there is an added pragmatic issue regarding the likely effectiveness of any particular intervention. Under what circumstances does outside intervention (including military intervention) prevent ethnic persecution and impose a durable solution, and when are such efforts futile? Will countries such as the United States, France, India, or Nigeria be willing to commit their soldiers and economic resources on a sustained basis to support future peacekeeping operations? How many casualties among their own soldiers are peacekeeping nations prepared to accept?[105]

In the end, governments contemplating a humanitarian intervention have to weigh their own national interests and the costs of intervention against their commitment to sustaining human rights abroad. Most nations are reluctant to risk their soldiers' lives for humanitarian purposes. A relatively small number of American soldiers (18) brutally killed in 1993 during a mission to restore order and distribute food in war-torn Somalia shocked U.S. public opinion and caused President Clinton to withdraw the remaining American troops. Only one year later, government leaders in Washington, Paris, and other Western capitals were warned that an ethnic massacre was likely to unfold in Rwanda. Sobered by the recently failed intervention in Somalia and unsure how well they could prevent genocide, they decided against intervention. Some analysts insist that the United Nations or the United States or France could have saved many thousand lives if they had quickly sent a military force to quell the violence.[106] Others disagree, arguing that the Rwandan genocide took place so quickly (most of the deaths occurring within a few weeks) that intervention could not have arrived in time to save most of the victims.[107] More recently, the

United Nations, African nations, and the Western powers have lamented the genocidal warfare unleashed against non-Arab minorities in Darfur (a region of Sudan). Only after nearly 2 million people had fled Darfur to squalid and dangerous refugee camps and some 200,000 had died (largely of starvation) did the African Union send a small and ineffective military force, with the acquiescence of the Sudanese government. The United Nations has been even slower to take action and only in mid-2007 did there seem to be very slow and limited progress toward dispatching a larger U.N. force.

For the most part, peacekeeping forces have been sent only to enforce or monitor settlements that the warring factions had already negotiated (such as recent U.N. and West African peacekeeping missions in Liberia, Sierra Leone, and Ivory Coast), and only after prolonged conflict had already cost thousands of lives. At other times, when world opinion has forced the host government to accept external intervention, such as United Nations intervention in East Timor (then a part of Indonesia) and Sudan, again troops have normally only been sent *after* the worst outrages had already been committed.

To be sure, outside forces occasionally have imposed resolutions on seemingly intractable ethnic conflicts. In such cases, the intervening power is often a neighboring state that either has ties to one of the warring ethnic factions or has a strategic interest in the country it invades. Such was the case with India's intercession on behalf of the Bengalis in East Pakistan. Without that intervention, the nation of Bangladesh could not have been born. The Turkish invasion of Cyprus imposed an ethnic settlement by partitioning the island's Greek and Turkish communities. Recent examples of intervention by *non*-neighboring nations include the U.S. and British protection of the Kurdish enclave in northern Iraq during the 1990s. In Central Europe, NATO's bombing of Serbia in 1999 forced that government to cease its attacks on Kosovo's Albanian population and to accept NATO peacekeepers. But NATO intervention was stimulated by the West's earlier, embarrassing refusal to halt ethnic cleansing in Bosnia that had left hundreds of thousands dead. Even in Kosovo, the West only employed bombing missions (not ground action), posing minimal risk to their forces.

Not only do international interventions frequently come too late, but they often end badly. While the Iraqi Kurds have benefited greatly from America's two wars against their oppressor, Saddam Hussein, a prior U.S. intervention had devastating results. In 1974, the American CIA and Iran supported a Kurdish rebellion against the Iraqi government. But, for Washington, Kurdish interests were secondary to its own policy objective—supporting Iran's royal government, which at that time was America's ally and Iraq's enemy. The following year, however, the Shah of Iran temporarily resolved his differences with Iraq and withdrew his support for the Kurdish insurrection. The CIA then also terminated its assistance to the rebels and the insurrection collapsed. Thousands of Iraqi Kurds were killed or driven from their homes.[108] But, Washington's behavior was not unique. Most countries—especially powerful ones with a broad international agenda—will only assist persecuted ethnic groups if that help does not conflict with their own national interests. Indeed, some outside interventions have intentionally intensified ethnic conflicts. For example, from the late 1990s to 2003, as many as nine African nations, particularly Rwanda and Uganda, intervened in the Congo's ethnic conflict, which pitted the Congolese government against Congolese Hutus and some 2 million Hutus who had just fled Rwanda. In what some have called "Africa's World War," perhaps 5 million people died (either from malnutrition, disease, or warfare) in a conflict that went largely unnoticed in the West (and which continues to erupt periodically). While the loss of life would have been horrifying no matter what, the Ugandan and Rwandan interventions surely added to the death toll.[109]

As we have seen, India's attempt to settle the Tamil–Sinhalese conflict in Sri Lanka ended disastrously. Not only did it fail to resolve the civil war, but it led subsequently to the assassination of India's Prime Minister Rajiv Gandhi by a Tamil Tiger suicide bomber. Foreign intervention did halt ethnic violence in the former Yugoslavia (Bosnia and Kosovo), but peacekeeping troops now face an indefinite stay. Finally, sometimes minority groups wishing to secede from their country receive help from neighboring countries with whom they share an ethnic identity. Somali rebels in the Ethiopian region of Ogaden have received help over the years from neighboring Somalia. In South Asia, the Pakistani military has aided Islamic secessionists in the Indian, predominantly Muslim, state of Kashmir. In all these cases outside intervention may merely have thrown gasoline on the fire of existing ethnic strife.

In short, outside interventions frequently fail to resolve ethnic conflicts. Furthermore, even when they are well intentioned, outside powers are often unwilling or unable to "stay the course." Thus, Glynne Evans notes:

> A half-hearted [outside] military response [to ethnic conflict] without any underlying political action is a poor option. . . . Conflicts with a high degree of ethnic mobilization last for generations rather than years, and are intense in their impact . . . as neighbors turn on neighbors. An intervention for humanitarian purposes in such cases becomes a major military commitment, and one of long duration.[110]

Events in countries such as the Congo, Rwanda, and Sudan suggest that this is a commitment that outside powers are rarely prepared to make.

Outside Intervention in Iraq: The Effect of the U.S. Occupation on Kurdish Autonomy

While, the purpose of the U.S. invasion of Iraq surely was not to resolve ethnic conflicts, the defeat of Saddam Hussein's Sunni-dominated dictatorship unleashed formerly repressed ethnic grievances. Having previously discussed the intense conflicts between Shi'a and Sunni Muslims, we can now turn to the effects of foreign intervention on Kurdish national aspirations. Iraq is home to perhaps 5 million Kurds (the precise figure is in dispute), the world's third largest Kurdish community, after Turkey and Iran. Living primarily in the country's mountainous northeast, they constitute the majority population in three of Iraq's eighteen provinces.[111] Under the Ottoman Empire, which governed much of Iraq and the Middle East from the sixteenth to the early twentieth centuries, ethnic minorities were treated relatively fairly. Hence, Kurdish nationalism did not really blossom until Ottoman rule collapsed after World War I. At that time, several victorious nations—Britain, France, and Italy—signed the short-lived Treaty of Severe (1920), which promised the creation of an autonomous or independent Kurdistan.[112] Yet, just three years later, the Treaty of Lausanne terminated that commitment. Because the newly created Turkish and Iraqi states viewed the Kurds as a threat, the Kurdish dream of autonomy or independence remained unfulfilled.

When the Iraqi monarchy was overthrown in 1958, the new government briefly allowed Kurdish culture to flourish. By 1960, however, the new republican regime initiated a 15-year campaign to give Arabs a greater foothold in Kurdish regions. The program involved removing large numbers of Kurds from their homelands to other parts of the country, destroying Kurdish villages, and moving Arabs into historically Kurdish regions. In 1980, only a year after Iran's Islamic revolution had toppled the Shah, Iraq and Iran began a brutal, decade-long war. Because Iraq's Kurds largely supported Iran, Saddam implemented a genocidal campaign against them (called *"al-Anfal"*) during the 1980s. During that operation, the Iraqi military was responsible for "the first documented instances of a government employing chemical weapons against its own civilian population."[113] In total, the Saddam dictatorship is believed to have killed over 300,000 Kurds, more than half of them during al-Anfal.[114] Millions more were displaced from their homes.

As we have seen, following the Gulf War, the Kurds, like the Shi'a Arabs in the South, rebelled against Saddam Hussein's dictatorship. Quickly, however, the armed forces recaptured the towns that had fallen to the rebels, forcing over 1 million Kurds to flee toward or across Iraq's borders with Turkey and Iran. When Turkey refused to allow them in and numerous refugees died of exposure in the high mountains, the European Community proposed, and the United States supported, the creation of a U.N.-protected, Kurdish enclave within Iraq. Under "Operation Provide Comfort," several Western nations placed troops on the ground and used air power to establish a "no-fly zone" prohibiting Iraqi planes from flying north of the 36th parallel, thereby effectively creating the autonomous region that the Kurds had so long yearned for. The United States and its allies soon withdrew their ground troops, but continued to provide aid while maintaining the no-fly zone. Thousands of Kurdish families returned to the region and established democratic political institutions, including the election of a Kurdish National Assembly in 1992. Although feuding between the two major Kurdish political parties temporarily split the autonomous zone, those two "governments" subsequently reunited.

During the 2003 invasion of Iraq, U.S. forces received valuable military and intelligence support from Kurdish militias. The ouster of Saddam Hussein's regime raised the issue of Kurdish participation in postwar Iraq. In deference to U.S. pressure and Turkey's adamant opposition to a neighboring Kurdish state, the Kurdish political and military leadership provisionally foreswore ambitions for an independent Kurdistan but demanded substantial autonomy in the new political order. Yet, Phebe Marr, a leading Middle-East expert, notes that in her many interviews of Kurdish leaders during the past 15 years, all but one of them identified themselves as Kurds first and Iraqis second.[115] Iraq's interim constitution (2004), the electoral rules for the 2005 referendum on a new constitution, and the 2005 constitution itself all gave the

Kurdish and Sunni minorities considerable power to block legislation that they believed adversely affected them.

Currently the future of the Iraqi Kurdish community remains uncertain. Once unified by their opposition to Saddam regime, Kurds and Shi'a each have a distinct vision for Iraq's political future. While Shi'ite leaders support the principle of majority rule, Kurdish representatives are more concerned with protecting minority rights. In sum, although foreign intervention—the Gulf War and current war in Iraq—has benefited the Kurdish and Shi'a populations in many ways, it remains to be seen whether they can work out a way of living peacefully with each other and with their Sunni antagonists.

Settlement through Exhaustion

Finally, many ethnic conflicts have been resolved less through statecraft, constitutional arrangements, or external intervention than through the exhaustion of the warring parties. Although the Arab League helped negotiate an end to Lebanon's lengthy civil war, it was the weariness of the Lebanese, after the virtual destruction of Beirut, that permitted a settlement (even though some 15 years later that may be unraveling). Similarly, although the Ugandan government continues to clash periodically with the Acholi and Langi tribes, conflict has been held in check because Ugandans do not want to return to the ethnically based bloodshed of the Amin and Obote eras. In Mozambique, Angola, Liberia, and Sierra Leone, exhaustion helped drive the warring factions toward United Nations—brokered peace treaties that halted their long and bitter civil wars. And, in Sudan, a similar process contributed to the end of a 21-year war between the Arab-dominated national government and the Black (non-Muslim) population of the south.

Toward a Peaceful Resolution of Conflict

If developing nations are to avoid the horrors of civil war, secession, and foreign intervention, they must arrive at legal, political, and economic solutions that can constrain ethnic tensions. A conference of American academics and foreign assistance officials proposed the following measures:

- Writing a new constitution [that] offers the possibility of creating new institutional arrangements, such as federalism, for power sharing between . . . ethnic groups.
- Establishing protection for ethnic minority rights not only through constitutional and legal guarantees but also through civic education.
- Creating electoral systems with incentives for cooperation and accommodation among groups.[116]

Such institutional goals, though clearly reasonable, are more easily set out than achieved. More difficult still is the task of repairing the damage done to plural societies that have been torn apart by bloody conflict (e.g., Rwanda, Kashmir, and Lebanon) or by decades of prejudice and segregation (South Africa). Not long after South Africa's new, multiracial regime was installed in 1994, Nelson Mandela's administration created a Truth and Reconciliation Commission, before which perpetrators of racially based violence and injustices were invited to confess their crimes in return for amnesty.[117] The goal of the Commission was to further unearth the crimes of apartheid and, more importantly, to allow the nation's races to live to together more harmoniously. Yet, as one observer of the Commission's hearings has suggested, in countries that have experienced systematic repression or extensive ethnic violence, reconciliation—the creation of harmony between formerly hostile parties— may be too much to hope for.[118] A more realistic goal, he suggests, may be establishing the basis for *coexistence* between these groups. Toward this end, governments or international agencies trying to assist countries previously devastated by ethnic violence need to create trauma centers for the survivors of atrocities, multicultural educational programs, contact programs that try to establish a dialogue between erstwhile perpetrators and victims of ethnic vio- lence, and cross-ethnic economic development programs, all designed to help former antagonists coexist. While, as we might expect, such efforts have had mixed records of success, they are worth trying.[119]

CONCLUSION: ETHNIC PLURALISM AND DEMOCRACY

We have seen that, while in the end modern plural societies (such as Belgium and Canada) are more capable of resolving ethnic tensions peacefully, in the shorter term early modernization has intensified such conflicts in many LDCs. But, how has the spread of Third World democracy affected ethnic relations?

Crafting peaceful solutions for multicultural societies remains one of the greatest challenges facing Third World leaders. Still, there is some basis for hope. The frequency and intensity of ethnic conflicts peaked during the late 1980s and early 1990s and have decreased modestly since that time. Although Africa has remained home to some of the world's most brutal conflicts (Sierra Leone, Sudan, the Congo), it has also enjoyed the most progress of late in bringing ethno-warfare to a halt. In fact, most of the continent's remaining ethnic wars are conflicts that date back to the mid-1990s or earlier, while fewer new ones have emerged as of late. Realizing that their countries were being destroyed by eth- nic hostilities and decades of related economic decay, a number of governments and rebel groups in the region have become more accommodating.

During the 1970s and 1980s, increased ethnic violence in the developing world and the former communist states of Eastern Europe often coincided with the spread of democratic government. This raised two questions about the rela- tionship between democracy and ethnic politics: first, are multiethnic countries less likely to maintain democracy than are culturally homogenous societies? Second, do the growth of citizen participation and the creation of democratic government intensify conflict between ethnic communities?

The first question can be answered relatively easily. Democracy *is* clearly harder, though far from impossible, to establish and maintain in multiethnic countries. We have seen, for example, how Lebanon, long considered the most democratic Arab country, was devastated by ethnic civil war. Looking at democ- racy's failure to take root in most of Africa and Asia from the 1960s to the 1980s, Alvin Rabushka and Kenneth Shepsle concluded that ethnic antagonisms had created important obstacles to democratization. Democracy, they argued, "is simply not viable in an environment of intense ethnic preference."[120] Here they referred to societies in which powerful ethnic groups receive special privileges while others suffer discrimination.

An examination of both economically developed nations and LDCs reveals that democracy has fared best in countries that are most ethnically homogeneous (such as Botswana, Iceland, Uruguay, and Japan) and in countries of "new settlement" (including the United States, Canada, and Australia) populated primarily by immigrants and their descendants, who created a new common culture.[121] In Africa, Asia, and the Middle East, where many countries labor with strong ethnic divides, the growth of democracy and mass political participation may unleash communal hostilities, sometimes intensified by opportunistic politicians who use group fears to build a political base.

Ethnic pluralism poses a particular obstacle to democracy in poorer countries, where various groups must contend for limited government resources (schools, roads, civil service jobs, and the like) in the "politics of scarcity." But although democracy is more difficult to achieve in plural societies, it is not impossible even in very poor nations. Despite its history of religiously based violence, India, one of the world's most ethnically diverse countries, has maintained democratic government for most of its half-century of independence. Trinidad-Tobago, a country divided by religion and race, is among the Third World's most democratic nations.

To be sure, the initial transition to democracy frequently intensifies existing ethnic animosities. Newly formed political parties often base their support in competing ethnic communities. Politicians, even those opposed to violence, are tempted to use ethnic appeals as a means of gaining public support. As public resources are distributed through more transparent legislative decisions, ethnically based interest groups and political parties fight for their fair share. Some analysts warn that "the opening of democratic space throws up many groups pulling in different directions, that it causes demand overload, systematic breakdown and even violent conflict," a danger particularly relevant in societies with deep ethnic tensions prior to their democratic transitions.[122] That danger is greatest in strict majoritarian democracies in which a single ethnic group or allied ethnicities can dominate parliamentary or presidential elections without affording constitutional or other institutional protections to minority groups. Thus, the Carnegie Commission on Preventing Deadly Conflict concluded that

> In societies with deep ethnic divisions and little experience with democratic government and the rule of law [a common phenomenon in Africa, Asia and the Middle East], strict majoritarian democracy can be self-defeating. Where ethnic identities are strong and national identity weak, populations may vote largely on ethnic lines. Domination by one ethnic group can lead to a tyranny of the majority.[123]

But this merely indicates the importance of limiting majoritarian rule in democratic, multiethnic societies. It does not suggest that authoritarian government is preferable in such situations. Indeed, in the long run the only way ethnicities can resolve their differences is through open discussion and bargaining in a relatively democratic political arena, as long as majority rule is tempered by constitutional guarantees of human rights, consociational arrangements, or other institutional protections for minorities such as those previously discussed.[124]

Although dictatorships in Yugoslavia and the Soviet Union were able to repress ethnic conflicts for many years, in the end they actually intensified these grievances by denying their existence, silencing them, and failing to deal with them. After the fall of communism, long-repressed antagonisms in Croatia, Bosnia, Kosovo, and Chechnya burst to the surface, producing civil war or lesser forms of violence. Elsewhere, dictators such as Laurent Kabila (the Congo), Suharto (Indonesia), and Saddam Hussein (Iraq) presided over ethnic massacres that would have been unthinkable in a democracy monitored by public opinion and a free press.

Conversely, democratic politicians are open to interest group pressure from ethnic minorities and, hence, are more likely to settle disputes peacefully before they degenerate into violence. Indeed, the recent study of "minorities at risk" throughout the world revealed that democratic regimes are more likely than dictatorships to negotiate peaceful settlements of ethnic warfare. And during the 1990s, political discrimination and, to a lesser degree, economic discrimination against ethnic minorities were more likely to decline in democracies than under authoritarian governments.[125] In short, to accommodate ethnic pluralism and resolve tensions, what is needed is democratic, mature, and enlightened political leadership, a spirit of compromise, and the implementation of politically negotiated solutions such as federalism and consociational democracy.

DISCUSSION QUESTIONS

1. What do we mean by *ethnicity*, and what are some of the most important types of ethnic identification?
2. Discuss the effect that modernization has had on ethnic identification and ethnic conflict.
3. How might outside intervention reduce or increase ethnic tension? Cite specific successful examples of such intervention as well as some failures.
4. Discuss the ethnic identity of Middle Eastern Kurds and how their aspirations have created political divisions in Turkey, Iran, and Iraq during the past decades. How has American military intervention affected the status of the Kurds in Iraq?
5. Discuss the effects of Saddam Hussein's government on Shi'a-Sunni relations in Iraq. What effect did Saddam's fall from power have on relations between these two religious communities? What do you feel is likely to happen to Shi'a-Sunni relations after the U.S. and allied troops withdraw from Iraq?
6. Discuss how a country's transition to democracy might increase ethnic tensions in some cases and decrease it in others?
7. What are some reasons that might explain why major civil strife related to ethnicity has declined in the last 10 to 15 years?

NOTES

1. Human Rights Watch, *Darfur Destroyed: Ethnic Cleansing by Government and Militia Forces in Western Sudan* 16, no. 6 (A) (May 2004), 1; on the earlier civil war in the south, see Douglas Hamilton Johnson, *The Root Causes of Sudan's Civil Wars* (Bloomington: Indiana University Press, 2003).

2. Eric Hobsbawm, *The Age of Extremes* (New York: Vintage Books, 1996), 50.

3. Quoted in Yueh-Ting Lee, Fathali Moghaddam, Clark McCauley, and Stephen Worchel, "The Global Challenge of Ethnic and Cultural Conflict," in *The Psychology of Ethnic*

and Cultural Conflict, eds. Y. Lee, C. McCauley, F. Moghaddam, and S. Worchel (Westport, CT: Praeger, 2004), 3.

4. Crawford Young, *The Politics of Cultural Pluralism* (Madison: University of Wisconsin Press, 1976), 23–26. The quotation appears on p. 23.

5. Ted Robert Gurr, "Preface" and "Long War, Short Peace: The Rise and Decline of Ethnopolitical Conflict at the End of the Cold War," in *Peoples versus States: Minorities at Risk in the New Century*, ed. Ted Gurr (Washington, DC: United States Institute of Peace Press, 2000), xiii and 27–56; David Carment and Frank Harvey, *Using Force to Prevent Ethnic Violence* (Westport, CT: Praeger, 2001), 5.

6. For an attack on such gloom and doom prophecies, see Yahya Sadowski, *The Myth of Global Chaos* (Washington, DC: The Brookings Institution, 1998), esp. chap. 10.

7. Analysis of the years 1958 to 1966, for example, shows that of 164 conflicts with significant violence, only 15 involved clashes between 2 or more states. Most involved ethnic conflict within countries. See Abdul A. Said and Luiz R. Simmons, "The Ethnic Factor in World Politics," in *Ethnicity in an International Context*, eds. Said and Simmons (New Brunswick, NJ: Transaction Books, 1976), 16.

8. Monica Duffy Toft, *The Geography of Ethnic Violence: Identity, Interests, and the Indivisibility of Territory* (Princeton, NJ: Princeton University Press, 2003); see also, Peter Wallensteen and Margareta Sollenberg, "Armed Conflicts, Conflict Termination, and Peace Agreements, 1989–1996," *Journal of Peace Research* 34, no. 3 (1997), 339–358.

9. David Bloomfield and Ben Reilly, eds. *Democracy and Deep-rooted Conflict: Options for Negotiations* (Stockholm: International Institute for Democracy and Electoral Assistance, 1998), 4.

10. During this period, only two or three international conflicts—the Iran–Iraq War, the Soviet war in Afghanistan, and perhaps the current Iraq War—had comparable death tolls. Ironically, the last two were followed by internal ethnic violence. Of course, some brutal civil wars, such as those in El Salvador and Nicaragua, have not been ethnically based.

11. One study estimated that there were 10 million deaths as of the early 1970s. Harold Isaacs, *Idols of the Tribe: Group Identity and Political Change* (New York: Harper & Row, 1975), 3. Millions more have died since that time in the former Yugoslavia, Chechnya, Sudan, Mozambique, Angola, the Congo, Rwanda, Burundi, Ethiopia, India, Iraq, Guatemala, Afghanistan, and elsewhere. In the Congo alone some 5 million people have died directly or indirectly (starvation) in the country's ongoing ethnic conflict.

12. Colin H. Kahl, *State, Scarcity, and Civil Strife in the Developing World* (Princeton, NJ: Princeton University Press, 2006).

13. Gurr, *Peoples versus States*, 10–11.

14. First popularized by renowned social psychologist, G.W. Allport 50 years ago—see Allport, *The Nature of Prejudice* (Cambridge, MA: Addison-Wesley Press, 1954)—the hypothesis has quite recently been referred to as "one of the most long-lived and successful ideas in the history of social psychology." See M. B. Brewer and R. J. Brown, "Intergroup Relations," in *Handbook of Social Psychology* (Vol. 2), eds. S. T. Fiske and G. Lindzey (Boston: McGraw-Hill, 1998).

15. Gurr, *Peoples versus States*, 5.

16. Donald Rothchild and Victor A. Olorunsola, "Managing Competing State and Ethnic Claims," in *State versus Ethnic Claims: African Policy Dilemmas*, eds. Rothchild and Olorunsola (Boulder, CO: Westview Press, 1983), 20.

17. Quoted in Francine Friedman, *The Bosnian Muslims: Denial of a Nation* (Boulder, CO: Westview Press, 1996), 1; For a discussion of competing definitions of ethnicity and the factors that cause ethnic groups to feel a common self-identity, see Donald G. Ellis, *Transforming Conflict: Communication and Ethnopolitical Conflict* (Lanham, MD: Rowman and Littlefield Publishers, 2006), 32–35.

18. Quoted in David A. Lake and Donald Rothchild, "Spreading Fear: The Genesis of Transnational Ethnic Conflict," in *The International Spread of Ethnic Conflict*, eds. Lake and Rothchild (Princeton, NJ: Princeton University Press, 1998), 7.

19. Cynthia Enloe, *Ethnic Conflict and Political Development* (Boston: Little, Brown, 1973), 15.

20. Charles W. Anderson, Fred R. von der Mehden, and Crawford Young, *Issues of Political Development*, 2nd ed. (Upper Saddle River, NJ: Prentice Hall, 1974), 31–33; Crawford Young, *Politics in the Congo* (Princeton, NJ: Princeton University Press, 1965), chap. 11.

21. Donald Horowitz, *A Democratic South Africa? Constitutional Engineering in a Divided Society* (Berkeley: University of California Press, 1991), 44–48.

22. Young, *Cultural Pluralism*, 20.

23. Uri Ra'anan, "Nation and State: Order Out of Chaos," in *State and Nation in Multi-ethnic Societies*, ed. Ra'anan et al. (Manchester, England, and New York: Manchester University Press, 1991), 4–7.

24. Toft, *The Geography of Ethnic Violence*, 17, 149–152.

25. Said and Simmons, *Ethnicity in an International Context*, 10. With the spread of

migration across state borders, even countries like Denmark and Norway are no longer fully homogeneous (each of them home to a growing number of Third World and Eastern European immigrants).

26. Scholars specializing in African culture and politics generally reject the use of the term *tribe* to describe the region's various cultural-linguistic groups; they prefer the term *ethnicity*. This book uses the word *tribe* because it is more familiar to readers and is still used in much of the ethnic literature. It also avoids confusion with the more broadly used meaning of the word *ethnicity*. More will be said of this later in the chapter.

27. Omo Omoruyi, "State Creation and Ethnicity in a Federal (Plural) System: Nigeria's Search for Parity," in *Ethnicity, Politics, and Development*, eds. Dennis L. Thompson and Dov Ronen (Boulder, CO: Lynne Rienner Publishers, 1986), 120. Because social scientists do not always agree on what constitutes a distinct ethnic group, other calculations differ.

28. Jacques Bertrand, *Nationalism and Ethnic Conflict in Indonesia* (Cambridge, England and New York: Cambridge University Press, 2004), 135–144.

29. Crawford Young, "Comparative Claims to Political Sovereignty: Biafra, Katanga, Eritrea," in *State versus Ethnic Claims*, 211–219.

30. On Ethiopia and the secessionist wars, see Christopher Clapham, *Transformation and Continuity in Revolutionary Ethiopia* (Cambridge, England: Cambridge University Press, 1988), and J. Markakis, *National and Class Conflict in the Horn of Africa* (Cambridge, England: Cambridge University Press, 1987). Subsequent events have superseded the material in both books.

31. Scholars such as Crawford Young maintain that "caste, race, and religion belong to a larger genus . . . called cultural pluralism." I will not discuss caste as an ethnic category because it exists only in India and a handful of other countries.

32. John Breuilly, *Nationalism and the State* (Manchester, England: Manchester University Press, 1982), 3.

33. Many Kurdish and non-Kurdish scholars dispute the Kurdish nationalists' assertion that there is a single Kurdish language with multiple dialects. They argue that the variations in different Kurdish languages are too great to call them part of a single language. Even so, the languages or dialects are closely related to each other and are distinct from the Turkish, Arabic, and Persian languages that predominate in the Kurds' home countries (though Kurdish is somewhat related to Persian). See Nader Entessan, "Ethnicity and Ethnic Challenges in the Middle East," in *Ethnicity and Governance in the Third World*, eds. John Mukum Mbaku, Pita Ogaba Agbese, and Mwangi S. Kimenyi (Hants, England: Ashgate Publishing, 2001), 159.

34. David Brown, *Contemporary Nationalism: Civic, Ethnocultural and Multicultural Politics* (London and New York: Routledge, 2000), 70–88.

35. For a helpful analysis of Tamil-Sinhalese conflict in Sri Lanka, see A. Jeyaratnam Wilson, *Sri Lankan Tamil Nationalism* (Vancouver: University of British Columbia Press, 2000).

36. Appapillai Amirdhalingam, quoted in Eller, *From Culture to Ethnicity to Conflict*, 123.

37. S. W. R. de A. Samarasinghe, "The Dynamics of Separatism: The Case of Sri Lanka," and K. M. de Silva, "Separatism in Sri Lanka: The Traditional Homelands of the Tamils," in *Secessionist Movements in Comparative Perspective*, eds. Ralph R. Premdas, S. W. R. de A. Samarasinghe, and Alan B. Anderson (London: Pinter Publishers, 1990), 32–67; also, K. M. de Silva, *Managing Ethnic Tensions in Multi-Ethnic Societies: Sri Lanka 1880–1985* (Lanham, MD: University Press of America, 1986).

38. Eller, *From Culture to Ethnicity to Conflict*, 130–132.

39. *Eelam* is the Tamil word for Sri Lanka.

40. For a blistering criticism of the Indian intervention, see Chris Smith, "South Asia's Enduring War," in *Creating Peace in Sri Lanka: Civil War and Reconciliation*, ed. Robert I. Rothberg (Washington, D.C.: Brookings Institution Press, 1999), 19–25.

41. "Sri Lanka Toll Mounts amid Bloodshed," *Associated Press* (May 24, 2007) http://www.canada.com/topics/news/world/s; *New York Times*, "Sri Lanka's Scars Trace Lines of War Without End," (June 15, 2007). In addition, an estimated 800,000 Tamils have fled the country.

42. Aidan Southall, "The Illusion of Tribe," in *The Passing of Tribal Man in Africa, Journal of African and Asian Studies* 5 (special issue), nos. 1–2 (January–April 1970), 28–50. Cited by Young, *Politics of Cultural Pluralism*, 19.

43. Milton Obote, *Proposals for New Methods of Election of Representatives of the People to Parliament* (Kampala, Uganda: Milton Obote Foundation, 1970), 6. Quoted in Donald Rothchild, "Hegemonial Exchange: An Alternative Model for Managing Conflict in Middle Africa," in *Ethnicity, Politics and Development*, 77. Several scholars in that volume use the term *tribe*, as does Enloe, *Ethnic Conflict*.

44. Pippa Norris and Robert Mates, "Does Ethnicity Determine Support for the Governing Party? The Structural and Attitudinal Basis of Partisan Identification in Twelve African Nations" (Cambridge, MA: Working Paper, Kennedy

School of Government, Harvard University, 2003). The data analyzed came from the Afrobarometer surveys.

45. Dov Ronen, *The Quest for Self Determination* (New Haven, CT: Yale University Press, 1976), 79–86.

46. Young, "Comparative Claims to Political Sovereignty," 204–211; Enloe, *Ethnic Conflict*, 89–92.

47. Frederick Forsyth, *The Biafran Story* (Baltimore, MD: Penguin Books, 1969).

48. See Toyin Falola, *Violence in Nigeria: The Crisis of Religious Politics and Secular Ideology* (Rochester, NY: University of Rochester Press, 1998), 193–226.

49. Basil Davidson, *The Black Man's Burden* (New York: Times Books, 1992), 250.

50. Gérard Prunier, *The Rwanda Crisis, 1959–1994* (London: Hurst & Company, 1995) offers an excellent account of the genocide and the events leading up to it. Prunier's book, written fairly soon after the events, estimates the number of deaths at 500,000. Experts have debated the true number, but most reputable studies put the figure at closer to 800,000. See Gendercide Watch, "Case Study in Genocide: Rwanda, 1994," www.gendercide.org/case_rwanda.html.

51. Anderson, von der Mehden, and Young, *Issues of Political Development*, 21.

52. Horowitz, *A Democratic South Africa*, 47.

53. Khehla Shubane, "South Africa: A New Government in the Making?" *Current History* 91 (May 1992), 202–207; Pauline H. Baker, "South Africa on the Move," *Current History* 89 (May 1990), 197–200, 232–233.

54. Jacob T. Levey, *The Multiculturalism of Fear* (Oxford and New York: Oxford University Press, 2000), 179.

55. *New York Times* (December 8, 1992).

56. *New York Times* (July 27, 2002). For a further discussion of violence by Hindu extremists, see Rubal Oza, "The Geography of Hindu Right-Wing Violence in India," in *Violent Geographies: Fear, Terror, and Political Violence*, eds. Derek Gregory and Allan Pred (New York: Routledge, 2007), 153–174.

57. Cited in T. Walker Wallbank, *A Short History of India and Pakistan* (New York: Mentor, 1958), 196.

58. Bernard E. Brown, "The Government of India," in *Introduction to Comparative Government*, 2nd ed., eds. Michael Curtis et al. (New York: HarperCollins, 1990), 479–480; Robert L. Hardgrave Jr., *India: Government and Politics in a Developing Nation*, 3rd ed. (New York: Harcourt Brace Jovanovich, 1980), 40–42. Hardgrave offers a more conservative estimate of half a million

dead. For personal accounts of the violence that followed partition, especially the recollections of women, see Urvashi Butalia, *The Other Side of Silence: Voices from the Partition of India* (Durham, NC: The Duke University Press, 2000).

59. Originating in the fifteenth century, the Sikh religion is related to both the Hindu and the Islamic religions.

60. Sikhs have a long military tradition and were heavily recruited into the colonial army by the British. Hence, they have long been over-represented, relative to their population size, in the Indian armed forces and security forces. While Sikhs constitute less than 3 percent of India's population, they represented about 8–9 percent of the military at that time and more than 12 percent of the army combat troops.

61. Latif Abul-Husn, *The Lebanese Conflict: Looking Inward* (Boulder, CO: Lynne Rienner Publishers, 1998), 29–44.

62. Elizabeth Picard, "Political Identities and Communal Identities: Shifting Mobilization among the Lebanese Shi'a Through Ten Years of War, 1975–1985," in *Ethnicity, Politics, and Development*, 159–175. In the absence of dependable census information, estimates of Lebanon's religious composition vary widely.

63. Ronald D. McLaurin, "Lebanon: Into or Out of Oblivion?" *Current History* 91 (January 1992), 29–30.

64. Latif Abul-Husn, *The Lebanese Conflict;* Carole H. Dagher, *Bringing Down the Walls: Lebanon's Postwar Challenge* (New York: St. Martin's Press, 2000).

65. Vali Nasr, *The Shi'a Revival: How Conflicts within Islam Will Shape the Future* (New York: W. W. Norton, 2006).

66. Ibid.

67. Robert Pape, Director of the University of Chicago's Project on Suicide Terrorism, quoted on "Spate of Suicide Bombings Threatens Iraq 'Surge,'" National Public Radio (NPR), *All Things Considered*, (May 2, 2007). Sunni insurgents have also killed many American soldiers, but most of these have come from hidden roadside bombs, not suicide bombings.

68. Nasr, *The Shi'a Revival*, 195.

69. Of course, America's image as a successful melting pot has frequently been overstated. For example, racial prejudice, though much diminished in recent decades, continues to divide American society. In recent decades, many Hispanic immigrants have found it difficult to integrate into the mainstream of American life, and there is considerable prejudice against them, as evidenced by some of the recent debate on illegal immigration .

70. Young, *Cultural Pluralism*, 65.

71. Anderson, von der Mehden, and Young, *Issues*, 29.

72. A similar process is currently taking place in Eastern Europe, where the collapse of the Soviet empire and the end of authoritarian communist regimes have unleashed ethnic conflict in Bosnia, the former Soviet Union, and elsewhere.

73. Karl W. Deutsch, *Nationalism, and Social Communication* (Boston: MIT Press and John Wiley and Sons, 1953).

74. This author has heard several racist comments in his three visits to Cuba. The Cuban government tends to understate the problem and has been much more explicit in its campaigns against sexism than it has against racism. The regime seems to believe that pre-Revolutionary racial divisions were merely surrogates for class divisions. Consequently, it erroneously maintains that the social and economic gains the Revolution brought to the lower classes have, by themselves, ended racism.

75. Gordon Means, "Ethnic Preference Policies in Malaysia," in *Ethnic Preference and Public Policy in Developing States*, eds. Neil Nevitte and Charles H. Kennedy (Boulder, CO: Lynne Rienner Publishers, 1986), 95–115; Young, *Cultural Pluralism*, 121–124.

76. The designation *East Indian* is used in Trinidad, Guyana, and other Caribbean nations to distinguish them from indigenous American Indians (Native Americans). The country's official name is Trinidad and Tobago. But elsewhere in this text, especially when the country is included in a list of nations, I refer to it as Trinidad-Tobago so as to prevent the reader from thinking that these are two countries. As about 95 percent of the nation's population lives in Trinidad (a much larger island than Tobago), the country is often referred to simply as Trinidad.

77. Bridget Brereton, "The Foundations of Prejudice: Indians and Africans in 19th Century Trinidad," *Caribbean Issues* 1, no. 1 (1974), 15–28; John Gaffar LaGuerre, "Race Relations in Trinidad and Tobago," in *Trinidad and Tobago: The Independence Experience, 1962–1987*, ed. Selwyn Ryan (St. Augustine, Trinidad: University of the West Indies, 1988), 195.

78. Selwyn D. Ryan, *Race and Nationalism in Trinidad and Tobago* (Toronto: University of Toronto Press, 1972).

79. Kevin Yelvington, "Trinidad and Tobago, 1988–89," in *Latin American and Caribbean Contemporary Record*, eds. James Malloy and Eduardo Gamarra (New York: Holmes and Meier, 1991).

80. However, in recent years a surge in Indian cultural pride and political influence has reversed that trend. For the first time, government bureaucrats in Bolivia, Ecuador, and Peru can be seen wearing indigenous dress and speaking Aymara or Quechua, though they still conduct much of their work in Spanish. And bilingual education has spread in many indigenous areas.

81. For a discussion of rising Indian political mobilization and influence in Bolivia, Ecuador, and Peru, see "A Political Awakening," *The Economist* (February 19, 2004) reprinted on http://www.economist.com/world. And, as we will note, in recent years Bolivia and Peru have elected their first indigenous presidents.

82. Howard Handelman, "The Origins of the Ecuadorian Bourgeoisie: A Generational Transformation," paper presented at the XVII International Congress of the Latin American Studies Association, Los Angeles, 1992.

83. *New York Times*, "Multiracial Brazil Planning Quotas for Blacks," (October 2, 2001) and "Racial Quotas in Brazil Touch Off Fierce Debate," (April 5, 2003).

84. Susanne Jonas, *The Battle for Guatemala* (Boulder, CO: Westview Press, 1991).

85. D. Scott Palmer, *The Shining Path of Peru* (New York: St. Martin's Press, 1992).

86. Elsewhere, there are countries, such as Bosnia, where the Muslim community is more affluent, educated, and modern than the Christian population.

87. For an analysis of elite manipulation as a cause of ethnic conflict, see Paul Brass, *Ethnicity and Nationalism: Theory and Comparison* (New Delhi, India: Sage Publications, 1991).

88. V. P. Gagnon Jr., "Ethnic Nationalism and International Conflict: The Case of Serbia," *International Security* 19, no. 3 (Winter 1994/95), 130–166.

89. J. Isawa Elaigwu and Victor A. Olorunsola, "Federalism and the Politics of Compromise," in *State versus Ethnic Claims*, 282.

90. Enloe, *Ethnic Conflict*, 89–134. Of course, federalism is not necessarily ethnically based, as evidenced by the United States.

91. Ibid., 111.

92. Young, "Comparative Claims to Political Sovereignty."

93. Consociationalism can exist among conflicting groups other than ethnicities, but we confine our discussion of it to that area.

94. Arend Lijphart, *Democracy in Plural Societies* (New Haven, CT: Yale University Press, 1977), 25–40.

95. Arend Lijphart, "The Power-Sharing Approach," in *Conflict and Peacemaking in Multiethnic Societies*, ed. Joseph V. Montville (Lexington, MA: Lexington Books, 1990), 497.

96. Ralph R. Premdas, "Secessionist Movements in Comparative Perspective," in *Secessionist Movements*, 12.

97. The only amicable secession that comes to mind took place in Central Europe where, not long after the collapse of Czechoslovakia's communist regime, the Czech Republic acceded to the Slovakian demand that the country be split in two.

98. Ibid., 14–16.

99. Kurdish leaders have claimed that their people number 35 million, but this is an exaggeration. On the other hand, national governments offer figures that are generally too low. Laura Donnandieu Aguado, "The National Liberation Movement of the Kurds in the Middle East," in *Secessionist Movements;* Nader Entessar, *Kurdish Ethnonationalism* (Boulder, CO: Lynne Rienner Publishers, 1992), 1–10; D. McDowall, *A Modern History of the Kurds*, revised ed. (London: I. B. Tauris, 2000), 3–18.

100. The Kurds have achieved virtual autonomy in Iraq and exercise considerable influence in that country's national government. But raids across the Turkish border by soldiers of the Kurdistan Workers Party (PKK) from their camps in Iraq have provoked Turkish military retaliation and the danger of a full-blown Turkish invasion.

101. Daniel Patrick Moynihan, *Pandemonium: Ethnicity in International Politics* (Oxford, England and New York: Oxford University Press, 1993).

102. Gurr, *People versus States*, 276.

103. Samantha Power, "Bystander to Genocide," *The Atlantic Monthly* 288, no. 2 (September 2001), 84–108, ww.theatlantic.com/doc/200109/power- genocide; see also the *Frontline* documentary on PBS entitled "The Triumph of Evil," www.pbs.org/ wgbh/pages/shows/evil.

104. Edward Luttwak, "If Bosnians Were Dolphins . . . ," *Commentary* 96 (October 1993), 27.

105. See, for example, Samantha Power, "Bystanders to Genocide"; Romeo Dallaire, *Shake Hands with the Devil: The Failure of Humanity in Rwanda* (Toronto: Random House Canada, 2003). General Dallaire was the military commander of a small U.N. military mission in Rwanda. He tried, in vain, to get the United Nations to send him reinforcements to quell the genocide. Instead, the U.N. pulled Dallaire's troops out.

106. These include Alan J. Kuperman, "Rwanda in Retrospect," *Foreign Affairs* (January/February, 2000); Alan K. Kuperman, *The Limits of Humanitarian Intervention: Genocide in Rwanda* (Washington, DC: Brookings Institution Press, 2001).

107. Carment and Harvey, *Using Force to Prevent Ethnic Violence.*

108. Entessar, *Kurdish Ethnonationalism*, 119–127. The Pike Commission of the U.S. House of Representatives revealed details of America's support for the abortive Kurdish revolt.

109. Global Security.Com, "Congo Civil War," http://www.globalsecurity.org/military/world/war/congo.htm.

110. Glynne Evans, *Responding to Crises in the African Great Lakes* (New York: Oxford University Press, Adelphia Paper 33, 1997), 75.

111. Carole O'Leary, "The Kurds of Iraq: Recent History, Future Prospects," *The Middle East Review of International Affairs* 6, no. 4 (December 2002).

112. G. Fuller, "Turkey's Restive Kurds: The Challenge of Multiethnicity," in *Ethnic Conflict and International Politics in the Middle East*, ed. Leonard Binder (Gainesville: University of Florida Press, 1999), 225.

113. Human Rights Watch, *1993 Report on the Anfal*, http://hrw.org/reports/1993/iraqanfal/ANFAL1.htm, chap. 1, p. 3; J. Ciment, *The Kurds: State and Minority in Turkey, Iraq and Iran* (New York: Facts on File, 1996), 62–63. Although the Geneva Protocol of 1925 banned chemical weapons, both sides used them in the Iraq–Iran war. When Saddam was tried by a war crimes' tribunal in 2004, he claimed, as he had before, that these gas attacks were the work of Iran. And, there is evidence that Iranian chemical shells may have killed Iraqi civilians at other times. Yet, independent observers agree that, on March 16, 1988, Iraqi aircraft shelled the Kurdish city of Halabja with chemical weapons, leaving 5,000 dead and 7,000 injured or with long-term illnesses.

114. "Babies Found in Iraqi Mass Graves," BBC *News* (October 13, 2004), http://news.bbc.co.uk/2/hi/middle_east/3738368.stm.

115. Phebe Marr, "Kurds and Arabs, Sunnis and Shiites: Can an Iraqi Identity be Salvaged?" in *Religion and Nationalism in Iraq*, eds. David Little and Donald K. Swearer (Cambridge, MA: Harvard University Press, 2006), 66.

116. Project on Democratization, *Democratization and Ethnic Conflict* (Washington, DC: National Academy Press, 1992), 16.

117. J. Edelstein, *Truth and Lies: Stories from the Truth and Reconciliation Commission in South Africa* (New York: New Press, 2001).

118. Michael Ignatieff, "Afterward: Reflections on Coexistence," in *Imagine Coexistence: Restoring Humanity After Violent Ethnic Conflict*, eds. Antonia Chayes and Martha Minnow (San Francisco: Jossey-Bass, 2003), 325–333.

119. Chayes and Minnow, *Imagine Coexistence.*

120. From *Politics in Plural Societies,* quoted in Larry Diamond and Marc F. Plattner, eds. *Nationalism, Ethnic Conflict, and Democracy* (Baltimore, MD: Johns Hopkins University Press, 1994), xix.

121. Francis Fukuyama, "Comments on Nationalism and Democracy," in *Nationalism, Ethnic Conflict and Democracy,* 23–28.

122. This quote, summarizing such pessimistic analyses, comes from Claude Ake, "Why Humanitarian Emergencies Occur: Insights from the Interface of State, Democracy and Civil Society," *Research for Action* 31 (1997), 8.

123. Quoted in Robin Luckham, Anne Marie Goetz and Mary Kaldor, "Democratic Institutions and Democratic Politics," in *Can Democracy Be Designed: The Politics of Institutional Choice in Conflict-torn Societies,* eds. Sunil Bastian and Robin Luckham (London and New York: Zed Books, 2003), 43.

124. That argument is presented in a number of essays in Bastian and Luckham, ed., *Can Democracy be Designed?*

125. Gurr, *People versus States,* 152–163, 169, 204.

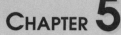
WOMEN AND DEVELOPMENT

A Chinese adage observes that "Women Hold Up Half the Sky." Yet for many years, scholars, Third World governments, and Western development agencies appeared strangely oblivious to women's role in the modernization process. Most early studies of political and economic change in the LDCs said little or nothing about women's issues. In the past few decades, however, three factors have contributed to a new understanding of women in developing nations: the emergence of feminist or gender-related social science research; policy planners with heightened awareness of how women play a distinct and important role in national development; and the growing political empowerment of women in many parts of the developing world. Like examinations of ethnicity and class, gender analysis provides a greater understanding of underdevelopment. Economic planners, for example, have found that women in less-developed countries are concentrated in certain occupations and face barriers to entering others. Poorer women work primarily in agriculture or the semi-legal underground, urban economy known as the "informal sector" (discussed below).[1] Those who work in industry are disproportionately employed in labor-intensive and lower-wage industries such as apparel and electronics in the Far East and Southeast Asia and assembly plants in Mexico and the Caribbean. Like their counterparts in developed nations, female professionals are overrepresented in such nurturing professions as nursing and teaching. In a sample of Asian and Latin American countries—including China, Indonesia, Thailand, Argentina, Brazil, Chile, and Peru—women made up roughly half of the professional and technical workers, but less than 20 percent of the administrative and managerial employees.[2] These divisions between "women's work" and "men's work" have obvious economic and political implications, with women's jobs usually earning lower wages or salaries and wielding less power. At the same time, women are also greatly underrepresented in the political arena. Not only do they hold far fewer government posts than do men, but their share also diminishes as one moves up the pyramid of power.

Although evidence of gender inequality and exploitation exists in most societies, the problem is more severe in many parts of the developing world. In its most horrifying form, the list of injustices includes forced and painful female genital mutilation (so-called "female circumcision") in parts of Africa; the sale of child brides for dowries in Bangladesh; wife beatings in Zambia and the Andes; the murders of some 5,000 Indian women annually, committed by husbands who were dissatisfied with the size of their dowries; courts that condone "honor killings" of women suspected of extramarital relations; and economic deprivation that forces large numbers of women into prostitution. Not long ago, a village tribal council in rural Pakistan found a 12-year-old boy guilty of having a sexual relationship with a higher-class woman (a relationship that government investigators later concluded had never happened). As punishment for the alleged behavior, the council ordered four of the woman's male relatives to gang-rape the boy's adult sister. Villagers did nothing to stop it.[3] Until recently (2006), Pakistani law required a woman who said that she had been raped to produce four *male* witnesses to substantiate her claim, an obviously impossible task in almost all situations. Worse yet, if she could not produce those witnesses, she could be charged with adultery. If convicted, she could be flogged, imprisoned, or, even, stoned to death. In one infamous case, 18-year old Safia Bibi was raped by her employer. Because she was blind and unable to see or identify her rapist and because she was pregnant, she was convicted of adultery and sentenced to 30 lashes. Only after her case provoked international outrage did a Pakistani court acquit her.[4] Although the West African nation of Guinea criminalized female circumcision in 1965, theoretically punishable by possible imprisonment for life or execution, for at least 40 years not a single case came to trial, and 99 percent of Guinean women continued to undergo this painful practice. Such nonenforcement is commonly the fate of women's rights legislation in Africa.[5] The persistence of such customs is complicated by the fact that so many women in these societies subscribe to these traditions. In Africa, the many older women who carry out those circumcisions support the persistence of female genital mutilation. Despite the seemingly obvious repression of women (such as honor killings) in many Islamic societies, a Gallup Poll of several thousand women in Pakistan and seven other Muslim nations in the Middle East and Asia revealed that the majority did not consider themselves oppressed and did not list gender discrimination among the most serious problems facing their country.[6]

Less chilling, but no less significant, examples of gender inequality include divorce laws that greatly favor husbands; barriers to women seeking commercial credit for small businesses; the "double day" that working women typically face (coming home after a day's work and having to do most of the housework and child care); and restricted opportunities for women in government, the professions, and better-paid, blue-collar jobs.

But the study of women in the developing world is by no means confined to issues of inequality and victimization. After years of neglect, many international agencies and government planners have begun to recognize women's special status and particular needs in development projects. Nor have women always been passive subjects who are victimized or "acted upon." Their political activity has ranged from the quiet subversion common to many oppressed groups to a more vigorous assertion of their political, economic, and social rights. A growing body of scholarly literature now focuses on women's *empowerment*. Throughout Latin America, for example, women have played a decisive role in independent, grassroots political organizations known as "new social movements (NSMs)" that have burst upon the scene since the 1970s. Focusing on gender issues, human rights, poverty, and a range of other concerns, NSMs have provided an important alternative to political parties, labor unions, and other mainstream political organizations.[7] Elsewhere, revolutionary movements in countries such as El Salvador, Nicaragua, and China have opened up opportunities for female activism and leadership that had not existed previously. In nations as diverse as Bangladesh, India, Nicaragua, Pakistan, Panama, and the Philippines, women have headed their national governments. And during the past 15 years a growing number of developing countries have reserved seats for women in national, state, and local legislatures, while other nations have introduced gender quotas for those offices. Such measures have increased the number of female political leaders dramatically in many LDCs. All of these aspects of female economic and political activity deserve our attention.

THE POLITICAL AND SOCIOECONOMIC STATUS OF THIRD WORLD WOMEN

One of the notable problems in much of the developing world is that women have far fewer educational opportunities and lower literacy rates than men. In the most extreme case, Afghanistan's Taliban government (1996–2001) prohibited girls and women from attending school.[8] Because education and literacy substantially influence income, health practices, and political participation, gender gaps in education impact many other important facets of political and economic life. We know, for example, that as average educational levels for women rise, birth rates, and family size tend to decline.

Table 5.1 compares the literacy rates of men and women in the major regions of the Third World. The first column of data presents the overall adult literacy rate for each region. The next two columns indicate the literacy rate for each of the sexes, while the last column expresses the female literacy rate as a percentage of the male's. The greater the literacy gap between the sexes, the lower the percentage in that column. The table reveals that South and West Asia (including Afghanistan, Bangladesh, India, and Pakistan) and the Arab world have the greatest gender gaps in literacy, with Sub-Saharan Africa slightly ahead of those regions. Indeed, in South and West Asia women are only 66 percent as likely as men to read and write. On the other hand, Latin America and the Caribbean have essentially eliminated this gender gap, while East Asia is only slightly behind.

TABLE 5.1   Women's Literacy Rates Compared to Men's

Region	Adult Literacy (Percent)	Female Adult Literacy (Percent)	Male Adult Literacy (Percent)	Female Literacy as a Percent of Male
Third World	77.0	70.2	83.6	84
Arab States	69.7	58.9	80.2	73
East Asia	˙91.7	88.1	95.2	93
Latin America and the Caribbean	•90.3	89.5	91.1	98
South and West Asia	58.7	46.3	70.5	66
Sub-Saharan Africa	61.2	53.3	69.5	77

Source: UNESCO Institute for Statistics (September 2006), http://www.uis.unesco.org.

TABLE 5.2   Measures of Gender Empowerment

Country (HDI Rank)	Gender Empowerment Measure (Rank)	Percentage of Members of Parliament (Lower House) Who Are Women
Norway (1)	.932 (1)	37.9%
United States (8)	.808 (12)	16.3
Mexico (53)	.597 (35)	22.6
Tanzania (162)	.597 (36)	30.4
Chile (38)	.506 (52)	15.0
South Korea (26)	.502 (53)	13.4
Malaysia (61)	.500 (55)	9.1
Iran (96)	.326 (71)	4.1
Yemen (153)	.128 (75)	0.3

Sources: United Nations Development Programme (UNDP), *Human Development Report 2006*, http://www.undp.org; Inter-Parliamentary Union, *Women in National Parliaments* (March 31, 2007), www.ipu.org/.

Table 5.2 turns our attention from regional literacy data to measures of women's political and economic influence in selected countries. Two developed nations—Norway and the United States—are included for the sake of comparison. The number in parentheses after each country's name and after each nation's Gender Empowerment Measure (GEM) indicates, respectively, that country's HDI and GEM ranking relative to other countries. The GEM shown in the first data column is a composite *index* indicating how commonly women hold significant positions in the country's political system and in its private sector. The highest GEM possible (i.e., the highest level of female political and economic empowerment) is 1.0, and the lowest possible score is 0.0. Thus, with a score of .932, Norway had the highest GEM in the world, while the United States (.808) ranked 12th worldwide. Yemen's score of .128 placed it 75th and last among countries that have data available on GEMs. Note that GEM scores are available for less than half of the countries in the United Nations Development Program (UNDP) database (75 of 177 countries), with no GEM data for most of the poorest LDCs. HDI rankings, though also unavailable for many nations, do exist for a nearly twice as many countries (136). So, a country whose HDI ranks 70th (out of the more than 190 countries reporting HDIs) falls in above the middle of its peers. If, on the other hand, its GEM ranked 65th, it would have one of the lowest scores among the 75 countries that had GEM scores.

Modernization theory suggests that the most developed nations in this table—Norway and the United States—should have the highest GEMs. That is, we would expect that as countries modernize, their economic and political gender gaps should narrow. For the most part, the evidence here (as well as data for nations not in the table) supports that hypothesis. As expected, the higher a country's educational level, life expectancy, and per capita income (its HDI), the higher it *tends* to rank on its GEM. But there are some notable exceptions to that pattern. The most glaring "overachiever" in the group shown in Table 5.2

is Tanzania. Although it is one of the world's poorest nations and ranks near the bottom in HDI (162nd), Tanzania had a strong GEM, ranking well ahead of far more affluent countries with stronger HDIs, such as South Korea and Chile (Table 5.2). Conversely, South Korea, with one of the world most dynamic economies and an HDI that ranks it among the top 15 percent in the world (i.e., 26th of some 190 countries), has a GEM that falls near the bottom third of the 75 nations reporting that measure, well behind much poorer countries such as Tanzania and Mexico, and barely ahead of Malaysia. This suggests that other factors besides economic development and education—such as cultural values and political ideology—also influence the position of women in society.

The last column in Table 5.2 speaks more directly to the influence and representation of women in national politics. It shows what percentage of the seats in the lower (normally, more powerful) house of the national parliament (or congress) were filled by women as of early 2007. The proportion of women in Norway's parliament (almost 38 percent) far surpasses the United States as well as other developed nations—such as Canada, France, and Japan—not shown in this table.[9] Contrary to expectation, Mexico's Chamber of Deputies and, especially, Tanzania's parliament have more women (22.6 and 30.4 percent, respectively) than the U.S. House of Representatives (16.3 percent) or the lower house of parliament in Italy, Ireland, or Japan (not shown). More predictably, the Muslim states of Iran, Malaysia, and, especially, Yemen lagged behind, well below the worldwide average of 17.2 percent female representation.

Colonization, Westernization, Modernization, and the Economic Status of Women

How was the status of women altered when Africa, Asia, and the Middle East were colonized or otherwise brought into the orbit of Western economic and military power? How have women been affected subsequently by the transition from traditional to modern society? Westerners often associate traditional social and economic systems with rigid religious and cultural values that relegate women to an inferior rank. That notion may lead us to assume that European colonization of Africa and Asia and the subsequent spread of Western-style modernization offered women greater opportunities and improved social status. But while modernization theory would have us believe that urbanization, industrialization, and the diffusion of Western values have an emancipating effect, "feminist scholars have produced a wealth of literature that maintains that political and economic modernization had many negative effects on women," at least initially.[10]

Although the status of women in pre-colonial (largely rural) Africa varied from place to place, oftentimes European colonialism undermined women's social position. For one thing, colonial rule was imposed at a time (the nineteenth century) when Victorian England and other European societies had rather restricted views of women's roles.[11] Therefore, many colonial administrations treated women less equitably than traditional institutions had. In West African cultures, for example, women sometimes served as chiefs or held other important political positions. However, as the influence of such traditional leadership posts declined, first under colonialism and then after independence, such women lost their authority to male-dominated colonial and national govern-ments. Among the Nigerian Ibos, for example, women had exercised significant political power prior to the British conquest. Colonial administrators, however, viewed politics as "a man's concern" and, consequently, downgraded female political influence.[12]

The commercialization of agriculture frequently reduced women's *economic* power as well. In Asia and Africa, commercialization often led colonial govern-ments to grant peasants legal titles to their farm land. In some regions that process transferred plots that had been unofficially controlled by women to male ownership.[13] In addition, as families moved from subsistence agriculture (for family consumption) to commercial agriculture, and as commercial plantations were developed by foreigners, men were more likely than women to be hired as plantation workers. Commercialization also made farmers more dependent on the state for credit and for technical training. In both the colonial era and in the early decades of independence, women were usually frozen out of such aid. In Uganda, for example, even though female farmers often had begun the earliest commercial cotton cultivation, the British administrator in charge of agriculture declared that "cotton growing [can] not be left to the women and old people."[14] Thus, as new agricultural technologies were introduced, they were taught prima-rily to men, ultimately driving women off the land. After independence, most African and Asian governments continued this pattern, as extension agents offered modern technologies, credits, and other assistance primarily to men.

Just as modernization theorists and radical feminists hold different views of colonialism, they also disagree on how subsequent modernization has affected the lives of Third World women. Modernization theory contrasts the egalitarian values of modern culture with the allegedly sexist perspectives of traditional societies. Radical feminists, many of whom subscribe to depend-ency theory, counter that in many instances industrialization, urbanization, and the spread of world capitalism have *widened* the gender gap or otherwise dis-advantaged women. How might we reconcile these opposing viewpoints? The evidence suggests that modernization positively affects women's status over the long run, but is often harmful in the short-to-medium term. Gender gaps in education, literacy, income, and economic/political influence are generally narrower in developed nations than in the LDCs (see Tables 5.2 and 5.3). Economic growth eventually creates new opportunities for women. And expanded educational systems usually offer them additional opportunities while creating more egalitarian values and gender roles. For example, in East Asia, the world's fastest growing regional economy, women's share of the labor force has increased in seven of the eight countries with the region's highest rates of economic growth (all but Thailand), rising substantially in four of them (Singapore, South Korea, Malaysia, and Indonesia). Elsewhere, high-growth nations have narrowed their gender gaps in education and literacy.

But, as noted, the early stages of the transition to modernity often produce particular hardships for women. The discussion that follows focuses on the negative initial effects of economic growth, neoliberal economic reforms, and other elements of modernization. Policy makers and planners need to address these problems. However, they should not obscure the fact that, in the long term, modernization offers women the best hope for equality. The task, then, is to reduce the short-term pain and increase the likelihood of long-term gain.

TABLE 5.3   The Proportion of Women in National Parliaments (Regional Averages)

Region	Single House or Lower House (Percent)	Upper House or Senate (Percent)	Both Houses Combined (Percent)
Nordic European Countries	41.7	—	39.7
Europe excluding Nordic countries	17.7	17.5	17.7
The Americas	20.0	19.3	19.9
Asia	16.5	15.7	16.4
Sub-Saharan Africa	16.8	18.0	16.9
Arab States	9.5	6.3	8.8

Source: Inter-Parliamentary Union, *Women in National Parliaments* (March 31, 2007), www.ipu.org/.

Women in the Economy: Rural and Urban

Women are critical players in Third World agriculture. A recent publication by the Food and Agriculture Organization (FAO) of the United Nations estimates that "women produce between 60 and 80 percent of the food in most developing countries."[15] Particularly in Africa, the percentage of female farmers has grown substantially in recent decades. In its article on "The Feminization of Agriculture," the FAO points out that "war, sickness and death from HIV/AIDS have reduced rural male populations" as has male migration from the countryside to cities at home and abroad.[16] But despite the predominance of female farming in most of the LDCs, Nici Nelson noted years ago that "too little attention has been given by researchers and administrators or planners to women and the roles they play in rural society."[17] Even though male "heads of household" are increasingly employed off the family farm, leaving its cultivation to their wives, government planners have often clung to "the myth of the ever-present male head" while neglecting female farmers.[18]

In the years since the United Nations' Decade for Women (1975–1985), international agencies and Third World governments have become more aware of women's role in rural development. The World Bank, the United States Agency for International Development (USAID)—the government agency that administers U.S. economic and humanitarian assistance to developing nations—and many nongovernmental organizations (NGOs) recognized the need to address the roles of rural as well as urban women. For example, USAID established an office for Women in Development (WID) to better address women's needs in U.S. foreign aid projects. Subsequently, the United Nations issued "FAO's Plan of Action for Women in Development (WID), 1996–2001." But, the development community has struggled to find an approach that best serves women's needs. Critics of the WID strategy charged that it addressed women's issues in isolation—for example, domestic violence, low female school enrollment—thereby failing to get at the root causes of these problems. Instead, NGOs such as Oxfam now favor a strategy called Gender and Development (GAD), which looks comprehensively at problems, such as high student dropout rates. By examining power relationships between genders, the GAD perspective seeks to explain why such problems affect females more severely than males. But, while development agencies have become more sensitive to the special problems of poor women in the LDCs (urban and rural), and while there have been many successful development projects that reflect this sensitivity, progress overall has been limited. One expert estimates that "two thirds of the poor in Asia [still] are women," with similar statistics in most of the developing world.[19] Furthermore, the FAO laments the fact that "gender bias and gender blindness persist: farmers are still generally perceived as 'male' by policy makers, development planners, and agricultural service deliverers. For this reason, women find it more difficult than men to gain access to valuable resources such as land, credit and agricultural inputs, technology, extension, training and services that would enhance their production capacity."[20]

During the past half-century in most developing countries, there has been an enormous population shift from the countryside to the cities (see Chapter 7). As we have noted, modernization theorists had expected that urbanization—often accompanied by increased industrialization, literacy, and exposure to the mass media—would offer women greater occupational and educational opportunities, thereby enhancing their status. In many Latin American nations, women have constituted a majority of the migrants to urban centers. But while many of them have benefited, a large portion has been left behind. Once arrived in the city, most women are only able to secure low-end jobs. Indeed, the most common type of employment among female migrants is domestic service, for which they generally earn the legal minimum wage or lower. At one time 25 percent of all women in the Mexican urban work force were either maids in private homes or cleaning women in commercial establishments and hotels.[21] Another important source of employment is the so-called "informal sector"—including street vending, employment in "sweet shops," and doing "piece-work" at home for contractors, all of which defy government regulation.[22] According to data compiled by the U.N.'s International Labor Organization (ILO), about two-thirds of the women in Third World cities work in the informal sector. They comprise some 30–90 percent of all street vendors (depending on the country) and 35–80 percent of all home-based workers.[23] Although some informal-sector workers earn higher incomes than do blue-collar laborers in the modern economy, many others fall below the poverty line. Finally, in newly industrializing countries, women are frequently employed in low-wage manufacturing. Over time, as factories become more technologically sophisticated and as wages rise, the percentage of female employees in those firms tends to decline.[24]

In East Asia, the industrial boom since the 1980s has created many new jobs for women, particularly in labor-intensive industries such as apparel and electronics. Many of those firms prefer to hire young unmarried women for several reasons: the jobs frequently require manual dexterity, a skill that employers associate with women; because they are not the principal breadwinners in their families, young women are usually willing to work for lower wages; and, finally, women are less likely to join unions or participate in strikes. During the late 1990s, Asia's economic crisis caused numerous plant closings and layoffs. Women were often the first fired because most employers believed that men needed their jobs in order to support their families. The crisis also forced many poor and middle-class families to take their daughters out of school in order to save the costs of school uniforms, educational fees, and tuition. Indeed, at the height of the crisis, Indonesian girls were six times more likely than boys to drop out of school before the fourth grade.[25]

As we have seen (Table 5.1), in most developing regions women tend to have fewer educational opportunities than men, a deficit that later limits their occupational opportunities. All too often, poverty and a lack of vocational skills force desperate women into prostitution. Despite Thailand's economic boom since the mid-1960s, continuing rural poverty has driven many young female migrants into Bangkok's thriving "sex tourism" industry. One study of Manila (the Philippines) and Bangkok (Thailand) revealed that 7–9 percent of female employment in those two cities was "prostitution related."[26] Some desperately poor families in that region have sold young daughters to brothels or given them as collateral for loans. A study of Southeast Asia by the U.N.'s ILO estimated the number of sex workers shortly before the crisis to be 140,000 to 230,000 in Indonesia, 43,000 to 142,000 in Malaysia, and 200,000 to 300,000 in Thailand. In the economically depressed Philippines, the situation was even worse as "the estimated 400,000 to 500,000 prostitutes in the country *approximated the number of its manufacturing workers* (italics added)." The situation worsened considerably during the Asian financial crisis when many employed in other areas needed to supplement their income: "the number of Southeast Asians earning a living directly or indirectly from prostitution—including waitresses, security guards, escort services, tour agencies—could easily [have] reached 'several millions.'"[27] That number may have declined since 1998, when East and Southeast Asia resumed rapid growth, but it remains disturbingly high. While some sex workers enter the trade voluntarily, others (including underage girls) do not. A 2001 State Department report on the status of women notes a survey by a human-rights NGO in Cambodia that "found that 40 percent of women and girls who work as prostitutes do so voluntarily, while 60 percent have been forced to work as prostitutes or have been deceived into prostitution."[28] In the squatter settlements of Kenya's capital, Nairobi, impoverished women are rarely equipped to gain employment in the economy's modern sector. Consequently, illegal brewing of beer and prostitution have been the two major sources of female employment.[29]

While these studies document the severe problems that often accompany Third World modernization, it is important to recognize that economic growth, most notably in East Asia, has improved the incomes of millions of other underprivileged women who are newly employed in the modern sector of the economy. This is particularly true in the countries where their educational opportunities also have improved.[30] Among the developing world's middle- and upper-class women, the advantages of higher class status often mitigate the educational and career disadvantages of being female. In Asia and Latin America, the number of woman professionals and businesswomen has increased rapidly in recent decades. At the university level, the gender gap has narrowed considerably as well. In Brazil, for example, the number of female university students has grown far more quickly than have the ranks of men. And in some LDCs today—including, Muslim Kuwait—women university students outnumber men. Still, for now, "women [remain] vastly under-represented in government, business, political and social institutions."[31]

WOMEN AND POLITICS

Many of the same traditions and prejudices that have undermined women's socioeconomic positions have also disadvantaged them politically. In Latin America, for example, women won the right to vote substantially later than they did in industrialized democracies. Whereas the United States and most European democracies legalized female suffrage in the first two decades of the twentieth century, only 7 of 20 Latin American countries allowed women to vote before the close of World War II.[32] Ecuador was the first nation in that region to extend the franchise (1929) and Paraguay the last (1961).[33] In Africa and Asia the situation was different. Because most of the countries in those regions only became independent in the decades after World War II, when female suffrage was a universally accepted principle, women were normally enfranchised from the start of self-rule. However, Arab Gulf States such as Bahrain only enfranchised women in 2001, while Kuwait did the same in 2005. Today, Third World women generally still vote at a lower rate than men, but that gender gap is narrowing.[34]

In many parts of Africa, Asia, and the Middle East, traditional cultural values have limited women's political participation and activism.[35] One study of transitional Hindu families in India (partly traditional and partly modernized) revealed an important generational difference between women who had completed a university education at the time of national independence and their more traditional mothers. The women analyzed in this study were the daughters of Westernized fathers who had worked for the colonial civil service and who had been quite politically involved. Yet, their mothers generally spoke no English, believed in female submissiveness, and were quite apolitical.[36] In contrast, the university-educated daughters were far more politically involved than their mothers. In the absence of such educational opportunities, political participation levels remain low for the vast majority of women in South Asia, the Middle East, and much of Africa, who lack the resources available to more affluent women.

Indeed, social class correlates particularly strongly with female political participation in the LDCs. In many developing countries, highly educated and westernized women born to elite families are as likely to hold important political offices as are Western women. It is worth noting, for example, that all the countries of the Indian subcontinent—India, Pakistan, and Bangladesh—as well as neighboring Sri Lanka have had female prime ministers (including the recently assassinated Pakistani leader, Benazir Bhutto), a record not nearly equaled in North America or most of Western Europe. The first woman president of the United Nations General Assembly and the first female chair of the Security Council were both from Africa, not the advanced, industrial nations.[37] As of 2007, a total of 17 Latin American and Caribbean countries had a higher percentage of women in parliament or congress than did the United States. In a number of African countries—Rwanda, Mozambique, South Africa, Burundi, Tanzania, Uganda, the Seychelles, and Namibia—women constitute at least 25 percent of the "members of parliament" (MPs), all exceeding the United States, with Rwanda leading the world at 49 percent.[38]

Because the developing world encompasses so wide a variety of cultural traditions, and because social change has impinged so differently on the various social classes and sectors within individual nations, there can be no simple generalizations about the way in which modernization has influenced women's political status. Modernization theory would lead us to expect that more socially and economically developed countries would be quicker to grant political rights to women. If we look at Latin America, however, we find little correlation between a country's literacy rate and the year in which it granted suffrage to women.[39] Thus, the spread of education alone does not guarantee women greater political equality. On the other hand, in countries such as Rwanda, Mozambique, South Africa, Argentina, Costa Rica, and Cuba, conscious efforts to change traditional values and/or the creation of reserved seats and quotas for women in parliament have given women substantially greater political opportunities and have advanced gender equity.[40]

Women's Political Activism at the Grass Roots

It is possible that women exert the greatest influence on Third World politics when acting through grass-roots organizations in their own neighborhoods and communities. Community-based groups afford them opportunities for participation and leadership normally absent at the national or regional level. For one thing, these groups typically focus on issues that are of immediate importance to underprivileged women such as housing, health care, potable drinking water, and education. Furthermore, neighborhood and village organizations are more accessible to poor women, who have no day care for their young children and often cannot travel far from home. Hence, many women who have been excluded from mainstream political parties, interest groups, and government institutions are attracted to community groups because of their accessibility and their relevance to their own lives.

In recent decades a range of grass-roots organizations representing poor and middle-class women has emerged in much of the developing world. Some represent women exclusively, while others include members of both sexes but are led by women or contain women's wings.[41] Jana Everett examined several Indian community groups in urban and rural settings, finding important similarities and differences. Both urban and rural groups were initially led by politically experienced, middle-class women committed to organizing the poor. And in both locations, as low-income women became more involved in neighborhood activities, their political awareness, confidence, and assertiveness grew, stimulating, in turn, greater participation in the broader political system.[42]

But, the goals and tactics used by these groups varied. For example, Everett found that the rural, grass-roots groups were more likely than urban organizations to stage demonstrations and other types of protest and they were more prone to demand redistributive economic remedies such as land reform. In comparison, urban women's groups were more moderate in their tactics and often in their goals. Armita Basu's study of female rural protests in the Indian state of Maharashtra also noted their militancy. In one case, when a woman villager complained that the local police had ignored her charges against a landlord who had beaten her severely, a crowd of 300 women and 150 men "smeared [the landlord's] face with cow dung . . . and paraded him through the surrounding villages."[43] The rural women's greater aggressiveness likely resulted from the more hostile political atmosphere they confronted. Because village political and economic elites are usually less willing than their urban counterparts to redress lower-class grievances through normal political channels, these women were forced to use more radical tactics.

Social movements often develop as a response to a specific crisis or danger. For example, the 1985 earthquake that destroyed large sections of Mexico City had a particularly devastating effect on seamstresses in the city's apparel industry. The quake hit early in the morning when most residents had not yet left home for work. But seamstresses work longer hours, so many of them were already at their machines when the earthquake occurred and they were trapped under rubble at their places of employment. To their horror, some found that their employers were more interested in saving their sewing machines than in bringing out trapped workers. The clothing workers subsequently formed their own labor union led by women from their own ranks, independent of the government-affiliated federation to which most Mexican unions belong. With more honest leadership than is typically found in the Mexican labor movement, the new union not only has bargained with employers and the government for better working conditions but has also provided day care and related services for its members.

In Latin America, opposition to the authoritarian military governments that governed much of the region during the 1970s and 1980s was a major catalyst for grass-roots political activity. In Argentina, Brazil, Chile, and Uruguay, bureaucratic-authoritarian (BA) regimes halted the electoral process, banned leftist political parties and unions, and arrested, tortured, and killed many suspected "subversives" (see Chapter 9). At the same time, a major debt crisis in the 1980s, coupled with harsh government economic remedies, produced the region's worst recession since the 1930s and a precipitous decline in mass living standards (Chapter 10). Women played an important role in anti-authoritarian social movements, which helped pave the way for the restoration of democracy in the 1980s and 1990s.

The women's movement incorporated three types of political organizations, all largely urban based. First were feminist groups, primarily led by middle-class women. They included many professionals who previously had been active in leftist political parties, but had become disillusioned by the left's disinterest in women's issues at that time. A second type, neighborhood organizations, represented women from the urban slums. In the face of the region's severe economic crisis, poor women organized self-help groups to run communal kitchens, infant nutrition centers, and other antipoverty groups. Though not initially highly politicized, many of these groups radicalized over time as they demanded more equitable distribution of state resources and the restoration of democracy. Finally, a third strand of the women's movement campaigned for human rights. Argentina's "Mothers of the Plaza de Mayo" regularly marched in defiance of government restrictions to demand an accounting of their missing children and grandchildren who had disappeared at the hands of the police or armed forces. Responding to state-sponsored imprisonments, torture, and assassinations, women's groups in Brazil, Chile, and Uruguay became a major component of the human rights movement. This was the most socially integrated branch of the women's movement, bringing together participants from the middle and working classes. Often they also joined forces with other human rights activists in the Catholic Church and Christian Base Communities.[44]

One of the most politically influential women's movements emerged in Brazil. Several factors contributed to this phenomenon. First was the rapid expansion of women's educational opportunities from the early 1960s through the 1980s. Between 1969 and 1975 alone, while the number of men attending Brazilian universities doubled, the number of women increased fivefold. By 1980, women constituted nearly half of the country's university students. They also accounted for a growing proportion of Brazil's professionals, their numbers swelling from 19,000 in 1970 to more than 95,000 in 1980.[45] Often paid significantly less than their male counterparts, they became the nucleus of the new feminist movement. Their leaders were highly politicized, many of them having been active in leftist political parties prior to the military takeovers. When government repression forced many of these militants into exile, they frequently resettled in Western Europe or Chile, where they were influenced by older and more sophisticated feminist organizations. Years later, when Brazil's political system began to open up, these exiles returned home to organize.

Second, in the absence of democratic elections, grass-roots movements such as tenants' associations offered the urban poor one of the only opportunities to pressure the government. In slums and shantytowns, radical priests, nuns, and parishioners—motivated by liberation theology—organized Christian Base Communities, which combined religious values with social activism. Leftist secular groups also helped to organize the poor. One study of neighborhood, grass-roots organizations in São Paulo, Brazil's largest city, revealed that most members and leaders were women.[46] Typically, such organizations first focused on their rank-and-file's immediate economic needs—jobs, health care, and food—rather than feminist issues. Indeed, among their allies, many Church leaders were hostile to feminism while leftist groups were less concerned about gender divisions than class conflict. In time, however, many poor women came to share "middle-class" feminist concerns regarding household equality, domestic abuse, and aggressively macho behavior by male household heads.

In the late 1970s, the third strand of the women's movement emerged: human rights groups protesting government repression. Progressive political party and Catholic Church activists often assumed leadership roles. Interestingly, this was one of the few instances in which women's organizations had an advantage over similar groups led by men. Because the government viewed women as inherently less political than men and, hence, less dangerous, they allowed women's human rights groups greater freedom than they gave other protest movements. As the Brazilian military government engineered a transition to democracy in the 1980s, female voters and politicians played important roles in the PMDB, the major opposition party. Ironically, the restoration of democracy reduced the motivation for unity among the disparate wings of the women's movement and weakened them in other ways. As middle-class leaders and militants became increasingly involved in the restored democratic system, they often lost contacts with community groups representing the urban poor. Thus, ironically, in Brazil and elsewhere, the restoration of democracy demobilized many lower-income women and often temporarily weakened the women's movement. More recently, however, the explosion of private voluntary groups (NGOs) in developing areas worldwide has created new opportunities for women's grass-roots political participation. As their name suggests, NGOs are independent of government control. Many try to influence public policy in areas such as democratization, human rights, women's rights, environmental protection, housing, health care, and education. Compared to the earlier social movements, NGOs tend to be more specialized, more professionalized, better funded, and "more respectable." The best-known and financed groups operate internationally, including the International Red Cross, Amnesty International, Greenpeace, and Oxfam. But most NGOs are limited to the local or, perhaps, national level, where many of them try to mobilize popular support and influence government policy. In the LDCs, they have contributed enormously to the expansion of civil society, particularly in democratizing societies, where they often provide a political voice to otherwise powerless groups seeking reform. In countries such as Chile, Peru, India, and Thailand, they have helped expand women's political rights and economic opportunities.

Women as National Political Leaders

In political systems throughout the world (except perhaps the Northern European Nordic nations), women are severely underrepresented in political leadership positions. The Third World is surely no exception. In the mid-1980s, for example, only 6 percent of Africa's national legislators and only 2 percent of its cabinet members were women. Despite dramatic gains since then, women remain greatly underrepresented in major government offices in most LDCs. Looking at the whole world, "United Nations surveys repeatedly show that even in countries where women are active professionally, their level of responsibility as policy makers and planners [has usually been] low."[47] Furthermore, a disproportionate number of the women who *have* reached national leadership positions have been restricted to posts commonly associated with female qualities. For example, most of the African women who have held cabinet posts in the recent past served as ministers of education, women's affairs, health, or social welfare—areas traditionally believed to be suited for women's "nurturing role."[48]

Some 30 years ago, a study of Chilean and Peruvian female political leaders revealed a pattern common to much of Latin America. Female political leaders were forced to legitimize their activism outside the home by presenting themselves as *supermadres* ("supermothers") who were using their political position to nurture their constituents (their extended family). Argentina's legendary political leader, Eva Perón (Evita), had painted that image eloquently years earlier:

> In this great house of the Motherland [Argentina], I am just like any other woman in any other of the innumerable houses of my people. Just like all of them I rise early thinking about my husband and about my children . . . I so truly feel myself the mother of my people.[49]

Elsa Chaney's survey of 167 Chilean and Peruvian woman government officials showed that half of them felt that certain government posts (such as education and health) were more appropriate for women, while others should be held by men (Finance and Defense, for example). Only 13 percent of the women politicians interviewed believed that gender should be irrelevant to the type of political post one holds, while another 37 percent were ambivalent.[50] Of course, it is not only in developing nations that women have frequently been confined to political positions associated with gender stereotypes. Until the 1990s, female cabinet members in the United States generally presided over such departments as Labor, Education, and Health and Human Services. More recently, however, Presidents Clinton and Bush broke that mold by appointing women as Attorney General, Secretary of State, and National Security Advisor, all previously male preserves. In the LDCs, a similarly groundbreaking appointment took place in 2002 when Michelle Bachelet was named Chile's Minister of Defense (she subsequently was elected Chile's first woman president). Since that time women have headed the defense ministry in several Latin American nations, including Argentina, Colombia, Uruguay, and a second time in Chile. Indeed, in much of the developing world the role of women in national politics has expanded tremendously in recent years, and their range of government positions has broadened.

Still, even today, female political leaders are constrained by a somewhat permeable "glass ceiling" that concentrates them at lower levels. Thus, women are generally more likely to be elected to local or state legislatures than to the national parliament. In 1993, India passed a constitutional amendment reserving one-third of the seats in all local assemblies (village councils, etc.) for women.[51] Since 1995, however, repeated efforts to extend that quota to parliament have failed.

Of course, the ability of female political leaders to rise to the very top of several South Asian governments in recent decades is striking, particularly in light of the generally lamentable position of women in their broader societies. All three nations on the Indian subcontinent, as well as neighboring Sri Lanka, have been led by women prime ministers. The most prominent member of this group was Indira Gandhi, who served four terms as prime minister (1966–1977 and 1980–1984) and dominated Indian politics from 1966 until her assassination in 1984, when she was succeeded by her son Rajiv. In 1998, Rajiv's widow (he was assassinated as well, in 1991), Sonia Gandhi, assumed the leadership of the Congress Party (the nation's most powerful party for most of the last 60 years). Six years later, she led the party back to power but declined the position of prime minister because of vehement opposition-party objections—objections not related to her being a woman, but rather to the fact that she was born and raised in Italy and still speaks Hindi somewhat haltingly.[52]

In recent decades, women have served as prime ministers or presidents in Pakistan (Benazir Bhutto), Sri Lanka (Prime Minister Sirimavo Bandaranaike, the world's first female head of government in the twentieth century and her daughter (President Chandrika Kumaratunga), and Bangladesh (Begum Khaleda Zia and her rival Sheikh Hasina Wajed alternated as prime minister from 1991 to 2006). Elsewhere in Asia, prominent female political leaders have included the Philippines' former president Corazón Aquino and its recently reelected president Gloria Macapagal Arroyo; former Indonesian President Megawati Sukarnoputri; South Korean Prime Minister Han Myung Sook; Congress Party leader Sonia Gandhi; and Burmese opposition leader Daw Aung San Suu Kyi, winner of the 1991 Nobel Peace Prize.[53]

No other developing region matches Asia's array of female leaders, but, in addition to Eva Perón (who never held elective office), Latin America and the

Caribbean have produced the current Chilean President Michelle Bachelet and several former presidents—Mireya Moscoso Rodríguez (Panama), Isabel Perón (Argentina), Violeta Chamorro (Nicaragua), Janet Jagan (Guyana), and Ertha Pascal-Trouillot (Haiti's provisional president). Western hemisphere nations with female prime ministers have included Bermuda, Bolivia, Dominica, Guyana, Haiti, Jamaica, and Peru.

In 2006, Ellen Johnson-Sirleaf became Africa's first popularly elected female president. Women have also briefly held the post of prime minister in Burundi, the Central African Republic, Rwanda, and Senegal. They served for two years or more in the Democratic Republic of Sâo Tomé e Principe and in Mozambique. Yet, although several Sub-Saharan African parliaments have among the highest percentage of women in the world (discussed below), that region has had far fewer woman heads of government or heads of state than either Asia or Latin America.

Several caveats must be raised, however, regarding the political success of women leaders in Asia and Latin America. First, a number of them only served briefly as interim leaders. Second, most emerged from a tiny elite of highly educated, upper-class women from powerful families and, therefore, were not representative of women's societal status generally. Thus, for example, Pakistan's Benazir Bhutto and Burma's Aung San Suu Kyi were educated at Harvard and/or Oxford universities (Bhutto attended both). Corazón Aquino belonged to one of the Philippines' more powerful land-owning families. Finally, many of the most enduring and influential leaders, particularly in Asia, have been the wives, widows, or daughters of charismatic national leaders: Indira Gandhi was the daughter of India's legendary first prime minister, Jawaharlal Nehru; Aung San Suu Kyi's father was the founder of modern Burma (Myanmar); Indonesian President Megawati Sukarnoputri was the daughter of President Sukarno, that country's first president and founding father; Filipino President Gloria Macapagal Arroyo's father had also been president; former Pakistani Prime Minister Benazir Bhutto's father preceded her as prime minister. In Latin America and the Caribbean, three of the ten women who have held the posts of president or prime minister have been the wives or widows of earlier presidents: Isabel Martínez de Perón (Argentina), Janet Jagan (Guyana), and Mireya Elisa Moscoso de Arias (Panama).

Indeed, a shocking number of female government leaders in the developing world, most notably in Asia, have been the widows (or daughters) of assassinated political leaders. Sri Lankan Prime Minister Sirimavo Bandaranaike was the widow of a slain prime minister, while the country's current president, Chandrika Kumaratunga, endured the political assassinations of both her father and her husband (30 years apart). Former President Corazón Aquino, hero of the Filipino democracy movement, was the widow of an assassinated opposition leader. Bangladesh's two prime ministers from 1991 to 2006 were, respectively, the widow of a slain prime minister and the daughter of another. Benazir Bhutto's father, a former prime minister, was ousted and then hung by the Pakistani armed forces. In Myanmar, democracy leader Aung San Suu Kyi's father, General Aung San, was assassinated when she was a child. And in the Americas, former Nicaraguan President Violeta Chamorro was the widow of a famed newspaper editor whose assassination sparked the Nicaraguan Revolution.[54]

This does not imply that these women lacked political ability or leadership qualities. Indira Gandhi was recognized as one of the world's most accomplished political leaders, and Violeta Chamorro helped heal the wounds of her country's civil war. After Sri Lanka's Sirimavo Bandaranaike succeeded her assassinated husband as prime minister, she dominated that country's political system for the next three decades. Current Philippine President Gloria Macapagal Arroyo was an economics professor, finance minister, and vice president before becoming president.[55] Still, no matter how highly skilled they have been, most female political leaders in the LDCs, particularly in Asia, have been able to reach the top of their political system only as heirs to their fathers or husbands. For now, then, a glass ceiling on government leadership remains in place for most Third World women, with the notable exception of some members of the political and socioeconomic elites.

Reserved Seats and Quotas: Female Representation in Parliament and the Cabinet

Since women account for slightly over half the population of most nations, gender-neutral political systems would presumably produce a corresponding percentage of female representatives in important institutions such as the national legislature (hereafter referred to generically as "parliament" even when it bears another name such as "congress"). Yet, today only about one in six members of parliament (MPs) worldwide are women and rarely does that proportion exceed one in three.[56] As the first data column in Table 5.3 indicates, the Nordic nations (Denmark, Finland, Iceland, Norway, and Sweden) are far ahead of any other region, with more than 40 percent female representation.[57] In less-developed regions, representation in the lower (more powerful) house of parliament varies from a high of 20 percent in the Americas to a mere 9.5 percent in the Arab states.[58] But, somewhat surprisingly, when we set aside the Nordic countries (at the high end of all nations) and the Arab nations (at the low end of the spectrum), we find that the percentage of women MPs in Asia and Sub-Saharan Africa (Africa other than the handful of Arab countries in North Africa) is about the same as in Europe and the United States. And, Latin America has a higher percentage of women in "parliament" than either the United States or Europe. The rise in female representation in Latin America over the past two decades has been achieved primarily through the introduction of gender quotas in many of the region's legislatures (discussed below).

From 1996 to 2007, the number of women MPs worldwide rose from 10.1 to 17.2 percent. Gains in the LDCs during that period were sharpest in the Arab world (though it still has the world's lowest rate of female representation, it doubled its percentage in 11 years) and slowest in Asia (up only slightly from 13.1 to 16.5 percent over that period, allowing Latin America to pass it as the Third World's leader). Despite significant improvements, however, women remain severely underrepresented in virtually all parts of the world. Several social, economic, and cultural factors help account for this. Pippa Norris and Joni Lovenduski have argued that the number of women in elected office depends on various factors affecting "supply and demand."[59]

Supply refers to the number of women who meet the typical socioeconomic levels of public officeholders in their country. Because Third World women generally have lower levels of education, lower status, and, most important, fewer economic resources—all factors closely related to political success—they are able to "supply" fewer viable candidates for office. Indeed, Rae Lesser Blumberg's research in several regions of the world indicates that "the most important variable . . . affecting the level of [political] equality [or inequality] between men and women is economic power" as defined by their relative control over income and economic resources.[60] On the "demand" side (a measure of society's interest in having female political representation), cultural prejudices about women, most blatant in the Islamic states of the Middle East, further reduce female political representation.

In the past two decades, as women's educational levels have risen in most of the developing world, as they have entered the professions in greater numbers, and as cultural prejudices have diminished somewhat in many developing countries, both the supply of and demand for potential women officeholders have increased. However, the most important change in recent years has been on the demand side—the introduction of gender-based reserved seats and quotas for parliament itself or for the lists of candidates presented by competing political parties. Since 1991, gender-quota laws relevant to parliament have been passed in at least 20 countries, 14 of them LDCs. Interestingly, Latin America, a region commonly known for its *machismo*, has predominated, with 12 nations having adopted gender quotas since Argentina led the way in 1991 (soon to be followed by Bolivia, Brazil, Costa Rica, the Dominican Republic, Ecuador, Guyana, Mexico, Panama, Paraguay, Peru, and Venezuela).[61] Across the region, the percentage of female representatives jumped from 9.36 in 1997 to 20.00 in 2007.

Legislated and voluntary attempts to raise the proportion of women in national parliaments have taken several forms. The most direct and intrusive method is to *reserve* a designated number of parliamentary seats for women. In Bangladesh, for example, the 1972 constitution set aside 15 seats in parliament exclusively for women (though women could also run for regular seats). That was later raised to 30 seats before the quota amendment lapsed in 2001 and the number of women MPs (elected through normal channels) plunged to six (just 2 percent of all seats) in the following election. A 2004 constitutional amendment reinstated reserved seats and raised the number to 45 (13 percent of all MPs). However, women filling these "reserved seats" were not directly elected by the voters but, rather, were chosen by the regularly elected (almost exclusively male) MPs. Bangladeshi political parties divided these reserved seats in direct proportion to the percentage of seats each party had won in the most recently concluded national election.[62] Similarly, Morocco has reserved 10 percent of its parliamentary seats for women, while Tanzania has reserved 20 percent. Several other African nations, including Botswana, Rwanda, Eritrea, Sudan, Tanzania, Zimbabwe, Lesotho, Burkina Faso, and Uganda, also have reserved women's seats as have Jordan, Pakistan, and Taiwan. Moreover, while Rwanda reserves 30 percent of its parliamentary seats for women, female candidates in the last national election won an additional 19 percent of the seats by defeating male opponents in contests for non-reserved seats. As of early 2007, only 10 countries (all of them LDCs) had reserved seats for women in the lower house, including Afghanistan and Iraq, which included these set-asides in their recently issued constitutions under pressure from the United States.

Reserving seats for women is the most direct and certain means of guaranteeing greater female representation in parliament or (in cases such as India and Tanzania) in local government councils. Many democratic reformers, however, object to the practice because it creates a legal entitlement for women that men do not enjoy and because the women filling these seats frequently are not directly elected by the voters (as we have seen in Bangladesh).[63] Interestingly, many women's advocacy groups also oppose the practice. For one thing, the number of reserved seats usually is rather low (only 6 of 110 parliamentary seats in Jordan, for example). Also, while women are allowed to run in the regular parliamentary elections as well, the process of reserving seats creates its own glass ceiling if political leaders or voters feel that such set-asides have already given women their "fair share." Political parties then feel no obligation to be inclusive when choosing their regular slate of parliamentary candidates. Furthermore, opponents argue, because the women holding reserved seats in 7 of the 12 countries with such set-asides are not directly elected by the voters, but, rather, are picked by predominantly male political leaders, they are beholden to the male power structure and unlikely to challenge it. Finally, female MPs holding reserved seats lack the legitimacy that an open election confers on their fellow parliamentarians. In short, the system generally smacks of tokenism and is frequently, though not exclusively, introduced in countries such as Morocco and Jordan where women's political power is very limited, where the number of reserved seats is rather small, and where few, if any, women win regularly contested parliamentary races.[64] On the other hand, if a significant amount of seats are reserved for women, the effect can be dramatic. In Eritrea, 30 percent of the seats in both the national and the regional legislatures are reserved for women.

Another means of reducing gender underrepresentation is the creation of quotas for the slates of parliamentary *candidates* in general elections. Quotas may take two forms. First, individual political parties may voluntarily guarantee that their slate of parliamentary candidates will contain a certain percentage of women. In Europe, for example, the first major gains for female parliamentary representation came in Scandinavia when that region's socialist parties (often the largest party in those countries) agreed to gender quotas. In the Third World, the most successful example of voluntary quotas has been in South Africa's dominant party, the African National Congress (ANC).

The second type of candidate quota is legislated and is either mandatory or penalizes noncomplying parties by imposing fines or withholding government campaign funds. As we have seen, a dozen Latin American countries, and a few other LDCs, passed some form of a gender quota during the wave of democratic transitions in the 1990s. Typically, quotas of either type commit parties to nominate women in 30 percent of the parliamentary races, which is the proportion that seems to be the threshold for producing government policies that are friendlier to women's interests.

The goal of quotas is purportedly to give women a greater opportunity to hold regularly elected seats rather than fill seats specially reserved for them. But candidate quotas, particularly when legislatively imposed, are frequently ineffective because their objective is easily circumvented if women are largely nominated in electoral contests that they are unlikely to win. In electoral systems that choose a single legislative representative from each district (Single-Member Districts or SMD as in the United States), gender quotas are often undermined when political parties primarily nominate women in districts that those parties have little chance or expectation of winning. Similarly, in countries that elect their parliament through proportional representation—that is, parties present voters with a choice between competing lists of candidates—women are often placed at the bottom of the party's list where they are unlikely to be elected.

Outside the English-speaking world, most electoral democracies use some form of proportional representation (PR) to elect their parliament. To understand how PR works, let us imagine a country with a 500-seat parliament divided into 25 electoral districts (assuming here that they have roughly equivalent populations), each of which elects 20 MPs. The national parties each nominate a "party list" of 20 candidates in each district, with candidates usually ranked from 1 through 20. Rather than vote for a single candidate, as Americans do when they vote for the House of Representatives, voters in PR elections vote for an entire party list. Seats are then allocated in proportion to the percentage of votes that each list receives. Thus if the Party X's list, for example, were to receive 40 percent of the votes in district 1, they would win 40 percent of the seats in that district (i.e., eight seats). But which eight of the party's 20 listed candidates would go to parliament? It would be those who were ranked first through eight on the party's list prior to the election. If we further imagine that a quota law requires that at least 35 percent of each party's candidates be women (i.e., at least seven in each district), the number of women who actually are elected would still depend on where they had been ranked on the party list. Because the record shows that in most countries women tend to be placed lower down on the candidate lists, even with the high quota requirement, all eight of that party's victorious candidates could be men if all of the female candidates had been ranked in the bottom half of the list.

To put teeth into a legislated quota system and prevent dumping of women candidates into hopeless positions at the bottom of the party lists or in single-member districts that the party knows it cannot win, countries such as Argentina passed electoral laws requiring so-called zipper-style quotas. That means each party must not only meet its quota of female candidates, but it must also alternate male and female candidates, according to that quota percentage from the top of the list downward. In other words, if a country has a zipper-style quota of 33 percent, women candidates would have to occupy every third position on the list from the top rank on down.

In general, since 1991 the spread of legally mandated quotas, of whatever type, has contributed substantially to the increase in female MPs worldwide. In 10 Latin American countries that enacted quotas from 1991 to 1997, the number of women in parliament rose by an average of 8 percent in the very next national election.[65] However, results have been most impressive when electoral laws mandates zipper-style quotas or their equivalent. For example, in the first election after Ecuador passed its 1997 zipper-style quota law, female representation in parliament jumped from 4 to 15 percent. Similarly, when Costa Rica's Supreme Court strengthened that country's quota law by insisting that women be proportionally included in competitive races, the percentage of women in the national Legislative Assembly rose from 19 percent in 1997 (already higher than in the U.S. Congress at that time) to 35 percent in 2002. Also, when the ANC took power and voluntarily adopted a gender quota, the percentage of women MPs in South Africa rose from only 141st highest in the world in 1994 to 11th highest in 2004. On the other hand, even though Venezuela's electoral law established a women's quota of 30 percent on each party's candidate list, the absence of regulations governing rankings helps explain why women won less than 10 percent of the seats in the 2000 recent parliamentary election and only 19 percent in 2005 (a very respectable number, but well below the target of 30 percent).

Ultimately, the issue of reserved seats and candidate quotas raises another fundamental question. How much difference does increased female representation have on government policy? Women's rights advocates argue that legislatures with significantly higher female membership are more prone to address issues such as gender bias in the economy, child care, education, and equitable divorce law and are more likely to produce legislation in these areas that are beneficial to women. In fact, most analysts agree that even a substantial increase in female representation at very low levels—for example, the tripling of female representation in Arab parliaments over a 10-year period (1997–2007)—is still unlikely to affect government policy because, in this case, women still hold under 10 percent of parliamentary seats. Instead, as I have indicated, the evidence suggests that women usually need to achieve a critical mass of 30 percent of the seats in the national legislature in order to influence policy. If representation falls substantially below that figure, women MPs tend to be co-opted or are simply ineffective in pressing "women's issues." As representation reaches that threshold, however, parliaments are more likely to pass "women-friendly" legislation. It is for this reason that the Inter-Parliamentary Union endorses 30-percent quotas and why most quota legislation sets that mark. It is important to keep in mind, however, that while female legislators tend to be of one mind on issues such as domestic violence, they may be very split, particularly in Latin America, on other issues such as abortion.

In spite of recent gains, as of mid-2007 there were still only 18 countries in the world that have reached that 30 percent target (though 6–10 other countries came close). Of those, half are LDCs. Rwanda is the only country in the world with full gender parity.[66] The other eight LDCs achieving 30 percent target are Costa Rica (39 percent), Cuba (36 percent), Argentina (35 percent), Mozambique (35 percent), South Africa (33 percent), Burundi (31 percent), Tanzania (30 percent), and Uganda (30 percent).[67]

Elections through proportional representation with closed lists (i.e., each political party ranks the candidates on its list and voters have no direct role in deciding that ranking) benefit women candidates significantly more than single-member districts do. Effective gender quotas are very difficult legislate in a SMD system unless there are a large number of seats reserved for women. Worldwide, 13 of the 14 countries with competitive elections and 30-percent female representation or more use PR exclusively and the other (Germany) uses a combination of both systems. Of the six LDCs in that group, Costa Rica and Argentina have legally mandated (zipper-style) quotas for all party candidate lists; Mozambique and South Africa have voluntary, party quotas; Rwanda has both legal quotas and reserved seats; and Cuba has neither, but there is only one legal party (the Communist Party) so the government and the ruling party determine its nominees. Finally, of the five countries using quotas, all use zipper-style quotas or something similar (Costa Rica). As we have noted, without a zipper-style requirement, party leaders typically undermine quota systems by relegating women to the bottom of candidate lists.

While the percentage of women in parliament is a useful measure of their influence in national politics, their share of cabinet posts is perhaps more significant. Cabinet ministers normally operate at the center of political power and are among the nation's most influential political figures.[68] Although women have held a relatively small percentage of ministerial posts in most countries (even lower than their share of parliamentary seats), their numbers have grown significantly over the past two decades. Between 1987 and 2004, the proportion of women ministers worldwide more than tripled, from a mere 3.4 to 11.3 percent.[69] That figure has continued to grow since that time. In general, European cabinets have greater female representation than their Third World counterparts, with three governments (Sweden, Spain, and France) currently fielding cabinets with equal numbers of women and men, as a matter of government gender policy (but not legally required). However, from 2000 to 2006, the proportion of women ministers in Latin America grew from 14 to 21 percent, giving that region a level of female representation comparable to Western Europe and the United States. In fact, as of early 2007, women held 50 percent of the cabinet posts in Chile (appointed by a female president) and about 40 percent in Paraguay and Peru (a level also reached briefly in Colombia).[70] Indeed, the percentage of women cabinet members in Latin America slightly exceeds that region's percentage of female MPs. Women are less well represented in Asian cabinets. For example, in Thailand, Pakistan, and Indonesia, they typically have held fewer than 5 percent of ministerial posts. Arab nations trail far behind any other region, just as they trailed on women MPs, GEM scores, and female literacy rates.

Until recently, the types of cabinet posts occupied by women conformed to gender stereotypes. In a 1999 study of 190 countries throughout the world, the Inter-Parliamentary Union found that women were Ministers of Women's Affairs in 25 percent of the countries. They frequently headed the Ministers of Social Affairs (23 percent), Health (16 percent), Environment (15 percent), Family Affairs (14 percent), Labor (13 percent), Education, and Justice (both 12 percent)—mostly "nurturing positions." However, women held the following ministerial positions in fewer than 5 percent of the countries: Defense, Health, Agriculture, and Science and Technology.[71] Undoubtedly, such gendering of cabinet posts has diminished somewhat since that time.

Earlier in this chapter, we noted the growing number of women prime ministers and presidents in the LDCs, most notably in South Asia. While we might assume that gains for women at the pinnacle of government would either reflect or cause broader political gains in female political representation—as it has, for example, in the Nordic countries—this has not necessarily been true in less-developed countries. Sri Lanka and Bangladesh show the most glaring inconsistencies. Women have served for extended periods as either president or prime minister of Sri Lanka, while Bangladesh saw two women alternate as prime minister from 1991 to 2006. Yet Sri Lanka's parliament currently has only 4.4 percent female representation, less than one-third the international average and, until reserved seats were reintroduced in 2004,

Bangladesh had one of the world's lowest rates of female MPs (2 percent). With those 45 new reserved seats the number of women MPs rose from 7 to 52 (15 percent). Similarly, in India, having a woman dominate the political system for many years failed to generate more opportunities for women at the parliamentary level (Indian women currently have about half the international average). In fact, during her long tenure in office, Indira Gandhi proposed little to advance women's political representation. It was only after her assassination and the transfer of power to her son, Rajiv, that the parliament passed a 30 percent quota for women in local government. Female representation in parliament (where there is no gender quota) is currently a rather low 8 percent.

Although electoral mechanisms such as quotas and reserved seats are the most important factors associated with greater female representation in parliament, social, cultural, and historical forces may also play a role. Indeed, these elements often explain why a particular country adopts quotas or reserved seats in the first place. For example, in Scandinavia, the culture's strong emphasis on gender (and class) equality produced a very high number of female MPs even before many major parties adopted voluntary quotas. And it was that same societal commitment to gender equality that led Norwegian and Swedish political parties to commit to such quotas. Denmark's parties abandoned gender quotas in 1996 (after enforcing them for nearly two decades), yet, even without the benefit of quotas, women continue to hold 37 percent of parliamentary seats, one of the world's highest percentages.

In Africa, many of the nations with parliamentary gender quotas are "post-conflict" states. That is to say, they are countries such as Mozambique, Namibia, and Rwanda, which had endured bloody civil wars, or South Africa, which had experienced a long and difficult struggle for majority rule. All of them also have some of the world's highest representations of women MPs, ranging from 27 percent (Namibia) to 49 percent (Rwanda). While past conflicts produced enormous suffering and death, they also provided "new opportunities to articulate debate about gender politics as well as for individual women to live in a different way."[72] In countries such as South Africa, women played an important role in the liberation struggle, providing them and the organizations that represent them (such as the women's branch of South Africa's ANC) greater access to the centers of political power. In countries such as Mozambique and Uganda, where so many men fought and died in civil wars, women had to assume greater responsibilities at home and in their local villages or neighborhoods.

Women and Revolutionary Change

The political, economic, and social changes brought about by Third World revolutions often present women with rather unique opportunities that merit special attention. For one thing, revolutions tend to alter or destroy many of the traditional social structures and values that had previously oppressed women. When the communists came to power in China, for example, they eliminated the last vestiges of foot binding for young women and prohibited the sale of women and girls as wives, concubines, or prostitutes.[73] At the same time, many revolutionary armies and parties have created new social structures that are more open to women and offer greater opportunities for upward mobility. For example, women held important military command positions in both the

Nicaraguan Sandinista army and the Salvadorian FMLN during their guerrilla struggles. In South Africa and Namibia, many women now serving in parliament initially developed their political skills in their country's national liberation movement (respectively the ANC and SWAPO).

Indeed, because of their need for military recruits and their willingness to violate traditional gender roles, many guerrilla armies have included significant numbers of women. For example, in the Eritrean People's Liberation Front (ELF), which engaged in a successful 30-year struggle for independence from Ethiopia, women constituted some 30 percent of the army and 11 percent of the delegates to the first ELF Congress.[74] Similarly, women made up an estimated 20–30 percent of the Sandinista forces in Nicaragua, perhaps 25 percent of Uruguay's Tupamaros, and a significant proportion of the FMLN guerrillas in El Salvador.[75] Because these guerrilla armies usually played a central political role after the revolutionary party took power as well, their substantial gender equality transferred to other political institutions and to the broader society.

After the communist victory in China, Party Chairman Mao Zedong and the All-China Women's Federation assigned women an important role in rebuilding the nation's economy.[76] Consequently, many women who had long been confined to their homes entered the work force, not because of any feminist agenda but because the government needed to reconstruct an economy devastated by three decades of war. But while these opportunities to work outside the home obviously benefited women, they failed to attain the occupational equality promised by the government. In both collective farms and industry, women continued to hold the less-skilled, lower-paying jobs.

Radical regimes in such countries as China, Vietnam, and Cuba try to transform traditional cultural values through education and propaganda. Combating long-standing prejudices against women is a part of that process. But even revolutionary societies find it difficult to eradicate long-standing sexist attitudes. Although China's 1950 Marriage Law decreed that women could wed only of their own free will and also granted women equal rights within the family, enforcement of those provisions has often been spotty, especially in rural areas. Furthermore, during the Maoist era (1949–1976) the government's commitment to these new values varied considerably, as the country swung back and forth between periods of ideological fervor and pragmatism. During radical phases, such as the Great Leap Forward and the Cultural Revolution, state policy supported female liberation and lambasted traditional male prejudices. In between these turbulent periods of mass mobilization, however, when party leaders wished to restore stability, the government reverted to more traditional values, extolling the importance of motherhood and family.

Since Mao's death (1976), the government's more pragmatic policies have stressed economic growth more than gender or social class equality. As many state-owned factories phase out guaranteed lifetime employment (the "iron rice bowl") in their quest for higher efficiency, women are likely to be the first workers fired. It is in the Chinese countryside, however, that one finds the most blatant remnants of sexist values as villagers respond to stringent state policies aimed at controlling population growth in this nation of 1.4 billion people. Since the late 1970s, the government has pressured or even forced Chinese urban families to have no more than one child and rural families to have no more than two, denying them many government benefits if they exceed that number, and rewarding them if they satisfy the policy. Statistics on births indicate that the single-child policy has succeeded well in lowering China's birth rate, especially in the cities, but has also had a terrible unintended consequence. In 2007 the Chinese government announced that there were 119 registered boy births for every 100 registered girls.[77] As the normal gender ratio worldwide is about 106 male births to 100 female, China's huge gender gap (by far the largest in the world), raises the question of what happened to "the missing girls." Particularly in rural regions, where daughters are less valued than sons, many new-born girls are either not officially registered or are abandoned to orphanages. Many others, however, have fallen victim to infanticide, the murder of female babies by parents who want their only child to be a boy.[78] Similarly, girls represent a disproportionate share of the abandoned children in rural orphanages. Indeed, because of the enormous overrepresentation of girls in the nation's orphanages, more than 95 percent of Chinese children put up for foreign adoption are female.

Cuba's revolutionary government has also tried to improve the status of women and change traditionally sexist cultural values. In 1960 the Federation of Cuban Women (FMC) was created to mobilize women in support of the revolution and to give them a voice in the political process. Because Vilma Espín, the federation's leader from 1960 until her death in 2007, was married to Fidel Casto's brother, Raúl (currently Cuba's acting leader) and served for decades as an unofficial "first lady" to divorced President Fidel Castro, the FMC had a direct line to the center of state power. Espín also had a distinguished career as a guerrilla officer in Cuba's revolutionary conflict. Officially representing 70 percent of Cuban women, the FMC encouraged its members to support the government and to enter the Cuban work force. Thus, during the first decade of the revolutionary government, the proportion of women in the work force rose from 17.8 to 30.9 percent, with even more impressive gains in the professions.[79] In the political arena, women have been particularly active in the neighborhood-based Committees for the Defense of the Revolution (CDRs). These Committees (to which some 80 percent of Cuban adults belong) promote revolutionary values, including gender equality. At their meetings, men who refuse to let their wives work or who do not put in their share of the housework sometimes find themselves criticized for machismo (perhaps by their own wives) and chastised by their peers for such nonrevolutionary values. By the early 1980s, women represented half the local CDR leaders, 46 percent of the leaders of labor union locals, and 22 percent of the delegates to the National Assembly, the nation's congress.[80] Female representation in congress has since risen to 36 percent, one of the highest rates in the world.

But revolutions are no panacea for women's problems. Often radical rhetoric exceeds actual accomplishments. Like China, Cuba demonstrates that even egalitarian revolutions fail to achieve full gender equality. Thus, despite their prominence in local CDRs, labor unions, and the National Assembly, Cuban women have rarely penetrated the top ranks of national political leadership, such as the State Council (the equivalent of the president's cabinet) or the Communist Party's Central Committee and Politburo. Because the National Assembly routinely passes all policy proposals from the Communist Party, it is in the party's leadership that real power lies. An analysis in the early 1980s showed that only 8.9 percent of Central Committee members were female.[81] Cuba's Family Code (the law governing family relations), passed decades ago, requires spouses to contribute equally to domestic chores (child care, cooking, cleaning, etc.). While almost all Cuban men claim to subscribe to its regulations, most of them fail to contribute their fair share of housework. Change has been limited by ingrained male attitudes (*machismo*) and by most women's understandable reluctance to complain to their neighbors in the local CDR about their husband's noncompliance with the Code. As one observer noted, "It must take an extremely confident woman to bring her husband to public censure for failure to honor the code."[82] As in other revolutionary societies, traditional cultural values concerning gender roles have been hard to change.

THE STATUS OF WOMEN: THE ROLES OF MODERNIZATION, GLOBALIZATION, AND REGIME TYPE

Our analysis has revealed that the political and economic status of Third World women is far from uniform. Their situation varies considerably from world region to region and country to country. Furthermore, even within particular countries, women's standings differ considerably, depending on their social class and ethnicity. Three factors are particularly influential: the country's dominant cultural values, the level of socioeconomic modernization, and the type of political regime in place.

Culture, including religious values, sets baseline boundaries for women and affects the opportunities available to them. This is most obvious in fundamentalist Islamist countries such as Afghanistan (even after the Taliban), Iran, Sudan, and Saudi Arabia. The Taliban government prohibited women from working outside the household and virtually confined them to their homes. These restrictions imposed particular hardships on widows, who were unable to support their families even by begging. At the same time, these measures also deprived one of the world's poorest nations of badly needed teachers and health care workers. While educational and professional opportunities exist for the female elite in Saudi Arabia, most Saudi women are marginalized from the mainstream of political, social, and economic life. And, even women professionals in Saudi Arabia are barred from activities such as driving a car. Political leadership in all these fundamentalist countries is an exclusively male preserve. Cultural restraints are more subtle in East Asia, but even in modern societies such as Singapore and South Korea women are underrepresented at universities, in the business world, and in politics.

Yet, despite these religious and cultural restrictions, women have made some notable gains, sometimes in surprising places. In Algeria, where a 1992 military coup had headed off an expected Islamist victory in the nation's parliamentary elections, the resulting civil war between fundamentalist militias and the armed forces (1992–2002) caused an estimated 100,000–150,000 deaths. Many more Algerians (particularly men) emigrated to Europe, leaving the country with serious labor shortages. Stimulated more by necessity and opportunity than by any government plan, women filled many of the gaps. Today, women make up 70 percent of Algeria's lawyers, 60 percent of university students, and most of the country's doctors. In all, they still represent only 20 percent of the nation's work force, but that is twice as high as the rate 20–25 years ago.[83]

Contrary to modernization theory, and true to radical feminist analysis, socioeconomic modernization has often adversely affected women in the LDCs in the short-to-medium term. In Africa, for example, the commercialization and mechanization of agriculture have benefited male cultivators disproportionately, often at the expense of women farmers. In East and Southeast Asia, rapid industrialization based on cheap labor has produced higher wages for some female laborers, but exploitation of others.[84] Yet, while modernization may initially impact poor women negatively, longer-term effects are generally beneficial. A growing middle class, wider educational opportunities, and higher rates of literacy make women more aware of their rights and opportunities, while increasing their capacity to defend these gains. Socioeconomic development also tends to create more egalitarian values within society. It is not coincidental that the more modernized nations of Latin America—including Argentina, Chile, Mexico, and Uruguay—have the largest number of female political leaders and professionals, just as the most economically advanced nations of Europe generally have the greatest opportunities for women.

Like many other political movements, the feminist movement has extended into the Third World through the mass media and the demonstration effect. In many developing nations, women's rights movements have emerged where none had existed, or were even conceivable, a decade or two before. Educated women in more traditional societies such as Bolivia and Jordan are often influenced by the women's movements in more progressive, neighboring societies such as Chile and Lebanon. However, these new movements generally have taken on a distinct character, distinguishing them from Western feminism. The women's movement was born in the Western world only four decades ago, and one can only speculate about its possible influence in the developing world three decades from now.

Finally, the status of women is shaped by the type of political regime and economic system prevailing in a country at a particular time. Women tend to fare more poorly under right-wing, authoritarian military regimes, such as those that dominated much of South America in the 1970s and early 1980s, and benefit more from revolutionary or democratic leftist regimes. Thus, for example, in countries such as Chile (like Sweden, Spain, and Norway), socialist and social democratic political parties have taken the lead in promoting increased female political representation. At the same time, however, while women suffered under the military dictatorships in South America, they also gained considerable political experience in social movements that defended human rights and petitioned for improved social services. Many radical regimes that are ideologically committed to equality have championed women's rights. However, while revolutionary change in countries such as China, Vietnam, Cuba, and Nicaragua benefited women in many ways, significant gender inequalities have persisted. Sometimes, that inequality simply reflects the resiliency of deeply entrenched cultural values or continued male dominance of the political system. Often it is also linked to the common Marxist belief that all societal inequalities—whether related to gender, race, or religion—are derived from class divisions. That article of faith has caused regimes such as Cuba's to underestimate gender-related problems by erroneously assuming that the destruction of capitalism had, by itself, undermined gender discrimination.

Given that full gender equality does not exist even in the most advanced industrialized democracies (only small, mostly Nordic, northern European democracies come close), it seems unlikely that socioeconomic modernization or the spread of democratic norms will automatically bring gender equality to the developing world. Future economic development can be expected to produce both negative and positive consequences. In the short run, economic modernization, particularly in agriculture, will likely harm many low-income women. In countries suffering severe economic difficulties, such as debt crises, or those experiencing civil conflict, women will doubtless continue to bear a disproportionate share of the burden. And the spread of Islamic fundamentalism in many parts of the Middle East and Africa does not bode well for women's rights in those nations. In the long term, however, economic modernization, higher educational levels, and modern values seem to offer Third World women their best hope.

CONCLUSION: DEMOCRACY AND THE ROLE OF WOMEN IN SOCIETY

Because democratic ideology endorses equal opportunity and equal rights for *all* citizens, we might expect the Third Wave of democracy during the final decades of the twentieth century to have advanced gender equity. Yet our discussion of revolutionary societies revealed that nondemocratic governments have sometimes promoted women's rights more successfully than their democratic counterparts. Many revolutionary regimes have established quotas for female participation in the national legislature, improved the legal status of women, banned oppressive traditional customs (the binding of Chinese women's feet, for example), and, to some degree, infused respect for women's rights into the new political culture. Thus, a good case can certainly be made, for example, that the revolutionary governments in China, Cuba, and Mozambique have advanced the cause of gender equality more effectively than the democratic governments of Brazil or India. It is also true that the Eastern European transition from communism to democracy brought a precipitous drop in the percentage of women elected to parliament.[85]

But most authoritarian governments are neither radical nor committed to women's rights. Women's issues have fared poorly in fundamentalist and most conservative authoritarian regimes. As we have noted, Afghanistan's Islamist government kept women veiled and confined.[86] In countries such as Chile, Nigeria, and Pakistan, repressive military dictatorships did little to improve women's status.

How was the wave of democratization that swept through the developing world in the closing decades of the twentieth century influenced by women and how did the emergence of democracy affect women's economic and political standing? In a number of Asian and Latin American nations, women's social movements helped topple repressive regimes. For example, mass demonstrations by Indonesian women's groups in 1998 contributed to the fall of the Suharto dictatorship. As we have seen, women played an important role in the struggle for democracy in several Latin American countries. Often they were able to demonstrate for change in the streets when men could not. Yet, the return of male-dominated political parties and interests groups to political center stage during the subsequent democratic transitions often marginalized grass-roots groups and NGOs in which women had played a major role. Thus, as Marta Htun has observed, the restoration of democracy had contradictory effects on women's political participation:

> The return to civilian rule and the consolidation of democratic governance created many more opportunities for women to be politically active, but also reduced the comparative advantage of gender-specific organizations as conduits for social demands. As a result, many women who had entered politics during the struggle against authoritarian rule left gender-specific organizations for political parties and other "traditional" organizations like labor unions.[87]

Bang-Soon L. Yoon has examined the effects of democratization on gender politics in South Korea. There, too, women had played an important role in the mass protests against the military government, working particularly through their labor unions. The transition to democracy in the late 1980s failed to raise the comparatively small percentage of women in the National Assembly, judiciary, and bureaucracy.[88] But, on the other hand, spurred to action by emerging women's groups, the South Korean National Assembly became more attentive to legislation affecting women, including two Equal Employment Acts (1989 and 1995), the Child Care Act (1990), and the Law on Prevention of Family Violence and Protection of Victims (1997).

However, while the transition to democracy may not lead to immediate gains for women, and while there may even be some initial setbacks, in time democratic governments tend to better advance women's rights and opportunities, particularly when democracy is coupled with social and economic development. We have noted that some authoritarian regimes have made gender equality an important component of their domestic policies (Cuba), while others have enforced a system of inequality (Saudi Arabia). Similarly, some Third World democracies have a strong record regarding women's rights and equity (Argentina), while others have done poorly (Brazil). In order to systematically compare democratic and nondemocratic developing countries, we will examine how each group performs on important indicators of women's empowerment and women's living standards. The first indicator is the Gender Empowerment Measure (GEM). As discussed earlier in this chapter, this is a measure of female economic and political empowerment. Specifically, it measures "the extent of women's political participation and decision making, economic participation and decision-making power, and the power exerted by women over economic resources."[89]

The second indicator is the Gender-Related Development Index (GDI). In Chapter 1 we learned that the Human Development Index is a composite measure of a nation's school enrollment, literacy, life expectancy, and per-capita income. The GDI breaks down the national HDI into separate indices for the male and female populations and then compares the two. This provides an excellent measure of the gender gap for education, income, and health. A GDI score of 1.000 would mean that the country's men and women are totally equal in these areas. The lower the GDI, the greater the extent of gender inequality. Among all of the countries in the world for which data are available, we find that Norway has the world's highest score for both GEM (.932) and GDI (.962). At the other end of the spectrum, Yemen has the lowest GEM (.128) and Niger the lowest GDI (.292).

Earlier we noted data on GEMs are available for fewer than half the countries in the UNDP database. The GDI data were much more complete—136 nations—but still left out more than 20 percent of the countries. Most of the omitted countries are in the Third World, particularly the poorest developing nations. That said, the data available clearly indicate that gender equality is greatest in the most advanced industrial democracies. For example, the 17 countries with the highest GEM scores (Norway through Ireland) are all economically advanced Western democracies, while the 21 lowest GEM scores were all from the Third World (17) or the former Soviet Bloc (4). That pattern is even stronger in the GDI scores. The problem is that these gaps likely reflected the effects of two different factors: first, more socioeconomically advanced countries are more likely than poor countries to have greater gender equality; second, social and economic conditions aside, democracies seem to achieve greater gender equality. When simply comparing rankings for the two indices, it is impossible to know how much of the gap in GEM and GDI scores was due to income and education differences and how much was determined by the country's level of democracy.

In order to reduce the effect of socioeconomic development on the two gender-related indices, Table 5.4 examines only Third World countries. All of the nations in the table were ranked, using the Freedom House evaluations, as either Free (Liberal Democracies), Partly Free, or Not Free. Then, they were divided into two groups based on their GEM scores (High or Low) and two corresponding groups based on their GDI scores. Are liberal democracies more likely to have high GEM and GDI scores than partial democracies or non-democracies are?

1. Overall, 19 LDCs had GEM indices higher than .500—ranging from Botswana (.501) up to Singapore (.707)—and were classified as *High GEM* nations. Of this group, 63 percent were Liberal Democracies, 37 percent were Partly Free, and not a single one was Not Free. (See Table 5.4.)
2. A total of 16 countries had *Low GEM* scores—ranging from Malaysia (.500) down to Yemen (.128). Of that group, only 19 percent were liberal democracies, 37 percent were Partly Free, and 44 percent were Not Free.

Looking at the data in terms of regime types (i.e., looking down the columns, rather than across the rows), 12 of 15 liberal democracies (80 percent) had high GEM scores, compared to only 7 of 13 Partly Free nations (54 percent). Of the seven countries that were Not Free, not a single one had a high GEM score.

TABLE 5.4   Gender Equality: Democratic and Nondemocratic LDCs Compared

Degree of Gender Equality	Liberal Democracies Percent (Number of Cases)	Partly Free Percent (Number)	Not Free Percent (Number)
High GEM Scores	63 (12)	37 (7)	0
Low Gem Scores	19 (3)	37 (6)	44 (7)
High GDI Scores	55 (11)	30 (6)	15 (3)
Low GDI Scores	15 (3)	55 (11)	30 (6)

Source: Data are extrapolated from UNDP, *Human Development Report 2006*, Statistics, http://hdr.undp.org/hdr2006/.

Turning to the other gender-based index, Table 5.4 examines the 20 Third World nations with the highest GDI scores and compares them to the 20 LDCs with the lowest scores.

1. Here again the correlation of index scores and level of democracy is quite striking. Among the *High GDI* nations, 55 percent were liberal democracies, 30 percent were Partly Free, and only 15 percent were Not Free.
2. Of the 20 *Low GDI* nations, only 15 percent were liberal democracies, 55 percent were Partly Free, and 30 percent were Not Free.

Again, reading the table down instead of across, 79 percent of the liberal democracies had High GDI scores, while only 35 percent of the Partly Free countries and 33 percent of those that were Not Free did as well.

These data strongly suggest, then, that more democratic LDCs are more likely to achieve greater gender equality than less democratic states are. The data in Table 5.4 are not definitive for two reasons. First, and most importantly, there were no GEM scores for the majority of the LDCs, while GDI scores were unavailable over one-fourth of the developing nations. Many of these were small island nations, but the group with missing data also included China, Cuba, India, Indonesia, Nigeria, Sudan, Vietnam, and other major countries. We do not know exactly how their GEM and GDI scores would have affected the correlations with democracy if the data were available. Second, we have not statistically controlled for variations between more socioeconomically developed Third World countries, such as South Korea and Singapore, and impoverished ones, such as Mali and Sierra Leone.[90] An eye-balling of the countries with no data as well as the socioeconomic levels of countries included in the table suggests that these possible objections do not undermine the relationship. For example, the group of countries with high GEM scores included several comparatively poorer LDCs such as Ecuador, El Salvador, and Peru, while the low GEM group included several comparatively affluent nations, such as the United Arab Emirates and Turkey. Thus it is unlikely that the correlation between democracy and gender equality is spurious or that it can be explained by socioeconomic factors.

There is reason to believe, then, that democratic government gives women greater social and economic opportunities because they are able to mobilize politically, lobby government officials, and otherwise voice their concerns through democratic channels. At the same time they are more likely to be heard by a free press and by politicians who want to be reelected.

DISCUSSION QUESTIONS

1. Explain how the focus of research on gender in the developing world has moved from the study of oppression to the study of empowerment. What does this change reflect?
2. Consulting with the UNDP website at http://www.undp.org enables you to compare a country's HDI score and its Gender Empowerment Measure (GEM)

score. What relationship does there seem to be between those two scores? Identify several countries that have wide discrepancies (in either direction) between their HDI and GEM scores and offer your best explanation for these wide differences.

3. Discuss the ways in which modernization has affected women of differing social status in distinct ways.

4. What is the most common characteristic of female heads of government in the Third World? To what extent has their assumption of power substantially improved the status of other women in their nations?

5. Discuss the different ways in which *quota systems* have been used to increase female representation in national legislatures and explain how quotas differ from a system of reserved seats.

6. Discuss how the percentage of women in a nation's parliament is affected by "supply and demand."

7. Compare the records of Third World democracies to those of authoritarian LDCs in term of how well each group has promoted gender equality in politics and in the workplace.

NOTES

1. The informal sector, which includes a large number of street vendors and small businesses, is the part of the economy that is "unregulated by the institutions of society [most notably the state], in a legal and social environment in which similar activities are regulated" and taxed. In other words, the informal sector encompasses otherwise legal activities (not criminal operations or prostitution) but operates outside the spheres of tax collection, government labor and safety regulations, and the like. In many developing countries, it represents 30–50 percent of the urban work force. See Manuel Castells and Alejandro Portes, "World Underneath: The Origins, Dynamics and Effects of the Informal Economy," in *The Informal Economy: Studies in Advanced and Developing Economies*, eds. Alejandro Portes, Manuel Castells, and Lauren A. Benton (Baltimore, MD: The Johns Hopkins University Press, 1989), 12. Of course, many men work in the informal sector, but women are disproportionately represented.

2. United Nations Development Programme data cited in Jennifer L. Troutner and Peter H. Smith, "Empowering Women: Agency, Structure, and Comparative Perspective," in *Promises of Empowerment: Women in Asia and Latin America*, eds. Peter H. Smith, Jennifer L. Troutner, and Christine Hünefeldt (Lanham, MD: Rowman & Littlefield Publishers, 2004), 26.

3. *New York Times*, July 6, 2002 and July 17, 2002. Indeed, the trial was probably held to intimidate and silence her young brother, who had been sodomized by members of the

wealthy family. The event was so extreme and so shocked Pakistani public opinion that the national government paid the victim compensation of $8,200 while bringing the perpetrators to trial. More generally, however, ordinary rape, including gang rape, is widespread in Pakistan, especially the province of Punjab where this incident took place, and is usually not reported to the authorities. A woman is raped every two hours in Pakistan (and gang raped on an average of once every four days in the state of Punjab), with only about a quarter of the cases being reported to the police.

4. *New York Times*, "Vendetta Rapes Continues as Pakistan Resists Change," (October 14, 2006 and November 16, 2006); Human Rights Watch, "Discrimination under the Hudood Law," http://www.hrw.org/about/projects/womre/General-90.htm.

5. *New York Times*, "Women's Rights Laws and African Custom Clash," (December 20, 2005).

6. *New York Times*, "Muslim Women Don't See Themselves as Oppressed, Survey Shows," (June 8, 2006).

7. Arturo Escobar and Sonia E. Alvarez, eds., *The Making of Social Movements in Latin America: Identity, Strategy and Democracy* (Boulder, CO: Westview Press, 1992); June Nash, "Women's Social Movements in Latin America," *Gender and Society* 4, no. 3 (September 1990), 338–353.

8. Women also were prohibited from working outside the home even if the family had no male breadwinner.

9. Inter-Parliamentary Union, *Women in National Parliaments* (March 31, 2007), www.ipu.org/. Four of the six Nordic nations (Sweden, Norway, Finland, and Denmark) had parliaments with over 37 percent female representation and ranked among the six most sexually equal countries in the world. Sweden topped the list with women constituting over 47 percent of all MPs, practically full gender equality. Iceland, the *lowest* ranking Nordic country, still ranked 10th in the world with 33 percent female representation.

10. Sonia E. Alvarez, *Engendering Democracy in Brazil: Women's Movements in Transition Politics* (Princeton, NJ: Princeton University Press, 1990), 4, fn. 2.

11. Paul Cammack, David Pool, and William Tordoff, *Third World Politics: A Comparative Introduction* (Baltimore, MD: The Johns Hopkins University Press, 1988), 184–193.

12. Leith Mullings, "Women and Economic Change in Africa," in *Women in Africa: Studies in Social and Economic Change*, eds. Nancy J. Hafkin and Edna G. Bray (Stanford, CA: Stanford University Press, 1976), 239–264.

13. Margo Lovett, "Gender Relations, Class Formation, and the Colonial State in Africa," in *Women and the State in Africa*, eds. Jane L. Parpart and Kathleen A. Staudt (Boulder, CO: Lynne Rienner Publishers, 1989), 37–39.

14. Ester Boserup, *Women's Role in Economic Development* (London: George Allen and Unwin, 1970), 54.

15. FAO, "Gender and Food Security: Agriculture," http://www.fao.org/Gender/en/agri-e.htm.

16. FAO, "The Feminization of Agriculture," http://www.fao.org/Gender/en/agrib2-e.htm. Only some LDCs have substantial migration from the countryside to foreign countries. These include Mexico, El Salvador, Guatemala, Algeria, Morocco, and Tunisia.

17. Nici Nelson, *Why Has Development Neglected Rural Women?* (Oxford, England: Pergamon Press, 1979), 4.

18. Ibid., 45–47.

19. Mandy Woodhouse, "Gender Mainstreaming . . ." (Siem Reap, Cambodia: Paper presented at a 2003 conference Gender and Poverty Reduction Strategies). For extended discussion of the WID versus GAD strategies, see Jane S. Jaquette and Gale Summerfield, eds., *Women and Gender Equity in Development Theory and Practice* (Durham, NC: Duke University Press, 2006), especially, 17–70.

20. FAO, "Gender and Food Security." Some microcredit institutions (banks or coops making small loans, as little as $5, to the poor with no need for collateral) have challenged that pattern by making credit more readily available to women. The most famous of these, the Grameen Bank (meaning "bank to the villages"), started in Bangladesh and has served as a model for similar microcredit groups in 43 other developing countries. In Bangladesh, 97 percent of its more than 7 million borrowers currently are women.

21. Gloria González Salazar, "Participation of Women in the Mexican Labor Force," in *Sex and Class in Latin America*, eds. June Nash and Helen I. Safa (New York: J. F. Bergin Publishers, 1980), 187.

22. See footnote 1 of this chapter for a detailed definition of this term.

23. Ruth Pearson, "Reassessing Paid Work and Women's Employment: Lessons from the Global Economy," in *Feminisms in Development*, ed. Andrea Cornwall, Elizabeth Harrison, and Ann Whitehead (London: Zed Books, 2007), 202–203.

24. Heleieth I. B. Saffioti, "Technological Change in Brazil: Its Effect on Men and Women in Two Firms," in *Women and Change in Latin America*, eds. June Nash and Helen I. Safa (South Hadley, MA: Bergin & Garvey Publishers, 1985), 110–111; Commack, Pool, and Tordoff, *Third World Politics*, 195–196.

25. *New York Times*, June 11, 1998.

26. Cited in Alan Gilbert and Josef Gugler, *Cities, Poverty and Development: Urbanization in the Third World*, 2nd ed. (New York: Oxford University Press, 1992), 104, fn. 29.

27. Johanna Son, "South-east Asia: Sex Industry Thrives, But States Look Away," *InterPress News Service* (IPS) (August 19, 1998), which draws on the recent ILO study. http://www.aegis.com/news/ips/1998/IP980803.html.

28. *Women and Human Rights*—U.S. Department of State report (released by the Bureau of Democracy, Human Rights and Labor, U.S. Department of State, February 2001).

29. Nici Nelson, "How Women and Men Get By: The Sexual Division of Labour in the Informal Sector of a Nairobi Squatter Settlement," in *The Urbanization of the Third World*, ed. Josef Gugler (New York: Oxford University Press, 1988), 183–203.

30. Shahnaz Kazi, "Some Measures of the Status of Women in the Course of Development in South Asia," in *Women in Development in South Asia*, ed. V. Kanesalingam (New Delhi, India: Macmillan India Limited, 1989), 19–52.

31. Sonia Nunes Jorge, "Gender-Aware Guidelines for Policy-Making and Regulatory

Agencies" (Geneva: ITU Telecommunication Development Bureau Task Force on Gender Issues, 2001), 1.

32. New Zealand was the first country to grant women voting rights, in 1893. Female suffrage was enacted at the United States federal level in 1920 at about the same time as in most West European democracies. On the other hand, women were not able to vote in Swiss national elections until 1971, or in the small European state of Liechtenstein until 1984.

33. On women's suffrage in Europe and the United States, see Vicky Randall, *Women and Politics: An International Perspective*, 2nd ed. (Chicago: University of Chicago Press, 1987), 5, 51, 209–211; on Latin America, see Jane Jaquette, "Female Political Participation in Latin America," in *Sex and Class in Latin America*, 223; also, Francesca Miller, *Latin American Women and the Search for Social Justice* (Hanover, NH: University Press of New England, 1991), 96–101.

34. World Bank, *Engendering Development*, 57.

35. See, for example, Ellen Gruenbaum, "Sudanese Women and the Islamist State," in *Women and Power in the Middle East*, eds. Suad Joseph and Susan Slyomovics (Philadelphia: University of Pennsylvania Press, 2001), 115–125. Other chapters in the volume paint a less pessimistic picture, such as the one on Palestinian women in the political system and workplace.

36. Rama Mehta, *The Western Educated Hindu Woman* (New York: Asia Publishing House, 1970), 16–32.

37. Judith Van Allen, "Memsahib, Militante, Femme Libre: Political and Apolitical Styles of Modern African Women," in *Women in Politics*, ed. Jane S. Jaquette (New York: John Wiley and Sons, 1974), 310.

38. Inter-Parliamentary Union, "Women in Parliament," www.ipu.org; see also, Gretchen Bauer and Hannah E. Britton, ed., *Women in African Parliaments* (Boulder: CO: Lynne Rienner Publishers, 2006).

39. Jaquette, "Female Political Participation," 223.

40. See Jo Ann Aviel, "Changing the Political Role of Women: A Costa Rican Case Study," in *Women in Politics*, 281–303.

41. See Amy Conger Lind, "Power, Gender and Development: Popular Women's Organizations and the Politics of Needs in Ecuador," in *The Making of Social Movements*, 134–149.

42. Jana Everett, "Incorporation versus Conflict: Lower Class Women, Collective Action, and the State in India," in *Women, the*

State and Development, eds. Sue Ellen M. Charlton, Jana Everett, and Kathleen Staudt (Albany: State University of New York Press, 1989), 163.

43. Armita Basu, *Two Faces of Protest: Contrasting Modes of Women's Activism* (Berkeley: University of California Press, 1992), 3.

44. Jane S. Jaquette, "Introduction" in *The Women's Movement in Latin America: Feminism and the Transition to Democracy*, ed. Jane S. Jaquette (Boston: Unwin Hyman, 1989), 6. This section draws heavily on Jaquette's book and Alvarez, *Engendering Democracy in Brazil*.

45. Sonia E. Alvarez, "Women's Movements and Gender Politics in the Brazilian Transition," in *The Women's Movement in Latin America*, 19–20; see also Alvarez, *Engendering Democracy in Brazil*.

46. Teresa Pires de Rio Caldeira, "Women, Daily Life and Politics," in *Women and Social Change in Latin America*, 47–79.

47. Elsa M. Chaney, *Supermadre: Women in Politics in Latin America* (Austin: University of Texas Press, 1979), 4.

48. Jane L. Parpart and Kathleen A. Staudt, "Women and the State in Africa," in *Women and the State in Africa*, 8.

49. Quoted in Chaney, *Supermadre*, 21.

50. Ibid., 141.

51. Suranjana Gupta, "Transforming Governance Agendas: Insights from Grass-roots Women's Initiatives in Local Government in Two Districts in India," in *Gender, Globalization, and Democratization*, eds. Rita Mae Kelly et al. (Lanham, MD: Rowan & Littlefield, 2001), 195–204.

52. "Sonia Gandhi turns down PM post," *BBC* (May 18, 2004), http://news.bbc.co.uk/2/hi/south_asia/3721863.stm; see also "Profile: Sonia Gandhi," *BBC* (May 18, 2004), http://news.bbc.co.uk/1/hi/world/south_asia/3546851.stm.

53. San Suu Kyi rightfully should have been included in the list of Asian prime ministers because she led her National League for Democracy party to an overwhelming victory in the 1990 national elections, but the results were annulled by the military and she has been under house arrest most of the time since 1989. Few observers doubt that she would be elected handily in any free election that would be held in Myanmar. For a constantly update list of women prime ministers worldwide, see "Women Prime Ministers," http://www.terra.es/personal2/monolith/00women3.htm.

54. The United States had a similar pattern until recently. Vicky Randall points out that between 1917 and 1976, 73 percent of female

senators, 50 percent of women congressional representatives (and almost all female governors) were the widows of men who had held those seats. See *Women and Politics*, 132.

55. To be sure, some of the previously mentioned women leaders, most notably Isabel Perón, were far less capable.

56. For current data on this subject, see Inter-Parliamentary Union's website, www.ipu.org and IDEA (the International Institute for Democracy and Electoral Assistance), *Global Database of Quotas for Women*, http://www.quotaproject.org. Unless otherwise cited, all the data presented here on female representation in parliament come from these two sources.

57. Unlike the United States, where both houses of Congress have roughly equal powers, in most national legislatures the upper house of parliament or congress has limited powers. For example, it is almost always the lower house that elects the prime minister. Nordic parliaments and a number elsewhere do not even have an upper house.

58. On the powers of the two houses of parliament, see endnote 57. "The Americas" refers to Canada, the United States, and more than 30 Latin American and Caribbean nations. Thus, its two First World nations have little effect on the regional average. Moreover, while Latin America and Caribbean legislatures had slightly lower female representation than Canada's 23.6 percent, they were actually substantially ahead of the U.S. Congress's 14.2 percent.

59. Pippa Norris and Joni Lovenduski, *Political Recruitment: Gender, Race and Class in the British Parliament* (Cambridge, England: Cambridge University Press, 1994).

60. Rae Lesser Blumberg, "Climbing the Pyramids of Power: Alternative Routes to Women's Empowerment and Activism," in *Promises of Empowerment*, 60.

61. Lisa Baldez, "Election Bodies: The Gender Quota Law for Legislative Candidates in Mexico," (Philadelphia, PA: Paper presented at the convention of the American Political Science Association, August 28–31, 2003), 32.

62. "BD women unlikely to gain more power," Internet Edition of *Dawn* (Pakistani English-language newspaper), June 11, 2004. See http://www.dawn.com/2004/06/11/int12.htm.

63. As of 2003, women were appointed by another body to reserved seats in 7 of 12 countries and were elected in only 5. Opponents have also challenged the system in a number of countries on the grounds that it violates the principle of "equal treatment" of the sexes.

Defenders, who have been supported by the courts in Mexico and elsewhere, argue that since men held most of the parliamentary seats under the previous system, they obviously have no need for equal protection.

64. For example, in Morocco's last parliamentary elections, women had 30 seats reserved, but managed to win only 5 more seats in the 295 regularly contested races. In Jordan's last election, 6 seats were reserved for women, but not a single additional woman was victorious in any of the nation's 104 regularly contested contests. Those six women were not popularly elected, but rather were appointed to their seats by the king.

65. Mala Htun, "Women and Democracy," in *Constructing Democratic Governance in Latin America*, eds. Jorge L. Domínguez and Michael Shifter (Baltimore, MD: The Johns Hopkins University Press, 2003), 122; Mala Htun and Mark P. Jones, "Engendering the Right to Participate in Decision-Making: Electoral Quotas and Women's Leadership in Latin America," in *Gender, and the Politics of Rights and Democracy in Latin America*, eds. Nikki Craske and Maxine Molyneux (New York: Palgrave, 2002), 241.

66. In the economically developed nations, only Sweden comes close to parity with 45 percent representation in its single-house parliament. The other developed countries that have reached the 30 percent mark are, in descending order of representation, Finland, Norway, Denmark, the Netherlands, Spain, Belgium, Iceland, Austria, New Zealand, and Germany.

67. Among South Africa's parties, only the African National Congress has a self-imposed quota. But since it holds almost three-quarters of all seats in parliament, the total percentage of women in parliament is relatively high. See Women's Environment & Development Organization (WEDO), "*Getting the Balance Right in National Parliaments*. See www.wedo.org or www.wedo.org/balance.htm.

68. In purely presidential systems such as in the United States, there is a separation of powers between the executive and legislative branches, excluding congressional participation in the cabinet. However, most of the world's nations have parliamentary systems (normally headed by a prime minister), which join the two branches of government so that cabinet members are either exclusively or significantly drawn from the parliament. In countries using the British "Westminster" model of government, appointment to the cabinet is the pinnacle of a parliamentary representative's political career.

69. 2004 Global Summit of Women Report: *Women in [sic!] Leaders Worldwide* (June, 2004), http://www.globewomen.com/summit/2004/GSW2004Report.htm.

70. Inter-American Bank Press Release (March 27, 2007).

71. Cited in Maria Escobar-Lemmon and Michelle M. Taylor-Robinson, "Women Ministers in Latin American Government: When, Where, and Why" (paper presented at the conference on Pathways to Power: Political Recruitment and Democracy in Latin America, Clemson University, 2004), 2.

72. Donna Pankhurst, "Women and Politics in Africa: The Case of Uganda," in *Women, Politics, and Change*, ed. Karen Ross (Oxford, England: Oxford University Press, 2002), 127.

73. Delia Davin, "Chinese Models of Development and Their Implications for Women," in *Women, Development, and Survival in the Third World*, ed. Haleh Afshar (New York: Longman, 1991), 32.

74. National Union of Eritrean Women, "Women and Revolution in Eritrea," in *Third World: Second Sex*, ed. Miranda Davis (London: Zed Press, 1983), 114.

75. *Envio* (Managua) 6, p. 78, quoted in Mary Stead, "Women, War and Underdevelopment in Nicaragua," *Women, Development and Survival*, 53; Randall, *Woman and Politics*, 61.

76. Bee-Lan Chan Wang, "Chinese Women: The Relative Influences of Ideological Revolution, Economic Growth and Cultural Change," in *Comparative Perspectives of Third World Women: The Impact of Race, Sex and Class*, ed. Beverly Lindsay (New York: Praeger, 1980), 99–104; see also Delia Davin, "Chinese Models of Development," in *Women, Development and Survival*.

77. *New York Times* (January 12, 2007).

78. John Pomfret, "In China's Countryside: It's a Boy! Too Often," *Washington Post* (May 29, 2001). An estimated 80 percent of female infanticide (also called gendercide) in the world occurs in China and India. In India the government does not limit the number of children a couple can have, but many families voluntarily limit themselves to one or two children in order to concentrate their economic resources on fewer children. Because India, like China, has a strong cultural preference for male children, many middle-class families choose to abort female fetuses. One recent study estimates that millions of female fetuses in India have been aborted in recent years.

79. Isabel Larguia and John Domoulin, "Women's Equality in the Cuban Revolution," in *Women and Change in Latin America*, 344, 363.

80. Ibid., 360. There is extensive literature on women in revolutionary Cuba, most of it written from a strongly pro-revolutionary perspective. See Margaret E. Leahy, *Development Strategies and the Status of Women* (Boulder, CO: Lynne Rienner Publishers, 1986), 91–116; Lois M. Smith and Alfred Padula, "The Cuban Family in the 1980s," in *Transformation and Struggle: Cuba Faces the 1990s*, eds. Sandor Halebsky and John M. Kirk (New York: Praeger, 1990), 176–188; and Max Azicri, "Women's Development through Revolutionary Mobilization," in *The Cuba Reader: The Making of a Revolutionary Society*, eds. Philip Brenner et al. (New York: Grove Press, 1989), 457–470. For a more critical viewpoint, see Julie Marie Bunck, "The Cuban Revolution and Women's Rights," in *Cuban Communism*, 7th ed., ed. Irving Louis Horowitz (New Brunswick, NJ: Transaction Publishers, 1989), 443–465.

81. Randall, *Women and Politics*, 103.

82. Johnetta Cole, "Women in Cuba," in *Comparative Perspectives of Third World Women*, 176.

83. *New York Times*, "A Quiet Revolution in Algeria: Gains by Women" (May 26, 2007).

84. Linda Y. C. Lim, "Capitalism, Imperialism and Patriarchy: The Dilemma of Third World Women in Multinational Factories," in *Women, Men and the International Division of Labor*, eds. June Nash and María Patricia Fernández-Kelly (Albany, NY: SUNY Press, 1983).

85. World Bank, *Engendering Development*, 58.

86. For personal accounts by Afghan women, see Deborah Ellis, *Women of the Afghan War* (Westport, CT: Praeger, 2000).

87. Htun, "Women and Democracy," 125.

88. Bang-Soon L. Yoon, "Democratization and Gender Politics in South Korea," in *Gender, Globalization, and Democratization*, 174–176.

89. UNDP, *Human Development Report 2006*. http://hdr.undp.org/hdr2006/statistics/indices/.

90. A more rigorous statistical analysis would have employed regression analysis to control for the effects of socioeconomic development, but likely would not have been meaningful to most undergraduates.

CHAPTER 6

AGRARIAN REFORM AND THE POLITICS OF RURAL CHANGE

When we speak of "the people" of Africa and Asia, in large part we are talking about the peasantry—poor farmers living in a traditional culture. Despite substantial urbanization in recent decades, at the present time slightly over half the population of the Third World remains rural.[1] It is in the countryside where some of the worst aspects of political and economic underdevelopment prevail. In nations as distinct as China and Mexico, rural annual incomes are only 20–25 percent as high as urban earnings. Sharp urban–rural gaps also persist in literacy, health care, and life expectancy. Rural villagers are less likely than their urban counterparts to have safe drinking water, electricity, and schools.

While the proportion of the Third World's overall population living in the countryside is substantially higher than in developed nations, the percentage varies greatly from country to country: from under 12 percent in Chile, Uruguay, and Venezuela to over 80 percent in Cambodia, Ethiopia, and Nepal. In all, more than 1 billion rural inhabitants live in "absolute poverty," defined as suffering from very inadequate housing, pervasive illiteracy, malnutrition, and high rates of infant mortality.[2] But, in the world's poorest nations—including Malawi, the Congo, Bangladesh, and Haiti—the number of rural residents living in absolute poverty exceeds 80 percent.[3] Looking at rural poverty from a different perspective, of the approximately 1.2 billion people currently living in extreme poverty worldwide (earning less than $1 per day), about 65 percent live in the countryside, with that proportion rising to over 90 percent in countries such as Bangladesh.[4]

In most of the developing world, political and economic powers are concentrated in the cities. Consequently, government policy—on issues ranging from social expenditures to agricultural pricing—has a predictable urban bias. As noted in Chapter 1, modernization theory argues that as countries develop, modern values and institutions will spread from the cities to the countryside, and the gap between the two will narrow. Conversely, dependency theorists maintain that the links between urban and rural areas replicate the exploitative international relationship between the industrialized core (the First World) and the periphery (the LDCs).[5] What is certain is that resolving the political and economic tensions *between* urban and rural areas and reducing the vast inequalities *within* the countryside, the major subjects of this chapter, remain among the most important challenges facing many developing nations.

RURAL CLASS STRUCTURES

Within the countryside, there are generally substantial disparities in access to, and ownership of, farmland. Particularly in Latin America and parts of South Asia, agricultural property tends to be concentrated in a relatively small number of hands. These inequalities have contributed to rural poverty and created rigid class systems in countries such as El Salvador, Colombia, the Philippines, and parts of India. African nations—with notable exceptions such as South Africa, Morocco, and Kenya—tend to have a more equitable pattern of land distribution, though they still suffer from sharp urban–rural gaps and intense rural poverty. East Asia (excepting the Philippines) has the most equitably distribution of farmland.

At the apex of the rural class system stand the large and powerful landowners, sometimes known as the *oligarchy*. Major Filipino sugar growers and Argentine cattle barons, for example, have historically exercised considerable political power in national politics. In El Salvador, the most influential coffee producers dominated the country's political system for most of the twentieth century. Land concentration has been most intense in Latin America, with its tradition of large estates (*latifundia*) dating back to the Spanish colonial era and the early years of independence. In the Philippines, Sri Lanka, Pakistan, and Bangladesh, along with parts of India, Indonesia, and Thailand, reactionary landed elites have also contributed to rural backwardness and poverty.

Since the middle of the twentieth century, the economic and political power of rural landlords has declined considerably in many LDCs. In the most dramatic cases, radical revolutions in countries such as China and Vietnam stripped landlords of their property. Revolutionary governments sometimes killed many of them and sent others to prison camps for "political reeducation." Elsewhere, nonrevolutionary and relatively peaceful agrarian reforms undermined the rural elites of Peru and South Korea.[6] In industrializing nations such as Brazil and Thailand, over time the economic importance of agribusiness has diminished relative to the industrial and commercial sectors. Therefore, many wealthy landowning families have diversified into other parts of the economy or have left agriculture entirely.

At the local and regional levels, however, landlords in Latin America and much of Asia continue to exercise considerable power. For example, upper-caste farmers in the Indian state of Bihar and large cattle ranchers in the Brazilian interior retain virtually unchallenged supremacy. At times they have intimidated, or even murdered, peasant organizers and union leaders without fear of legal sanctions. Such was the fate of Chico Mendes, the celebrated Brazilian union leader who had organized Amazonian rubber-tree tappers against the powerful ranchers who were clearing the forest and destroying the local habitat. Despite Mendes's impressive international stature (the Turner broadcasting network and various U.S. senators had honored him, for example,) and despite his links to influential American environmental groups, local landlords still hired gunmen to assassinate him. Only after a sustained international outcry were his murderers brought to trial. They were convicted, but after serving several years were able to walk out of prison and stay at large for three years. Hundreds of lesser-known Brazilians have been killed on orders from powerful landlords, crimes that often go unpunished.

On the rung beneath the landed elite, we find middle-sized landlords and "rich" peasants. The second group (sometimes called *kulaks*) consists of peasants who, unlike small landlords, still work on the land themselves. However, unlike poorer peasants, *kulaks* can afford to hire additional peasant labor to work with them. While neither middle-sized landlords nor rich peasants belong to the national power elite, they exercise considerable local political influence in countries such as India. Indeed, in much of Asia, where the biggest agricultural holdings are not nearly as large as those in Latin America, these two groups are a potent political force. Extended family networks typically magnify their influence.

Finally, at the bottom of the socioeconomic ladder, the rural poor—including peasants who own small plots of land, tenant farmers, and farm workers—are generally the Third World's most impoverished and powerless occupational group. *Peasants* are defined as family farmers (mostly poor) who maintain traditional lifestyles that are distinct from those of city dwellers. Because they are often poor and poorly educated, many peasants lack the means to transport their crops to market themselves, lack ready access to credit, and do not know how to deal with the legal proceedings that they may encounter. As a result, they depend on merchants, moneylenders, lawyers, and government bureaucrats, all of whom frequently exploit them. Their links to the outside world—including the government, the military, the church, and the market economy—are largely dependent upon individuals and institutions outside the peasants' community.[7] Thus, as Eric Wolf has noted, "Peasant denotes an asymmetrical structural relationship between the producers of surplus [peasants] and controllers [including landlords, merchants, and tax collectors]."[8]

We may further subdivide poor peasants into two subgroups: those who own small plots of land for family cultivation (smallholders) and those who are landless. The ranks of the landless, in turn, include tenant farmers (who enter into various types of rental arrangements with landlords) and farm wage laborers. However, these categories are not mutually exclusive. Smallholders, for example, may also supplement their incomes by working as farm laborers or renting additional land as tenants. Generally, it is the landless that constitute the poorest of the rural poor. While they represent a mere 10 percent of all agricultural families in countries such as Kenya and Sierra Leone, their numbers rise to 25–35 percent in Mexico, Peru, Turkey, and Cameroon and to 50–70 percent in India, Pakistan, the Philippines, the Dominican Republic, and Brazil.[9] Not surprisingly, in parts of Asia and Latin America, where concentration of land ownership and associated peasant landlessness are particularly notable, the issue of land reform was long at the center of rural politics.

PEASANT POLITICS

Despite their vast numbers, peasants often play a muted role in Third World politics. Because most LDCs did not have competitive national elections until recently, those numbers have not readily converted into political influence. The peasantry's political leverage is also limited by poverty, lack of education, dependence on outsiders, and physical isolation from the centers of national power and from peasants elsewhere in the country. Cultural values stressing caution and conservatism may further constrain peasant political behavior. Karl Marx's analysis of nineteenth-century European rural society questioned the peasants' capacity for political change or revolution. Writing on the French peasantry, he derided their alleged lack of solidarity and class consciousness, and disparagingly referred to them as a "sack of potatoes." Dismayed by their apparent conservatism, he dismissed peasants as "the class that represents the barbarism in civilization."[10] In the twentieth century, Robert Redfield's classic study of Third World peasants portrayed them somewhat similarly. "In every part of the world," he argued, "generally speaking, peasants have been a conservative factor in social change, a brake on revolution."[11]

Indeed, over the years anthropological research has frequently depicted peasant political culture as fatalistic and atomized. Hence, most of them allegedly doubt that collective political action can better their own fate.[12] Discussing the reaction of Indian villagers to local government authorities, Phyllis Arora describes a sense of powerlessness resulting in political apathy. "Helplessness is . . . evoked by the presence of the district officer. The peasant tends to feel that all he [or she] can do before such authority . . . is petition for redress of grievances. . . . In the ultimate analysis, however, . . . the peasant feels at the mercy of the whims of the [political] authorities."[13] In the 1990s, Western journalists, visiting peasant communities in China not long after massive urban protests against the government, noted the villagers' lack of political involvement and their insulation from national political debate.[14]

No doubt, peasants typically *are* wary of radical change and respectful of community traditions. To some extent, this conservatism reflects a suspicion of outside values—distrust frequently grounded in religious beliefs and other long-standing traditions. Indeed, the maintenance of a distinct peasant culture depends, to some extent, on the rejection of external influences. But peasant suspicion of social change is frequently understandable and rational. Struggling on the margins of economic survival, the rural poor have found that the commercialization and mechanization of agriculture, as well as other aspects of rural modernization, have often had a negative impact on their lives. In rural Pakistan, for example, the introduction of tractors improved the output and income of the farmers who could afford them. As a consequence, however, many poorer tenant farmers who could not compete were forced off their plots, concentrating land into fewer hands.[15] Political changes may also be threatening. For example, when outside activists have organized them to challenge local injustices, peasants have often been ruthlessly repressed. Small wonder, then, that they may be suspicious of change, including any challenge to the power structure.

This does not mean, however, that they are incapable of standing up to landlords and government authorities who wrong them. Far from it! Examples of peasant resistance are commonplace, ranging from the most restrained to the most radical. James C. Scott has demonstrated that many peasants in Southeast Asia who appear to accept the established order actually engage in unobtrusive "everyday forms of resistance," such as theft and vandalism against their landlords, foot dragging, and false deference.[16] Elsewhere, peasants have presented their political demands more openly and aggressively. Contrary to Marx's expectations, the supposedly conservative peasantry has been a critical actor in most twentieth-century revolutions, including communist upheavals in Russia,

China, Vietnam, and Cuba, as well as in noncommunist insurgencies in Bolivia and Mexico.[17] More recently, they have been the backbone of guerrilla movements in the Philippines, Cambodia, Colombia, El Salvador, Peru, Nepal, and parts of India. In the mid-1990s, *Zapatista* rebels from the indigenous communities of Chiapas, Mexico, established a de facto zone of self-rule, and forced the government to the negotiating table. And in many other LDCs, ranging from India to Ecuador, well-organized peasant groups also have become influential actors in democratic political systems.

We will examine the role of the peasantry in revolutionary movements in greater detail in Chapter 8. For now, however, suffice it to say that peasants are not inherently conservative or radical. Rather, they vary considerably in their ideological propensities and their capacity for collective political action. To understand why so many peasants accept the political status quo, while others choose to resist or even rebel, we must first examine the relationship between the powerful and the weak in the countryside. Although landlords in traditional settings frequently exploit their tenants or neighboring smallholders, mutually understood boundaries normally limit the extent of that exploitation. Links between landlords and peasants are usually grounded in long-standing patron–client relationships involving reciprocal obligations. Despite the landlords' superior power, these relationships are not always exploitative. For example, landowners frequently provide their tenants with land and financial credit in return for labor on their estate. And they may fund religious festivals or serve as godparents of their tenants' children.

As long as landlords and other members of the rural power elite fulfill their obligations, peasants generally accept the traditional order despite its many injustices. However, should rural modernization and the commercialization of agriculture induce rural patrons to cease discharging their traditional responsibilities, the peasantry may conclude that the previously existing "moral economy" has failed them.[18] In other cases rural modernization may give larger landlords (who can afford farm machinery and irrigation pumps) a competitive advantage over peasants (who cannot afford them) and eventually force the smallholders off the land. Eric Wolf has noted that the transition from feudal or semifeudal rural relations to capitalist economic arrangements frequently strips the peasantry of the certainty and protection afforded them by the old order. Frequently, the result is rural upheaval. Thus, he argued, communist revolutions in China, Vietnam, Cuba, and other Third World nations originated with the threats to the peasants' traditional way of life posed by the rise of rural capitalism.[19] This in no way suggests that rural modernization and the transition to capitalism *always* radicalize the peasantry or drive them to revolutionary activity. But when peasants feel that their traditional way of life is threatened, they will resist change or at least try to channel it into forms more beneficial to their interests. How effectively they engage in collective political action and how radical or moderate their demands are depend on various factors: the extent to which they perceive themselves to be exploited; how desperate their economic condition is; the degree of internal cohesion and cooperation within their communities; their ability to form political linkages with peasants in neighboring villages or in other parts of the country; the extent to which they forge political ties with nonpeasant groups and leaders; the type of outside groups with whom they ally (be it the Catholic Church in the Philippines or

Maoist revolutionaries in parts of rural India); the responsiveness of the political system to their demands; and the types of political options that the political order affords them.

The last two factors suggest that the probability of radical peasant insurrection depends as much on the quality of a country's political system as it does on the nature of the peasantry. Given a meaningful opportunity to implement change peacefully, peasants rarely opt for revolution. Rebellion—which brings obvious dangers to their own lives and to the lives of their families—is an act of desperation normally entered into only when other options are unavailable. It is perhaps for that reason that no democratic political system has ever fallen to revolutionary insurgency.

In recent decades, the spread of the mass media throughout the countryside, increased rural educational levels, and the broadening of voting rights in many LDCs (such as extension of the vote to illiterates) have greatly increased the political influence of peasant voters in electoral democracies. In countries such as India, South Korea, Turkey, Nicaragua, and Ecuador, politicians must now consider the interests of the rural poor more seriously. With rising educational levels and more information at their disposal, peasants can more effectively press their demands. Still, such voting power is of little use in the many nondemocratic nations that remain in Africa, the Middle East, and Asia. And even in competitive party systems, the peasantry's political power is not proportional to their numbers.

Ultimately, the range of peasant political activity runs the gamut from the far Left to the far Right, from peaceful to violent. As Samuel Huntington has noted, "The peasantry . . . may be the bulwark of the status quo or the shock troops of revolution. Which role the peasant plays is determined by the extent to which the existing system meets his immediate economic and material needs as he sees them."[20] In India, many peasants vote for the BJP—the conservative Hindu fundamentalist party (see Chapter 3). In Latin America, on the other hand, peasants often vote for moderately left-of-center candidates. And in countries such as China, Vietnam, Nicaragua, and Colombia, still other peasants have supported revolutionary insurrections. Whatever their political inclinations, the peasants' economic and political concerns usually revolve around four broad issues: the prices they receive for their crops, consumer prices, taxes, and the availability of land.[21] The issue of land has been the most volatile and the most critical to the political stability of many Third World nations, and it is to this issue that we now turn our attention.

THE POLITICS OF AGRARIAN REFORM

In those areas of the Third World where land ownership is highly concentrated, the issue of agrarian reform has long been an issue in the national political debate. To be sure, the pressure for reform has waxed and waned and other models of rural development have become more popular in recent decades. Still, the problem lingers in many Third World countries. Normally, it involves redistribution of farmland from landlords to landless peasants or to smallholders who need it to support their families. In other instances, it entails distribution of public property, including previously uncultivated lands. To stand a real chance of increasing agricultural production, improving rural living standards, and establishing political stability, however, government land redistribution must be accompanied by supplementary aid to its program beneficiaries. This aid includes technical assistance for farming, commercial credits, transportation, and enhanced access to markets. Unfortunately, agrarian reform programs often fail to provide sufficient support. Furthermore, the amount of land distributed is frequently inadequate to meet the peasants' needs. Agrarian reforms introduced by revolutionary regimes sweep out the old systems of inequality, but often create new forms of land ownership or management dominated by the state that fail to live up to the peasants' expectations. Thus, with notable exceptions such as Japan, Taiwan, and South Korea, land reform programs frequently have fallen short of their goals.

Patterns of Land Concentration

In much of Third World, especially Asia, landless peasants constitute a large portion of the rural population. In Bangladesh, for example, about half the rural population is landless. The proportion in India is about 40 percent. In Brazil there are about 5 million landless rural families. In addition, millions of peasant smallholders own plots too small to support their families adequately. In countries such as Bangladesh, Rwanda, El Salvador, and Peru, the ratio of rural families to arable land is so high that even an equitable distribution of farmland would fail to meet all the peasants' needs. But in many LDCs, where the ratio of rural families to arable land is more favorable, landlessness and land shortages are caused by the concentration of agricultural land in a small number of hands.

Maldistribution of land is most pronounced in Latin America, where large estates, sometimes measuring thousands of acres, contain a substantial proportion of the region's farmland. In Brazil, for example, a mere 2 percent of the nation's farms, each exceeding 1,000 hectares (2,500 acres), have owned more than 55 percent of all farmland.[22] Vast cattle and citrus estates have been cut out of the Amazonian interior, some covering several hundred thousand acres. In the Dominican Republic, where holdings are not nearly as vast, farms larger than 50 hectares in size have constituted less than 2 percent of the nation's agricultural units; nevertheless, they too have controlled more than 55 percent of the country's farmland. The largest of these estates—those exceeding 500 hectares—represented a mere 0.1 percent of all Dominican farms but held 27 percent of the nation's agricultural land. At the other end of the spectrum, peasant smallholders (owning units of 5 hectares or less) owned nearly 82 percent of the country's farms, which covered merely 12.2 percent of all farmland.[23] Similar patterns have prevailed in much of Latin America. Prior to the 1979 Sandinista revolution, an astounding 43 percent of Nicaragua's rural families were landless. Yet a mere 2 percent of the rural population owned 36 percent of the land, including a full 20 percent of Nicaragua's farmland belonging to the ruling Somoza family.[24]

With different historical traditions and far higher population density, Asia does not have agricultural estates of the same magnitude. In nations such as Indonesia, India, and Pakistan, farm holdings have rarely exceeded 50 hectares.[25] Still, in many cases a high proportion of farmland is concentrated in relatively few hands. For example, in Bangladesh, one of the world's most densely populated countries, the largest farms are relatively small, rarely exceeding 5–10 hectares. Yet less than 3 percent of the nation's rural households controlled more than 25 percent of the country's agricultural land. In the Philippines, virtually identical data showed 3.4 percent of the country's farms accounting for 26 percent of the land.[26]

The Case for Agrarian Reform

Given the powerful interests opposing land redistribution, supporters of agrarian reform have needed to defend their objectives on several grounds, including social justice and equity, greater political stability, improved agricultural productivity, economic growth, and preservation of the environment. An examination of each of these arguments reveals the complexity of the debate.

Social Justice   Because of the concentration of agricultural holdings in Latin America and parts of Africa and Asia, many analysts feel there is a *prima facie* case for some form of land redistribution based on social justice and human rights.[27] As previously noted, the millions of rural families with little or no land are among the poorest of the Third World's poor. They are trapped in a web of poverty, malnutrition, and illiteracy from which few escape. Usually they are politically powerless as well, controlled by landlords or local political bosses. For those peasants, agrarian reform is a fundamental step toward achieving greater political and socioeconomic justice.[28]

Political Stability   From the perspective of government policy makers, perhaps a more compelling justification of agrarian reform has been curtailing peasant unrest. Samuel Huntington has starkly linked land reform to political stability:

> Where the conditions of land tenure are equitable and provide a viable living for the peasant, revolution is unlikely. Where they are inequitable and where the peasant lives in poverty and suffering, revolution is likely, if not inevitable, unless the government takes prompt measures to remedy those conditions.[29]

Indeed, statistical analyses indicate that the likelihood of revolutionary activity in developing countries increases where farmland is very unequally distributed and where there is a high percentage of landless peasants.[30] Without the threat of peasant unrest, however, most policy makers have been relatively indifferent to the injustices of land tenure patterns. Ironically, then, the end of the Cold War, and with it the threat of communist insurrection, has reduced U.S. interest in promoting land reform, as it had done, for example, in El Salvador during the 1980s and in South Korea decades earlier.

Productivity   One of the most hotly debated aspects of land reform is its effect on agricultural productivity. Opponents of reform maintain that land redistribution lowers agricultural output, thereby diminishing food supplies for the cities and curtailing export earnings. Citing "economies of scale," they argue that large agricultural units are generally more productive because they are more easily mechanized and use rural infrastructure (such as irrigation and roads) more effectively. Second, they insist that peasant cultivators have less technical knowledge than large landowners and are, therefore, less-productive farmers.

Advocates of agrarian reform counter that, in fact, smallholders are generally more efficient producers than larger landlords. Although a growing number of large landowners currently study agricultural sciences and employ modern productive techniques, many of the landed elite still farm their land ineffectively. For example, in Latin America, where land is an important source of prestige and political power, landlords have often owned more land than they can efficiently cultivate. Peasant cultivators, on the other hand, tend to farm their plots very intensively because their families' living standards depend on raising productivity. This does not mean that small, peasant-run units are *always* more efficient. Peasant beneficiaries of land reform in some regions lack necessary skills for owning their own plots. Consequently, land transfers in such cases sometimes have caused short-term declines in efficiency.[31] In such cases the beneficiaries of land reform may require supplemental government assistance as they become landowners.

The comparative efficiency of landlords and smallholders also varies according to which crop or animal they are raising. For example, production of meat, wheat, and sugar are more likely to benefit from economies of scale (i.e., output per acre will usually rise significantly as the result of capital investment). On the other hand, most of the grains, tubers, fruits, and vegetables that constitute the core of Third World food consumption, along with some exports such as coffee, do best with labor-intensive cultivation on small farm units. These variations notwithstanding, data collected in Asia and Latin America reveal that labor-intensive smallholders (peasants who invest large amounts of physical labor) generally have higher yields per acre than large-scale, capital-intensive (mechanized) producers.[32]

The economic efficiency of small farms may surprise many Americans accustomed to believing that larger units are inherently more productive. But in underdeveloped rural societies with a surplus of labor (i.e., many people who are underemployed and who will work for low wages), it is often more cost effective to use family or hired labor intensively rather than invest in machinery. Out of economic necessity, peasant cultivators work hard, exploiting their own family labor. On the other hand, most large estates are farmed by tenants or hired laborers, neither of whom gain from raising productivity. That difference in motivation helps explain why the agricultural yields of peasant landowners in Japan, South Korea, and Taiwan and of near-owners in China are generally over twice as high as those of Filipino tenant farmers with comparable plots of land but less motivation to raise productivity.[33]

In recent decades, the disparity between large and small units in agricultural productivity has diminished. By using more advanced technology such as high-yield seeds and complementary irrigation, some large farmers have narrowed the efficiency gap.[34] But even if large farm units were more efficient, smallholding operations would still be more productive to society than large landlords in other ways. For example, large landowners tend to import a sizable portion of their machinery, fuel, and chemicals, thereby expending much of the country's scarce foreign exchange. On the other hand, peasant farms draw upon family labor, a cheap input found in abundance. It is for this reason that the former president of the Overseas Development Council argued that "a land and capital scarce (but population plentiful) country should favor 40 two-and-a-half acre farms over a single-owner 100-acre farm in order to make optimum use of available land, labor, and capital."[35]

Economic Growth   In addition to its positive effect on agricultural productivity, land redistribution often brings broader benefits to the economies of
developing areas. In countries such as Bolivia and Cuba, agrarian reform gave
peasants a greater economic stake in the countryside, thereby reducing rural-to-
urban migration and alleviating the tremendous strain on resources experienced
by so many Third World cities (see Chapter 7).

When successfully implemented, land reform improves the living standards
of the rural poor. And, as their purchasing power increases, they consume more
of their country's manufactured goods, thereby stimulating industrial growth.[36]
Indeed, Japan's, Taiwan's, and South Korea's postwar economic booms followed
closely on the heels of land reforms.[37] At the same time reform also reduced
income equality in those East Asian nations. That equality has brought political stability and supported rapid economic growth. In contrast, Latin America's pattern
of concentrated land ownership has contributed to the region's highly inequitable
income distribution, widespread rural poverty, and lower economic growth.

Environmental Preservation   Another, more-recent argument for agrarian
reform relates to environmental protection. For example, Brazilian ranchers and
farmers deliberately burn tracts of the Amazonian rainforest to clear land for agriculture, annually destroying an area equal to the size of New Jersey. The fires are
so vast that they contribute to the *greenhouse effect* on world climate. Although large
landowners create a substantial portion of this burn-off, peasant settlers also contribute. Driven out of the nation's poorest regions by desperation, land-hungry
peasants colonize the jungle in search of a better life. Once there, however, they dis-
cover that cleared jungle soil quickly loses its nutrients. So, they must soon move
on, clearing yet more forest land. Land reform in Brazil's nonforested regions
would reduce landlessness and give tenant farmers a greater stake in the land they
farm, thus reducing migration to the Amazonian basin.

Environmentalists advance similar arguments for land reform in other
parts of the world. For example, Bangladesh's severe population pressure and
concentrated land ownership have forced many poor farmers to push the fron-
tiers of agriculture beyond the ecologically desirable limits. In their search for
farmland, landless peasants often move to coastal regions unsafe for habitation.
There they fall victim to the typhoons that periodically sweep across the region,
killing thousands of people.

TYPES OF AGRARIAN REFORM

In the past century, various forces brought about agrarian reform. At times
reform followed foreign occupation or pressure; occasionally it resulted from
peasant-based revolutions; and sometimes it was introduced by national governments anxious to garner peasant support and maintain political tranquility.
In each case, the underlying forces that stimulated reform have influenced the
type of program that emerged.

Externally Imposed Reform

The most successful externally imposed reforms occurred in East Asia after
World War II. In Japan, the U.S. occupation command limited land ownership

to 10 acres, transferred 41 percent of the country's farmland from landlords to their tenants, and controlled rents for the remaining tenant population. The number of landless peasants fell from 28 to 10 percent of the rural population, making the countryside a bastion of stability.[38] In Taiwan and South Korea, U.S. pressure encouraged similar reforms designed to avert rural unrest. Farm ownership was limited to small parcels, and about one-third of each country's farmland was transferred to tenants, some 60 percent of whom benefited from the land transfers.[39] In all three nations, the transformation of rural society was enormously successful, raising agricultural productivity, improving rural living standards, and strengthening political stability. Consequently, East Asia's agrarian reforms have served as benchmarks in evaluating programs elsewhere in the world.

In view of these impressive early achievements, it is striking how infrequently and ineffectively Washington has promoted Third World land reform since that time. In retrospect, it appears that there were three unique conditions in postwar East Asia that have rarely been reproduced subsequently. First was the depth of American commitment to reform. At the start of the Cold War, fearing that peasant-based revolutions would spread from China to other Far Eastern nations, American policy makers endorsed land reform as the best way to contain communism. A second unique condition was the enormous pressure that the United States could exert on those East Asian governments in the years following World War II. The Japanese were under U.S. military occupation, while the South Korean and Taiwanese governments were deeply beholden to the United States for liberating them from Japan and then protecting them from their communist neighbors (North Korea and China). In subsequent years, the United States lacked comparable influence. Although it favored land reform in South Vietnam (in the 1960s) and Central America (1980s), it was unwilling or unable to exert sufficient pressure on their conservative governments to achieve effective programs.

This leads us to East Asia's last unique characteristic: its land-owning elites were so weakened at the end of World War II that they were ill-equipped to defend their own interests. The situation was most stark in Japan following its surrender to U.S. forces at the close of the war. As the occupying power, the United States could impose its will on the country's previously powerful rural landlords. Moreover, key Japanese political leaders, working with the U.S. high command, agreed that agrarian reform was necessary.[40] In South Korea, many of the country's landlords had collaborated with Japan during its 35 years of occupation. Hence, when Japanese occupation ended at the close of World War II, the Korean landed elite had little legitimacy or political influence. And in Taiwan—where the Kuomintang (KMT) regime had fled after being driven out of China by the revolutionary army—government leaders recognized that their earlier failure to implement agrarian reform on the Chinese mainland had contributed to the communist victory there. So, prodded by the United States, the KMT was ready to reform the Taiwanese countryside.

But, in the decades that followed, U.S. efforts on behalf of land reform were far less effective. Within the nations of Southeast Asia and Central America, large landlords used their extensive political power to obstruct rural reform. At the same time, when peasant unrest erupted in countries such as South Vietnam and El Salvador, the United States lacked the capacity, or perhaps the will, to promote real reform in the face of determined opposition by conservative elites.

Revolutionary Transformation

From the Mexican and Chinese revolutions through more recent insurgencies in the Philippines, El Salvador, Colombia, and Nepal, most twentieth-century insurrections were peasant based (Chapter 8). Therefore, agrarian reform was a fundamental rallying cry in both Marxist revolutions (China, Vietnam, Cuba, and Nicaragua) and non-Marxist insurgencies (Mexico, Bolivia, and Algeria). In the 1930s and 1940s, for example, the Chinese communists gained considerable peasant support by transferring land to the rural poor. Following their victories in Nicaragua, Vietnam, and Cuba, revolutionary parties also implemented far-reaching land redistribution.

After coming to power in 1949, the Chinese communists distributed almost half of the country's arable land to about 60 million peasant households, totaling over half the nation's population. Like the U.S.-sponsored reforms in East Asia (Japan, South Korea, and Taiwan), China's agrarian reform initially disbursed the land to peasant smallholders. But, soon convinced that privately owned peasant plots would reintroduce rural inequalities and class divisions, the government forced the peasantry to join state-directed cooperatives.[41]

Because they had vanquished the rural upper class, revolutionary governments are freer to redistribute large amounts of land. In countries such as Cuba, Nicaragua, and Vietnam, the government either converted property belonging to the defeated rural aristocracy to state farms or distributed it to peasant smallholders. Similarly, following their anticolonial revolutions, Algeria and Kenya redistributed farmland belonging to the ousted European settlers. In Mexico, some 40 percent of peasant families benefited from agrarian reform, receiving more than 40 percent of the country's agricultural and forest areas. Eighty percent of Bolivia's farmland was transferred to three-fourths of its rural families.[42]

While revolutionary reforms are generally more far-reaching than any of the other approaches discussed in this chapter, the way in which those governments implement land reform frequently does not please the peasant recipients. Marxist regimes have frequently converted the land of both the vanquished landlords and the victorious peasantry into large collective or cooperative farms dominated by the state, rather than breaking up the landlords' holdings into the type of peasant smallholdings created in the East Asian model. To be sure, Cuba and some other Marxist regimes have allowed a parallel sector of peasant-owned farms. But, until recently the Cuban government offered material incentives and social pressures to convince peasant smallholders to sell their land to the state. Elsewhere, other revolutionary regimes have been more authoritarian, crushing any resistance to collectivization, often with a tremendous loss of life. Eric Wolf points out the irony of forced collectivization in countries such as the Soviet Union, China, and Vietnam. Peasants, he notes, supported and fought for Marxist revolutions in hopes of getting a plot of land for their family. Yet after they had risked their lives to bring the revolution to power, the government coerced them into collectivizing their farms.[43] The results have often been disastrous. Frequently these programs have resulted in famines for one or more of the following reasons: the government purposely cuts food supplies to parts of the countryside to starve peasants resisting collectivization into submission (the Soviet Union in the 1920s and Ethiopia in the 1980s); the initial chaos caused by forced collectivization resulted in sharp declines in food production (China); the ongoing inefficiencies of collective farming also create severe shortages (North Korea). The loss of lives resulting from forced collectivization in those countries numbered in the millions.

China illustrates the dangers of forced collectivization, not only at the time the peasants were coerced into joining collective farms but years later as well. As we have noted, a brief period of family farming soon gave way to collective farming. The process reached its apex during the Great Leap Forward (1958–1961), when the government created huge agricultural communes. Overcentralization of agricultural decision making and poorly informed government policies caused enormous food shortages. In the massive famine that resulted, perhaps 25 million people died of starvation or disease.[44] Although the government eventually abandoned its plans for huge communes, it expanded collective farming once again during the Chinese Cultural Revolution (1966–1976).

Several factors motivated Marxist regimes' preference for collective farming, whether through state farms or state-directed peasant cooperatives. A fundamental objective was to establish state control over agriculture, so that government administrators could dictate which crops peasants grew and what they were paid for them. In China, for example, the government required agricultural communes to concentrate on the production of basic food grains such as rice and wheat, which were then sold to the general public at controlled prices. From a political standpoint, communist governments believed that collectivization was a means of controlling the peasants' individualistic impulses and reorienting them toward the public good. Arguing that private farming inevitably leads to inequalities between villagers and creates a "bourgeois mentality" among peasant smallholders, government leaders dismissed family farming as an undesired form of capitalism.[45] Finally, supporters of collectivization maintained that large, centrally controlled farms were more efficient than smallholdings.

To be sure, large state farms *are* often more efficient in one respect. They facilitate government delivery of social service. Thus, it is easier to deliver clean water, medical care, and schools to large collective farms than to provide these services to widely scattered private farms. However, the assumption that large state farms are more efficient *producers* than peasant smallholdings was usually quite mistaken. In fact production data from Cuba, Ethiopia, Nicaragua, and China demonstrate that, for most crops, private peasant plots have *higher* yields per acre than collective farms do.[46]

Peasant plots are generally more productive than collective farms for the same reason that they tend to outperform large private farms in capitalist LDCs. Because their standard of living is tied directly to how much they produce, peasant smallholders are highly motivated to work intensely and to do whatever it takes to raise output. On the other hand, state farm employees receive the same wage no matter how hard or how little they work. Small wonder that a number of years ago the Cuban government admitted that the average state farm worker, while being paid to work an eight-hour day, actually worked about four. Government research revealed that they spent the remaining time taking breaks or, in some cases, illegally moonlighting as workers for nearby private farmers.

In recent decades, faced with growing evidence that peasant smallholdings are more productive than collective farms, many of the Third World's remaining communist governments have set aside their ideological preferences and accepted more pragmatic policies. When Deng Xiaoping succeeded Mao Zedong as China's political leader, he introduced the "Household Responsibility System," which converted China's farm communes back to peasant-controlled, essentially private farms.[47] In what amounted to a second agrarian reform (or, as one expert called it, "a second revolution"), the government broke up large communal farms and distributed the land to the peasants as family plots. The ensuing "unleashing [of] the entrepreneurial talents of China's peasants" led to striking gains in farm productivity. From 1980 to 1984 alone, the value of agricultural output rose an astonishing 40 percent.[48] That surge was a major factor contributing to a vast improvement in rural living standards from the early 1980s to the mid-1990s. More recently, other revolutionary and reformed-Marxist regimes in Asia, most notably Vietnam, have also decollectivized agriculture.

In Nicaragua, agrarian reform officials in the Sandinista revolutionary government initially preferred state farms over any other type of agricultural unit. They saw peasant-run cooperatives as next best, and ranked private smallholdings last. Not surprisingly, surveys showed that the peasants' preferred rankings were exactly the opposite. During the economic crisis of the 1980s, the government, which was more pragmatic and less ideologically rigid than most Marxist regimes, conceded that peasant farms were more efficient. Moreover, as it fought a bitter civil war with the Contras (U.S.-backed anti-revolutionary guerrillas), the government realized that giving land to family farms would give peasant recipients incentive to support the Sandinista army. Consequently, the regime altered its priorities to accommodate peasant preferences.[49] Similarly, during its severe economic crisis in the 1990s, Cuba's government reversed gears and converted many of the country's centrally run agricultural cooperatives into family-run units. Cuba's president, Raúl Castro, allegedly favors a more intensive shift to private farming similar to China's reforms.

Moderate Reformism

Most agrarian reform programs stem neither from foreign intervention nor revolution. Countries such as Egypt, Iran, India, Bangladesh, Zimbabwe, Chile, Venezuela, and Peru have redistributed agricultural land in various ways. In each case, however, the government introduced reform as a means of soliciting peasant support. Following the Cuban revolution, the United States and various Latin American governments concluded that the region needed rural reform in order to contain the spread of peasant unrest. Chile, Venezuela, and Peru all enacted moderate land reform programs in the 1960s. Twenty years later, the challenge of guerrilla insurgency prompted limited reform in El Salvador.

Elsewhere, the abolition of literacy requirements for voting and rising rural literacy rates have enfranchised a growing numbers of peasants, creating pressure for rural reform. Once minor players in the electoral process, in many countries peasants have become an important voting constituency, wooed by competing political parties. Running on platforms calling for agrarian reform, Chile's Christian Democratic Party, Peru's *Acción Popular*, and Venezuela's

Acción Democrática all won national elections in the past with the help of broad peasant support. Once in office, all these governments introduced land reforms of varying magnitudes.[50] Similarly, in Asia, some mix of incipient rural unrest and electoral politics contributed to modest reforms in the Philippines and parts of India, including the states of Kerala and West Bengal.[51]

Moderate reformism has one obvious advantage. It is relatively free of the violence and excesses often associated with revolutionary programs. But with rare exception, its scope is far more limited than either externally induced redistribution or revolutionary change. For example, revolutions in Cuba, Bolivia, Mexico, and Nicaragua introduced Latin America's most extensive land redistribution programs, far exceeding moderate reformism.[52] Similarly, reformism in Asia (Bangladesh, Thailand, the Philippines, and India) has also produced meager results when compared to revolutionary land redistributions in China and Vietnam.

Reformism generally produces a less-sweeping agrarian transformation because the government must deal with landed elites who are still strong enough to limit the scope of change.[53] For example, reformist programs generally grant monetary compensation to landlords who have lost property. Because most Third World governments are strapped for funds and have other important spending needs, those payments limit the scope of land redistribution. In addition, bureaucratic obstacles and court challenges frequently slow the pace of land redistribution to a crawl.

One notable exception to this pattern was the Peruvian agrarian reform. There, the government implemented a sweeping reform in the absence of either external pressure or internal revolution. A left-leaning, nationalist military government led by General Juan Velasco expropriated most of the country's large agricultural and ranching estates, turning them over to the peasants and farm laborers who had been working on them. The military regime had the power to sweep aside objections from Peru's rural oligarchy, a group despised by Velasco and his team. In all, it transferred approximately 40 percent of the country's farmland to 30 percent of the nation's peasant families.[54] Initially, most of the land was organized into cooperatives, but subsequently, as administrative and labor problems arose, most co-ops were subdivided and converted into peasant smallholdings.[55]

Ultimately, however, the military's agrarian reform failed to reduce Peru's pervasive rural poverty (discussed below). What it did accomplish was to destroy the once-considerable power of the landowning class and thereby transform the country's political and economic structure. The virtually unchallenged power of a military dictatorship, like the might of a revolutionary regime, allowed the government to ignore the demands of the rural aristocracy in a way that a democratic government never could. However, no other military government in Latin America has been equally dedicated to comprehensive rural change.[56]

In contrast, democratic governments, no matter how committed to helping the peasantry, cannot launch that type of frontal assault on the landed elite. For example, Venezuela's democratically elected *Acción Democrática* government, with strong backing from peasant voters, introduced a relatively ambitious agrarian reform. But because of political and financial restraints, much of the land transferred was previously uncultivated public property in the nation's jungle regions. Although this transfer permitted the government to sidestep landlord objections, such land was typically of marginal quality and not very accessible.

The Limits of Agrarian Reform

While the experiences of Taiwan, South Korea, Cuba, and China demonstrate that agrarian reform can substantially improve peasant living standards, few programs elsewhere have matched their success. Peru illustrates how even sweeping change initiated by a well-intentioned government may not achieve its objectives. That program transferred a relatively high proportion of national farmland to the peasantry compared to other Latin American agrarian reforms, comparable to revolutionary transformations in Cuba, Mexico, and Nicaragua. The military regime stripped powerful Andean and coastal landlords of their land and its associated political power, undercutting an elite that had once dominated the countryside. Yet these radical changes failed to improve peasant living standards as anticipated. The military's attempts at rural political change were often heavy-handed and counterproductive. But even if the government had better executed its reforms, expropriating the nation's largest haciendas and plantations would not have provided enough land to satisfy the peasants' requirements. There simply was not enough arable farmland to go around. Ultimately, less than one-third of the rural families in need received any land, and the poorest of the poor were frequently overlooked.[57] Even most of the program's beneficiaries found that their added land was insufficient to alleviate their deep poverty.

While the military regime narrowed the gap between rich and poor in the countryside, it did nothing to bridge the more important gulf between rural and urban living standards. As in most LDCs, the nation's economic structure has long favored the urban population over the peasantry. Despite substantial poverty in the cities, average urban income remains several times higher than rural earnings. Consequently, a substantial improvement in peasant living standards is impossible without a shift of wealth and government resources from urban areas to the countryside. Given the tremendous political power of the urban upper class, middle class, and organized working class, such a transfer of wealth and resources was more than even the armed forces were prepared to implement. Absent that change, agrarian reform merely redistributed poverty within the countryside.

Revolutionary agrarian reforms have limitations as well. Mexico still suffers from substantial rural poverty and landlessness, despite a reform that affected half the nation's peasants and a similar proportion of agricultural land. Beginning in the 1930s, the government organized reform beneficiaries into *ejidos*, cooperative units designed to channel state aid to the peasantry and increase their productivity. Following World War II, however, government agricultural policy changed in favor of larger commercial farms, failing to channel adequate credits, infrastructure, and technology to the *ejidos*. As a consequence, poor farmers were unable to compete in the marketplace. Many lost their farms and poured into the nation's cities or across the border to the United States. Since 1970, the government has developed several programs designed to bolster peasant agriculture. While these programs have had some positive impact, they were cut short after 1982 by the country's debt crisis and severe economic recession.[58] Current government policies encourage the privatization of the *ejidos'* communal property. This may benefit the most productive peasants, because they may now buy and sell land more readily. However, it also forces less-competitive peasants off their family plots into Mexico's already overcrowded cities or across the U.S. border.

The shortcomings of reform efforts in Mexico and Peru do not suggest that agrarian reform is without value. Rather, they indicate that redistribution of land must be supported by additional government measures if it is to be effective. Evidence from elsewhere in Latin America and from South Asia indicates that successful reform programs usually require some degree of peasant organization and mobilization.[59] That is to say, the state is more likely to provide land recipients with needed technical assistance, infrastructure, education, and financial credit if it is pressured to do so by effective peasant organizations. Government also needs to allow peasants a fair price for their crops.[60] The administrative apparatus governing reform must be simple, and peasant beneficiaries must be given a strong role in the decision-making process. In countries where rural elites maintain substantial political power, landlords losing property must receive reasonable payments if the program is to be politically viable. At the same time, peasant beneficiaries must only pay an amount they can afford if the program is to be economically feasible for them.[61] Wherever possible, Third World governments must reduce the tremendous gap that typically separates urban and rural living standards.

In recent years a number of LDCs have introduced or continued land reform programs. Most programs, however, are very limited or exist in name only. Only a few governments are implementing significant reforms. In Venezuela, Hugo Chavez's leftist government has introduced a program to redistribute currently unused state and private lands to needy peasant families and to urban migrants who wish to return to the countryside. Venezuela's situation is uniquely favorable to rural reform in a number of ways: the rural population is very small (about 10 percent of the national total); the country has low population density with significant government land holdings (though much of that is unusable for agriculture); and, the boom in petroleum prices has given the state substantial economic resources. Despite all these advantages and despite the existence of a powerful reform-oriented government, so far the number of beneficiaries has been modest and only state-owned land has been touched. Elsewhere in Latin America, Bolivia's government, led by Chavez's ally, Evo Morales, issued an executive order for land redistribution in 2006 and later pushed a potentially far-reaching reform bill through Congress. It calls for the "expropriation of lands [that] do not serve a just social-economic function." Because Morales' primary political support comes from Bolivia's peasants, the effects of the reform are likely to be far-reaching, but it is still too early to judge its effectiveness.

Elsewhere in the developing world, modest land reform programs have been implemented in the Philippines and South Africa, but they have only touched the surface. The same can be said of a large number of reforms in Asia, Africa, and the Middle East. Zimbabwe's broader reform program has transferred land held by Whites, since the colonial era, to the Black rural population. However, this program has been plagued by a number of serious problems.

The Mugabe government seems more interested in using agrarian reform for political gain than for improving rural conditions. It has distributed land primarily to government supporters without regard to the recipients' qualifications or need. The government has often encouraged its militants to seize land violently, thereby leading many large landowners to cease investing in production. Finally, because the farms seized so far and those in danger of future expropriation produce much of Zimbabwe's food exports, and because rural production has been badly disrupted, the national economy has suffered. Domestic food production has fallen as well. In contrast, mindful of the violence and econmic problems generated by agrarian reform programs in Zimbabwe and elsewhere, South Africa's government has moved very cautiously in redistributing land owned by wealthy White farmers to Black peasants. As a result, many rural Blacks complain that the government has not moved fast enough and that their living conditions have not improved significantly since the end of White rule.

Finally, in recent decades a very different type of land reform has taken place in several communist nations that have been moving in the direction of free-market economies. Farmlands that had been seized from big landowners during their revolutions and turned into state farms or state-controlled peasant cooperatives have been decollectivized and broken into smaller, peasant-owned farms. As we have seen, the most extensive reform of this kind was in China during the 1970s and 1980s under the "Household Responsibility System." Since the end of the 1980s, Vietnam has carried out a comparable agrarian decollectivization program. And, a similar process has taken place in the privatization of state-controlled farmland in Russia and the former communist nations of Eastern Europe.

Even the most intelligently executed reform programs, however, will not be equally successful in each country. In nations such as Peru, El Salvador, and Bangladesh, there simply is not enough quality land to satisfy peasant needs. In such cases, the government and the private sector need to create alternative employment for the rural poor in other sectors of the economy. Ultimately, each nation's agrarian-reform package must be carefully designed to meet its own specific needs.

OTHER APPROACHES AND ISSUES

For the past 30 years, few governments have introduced significant agrarian reform programs, with some notable exceptions, such as Nicaragua, El Salvador, possibly Bolivia, and, in a more controversial form, Zimbabwe. Critics on the Right have long believed land redistribution programs undermine allegedly more efficient, large-scale agribusiness. Critics on the Left have found the fruits of moderate reformism disappointing, claiming that often it has benefited capitalists and state bureaucracies more than it has the peasantry.[62] And, powerful urban interests fear agrarian reform will curtail agricultural production. In many ways, rural pressures for reform have diminished. Increasing numbers of peasants have migrated to the cities, no longer demanding change in the countryside. Most governments now attach less importance to peasant agriculture than to large export-oriented commercial farming, which earns the nation foreign exchange. While modest land redistribution programs continue in some LDCs, for now at least, efforts at rural reform have shifted to other issues and other types of programs.

Crop Pricing

In addition to lacking sufficient farmland, peasants often have suffered from unfavorable government price policies. Anxious to ensure a supply of cheap food for their urban populations, many governments, particularly in Africa and the Middle East, have imposed price controls on basic commodities such as rice, potatoes, and sugar. Price controls were also designed to promote industrialization by providing workers with cheap food, thereby helping employers keep wages down and permitting more capital investment.[63] But by holding crop prices below their free-market levels, these controls further impoverished peasant producers.

In Africa, governments have also commonly controlled the price of export crops, extracting the gap between what they have paid farmers and the higher world-market price as a de facto tax. One early study found that African farmers often received less than two-thirds, and in some cases less than half, of the value of their export crops.[64] Although designed to provide the urban poor and the middle class with cheaper food and to generate government revenues from exports, price controls ultimately have had perverse effects. They particularly damage poor farmers and reduce the supply of basic foods by creating disincentives to production. In Egypt, for example, when the government controlled the price of basic food grains, large landlords either evaded government controls or, more commonly, reduced the supply of badly needed grains by switching to other, uncontrolled crops. Peasants were less capable of switching crops and thus suffered declining incomes.[65] Throughout Africa, price controls reduced food output by driving many farmers out of business and removing production incentives for the rest. For decades, per-capita food production has declined, and the continent has become increasingly dependent on food imports and foreign aid. While there is no single cause for that deterioration, one study of African famine argues that government price controls and inefficient government bureaucracies have aggravated the problem.[66]

Unfortunately, once governments embarked on the path of commodity price regulation, they were soon caught in a conflict between short-term political pressures and long-term production needs. The immediate effect of price deregulation would be sharp increases in basic food prices. Governments that removed price controls (often in response to external pressures from the IMF) frequently faced urban protests and riots by irate urban consumers. Not surprisingly, for many years few administrations were willing to risk such unrest, particularly because the urban middle class, a group adversely affected by price hikes on food, is usually a vital pillar of government support. In the end, however, better crop prices should stimulate greater food production, ultimately leading prices to the consumer to start falling, though not necessarily to their prior low. More recently, as many developing nations have introduced neoliberal economic policies (reducing or eliminating government economic intervention), more and more are eliminating price controls (see Chapter 10).[67]

CONCLUSION: DEMOCRACY AND RURAL REFORM

For decades, Third World development policies have generally emphasized industrial growth and urban modernization, often to the detriment of the rural sector. In many cases the consequences have been stagnant agricultural production, rising food imports, rural poverty, and heavy rural-to-urban migration. In some instances, rural poverty has led to peasant insurrection. Most notably in Africa and Latin America, pro-urban government biases, along with the forces of capitalist development, have driven many peasants into the rural or urban working class in a process known as *proletarianization*.[68] Many pessimistic scholars have predicted the inevitable spread of large mechanized farms to the detriment of peasant family farming.

More recently, research in countries such as Bolivia, Ecuador, and Colombia has revealed that, in at least some regions, innovative peasants have adapted skillfully to the forces of rural capitalism and modernization. Many have taken advantage of new commercial opportunities to compete successfully in the marketplace.[69] In Africa and Asia, peasant smallholders remain an even greater component of rural society. Rather than abandoning the peasantry as a relic of history, Third World governments and international agencies need to promote balanced economic and political development that gives proper weight to the rural sector and its peasant population.

The relationship between democracy and rural reform is somewhat paradoxical. On the one hand, democratic governments such as Venezuela, which carried out agrarian reform and other forms of assistance to the rural poor, broadened their base of political support. As we noted earlier, experts such as Samuel Huntington argued during the Cold War that agrarian reform was a Third World nation's best defense against revolution. However, the fact remains that the most far-reaching land reforms in the past century were implemented by revolutionary regimes in China, Vietnam, Mexico, Bolivia, Cuba, and Nicaragua, rather than by democratic governments. Military regimes redistributed significant amounts of land in Peru and Egypt. Authoritarian governments under pressure from the United States implemented South Korea's and Taiwan's reforms. By contrast, in democratic countries such as Brazil, India, and, more recently, the Philippines, landlords have been so powerful as a lobbying group and pillar of major political parties that they have blocked substantial reforms from becoming law.

Institutions such as the U.N.'s Food and Agricultural Organization (FAO) continue to support agrarian reform in the LDCs and to push for its expansion. Arguing that current agricultural policies stress increased production to the exclusion of other important needs, such as improving the living standard of the rural poor and sustaining the environment, FAO endorses agrarian reform as a key component of those objectives. As they noted at a 2006 conference on agrarian reform and rural development:

> While globalization, industrialization, and (often subsidized) commercial agriculture are creating wealth for some, they are also dramatically increasing the socio-economic disparities within and between countries, further exacerbating land concentration . . . Investment has tended to favor the development of the industrial, urban and service and often military sectors, at the expense of agriculture and rural development.[70]

Countries such as Brazil, the Philippines, and Burkina Faso have recently worked with FAO on modest agrarian reform programs. Still, with the threat of communist revolution no longer facing most developing nations, the prospect of major land redistribution in the Third World currently seems remote. But if the LDCs are to prevent unmanageable rural-to-urban migration and potential rural violence, their governments will have to find other ways to improve the lives of the rural poor.

DISCUSSION QUESTIONS

1. Many analysts have described Third World peasants as conservative or apolitical, yet they have been major players in revolutionary movements. How can those two images be reconciled?
2. What major arguments have been raised for and against agrarian reform programs in the developing world?
3. Describe the different types of agrarian reform programs that have been introduced. Briefly discuss some of the advantages and disadvantages of each type of reform.
4. What are the reasons why major agrarian reform programs are unlikely in the near future?
5. How have government crop-pricing policies often disadvantaged the rural producer and inhibited production?
6. Although Third World agrarian reform programs have fallen out of favor in contemporary government policies, there are those who still argue for their value. What are some current arguments for restarting agrarian reform in the developing world?

NOTES

1. All of the statistics in this and the following paragraph come from United Nations Population Division, *World Urbanization Prospects: The 2005 Revision Population Database*, http://esa.un.org/unup/. As of 2005, the figure was 57 percent and is now probably about 55 percent.

2. Scholarly estimates of rural poverty levels are imprecise and vary from study to study. They are basically educated estimates than can serve as guideposts.

3. Figures are extrapolated (i.e., updated) from earlier data in M. Riad El-Ghonemy, *The Political Economy of Rural Poverty* (London: Routledge and Kegan Paul, 1990), 302–303, and 17–19.

4. Mahmood Hasan Khan, *Rural Poverty in Developing Countries: Implications for Public Policy* (Washington, DC: IMF Economic Issues, no. 26, 2001).

5. Alain de Janvry, *The Agrarian Question and Reformism in Latin America* (Baltimore, MD: Johns Hopkins University Press, 1981), 7–60.

6. The terms *agrarian reform* and *land reform* are often used interchangeably. Technically, *land*

reform refers only to the redistribution of land to needy peasants or laborers. *Agrarian reform* is a broader process, which encompasses financial and technical aid, infrastructure, and the like that are normally needed to go with land redistribution if it is to be effective.

7. George Foster, "Introduction: What Is a Peasant?" in *Peasant Society*, eds. Jack Potter, George Foster, and May Diaz (Boston: Little, Brown, 1967); Teodor Shanin, "The Nature and Logic of the Peasant Economy," *Journal of Peasant Studies*, vol. 1, no. 1–2 (1974).

8. Eric R. Wolf, *Peasants* (Upper Saddle River, NJ: Prentice Hall, 1966), 10.

9. Roy L. Prosterman and Jeffrey M. Riedinger, *Land Reform and Democratic Development* (Baltimore, MD: Johns Hopkins University Press, 1987), 41. Undoubtedly, those figures have changed in the last twenty years (in both directions), but they are still useful for cross-national comparisons.

10. Karl Marx, *Capital*. Quoted in Teodor Shanin, "Peasantry as a Political Factor," *Sociological Review*, vol. 14 (March 1966) 6. See also, Marx,

The Eighteenth Brumaire of Louis Bonaparte (New York: International Publishers, 1964).

11. Robert Redfield, *Peasant Society and Culture: An Anthropological Approach* (Chicago: University of Chicago Press, 1965), 77.

12. See, for example, George M. Foster, "Peasant Society and the Image of the Limited Good," *American Anthropologist*, vol. 67 (April 1965), 293–315.

13. Phyllis Arora, "Patterns of Political Response in Indian Peasant Society," *Western Political Quarterly*, vol. 20 (September 1967), 654.

14. See, for example, *New York Times*, July 4, 1993.

15. Ronald J. Herring and Charles R. Kennedy Jr., "The Political Economy of Farm Mechanization Policy: Tractors in Pakistan," in *Food, Politics and Agricultural Development: Case Studies in the Public Policy of Rural Modernization*, eds. Raymond F. Hopkins, Donald J. Pachula, and Ross B. Talbot (Boulder, CO: Westview Press, 1979), 193–226.

16. James C. Scott, *Weapons of the Week: Everyday Forms of Peasant Resistance* (New Haven, CT: Yale University Press, 1986).

17. One of the most insightful books on the role of the peasantry in twentieth-century revolutions is Eric R. Wolf, *Peasant Wars of the Twentieth Century* (New York: Harper & Row, 1969).

18. James C. Scott, *The Moral Economy of the Peasant: Rebellion and Subsistence in Southeast Asia* (New Haven, CT: Yale University Press, 1976); James C. Scott and Benedict J. Kirkvliet, *How Traditional Rural Patrons Lose Their Legitimacy* (Madison: University of Wisconsin, Land Tenure Center, 1975).

19. Wolf, *Peasant Wars*.

20. Samuel P. Huntington, *Political Order in Changing Societies* (New Haven, CT: Yale University Press, 1968), 375.

21. Ibid.

22. Hectares, rather than acres, are the standard measurement of farmland area in most of the world. One hectare is equivalent to 2.47 acres; Anthony L. Hall, "Land Tenure and Land Reform in Brazil," in *Agrarian Reform and Grassroots Development*, eds. Roy L. Prosterman, Mary N. Temple, and Timothy M. Hanstad (Boulder, CO: Lynne Rienner Publishers, 1990), 206.

23. Carrie A. Meyer, *Land Reform in Latin America: The Dominican Case* (New York: Praeger, 1989), 38.

24. Rupert W. Scofield, "Land Reform in Central America," in *Agrarian Reform and Grassroots Development*, 154–155.

25. D. P. Chaudhri, "New Technologies and Income Distribution in Agriculture," in *Peasants, Landlords and Governments: Agrarian Reform in the Third World*, ed. David Lehmann (New York: Holmes and Meier, 1974), 173; Howard Handelman, "Introduction," in *The Politics of Agrarian Change in Asia and Latin America*, ed. Howard Handelman (Bloomington: Indiana University Press, 1981), 4.

26. F. Tomasson Jannuzi and James T. Peach, "Bangladesh: A Strategy for Agrarian Reform," and Jeffrey Riedinger, "Philippine Land Reform in the 1980s," in *Agrarian Reform and Grassroots Development*, 84, 91.

27. Henry Shue, *Basic Human Rights: Subsistence, Affluence, and U.S. Foreign Policy* (Princeton, NJ: Princeton University Press, 1980). For a discussion of the moral issues, see Joseph S. Nye Jr., "Ethical Dimensions of International Involvement in Land Reform," in *International Dimensions of Land Reform*, ed. John D. Montgomery (Boulder, CO: Westview Press, 1984), 7–29.

28. Keith Griffin, *Land Concentration and Rural Poverty*, 2nd ed. (London: Macmillan, 1981), 10.

29. Huntington, *Political Order*, 375.

30. Bruce M. Russet, "Inequality and Instability: The Relation of Land Tenure to Politics," *World Politics*, vol. 16 (April 1964), 442–454; Prosterman and Riedinger, *Land Reform*, 24.

31. William Thiesenhusen, "Introduction," in *Searching for Agrarian Reform in Latin America*, ed. William Thiesenhusen (Boston: Unwin Hyman, 1989), 18.

32. Ibid., 16–20; Peter Dorner, *Latin American Land Reforms in Theory and Practice* (Madison: University of Wisconsin Press, 1992), 21–29; R. Albert Berry, "Land Reform and the Adequacy of World Food Production," in *International Dimensions*, 63–87.

33. Riedinger, "Philippine Land Reform," 19.

34. Dorner, *Latin American Land Reforms*, 23–25; Berry, "Land Reform," 72; Michael R. Carter and Jon Jonakin, *The Economic Case for Land Reform: An Assessment of 'Farm Size/Productivity' Relations and Its Impact on Policy* (Madison: University of Wisconsin, Department of Agricultural Economics, 1989), quoted in Dorner, *Latin American Land Reforms*.

35. James Grant, "Development: The End of Trickle Down," *Foreign Policy*, vol. 12 (Fall 1973), 43–65.

36. Bruce F. Johnston and John W. Mellor, "The Role of Agriculture in Economic Development," *American Economic Review*, vol. 51 (September 1961), 566–593.

37. Dorner, *Latin American Land Reforms*, 29–31.

38. Ronald P. Dore, *Land Reform in Japan* (London: Oxford University Press, 1959); Mikiso Hande, *Modern Japan* (Boulder, CO: Westview Press, 1986), 347–348.

39. Shirley W. Y. Kuo, Gustav Ranis, and John C. H. Fei, *The Taiwan Success Story: Rapid Growth with Improved Distribution in the Republic of China, 1952–1979* (Boulder, CO: Westview Press, 1981); Gregory Henderson, *Korea: Politics of the Vortex* (Cambridge, MA: Harvard University Press, 1968).

40. Dore, *Land Reform in Japan*, 147–148.

41. John W. Bruce and Paula Harrell, "Land Reform in the People's Republic of China: 1978–1988," *Land Tenure Center Research Paper No. 100* (University of Wisconsin-Madison, 1989), 3–4; Vivienne Shue, *Peasant China in Transition— The Dynamics of Development Toward Socialism, 1949–56* (Berkeley: University of California Press, 1980).

42. Thiesenhusen, *Searching for Agrarian Reform*, 10–11.

43. Wolf, *Peasant Wars*.

44. Harry Harding, *China's Second Revolution* (Washington, DC: Brookings Institution, 1987), 12; Suzanne Ogden, *China's Unresolved Issues* (Englewood Cliffs, NJ: Prentice Hall, 1989), 46–50; Nicholas Lardy, *Agriculture in China's Modern Economic Development* (Cambridge, England: Cambridge University Press, 1983). Amartya Sen, a Nobel Prize winner in economics, maintains that the death toll may have reached 40 million. Amazingly, not only was this kept secret from the outside world, but even Chinese citizens did not know the extent of the tragedy, particularly if they lived in cities less affected by the famine.

45. There were exceptions to this pattern, particularly outside the Third World. Poland and Yugoslavia, for example, did not collectivize agriculture during the communist era. Nicaragua and, especially, Cuba established a large collectivized sector (primarily peasant cooperatives), but allowed many smallholders to keep their land.

46. For a crop-by-crop analysis of state and private sector farm productivity in Cuba, see Nancy Forster, "Cuban Agricultural Productivity," in *Cuban Communism*, 7th ed., ed. Irving Louis Horowitz (New Brunswick, NJ: Transaction, 1989), 235–255.

47. Nicholas Lardy, "Agricultural Reforms in China," *Journal of International Affairs* (Winter 1986), 91–104. Deng announced the program in 1978, but the government did not begin implementing it until 1980.

48. Harding, *China's Second Revolution*, 106.

49. Forrest D. Colburn, *Post-Revolutionary Nicaragua: State, Class and the Dilemmas of Agrarian Policy* (Berkeley: University of California Press, 1986), and Laura J. Enríquez, *Harvesting Change: Labor and Agrarian Reform in Nicaragua* (Chapel

Hill: University of North Carolina Press, 1991), offer contrasting analyses.

50. David Lehmann, "Agrarian Reform in Chile, 1965–1972: An Essay in Contradictions," in *Peasants, Landlords and Governments*, 71–119; Marion R. Brown, "Radical Reformism in Chile: 1964–1973," in *Searching for Agrarian Reform*, 216–239.

51. Riedinger, "Philippine Land Reform," and Ronald Herring, "Explaining Anomalies in Land Reform: Lessons from South India," in *Agrarian Reform and Grassroots Development*, 15–75; K. N. Raj and Michael Tharakan, "Agrarian Reform in Kerala and Its Impact on the Rural Economy," and Ajit Kumar Ghose, "Agrarian Reform in West Bengal," in *Agrarian Reform in Contemporary Developing Countries*, ed. Ajit Kumar Ghose (New York: St. Martin's Press, 1983), 31–137.

52. Thiesenhusen, "Introduction," *Searching for Agrarian Reform*, 1–41; Meyer, *Land Reform in Latin America*, 4. Thiesenhusen and Meyer each calculate the percentage of farmland redistributed and the percentage of rural families benefiting. Although they use somewhat different time periods and Meyer analyzes a wider sample of nations, they arrive at very similar rankings.

53. de Janvry, *The Agrarian Question*.

54. Howard Handelman, "Peasants, Landlords and Bureaucrats: The Politics of Agrarian Reform in Peru," in *The Politics of Agrarian Change*, 103–125; Cristóbal Kay, "The Agrarian Reform in Peru: An Assessment," in *Agrarian Reform in Contemporary Developing Countries*, 185–239.

55. Michael Carter and Elena Alvarez, "Changing Paths: The Decollectivization of Agrarian Reform Agriculture in Coastal Peru," in *Searching for Agrarian Reform*, 156–187.

56. Agrarian reforms enacted by the Ecuadorian and Panamanian militaries were far more modest.

57. Howard Handelman, "Peasants, Landlords and Bureaucrats," 103–125; Kay, "The Agrarian Reform in Peru," 185–239.

58. Merilee S. Grindle, *Searching for Rural Development: Labor Migration and Employment in Mexico* (Ithaca, NY: Cornell University Press, 1988); Grindle, "Agrarian Reform in Mexico: A Cautionary Tale," in *Agrarian Reform and Grassroots Development*, 179–204; Steven E. Sanderson, *The Transformation of Mexican Agriculture* (Princeton, NJ: Princeton University Press, 1986); Frank Meissner, "The Mexican Food System (SAM)—A Strategy for Sowing Petroleum," and M. R. Redclift, "The Mexican Food System (SAM)—Sowing Subsidies, Reaping Apathy," *Food Policy*, vol. 6, no. 4 (November 1981), 219–235.

59. Ronald J. Herring, "Explaining Anomalies in Agrarian Reform: Lessons from South Asia," in *Agrarian Reform and Grassroots Development*, 73.

60. Thiesenhusen, "Conclusions," in *Searching for Agrarian Reform*, 483–503.

61. Prosterman and Riedinger, *Land Reform and Democratic Development*, 177–202.

62. de Janvry, *The Agrarian Question*; Merilee S. Grindle, *State and Countryside: Development Policy and Agrarian Politics in Latin America* (Baltimore, MD: Johns Hopkins University Press, 1986).

63. Charles Harvey, ed. *Agricultural Pricing Policy in Africa* (London: Macmillan, 1988), 2.

64. Robert H. Bates, *Markets and States in Tropical Africa: The Political Basis of Agricultural Policy* (Berkeley: University of California Press, 1981), 29; see also Michael J. Lofchie, *The Policy Factor: Agricultural Performance in Kenya and Tanzania* (Boulder, CO: Lynne Rienner Publishers, 1989), 57–59.

65. Marvin G. Weinbaum, *Food, Development, and Politics in the Middle East* (Boulder, CO: Westview Press, 1982), 61.

66. Michael F. Lofchie, "Africa's Agricultural Crisis: An Overview," and Robert H. Bates, "The Regulation of Rural Markets in Africa," in *Africa's Agrarian Crisis: The Roots of Famine*, eds. Stephen K. Commins, Michael F. Lofchie, and Rhys Payne (Boulder, CO: Lynne Rienner Publishers, 1986), 3–19, 37–54.

67. Neoliberalism rejects much of the state intervention in the economy that was prevalent in many developing economies and instead favors free-market mechanisms. For a more extensive discussion of these issues, see Chapter 10.

68. de Janvry, *The Agrarian Question*; David Goodman and Michael Redclift, *From Peasant to Proletarian: Capitalist Development and Agricultural Transitions* (Oxford, England: Basil Blackwell, 1981).

69. This is most impressively demonstrated in Nola Reinhardt, *Our Daily Bread: The Peasant Question and Family Farming in the Colombian Andes* (Berkeley: University of California Press, 1988). See also Lesley Gill, *Peasants, Entrepreneurs and Social Change: Frontier Development in Lowland Bolivia* (Boulder, CO: Westview Press, 1987).

70. F72 and Rural Development, (March 7–10, 2006), "FAO's Contribution to Good Policies and Practices in Agrarian Reform and Rural Development: A Brief Overview," p. 3, http://www.fao.org/participation/bibdb/retrieval/det_scr.asp?unid=5800&langsel=en.

CHAPTER 7

RAPID URBANIZATION AND THE POLITICS OF THE URBAN POOR

Each day, in the villages of Bangladesh, China, Kenya, Egypt, and Bolivia, thousands of young men and women pack up their meager belongings and board buses, trucks, or trains for the long trip to Dhaka, Shanghai, Nairobi, Cairo, or La Paz. Often they travel alone, sometimes with family or friends. They are a part of one of the largest and most dramatic tides of human migration in world history. In China alone, some 300 million rural villagers are likely to migrate to urban centers over the next two to three decades. Despairing of any hope for a better life in the countryside and seeking new opportunities for themselves and their children, millions of villagers leave the world they have known for the uncertainties of the city. In Africa, refugees fleeing civil wars and famine have augmented these legions of migrants. In the aftermath of Rwanda's ethnic genocide, the country's urban population grew by an astounding 11.6 percent *annually* from 2000 to 2005. By 2030, the proportion of that county's population living in cities will have climbed from only 18.3 percent (in 2003) to 58.5 percent.[1]

Most migrants maintain close links with their rural roots long after they have left the countryside. Some come intending to accumulate savings and eventually return to their villages. "Others alternate between city and country in a permanent pendular pattern."[2] Indeed, in many parts of West Africa and Southeast Asia, more than half the urban migrants are temporary, including those who repeatedly circulate between village and city.[3] In China, where until recently government restrictions made it very difficult to migrate, most new migrants live in a bureaucratic limbo without assurance of permanence. Known as China's "floating population," these relatively temporary migrants number 100 million people or more. Some stay permanently, though most do not. Although not officially counted as part of the urban population (because their residency documents officially restrict their residence to their home villages), they actually account for about one-fifth of China's city residents at any given time.[4] In contrast, Latin America's cityward migrants tend to settle permanently. Whatever their initial aspirations, they continue to crowd the urban slums and shantytowns they have come to call home.

Swelled by both internal (natural) population growth and the influx of migrants in recent decades, many Third World cities have mushroomed in size and will continue to grow rapidly in the coming years (see Tables 7.1 through 7.3). The magnitude of that expansion has placed tremendous strains on public services, housing, public health, and personal safety in these large cities. In Latin America, the *rate* of growth (in percentage terms) was most rapid in the middle of

TABLE 7.1   Percentage of the World's Population in Urban Areas by Region, 2003–2030

Region	Percentage Urban 1980	Percentage Urban 2005	Projected Percentage Urban 2030	Annual Rate of Urban Growth (Percent)	
				1950–2005	*2005–2030*
Developed Regions[a]	69	75	82	1.17[b]	0.16[b]
Third World[c]	30	43	57	—	—
Africa	28	40	54	4.29	3.04
Asia	26	40	55	3.44	2.12
Latin America and the Caribbean	65	78	85	3.31	1.35

[a]Europe, North America, Australia, New Zealand, and Japan.

[b]Europe only.

[c]Africa, Asia (except Japan), and Latin America.

Source: United Nations Population Information Network, *World Population Prospects* (2003 and 2005), http://esa.un.org/unpp/.

the twentieth century. Thus, in just a single decade (1950–1960), the populations of Bogotá (Colombia) and Caracas (Venezuela) doubled, while Lima (Peru) nearly tripled. Since the 1970s, the rate of growth in the region's largest metropolises has slowed, but in absolute terms, there is still considerable migration to both primary and secondary cities. African cities, though starting from a smaller base, expanded at an even faster pace. Between 1960 and 1983, Kinshasa (Congo) grew by nearly 600 percent and Abidjan (Côte d'Ivoire) by more than 800 percent.[5] Today, a number of cities in the LDCs continue to double their populations in two decades or less (Table 7.3).

TABLE 7.2   Percentage of the Population in Urban Areas by Country, 1975–2015

Country	Percentage Urban 1975	Percentage Urban 2004	Percentage Urban 2015 (estimate)
Egypt	44	43	45
Ethiopia	10	16	19
Nigeria	23	47	56
China	17	40	49
Indonesia	19	47	59
Brazil	62	84	88
Chile	78	87	90
Dominican Republic	46	66	74

Source: United Nations Development Programme, *Human Development Report, 2006,* "Urban Population," http://hdr.undp.org/hdr2006/statistics/indicators/41.html.

TABLE 7.3   Populations of Third World Metropolitan Areas, 1995–2015

City	Population	
	1995	*2015 (estimate)*
Mexico City	16,562,000	19,180,000
Tegucigalpa	995,000	2,016,000
Santiago	4,891,000	6,066,000
Cairo	9,690,000	16,530,000
Casablanca	3,101,000	4,835,000
Addis Ababa	2,431,000	6,578,000
Lagos	10,287,000	24,640,000
Bangkok	6,547,000	9,844,000
Dhaka	8,545,000	19,486,000

Source: United Nations Development Programme, *Human Development Report, 1998* (New York: Oxford University Press, 1998), 174–175.

In 1970, Third World cities contained 675 million people. That figure nearly tripled to 1.9 billion by the year 2000 and is expected to reach some 4 billion in 2025.[6] A recent U.N. study projects that the *world* population of towns *and* cities will surpass the rural population for the first time in 2008 and will increase from 3.3 billion people in that year to 5 billion by 2030.[7] There is some debate among demographers as to what proportion of the growth to this point has been caused by natural increases and what percentage has been the product of rural-to-urban migration. The evidence indicates that about half the urban population explosion has come from each of those two sources, with a higher proportion attributable to migration in Africa and a greater percentage to natural increases in Asia.[8] As a consequence, the developing nations, not long ago predominantly rural, will soon be half urban and will be nearly 60 percent urban by 2030 (see Table 7.1).

Latin America and the Caribbean are by far the most urbanized areas in the developing world (Table 7.1). In 2005, the portion of their total population living in cities (78 percent) was slightly larger than in the world's more developed nations (Europe, North America, Oceana, and Japan). Today, Mexico City, with some 19 million people, is already the world's second largest metropolitan area. Sao Paulo, Brazil (4th largest), and Buenos Aires, Argentina (8th), are not far behind.[9] To be sure, poor Central American countries such as Honduras are still less than half urban, but more than 87 percent of Chile's national population now live in cities (Table 7.2).

With city dwellers now accounting for only about 40 percent of their populations, Africa and Asia (Table 7.1, column 2) are considerably less urban than Latin America. At the same time, however, their cities have been growing far more rapidly since 1950, especially Africa's (last two columns). In 1960, Casablanca (Morocco) and Cairo (Egypt) were the only African cities with populations greater than 1 million. Twenty-three years later, nine cities in the region exceeded that size.[10] As Table 7.3 indicates, in many Sub-Saharan African metropolises—such as Addis Ababa (Ethiopia) and Lagos (Nigeria)—populations continue to explode. Indeed, Lagos is expected to have a population of nearly 25 million by 2015, making it one of the world's largest mega-city. In all, between 1950 and 2005, African cities grew at an average annual rate of 4.29 percent (Table 7.1), while Latin America—its most rapid rural-to-urban migration behind it—will see its annual urban growth rate fall from 3.31 percent (in the period 1950–2005) to only 1.35 percent in the coming 25 years or so. Within each region, the proportion of people residing in cities varies considerably from country to country (Table 7.2). At one end of the spectrum, Ethiopia remained only 16 percent urban in 2004. However, North African countries had much larger urban populations, including more than 40 percent of Egypt's national total. Moreover, some Sub-Saharan nations, including Nigeria, already have substantial urban populations as well.

Most of Asia's largest countries—including Bangladesh, India, Pakistan, and Thailand—are still at least two-thirds rural (China is close to that figure). Yet huge metropolitan areas such as Jakarta (Indonesia), Karachi (Pakistan), New Delhi, Mumbai—formerly Bombay—and Calcutta (the last three in India) now have populations exceeding 10 million. During the second half of the twentieth century, most of these urban giants leapfrogged past Paris, London, and Chicago. While the nation of Bangladesh is currently only about 20 to 25 percent urban, the population of its mega-city, Dhaka, will have more than doubled between 1995 and 2015, reaching nearly 20 million people in the coming decade (Table 7.3).

THE POLITICAL CONSEQUENCES OF URBAN GROWTH

In fact, the Third World's enormous *rate* of urban growth since the middle of the twentieth century is not without precedent. According to one estimate, the proportion of the LDCs' total population living in cities grew from 16.7 percent in 1950 to 28.0 percent in 1975 (and 42 percent in 2003). But, from 1875 to 1900, the West's urban population increased from 17.2 to 26.1 percent, a percentage change of similar magnitude.[11] What makes the current urban explosion unique, however, is the sheer volume of people involved. The *total* population of the developing world is much larger today than that of nineteenth-century Europe and North America. Thus, it is one thing for a nineteenth-century European city to grow from 80,000 to 400,000 people in a 25-year period. It is quite another for Seoul (South Korea) to mushroom from 1 million to nearly 7 million, for Kinshasa (Congo) to spiral from 400,000 to more than 2.5 million, or Lagos from 10 million to more than 25 million in the same number of years. Massive population shifts such as these obviously pose especially daunting challenges to urban housing, sanitation, education, and transportation needs.

This chapter examines two important aspects of urban politics in the developing world. First, it looks at the problems that exploding urban populations present to political leaders and government planners. Specifically, it asks how poor countries can provide city dwellers with needed jobs, housing, sanitation, and other services, while also protecting them from crime. What is the government's role in those areas, and how do state policies interact with private sector activities and self-help efforts? Second, we examine the political attitudes and behavior of city dwellers in the LDCs, focusing particularly on the politics of the urban poor. To what extent do the inhabitants of urban shantytowns and slums have political orientations that are distinct from both those of the rural poor and those of the urban middle and upper classes? Is rapid urbanization likely to contribute to political development, or does it carry the seeds of political instability?

THE STRUGGLE FOR EMPLOYMENT

Contemporary Third World urbanization differs from the West's earlier experience not only in its magnitude but also in its economic context. The nineteenth-century urban revolution in Europe and North America occurred at the dawn of an era of unprecedented industrialization and economic growth. Modern capitalism was coming of age and could accommodate, indeed needed, the wave of migrant and immigrant laborers. By contrast, the economies of most contemporary LDCs have failed to provide sufficient employment to their growing urban work force.

To be sure, many people do find jobs, and some low-income workers achieve impressive upward mobility. For example, one study of Howrah, an industrial city in West Bengal, found that "several hundred men who started with almost nothing now own factories large enough to employ twenty-five [or more] workers," placing them "among the richest people in the community."[12] We can find similar examples in much of the developing world. Still, these are exceptional cases. Many others have achieved success that is more limited. For most of the urban poor, however, economic survival remains an ongoing struggle. Even during Mexico's economic boom in the 1960s and 1970s, the country's expanding modern sector was able to provide regular employment for only about half the people seeking to enter the urban work force. The debt crisis and severe recession that gripped Africa and Latin America during the 1980s and parts of Asia in the late 1990s exacerbated the problem, as industrial employment in many countries plummeted. Hyperinflation in many Sub-Saharan African countries has meant that even most regularly employed people do not have salaries or wages high enough to support their families.

Most of those unable to find work in the formal sector of the urban economy (factories, the civil service, modern commercial enterprises) and those whose formal-sector paychecks cannot feed or house their families have turned to the informal economy for employment. As noted in Chapter 5, that sector is defined as the part of the economy that is "unregulated by the institutions of society [most notably the state], in a legal and social environment in which similar activities are regulated" and taxed.[13] A large proportion of the workers in the informal economy are self-employed in occupations ranging from garbage recyclers to shoeshine boys, street vendors, mechanics, electricians, plumbers, and drivers of unlicensed taxis.

Of course, informal sector activity is not limited to the developing world. In recent years, cities such as New York, Los Angeles, and Milan have seen substantial expansion in the number of unlicensed street vendors, underground sweatshops, and other illegal or unlicensed activities. In the Third World, however, the informal economy represents a far greater proportion of total urban employment. During the 1970s, for example, it constituted some 35 percent of the urban work force in Malaysia; 44 percent in Nairobi

(Kenya); 45 percent in Jakarta; and 60 percent in urban Peru.[14] In many countries, those percentages rose significantly because of the economic crises of the 1980s and late 1990s.

In the vast garbage dumps of Cairo, hordes of entrepreneurs sift through the refuse looking to recycle marketable waste. At night, on the streets of Rio de Janeiro and Nairobi thousands of prostitutes search for customers. On the commercial boulevards of Manila (Philippines) and Mexico City, an army of street vendors sells food, household appliances, and bootleg DVDs. In Lagos and Lahore (Pakistan), shoemakers and carpenters, working out of their homes, sell their wares to appreciative clients. All belong to the informal economy. While outside observers once assumed that people working in this sector were particularly impoverished, we now know that their earning power varies greatly and that some have higher incomes than the average factory worker.[15] To cite one admittedly atypical example, during Nicaragua's runaway inflation in the 1980s, street vendors selling Coca-Cola made more in a few hours than government white-collar employees earned in a week. A more representative study of Montevideo (Uruguay) found that laborers in the formal and informal sectors had comparable incomes.[16]

Social scientists have extensively debated the informal economy's merits and faults. Critics point out that its workers are not protected by minimum wage laws and lack access to government health and welfare programs. Proponents respond that the informal economy not only employs vast numbers of people who would otherwise have nothing, but also contributes a substantial proportion of the Third World's consumer goods and services. In a book that has been very influential in Latin American political circles, Peruvian author Hernando de Soto argues that Third World governments should cease trying to regulate and license the informal sector and instead allow it to flourish and expand.[17]

While the informal sector represents concrete small-scale efforts by the poor (and the "not so poor") to create employment, the government's involvement in the job market has usually been more indirect. Only in communist countries such as China and Cuba is the state a primary urban employer. Because they consider employment to be a fundamental worker's right, until recently many communist governments created as many jobs as necessary to achieve full, or nearly full, employment, no matter how economically inefficient many of these jobs might be. Often they also restricted migration, prohibiting people from moving into cities unless they already had employment lined up (though these regulations have been ineffective in China as of late). Governments in capitalist LDCs, on the other hand, reject the role of "employer of last resort" and do not limit urban migration. They may occasionally institute public works projects specifically designed to create employment, but such efforts are normally quite limited.

Instead, nonsocialist, Third World governments primarily influence urban employment indirectly through their broader national macroeconomic policies.[18] Ideally, wise government policies should stimulate economic growth and generate new jobs. Two areas of economic policy particularly influence job creation: industrialization strategy and the containment of inflation. Differences in government industrialization policies led to very different employment outcomes in Latin America and East Asia.

Starting as early as the 1930s and 1940s, some Latin American governments began stimulating economic development through import-substituting industrialization (ISI).[19] The governments of Argentina, Brazil, and Mexico, for example, created tariff walls against competing imports and offered fiscal stimuli to nourish local industries that produced consumer goods for the domestic market. Items such as clothing, appliances, and even automobiles, which had previously been imported, were largely manufactured locally instead. One of ISI's many goals was to create industrial employment for the urban working class. Consequently, from the 1940s into the 1970s, labor unions and industrialists, despite their differences on a host of other issues, united behind state policies supporting ISI.

ISI created many comparatively well-paid blue-collar jobs, but their numbers remained rather small relative to the vast army of unskilled laborers. Domestic markets simply were not large enough to generate a sufficient number of industrial jobs, and the region's highly protected industries, facing little external competition, had few economic incentives to improve product quality or manufacturing efficiency. Therefore, their products were unable to compete in the international market and exports lagged. By the late 1970s, Latin America's industrial economies began to stagnate (see Chapter 10).

In contrast, East Asian governments in Hong Kong, Singapore, South Korea, Taiwan, Thailand, and Malaysia, which had first stimulated industrialization through import-substituting policies, soon lowered or removed protective tariffs, forcing domestic manufacturers to compete with foreign imports. That competition forced firms to produce goods whose quality and price made them competitive, not only at home but also in the export market. Though the East Asian export-led model was initially based on the exploitation of a poorly paid work force, in many of the region's countries (including South Korea, Taiwan, and Singapore) labor-intensive industries eventually generated so large a demand for labor that they drove up local wage scales. More recently, Latin American countries such as Brazil, Chile, Colombia, and Mexico have sought to emulate East Asia's export-led model, with some success.[20] But, while these countries have increased their industrial exports considerably in the past 20 years, job creation has still lagged behind because Latin American export industries tend to be more capital-intensive and less labor-intensive.

Beginning in the early 1980s, many LDCs faced the dual problems of rampant inflation and stagnant economic growth. Because solutions to each of those problems often conflicted, at least in the short run, governments had to decide which challenge to tackle first and how to confront it. Encouraged or pressured by the International Monetary Fund (IMF), the World Bank, and private lenders, many heavily indebted African and Latin American countries first adopted macroeconomic policies designed to slash inflation rates. To do so, they reduced (or tried to reduce) large budgetary and trade deficits by slashing government spending and public sector employment, devaluing the national currency, and privatizing state enterprises (selling them to private investors). In the late 1990s, East and Southeast Asian governments had to devalue their currencies as well.

Although stabilization and adjustment policies such as these may be beneficial in the long run (actually their record is somewhat mixed), they always drive unemployment up sharply in the short run. Moreover, while austerity programs

in countries such as Argentina, Ghana, Morocco, and Peru have curtailed inflation, they generally have been slow or unable to reinvigorate employment. In the
1990s, government economic adjustment policies in Thailand, Indonesia, and
Malaysia caused substantial unemployment and declining living standards.

Government policy also affects the urban employment market in yet
another important way—expanding or contracting state bureaucracies and semi-
autonomous, state-owned enterprises known as *parastatals*. Throughout Africa,
government bureaucracies and parastatals have traditionally employed far more
people than they needed. Ten people often do the work of six. They have been
overstaffed for two important political reasons: they provide work for potentially
volatile white- and blue-collar workers unable to find jobs in the weak private
sector, and they are a source of patronage for government or political party supporters. For example, at the start of the 1990s, some 40 percent of all government
employees in Sierra Leone were "ghosts," employees on the government payroll
who never showed up for work. The government's inclination to hire an excessive
number of bureaucrats, pervasive throughout the Third World, primarily benefits
the urban middle class rather than the poor, who lack the necessary education
for these positions. However, parastatals (including agricultural marketing
operations, electric power plants, telephone companies, railroads, and other state
business enterprises) employ both blue- and white-collar workers, thereby benefiting working-class and middle-class constituencies.

In recent decades, the IMF and other international lenders have induced
debt-ridden African governments to pare their payrolls substantially. As a
result, in countries such as Ghana and Uganda, the government fired thousands of ghost employees.[21] Austerity measures in Latin America also have
required sharp cuts in government employment. In addition, the government
sold many parastatals to private investors, who had no incentives to maintain
unneeded workers. Following the sale of Mexico's state steel industry, for
example, the new private owners laid off more than half the work force.[22]

Thus, at least for the near future, the shrinking state sector will offer little
relief for the growing number of urban job seekers. For decades, the expansion
of labor-intensive industries in the private sector provided substantial private
sector employment in East and Southeast Asia. However, the region's 1997 economic crisis led to widespread plant closings. In recent years, Asian economies
have recovered. On the other hand, manufacturing in Latin America has often
been more capital-intensive, generating fewer jobs. In Africa, where most
economies performed rather poorly for decades (though many have been growing nicely in recent years) and the size of the industrial sector has remained
quite limited, the informal sector will continue providing a substantial proportion of urban employment.

THE STRUGGLE FOR HOUSING AMONG THE URBAN POOR

Of all the problems facing the urban poor, particularly the wave of new migrants,
none is more serious than finding adequate housing. With many metropolitan
areas doubling in size every 10–25 years, private-sector housing cannot possibly
expand fast enough to meet the need. Moreover, most of the new homes and
apartment houses built for private sale or rental are built for the middle and

upper classes, because low-income housing is not profitable enough to attract significant investment. At the same time, while many Third World governments have invested in public housing, little of that reaches the poor either. Therefore, lacking adequate options in the private or state sectors, a lot of the urban poor live in squatter settlements and other forms of "self-help" (occupant-built) housing, collectively called "spontaneous shelter."[23] Many others crowd into existing urban slums (decaying tenements). The poorest city dwellers, lacking even the resources to rent or build, are often homeless, residing in doorways, unused construction material, or the like. In Cairo, several hundred thousand people, with nowhere else to go, live amidst cemetery tombs.[24]

In all, the total number of slum dwellers (either living in squatter settlements or dilapidated older housing) and homeless persons account for close to half the population of Third World cities. UN data from earlier in the decade indicate that about 30 percent of the urban population in North Africa, Latin America, and the Caribbean live in slum (sub-standard) housing. That number rises to 57 percent in South Asia (including Bangladesh, India, Iran, and Pakistan) and 72 percent in Sub-Saharan Africa. Looking at individual nations, about 40 percent of the urban population live in slums in Brazil, Egypt, and Turkey. In urban India the proportion of slum dwellers is about 55 percent. About 70–80 percent of urban residents live in slums in Kenya, Pakistan, and Nigeria, while that figure jumps to 86 percent in Haiti and 98 percent in Afghanistan.[25] Millions of the Third World's urban residents have no direct access to clean water or sanitation facilities.

Today, the availability of basic urban services in low-income neighborhoods varies considerably from region to region. For example, a recent study of eight low-income neighborhoods in Latin America—in Rio de Janeiro and Aracajo (Brazil) as well as Santiago and Temuco (Chile)—found that nearly all of the inhabitants had running water and electricity. On the other hand, a parallel study of eight poor, African neighborhoods—in the cities of Abidjan and Man (both in Côte d'Ivoire) and Nairobi and Kisumu (Kenya)—revealed that almost all the residents had to buy their drinking water in cans (a minority had nearby wells, while virtually no families had tap water in their homes). Similarly, very few homes in any of the eight African neighborhoods had electricity, which was either unavailable or too expensive.[26] In light of these glaring needs, developing nations frequently have sought appropriate state responses.

Public Housing and the Role of the State

Throughout the developing world, many governments have constructed public housing to alleviate housing shortages. In China, workers in state enterprises are assigned apartments linked to their employment. Cuba's revolutionary regime has built large apartment blocks housing 25,000 to 40,000 persons on the outskirts of its largest cities.[27] During Venezuela's petroleum boom, the government constructed as many as 34,000 urban housing units annually.[28] In the 1960s and 1970s, various African governments established housing agencies with far more limited resources. One of the continent's most ambitious programs was in the Côte d'Ivoire, where some 40,000 units were constructed during the 1970s, almost all in the capital city of Abidjan. By the close of that decade, the Kenyan government was building more than 3,000 units annually.[29]

In time, however, it has become clear that public housing cannot provide sufficient shelter for the poor, and, in some cases, it actually worsens their plight. In the capital cities of India, Senegal, and Nigeria, for example, many government housing projects were designed to eradicate urban blight. Prior to their construction, "unsightly," low-income housing had been demolished, so that the city could become more aesthetically pleasing to the political elite, urban planners, middle-class residents, and foreign tourists. However, rarely did the poor families who had been evicted from their homes subsequently secure residence in the newly constructed public housing projects built in their place. Even those who received alternate housing were usually relocated on the edges of town, far removed from their workplace. Diana Patel describes how Zimbabwe's government periodically ousted the same squatters from their settlements in different parts of the nation's capital, in effect "chasing them around town." Many government planners, viewing these shacks through middle-class lenses, believed that unless the squatters could afford "decent" urban housing with plumbing and multiple rooms for their families, they would be better off returning to the countryside.[30]

In fact, most of the new public housing projects do not help the needy. In order for the government to recoup its construction costs, it must sell or rent the new housing units at higher rates than the urban poor can afford. Consequently, the state faces two options: it can subsidize rents and mortgages to bring their cost down to a level that the poor can afford, or it can rent or sell the dwellings to those who can better afford them, namely the middle class.

Despite its obvious potential as a welfare benefit for the poor, subsidized housing has several drawbacks. First, it is simply too costly for most developing nations to sustain even if they would like to do so. For example, following the Cuban revolution, the government committed itself to various programs designed to serve workers and the poor—including public health, education, and housing. "Early housing policies reflected Fidel Castro's belief that nothing was too good for the working class."[31] Housing projects such as Santiago's José Martí provided schools, day-care centers, theaters, clinics, and stores for its 40,000 inhabitants. However, by lavishing excessively "luxurious" housing on early recipients, the government soon ran out of funds for the many others needing shelter. Thus, the East Havana project, planned for 100,000 dwelling units, ultimately contained only 1,500. Even though the state lacked the resources to meet the country's housing needs, it discouraged or prohibited private and self-help housing (i.e., units built by the owner) until recently.[32] Not surprisingly, Cuba, like most Marxist regimes, has suffered chronic housing shortages.[33]

Second, in many LDCs subsidized housing has become a political plum, with allocations based on the applicants' activism on behalf of the government or ruling party, rather than their need. Because political patronage plays such an important role, police officers, government bureaucrats, teachers, and activists in the ruling party are the first served.[34] Consequently, residents in state housing are generally middle class (or lower middle class). They not only can better afford the rents, which reduces the extent of government housing subsidies, but they also have the political influence to acquire this valuable resource.

Singapore and Hong Kong are among the very few cities that have constructed extensive low-income public housing. However, they are very atypical in two respects. First, because they are unusually densely populated and have very little unused land on which to expand, high-rise projects are the only possible means of housing large numbers of people. Second, the two cities are among the Third World's most affluent and, hence, can afford the cost of extensive subsidized housing. With the exception of the oil-rich Gulf States, other developing nations lack the budgetary resources to make a serious dent in their housing shortage. Consequently, most analysts feel that limited state funds would be more effective helping a larger number of beneficiaries in a less costly way. Macroeconomic policy changes have also lowered the scale of public housing in recent decades, as many LDCs have introduced neoliberal economic policies, which reduce the role of the state in society more broadly (see Chapter 10).

Spontaneous Housing

For years, many social scientists and urban planners have maintained that the most effective remedy for housing shortfalls in Third World cities is spontaneous (or self-help) shelter—including the very shantytowns and squatter settlements that are so frequently viewed as a blight. In cities throughout the developing world, the poor have built their own homes, sometimes with hired or volunteer assistance. While living in these dwellings, many proprietors, particularly in Africa, also rent space to tenants. In some cases, the owners are squatters, living on land that has been occupied illegally, though often with the compliance of government authorities.[35] Others, residing in so-called "pirate settlements," have purchased their lots from land speculators but lack ownership titles because their community does not conform to government zoning requirements.[36]

Spontaneous housing settlements range in size from a few isolated homes to communities of many thousands. For example, on the dried-up marshlands outside Mexico City, the municipality of Netzahualcóyotl began as a pirate settlement in the 1940s. By 1970 it housed 600,000 people.[37] An organized protest eventually persuaded the government to provide badly needed urban services and grant the squatters legal title to their homes. Elsewhere, up to 40 percent of Nairobi's population and one-fourth to one-third of the inhabitants of Jakarta, Karachi, and Lima live in squatter settlements.[38] These homes, argued John F. C. Turner, have erroneously been viewed as a problem, when, in fact, they are a major part of the solution to urban housing needs.[39] Rather than building public housing, he insisted, Third World governments can serve many more people by removing legal and political obstacles to spontaneous housing settlements and helping their residents upgrade the dwellings they have built.

Self-built homes have several important advantages over public housing.[40] First, they actually serve the poor, whereas most public housing does not. Second, they afford occupants the opportunity to upgrade their homes continuously. For example, in Lima's vast network of shantytowns, one can observe many wood and straw shacks whose owners are building brick walls around them, slowly constructing a better home as funds become available. Third, precisely because they are self-built, these homes better address the needs and desires of their owners than do units built by government planners. Finally, squatter settlements have the "churches, bars, and neighborhood stores that help create a sense of community" that is too often lacking in large, impersonal public housing projects.[41] Given these advantages, proponents of spontaneous housing argue that the state's most constructive role would be to stop evicting illegal squatters and grant them land titles and other assistance needed to improve their homes. In 2003, Brazil's reformist government announced plans to give several million urban squatters title to their homes. Proponents of the plan expect that it will give millions of families greater access to utilities, mail delivery, and credit. Many obstacles, however, including problems of competing ownership claims, remain to be ironed out.[42]

Sites-and-Services Programs

Other analysts who favored a more active role for the state viewed the Turner thesis as a convenient excuse for governments that did not wish to spend much on the poor. Championing self-help housing, charged these critics, merely perpetuated the status quo, and allowed the state to direct its limited housing resources toward the middle class.[43]

Ultimately, however, many Third World governments, the World Bank, and other foreign aid donors have pursued a middle ground between providing expensive, fully built public housing units and a laissez faire policy that leaves the government with little role to play. In countries as diverse as Colombia, India, Malawi, and Turkey, the state has sold or rented parcels of land to the poor with basic services such as running water, sewage, and electricity. Buyers then build their own homes on the sites as they do with spontaneous housing. In some cases, governments provide credit, technical assistance, or low-cost construction materials.[44]

These "sites-and-services" programs have several obvious advantages. First, they allow the government to steer self built housing to locations that are safer and more environmentally sound. By contrast, unregulated spontaneous shelters in Caracas illustrate the dangers of unzoned squatter settlements. There, more than half a million people live on precarious hillsides in shacks that are sometimes washed away during the rainy season by mudslides. Second, in contrast to many sprawling squatter communities, inhabitants of sites-and-services settlements have electricity, sanitation, and other basic services from the outset. Furthermore, although occupants must purchase their sites, the lots are far more affordable than are fully built, state housing units.

Critics of sites-and-services programs concede that the communities developed on those sites are generally healthier, safer, and more aesthetically pleasing than spontaneous shelter, but they point out that they still fail to help the very poor, who cannot afford even these lots. In addition, they charge that these programs draw away the most talented and successful residents of existing slums and shantytowns, thereby leaving the older communities bereft of leadership. Moreover, they note that governments tend to locate sites-and-services projects in remote areas of town in order to remove the poor from downtown business areas. Consequently, their inhabitants live far from their jobs and from important urban facilities.[45]

Such criticisms notwithstanding, we have seen that sites-and-services programs have some clear advantages over unaided spontaneous shelters and clearly benefit the poor more than fully built public housing does. Unfortunately, these programs often have not been self-financing (i.e., government income from the rent or sale of lots has not covered costs). Consequently, during the periodic economic crises that LDCs have faced over the years, many governments have abandoned them, once again leaving the poor to fend for themselves. Finally, in time, both sites-and-services programs and unregulated squatter settlements have faced a growing obstacle—because of increasing urban sprawl, cities have ever-diminishing space for any type of self-built housing.[46]

THE STRUGGLE AGAINST URBAN CRIME

Escalating levels of crime have been a problem in many Latin American and African urban centers, though East Asia's major cities are generally safer than cities of comparable size in the United States.[47] In cities such as Rio de Janeiro and Nairobi, large, well-armed youth gangs escalate the level of violence. For example, in Nairobi's massive Mathare slum (housing some 500,000 people), a recent war between two ethnically (tribally) based gangs resulted in 10 deaths and 600 homes burned to the ground in a period of five days. Thousands of families fled Mathare, seeking shelter in makeshift refugee camps in other parts of Nairobi.[48] Thus, crime is more than a personal concern. It has become an important political issue in a number of LDCs, with periodic mass demonstrations demanding more effective government measures against robbery and violent crime. Just as in the United States and other industrialized nations, the origins of criminal activity lie, in large part, in poverty, discrimination, income inequality, inadequate schools, and broken families. Its victims come from all social classes—poor, middle class, and, less frequently, the rich. However, throughout the world, the urban poor represent a disproportionate percentage of the perpetrators and the victims of crime. The confluence of poverty, inequality, and social decay helps explain why violent crime rates in Africa and Latin America are generally much higher than in economically developed nations.

Nevertheless, many countries and regions do not fit that pattern. For example, the rates of homicide and rape (per capita) are a good deal higher in the United States than in most other highly developed countries (including Canada, Japan, and Western Europe) and even exceed the rates in such Third World countries as South Korea, Indonesia, Hong Kong, Malaysia, Singapore, Tunisia, and Kuwait. Conversely, despite the considerable poverty in much of Asia, violent crime rates for many countries in that continent are not only substantially lower than in the United States, but often even lower than in Western Europe.[49] Indeed, the United States has a homicide rate about five times as high as Indonesia's, four times as high as Tunisia's, and two to three times as high as South Korea's and Chile's.[50] One possible explanation for these anomalies is that income *inequality* seems to be as much or more a factor in promoting crime as is the *absolute* rate of poverty. Countries such as the United States, South Africa, and Brazil—with particularly high levels of income inequality—tend to have higher violent crime rates than other countries with comparable or lower per capita incomes but lower inequality.

In general, however, African and Latin American countries (often both poor and unequal) tend to suffer from very high crime rates, particularly in their urban centers. South Africa, with one of the world's more inequitable income distributions (a vestige of its *apartheid* past), currently has the world's second highest homicide rate (behind Colombia) and the highest level of rape.[51] Rio de Janeiro is among the world's leaders in robbery and sexual assaults, while Bogotá, Kingston (Jamaica), Kampala (Uganda), and Gaborone (Botswana) all suffer from exceptionally high levels of violent crime. Of course, crime rates within each continent and region vary considerably from country to country. However, the variation is greatest within Latin America and the Caribbean. Thus, Colombia, Venezuela, Jamaica, and Mexico have some of the world's highest murder rates (ranging from three to fourteen times the U.S. level). At the same time, however, Argentina (at least until recently), Chile, Costa Rica, Cuba, and Uruguay have relatively moderate homicide rates.[52]

Cross-national comparisons of homicide rates are informative, but should be used with caution. For example, in some Muslim countries, so-called "honor killings" (murders committed by male family members against women relatives whose relationships with unapproved outsiders have allegedly dishonored the family) are legal or unofficially accepted and, therefore, not included in the homicide statistics (see Chapter 5). At the same time, industrialized nations have far superior medical facilities (including trauma centers), so that many victims who die in countries such as Brazil survive in American or French hospitals and do not add to the murder rate. In general, the homicide statistics released by groups such as the United Nations are fairly consistent with each other (e.g., all data sources agree that Colombia and Mexico have high murder rates, while Saudi Arabia and Indonesia have low rates). Nevertheless, minor disparities between individual countries, such as Portugal and Malaysia, may merely result from data-gathering issues rather than real differences. Table 7.4 offers a different means of measuring and comparing crime rates. During the 1990s, researchers conducted surveys in cities located in the major regions of the world. Rather than accepting official crime statistics, the study asked respondents whether they had been a victim of crime in the previous five years. The table reflects the percentage of the urban population that claimed to have been victimized during that period. The last column indicates the percentage of

TABLE 7.4 Percentage of the Urban Population Victimized by Crime within the Previous Five Years

Region	Victims of Violent Crimes[a] (Other than Homicide)	Victims of All Crimes (Other than Homicide)
Western Europe	15%	60%
North America	20	65
South America	31	68
Asia	11	44
Africa	33	76

[a]Rape, assault, muggings, grievous bodily harm. These data were generated by interviews of victims and nonvictims. Obviously murder victims could not be interviewed and, hence, homicides could not be included.

Source: Franz Vanderschueren, "From Violence to Security and Justice in Cities," *Environment and Urbanization,* vol. 8, no.1 (April, 1996), 94.

the population that had been a victim of any kind of crime. The first data column indicates what percentage of the respondents had suffered violent crimes. Note that these figures do not include homicide because the data were obtained through interviews, and existing survey techniques do not enable us to interview murder victims.

Table 7.4 reveals that, as indicated by our prior discussion, crime rates are much lower in Asia than in any other region. "Only" 44 percent of all respondents had been crime victims in the previous five years, considerably lower than the 65 percent in North America and 76 percent in Africa. Violent crimes were also far less common in Asia, with only 11 percent of the population victimized, about half the rate in North America and one-third the level of South America and Africa. Europe was the next safest region, with South America and Africa suffering the highest rates of violent crime.

In addition to normal criminal activity, residents of many cities must deal with "government crime" in the form of corruption. In many Mexican cities, for example, the police will not respond to a homeowner's report of a burglary unless he or she has previously paid the local police officer a small monthly bribe for protection. In polls conducted during the late 1990s, only 0.1 percent of British residents (one in a thousand) and 0.2 percent of Americans responded that they had been asked to pay a bribe to a government official (including police) during that year or expected to be asked to pay one before the end of the year. That proportion increased to 19.5 percent in Kampala (Uganda), 29.9 percent in Jakarta (Indonesia), and 59.1 percent in Tirana (Albania).[53] The situation is even more precarious when police are closely linked to violent criminal activities. In 2004, hundreds of thousands marched in Buenos Aires (Argentina) and Mexico City to protest extensive police involvement in their cities' alarmingly high (and rising) rates of kidnapping. In Buenos Aires, the extent of criminal activity by the police is so great that it resisted the best efforts of reformist President Néstor Kirchner to clean it up. As one Argentine sociologist has explained:

> Each division [of the Buenos Aires police department] dedicates itself to the area of crime that it is supposed to be fighting. The robbery division steals and robs, the narcotics division traffics drugs, auto theft controls the stealing of cars and the chop shops, and those in fraud and bunko, defraud and swindle.[54]

All too sadly, the same can be said of police forces in many other Third World capitals. Rampant crime and, especially, widespread police corruption not only threaten the security of all city dwellers (regardless of economic status) but undermine the government's legitimacy.

THE POLITICS OF THE URBAN POOR: CONFLICTING IMAGES

How do the urban poor react politically to their daily struggle for jobs, shelter, and personal safety? Their political attitudes and behavior, like those of the peasantry, have been depicted in sharply conflicting ways.[55] When political scientists and sociologists first noted the flood of cityward migration and urban growth in the developing countries, many viewed the sprawling slums and squatter settlements as potential hotbeds of unrest or revolution. In one of the most influential early works on Third World politics, James Coleman warned that, "there exist in most urban centers elements predisposed to anomic activity."[56] Samuel Huntington maintained that the first generation of urban migrants was unlikely to challenge the existing order, but their children often would: "At some point, the slums [and shantytowns] of Rio and Lima are likely to be swept by social violence, as the children of the city demand the rewards of the city."[57] And economist Barbara Ward, taking note of shantytown poverty and the rise of radical urban movements, insisted that "unchecked left to grow and fester, there is here enough explosive material to produce . . . bitter class conflict . . . erupting in guerrilla warfare, and threatening, ultimately, the security even of the comfortable West."[58]

As we will see, the urban poor have, indeed, contributed to several recent Third World revolutions. In addition, rioting over food prices and bus fares has shaken such cities as Algiers, Amman (Jordan), Cairo, Caracas, Lima, and Santo Domingo (Dominican Republic). Nonetheless, the urban conflagrations that many had expected have been rare. For the most part, the poor have shunned violence. Indeed, they have been as likely to vote for right-wing or centrist political candidates as for radicals. Initial expectations of a violent or radicalized urban lower class were based largely on erroneous premises. To be sure, many urban migrants came to the cities with raised expectations and heightened political sensitivities. Nevertheless, horrendous as the slums of Cairo, Calcutta, or Karachi may appear to the Western observer, migrants often find them preferable to their previous dwellings in the countryside. In fact, the urban poor are far more likely than their rural counterparts to enjoy electricity, sewage, tap water, and nearby schools. In many countries, urban migration provides an escape from semi-feudal social controls or ethnic civil war. Small wonder that surveys of migrants to Ankara, Baghdad, Bogotá, Mexico City, Rio de Janeiro, and other cities have indicated that most respondents feel better off in their urban hovels than they had in their rural villages.[59] A study of 13 low-income neighborhoods in Bogotá, Valencia (Venezuela), and Mexico City revealed that between 64 and 76 percent of those surveyed believed that their settlement was "a good place to live," while only 11–31 percent felt they lived in a "bad place."[60] Undoubtedly, severe economic recession since the early 1980s, which sharply lowered urban living standards in Africa, Latin America, and parts of Asia, gave the urban poor a more jaundiced view of their condition. Yet survey research in Latin America has usually indicated that even when the urban poor do not feel their own lives have improved, most remain optimistic about the future and about prospects for their children.[61]

When early expectations of urban radicalism and violence generally failed to materialize, some scholars jumped to opposite conclusions. For example, based on his studies of low-income neighborhoods in Mexico and Puerto Rico, anthropologist Oscar Lewis concluded that most of the urban poor are prisoners of a "culture of poverty." Lewis described a sub-proletariat that lacks class consciousness, economic and political organization, or long-term aspirations. While distrustful of government, they feel powerless and fatalistic about effecting change. The culture of poverty, Lewis argued, is inherently apolitical and, hence, quite unlikely to generate radical or revolutionary activity.[62]

A related body of literature described the urban poor as "marginal"—outside the mainstream of the nation's political and economic life. Consequently, many analysts perceived a vicious cycle in which the exclusion of the poor increases their political apathy, which, in turn, isolates them further. They demonstrate a "lack of active participation due to the fact that . . . marginal groups make no decisions; they do not contribute to the molding of society."[63] Like the victims of Lewis's culture of poverty, marginals allegedly show little class consciousness or capacity for long-term collective action.

While it may be true that many poor city dwellers feel incapable of advancing their lives or influencing the political and economic systems—often with good reason—survey research suggests that they do not necessarily suffer from the apathy or helplessness that scholars such as Lewis ascribed to them. Levels of fatalism and optimism undoubtedly vary from place to place and from time to time, depending on both the community's cultural values and its socioeconomic experiences. That is, those living in a country that has been enjoying rapid economic growth, some of which has percolated down to the urban poor, should logically be more optimistic about the future than are those in stagnant or inequitable economies. When poor urbanites in Côte d'Ivoire and Kenya—two low-income African countries—were asked whether they believed that "when a person is born, the success he/she is going to have is already decided" (an obvious measure of fatalism), nearly 60 percent of them strongly agreed and an additional 11 percent agreed somewhat. In Brazil, a much more economically developed country with one of the world's most unequal income distributions, only about 15 percent strongly agreed, but some 30 percent agreed somewhat. Finally, in Chile, which has experienced the most rapid economic growth in Latin America since the start of the 1990s and has enjoyed a sharp decline in urban poverty, a mere 4 percent of the respondents strongly agreed while only 15 percent agreed somewhat.[64] In short, the level of fatalism or optimism among the urban poor varies considerably across nations and seems to correspond to objective economic conditions more than to any culturally embedded values.

Just as initial predictions of radicalism and political violence among the urban lower class have turned out to be greatly exaggerated, so too have assertions that the poor are invariably apathetic and fatalistic. To be sure, most low-income communities are not highly politicized. In his study of the poor in Guatemala City, Bryan R. Roberts found that "they claim to avoid politics in their local work, and to them the term 'politician' is synonymous with deceit and corruption."[65] Such perceptions are not the result of apathy or fatalism, however, but stem rather from the realistically "perceived impracticality of changing the existing order" in most Third World countries and, in some cases, such as Guatemala, from a repressive political climate.[66] On the other hand, when given the opportunity to organize (i.e., when their political activity is not repressed) and when there is a realistic chance of attaining some benefits from the political system, many low-income communities have seized the opportunity. Studies of Caracas, Lima, and Rio, for example, have described a number of poor neighborhoods with extensive political cooperation and organization. Moreover, their community leaders often have a keen sense of how to manipulate the political system.

In time, social scientists came to question the concepts of marginality and the culture of poverty.[67] In the previously mentioned survey of poor neighborhoods in four African cities (in Côte d'Ivoire and Kenya) and four Latin American cities (in Brazil and Chile), political attitudes, levels of political interest, and political knowledge varied considerably. In all four countries, a majority of the people surveyed responded that they were not interested in politics. The portion of those expressing "no interest" ranged from 51 percent in Brazil to 62 and 63 percent in Côte d'Ivoire and Chile.[68] The Chilean figures are noteworthy since 25–30 years earlier the shantytowns of Chile's largest cities were among the most politicized and radicalized in the world. However, 17 years of repressive military dictatorship, during which many left-wing political activists were jailed or killed, had caused many Chileans to disengage from politics.

Yet, despite their professed disinterest, many of the urban poor in these four countries were rather well informed and communicative about politics. In Chile, Côte d'Ivoire, and Kenya roughly half of them reported talking occasionally with other people "about the problems which [their] country has to face today."[69] That proportion rose to almost two-thirds in Brazil. Moreover, about half of those surveyed in Chile and Côte d'Ivoire claimed that they regularly followed political news. In Brazil and Kenya, that portion fell to about one-third. When asked to name important government leaders, respondents were generally quite knowledgeable. In all four nations, most people were able to name the president of their country (ranging from 69 percent in Brazil to 94 and 96 percent in Kenya and Chile). Moreover, about half the respondents in Chile and Kenya, and two-thirds in Brazil and Côte d'Ivoire could also name the mayor of their town. Most impressively, more than 70 percent of the poor Kenyans and Ivorians could name the president of at least one *other* African country, while almost half the Chileans could name the president of another Latin American country (Brazilians were less knowledgeable). One suspects that these figures exceed the percentage of Americans who can name the president of Mexico or the prime minister of Canada. In short, these low-income city dwellers seemed to have a greater interest in politics than they were willing to admit. On the other hand, perhaps, the question regarding their level of political interest had a different meaning to them than it did to the people conducting the survey.

On the negative side of the ledger, in all four countries the urban poor tended to take a rather dim view of their political system and their elected representatives. More than 80 percent of those surveyed in each of the four countries believed, that "those we elect to parliament lose touch with people pretty quickly," with that number reaching 94 percent in Chile. When asked whether they believed that "public officials care what people like me think," a significant majority in all of the eight cities said "no." The number who believed that public officials *do* care ranged from a low of 15 percent in Chile to a high of 40 percent in Côte d'Ivoire. Perhaps most surprisingly, Ivorians, living in a country that was not democratic, were most positive about their public officials (the poll took place prior to the outbreak of that country's bloody civil war). On the other hand, Chileans, who live in the most democratic and politically responsive of the four nations, were least likely by far to believe that their government officials care about them and were also least likely to believe that their parliamentary representative keeps in touch with their low-income constituents. Perhaps Chileans had harbored unrealistically high expectations of their new political leaders since the time democracy was restored in 1990, ending General Pinochet's 17-year dictatorship. Another important factor may be that Chilean parties, renowned prior to the dictatorship for their strong linkages to the lower classes, have become more elitist and distant after the return of democracy.

Thus, even that limited sample of Third World cities reveals a wide variety of political attitudes among the urban poor. Similarly, while the poor neighborhoods of, say, Santiago in 1973 or Tehran (Iran) in 1979 may have boiled with unrest, the same neighborhoods may be tranquil or even passive years later. Clearly, a more nuanced view of Third World urban politics requires us to ask: Under what circumstances do the poor organize politically? What goals do they seek, and how do they pursue them? What factors determine whether their political organization is peaceful or violent, conservative or radical, reformist or revolutionary?

FORMS OF POLITICAL EXPRESSION AMONG THE URBAN POOR

Political scientists have long understood that the urban poor tend to be more politically informed and more politically active than their rural counterparts are. Indeed, early scholarship on the Third World used a nation's level of urbanization as an indirect indicator of its level of political participation.[70] Lower-income city residents have higher levels of literacy than peasants do, greater exposure to the mass media, and more contact with political campaigns and rallies. This does not mean, however, that most of them are highly politicized. To the contrary, many of them are indifferent, apathetic, or even fatalistic about political events.[71] Nor does it even mean that political activists in the community are necessarily radical, indignant about economic conditions, or prone to violent protest. What it does mean is that the urban poor generally vote in higher numbers than the peasantry. Furthermore, it means that many low-income neighborhoods carefully calculate what benefits they can secure from the political system and then organize to secure them. Contrary to initial expectations that the disoriented and frustrated urban poor would riot and rebel, they have tended, instead, to be rather pragmatic and careful in their political behavior.

Individual Political Behavior

For most slum and shantytown dwellers, opportunities for individual political activity are rather restricted. Until recently, voting has had a limited political impact in most developing nations. Even with the impressive spread of Third World democracy during the past decades, most countries in Africa and the Middle East, and many in Asia, are still dominated by a single party, with manipulated elections. Moreover, while candidates in Third World electoral democracies may court the votes of the urban poor, those voters are often forgotten between elections.

An alternative, often more fruitful, type of individual political activity takes the form of *clientelism*. As many observers have noted, members of the urban lower class often seek to advance their interests by attaching themselves to a patron, within the government, or an influential political party, or an organized movement.[72] Clientelism (patron–client relationships) involves "the dispensing of public resources as favors by political power holders/seekers and their respective parties, in exchange for votes or other forms of popular support."[73] While offering concrete advantages to the less-powerful partner (the client), clientelism is at its heart "a strategy of elite-controlled political participation fostering the status quo."[74] Among the urban poor, potentially frustrated or radicalized individuals and groups are often co-opted into the political system with the lure of immediate, though limited, gains.

Of course, patron–client relations were also typical tools of American urban political machines in the late nineteenth and early twentieth centuries. Political parties aided recently arrived immigrants or, less frequently, African-American migrants from the South by offering them help in the form of jobs, Christmas turkeys, or assistance with local authorities, all in exchange for their support at the polls. Today, in countries throughout the Third World, the poor use clientelistic relations with such patrons to secure credit, government employment, and other economic goods from governing political parties or local politicians. Even in electoral democracies, such as India, Uruguay, and the Philippines, political bosses garner votes and volunteers largely through patronage.

For most of the urban poor, however, collective rather than individual activity appears to be the most productive form of political participation. Many low-income neighborhoods have organized rather effectively to extract benefits from the political system. Often, one of their first goals is to secure land titles for their homes along with basic services such as sanitation, sewage, tap water, schools, and paved streets.

Collective Goals: Housing and Urban Services

On the outskirts of Lima, Peru, several million people live in squatter communities. Originally, these settlements were born out of organized invasions of unoccupied land—either government property or land whose ownership had been in dispute:

> Some invasions involve relatively small groups of families who cooperate on an informal basis shortly before the occupation of the land. Others involve hundreds of families and are planned with great care. The leaders of these invasions often organize well before the invasion occurs and meet many times to recruit members, choose a site, and plan the occupation itself.[75]

Although these land seizures were obviously illegal, David Collier found that nearly half of the oldest ones were conducted with explicit or tacit government approval.[76] While the authorities did not want this phenomenon to get out of hand, they understood that permitting a controlled number of invasions onto low-value land (much of it public) enabled the poor to build their own homes with little cost to the state and defused a potentially explosive situation. There were political benefits to be gained as well. By protecting the invaders from police eviction, a political leader or a party could garner future electoral support from that community. In many cases, squatters paid off local authorities prior to their invasions.

When Peru's leftist military regime seized power, it was anxious to mobilize the urban poor but, at the same time, to reduce spontaneous grass-roots political activity. The generals issued an urban reform law legalizing most existing squatter communities. They tried to mobilize, yet control, the poor through SINAMOS, a state-controlled political organization for the rural and urban masses. However, they also took a tougher stance against new land invasions. Henry Dietz's study of six poor neighborhoods in Lima demonstrates that community leaders in several locations were quite adept at moving from Peru's earlier competitive electoral politics to the new rules of enlightened authoritarianism.[77] Mobilized neighborhoods used an impressive array of tactics to secure assistance from the military regime. These included working through SINAMOS, enlisting the aid of a sympathetic Catholic bishop whom the church had assigned to the shantytowns, gaining the support of foreign nongovernmental organizations (NGOs), publishing letters in major newspapers, pressuring local government bureaucrats, and directly petitioning the president.

Lima's squatter settlements have long attracted scholarly interest because of their unusually high level of political activity. Still, research elsewhere in Latin America has found similar ties between poor neighborhoods and the state.[78] For example, in her study of low-income neighborhoods in Mexico City, Susan Eckstein described how community leaders tied themselves to the then-ruling party (the PRI) and became the links between the government and the grass roots. Because these community organizations were controlled from the top down and tended to be short-lived, Eckstein was skeptical about how much the poor really gained by operating through Mexico's clientelistic system. Still, she conceded that, over the years, poor neighborhoods had successfully petitioned the government for such benefits as running water, electricity, local food markets, schools, and public transportation.[79] Following the National Action Party's presidential victory in 2000 and Mexico's transition to democracy, many low-income neighborhoods have been forced to establish new clientelistic relationships.

The politics of low-income neighborhoods throughout the developing world tends to resemble Peru's and Mexico's in two important respects: the scope of each group's claims and its relationship to the national political system. Studies of urban politics in India, Pakistan, the Philippines, and other LDCs find that the demands of the poor are usually limited and pragmatic.[80] At times the goals are just defensive, for example, merely trying to avoid eviction from illegal settlements. Their political objectives frequently focus on housing. However, as John Turner suggested, urban squatters rarely want the government to build homes for them, desiring only the means to do it themselves.[81] Some neighborhoods may ask for a medical clinic, a market, or a preschool lunch program. None of these objectives, however, involves a fundamental challenge to the political system or a major redistribution of economic resources.

These limited demands are intimately related to the nature of political organization in low-income neighborhoods. Patron–client links to the state, powerful political parties, or political bosses filter political inputs from the poor. Political organizations among the urban poor are often based in particular neighborhoods; or they may be tied to ethnic, religious, or racial identities; or they may simply be formed around powerful political figures. In the slums of Madras, India, where politics is closely linked to the film industry, clientelistic organizations grow out of local fan clubs for politically active movie stars.[82]

Whatever its base, patron–client politics inherently reinforces the status quo. In return for votes or other forms of political support, the state or political party delivers some of the goods or services that residents need. In many cases, a neighborhood's rewards are very paltry. Elsewhere, political systems are far more generous. In either case, however, the state or local political bosses engage in "divide and rule" politics, as poor urban districts compete with each other for limited government resources.[83]

Critics of clientelistic politics stress the limits of the benefits gained by poor neighborhoods. While some communities get water, electricity, or medical clinics, many others are left out. Moreover, even successful neighborhoods find it difficult to maintain pressure on the system for an extended period because their political organizations generally atrophy after a number of years. Consequently, as Alan Gilbert and Peter Ward charge, "The [the government's] main aim [in supporting] community-action programs is less to improve conditions for the poor . . . than to legitimate the state . . . to help maintain existing power relations in society."[84] As an alternative to clientelism, its critics favor a more independent, and perhaps more radical, form of mobilization that would raise the urban poor's political consciousness and lead to more sweeping redistributive policies benefiting far more people.

Other analysts, however, hold a more positive view of clientelism. While recognizing its shortcomings, they insist that the benefits that it brings are clearly better than nothing. Viewed in the broader context of society's tremendous inequalities, paved streets, clean drinking water, a clinic, or a food market may not seem like sufficient improvements to some outside observers. Nevertheless, the low-income neighborhoods that receive them appreciate their value. A radical regime might redistribute more to the poor, but, particularly today, that is normally not a viable option.[85]

The benefits of clientelism vary from country to country, depending on the nature of the political system and the health of the economy. In relatively open and democratic systems, the poor have broader opportunities to organize, demonstrate, petition, and vote. Clearly, their capacity to *demand* rewards from the state is usually greater than under authoritarian regimes. At the same time, the benefits clientelistic systems can allocate to low-income neighborhoods are also constrained by the state's economic resources. During their petroleum booms, the Mexican and Venezuelan governments could be more generous to the urban poor. Even in more difficult economic times, the Mexican government has used revenues from the sale of state enterprises to finance public works projects in urban slums. Currently, Venezuela's petroleum wealth enables Hugo Chavez to finance extensive anti-poverty programs, which have helped him build strong support among the urban poor. Conversely, the remaining dictatorships in Sub-Saharan Africa, such as Zimbabwe, have neither the economic resources nor the political will to aid their impoverished urban neighborhoods.

During the 1980s, a number of independent, grass-roots organizations emerged in the poor neighborhoods of Brazil, Chile, Mexico, and other Latin American countries. Known as "new social movements," they avoided clientelistic linkages with the government or political parties, keeping independent even of leftist parties. For example, following Mexico City's immense earthquake in 1985, slum dwellers, frustrated by the ineptitude of the government's reconstruction efforts, formed an effective network of self-help associations. In Monterrey, radicalized squatters in the community of *Tierra y Libertad* (Land and Liberty) hijacked several buses, forcing the public transport company to extend its routes further into their neighborhood.[86] Ultimately, however, these independent movements had limited life spans. By the 1990s, they were overshadowed by President Carlos Salinas's public works network for low-income neighborhoods known as the National Solidarity Program. Using traditional clientelistic techniques, his administration won the support of many poor neighborhoods by establishing new schools, clinics, and the like through government-affiliated groups. When the Mexican economy plummeted after Salinas left office, those programs were cut back.

Whatever the merits or limits of clientelism, its scope and range refute prior assumptions about the politics of the urban poor. On the one hand, the sometimes delicate and complex patron–client negotiations that they frequently involve demonstrate that many low-income neighborhood leaders are more politically skilled than some outside analysts had believed. While many of the urban poor suffer from fatalism and excessive individualism, others are capable of sophisticated political organization and tough bargaining with the state or political parties. On the other hand, the poor rarely engage in the kind of revolutionary activity, violent upheavals, or radical politics that some political scientists had expected. During the 1980s and early 1990s, when living standards declined precipitously in much of the Third World, there was some increase in protest activity.[87] Nevertheless, the extent of rioting and social unrest remained surprisingly limited. Similarly, the slums of Bangkok and Kuala Lumpur (Malaysia) have remained politically peaceful despite East Asia's recent financial crisis. To be sure, Indonesia's economic slide produced widespread urban rioting that helped topple the Sukarno dictatorship in 1998. However, it was primarily university students, not the poor, who first demonstrated against the government. Jakarta's slum dwellers more often vented their fury, instead, against the affluent Chinese minority.

Radical Political Behavior

While most of the Third World's urban poor have favored moderate and pragmatic forms of political expression, there have been important exceptions. In some countries, such as Chile in the early 1970s, Peru in the 1980s, and El Salvador since the mid-1990s, low-income neighborhoods have voted in substantial numbers for Marxist political candidates. And, in a few cases, residents of urban slums and shantytowns have been important players in revolutionary upheavals. In 1970, Salvador Allende, candidate of Chile's leftist Popular Unity (UP) coalition, became the developing world's first democratically elected Marxist president. Allende received considerable electoral support in the *campamentos* (squatter settlements) that ring the capital city of Santiago. In fact, a number of *campamentos* were politically organized by the UP or by the MIR (Leftist Revolutionary Movement), a group to the left of the UP that periodically engaged in armed action.[88] In 1983, the poor of Lima played a major role in electing a Marxist mayor, Alfonso Barrantes. These examples, as well as the Communist Party's electoral successes in several Indian cities, indicate that the poor do support radical political parties under certain circumstances.

However, those parties must have a realistic chance of winning at the local or national level so that they can be in a position to deliver tangible benefits to their supporters. Thus, even radical voting is often based on very pragmatic calculations. Not long after supporting Barrantes for mayor, Lima's poor rejected him for the post of national president, believing that his moderate Marxist might work in Lima but were not viable at the national level.[89]

More often, the urban poor are attracted to charismatic populists (such as Venezuelan president Hugo Chávez) or to moderate leftists (such as Brazilian President Luiz Inácio Lula da Silva). Squatters or slum dwellers are even less likely to embrace urban guerrillas or other revolutionary movements. Teodoro Petkoff, a former leader of the Venezuelan communists' urban guerrilla wing, noted that even residents of Caracas's poor barrios who belonged to leftist unions rejected the guerrillas. Blue-collar workers often elected communist union representatives in those days, Petkoff observed, because they felt that union militants would deliver more at the bargaining table. On the other hand, in national elections, the urban poor were more likely to vote for the two mainstream parties (Social Democrats and Christian Democrats) or even the country's former right-wing dictator, all of whom had a better track record of delivering rewards to their supporters.[90] Talton Ray's study of barrio politics explains why the residents were unlikely to support the armed insurrection of the Armed Forces of National Liberation (Fuerza Armada de Liberación Nacional or FALN):

> The FALN's urban guerrilla warfare proved to be a grave tactical error . . . [creating a] mood of revulsion . . . in the barrios. Terrorist activities struck much too close to home. . . . Almost all of the murdered policemen [killed by the FALN] were barrio residents.[91]

In the 1980s and 1990s, Peru's *Sendero Luminoso* (Shining Path) guerrillas had some success in the shantytowns of Lima. However, in view of Sendero's terrorist intimidation tactics against both the peasantry and the urban poor, there is reason to believe that the group inspired more fear and acquiescence than support. When the popular vice-mayor of one of Peru's largest and most radical shantytowns, Villa El Salvador, tried to keep the Shining Path out of her community, she was brutally assassinated. In any event, Sendero activists in both the countryside and urban shantytowns were more often students and teachers, rather than the poor themselves.

This is not to suggest that the urban poor never support revolutions. Josef Gugler notes that during the second half of the twentieth century the cities played a central role in four of the Third World's revolutions—Bolivia, Cuba, Iran, and Nicaragua.[92] However, in all but Nicaragua, where mass demonstrations by the urban poor were crucial for the revolutionary victory, other social classes took the lead in the cities: miners, unionized blue-collar workers, artisans, the lower-middle class, and the national police in Bolivia; students and university graduates in Cuba; theology students and petroleum workers in Iran. In contrast, Douglas Butterworth's study of the former inhabitants of a Havana slum, *Las Yaguas*, conducted almost 20 years after the revolutionary victory, found that most respondents were barely aware of Fidel Castro's existence during his rise to power.[93]

CONCLUSION: FUTURE URBAN GROWTH
AND DEMOCRATIC POLITICS

While the *rate* of urbanization has slowed in parts of the Third World, *absolute increases* in urban populations will be greater than ever in the coming decades (Tables 7.2 and 7.3). Thus, governments will have to heed urban needs, including those of the poor. Still, even with the best-intentioned public policies, developing economies will be hard pressed to provide sufficient jobs, housing, sanitation, and social services. Economic crises such as Latin America's and Africa's in the 1980s and East Asia's in the late 1990s have made the task all the more difficult. Urban crime, pollution, and AIDS will add tremendously to the burdens on the political-economic systems. In countries such as South Africa, Guatemala, and Iraq, the fall of authoritarian regimes has led to a surge in crime.

Given the current weakness of the radical Left, however, and the tendency of the poor to engage in adaptive behavior, urban unrest is more likely to express itself in occasional rioting than in mass insurrection or revolution. Perhaps the one exception may be in the Middle East, where segments of the urban lower and middle classes may turn to militant Islamic fundamentalism, as many have already done in Algeria, Egypt, Iran, and Iraq. Elsewhere, crime and drug usage are more likely than radical politics to threaten stability in the proximate future. In the long run, Third World governments may be able to cope with these problems if they can generate sustained economic growth. In the short term, however, the possibility of increased state repression persists in many countries as the military and middle class become fearful of urban crime or disorder.

We have noted previously that poor urban neighborhoods generally receive more government assistance from democratic governments than from authoritarian ones. In countries where there has been an enduring transformation from dictatorship to democracy, the urban poor will have to refine their strategies for securing state resources. Similarly, if newly democratic governments are to endure, they will need to become more responsive to the poor and more cognizant of the vast inequalities that plague Third World cities. Studies of urban slums and shantytowns generally suggest that while the poor are not as radical or even potentially radical as once thought, they are not necessarily committed to democratic values either. Faced with rising crime rates and economic barriers they may become disillusioned with democracy (Chapter 2). Democratic governments will have to prove to them that they are more helpful than alternative authoritarian regimes. In addition, political institutions of all kinds need to spread democratic cultural values among the urban poor.

DISCUSSION QUESTIONS

1. How have Third World governments provided urban housing? To what extent have such efforts benefited or hurt the urban poor?
2. Describe the advantages and limitations of spontaneous housing. In what ways are sites-and-services programs an improvement over spontaneous housing? Are there disadvantages to sites-and-services programs?

3. Discuss the political orientations of the urban poor. What does survey research tell us about the way that the urban poor look at their present circumstances and their view of the prospects of improving them?
4. Discuss the role of clientelism (patron–client relationships) in the politics of the urban poor.
5. Discuss the growth of urban crime in the Third World, the major obstacles to reducing crime, and the possible political consequences of rising crime rates.
6. Is rapid urban growth (linked to migration) beneficial or harmful in developing democratic government?

NOTES

1. United Nations, Department of Economic and Social Affairs, Population Division, "Urban and Rural Areas, 2003," http://www.un.org/esa/population/publications/wup2003/2003 Urban_Rural.pdf.

2. Stella Lowder, *The Geography of Third World Cities* (New York: Barnes and Noble, 1986), 19.

3. Sally Findley, "The Third World City," in *Third World Cities*, eds. John Kasarda and Allan Parnell (Newbury Park, CA: Sage Publications, 1993), 14–16.

4. Thus, while China officially has an urban population of about 500 million (or 39 percent of the nation's total), in fact, when the floating population is added in, there are actually more than 600 million city dwellers. See, Beatriz Carrillo Garcia, "Rural-Urban Migration in China: Temporary Migrants in Search of Permanent Settlement," *Portal*, vol. 1, no. 2 (July 2004), 1–12; also, Arianne M. Gaetano and Tamara Jacka, eds., *On the Move: Women and Rural-to-Urban Migration in Contemporary China* (New York: Columbia University Press, 2004).

5. R. A. Obudho, "Urbanization and Urban Development Strategies in East Africa," in *Urban Management*, ed. G. Shabbir Cheema (New York: Praeger, 1993), figures extrapolated from Table 4.2, p. 84.

6. Cheema, "The Challenge of Urban Management," in *Urban Management*, 2.

7. United Nations Population Fund, *"State of World Population: 2007: Unleashing the Potential of Urban Growth,"* as quoted in the *New York Times*, "U.N. Predicts Urban Population Explosion," (June 28, 2007).

8. David Drakakis-Smith, *Urbanization, Housing and the Development Process* (New York: St. Martin's Press, 1980), 6; Samuel Preston, "Urban Growth in Developing Countries," in *The Urbanization of the Third World*, ed. Josef Gugler (New York: Oxford University Press, 1988), 14–15. Preston, using earlier data, indicates a higher percentage of

increase due to natural growth; Findley, "The Third World City," 15, using more recent data, indicates a higher percentage of increase due to migration.

9. "Largest Cities in the United States & the World," http://www.mongabay.com/igapo/cities.htm. The data are drawn from the United Nations, with estimated future populations calculated by Mongabay. Data from different sources vary somewhat, particularly about projected populations, but agree on general tends. See Table 7.3 for population statistics for major metropolitan areas in other periods.

10. Obudho, "Urbanization and Urban Development Strategies," 84.

11. John V. Graumann, "Orders of Magnitude of the World's Urban and Rural Population in History," *United Nations Population Bulletin*, vol. 8 (1977), 16–33, quoted in Preston, "Urban Growth," 12.

12. Raymond Owens, "Peasant Entrepreneurs in an Industrial City," in *A Reader in Urban Sociology*, eds. M. S. A. Rao, Chandrashekar Bhat, and Laxmi Narayan Kadekar (New Delhi, India: Oriental Longman, 1991), 235.

13. Manuel Castells and Alejandro Portes, "World Underneath: The Origins, Dynamics and Effects of the Informal Economy," in *The Informal Economy: Studies in Advanced and Developing Economies*, eds. Alejandro Portes, Manuel Castells, and Lauren A. Benton (Baltimore, MD: Johns Hopkins University Press, 1989), 12.

14. Om Prakash Mathur, "Managing the Urban Informal Sector," in *Urban Management*, 179. The data are drawn from International Labor Organization (ILO) studies.

15. Alan Gilbert and Josef Gugler, *Cities, Poverty and Development*, 2d ed. (New York: Oxford University Press, 1992), 98. Gugler argues elsewhere that the composition of the informal economy is so diverse that it is not clear whether it can really be considered a single sector.

16. Alejandro Portes et al., "The Informal Sector in Uruguay," *World Development*, vol. 14 (1986), 727–741.

17. Hernando de Soto, *The Other Path* (New York: Harper & Row, 1989), translated from the Spanish edition.

18. Dennis Rondinelli and John Kasarda, "Job Creation Needs in Third World Cities," in *Third World Cities*, 92–120. I will discuss macroeconomic policy in detail in Chapter 10. The reader wishing to better understand the economic analysis offered briefly in this section is referred to that chapter.

19. Stephan Haggard, *Pathways from the Periphery* (Ithaca, NY: Cornell University Press, 1990).

20. Ibid.

21. Richard Sandbrook, *The Politics of African Economic Recovery* (New York: Cambridge University Press, 1993), 60–61.

22. *New York Times* (October 27, 1993).

23. While squatter settlements or shantytowns are poor neighborhoods, not everyone living in them is poor. Data from Istanbul, Rio, Caracas, and elsewhere show that some shantytown residents are white-collar workers or well-paid blue-collar workers. Better-off residents may live there because rents elsewhere are too high. Others have enjoyed upward mobility since settling there but stay because of attachments to friends and community. Still, most of the residents are poor.

24. Om P. Mathur, "Foreword" in Kamlesh Misra, *Housing the Poor in Third World Cities* (New Delhi, India: Concept Publishing Company, 1992), 6–8.

25. UN-Habitat (United Nations Human Settlements Programme), Statistics. http://ww2.unhabitat.org/programmes/guostatistics.asp.

26. Silvia Schmitt, "Housing Conditions and Policies," in *Poverty and Democracy*, eds. Dirk Berg-Schlosser and Norbert Kersting (London and New York: Zed Books, 2003), 61. In each of the four countries (Brazil, Chile, Côte d'Ivoire, Kenya), the study examined two poor urban neighborhoods in the nation's capital and two in smaller cities.

27. Fred Ward, *Inside Cuba Today* (New York: Crown, 1978), 36–38.

28. Howard Handelman, "The Role of the State in Sheltering the Urban Poor," in *Spontaneous Shelter*, ed. Carl V. Patton (Philadelphia: Temple University Press, 1988), 332–333.

29. Richard Stern, "Urban Housing in Africa: The Changing Role of Government Policy," in *Housing Africa's Urban Poor*, eds. Philip Amis and Peter Lloyd (Manchester, England: Manchester University Press, 1990), 36–39.

30. Diana Patel, "Government Policy and Squatter Settlements in Harare, Zimbabwe," in *Slum and Squatter Settlements in Sub-Saharan Africa*, eds. R. A. Obudho and Constance Mhlanga (New York: Praeger, 1988), 205–217.

31. Handelman, "The Role of the State," 339.

32. Some experts call Cuba's construction of so-called microbrigade units (houses built by teams of worker volunteers) self-help housing. However, construction crews are directed by the state, which designs the homes. Moreover, the workers did not build homes for themselves. Thus, in various ways, this housing does not conform to the self-help model discussed later in the chapter.

33. Gilbert and Gugler, *Cities, Poverty and Development*, 139.

34. Susan Eckstein, *The Poverty of Revolution: The State and the Urban Poor in Mexico*, 2d ed. (Princeton, NJ: Princeton University Press, 1988); Henry Dietz, *Poverty and Problem Solving Under Military Rule* (Austin: University of Texas Press, 1980), 41; Howard Handelman, *High-Rises and Shantytowns* (Hanover, NH: American University Field Staff, 1979), 17; B. Sanyal, "A Critical Look at the Housing Subsidies in Zambia," *Development and Change*, vol. 12 (1981), 409–440.

35. David Collier, *Squatters and Oligarchs* (Baltimore, MD: Johns Hopkins University Press, 1976).

36. Gilbert and Gugler, *Cities, Poverty and Development*, 123.

37. Alan Gilbert and Peter Ward, *Housing, the State, and the Poor* (New York: Cambridge University Press, 1985), 86–87.

38. Diana Lee-Smith, "Squatter Landlords in Nairobi," in *Housing Africa's Urban Poor*, 177; Douglas Butterworth and John Chance, *Latin American Urbanization* (New York: Cambridge University Press, 1981), 147; Collier, *Squatters and Oligarchs*, 27–28.

39. John F. C. Turner, "Barriers and Channels for Housing Development in Modernizing Countries," *Journal of the American Institute of Planners*, vol. 33 (May 1967), 167–181; John F. C. Turner and Robert Fichter, eds., *Freedom to Build* (New York: Macmillan, 1972); see also William Mangin, "Latin American Squatter Settlements: A Problem and a Solution," *Latin American Research Review*, vol. 2, no. 3 (1967), 65–98.

40. Gilbert and Gugler, *Cities, Poverty and Development*, 117–130; Carl Patton, "Prospects for the Future," in *Spontaneous Shelter*, 348–355.

41. Handelman, "The Role of the State," 328.

42. *New York Times* (April 19, 2003).

43. Peter Nientied and Jan van der Linden, "Approaches to Low-Income Housing in the Third World," in *The Urbanization of the Third World*, 138–156; R. Burgess, "Petty Commodity Housing or Dweller Control? A Critique of John Turner's Views on Housing Policy," *World Development*, vol. 6 (1978), 1105–1133.

44. Handelman, *High-Rises and Shantytowns*; A. A. Laquian, "Whither Site and Services," *Habitat*, vol. 2 (1977), 291–301; Thomas Pennant, "The Growth of Small-Scale Renting in Low-Income Housing in Malawi," in *Housing Africa's Urban Poor*, eds. Philip Amis and Peter Lloyd (Manchester, England: Manchester University Press, 1990), 196–200.

45. Ernest Alexander, "Informal Settlement in Latin America and Its Policy Implication," in *Spontaneous Shelter*, 131–133; Drakakis-Smith, *Urbanization, Housing and the Development Process*, 141–142; Jorge Hardoy and David Satterthwaite, *Shelter, Need and Response* (New York: John Wiley, 1981); Lisa Peattie, "Some Second Thoughts on Sites-and-Services," *Habitat International*, vol. 6 (Winter 1982), 131–139.

46. Gilbert and Ward, *Housing, the State, and the Poor*.

47. Portions of this section are drawn from Howard Handelman, *The Security and Insecurities of Democracy in the Third World*, vol. 12, no. 1 (Milwaukee: University of Wisconsin-Milwaukee, Global Studies Perspectives: Occasional Paper Series of the Center for International Education, 2004).

48. *New York Times*, "Chased by Gang Violence, Residents Flee Kenyan Slum" (November 10, 2006). In December 2007 and January 2008 this slum was the scene of violent, ethnically based protests against the apparently fraudulent vote tallies in the 2007 presidential election.

49. Andrew Morrison, Mayra Buvinic, and Michael Shifter, "The Violent Americas: Risk Factors, Consequences, and Policy Implications of Social and Domestic Violence," in *Crime and Violence in Latin America*, eds. Hugo Frühling and Joseph Tulchin (Washington, DC: Woodrow Wilson Center Press, 2003), 96.

50. National-level data are drawn from the *Seventh United Nations Survey of Crime Trends and Operations of Criminal Justice Systems, Covering the Period 1998–2000* (United Nations Office on Drugs and Crime, Centre for International Crime Prevention) as reported by Nationmaster.com. http://www.nationmaster.com/graph/cri_mur_percap-crime-murders-per-capita.

51. Jeffrey Herbst, "The Nature of South African Democracy: Political Dominance and Economic Inequality," in Theodore K. Rabb and Ezra N. Suleiman, eds., *The Making and Unmaking of Democracy: Lessons from History and World Politics* (New York and London: Routledge, 2003), 220–221.

52. *Seventh United Nations Survey of Crime*.

53. All the crime and corruption data in this paragraph come from the UNDP, *Human Development Report 2000*, 220–221.

54. *New York Times* (August 4, 2004).

55. Joan Nelson, *Access to Power* (Princeton, NJ: Princeton University Press, 1979), chap. 4; Howard Handelman, "The Political Mobilization of Urban Squatter Settlements," *Latin American Research Review*, vol. 10, no. 2 (1975), 35–72; Gilbert and Gugler, *Cities, Poverty and Development*, chap. 7.

56. James Coleman, "Conclusion: The Political Systems of Developing Nations," in *The Politics of Developing Areas*, eds. Gabriel Almond and James Coleman (Princeton, NJ: Princeton University Press, 1960), 537. Anomic activity is action not governed by social practices and values.

57. Samuel Huntington, *Political Order in Changing Societies* (New Haven, CT: Yale University Press, 1968), 283.

58. Barbara Ward, "Creating Man's Future Goals for a World of Plenty," *Saturday Review*, vol. 9 (August 1964), 192.

59. Joan Nelson, *Migrants, Urban Poverty, and Instability in Developing Nations* (Cambridge, MA: AMS Press and the Harvard University Center for International Affairs, 1969), 18–20; Eckstein, *The Poverty of Revolution*, 41.

60. Gilbert and Ward, *Housing, the State, and the Poor*, 215.

61. Ibid., 57–61.

62. Oscar Lewis, *The Children of Sanchez* (New York: Random House, 1961), and *La Vida* (New York: Random House, 1966).

63. Jorge Giusti, "Organizational Characteristics of the Latin American Urban Marginal Settler," *International Journal of Politics*, vol. 1, no. 1 (1971), 57.

64. Barbara Happe and Sylvia Schmit, "Political Culture," in *Poverty and Democracy*, eds. Berg-Schlosser and Kersting 130.

65. Bryan R. Roberts, *Organizing Strangers: Poor Families in Guatemala City* (Austin: University of Texas Press, 1973), 299.

66. Alejandro Portes and John Walton, *Urban Latin America* (Austin: University of Texas Press, 1976), 108.

67. Janice Perlman, *The Myth of Marginality* (Berkeley: University of California Press, 1976); William Mangin, "The Role of Regional

Associations in the Adaptation of Rural Migrants to Cities in Peru," in *Contemporary Cultures and Societies of Latin America*, eds. Dwight Heath and Richard Adams (New York: Random House, 1974).

68. Happe and Schmit, "Political Culture," in *Poverty and Democracy*, 125. All of the survey results that follow come from that chapter (pp. 121–152) or from Norbert Kersting and Jaime Sperberg, "Political Participation," in *Poverty and Democracy*, 153–180.

69. These surveys were conducted when Côte d'Ivoire (Ivory Coast) was at the tail end of a 40-year period of political stability and economic development (but not democracy). Not long afterwards (2002) a civil war began that split the country in half and left several thousand dead. Undoubtedly, the war (now over) and several military coups that preceded it changed Ivorian political attitudes, including their interest in politics.

70. Karl Deutsch, "Social Mobilization and Political Development," *American Political Science Review*, vol. 55 (September 1961), 493–514; Daniel Lerner, *The Passing of Traditional Society* (Glencoe, IL: Free Press, 1958).

71. Of course, even in highly educated industrialized democracies such as the United States, many citizens are also apolitical. Moreover, that political apathy often extends to members of the middle class.

72. Gilbert and Gugler, *Cities, Poverty and Development*, 180–187; S. N. Eisenstadt and L. Roninger, *Patrons, Clients and Friends* (New York: Cambridge University Press, 1984).

73. A. Bank, "Poverty, Politics and the Shaping of Urban Space: A Brazilian Example," *International Journal of Urban and Regional Research*, vol. 10, no. 4 (1986), 523.

74. Ibid.

75. Collier, *Squatters and Oligarchs*, 41.

76. Ibid., 44.

77. Dietz, *Poverty and Problem Solving Under Military Rule*.

78. Wayne Cornelius, *Politics and the Urban Poor in Mexico* (Stanford, CA: Stanford University Press, 1975); Gilbert and Ward, *Housing, the State and the Poor*, 189–196.

79. Eckstein, *The Poverty of Revolution*, chap. 3.

80. Frans Schuurman and Ton van Naerssen, eds., *Urban Social Movements in the Third World* (New York: Routledge, 1989).

81. Turner, "Barriers and Channels."

82. Joop de Wit, "Clientelism, Competition and Poverty: The Ineffectiveness of Local Organizations in a Madras Slum," in *Urban Social Movements in the Third World*, 63–90.

83. Jan van der Linden, "The Limits of Territorial Social Movements: The Case of Housing in Karachi," in *Urban Social Movements in the Third World*, 101.

84. Gilbert and Ward, *Housing, the State and the Poor*, 175.

85. Nor has the record of radical regimes been particularly impressive. Marxist governments often redistribute significant resources to the poor soon after taking power. However, with the notable exception of China, they generally have a poor record of economic growth. In Nicaragua, for example, the urban poor benefited initially from Sandinista welfare programs, but then saw their standard of living deteriorate sharply due to the U.S.-backed Contra war and the government's poor economic management. In other revolutions, such as Cuba's, experts disagree about how well the urban poor have fared in the long run.

86. Vivien Bennet, "The Evolution of Popular Movements in Mexico Between 1968 and 1988," in *The Making of Social Movements in Latin America*, eds. Arturo Escobar and Sonia Alvarez (Boulder, CO: Westview Press, 1992); Menno Vellinga, "Power and Independence: The Struggle for Identity and Integrity in Urban Social Movements," in *Urban Social Movements in the Third World*, 151–176.

87. Susan Eckstein, *Urbanization Revisited: Inner-City Slum of Hope and Squatter Settlement of Despair* (Storrs: University of Connecticut and Brown University Occasional Papers in Latin American Studies, 1989), 14.

88. Handelman, "The Political Mobilization of Urban Squatter Settlements: Santiago's Recent Experience," *Latin American Research Review*, vol. 10, no. 2 (1975), 35–72.

89. Henry Dietz, "Political Participation in the Barriadas: An Extension and Reexamination," *Comparative Political Studies*, vol. 18, no. 3 (1985), 323–355.

90. The author's conversations with Petkoff in 1976 and 1978. Petkoff left the Communist Party to help found a democratically oriented Marxist party called MAS. He was subsequently elected to Congress on the MAS ticket and in the late 1990s held an important cabinet position.

91. Talton Ray, *The Politics of the Barrios of Venezuela* (Berkeley: University of California Press, 1969), 132–133.

92. Josef Gugler, "The Urban Character of Contemporary Revolutions," in *The Urbanization of the Third World*, 399–412.

93. Douglas Butterworth, *The People of Buena Ventura* (Urbana: University of Illinois Press, 1980), 19–20.

CHAPTER 8

REVOLUTIONARY CHANGE

T he opening decades of the twentieth century ushered in the Mexican and Russian revolutions. The closing decades witnessed the collapse of Soviet communism, the transformation of the Chinese and Mexican revolutions, and the weakening of Cuba's revolutionary government.[1] No era in world history encompassed more revolutionary upheaval. Yet as the twenty-first century begins, the force that had once promised (or threatened) to transform the face of the Third World appears to be spent, at least for the time being.

Karl Marx, the foremost prophet of revolution, expected them to take place in industrialized European nations where the organized working class would rise up against the oppressive capitalist system. Instead, modern revolutionary movements have been largely a Third World phenomenon, fought primarily by the peasantry. And even Europe's internally generated communist revolutions—Russia and Yugoslavia—occurred in countries where capitalism and industrialization were relatively underdeveloped. The remaining communist regimes in Central Europe were installed by Soviet military intervention, not through national uprisings.

In the Third World, the appeal of revolutionary change has been its pledge of rapid and sweeping solutions to the problems of underdevelopment. It promised to end colonial rule, terminate dependency, protect national sovereignty, reduce social and economic inequalities, accelerate economic development, mobilize the population, and transform the political culture. Not surprisingly, many of the LDCs' poor and oppressed, along with numerous intellectuals and alienated members of the middle class, have found revolutionary platforms and ideologies quite appealing.

Some revolutionary governments—in China, Cuba, and Mexico, for example—were able to deliver on a number of their promises. Under Mao Zedong's leadership, the Chinese Communist Party redistributed land to the peasantry, industrialized the economy, and transformed the country into a world power. Fidel Castro's government implemented extensive land reform, an impressive adult literacy campaign, and significant public health programs. Mexico's revolutionary party reestablished national sovereignty over the country's natural resources, initiated agrarian reform, and transformed the nation into a Third World industrial power.

Often, however, these gains have come at great cost, including political repression, considerable human suffering, and rampant corruption. As a result of their revolution, the Chinese people now enjoy far better medical care, more education, and better living conditions than ever before. At the same time, however, some 30 million people starved to death in the 1950s due to the mistaken experiments of Mao's Great Leap Forward. Millions more suffered humiliation, imprisonment, or death (for some 400,000 people) during the ultra-radical period called the Cultural Revolution (1966–1976). Most communist governments had their *gulag* for real and imagined political opponents. In Vietnam, the revolutionary government sent many suspected dissidents to "reeducation" camps, and in Cuba a smaller, but still significant, number were imprisoned.

In the most unfortunate cases—Angola, Mozambique, and Cambodia (Kampuchea)—huge portions of the population died as the result of civil war or the regime's brutality, with little or nothing positive to show for it.[2] In Cambodia, the fanatical Khmer Rouge government killed more than a million people, including much of the country's educated class, while accomplishing nothing for its people. Over the years, even some of the more idealistic revolutionary regimes were transformed into corrupt bureaucracies, run by a new generation of opportunistic *apparatchiks* (party or government bureaucrats) who had never risked anything for the revolution's ideals.

After examining the meaning of the term "revolution" and classifying different types of twentieth-century revolutions, this chapter will discuss the causes of revolutionary upheavals, their principal sources of leadership and support, and the policy objectives of their leaders once in power. Finally, it will discuss the decline of the revolutionary model at the end of the twentieth century.

DEFINING REVOLUTION

Scholars have argued endlessly about what constitutes a revolution and whether particular upheavals such as the American Revolution or Iran's Islamic Revolution were, in fact, true social revolutions.[3] Thus, Chalmers Johnson notes, "half the battle will lie in answering the question, 'What is revolution?'"[4] In its broadest and least precise usage, the term is applied to any violent overthrow of government. Peter Calvert offers perhaps the most open-ended definition when he maintains that revolution is "simply a form of governmental change through violence."[5] Such a definition, however, seems too broad because it encompasses military coups and other upheavals that do little more than change the heads of government. Most scholars insist on a more rigorous definition, arguing that revolutions must bring fundamental political, economic, and social change. Thus, Samuel P. Huntington has suggested:

> A revolution is a rapid, fundamental, and violent domestic change in the dominant values and myths of society, in its political institutions, social structure, leadership and government activity and policies. Revolutions are thus to be distinguished from insurrections, revolts, coups and wars of independence.[6]

To be sure, it is frequently difficult to make the distinctions that Huntington proposes in the last sentence. For example, some "wars of independence" (sometimes called "wars of national liberation") such as Algeria's and Mozambique's are generally considered authentic social revolutions because they ushered in fundamental societal change.[7] On the other hand, Theda Skocpol accepts Huntington's starting definition but narrows it by claiming that "social revolutions are accompanied and in part effectuated through [massive] class upheavals."[8] She adds:

> Social revolutions are set apart from other sorts of conflicts by the combination of two coincidences: the coincidence of societal structural change with class upheaval; and the coincidence of the political with social transformation.[9]

Skocpol concedes that according to her more restrictive, class-based definition, only "a handful of successful social revolutions have ever occurred." The most clear-cut cases are the three she has studied in great detail: France (1789–1799), Russia (1917), and China (1911–1949). Other less-restrictive definitions of revolution apply to Mexico, Bolivia, Cuba, Nicaragua, Algeria, Ethiopia, Mozambique, Angola, Eritrea, Vietnam, Cambodia, Turkey, and Iran, among others. What is common to all of them is that insurgency brought sweeping changes to the country's political, economic, and social systems.

Because revolutions involve a fundamental transfer of political and economic power, rather than a mere change in political leaders (as is the case in most military coups), they are invariably violent. Not surprisingly, the government officials and social classes that have long held (and often abused) power and now face bleak futures invariably fight to stay on top. Should the revolutionaries triumph, old elites are then removed from power, new ones are installed, and at least in some respects, political, economic, and social participation broadens to include those further down the social and economic ladder. This does not imply that revolutionary governments are democratic. They virtually never are. But they are usually more broadly participatory and egalitarian than the regimes that they have toppled.

I classify as a revolution any insurgency that brings about these kinds of comprehensive political and socioeconomic changes. The insurrection may be rooted in class struggles (China and Nicaragua), as Skocpol insists, or, contrary to Huntington, it may be a war of national liberation (Algeria and Angola), as long as it overturns critical political and economic institutions and changes the country's underlying power structure and societal values. In fact, the borderline between nationalist and class-based revolutions is often difficult to discern. The Vietnamese revolution most clearly combined anticolonial and class struggle.[10] Moreover, even primarily class-based revolutions, such as China's, Mexico's, Cuba's, and Nicaragua's, had important nationalist, anti-imperialist components to them.

Revolutions may be Marxist (China, Russia, Vietnam, Cambodia, and Cuba), partly Marxist (Nicaragua), or non-Marxist (Mexico, Bolivia, Libya, and Iran). Marxism was particularly appealing to many revolutionaries because it promised the ideological rigor, "economic justice," and new political myths that they sought. But the revolutionary's vision of social justice need not be communist. It may also come from nationalism, Islam, or other ideologies and religions.

Revolutionaries generally come to power either through mass uprisings— featuring strikes, protest marches, and street riots (Russia, Bolivia, and Iran), guerrilla warfare (China, Vietnam, and Cuba), or a combination of both (Nicaragua). There have also been a few elite revolutions in which military officers or upper-level bureaucrats have overthrown the regime and instituted far-reaching socioeconomic changes that far transcended the objectives of mere coups.[11] Primary examples include Mustafa Kemal Ataturk's revolt in Turkey in 1919, Gamal Abdel Nasser's officers' revolt in Egypt in 1952, and Peru's "revolution from above" in 1968, all led by progressive military officers (see Chapter 9).

UNDERLYING CAUSES OF REVOLUTION

Just as experts have disagreed over the definition of revolution, they have also differed over the causes of revolutionary insurrection. Some theories focus on broad historical trends, including changes in the world order that make revolution possible or likely. Other explanations center on weaknesses in the *ancien régime* (the former political and socioeconomic systems), examining factors that caused the prerevolutionary state to fall. And yet others focus on the major players in Third World revolutions, particularly the peasantry, seeking the factors that cause them to revolt.

Inexorable Historical Forces

Karl Marx viewed revolution as an unstoppable historical force growing out of class inequalities that are rooted in the unequal ownership of the means of production. Those who command the economic system, he argued, control the state as well. Over time, however, subordinate classes will become alienated from the political-economic system and will attain sufficient political skills and vision (class consciousness) to overthrow the existing order. Thus, Marx maintained, that the ascendant *bourgeoisie* (property owners, including capitalists)— who had toppled the old order controlled by the aristocracy and landed oligarchy—had led the British "Revolution" (Civil War of 1640) and the French Revolution (1789). Both revolutions were part of a broader European transition from agrarian feudalism to industrial capitalism. Although Marx believed that this new capitalist order presented a more advanced and more productive historical stage, he argued that it depended on the exploitation of the working class (proletariat). In time, he predicted, as the exploitation of the proletariat became more apparent and as workers developed sufficient class consciousness, they would overthrow capitalism and install revolutionary socialism.[12]

More than any other revolutionary theorist, Marx influenced the course of history, because most of the twentieth century's major revolutionary leaders— including V. I. Lenin, Mao Zedong, Ho Chi Minh, Ché Guevara, and Fidel Castro—fervently believed in his ideology. His writings evoked the centrality of class struggle in most revolutionary movements. But as even sympathetic analysts have noted, "He was, first and foremost a nineteenth-century man" whose ideology was closely linked to the era in which he lived.[13] "Marx's theoretical approach," writes one contemporary Marxist sociologist, "enabled him to explain the past but failed him in his predictions."[14] Indeed, *no* country has ever had the succession of revolutions that he predicted, first capitalist, then socialist.[15] Instead, the major locus of modern revolution has been the Third World—not advanced capitalist nations—and the major protagonists have been peasants rather than industrial workers.

Mao Zedong, the father of the Chinese Revolution, accepted Marx's view of revolution as part of a historical dialectic.[16] Like other Third World Marxists, he viewed capitalist exploitation and the resulting class conflict as the root cause of communist upheavals. However, the Chinese communist party's military defeats in the 1920s convinced him that its orthodox commitment to proletariat revolution was not viable in a country in which the working class constituted such a small percentage of the population. Consequently, he reinterpreted Marxist revolutionary theory to make it more applicable to China and other parts of the developing world. Mao developed a theory of peasant-based struggle and a military strategy designed to encircle and conquer China's cities following a period of protracted rural guerrilla conflict.[17] The success of his strategy in the world's most populous country and its frequent use elsewhere in the Third World made Mao the most influential twentieth-century practitioner of revolutionary warfare.

In Vietnam and Cuba, Ho Chi Minh and Ché Guevara refined Mao's vision of "peoples' war" to make it more compatible with conditions in Southeast Asia and Latin America. While all of them demonstrated that communist revolutions could take place in countries that are not highly industrialized, those leaders still adhered to Marx's theory of history and his vision of class struggle.

Regime Decay

Even before the collapse of the Soviet bloc, it had become obvious that there was no *inevitable* march toward revolution and that, in fact, successful revolutions are rather rare and unique. Theta Skocpol argues that neither the repression of the masses nor the skills of revolutionary leadership alone can bring about successful social revolutions. These factors may be necessary, but they are not sufficient. Rather, true revolutions succeed only when international pressures such as war, economic competition, or an arms race undermine the state. The modernization of Britain and other European powers, she contends, created severe military and economic pressures on the LDCs within and outside Europe. Some of those states, such as royalist France, czarist Russia, and imperial China, were less able to adjust to these challenges and, hence, became more susceptible to revolutionary challenges.[18]

In the Russian case, excessive military entanglements, foreign indebtedness, and a disastrous military involvement in World War I undermined the czarist state. Successive military defeats in two wars—first by the Japanese (1905) and then by the Germans (1917)—did in the regime. Similarly, China's Manchu dynasty, having been fatally weakened first by European and then by Japanese imperialism, was toppled easily by Kuomintang (Nationalist) forces in 1911, who, in turn, were overthrown by the communists nearly 40 years later. Elsewhere, stronger regimes were able to withstand comparable challenges, but the Russian and Chinese states were too weak to marshal sufficient economic and military resources. Ultimately, disgruntled soldiers, workers, and peasants, led by "marginal elites" (university students and middle-class professionals alienated from the system), toppled the old order.[19] Ironically, just as military competition undermined the czarist government and set the stage for the Russian Revolution, some 70 years later the Soviet-American arms race weakened the Soviet Union and contributed to the collapse of the communist regime.

Thus, Skocpol and others have argued that the primary factor contributing to revolutionary transformation is not the revolutionary leadership's strategy, tactics, or zeal, but rather the internal rot of the decaying old order. For example, Japan's invasion of China prior to World War II undercut the legitimacy of the Kuomintang government. The Japanese occupation demonstrated that the Nationalist regime was too corrupt and incompetent to resist a foreign threat, while the communist People's Liberation Army (PLA) was far more effective. When the Chinese revolutionary war resumed after World War II, many of the areas in which the communists won major military victories were the same ones in which they had organized mass resistance against the Japanese.[20]

In fact, military defeats have frequently delegitimized the regime in power, setting the stage for subsequent revolutions. Thus, the destruction of the Ottoman empire in World War I and the Japanese capture of British, French, and Dutch colonies in Asia (including Burma, Vietnam, and Indonesia) during World War II all undermined the imperial or colonial governments' legitimacy and led, respectively, to the "Young Turks" military revolt in Turkey, the communist revolution in Vietnam, and various independence movements in South and Southeast Asia.[21] Similarly, Egypt's defeat by Israel (1948–1949) helped precipitate Colonel Nasser's revolution from above in that country.

War has the additional effect of disrupting peasant life, forcing many of them to seek a new social structure and physical protection offered by the revolutionary forces. For example, in accounts of life in rural China during its civil war and the Japanese invasion, "one is struck by the number of peasants . . . who had their routines upset through the [war-related] death of their kin before they joined revolutionary organizations."[22]

But factors other than military defeat may undermine governments. In Cuba and Nicaragua, prolonged dictatorships became obscenely corrupt. Fulgencio Batista rose from the rank of army sergeant in 1933 to become Cuba's dominant political actor over the next two decades. Under his administration and those of others he dominated, corruption infested all ranks of government. Batista's links to the American mafia helped turn Havana into a playground for affluent tourists seeking gambling and prostitution. For decades, members of the ruling Somoza dynasty commandeered a huge share of Nicaragua's economy. The National Guard—virtually the Somozas' personal army—enriched themselves (on a far lesser scale) as well. For example, when an earthquake leveled the nation's capital (Managua), the Guard intercepted and sold U.S. relief supplies.

A further factor undermining the legitimacy of both the Cuban and the Nicaraguan dictatorships was their subservience to the United States and the resulting affronts to national pride. Because the U.S. military had occupied both countries for years early in the twentieth century and because both subsequently remained in the American sphere of influence, this was a particularly sensitive issue. The occupying American Marines had installed Anastasio Somoza Sr., the family dynasty's founder, as the first commander of Nicaragua's hated National Guard (the country has no army), and he used that position subsequently to seize the presidency. Decades later, in the years preceding their Sandinista revolution, Nicaraguans derisively referred to his son President

Anastasio Somoza Jr., a graduate of West Point, as "the last Marine." In both Cuba and Nicaragua, the combination of rampant corruption and injuries to nationalist sensibilities united people across class lines—from peasants to students to business people—against the government. Lacking any real commitment to the regime, Batista's undisciplined army offered surprisingly little resistance to Fidel Castro's small guerrilla force. In Nicaragua, the National Guardsmen, knowing that they faced popular retribution if they lost power, put up a stronger fight against the Sandinista revolutionaries, but also fell relatively quickly.[23]

Revolutionary opportunities may also develop when the economy deteriorates, standards of living decline, and the government is unable to meet long-standing economic responsibilities to its population. For example, runaway inflation undermined support for China's Kuomintang government. Declining living standards also helped spark the Kenyan rebellion against British colonialism. Thus, maintains Charles Tilly, one cause of revolution is "the sudden failure of government to meet specific obligations which members of the subject population regarded as well established and crucial to their welfare."[24]

While Skocpol, Tilly, and others emphasize the decay of state authority at the *national* level, revolutions can also arise from the breakdown of authority at the *grass-roots* level. We observed earlier (Chapter 6) that a web of patron–client relationships linking peasants to their landlords and other local power brokers helps maintain stability in the countryside. Peasants will tolerate considerable injustice if the local landlord and the village political boss compensate by providing villagers with needed benefits, such as secure access to land, credit, and protection from harassment by the police. However, if the expansion of market forces makes rural patrons unwilling or unable to continue providing benefits that peasants had come to expect, then their authority will likely break down. At this point, the state may try to replace the traditional patrons by providing social services such as credit, technical assistance, schools, and clinics. If, however, government authorities fail to satisfy the peasants' needs as well, the rural poor may turn to revolutionary groups as their new patrons and protectors.

Challenges from Below

While revolutionary movements generally succeed only against discredited or weakened governments, they must also mount a well-organized and politically coherent challenge from below. Without that, the old regime, weak though it may be, will either cling to power (the Third World has numerous incompetent and discredited governments that linger on) or the society may collapse into disorder or anarchy (as in Somalia).

Charles Tilly contends that three things must happen before a revolutionary movement can succeed: first, the revolutionaries must establish themselves as an "alternative sovereignty"; that is, the rebel leadership must convince its would-be supporters that it can function as a viable alternative government. Second, a sizable portion of the population must support that revolutionary alternative. Finally, the established government must be incapable of suppressing the revolutionary opposition.[25] There are a number of well-known cases in which revolutionaries successfully established alternative sovereignties.

Following the collapse of Russia's czarist regime, the Bolsheviks (Communist Party) established a network of workers' soviets (local political committees) to challenge the sovereignty of Alexander Kerensky's moderate provisional government. Asia's protracted guerrilla wars also illustrate the phenomenon. During the Chinese Revolution, the PLA (the Communist Party's military arm) controlled "liberated zones" in which the communists distributed land to the peasants, organized military and political support, and demonstrated their ability to govern. The same was true of South Vietnam's National Liberation Front (Viet Cong).

But, even after understanding these broad preconditions for successful revolutionary activity, we still must ask what causes a revolution to break out in a particular country, at a particular time and not in others. Samuel Huntington maintains that the probability of a successful insurrection is determined by the balance of power between the capabilities of government political institutions, on the one hand, and the level of anti-government political and social mobilization, on the other. Most revolutions, he notes, occur neither in highly traditional societies nor in modern nations. Rather, they are most likely to erupt in modernizing countries—those in transition from traditional culture to modernity.[26] As greater urbanization, increased education and literacy, and expanded mass-media communication stimulate mass political mobilization, civil society (the network of organized groups independent of government control) makes increased demands on the political system. Unless the governing regime can create appropriate institutions capable of accommodating this increased political participation in a timely manner, the system will become overloaded and, hence, more unstable.

Huntington then distinguishes two distinct revolutionary patterns: a *Western* model in which "the political institutions of the old regime collapse followed by the mobilization of new groups into politics and then by the creation of new [revolutionary] political institutions" (i.e., regime decay precedes a full challenge from below); and an *Eastern* (Asian) revolutionary model that "begins with the mobilization of new groups into politics and the creation of new [revolutionary] political institutions and ends with the violent overthrow of the political institutions of the old order." The French, Russian, and Mexican revolutions fit the Western model, while communist revolutions in China and Vietnam followed the Eastern model.[27]

James C. Davies shifts our attention from the broad historical-social forces that make revolution possible to the question of why particular individuals choose to join a revolt or a revolution. He asserts that, contrary to what we might expect, people rarely rebel when they are experiencing prolonged or permanent suffering. "Far from making people revolutionaries, enduring poverty makes for concern with one's solitary self or solitary family, at best a resignation, or mute despair at worst."[28] To uncover the source of political upheavals, Davies combines economic and psychological explanations. Unlike Marx, Skocpol, or Tilly, his analysis lumps together mass revolutions with local uprisings and military "revolutions from above." Drawing upon historical data ranging from Dorr's Rebellion (an 1842 uprising in Rhode Island) to the Egyptian military revolution of 1952, he concludes that each upheaval took place after a period of sustained economic growth was followed by a sharp downturn. A diagram of that growth and subsequent downturn (Figure 8.1) produces what Davies called the

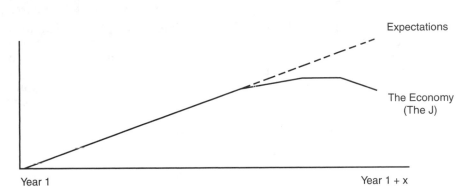

FIGURE 8.1   Davies's Psychological Model Showing the Gap Between People's Expectations and Economic Reality

"J-curve."[29] As a country's economy grows for a period of time, he suggests, people's expectations rise correspondingly (parallel to the long side of the J). However, those expectations continue to rise even after the economy experiences a downturn. What emerges is "an intolerable gap between what people want and what they get."[30] Davies argues that this economic J-curve also explains the American and French revolutions, the American Civil War, the rise of German Nazism, student unrest in the United States during the 1960s, and the African American civil rights movement.[31]

Using twentieth-century data from 17 LDCs, Raymond Tanter and Manus Midlarsky confirmed Davies's thesis in Asia and the Middle East but not in Latin America. Interestingly, their Asian and Middle Eastern cases also indicated that the higher the rate of economic growth prior to a downturn and the sharper the slide immediately preceding the outbreak of unrest, the longer and more violent the upheaval will be.[32]

Davies's theory is one of the most influential psychologically based explanations of revolutionary behavior. There is, however, an important limitation to his findings. He based his conclusions entirely on data from countries which had experienced revolts or revolutions. That raises the question of whether there are countries that experienced a J-curve in their economies (growth followed by a downturn) yet did not have social upheavals. In fact, Davies admits that there are. For example, he notes the absence of mass unrest in the United States during the Great Depression, a devastating economic downturn. The same holds true for many Latin American countries that enjoyed strong economic growth in the 1960s and 1970s followed by a precipitous decline in the 1980s. Argentina had a comparable cycle from 1990 to 1998. Thus, as Davies concedes, his theory identifies common but not sufficient conditions for unrest. Although a J-curve often leads to revolution, it does not necessarily do so.

Ted Gurr has also developed a psychological model examining the gap between expectations and reality. Like Davies, he examines various types of civil violence, not just revolution. Gurr argues that "the necessary precondition for violent civil conflict is relative deprivation defined as [the] actors' perception of the discrepancy between their value expectations [i.e., what people believe they deserve from life] and value capabilities . . . conditions that determine people's perceived chances of getting . . . what they . . . expect to attain."[33] In other words, *relative deprivation* is the gap between what people want or expect from life and what they actually get.

Unlike Davies's theory, however, Gurr's notion of relative deprivation is not solely economic. Thus, he posits that there is also a high probability of civil unrest if many people are deprived of an important, non-economic benefit that they have come to expect, or if they have suffered a blow to their status and their preferred social order. For example, although Westerners admired the Shah of Iran's attempts to modernize women's dress (prohibiting the veil) and improve their status, many of these changes violated the "preferred social order" of the nation's Shi'ite population. This, as we have seen, helped set the stage for the Islamist revolution. Furthermore, adds Gurr, the closer people are to attaining their goals, the greater will be their frustration if they fail to achieve them. Note, for example, the growing radicalization of Palestinians (expressed by the victory of the Islamist Hamas party in the most recent parliamentary elections) as the once-promising peace process between Israelis and the PLO had stalled and the dreams of a Palestinian state had faded.

Finally, Gurr maintains that the type of civil violence that a country experiences will depend on which segments of society are experiencing relative deprivation. If the poor alone feel frustrated, there may be political "turmoil" (spontaneous, disorganized violence) but not a revolution. Only if important elements of the middle class and the elite—more educated and politically experienced individuals who can provide political leadership—also suffer relative deprivation can there be revolutionary upheaval.

Causes of Revolution: A Summary

None of these theories of revolution offers a single "correct" explanation. For one thing, they often focus on different aspects of the question. For example, while Gurr and Davies ask why individuals join revolts or revolutionary movements, Skocpol focuses on the international economic and military factors that have weakened the state prior to successful revolutionary insurrections.

Clearly, revolutions are never inevitable and, in fact, successful revolutions are rare. While the causes of unrest may lie in relative deprivation and the regime's loss of legitimacy, the ultimate success or failure of revolutionary movements also depends on the relative military and political capabilities of the contending forces. Only by comparing the political-military strength of those who rebel with the state's capacity to defend itself can we understand why some revolutionary movements succeed while others fail.

As we have seen, revolutions often occur after a country has been defeated or badly weakened in war (Russia, China, Turkey, and Egypt) or after its government has been ousted temporarily (Europe's colonial regimes in Asia were removed by the Japanese during World War II). They may also take place when a government is particularly corrupt (Cuba and Nicaragua) or subservient to foreign powers (Cuba, Mexico, and Nicaragua). In all of these cases, the incumbent regime lost its legitimacy. Thus, the Russian czarist regime and China's Kuomintang government both fell when they proved incapable of defending their people's sovereignty. Similarly, Cuba's President Batista lost his legitimacy when he turned Havana into "the brothel of the Caribbean." And, the Shah of Iran lost his legitimacy after his Westernization program offended Iran's Islamic clerics. British, French, and Dutch colonial rule in Asia was secure as long as the indigenous population believed that Europeans were more powerful than they were and also better equipped to govern. When the Japanese ousted the colonial governments of Burma, Malaysia, Vietnam, and Indonesia, they demonstrated that Asian armed forces could defeat European powers. Once the Europeans lost their aura of invincibility, they were unable to reestablish sustained colonial rule after World War II.

Finally, the very authoritarianism of many Third World governments may ultimately undermine them. Cuba's Fulgencio Batista, the Shah of Iran, and Nicaragua's Anastasio Somoza Jr. illustrate that point. Because their governments had never been legitimized through free and honest elections, they could not convincingly claim to represent the people. Ignoring that problem during the Cold War, the United States supported authoritarian governments in countries such as El Salvador, Nicaragua, Chile, Zaire (Congo), South Korea, Iran, and Pakistan. Responding to criticisms by human rights groups, Washington argued that, whatever their faults, these repressive governments were the last remaining fire walls against communist subversion and the rise of totalitarianism. In truth, however, a democratic government offers the best inoculation against revolution. Indeed, no consolidated democracy has ever been toppled by a revolution.[34]

LEVELS OF POPULAR SUPPORT

Ché Guevara, the leading military strategist of the Cuban Revolution, once observed that those who undertake revolutions either win or die. Though perhaps overstating his point, Guevara's remark highlights the tremendous risk revolutionary fighters take, be they poor peasants or radicalized university students. Rebels almost always face superior fire power and a range of formidable state institutions (the police, the military, special intelligence units, etc.). Not surprisingly, most of the time the insurgents lose. One study counted 28 guerrilla movements in Latin America from 1956 to 1990. Of that total, only two succeeded (Cuba's July 26 movement and Nicaragua's Sandinistas).[35] Asia and Africa are also littered with the corpses of dead revolutionaries and failed insurgents. Even victorious revolutions, such as Vietnam's and China's, leave behind vast numbers of fallen rebel fighters and supporters. Those who survive often return home to devastated villages and suffering families. Not surprisingly, then, individual peasants, workers, students, and professionals do not take lightly the decision to join a revolutionary force.

What portion of the population must support a revolution if it is to succeed? What types of people are most likely to join the movement? The answer to the first question is ambiguous. There is no fixed or knowable percentage of the population that must support an insurrection in order for it to triumph. Following World War II, a majority of Ukrainians are believed to have supported a separatist movement fighting to end Russian control, yet that uprising was crushed by the powerful Soviet army. On the other hand, insurgencies elsewhere have succeeded with the active support of less than 20 percent of the civilian population.

Any evaluation of popular sentiment during a revolutionary upheaval needs to identify at least five different groups. First, there are those who strongly support the government and believe that their own fates are linked to the regime's survival. Government officials, military officers, landowners, and businesspeople with close links to the pre-revolutionary state normally fall in this category. It may also include ethnic groups tied to the regime (such as the Hmong people of Laos), people ideologically committed to the political system, and an assortment of others with a stake in preserving the status quo.

A second group in society also supports the government but more conditionally. For example, during the 1960s, most Venezuelans supported the government's battle against Marxist guerrillas. Even though many of them shared the guerrillas' disapproval of Venezuela's severe inequalities, sprawling shantytowns, and rural poverty, they were repelled by the rebels' use of violence and their failure to work within the country's recently achieved democratic framework.[36] Because the government's public support was broad but thin (i.e., many Venezuelans were conditional supporters), it could easily have lost its advantage had it used the repressive anti-guerrilla tactics so widely employed elsewhere in Latin America. By showing moderation, the government held its ground.

A third, often critical, segment of the population supports neither the revolutionaries nor the government. Its members are generally alienated and probably dislike both sides. In the 1980s and 1990s, many Peruvian Indian villages were victimized by the *Sendero Luminoso* (Shining Path) guerrillas, an extremely fanatical and brutal revolutionary Marxist movement. At the same time, these peasants also were often brutalized by the Peruvian army, which flagrantly violated their human rights. Not surprisingly, most peasants feared and hated both sides. Caught in the middle, for their own preservation they avoided taking sides, though some did join government-supported defense militias.

A fourth group—drawn primarily from the peasantry, workers, the urban poor, and alienated members of the middle class who sympathize with the revolutionary cause—occasionally lends support to the insurgents but does not actually join them. For example, sympathetic peasants in China, Cuba, and Vietnam offered intelligence information, food, and shelter to rebel guerrillas. In countries such as China and El Salvador, where the guerrillas controlled "liberated zones" for long periods of time, these support networks were very extensive. In other countries where the revolution was fought primarily through urban street protests rather than guerrilla war (Iran) and in revolutions with important urban and rural components (Mexico, Nicaragua), revolutionaries also depended on the sympathy and occasional support of the urban poor, workers, and the middle class.

Finally, there is a relatively small portion of the population that fully involves itself in the revolutionary struggle. In Cuba, Mexico, and Nicaragua, for example, committed students, teachers, and professionals assumed leadership positions. In those countries, as well as in China, Vietnam, and El Salvador, many peasants (including women and teenagers) become the revolution's foot soldiers. Given the enormous risks involved for the participants and their families, it is not surprising that only a small portion of the people took up arms. Some peasants joined out of desperation, because the armed forces had destroyed their farms or villages or because they feared being drafted into an army that they despised. Others were attracted to the revolutionaries' promises of a more just social order.

One can only guess the proportion of a particular country's population in each of these five groups at a particular point in time. Public opinion surveys in countries experiencing revolutionary upheavals are unlikely to elicit honest responses. But we do know that if they are to succeed, revolutionary movements must attract a core of firmly committed activists willing to risk their lives for the cause, as well as a larger circle of sympathizers. How large their numbers must be depends on the extent of government decay and loss of legitimacy. It also depends on how well-armed and committed government troops are, how effectively those troops fight, and how much foreign support they have. Thus, for example, Fidel Castro's small rural force of only a few hundred troops (supported by a comparable number of urban guerrillas) defeated Batista's much larger but dispirited army. On the other hand, El Salvador's FMLN—a far larger and better-equipped guerrilla army than Castro's—could not unseat a government that was bolstered by extensive American economic and military aid. Yet even the United States' commitment of massive military assistance and hundreds of thousands of American troops could not save the South Vietnamese government from the Viet Cong guerrillas and its North Vietnamese allies.

The people in the second category (mild government supporters) and the third (neutrals) are equally important targets for any revolutionary movement. In developing countries with substantial urban populations, governments can maintain power in the face of considerable peasant unrest and rural guerrilla activity as long as they control the cities and retain the support of the urban middle class, particularly civil servants, businesspeople, and professionals. These middle-class groups are not normally radical, but they can become disenchanted with particularly corrupt, repressive, or ineffectual regimes. In Iran, the tide turned in favor of the revolutionary mullahs when Tehran's bazaar shopkeepers lost confidence in the Shah's government.

Nicaragua's revolution also illustrates this point. Because the Somoza family had expropriated such a large share of the national economy, its greed not only damaged the poor but hurt the business community as well. As the Sandinista uprising spread and the National Guard became increasingly repressive, Nicaragua's private sector grew increasingly alienated from the government. Prominent business leaders—including the head of the country's Coca-Cola bottling plant, the nation's most prominent newspaper owner, and the directors of several important banks—demanded Anastasio Somoza Jr.'s resignation and organized business shutdowns to express their opposition. While most of these people were wary of the Sandinista movement (which made no secret of its leftist ideology), they shared its desire to oust the Somoza regime.[37]

While flying from Panama to Miami during the height of the insurrection, this author found himself seated next to the chief executive of an important Nicaraguan agrochemical plant. In the course of our conversation about events back home, he declared, "Somoza has to go. He's too damned corrupt and he's wrecking the country." "But what if reformist business leaders such as you have to share power with the [Marxist-oriented] Sandinistas after he falls?" I asked.[38] "I don't like those guys," he replied, "but if sharing power with them is what it takes to get rid of Somoza, then we'll have to do it." In the face of such broad ideological and cross-class opposition to the government, it was just a matter of time before the Somoza regime fell.

In short, if a revolutionary movement is to gain power, there must be wide-scale disaffection with the government, a disaffection that reaches beyond the ranks of the poor and the oppressed to the heart of the middle class and the business community. It is neither likely nor necessary for a large portion of those sectors to actively support the insurrection. For the revolution to succeed, it is only essential that some of them, including a highly committed core, do so, while many others, like the Nicaraguan business executive on the plane, simply cease supporting the government.

PEASANTS AS REVOLUTIONARIES

Let us now turn our attention to the ranks of committed revolutionary supporters, particularly the last group, revolutionary activists. With rare exception, Third World revolutions have been fought primarily by peasants. The Chinese Red Army and the Viet Cong, for example, consisted overwhelmingly of the rural poor. Indeed, almost all African and Asian revolutionary movements have been overwhelmingly rural in character. And even in Latin America's revolutions, where the urban populations often played key roles, peasants were also very important actors. Consequently, it is important to ask, "What factors induce peasants to risk joining a revolution, and what types of peasants join?"

Why Peasants Rebel

In our analysis of Third World rural society (Chapter 6), we noted that traditional peasant culture tends to be rather conservative. Because early economic modernization frequently affects them negatively, they have good reason to cling to tradition. But the intrusion of market forces into their communities sometimes so unsettles their world that it radicalizes them as they struggle to protect what they have. For one thing, increasing numbers of subsistence farmers (peasants producing primarily for their family's consumption) in a modernizing economy are induced or pressured to enter the commercial market for the first time. Once involved in commercial agriculture, however, they must deal with fluctuations in the price of their crops, including volatile shifts that they are ill-equipped to handle.

At the same time, rural landlords, whose precapitalist exploitation of local peasants had been somewhat constrained by their neofeudal obligations, now viewed their tenants merely as factors of production in the new market economy. In Latin America, many landlords who had previously funded their peons' *fiestas* or lent them money when they were in special need concluded that such expenditures were no longer financially prudent in the more competitive market environment. Other landlords entering the commercial market decided to mechanize production and evict tenant farmers from their land.

For all of these reasons, rural society's transition from neofeudal to capitalist production precipitated many of the twentieth century's Third World revolutions.[39] James Scott notes that the pain peasants suffered during that transformation was not merely economic or physical but also *moral*. To be sure, the precapitalist rural order had its share of grave injustices, but those inequities were somewhat mitigated by a web of reciprocal obligations between landlords and peasants and among peasants. It is the collapse of that "moral economy," Scott argues, that drives many peasants to revolution.[40] Similarly, as noted in Chapter 6, Eric Wolf insists that in countries as disparate as Cuba, Mexico, Algeria, Vietnam, and China, most peasant participants in revolutionary movements were not trying to create a new socialist order. Rather, they were seeking to restore the security of their old way of life.

Which Peasants Rebel

Even in a single country or region, peasants are not a homogeneous mass. Some of them, called *kulaks*, own larger plots of land and employ other peasants to work on their farms with them. Others are landless or own extremely small plots. And still others work as wage laborers on large estates or rent parcels of land from the landlord, paying their rent in cash, labor, or sharecropping.[41] Each group has distinct political and economic needs.

The peasants most threatened by the economic modernization of the countryside are the ones most likely to join local revolts or broader revolutionary movements. Analyzing data collected from 70 developing nations over a 22-year period, Jeffrey M. Paige found that the peasant groups most likely to join insurgencies were wage laborers and sharecroppers who worked for landlords who, in turn, earned all their income from their land.[42] Not only are these peasants particularly vulnerable to changing economic conditions, but their landlords are also less likely to grant them financial concessions because they depend exclusively on their farmland for their incomes. Research on Latin American guerrilla movements reveals that squatters (poor farmers illegally occupying land) and other peasants who face eviction from the land they cultivate are also more prone to rebel.[43]

But even peasants with more secure access to the land feel threatened by declining crop prices. For example, in Peru's Ayacucho province, the birthplace of the Shining Path (Sendero Luminoso) guerrilla movement, peasants experienced declining terms of trade for two decades; that is, the cost of the goods they consumed had been rising faster than the price of the crops that they sold. Caught in an ongoing financial squeeze, they felt increasingly insecure and, hence, became more receptive to the Shining Path's appeals.[44]

All of the peasants who are prone to support revolutions, then, have one element in common—they were threatened by the prospect of losing their land and/or their livelihood. Conversely, the most conservative peasants are those with secure title to their land holdings and relatively stable prices for their crops. It is for this reason that many analysts maintain that the best protection against rural revolution is an agrarian reform program that distributes land and offers the recipients secure titles and support services.

Peasant insurrections are also more likely to develop in areas that have historical traditions of rebellion. For example, the revolutionary forces in China, Vietnam, Cuba, Mexico, and Nicaragua all received their greatest support in regions that had traditions of peasant resistance, what one author calls a "rebellious culture."[45] Fidel Castro's home province of Oriente, known as "the cradle of the Cuban Revolution," had a long history of unrest dating back to nineteenth-century slave revolts against their owners and against Spanish colonial rule. China's Hunan province (Mao Zedong's home) and the area around the Sandinista stronghold of León also had rebellious traditions. Some revolutionary movements take root in areas without a record of prior rebellions but with a tradition of lawlessness and hostility toward the legal authorities. For example, Mexican revolutionary leader Pancho Villa operated in a region known for cattle rustling and other forms of social banditry. And Villa himself was a bandit turned revolutionary. Similarly, Castro's July 26 guerrillas based themselves in the Sierra Maestra mountains, a region with a history of smuggling, marijuana production, and banditry.

REVOLUTIONARY LEADERSHIP

Although peasants furnish the foot soldiers for revolutions, they rarely hold the highest leadership posts. They may stage spontaneous uprisings or even more extensive revolts on their own, but they usually lack the organizational and political skills needed to conduct a broader social revolution. Consequently, the top leadership and many of the mid-level revolutionary leaders are typically people with more education and greater political experience. To be sure, there are exceptions. Mexico's Emiliano Zapata was a horse trainer from a peasant family who only became literate as an adult.[46] Pancho Villa was also of humble origins. Today, peasants hold important leadership posts in the Colombian Revolutionary Armed Forces (FARC) guerrillas.[47] Ultimately, however, their lack of political experience and outside contacts usually prove costly. For example, Villa and Zapata jointly conquered Mexico City, the nation's capital, but then left it because neither man felt equipped to run the country.

More typically, then, the top revolutionary leadership comes from middle-class or even upper-class origins. In Latin America, for example, "they are drawn disproportionately from the intelligentsia, not only highly educated, but also largely involved in the production of theories."[48] Trained as a librarian, China's Mao Zedong was the son of a rural grain merchant. In Vietnam, Ho Chi Minh, the son of a rural school teacher, practiced a number of professions, including photography, while living in Paris, where he became a French Communist Party activist. Fidel Castro received a law degree at the University of Havana, where he was a leader in student politics. His father, a Spanish immigrant, had started life in Cuba as a worker, but eventually became a well-to-do landowner. Castro's comrade, Ché Guevara, was a doctor whose parents, though not rich, were of aristocratic background. Similarly, most of the nine *comandantes* who directed Nicaragua's Sandinista revolution came from solid middle- or upper-class families and were well educated. For example, President Daniel Ortega and his brother, Defense Minister Humberto Ortega, were the sons of an accountant-businessman. Luis Carrión, the son of a millionaire, had attended an American prep school. Only one *comandante*, Henry Ruiz, came from a poor urban family, and none were of peasant origin.[49] Finally, a Vietnamese Communist Party study of nearly 2,000 party activists (conducted after World War II, at the start of their long revolutionary struggle) revealed that 74 percent of them were either intellectuals or were from bourgeois families, while only 7 percent were workers, and 19 percent came from peasant families.[50]

These are remarkable statistics for a party trying to speak for the country's peasantry and working class.

Not surprisingly, a larger number of lower-ranking revolutionary leaders are of peasant or working class background. Compared to Latin America, more of the rural poor have held leadership positions in Asia's revolutionary governments (including China, Vietnam, and Cambodia), where peasants accounted for most of the country's population. During their two-decade revolutionary struggle and also after assuming power the Chinese Communist Party and the Red Army offered peasant activists unprecedented opportunities for upward mobility. Virtually from the date of its formation, the party gave peasants and children of peasants—heretofore at the bottom of the social ladder—preference for admission. And as recently as 1985, decades after it took power, one-third of all Communist Party members were peasants (some 25 percent of whom were illiterate).[51] Similarly, many of the lower- and middle-level guerrilla leaders in El Salvador and Peru were of peasant origin, although they had often left their villages to become teachers, health workers, or the like.

The educational and social gap separating aspiring revolutionary leaders from the peasant rank-and-file can be a considerable problem unless the leaders have a firm understanding of the local culture. Although Mao Zedong became an urban intellectual, his rural upbringing had given him an understanding of village life. Fidel Castro was certainly no peasant, but his childhood on his father's farm had familiarized him with the region's rural poor. And in Venezuela, several of the FALN commanders were sons of local landlords who traded on their father's patron–client ties to the local peasants.[52]

On the other hand, the rural poor often reject aspiring guerrilla activists who come to the countryside from the city, from other regions of the country, other countries, or other ethnic backgrounds. Given their history of exploitation, peasants tend to be understandably wary of outsiders. The wider the linguistic, cultural, or racial gaps between would-be revolutionary leaders and the local villagers, and the greater the peasants' prior suspicion of outsiders, the harder it is for aspiring organizers to break through that wall of distrust. In Cuba, where racial and ethnic divisions were relatively less severe, the peasants of the Sierra Maestra Mountains accepted a total outsider, Ché Guevara, a White, urban, middle-class Argentinean. So when he later ventured to Bolivia to spread the revolution, Guevara may have been ill-prepared for the substantial mistrust its Aymara Indian peasants felt toward White outsiders such as him. There, an anti-guerrilla unit of the Bolivian armed forces killed him, aided by the CIA and by local villagers who saw no reason to risk their safety for an outside agitator. Similarly, Hector Béjar, a failed Peruvian guerrilla leader, later wrote candidly in his memoirs about how he—a coastal, White journalist and poet—was unable to gain the trust of the highland Indians whom he had hoped to lead.[53]

REVOLUTIONARIES IN POWER

While many comparative studies have examined the causes of revolution, there is less cross-national research on the *policies* revolutionary regimes implement once in office. Perhaps guerrilla fighters in the hills have inspired more interest and romanticization (or fear) than have revolutionary bureaucrats in the corridors of power. The record suggests that Third World revolutions in the developing world have accomplished more than their detractors admit but less than their supporters claim.

A primary objective of Marxist and many non-Marxist revolutionary governments alike has been greater socioeconomic and political equality. That quest usually begins with the struggle for power itself, when revolutionary leaders use egalitarian appeals to garner support from downtrodden peasants and workers. Recognizing the critical importance of that support, Mao Zedong wrote that the peasantry is to the guerrilla army what water is to fish. To win their loyalty, the Red Army treated China's peasants with greater respect than other military forces or governments had.[54] Similarly, in Cuba, "the army's brutal treatment of the peasants" contrasted with "Castro's policy of paying for the food purchased from the peasants . . . and putting his [mostly urban] men to work in the . . . fields."[55]

Once in power, revolutionary governments continue to emphasize equality. In addition to redistributing land and other economic resources, they also introduce egalitarian cultural reforms. For example, at meetings of Cuba's Committees for the Defense of the Revolution (CDRs), neighbors may pressure husbands to share household tasks with their spouses. Efforts at economic and social egalitarianism have been more limited in non-Marxist revolutions. Still, insurgencies such as Bolivia's and Mexico's have somewhat improved the social status of the rural poor, including indigenous (Native American) peoples.

As we have seen, revolutions open up new channels of upward social mobility for peasants and workers who previously had few such opportunities. To be sure, we have noted that people from middle-class backgrounds hold most of the higher government and party posts. Nor do many party members from ethnic minorities hold the most powerful political positions. Thus, for example, there have been relatively few Blacks in Cuba's Communist Party politburo or ethnic minorities in China's. But many revolutionary activists from humble backgrounds *do* hold lower- and mid-level political positions that they could never have attained under the old order. Revolutionary parties and mass organizations such as Cuba's CDRs may give peasants and workers a greater sense of participation in the political system.

Finally, revolutions usually decrease their nation's level of economic inequality, though the degree of change varies from country to country. Agrarian reform programs in China, Vietnam, Bolivia, Cuba, Mexico, and Nicaragua redistributed land from the rural oligarchy to the peasantry.[56] Many Marxist regimes have offered guaranteed employment, state-supported medical care, subsidized housing and food, and other egalitarian measures, while also establishing more equitable income distribution . In contrast, more moderate revolutions in Bolivia and Mexico failed to reduce economic inequality.

To be sure, notable inequalities persist even in radical revolutionary societies. Disparities between rural and urban populations frequently decline but are never eliminated. As China implements free-market reforms, income inequality, down sharply in the 1980s, has increased sharply. In Cuba and Vietnam, professionals and skilled workers still earn much higher salaries than do peasants or unskilled blue-collar workers, even though that gap has narrowed. At the same time, a new form of inequality often seeps in, as newly entrenched party and government officials begin to appropriate special perquisites for themselves and their families. Many years ago, Milovan Djilas, a disillusioned former leader of Yugoslavia's communist government, complained about the rise of a "new class" in revolutionary regimes, an elite of party officials who enjoy special privileges and a better standard of living.[57] Today in China, the foremost Communist Party leaders are well known for their lavish lifestyles, while the children of the party cadre are despised for their arrogance and corruption. Despite these problems, however, revolutionary governments such as Cuba's and Vietnam's have substantially reduced the general level of social inequality.

Another major revolutionary objective has been mass political mobilization. As Samuel Huntington notes, "a full-scale revolution involves the rapid and violent destruction of existing political institutions, the mobilization of new groups into politics, and the creation of new political institutions."[58] Thus, in China, Vietnam, Cuba, and Nicaragua, government incentives and pressures induced a large portion of the population to join revolutionary support groups.[59] At one time, close to 90 percent of Cuban adults belonged to their neighborhood Committees for the Defense of the Revolution (CDRs). In the 1980s, substantial portions of the Nicaraguan population joined Sandinista Defense Committees (CDSs).

At its best, mass political mobilization has increased the government's capacity to build the economy by mobilizing volunteer labor or spreading labor discipline. At times, revolutionary support groups have also helped combat sexism, racism, and crime. At their worst, these groups have been used as vigilantes against alleged counterrevolutionaries and as agents of thought control. At Cuban CDR meetings, government spokespersons familiarize the members with current government political position, while citizens are encouraged to volunteer for projects such as planting neighborhood gardens, and are imbued with greater revolutionary consciousness.[60] But in Mao Zedong's China, mass mobilization often involved brutal political campaigns that called upon citizens to root out and punish alleged enemies of the revolution. Hundreds of thousands were persecuted, jailed, or killed during the government's Anti-Rightist Campaign (1957) and its Cultural Revolution (1966–1976).[61]

Mass mobilization can be used either to activate citizens who support the revolution's goals or to isolate and persecute those who do not. Most revolutionary regimes are led by a dominant party, such as the Chinese Communist Party or the Mexican PRI, which stands at the center of the mobilization process. Opposition parties are either prohibited or are only tolerated in a weakened condition. Among Marxist governments, only Nicaragua's Sandinistas allowed themselves to be voted out of office. Elsewhere, a number of non-Marxist revolutionary parties have lost favor over time. They may resort to fraud when faced with the prospect of losing (Mexico until 2000), cancel elections that the opposition is expected to win (Algeria), or hand over the reins of power and become just another competing party (Bolivia and, most recently, Mexico).

In short, while revolutionary regimes claim to speak for the people and often do in many respects, we have noted that they are hardly ever democratic. Because they view themselves as the *only* legitimate voice of the popular will and the *only* representatives of the general good, most radical regimes tend to regard opposition groups as enemies of the people who should not be given political space. Nicaragua's Sandinista government, a rare exception, allowed opposition parties and interest groups to function, though they were occasionally harassed. Although the opposition newspaper, *La Prensa*, was periodically censored or briefly shut down, it continued to vigorously, and sometimes outrageously, attack the government right up to the time its publisher, Violeta Chamorro, was elected the nation's president. For the most part, however, even communist governments that have opened up their economies to free-market reforms (China and Vietnam) have maintained a repressive political structure and remained intolerant of opposition voices.

While the first generation of revolutionary leaders often comes to power full of idealism, the next generation (or even the founding generation itself) frequently succumbs to the corruptions of power. In China and Vietnam—where rapid economic growth and the expansion of the private sector have opened up new opportunities for corruption—bribing the right state official is often a requirement for doing business.[62] Cubans, who had generally felt that their revolutionary officials had a higher standard of honesty than preceding governments, were shocked by the "Ochoa affair," which indicated that high-ranking military and security officers were involved in drug trafficking. Government corruption on a lesser scale has since become far more pervasive as a result of the severe economic scarcities of the 1990s.[63] And, after the Sandinistas left office, disillusioned Nicaraguans learned that top party officials had kept for themselves some of the luxurious mansions that had been confiscated from the Somoza regime. It is not that these revolutionary regimes are more corrupt than other Third World governments; often they are less so. Thus, *Transparency International*'s most recent ratings of international corruption rank both Cuba and China better than average (i.e., less corrupt than over half the countries on the list) and even better when compared to Third World countries only.[64] It is just that their supporters, many of whom made considerable sacrifices for the revolutionary cause, had expected more.

CONCLUSION: REVOLUTIONARY CHANGE AND DEMOCRACY

Throughout the twentieth century, revolutionary change was an important force in much of the Third World. That influence was probably greatest in Asia, where the Chinese Revolution transformed the lives of one-fifth of humanity and where revolutionary struggles in Vietnam, Laos, and Cambodia involved France and then the United States in major wars. Elsewhere in Asia, there have been failed communist insurgencies in the Philippines and Malaysia and, most recently, a partially successful one in Nepal. Most of Africa's revolutions have been wars of national liberation from European colonialism (Algeria, Kenya, and Namibia, among others) or secessionist wars (including Biafra, Eritrea, and southern Sudan). Military officers sometimes initiated from above class-related revolutions in Africa (such as Ethiopia's). Latin America had two non-Marxist insurrections (Bolivia and Mexico), two Marxist revolutions (Cuba and Nicaragua), and a number of unsuccessful revolutionary movements (Argentina, Colombia, El Salvador, Guatemala, Peru, Uruguay, and Venezuela). Both the revolutions and the failed insurgencies had spillover effects in neighboring countries. For example, the Cuban Revolution spawned various agrarian reform programs elsewhere in Latin America, often designed to avert "another Cuba." The Nicaraguan Revolution inspired both agrarian reform and intensified government repression in neighboring El Salvador.

However, in the past two decades the appeal of revolution, particularly Marxist revolution, has waned considerably. Indeed, today's world is a veritable graveyard of failed insurrections. The Soviet Union, once the fountainhead of communism, collapsed, and its most important successor state, Russia, struggles to overcome the errors of its Marxist-Leninist past. Communism is equally discredited in almost all of Eastern and Central Europe, where it held sway until recently. Cuba's government, like Nicaragua's before it, has seen its impressive initial gains in education, health care, and social equality partially eroded by an economic crisis from the late 1980s to the mid-1990s. Finally, in many other recently fallen as well as surviving revolutions (Marxist and non-Marxist alike), the scorecard of successes and failures is far more distressing. Countries such as Afghanistan, Angola, Cambodia, Ethiopia, and Mozambique have suffered enormous devastation with little or nothing to show for it.

Evaluating the quality of revolutionary change in the more successful revolutions is not easy, for it is influenced by the analyst's ideological lens and by the difficulty of isolating the effects of revolutionary policy from a host of other overlapping factors. For example, critics of the Chinese Revolution argue that the socioeconomic gains attained under Mao were achieved in spite of his radical policies, not because of them. They further insist that the country's rapid economic growth under Deng Xiaoping demonstrates the advantages of free-market reforms. Others maintain that Cuba's substantial progress in health care and education since its revolution has been no more substantial than Costa Rica's and, furthermore, that Cuba accomplished its gains because of massive Soviet aid over nearly 30 years.

On the other hand, more sympathetic observers note that Cuba achieved impressive educational and welfare progress in spite of the U.S. economic embargo and that the American-backed Contra war (coupled with a trade embargo) destroyed the Nicaraguan revolution's earlier economic and social accomplishments. At the same time, some analysts insist that China could never have achieved its market-based economic boom without the prior educational advances under revolutionary socialism. Neither side can definitively prove its position because too many determining factors make it impossible to establish clear causal relationships. In any event, while there may yet be future revolutions in the developing world, it is likely that *the age of revolution* is drawing to an end. The demise of Soviet and Central European communism exposed more clearly the deficiencies of Marxism-Leninism. So too have China's and Vietnam's introduction of free-market (capitalist) components into their economic systems.[65] As communism has been discredited even among some of its once-fervent supporters, it is unlikely to find many adherents willing to risk their lives fighting for its ideals. Marxist ideology, once chic among Third World intellectuals and political activists, has become far less fashionable.[66] At the end of the 1980s, facing defeat by its mujahadeen opponents, Afghanistan's ruling party, People's Democratic Party, renounced its Marxist ideology in a failed effort to maintain power. One of its leaders dismissed the party's long-standing communist stance by claiming that it had adopted that ideology at "a time when Marxism-Leninism was quite in fashion in underdeveloped countries." In Angola, where the governing party made a similar ideological conversion, the president explained that continuing to support the Marxist-Leninist model "would be rowing against the tide [of capitalist democracy]."[67] Similar transformations have occurred within Nicaragua's Sandinista party and El Salvador's FMLN, both former revolutionary movements that subsequently transformed themselves into democratic socialist political parties. In his unsuccessful 2001 campaign for the presidency and in his 2006 victory, Sandinista leader Daniel Ortega insisted that Jesus Christ, not Marx, was his first inspiration when he led the country's revolution more than 20 years earlier. Modifying his earlier leftist views, he declared that "in this new context, to which we had to adjust, the market economy plays its role."[68]

How many revolutionary upheavals will take place in the coming years is hard to predict, and the answer may be partly an issue of semantics (i.e., how we choose to define a revolution). However, now that colonialism has come to an end in Africa and Asia, there are few possibilities for wars of national liberation as we have known them. There still may be other mass-based revolutions in societies that suffer from severe socioeconomic inequalities, sharp rural–urban divisions, or repressive governments. However, as we have noted, the collapse of the Soviet bloc, the abandonment of Marxist economics in China and Vietnam, the failure of the Nicaraguan revolutionary government, and Cuba's economic problems have all substantially diminished the appeal of revolutionary Marxism. Thus, for example, El Salvador's FMLN guerrillas ended their 12-year revolutionary struggle, signed a peace treaty that promised some of the reforms that they had long fought for, and converted themselves into one of the leading political parties in the congress.

Future insurgencies are most likely to occur in Africa, the Middle East, and parts of Asia. Perhaps, there also will be scattered uprisings by indigenous peoples (Indians) in Latin America, as there already have been in Bolivia, Ecuador, and Peru. Fundamentalist Islamic upheavals are very likely in some of these regions. Whether these struggles can properly be called revolutions, however, is debatable. They satisfy neither Huntington's nor Skocpol's definitions. Hence, it is probably more accurate to call them civil wars, secessionist rebellions, religious uprisings, or ethnic conflicts, rather than revolutions. Successful revolutions, in the sense that Skocpol or even Huntington defines them, appear unlikely in the foreseeable future.

DISCUSSION QUESTIONS

1. What are some of the major factors that have led to the collapse of state power in a number of countries and the rise of revolutions?
2. What factors account for the declining likelihood of further Third World revolutions?
3. Discuss some of the psychological theories of revolution (i.e., the theories of James C. Davies and Ted Robert Gurr).
4. What segments of the population are most likely to support revolutionary movements, and how much support do such movements need in order to succeed?
5. Discuss some of the major accomplishments and failures of revolutionary governments.

NOTES

1. China's Leninist regime remains in place, but the government has abandoned the principles of Marxist economics and class politics.

2. In Angola and Mozambique, most of the killing was done by counterrevolutionary forces. For the hundreds of thousands of innocent civilians butchered, however, it mattered little which side killed them.

3. One classic study of historical change argues that the American War of Independence was not a revolution. See Barrington Moore Jr., *The Social Origins of Dictatorship and Democracy* (Boston: Beacon Press, 1966), 112. For a contrary view, see J. Franklin Jameson, *The American Revolution Considered as a Social Movement* (Boston: Beacon Press, 1956), 16–20, 32–35.

4. Chalmers Johnson, *Revolution and the Social System* (Stanford, CA: Hoover Institution, 1964), 2.

5. Peter Calvert, "Revolution: The Politics of Violence," *Political Studies*, vol. 15, no. 1 (1967), 2; and *Revolution and Counter Revolution* (Minneapolis: University of Minnesota Press, 1990).

6. Samuel P. Huntington, *Political Order in Changing Societies* (New Haven, CT: Yale University Press, 1968), 264. A similar definition was offered decades earlier in Sigmund Neumann, "The International Civil War," *World Politics*, vol. 1, no. 3 (April 1949), 333–334, fn. 1.

7. Norman R. Miller and Roderick R. Aya, *National Liberation: Revolution in the Third World* (New York: Free Press, 1971).

8. Theda Skocpol, "France, Russia, China: A Structural Analysis of Social Revolutions," *Comparative Studies in Society and History*, vol. 18, no. 2 (1976), 176.

9. Theda Skocpol, *States and Social Revolutions: A Comparative Analysis of France, Russia and China* (Cambridge, England: Cambridge University Press, 1979), 4.

10. John Walton distinguishes between the handful of "great revolutions" that satisfy Skocpol's definition and a larger number of "national revolts" that are based on class and nationality and that he feels are not particularly distinguishable from social revolutions. John Walton, *Reluctant Rebels* (New York: Columbia University Press, 1984), 1–36.

11. Ellen Kay Trimberger, "A Theory of Elite Revolutions," *Studies in Comparative International Development*, vol. 7, no. 3 (1972), 191–207; Ellen Kay Trimberger, *Revolution from Above: Military Bureaucrats and Development in Japan, Turkey, Egypt and Peru* (New Brunswick, NJ: Transaction Books, 1978).

12. Karl Marx and Frederick Engels, *Manifesto of the Communist Party* (New York: International Publishers, 1948).

13. A. S. Cohan, *Theories of Revolution* (London: Thomas Nelson and Sons, 1975), 72.

14. Irving M. Zeitlin, *Marxism: A Re-examination* (Princeton, NJ: Princeton University Press, 1967), 142.

15. In other words, no Marxist revolution has taken place in a country where capitalism was entrenched. By the end of the twentieth century, in a complete reversal of Marxist theory, communist regimes in the Soviet Union and Central Europe were changing to capitalism. It is still too early to know what form that transition will ultimately take in Russia and other former Soviet republics.

16. Marx's use of "dialectic," which he drew from the German philosopher G. W. F. Hegel, indicated that major ideas or historical forces (the thesis) are inevitably opposed by rival ideas or forces (the antithesis), and out of this struggle emerges a "synthesis" that draws upon both sides.

17. Stuart R. Schram, *The Political Thought of Mao Tse-tung* (New York: Praeger, 1969).

18. Skocpol, *States and Social Revolutions*.

19. Skocpol, "France, Russia, China."

20. Chalmers Johnson, *Peasant Nationalism and Communist Power* (Stanford, CA: Stanford University Press, 1962).

21. Johnson, *Revolution and the Social System*.

22. Joel Migdal, *Peasants, Politics and Revolution* (Princeton, NJ: Princeton University Press, 1974), 252.

23. Ramón L. Bonachea and Marta San Martín, *The Cuban Insurrection, 1952–1959* (New Brunswick, NJ: Transaction Books, 1974); Jorge L. Domínguez, *Cuba: Order and Revolution* (Cambridge, MA: Belknap Press of Harvard University Press, 1978), 93–95; John A. Booth, *The End and the Beginning: The Nicaraguan Revolution* (Boulder, CO: Westview Press, 1982).

24. Charles Tilly, *From Mobilization to Revolution* (New York: Addison-Wesley, 1978), 204–205.

25. Charles Tilly, "Does Modernization Breed Revolution?" *Comparative Politics*, vol. 5, no. 3 (April 1974), 425–447.

26. Huntington, *Political Order in Changing Societies*, 265.

27. Ibid., 266. Not all Asian revolutions followed the Eastern model, nor did all Latin American insurgencies conform to the Western model. The collapse of the Chinese imperial regime in 1911 fit

the Western model, while the Cuban Revolution (1959) followed the Eastern model, at least in part.

28. James C. Davies, "Toward a Theory of Revolution," *American Sociological Review*, vol. 27, no. 1 (February 1962), 7.

29. More precisely, the economic pattern he describes can be graphed as the letter "J" tipped over (Figure 8.1), with the long side representing the period of economic growth and the rounded part depicting the downturn.

30. James C. Davies, "Toward a Theory of Revolution," reprinted along with other articles on the causes of revolution in *When Men Revolt and Why*, ed. James C. Davies (New York: Free Press, 1971).

31. Ibid., and James C. Davies, "Revolution and the J-Curve," in *Violence in America: Historical and Comparative Perspectives, A Report Submitted to the National Commission on the Causes and Prevention of Violence*, eds. Hugh Davis Graham and Ted Robert Gurr (New York: New American Library, 1969), vol. 2, 547–577.

32. Raymond Tanter and Manus Midlarsky, "A Theory of Revolution," *Journal of Conflict Resolution*, vol. 11, no. 3 (1967), 264–280.

33. Ted Robert Gurr, "Psychological Factors in Civil Violence," *World Politics*, vol. 20, no. 2 (1967–1968), 252–253; see also Ted Robert Gurr, *Why Men Rebel* (Princeton, NJ: Princeton University Press, 1970).

34. The only case where a communist regime replaced a democratic government is in postwar Czechoslovakia. But that communist government took power through a Russian-backed coup, not through revolutionary insurgency.

35. Timothy P. Wickham-Crowley, *Guerrillas and Revolution in Latin America* (Princeton, NJ: Princeton University Press, 1992), 312. Revolutions and guerrilla wars are not synonymous, of course. In recent decades, however, virtually all revolutionary struggles have been fought by guerrillas in Latin America and other parts of the Third World.

36. One defining event, a guerrilla attack on a tourist train, alienated most Venezuelans. Ultimately, several guerrilla leaders renounced violence and, following a government amnesty, entered electoral politics. Teodoro Petkoff, a former guerrilla who has since enjoyed a distinguished career as a congressman, cabinet minister, and presidential candidate, told me in a 1978 interview that the Left's violent tactics had been a major error and had cost it considerable support.

37. Booth, *The End and the Beginning*.

38. Such an alliance was discussed in the American press and in both Washington and Nicaraguan political circles. Neither Nicaraguan businessmen nor the State Department harbored any illusions that they could keep the *Sandinistas* out of power at that point. However, they and the Carter administration hoped that the *Sandinistas* were not strong enough to hold power on their own. In fact, after rebels ousted the Somoza regime, the *Sandinista*-led government did initially include progressive business leaders, but they soon parted ways.

39. Eric R. Wolf, *Peasant Wars of the Twentieth Century* (New York: Harper & Row, 1969). For a discussion of similar factors in the capitalist transformation of Europe, see Karl Polanyi, *The Great Transformation* (New York: Rinehart, 1957).

40. James C. Scott, *The Moral Economy of the Peasant: Rebellion and Subsistence in Southeast Asia* (New Haven, CT: Yale University Press, 1976); James C. Scott and Benedict J. Kirkvliet, *How Traditional Rural Patrons Lose Legitimacy* (Madison: University of Wisconsin, Land Tenure Center, 1975).

41. Sharecroppers are tenant farmers who pay their rent by giving the landlord a percentage of their crop.

42. Jeffrey M. Paige, *Agrarian Revolution: Social Movements and Export Agriculture in the Underdeveloped World* (New York: Free Press, 1975), chaps. 1–2. Sharecroppers are defined in endnote 41.

43. Wickham-Crowley, *Guerrillas and Revolution*, chap. 6.

44. Cynthia McClintock, "*Sendero Luminoso*: Peru's Maoist Guerrillas," *Problems of Communism*, vol. 32, no. 5 (September–October 1983), 19–34.

45. Wickham-Crowley, *Guerrillas and Revolution*, 246–250; Wolf, *Peasant Wars*.

46. John Womack Jr., *Zapata and the Mexican Revolution* (New York: Vintage, 1968).

47. Wickham-Crowley, *Guerrillas and Revolution*, 145.

48. Ibid., 213; Alvin Gouldner, *The Future of Intellectuals and the Rise of the New Class* (New York: Seabury Press, 1979), 53–73.

49. Dennis Gilbert, *Sandinistas: The Party and the Revolution* (New York: B. Blackwell, 1988); for detailed information on the social backgrounds and occupations of a substantial number of Latin American guerrilla leaders, see Wickham-Crowley, *Guerrillas and Revolution*, 327–339.

50. Thomas H. Green, *Comparative Revolutionary Movements* (Upper Saddle River, NJ: Prentice Hall, 1974), 18.

51. Of course the percentages of peasants and illiterates in the party were still well below their

share of the general population, but they were higher than in most LDCs. Since the late 1980s, the educational level and professional training of mid-level party leaders has risen.

52. Wickham-Crowley, *Guerrillas and Revolution*, 143.

53. Hector Béjar, *Peru 1965: Notes on a Guerrilla Experience* (New York: Monthly Review Press, 1970).

54. Among the many writings on Maoist ideology and strategy, see Stuart R. Schram, *The Political Thought of Mao Tse-tung* (New York: Praeger, 1963); Arthur Cohen, *The Communism of Mao Tse-Tung* (Chicago: University of Chicago Press, 1964); Cohan, *Theories of Revolution*, 93–110.

55. Sebastian Balfour, *Fidel Castro* (New York: Longman, 1990), 49.

56. Peasants have been most pleased when they received individual family plots and far less satisfied when agrarian reform converted the old agricultural estates into cooperatives or state farms.

57. Milovan Djilas, *The New Class* (New York: Praeger, 1957).

58. Huntington, *Political Order in Changing Societies*, 266.

59. See, for example, William J. Duiker, *The Communist Road to Power in Vietnam*, 2d ed. (Boulder, CO: Westview Press, 1996).

60. Richard R. Fagen, *The Transformation of Political Culture in Cuba* (Stanford, CA: Stanford University Press, 1969); Domínguez, *Cuba: Order and Revolution*.

61. There is a voluminous literature on the Cultural Revolution. Liang Heng and Judith Shapiro, *Son of the Revolution* (New York: Vintage, 1983), offer a moving personal account of both the Anti-Rightist Campaign and the Cultural Revolution. See also K. S. Karol, *The Second Chinese Revolution* (New York: Hill and Wang, 1974); Jean Esmein, *The Chinese Cultural Revolution* (New York: Anchor Books, 1973); and Lowell Dittmer, *Liu Shao-ch'i and the Chinese Cultural Revolution* (Berkeley: University of California Press, 1974).

62. *The Guardian: Unlimited*, "Corruption: China's Mushrooming Problem" (August 3, 2007), http://www.guardian.co.uk/china/story/0,,2141185,00.html; *The Economist*, "Vietnam's Corruption" (September 12, 2002), 9.

63. Sergio Díaz-Briquets and Jorge Pérez López, *Corruption in Cuba: Castro and Beyond* (Austin: University of Texas Press, 2006). Because General Ochoa was convicted in a dubious "show trial" (13 days after his arrest), and because he was surely the victim of a power struggle, the extent of his guilt and that of his compatriots is unclear. However, most experts do believe he and other officers were involved in drug trafficking. There is also little doubt that there has been widespread corruption since the economic crisis of the 1990s.

64. "The 2996 Transparency International Corruption Perception Index," *Infoplease*, http://www.infoplease.com/ipa/A0781359.html.

65. Nicholas Nugent, *Vietnam: The Second Revolution* (Brighton, England: In Print Publishers, 1996), chaps. 5–6.

66. On this theme, see Forrest Colburn, *The Vogue of Revolution in Poor Countries* (Princeton, NJ: Princeton University Press, 1994).

67. Both quotations come from Colburn, *The Vogue of Revolution*, 89.

68. *New York Times* (September 6, 2001).

CHAPTER 9

SOLDIERS AND POLITICS

For many years, military governments were common in much of the developing world—most notably in Latin America, Africa, and the Middle East. More recently, as democracy has advanced in much of the Third World, military rule has become unusual. However, military men still govern countries such as Libya and Myanmar, and in many other developing nations the armed forces continue to exert considerable political influence.

Of course, men emerging from the military ranks occasionally head even the most advanced industrial democracies. American President Dwight Eisenhower, French President Charles de Gaulle, and Israeli Prime Minister Ariel Sharon all used distinguished military careers as stepping stones to the leadership of their nation. But each of them entered politics as a private citizen, having first retired from the armed forces. Moreover, they achieved high office through democratic elections, not military coups.

Over the years Third World politics has been distinguished by its high degree of military interference, either through direct rule or as a dominant interest group. Unlike their counterparts in industrialized democracies, soldiers in the LDCs have often rejected a dividing line between military and political activity. A pronouncement by the Indonesian armed forces prior to their assumption of power in the 1960s illustrates that perspective well:

> The army, which was born in the cauldron of the Revolution, has never been a dead instrument of the government, concerned exclusively with security matters. The army, as a fighter for freedom, cannot remain neutral toward the course of state policy, the quality of government, and the safety of the state.[1]

To be sure, there are countries such as India, Malaysia, Kenya, Tunisia, Mexico, and Costa Rica where the military has not ventured deeply into politics for decades. But, until the 1980s, such restraint was the exception rather than the rule. Indeed, until recently, the military's political involvement in most of the Third World was so pervasive that it was almost a defining characteristic of political underdevelopment.

One early study of military intervention revealed that the 59 developing nations scrutinized had experienced a total of 274 attempted military coups between 1946 and 1970.[2] Twenty-three of those countries witnessed five or more takeover attempts in that period. Bolivia and Venezuela led the way with 18 attempted coups each.[3] At the start of the 1980s, almost every country in South America—most notably Argentina, Brazil, Chile, and Peru—was governed by the armed forces. During that decade the military also dominated politics in much of Africa, including Algeria, Ghana, Nigeria, and Sudan.

Starting with the overthrow of Egyptian King Farouk by reformist military officers in 1952, Sudan's 1958 coup, and General Mobutu Sese Seko's 1960 takeover in the Congo (Kinshasa), the armed forces dominated the continent's politics. From 1958 to 1984, there were more than 62 successful and 60 failed coup attempts in Sub-Saharan Africa, affecting more than 80 percent of the nations in that region.[4] In 1982–1983 alone, Upper Volta (now Burkina Faso) experienced three military takeovers in only nine months! On average during the 1980s, military rulers governed 65 percent of Africa's population. Noting the absence of electoral change in the region for most of that period, one observer argued that "coups had become the functional equivalent of elections, virtually the sole manner of ousting incumbent political leaders."[5] As democracy began to grow in the 1980s, the number of coups on the continent (including North Africa) shrank somewhat from its high point during the previous decade (from 24 to 18), but rose again slightly in the 1990s. In all, Sub-Saharan Africa experienced 80 coups and 108 failed coup attempts from 1956 to 2001, affecting 41 of the region's 48 countries. Three African countries (including Nigeria, the continent's most populous nation) had six successful coups each.[6] One of them, Benin, experienced six coups in 10 years, an average of one military intervention every 20 months.

Military dominance was not nearly as prevalent in Asia, where India, Sri Lanka, and Malaysia, among others, were able to maintain relatively democratic civilian governments, while in the Philippines, Singapore, Taiwan, and China, authoritarian civilian rulers controlled the armed forces. Still, for much of the 1970s and 1980s, Pakistan, Bangladesh, Thailand, South Korea, and Indonesia were subjected to long periods of military dominance.

Although several Arab nations in North Africa (including Algeria, Libya, and Sudan) have often been controlled by the armed forces or by military strongmen, indirect military dominance is more common in the Middle East. President Husni Mubarak of Egypt and Syria's long-time strongman Hafez al-Assad (1970–2000) entered politics as military men. Elsewhere in the region, monarchies in Morocco, Jordan, Saudi Arabia, Kuwait, and the smaller Gulf States have, at least until now, successfully controlled the military.

The last 20–25 years has seen a sharp decline in the number of Third World military coups and military regimes. That change has been most dramatic in Latin America, where democratically elected government has become the norm. In 1990, the last extended military government in the region came to an end when Chile's freely elected government replaced General Augusto Pinochet's 17-year dictatorship. In a remarkable turnabout, armed forces coups have virtually ended in the region as it has enjoyed its longest period of democratic governance ever. In Asia, military regimes fell in countries such as Indonesia, Bangladesh, and South Korea. But, after having stepped down in favor of civilian governments, military rulers returned to power in Pakistan and Thailand, while in Bangladesh the armed forces indefinitely postponed national elections in 2007 and installed a caretaker government headed by civilians but dependent on military support. And, the military government in Myanmar endures as one of the oldest (since 1962) and most repressive dictatorships in the world. Even in Africa, where military government persisted into the 1990s, important transitions to civilian government have occurred in such nations as Nigeria and Ghana, leaving few military regimes in power. And, although coups remained common in Sub-Saharan Africa through the 1990s, from 2001 through 2006 there were only three successful military takeovers, all in very small nations (Sao Tome and Principe, Guinea-Bissau, and Mauritania). Today only a few Third World countries remain under formal military rule. However, there are others in which former leaders of the armed forces have become presidents in questionable elections.

While the number of Third World military governments has declined substantially, the armed forces continue to wield considerable political influence over many civilian regimes. As such, they may be able to veto the decisions of elected civilian officials in policy areas such as external defense and domestic security, and to influence appointments to important government posts.[7] In some countries, military leaders protect their own budgets, determine who serves as defense minister, or control military promotions. Thus, for example, although elected civilian presidents have governed Guatemala since 1985, any president still hesitates to pursue policies that threaten the army's interests. Similarly, when Corazón Aquino served as Philippine president, she regularly consulted on major issues with her military chief of staff, General Fidel Ramos, who subsequently was elected to succeeded her.[8] In a number of countries, such as Nigeria and Syria, the armed forces remain a powerful force in politics. On the other hand, in other nations once dominated by the military (such as Argentina and Brazil), the Generals now fully accept civilian control.

In order to examine military involvement in Third World politics and the changing nature of civil–military relations, this chapter explores a series of interrelated questions: What accounted for the high level of armed-forces political involvement in the past (and possibly again in the future)? How do the structures of military regimes differ from one another? What do the armed forces hope to accomplish when they seize power? How successful have military regimes been in achieving their political and economic goals? Is military rule generally beneficial or detrimental to economic and political development? What factors have induced military regimes to step down in recent decades? What political roles do the armed forces continue to play after the establishment or reestablishment of civilian rule? How can either long-standing or recently established civilian governments best control the military?

THE CAUSES OF MILITARY INTERVENTION

Political scientists have generally offered one of two alternative perspectives for explaining the frequency and nature of military intervention in developing countries. The first focuses on the *internal characteristics* of the armed forces themselves. The second stresses the broader *political environment* in which the military operates, most notably the weakness of civilian regimes.

The Nature of the Armed Forces

In early research on Third World politics, many analysts maintained that the armed forces enjoyed greater organizational cohesion and clarity of purpose than did civilian political institutions, hence their penchant for intervention. As one leading analyst concluded, "The ability of officers to intervene in domestic politics and produce stable leadership is [directly] related to internal [military] social cohesion."[9] Recognizing the importance of understanding the military's inner workings, scholars examined the class origins, educational levels, ideological orientations, and internal organization of the officer corps. These factors all seemed to affect the probability of military involvement in politics and to influence the officers' goals.

Obviously, the officers' education and training greatly influence their political values. In his highly influential book, *The Soldier and the State*, Samuel Huntington argued that a country wishing to keep the military out of politics must impart professional values to its officers.[10] Ideally, as military training and tactics become more sophisticated, officers develop specialized and complex military skills, while distancing themselves from politics. Under those circumstances, Huntington claimed, "a clear distinction in role and function exists between military and civilian leaders."[11] However, he warned, such a division of function only will develop if military training focuses on external threats such as wars with other nations. Should the focus of military education shift toward internal warfare—controlling guerrilla unrest or other civil insurrection—professionalization will not suffice to keep the military out of politics.[12]

Building on this theme, Alfred Stepan distinguished between "old" and "new" military professionalism. The former, typical of developed countries such as the United States, emphasizes skills relevant to "external security." As military officers train to repel foreign enemies, Stepan agreed, we can expect them to remove themselves from domestic politics. In many developing nations, however, military training (new professionalization) has primarily prepared officers for internal warfare against class- or ethnically-based insurgencies.

Following the Cuban Revolution, Latin American generals and U.S. policy makers shared a common concern about leftist guerrilla movements in the region. Training programs for Latin American officers at home and in the United States emphasized counterinsurgency techniques as well as "civic action" programs (e.g., road and school construction) designed to "win the hearts and minds" of the local population. American policy makers claimed that such preparation would provide the military with a professional mission in civilian society and thereby remove it from national politics. Almost invariably, however, teaching officers to deal with *internal* security threats involved them in the study of domestic political and economic issues, thereby drawing them into the political arena.[13] Not surprisingly, the number of military coups in the region soon escalated.

In a recent historical study of civilian relations with the military in various national settings, Michael Desch found that the level of civilian control over the armed forces correlates with the level of external threat that the country faces from a foreign adversary and the extent of any domestic threat from internal upheaval. He argues that civilian control over the military is likely to be strongest when the country faces a high external threat and a low internal threat. Conversely, civilian control is generally weakest when the country faces a low external threat and a high internal threat, precisely the situation that prevailed in many Latin American and African nations.[14]

The Nature of Civil Society

Although research into the internal structure and dynamics of the armed forces is very useful, it fails to tell the entire story. That is to say, we cannot ascertain the probability of military intervention in politics and the objectives of that intervention merely by evaluating internal military factors such as armed forces cohesion, size, or ideological orientation. For example, there is surprisingly little correlation between the military's size or its firepower, on the one hand, and its propensity to topple civilian governments, on the other. Indeed, Africa, home to some of the world's smallest militaries, has had one of the highest incidences of military rule. In Togo, an army of only 250 men and a small number of retirees from the former French colonial force carried out West Africa's first military coup. "In Dahomey [now called Benin], General Sogol [sic] who had come to power by a coup d'état, was [later] overthrown by sixty paratroopers."[15] Indeed, small and poorly armed military units executed several other takeovers in the region. In the closing years of the twentieth century, of nearly 45 African countries, 35 had armed forces of fewer than 30,000, and 23 of those had fewer than 10,000 men.[16] In contrast, China, India, Israel, Sweden, and the United States—with far larger, more skilled, and more internally cohesive militaries—have never experience a coup.

Ultimately, then, the military's propensity to intervene in politics is less a function of its own capabilities than a consequence of the weaknesses of civilian political institutions. As Huntington has insisted, "the most important causes of military intervention in politics are not military, but political and reflect, not the social and organizational characteristics of the military establishment, but the political and institutional structure of society."[17] Hence, the second group of explanatory theories focuses its attention on the nature of civil society.

If a civilian government enjoys substantial support from relevant elites, influential political parties, and the general public, and if it provides political stability and a healthy economy, it is relatively immune to military coups. Conversely, "in times of uncertainty and the breakdown of [civilian political] institutions, soldiers come into their own; when there is no other effective organization of society, even a small, weak army may take command over a large, unorganized mass."[18] In his classic study of civil–military relations, *The Man on Horseback*, Samuel E. Finer maintained that national political cultures could be ranked according to the following three criteria:

1. The extent of public support for the procedures used to transfer political power (such as elections) and for the corresponding belief that only those procedures are legitimate.
2. The degree of public awareness regarding the individuals and institutions holding sovereign authority, and the degree to which the population believes that no other person or group can legitimately hold that power.
3. The strength of civil society. That is, the extent to which citizens are organized into groups—such as labor unions, business associations, and churches—that act independently of the government.[19]

The stronger a nation's political culture supports those three factors, argued Finer, the lower the likelihood of military intervention. In short, countries are most capable of maintaining civilian rule when there is a wide consensus on the legitimacy of elected, civilian government and when there are independent, organized groups capable of defending that principle—even taking to the streets if need be.

If the government retains widespread citizen loyalty, even if coups are attempted, they will usually fail. An example from Eastern Europe demonstrates well what is possible when a civilian government enjoys greater legitimacy than its military opponents. In 1991, when Soviet generals and hardline communist civilian officials staged a coup aimed at ousting Soviet President Mikhail Gorbachev, thousands of civilians joined Russian President Boris Yeltsin in defending the Russian parliament with their bodies. At the same time, key commanders of the troops sent to take Moscow and St. Petersburg refused to support the rebellion. Thus, the coup d'état failed badly because Yeltsin's and Gorbachev's governments had sufficient legitimacy to survive. In contrast, the legitimacy of civilian regimes in many developing nations is low. Consequently, disgruntled military leaders have been more inclined to overthrow them, while loyalist troops and civilians have been less likely to risk their lives defending them.

Various factors may either enhance or undermine a civilian government's legitimacy. From an institutional perspective, civilian regimes are strongest when broadly based political parties support them. Where party systems are deeply entrenched in the fabric of society and elicit widespread support, the likelihood of military intervention is greatly diminished.[20] Indeed, a country's susceptibility to coups is influenced less by its level of democracy than by the degree to which its party system penetrates and organizes society. Thus, authoritarian governments in Mexico, Cuba, Taiwan, and China (all once or still dominated by a single party) have controlled the military as effectively as have multiparty systems in Jamaica and India. When placed under sufficient stress, however, not even a strong party system can fully immunize a political system from military interference. For example, during most of the twentieth century, vibrant, competitive parties in Uruguay and Chile shielded those countries from the military takeovers that plagued most of Latin America. By 1973, however, growing class conflict and political polarization had undermined the political order in both countries, ushering in authoritarian military regimes.

Civilian governments are most vulnerable when they are unable to maintain political stability, during periods of economic decay (particularly runaway inflation), and when they are widely perceived as corrupt. All these circumstances undermine their legitimacy and often increase popular expectations that military rule could improve conditions. In nations such as Nigeria, Thailand, and Pakistan, soon after taking power military leaders declared their intention to root out widespread corruption. In such cases, military intervention has sometimes, initially drawn broad support from civil society. Following severe economic and political crises in Argentina, Brazil, Chile, and Uruguay, the new military authoritarian regimes set out to crush leftist movements, restore social order, and reinvigorate the economy.

As modernization theory would lead us to believe, countries that are more socioeconomically developed are less likely to suffer military takeovers than their poorer neighbors.

Countries with per-capita GNPs of $1,000 or more [in 1995 dollars] do not [normally] have *successful* coups; countries with per-capita GNPs of $3,000 or more do not have coup *attempts*. The area between $1,000 and $3,000 per-capita GNP is where unsuccessful coups occur, while successful coups . . . were [most common] in countries with per-capita GNPs under $500.[21]

In short, a nation's propensity for military intervention reflects, in large part, the strength of its political institutions, the values of its political culture, and its level of economic development. Yet, these factors alone do not account for all the variations in civil–military relations. Elite values and behavior also play an important role. For example, India and Costa Rica, with political and socioeconomic circumstances comparable to those of their neighbors, have experienced far less military intervention in politics. The explanation may lie in the values of their political elites: elected officials, government bureaucrats, political party leaders, influential business people, and labor leaders, as well as military officers.

India illustrates this point well. Located near several countries with histories of military intervention (Pakistan, Bangladesh, Myanmar, Thailand), it has been governed exclusively by civilians since independence. There is little to suggest that the Indian public, still heavily rural and illiterate, has a political culture more modern or informed than that of its neighbors. Nor, until the 1990s, was its economy much more advanced (indeed it has trailed Thailand). It appears, however, that India's political elite has subscribed to the principles of civilian control more strongly than its neighboring counterparts have.

Elite values, however, may change more quickly than entire political cultures do. In a process of "political learning," a nation's civilian leaders may understand from prior experience how better to avert military coups. The armed forces governed Venezuela for much of the first half of the twentieth century. From 1959 into the mid-1990s, nearly four decades of elected government transformed the country into one of Latin America's most stable democracies until government corruption and a declining economy undermined the political establishment's legitimacy in the 1990s.[22] While a number of factors contributed to the prolonged period of civilian governance, one critical element was a change in the attitudes of political elites following the collapse of Venezuela's first experiment with democracy (1945–1948). Recognizing that political polarization had precipitated a 1948 military coup, leaders of the major political parties agreed to moderate their political conflict. In 1958, the foremost democratically oriented political parties signed the Pact of Punto Fijo, which increased interparty cooperation and set the basis for decades of civilian political dominance.[23] Viewed until recently as a model for democratic reform in the region, Venezuela was one of the only Latin American countries to avoid military rule in the 1970s and 1980s. Indeed, elite political pacts, often modeled after Punto Fijo, helped terminate civil wars and establish democratic government in several Central American countries.

By the end of the 1980s, however, Venezuela's deep economic crisis and its pervasive government corruption had severely eroded civilian support for the political parties that had dominated government since the interparty pact. Two unsuccessful coup attempts in 1992 received considerable popular approval and turned the coup's leader, Lieutenant Colonel Hugo Chávez, into a national hero, at least among the poor. Elected government has survived, but

Chávez, who spent two years in jail for his coup activity, easily won the 1998 presidential elections. The two political parties that had signed the Punto Fijo pact and had dominated Venezuelan politics for the next 40 years were practically wiped off the electoral map. Since then, Chávez has subverted some of the country's democratic institutions and given the armed forces a much greater foothold in politics (though a 2004 referendum on his presidency indicated that a substantial majority of the population continues to support his populist economic reforms). Still, while not a panacea, political pacts in Venezuela and elsewhere have often been a valuable tool for establishing more stable civilian government.

PROGRESSIVE SOLDIERS AND MILITARY CONSERVATIVES

Having examined the factors promoting or inhibiting military intervention, we will now consider the political behavior and policies of military regimes once they have established control. Given the disorder and conflict that characterize so many Third World civilian governments, we must ask whether military rule produces greater political stability and socioeconomic development, at least in the short run. Also, once in office, are the generals and colonels likely to be a force for progressive change or defenders of the status quo? Many of the foremost early modernization theorists felt strongly that the armed forces could contribute to development. Marion Levy was impressed by the military's alleged rationality, disciplined organization, and commitment to modern values. Taking their critics to task, he maintained that the armed forces might be "the most efficient type of organization for combining maximum rates of modernization with maximum levels of stability and control."[24] Lucian Pye also saw the military as one of the best-organized national institutions in otherwise "disorganized transitional societies." It was, said Pye, at the forefront of technical training and a leader in imparting the values of citizenship to the public.[25] For Manfred Halpern, the Middle Eastern military was "the vanguard of nationalism and social change."[26]

Positive evaluations such as these predominated in the early modernization literature.[27] They frequently were based on an idealized vision of the professional soldier: trained in modern organizational skills; nationalistic; and, above narrow tribal, class, and regional interests. At times these writings reflected the authors' strong preference for order and stability, coupled with the assumption that the military could bring order out of political and economic chaos. Occasionally, they drew on a few military success stories and projected them onto a larger screen. One early model was the Turkish military revolt led by Mustafa Kemal (Ataturk) in 1922. During the next two decades, Ataturk and his followers (the "Young Turks") modernized the country before eventually turning it over to civilian rule (see Chapter 3).[28] Another frequently cited military reformer was Egypt's Colonel Abdul Gamal Nasser, who rose to power in the 1950s seeking to reform his country's social and economic institutions while strengthening its military. Subsequent reformist militaries elsewhere in the developing world often have been labeled "Young Turks" or "Nasserites."

Over the years very different types of officers and even enlisted men have seized power, promising to modernize their country through industrialization, greater labor discipline, expanded education, agrarian reform, or other funda-mental changes. In countries such as Upper Volta, Libya, and Peru, left-wing militaries have promoted economic redistribution, greater state intervention in the economy, mass mobilization, and a struggle against imperialism. Conversely, conservative generals in Brazil, Chile, Indonesia, and South Korea repressed mass political participation while encouraging investment by domestic firms and multinational corporations (MNCs).

Why have some military regimes championed the poor, while others have supported wealthy corporate and landowning interests? To find the answer, we must examine the class origins of the officers' corps, the nation's level of socio-economic development, and the class alliances that emerge in the political system. Research in a range of LDCs has shown that officers often come from middle-class backgrounds, particularly in Asia and Latin America. Typically, their fathers were military officers, shopkeepers, merchants, mid-sized land owners, teachers, or civil servants.[29] Not surprisingly, then, military regimes have commonly identi-fied with the goals and aspirations of their nation's middle class.

But what are those goals, and what political ideologies and government policies have emerged from them? In the least developed Third World coun-tries, officers have often viewed economic elites, including large landowners and MNCs, as the source of their country's backwardness. The middle class fre-quently resents those same elites for obstructing its own rise to political and social prominence. In such a setting, both groups may perceive the relatively unmobilized lower class as a potential ally in the battle against the oligarchy. For example, soon after taking power, Peruvian General Juan Velasco blamed the traditional landowning class and Peru's international economic depend-ency for the nation's underdevelopment. In the following years, the military's ambitious land redistribution, shantytown reform, expropriations of property belonging to MNCs, expansion of the state economic sector, and mass mobiliza-tion greatly altered the country's political and economic landscape. Elsewhere, "General Omar Torrijos of Panama railed against oligarchical control and encouraged the lower class to participate in politics."[30] Muammar Qadhafi's government in Libya and a number of Marxist military regimes in Africa were cut from a similar cloth.

As a country modernizes, however, and as lower-class mobilization inten-sifies, the military confronts a changing political panorama. Urbanization, the spread of secondary and university education, and the development of more complex economies all enlarge and strengthen the middle class, enabling it to wrest a share of political power from the economic elites. At the same time, industrialization increases the size of the working class and enhances the trade union movement. Urbanization also creates a growing and sometimes militant shantytown population. And the commercialization of agriculture often trig-gers unrest in the countryside (see Chapter 6). Not surprisingly, the middle class (having achieved a share of political influence) and its military partners now come to see the more galvanized and politicized lower classes as a threat rather than a useful ally.

If left-wing political parties and trade unions have gained considerable mass support and if there has been growing political unrest, the military is even more likely to ally itself with the economic elite and to repress mass mobilization. In Chile, the election of Salvador Allende's Marxist government and the accompanying mobilization of workers, peasants, and urban poor polarized the country along class lines. In nearby Uruguay, the Left's electoral appeal was not as strong, but labor–industrial conflict was intense, and the Tupamaros, a potent urban guerrilla group, were engaged in a campaign of political kidnappings and insurgency. In both countries, the perceived threat of mass mobilization and an ascendant Left caused the military to topple long-standing democracies.

In short, then, the more underdeveloped a country is and the weaker its middle class, the higher the likelihood of having a left-of-center military.[31] However, notes Eric Nordlinger, "the soldiers who have power in countries with an established middle class . . . act as more or less ardent defenders of the status quo."[32] Similarly, Samuel Huntington observes:

> In the world of the oligarchy, the soldier is a radical; in the middle class world, he is a participant and arbitrator; as mass society looms on the horizon he becomes the guardian of the existing order. . . . The more advanced a society becomes, the more conservative and reactionary becomes the role of the military.[33]

The conservative military officers' concerns are not limited to leftist mass movements. They generally oppose any mobilization of lower-class groups that threaten the nation's stability. For example, in recent times, the Algerian and Pakistani armed forces (or at least portions of them) have stood in the way of mass mobilization by Islamic fundamentalists.

THE GOALS OF MILITARY REGIMES

Having observed the range of ideological orientations amongst military governments, we now examine the structures and goals of such regimes.

Personalistic Regimes

In the world's LDCs—those with low levels of military professionalization, limited mass political participation, extensive political corruption, and little semblance of representative government—military officers frequently seize power for their own personal enrichment and aggrandizement. Their governments tend to be personalistic; that is, a single charismatic officer with a strong personal following leads them. In order to bolster his support, however, the leader allows some government plunder to pass on to the military or civilian cliques surrounding him. "Legitimacy is secured through patronage, clientelistic alliances, [and] systemic intimidation."[34]

In Latin America, personalistic dictatorships were most common in the less developed political and economic systems of Central America and the Caribbean. One of the most prominent examples was the Somoza dynasty in Nicaragua. As leader of the country's National Guard (its only military force), General Anastasio Somoza Sr. overthrew the government in 1937, primarily seeking his own enrichment. Governing a small and impoverished nation, he amassed a fortune of several hundred million dollars at that time using state resources to purchase construction firms, urban real estate, electrical power plants, air and shipping lines, cement factories, and much of the nation's best farmland. Following Somoza's 1956 assassination, his political and financial empire passed to his two sons, who ruled the country in succession until the 1979 Sandinista revolution.[35] Other personalistic regimes in the Americas included the Batista government in Cuba (eventually toppled by Fidel Castro's revolutionary army) and Alfredo Stroessner's long-lived dictatorship in Paraguay. Batista had links to the mafia's gambling and prostitution operations in Havana. Stroessner and his associates enriched themselves by collaborating with international smugglers and drug dealers.[36]

Personalistic military regimes have been especially common in Sub-Saharan Africa, sometimes led by upwardly mobile junior officers or even enlisted men such as Ghana's Flight Sergeant Jerry Rawlings and Liberia's Sergeant-Major Samuel Doe. While some, like Rawlings, were well intentioned, most have done little to develop their countries. The most infamous personalistic dictators in the continent have been Uganda's Idi Amin Dada and the Central African Republic's Jean-Bédél Bokassa. Ironically, in light of his regime's enormous brutality, Amin initially justified his coup by pointing to the human rights violations of ousted President Obote. Enamored as much of power as of wealth, Amin played upon and exacerbated Uganda's ethnic divisions during his brutal eight-year reign (1971–1979). He not only expelled the country's sizable Asian population but also murdered an estimated 300,000 to 500,000 civilians, most notably members of the previously influential Langi and Acholi tribes. Seeing enemies at every turn, he even executed one of his wives. In an attempt to maintain absolute control over the armed forces, he purged or executed a large portion of the officers' corps, eventually creating an army composed largely of foreign troops (principally Sudanese and Zairian).[37]

Equally megalomaniacal, the Central African Republic's Marshal Bokassa unleashed a reign of death and terror on his country following his takeover in 1965. Plundering the treasury of one of the world's more impoverished nations, he concluded that the presidency was not a sufficiently exalted position, so he lavished millions of dollars on his own coronation as the country's new emperor. In time, Amin and Bokassa so outraged the world community that they were ousted through external intervention. Amin fell to a Tanzanian invasion, while a French-sponsored coup toppled Bokassa.[38]

Because most personalistic dictators lack a meaningful ideology or program to legitimize their regime, they typically must share some of the spoils with their military and civilian supporters in order to maintain themselves in office. For example, Zaire's President Mobutu, once Africa's most enduring military dictator (1965–1997), made himself one of the richest men on earth while opening up the floodgates of corruption to benefit his military and civil service. In this manner, he kept himself in office for decades while bankrupting the national government and destroying a once-dynamic economy. By the late 1990s, however, as the Zairian economy collapsed, his government unraveled, falling rapidly to a rebel force that, unfortunately, proved just as corrupt once they were in control.[39] More recently, warlords (regionally based, military/political bosses who loot the region they control) in Sierra Leone and Liberia overthrew the government with few goals other than looting the country. Warlords also have kept Somalia without a viable national government for some two decades. In Nicaragua, the Somoza dynasty maintained the National Guard's critical support by allowing its officers to enrich themselves. In the most egregious example, following an earthquake that devastated the nation's capital, Guard officers appropriated relief supplies sent from the United States and sold them for a profit.[40]

Institutional Military Regimes

As Third World political and economic systems modernize, corresponding changes take place in military institutions and attitudes. Frequently officers attend advanced military academies at home or abroad. Sometimes they enroll in specialized seminars with civilian leaders, establishing links with politicians, businesspeople, and academics. These programs more deeply expose military officers to their country's political and economic problems.

If these "new soldiers" seize power, they are likely to govern collectively rather than vest authority in the hands of a single leader. To be sure, some institutional military regimes often have been dominated by a single figure, such as Libya's Muammar Qadhafi, Indonesia's Suharto, Syria's Hafez Assad, and Chile's Augusto Pinochet. Like purely personalistic dictators, these men may be motivated by "covert ambition, fear, greed, and vanity."[41] Still, even in such cases, a substantial number of officers hold influential government positions (not just the paramount leader), and there is a degree of institutional decision making. In Indonesia, for example, active and retired military officers at one time held nearly half the positions in the national bureaucracy and some two-thirds of the provincial governorships.[42] In a like manner, the Argentine military dominated top positions in almost all government ministries during its most recent period in office. Furthermore, such institutional regimes' goals are broader than any single leader's ambitions.

Institutional military governments have generally been headed by collegial bodies such as Niger's Supreme Military Council or Myanmar's Revolutionary Council. Comparable councils or juntas have governed Algeria, Argentina, Brazil, Ethiopia, Thailand, Uruguay, and a host of other countries.[43] Typically, one active or retired officer serves as president and wields the most influence. Often, however, his term of office is limited. For example, their armed forces colleagues limited the presidents of military governments in Argentina and Brazil to a single term. In some countries, including South Korea, Brazil, and Indonesia, the armed forces tried to legitimize its rule by forming a government political party that ran candidates in tightly controlled elections. Often, candidates retire from active duty before standing for office. And in Egypt and Syria, military and civilian elites have joined together to form a ruling political party.[44]

Institutional military regimes can be as repressive and brutal as personalistic dictatorships—sometimes more so. Their day-to-day governing style, however, is more bureaucratic and sophisticated—commonly drawing on the talents of highly trained civilian technocrats.[45] Moreover, unlike self-aggrandizing personalistic leaders, they are more likely to support the aspirations of the middle class (from which most officers have sprung), more prone to espouse a coherent political ideology, and more likely to champion nationalistic causes.

Most institutional military governments pursue four broad objectives, or at least profess to do so. *First*, whatever their real motivations, they usually justify their seizure of power by denouncing the alleged corruption of the government they have ousted. Thus, when Bangladesh's Lieutenant General Hussain Muhammad Ershad led a 1982 army coup, he charged that the outgoing administration had "failed totally because of [its] petty selfishness . . . and unbounded corruption."[46] Incoming military leaders in Uruguay, Pakistan, Thailand, and much of Africa have made similar proclamations. All of them promised to clean up the mess.

A *second* goal—one rarely publicly articulated or acknowledged—is the advancement of military corporate interests. As Ruth First observed, while African coup leaders may claim to have acted for the good of the nation or other noble political purposes, "when the army acts, it generally acts for army reasons."[47] When officers are unhappy with their salaries, defense budgets, or the level of government arms purchases, they usually respond. They also react negatively to civilian "interference" in military affairs, such as deviating from normal officer promotion practices or lessening the armed forces' autonomy.

Ever since the 1960s—a decade featuring coups in Togo, Ghana, Mali, Congo-Brazzaville, and Algeria—a number of African armies have taken power to protect themselves from competing military units (such as presidential guards), to increase their troop strength, to raise their salaries, or to augment their budgets.[48] In South Asia, repeated coups in Bangladesh have been motivated by similar desires for greater military spending and by resentment against civilian interference in military promotions.[49] In Southeast Asia "neglect of [military] corporate interests" by civilian governments has only been "a *background factor* contributing to a general sense of alienation [among the armed forces] rather than an immediate cause of intervention." Still, armed forces concerns over the defense budget contributed to several coups in that region.[50]

A *third* common goal is maintaining or restoring order and stability. Institutional coups have often occurred during periods of civil unrest, guerrilla insurgencies, or civil war. For example, the army first involved itself deeply in South Korean politics when student demonstrations and labor unrest challenged the civilian administrations of Syngman Rhee and Chang Myon (though other factors also played a role). Thailand's many coups have frequently followed strikes and street demonstrations in Bangkok.

Military officers are particularly troubled by radical challenges to the political and economic order and by threats to the safety and integrity of the armed forces. During the early 1960s, Indonesia's civilian president, Sukarno, moved his regime leftward and became increasingly dependent on the country's large Communist Party, much to the discomfort of his conservative military commanders. Their fears intensified in 1965, when a small group of leftist officers assassinated Lieutenant General Achmad Yani and five other officers, claiming that these men had been plotting a coup against President Sukarno. The country's top military command responded with a massive attack against the communists, eventually killing some half million alleged party supporters. Many Indonesian civilians used the chaos as an opportunity to loot and kill members of the country's relatively prosperous Chinese minority. In time, army chief General Suharto ousted Sukarno and established a military dictatorship that lasted more than 30 years.[51]

Similarly, in Argentina, Brazil, Chile, and Uruguay, the generals' fear of leftist unions, guerrillas, or radical political parties prompted military dictatorships that lasted up to two decades.[52] In 1992, the Algerian armed forces terminated parliamentary elections that seemed certain to result in victory for the FIS (Islamic Salvation Front), a party of militant Islamic fundamentalists.

A *final* goal of many institutional military regimes has been to revive and stimulate the economy. As we have noted, coups frequently follow periods of rampant inflation, labor conflict, or economic stagnation. For example, a statistical analysis of military intervention in 38 Sub-Saharan African governments over a two-decade period revealed that coups were most likely to occur after an economic downturn.[53] Asian and Latin American coups have frequently followed similar patterns.

Third World militaries are particularly committed to industrialization. For one thing, industrial growth can provide them with arms and supplies that previously needed to be imported. In the least developed countries, such production may be limited to uniforms or rifles. On the other hand, in countries such as Brazil, Indonesia, and South Korea, highly advanced arms industries now produce planes, tanks, and sophisticated weaponry for both domestic consumption and export. Even when it has no direct military payoff, industrialization contributes to national pride and international prestige. Small wonder, then, that many Latin American and Asian countries have seen a political alliance between industrialists and the armed forces.[54]

Having reviewed the goals of institutional military governments in general, we now focus on two distinct regime types that have received considerable attention in recent years: the bureaucratic authoritarian regime and the revolutionary military regime. While each type has only comprised a minority of Third World military governments, they have had a significant impact, particularly in Latin America and Africa.

Bureaucratic Authoritarian Regimes Beginning with the Brazilian coup d'état of 1964, through the Argentine military takeovers of 1966 and 1976, to the 1973 coups in Uruguay and Chile, four of the most socioeconomically developed countries in South America succumbed to authoritarian rule. Furthermore, Chile and Uruguay had also been the most entrenched democracies in the region, free of military domination for decades. Thus, their coups contradicted the widely held assumption that both socioeconomic development and the creation of a strong party system limit military intervention.

Once in power, these regimes lasted longer than typical military governments in the region, a total of 14 years in Argentina, 12 years in Uruguay, 17 in Chile, and 21 in Brazil.[55] These dictatorships suspended political party activity for extended periods, crushed labor unions and other grass-roots organizations, prohibited strikes, and jailed and tortured many suspected political dissidents. In Argentina and Chile, thousands of people were murdered or "disappeared" (unofficially taken away, never to be seen again).

In a series of provocative writings, Argentine political scientist Guillermo O'Donnell referred to these military governments as "bureaucratic authoritarian (BA) regimes." Compared to previous military dictatorships, they had a more extensive bureaucratic structure that included like-minded civilian technocrats. They penetrated more deeply into civil society, established close links to the MNCs, and were particularly repressive.[56] O'Donnell focused on the closely related economic and political factors that explained the rise of these BA regimes in the most developed nations of Latin America. First, he argued, economic growth in these countries had come to a relative standstill because their economies had developed as far as they could with their available capital and technology. Further growth would require heavy investment in capital goods industries and new technologies, both of which only MNCs had the resources to provide. But the MNCs (as well as domestic companies) had been reluctant to invest because of the frequent labor strife, civil unrest, and leftist electoral strength. In turn, economic stagnation, high inflation, and declining living standards had prompted further leftist political activity and support.

Not surprisingly, growing radicalism among the poor and portions of the middle class, and the resulting political polarization of society deeply alarmed the armed forces. In Argentina, Chile, and Uruguay, urban guerrillas added to the perceived threat (in Brazil, an urban guerrilla movement blossomed *after* the military coup). The goals of the new BA regimes, then, were to crush leftist political parties, unions, and guerrilla movements; limit wages; create a "stable environment for investment"; and work closely with MNCs and domestic big business to control inflation and reinvigorate the economy. Beyond repressing the Left, the generals sought to depoliticize society and terminate most forms of political participation for an extended period. At the same time, BA regimes wanted to extend the role of the private sector and roll back state economic activity, including welfare programs, minimum wage guarantees, and public ownership of economic resources. Many of these objectives, of course, were consistent with the goals of other institutional military regimes discussed earlier. But BA goals entailed a more precise and elaborate "game plan" and a far more sweeping restructuring of society. Yet, despite many predictions that Latin America's BA regimes would become a model for the LDCs trying to enter an advanced state of industrialization, they proved to be an exception to the general pattern of Third World military takeovers. Still, the military governments that industrialized South Korea and Indonesia had many elements of the BA regime model.

Revolutionary Military Regimes   In a number of developing nations, the military pursued goals diametrically different than those of the conservative BA regimes. Rather than excluding most of the population from the political system, they instead *extended* political and economic participation to formerly excluded groups. At the same time, however, their authoritarian political structure tightly controlled mass participation.[57] In Africa, a number of Marxist military regimes proclaimed policies of cultural nationalism, anti-imperialism, peasant and working-class political mobilization, expansion of the state's economic role, and redistribution of economic resources to the poor.

Revolutionary coups have usually been led by radicalized officers from the middle ranks (Captains, Majors, Colonels), rather than Generals. In a speech outlining the goals of Upper Volta's military government, Captain Thomas Sankara articulated the Marxist rhetoric typical of such regimes:

> The triumph of the Revolution . . . is the crowning moment of the struggle of the Volta People against its internal enemies. It is a victory against international

imperialism and its internal allies. . . . These enemies of the people have been identified by the people in the forge of revolutionary action. They are: the bourgeoisie of Volta [and] . . . reactionary forces whose strength derives from the traditional feudal structures of our society. . . . The People in our revolution comprises: The working class . . . the petty bourgeoisie . . . the peasantry . . . [and] the lumpen proletariat.[58]

Military governments in Ethiopia, Sudan, Somalia, Congo-Brazzaville, Benin, and Madagascar made similarly radical declarations. Like most African military regimes, however, these governments have been led by men without significant political experience or advanced education. Consequently, their Marxist ideals were "self-taught, ideologically immature and crude, and riddled with inconsistencies."[59] For some of them, Marxism simply expressed their strong nationalism and distaste for the European nations that had colonized the continent. For others, revolutionary rhetoric came almost as an afterthought, a means of justifying their earlier seizure of power and authoritarian control. Thus, the government of Colonel Mengistu in Ethiopia, perhaps Africa's most prominent radical military regime, did not embrace Marxism-Leninism until it had been in office for three years. In Dahomey, General Mathieu Kerekou declared his government to be Marxist and created "revolution committees" simply as a pretext for spying on the civil service.[60]

In other world regions, leftist (though not Marxist) military regimes have governed countries as disparate as Libya, Myanmar, Panama, and Peru. Peru's military came to power seeking to curtail the influence of the rural oligarchy and incorporate the peasantry, working class, and urban poor into the political system.[61] Finally, military regimes in Panama and Ecuador introduced comparable, though far more modest, reform programs.

THE ACCOMPLISHMENTS AND FAILURES OF MILITARY REGIMES

How successfully have military governments achieved their goals and how well have they served their country? Little needs to be said about personalistic military dictatorships. With a few notable exceptions, they are rarely seriously interested in benefiting their country. Even those with broader goals have had blatantly self-serving objectives. Thus, it would be impossible to argue seriously that dictators such as Batista (Cuba), Somoza (Nicaragua), Stroessner (Paraguay), Amin (Uganda), or Bokassa (Central African Republic) contributed to the long-term political or economic growth of their nation. Consequently, the analysis in our next section focuses exclusively on the record of institutional military governments, which often had more serious intentions.

Combating Corruption

Let us first look at one of the most commonly professed objectives of institutional regimes—eliminating government corruption. Because government malfeasance is so pervasive in the Third World, denouncing corruption is a convenient means of legitimizing the armed forces' unconstitutional seizure of power. Yet, most soldiers in office prove every bit as corrupt as their predecessors, or more so. To be sure, a few military regimes have been quite honest, but they are the exceptions. As one leading scholar has observed:

> Every Nigerian and Ghanaian coup . . . has had as its prime goal the elimination of deeply ingrained corruption from society. Yet, not one military administration has made truly consistent efforts in that direction . . . or for that matter remained immune to it itself. . . . [Elsewhere in Africa] in two . . . military regimes—Guinea and Burkina Faso—nepotism and accumulation of wealth commenced the very day the officers' hierarchy took office.[62]

Ironically, the continent's constant military intervention has tended to increase corruption in the civilian governments that they oust. "The fear that [civilian] power may not last encourages the incoming politicians to grab what is grabbable."[63] In Asian nations such as Thailand and Indonesia, the military's record has been equally disappointing. Indeed, Harold Crouch has noted that "often military officers have already become entangled in this web [of corruption] even before the coup takes place."[64] In those few military governments that avoid *gross* corruption, the more modest lure of contraband automobiles and tax-supported vacation homes often proves irresistible. In short, even those military governments that seized power with noble intentions are generally soon corrupted.

Defending Corporate Interests

When it comes to pursuing their second major objective—advancing their own corporate interests—not surprisingly, military governments have been more successful, at least in the short term. More often than not, military rulers enhance the nation's defense budget. Unfortunately, however, those expenditures draw government resources away from badly needed programs such as health care and education.

Typically, military governments increase spending on armaments, military salaries, military housing, and officers' clubs. In much of Asia, officers have benefited from "lucrative public sector employment, foreign postings, and preferential treatment in the disbursal of governmental contracts."[65] After leading a coup in Libya, Colonel Qadhafi insured his officers' loyalty by doubling their salaries, thereby making them the highest paid army in the Third World. In their first five years in office, Uruguay's generals raised the military and security share of the national budget from 26.2 percent to more than 40 percent.[66] A parallel "bias in favor of army, police and civil-service salaries and benefits can be observed in practically every military regime in Africa."[67]

Throughout the LDCs, even when soldiers do not actually govern, the mere specter of intervention has often led civilian governments to bestow salary hikes and expensive weapon systems on the armed forces. For example, it would be very imprudent of elected leaders in the Philippines or Thailand to slash their country's defense budget. Even Malaysia and Singapore, with no history of coups d'état, pay their officers generously to keep them out of politics.[68] Similarly, Colombia and Venezuela, two of Latin America's most long-lived civilian governments (though military involvement in politics has risen sharply in both since the 1990s), have supported healthy defense budgets aimed at keeping the generals at bay.

But, although military rule may enlarge military budgets, it also damages the armed forces in the longer term by reducing their institutional cohesion. Eventually, generals, colonels, and admirals begin to squabble over resource allocation and other policy issues. As new economic and political challenges arise, they drive a wedge between the officers in command. Furthermore, even military regimes that took power with considerable popular support usually lose their legitimacy as they confront difficult economic and social problems. As a consequence, in some regions, most notably Sub-Saharan Africa, internal coups (one military faction ousting another) have produced a series of unstable military governments. Nearly half of Africa's twentieth-century coups and failed coup attempts sought to topple incumbent military regimes.[69] But, for the most part in the past one or two decades, Third World militaries have returned to the barracks to avoid further internal divisions, restoring the government to civilian hands.

Patterns in Military Spending

Unfortunately, the major "accomplishment" of most military governments in the LDCs—budgetary gains for the armed forces itself—is frequently the nation's loss. Military expenditures are frequently higher than their country can afford, thereby reducing badly needed social and economic investment. Countries in South America that have not fought an international war in decades have spent fortunes on naval vessels and state-of-the-art combat jets. And in Africa, home to many of the world's poorest countries, military budgets are particularly disproportionate to economic capacities. For example, in the 1980s, despite having per-capita national incomes well below half of Latin America's, African governments spent one-third more per soldier.[70] Africa's defense outlays generally declined from 1988 to 1998, but have increased sharply since (see Table 9.2).[71] Currently, defense consumes a disproportionate share of that continent's Gross Domestic Product (GDP) and thereby limits government spending on education, health care, rural development, and other social needs. In the 1990s, military budgets were particularly large in countries that were engaged in either internal or international warfare, such as Eritrea, Ethiopia, Uganda, Rwanda, Sudan, and Angola. For example, in 1999, when Eritrea, one of the world's poorest countries, was at war with Ethiopia, it devoted an astounding 37.5 percent of its GDP to military expenditures.

Table 9.1 demonstrates that, while some developing nations have tightly limited their military spending, others, particularly those facing external military threats or civil war, have enormous military budgets relative to their social expenditures. The table compares government spending on health and education with outlays for the military in four groups of countries: highly industrialized democracies (the United States and Japan), relatively wealthy Third World nations (Singapore), "middle-income" developing nations (Mexico, Ghana, and Jordan), and very poor LDCs (Burundi, Ethiopia, and Eritrea). The first data column indicates the percentage of each nation's GDP that was devoted to public welfare programs as measured by total government spending on health and

TABLE 9.1   Public Welfare (Health and Education) versus Military
Expenditures as a Percentage of GDP (2002)

Country	Health and Education Expenditures (% of GDP)	Military Expenditures (% of GDP)	Health and Education Spending as % of Military Spending
United States[a]	10.1	3.4	297
Japan[a]	9.5	1.0	950
Singapore[a]	4.8	5.2	92
Mexico[b]	6.9	0.5	1380
Ghana[b]	6.3	0.6	1050
Jordan[b]	9.2	8.4	109
Burundi[c]	6.6	5.2	126
Ethiopia[c]	5.0	7.6	66
Eritrea[c]	7.6	23.5	32

[a]High-income countries.
[b]Middle-income countries.
[c]Low-income countries.

Source: Stockholm International Peace Research Institute (SIPRI) 2004, http://www.sipri.org/.

education. The next column shows the percentage of each country's GDP spent on the armed forces. Obviously poorer countries, such as Ghana and Ethiopia, cannot possibly spend nearly as much money on either public welfare or the military as Singapore and Japan do. But, Table 9.1 enables us to compare each country's expenditures relative to the size of its economy (GDP). The last column in the table compares those two budget items, expressing welfare spending as a *percentage of military outlays.* If a country spends more on *welfare* than on the military (as the United States, Japan, Mexico, Ghana, and Burundi do), the figure in the last column will exceed 100 percent. On the other hand, if it spends more on the *military* than on welfare, the figure in that last column will be less than 100 percent. Thus, this column tells us that in 2002 the United States spent almost three times as much on health and education combined as on the military (297 percent). In contrast, Eritrea spent about three times as much on *the military* as it did on public welfare (32 percent).

As the first data column indicates, both Third World and industrialized countries devote widely varying proportions of their GDP to military spending. For example, in 2002, Eritrea, whose bloody war with Ethiopia (1998–2000) had recently ended, still devoted an enormous portion of its GDP—more than 23 percent—to the military. That was probably the highest percentage in the world and about 6–7 times the international average. Military expenditures also consumed a very high percentage of the GDP in Jordan (8.4 percent), and Ethiopia (7.6 percent), as well as a smaller, but considerable, share in Burundi and Singapore (both at 5.2 percent). All of these countries faced hostile or potentially hostile neighbors, while two (Ethiopia and Burundi) also confronted internal ethnic unrest. All of them had authoritarian governments of varying stripes. On the other hand, the armed forces consumed less than 1 percent of the GDP in Mexico and Ghana, countries that have recently democratized and that face no foreign or internal military threats. For the sake of comparison, while the absolute level of military spending by the United States has long dwarfed that of any other country in the world, its military budget as a percentage of national GDP was only a modest 3.4 percent. Japan's allocation was even lower (1 percent of GDP).

The last column—comparing public welfare with military spending—is particularly revealing. Undoubtedly, the poorest nations in the table (Burundi, Ethiopia, and Eritrea) had the greatest need for health and educational expenditures and could, therefore, least afford high military outlays. Yet, Eritrea and Ethiopia spent far more on the armed forces than on public welfare. Similarly, the ratio of welfare expenditures to military spending is far higher in the United States, Japan, Mexico, or Ghana than in Burundi. While Singapore had a high military budget relative to welfare spending, it is so much wealthier and healthier than the other Third World nations in the table that, in spite of its high military spending, it could still serve its citizens' health and education needs.

Throughout the developing world, civilian governments with strong control over the armed forces and low security threats have been best equipped to reduce military budgets substantially. As the Third Wave of democracy strengthened the legitimacy and authority of newly elected, civilian governments in the 1980s and 1990s, a number of LDCs made such cuts. For example, from 1983 to 1987, following the restoration of democracy in Argentina (not in the table), military spending fell by almost 50 percent.[72] From 1985 to 1993, defense expenditures as a share of GDP fell from 2.9 to 1.7 percent in Argentina, from 6.8 to 2.1 percent in Chile, and from 4.4 to 1.6 percent in El Salvador.[73] Military spending and manpower also declined in Central America in the 1980s, but rose again in the 1990s. Some nondemocratic governments also cut military outlays. Thus, military expenditures in Cambodia fell from 4.6 percent of GDP (in 1997) to 2.7 percent (2003).

For the most part, however, the demise of so many military governments during the 1980s and 1990s has *not* caused widespread cuts in defense spending, at least not since the mid-1990s. Table 9.2 indicates the *absolute* volume of military spending, as expressed in U.S. dollars, over an 18-year period in the principal regions of the Third World. Dollar allocations for all years have been converted to their equivalent value in 2005 dollars, thereby eliminating the effects of inflation. The last column in the table indicates the percentage changes in military spending, for each region between 1988 and 2006. Although military expenditures continue to represent a high percentage of the GDP in many Sub-Saharan African countries, that region was the only one where military spending (in constant dollars) was the same in 2006 as it had been 18 years earlier. While military budgets in that region had declined substantially between 1988 and 1998, they rebounded to 1988 levels during the next eight years. Military outlays in South America also fell from 1988 to 1998 (though only slightly), but grew again from 1998 to 2006, producing a net increase of 22 percent for the 18-year period. In the Middle East, expenditures increased far more sharply (80 percent overall), as a consequence of the continued Arab–Israeli conflict and a Gulf-State arms build-up fueled by fear of invasion by either Iraq or Iran. East Asian military budgets grew by an almost identical amount (81 percent). Here, the causes are less clear, but two factors were surely important: the region's booming economies enabled many East Asian nations

TABLE 9.2   Trends in Estimated Regional Military Expenditures, 1988–2006ᵃ

Region	1988	1998	2006	Percent Change 1988–2006
Sub-Saharan Africaᵇ	9.0	5.6	9.0	0
Central America	2.4	3.6	3.5	+46
South Americaᶜ	23.9ᵈ	23.2	29.1	+22
East Asiaᵉ	76.4ᵈ	100.0	138.0	+81
South Asia	15.0	20.2	30.7	+105
Middle Eastᶠ	40.2	49.3	72.5	+80

ᵃFigures are in billions of dollars (U.S.) at constant 2003 prices and exchange rates.
ᵇAfrican data exclude Angola, Benin, Equatorial Guinea, and Somalia.
ᶜSouth American data excludes Guyana.
ᵈEstimates.
ᵉEast Asian data exclude Myanmar, North Korea, and Vietnam
ᶠMiddle East data exclude Iraq and Qatar.

Source: Stockholm International Peace Research Institute (SIPRI), "*World and Regional Military Expenditure Estimates,*" http://www.sipri.org/contents/milap/milex/mex_wnr_table.html.

(especially China, South Korea, Taiwan, and Singapore) to spend more on state-of-the-art weaponry; and, growing concerns over North Korea's military power led that country's neighbors to further arm themselves. But, the biggest jump in military spending came in South Asia (105 percent), anchored by the arms race between India and Pakistan (both of whom developed nuclear weapons during that period).

Because these statistics do not distinguish between defense expenditures in democratic countries (including newly democratized nations) with those of military regimes, they fail to tell us whether the spread of democracy influenced military spending. However, they clearly suggest that military expenditures were influenced, not only by regime type (democratic or authoritarian), but by other factors as well, particularly by the extent of international and domestic conflict in the region. Countries such as Cambodia, El Salvador, and Ethiopia, which ended their civil wars, sharply cut their military expenditures (as a percentage of national GDP). Ethiopia slashed the size of its armed forces, Africa's largest at that time, from 438,000 in 1991 to 120,000 in 1996, while Mozambique and Nigeria made sizable cuts as well. However, in countries such as Chad and Sudan, where internal warfare has continued, troop strength has grown considerably.[74]

Finally, Table 9.3 presents statistics on trends in military spending (expressed as a percentage of national GDP) in two developed nations (France and Spain) and six Third World nations that have large military budgets. Recall that Table 9.2 demonstrated that the *absolute* level of military spending (expressed in constant dollars) has *increased* in all but one region of the developing world in the past 20 years. But, in every nation represented in Table 9.3, military outlays *as a percentage of GDP* have steadily *decreased* during that same period. What this means is that, although the actual amount of military spending rose for most nations after

TABLE 9.3   Trends in Military Expenditures as a Percentage of GDP, 1988–2005

Country	1988 (%)	1998 (%)	2005 (%)
France	3.6	2.7	2.5
Spain	2.0	1.3	1.1
India	3.6	2.8	2.8
Indonesia	2.0[a]	1.1	1.2[a]
Saudi Arabia	15.2	14.3	8.2
Brazil	2.5[a]	1.9[a]	1.6
Nigeria	0.8	0.9	0.7
Ethiopia	8.1	6.7	2.6

[a]Estimates.

Source: Stockholm International Peace Research Institute (SIPRI), *"The SIPRI Military Expenditure Data Base,"* http://first.sipri.org/non_first/milex.php.

1988, their GDPs typically grew faster. As Table 9.3 indicates, for some developing nations, such as Ethiopia, that decrease (from 8.1 percent of its GDP to 2.6) has been dramatic. While not *all* LDCs experienced as large a reduction, in the vast majority of them military outlays as a percentage of GDP have declined. Even in countries such as Saudi Arabia and Eritrea, which allocate an unusually large percentage of their GDPs to military expenditures, this trend has persisted. Critics insist that many LDCs (especially the poorest) still spend too much on the military relative to national welfare needs (as demonstrated in Table 9.1), but the tendency, at least for now, is for lower military budgets as a percentage of GDP.

Establishing Stability

Military officers almost always react negatively to popular unrest and political instability. For one thing, disorder violates their hierarchical view of society. Furthermore, it frequently threatens the interests of their middle-class and industrialist allies. In other instances, it poses an imminent danger to the military itself. The Generals and Colonels of Latin America, for example, have been keenly aware that Marxist revolutions in Cuba and Nicaragua destroyed the old military establishment. In Cuba a number of Batista's officers faced the firing squad, while in Nicaragua, many National Guardsmen were imprisoned or had to flee the country. In Chile and Brazil, leftist political leaders threatened the officers' hierarchical control of the armed forces. Similarly, the generals in Algeria felt endangered by the growing strength of Islamic fundamentalism. Even "revolutionary soldiers" in Ethiopia, Libya, and Peru preferred to dictate change from the top, with tight government controls over mass mobilization.

In many respects, military governments are particularly well suited for controlling civil unrest. They can use force with impunity to combat guerrilla insurrections, disperse street demonstrations, and ban strikes. In some cases, their extensive intelligence agencies, such as South Korea's KCIA and Chile's

DINA, enabled them to penetrate deeply into society to control dissent. The Argentine, Chilean, and Uruguayan armies used mass arrests, torture, and death squads to crush potent urban guerrilla movements. In Indonesia, the military destroyed one of the world's largest communist parties and later decimated various separatist movements.

But the generals restored order in these countries at a tremendous cost in human suffering. Some 20,000–30,000 people died in the Argentine army's "dirty war" against the Left, while many more were imprisoned and tortured. Students and other young people were the primary victims, many of them incorrectly identified as part of the militant opposition. In Chile, thousands of intellectuals and professionals fled the country, devastating one of the Third World's most advanced university systems and artistic communities. Some 3,000 Chileans died; many others were the victims of torture.[75] During Indonesia's "year of living dangerously," perhaps 500,000 communists and ethnic Chinese were massacred, while some 150,000 other people died subsequently (largely from starvation) in the army's struggle against East Timorian separatists.[76] Another 12,000 died in the separatist struggle in Aceh (or Ache).

Moreover, *in the longer term*, the military has not been particularly successful in providing political stability. To be sure, in several Asian and Latin American countries, state repression, coupled with technocratic development policies, has either co-opted or decimated opposition groups. In South Korea, sharply improved living standards and a gradual political transition paved the way to stable elected government. And in Argentina, Chile, and Uruguay, the BA regimes' brutality against radical movements convinced political leaders on both sides of the ideological spectrum (but especially the Left) to moderate their positions so as not to provoke further military intervention.

But these "successes" are the exception. Despite their brute strength, the armed forces' hold on power has generally been relatively brief. Eric Nordlinger's pioneering study of military governments found that, on average, they dissolved in five to seven years.[77] Karen Remmer's later work on 12 South American military regimes between 1960 and 1990 showed four to be quite durable (12–35 years); the remaining eight, however, averaged less than seven years in office.[78] Moreover, military rule, no matter what its accomplishments, ultimately impedes the maturation of political parties and other civilian institutions necessary for long-term stability.

In Africa, more often than not, coups have only led to further coups, hampering political development as they turn politics into a Hobbesian game. The brutal regime of Sergeant Samuel Doe exposed Liberia to a devastating civil war and a far more sinister ruler who fomented unspeakably brutal internal warfare at home and in nearby Sierra Leone. Military rule in Ethiopia and the Sudan only worsened ethnically based civil wars. Elsewhere, extended suppression of dissident groups in countries such as Myanmar will likely lead to greater upheavals after those regimes fall.

Economic Development

Earlier we noted that coups often are provoked by economic recessions or severe inflation. Consequently, many newly installed military governments promise to impose fiscal discipline and revitalize the economy. In South Korea,

Indonesia, Brazil, and Chile, for example, conservative military regimes curtailed union activity in order to suppress wage demands. By reducing strike activity and weakening unions the generals expected to lower inflation and attract multinational investment.

Proponents of military dictatorships assert that they can more easily make economic decisions consistent with the national interest because they need not pander to special interest groups. Critics counter that soldiers lack the expertise to manage an economy. Even when well intentioned, they tend to allocate excessive funds to defense and to wasteful chauvinistic projects. Examining the economic performance of specific military governments provides evidence to support both sides of the debate. South Korea demonstrated that a military government can oversee a very successful economic development program. Following General Park Chung Hee's seizure of power in 1961, the armed forces governed the country for more than 25 years. During that period, the Republic of Korea changed from an underdeveloped nation into one of the world's most dynamic industrial economies.[79] Moreover, the country enjoyed sustained economic growth while still maintaing very equitable income distribution. Indeed, economists frequently cite South Korea as a model of well-executed economic modernization.

Elsewhere in Asia, Indonesia's military also presided over rapid economic growth from the mid-1960s to late 1990s. During the 1970s and early 1980s, the Suharto dictatorship plowed back a portion of the country's extensive petroleum revenues into labor-intensive export industries. At the same time, rural development programs and mass education improved income distribution and, coupled with economic growth, substantially reduced the number of Indonesians living in poverty. Nearby Thailand, governed by the military for much of the last 70 years, also enjoyed an economic boom.[80] However, excessive borrowing, "crony capitalism" (plentiful government loans and contracts to politically connected businesspeople), and corruption contributed to a severe financial crisis in East and Southeast Asia in 1998 (see Chapter 10). Sharp GDP declines, plant closings, currency devaluations, and inflation set back many of the gains that the region had enjoyed in the preceding decades.

Two of Latin America's major bureaucratic-authoritarian regimes—Brazil and, especially, Chile—also had relatively successful economic records. After several false starts, Chile's probusiness, export-oriented policies ushered in a period of strong economic expansion with low inflation. Those achievements, however, followed a period of severe economic hardship, which forced the poor to bear a disproportionate share of the sacrifice. Under Chile's military dictatorship, as with other BA regimes, income distribution deteriorated. After the restoration of democracy in 1990, the civilian governments of Patricio Aylwin and Eduardo Frei maintained high growth rates while using targeted programs to reduce poverty. Following the restoration of democracy in the 1990s, a combination of high growth and remedial programs for those left behind halved the number of Chileans living in poverty.

Brazil's BA regime achieved dramatic economic growth during the late 1960s and 1970s, turning the country into an important industrial power. The benefits of that growth, however, were very poorly distributed, leaving many of the poor worse off than before. Moreover, Brazil's "economic miracle" was built on excessive foreign borrowing that turned the country into the Third

World's largest external debtor. Unlike Chile, civilian rule has not appreciably improved the economy since the military stepped down in 1985. Initially, deficit spending and poor planning brought back the hyperinflation that the generals had vowed to eradicate. President Fernando Henrique Cardoso brought inflation under control in the 1990s, but economic growth generally has been weak and the country's financial structure unstable. Cardoso's successor, President Luiz Inácio Lula da Silva, has vowed to alter the economic model introduced by the military in an attempt to better serve the needs of the poor, though he has maintained Cardoso's conservative fiscal policies.

But, many other Latin American military governments, including the BA regimes in Argentina and Uruguay, performed poorly in the economic sphere. They spent far too much on defense, borrowed excessively, were generally corrupt, and frequently failed to understand development economics. In Africa the armed forces' economic record has ranged from poor to disastrous.

Moving beyond evidence from individual cases such as these, some analysts have engaged in more systematic statistical analysis. Examining data on economic indicators such as growth rates and inflation, they have compared the economic performance of military and civilian governments in specific regions or throughout the Third World. These comparisons face a number of methodological problems. It is very difficult to control for the myriad of other factors that might explain why one set of governments has performed better than another.[81] For example, judging the performance of specific military regimes with the civilian governments that preceded or replaced them requires comparisons of economic performances during different time periods. Consequently, disparities may be caused by international economic conditions unrelated to regime type—such as oil prices or demand for Third World exports. Another problem is that economic policies introduced by one type of government may be responsible for the strong or weak performance of the government that replaces it. Thus, for example, the poor economic performance of many Latin American democracies in the 1980s was primarily caused by the excessive deficit spending and borrowing of the military regimes that preceded them. Valid answers, then, require sophisticated and informed analytical techniques.

For the most part, cross-national statistical research, controlling for other variables, has uncovered little difference between the economic growth rates of democratic and military regimes. But analysis of Sub-Saharan nations in the last half of the twentieth century indicated that economic growth and human development (including life expectancy and literacy) are lower under military governments than under their civilian counterparts. Karen Remmer's analysis of Latin America points to the problem, just discussed, of determining the cause and effect of government economic policies over time. She found that economies frequently decline right after the military has stepped down. She argues, however, that there is a lag between the time a government introduces an economic policy and when its effect emerges. So the military's economic policies obviously contributed to the economic difficulties inherited by their civilian successors.[82] Of course, if a new democratic government enjoys strong economic indicators in the early years of the transition, the outgoing military regime deserves some of the credit. Such was the case in Chile's democratic transition. It is worth noting that the military rulers with the best economic performance—South Korea, Indonesia, and Chile—recognizing the limits of their own skills, pursued the policy recommendations of civilian advisers.[83]

MILITARY WITHDRAWAL FROM POLITICS

Once the armed forces have become entrenched in the political system, dislodging them is usually no easy task. Domestic upheavals (Indonesia) or external intervention (Uganda) sometimes induce the military to withdraw from power. More often, however, the armed forces voluntarily relinquish power for one or more of the following reasons: having accomplished their major objectives, they see no value in retaining power; deteriorating economic conditions make continued rule unappealing; extended rule undermines internal military cohesion; or, the regime becomes so unpopular that staying in office would reduce the military's legitimacy as an institution.

Many military governments come into office as "caretakers" whose goal is to restore stability or solve a particular problem and then quickly return control to civilians. In Ecuador, for example, the armed forces frequently ousted elected leaders whom they considered too demagogic, too populist, or too incompetent. After ruling relatively briefly, they then voluntarily stepped down.

Because the perpetrators of institutional coups usually take power with expectations of augmented military budgets and accelerated economic growth, their interest in governing, not surprisingly, wanes when the economy turns sour. In countries such as Peru, Uruguay, and Thailand, economic downturns have convinced military governments to step down. Economic declines may also aggravate internal divisions within the armed forces.

In Sub-Saharan Africa, military rule may also aggravate ethnic divisions within the armed forces, particularly when officers from one tribe or religion dominate top government positions. For example, in Nigeria, the military's entry into the political arena unleashed four internal coups in a 10-year span, with ethnic tensions playing an important role. Two heads of government and a number of other senior officers were killed in the military's internal struggles. Some military governments, fearing similar deteriorations in armed forces' cohesiveness, have preferred to step down, leaving the nation's problems to civilians. In some countries, soldiers from one tribe or ethnic group may dominate the armed forces. For example, in Togo as of 2005, the Kabyé tribe made up only 25 percent of the country's population but constituted 70 percent of all soldiers and 90 percent of the officer corps. Ultimate power lay in the hands of a Kabyé dictator who had ruled the country for 38 years.[84]

Finally, just as military coups are most likely when civilian governments lack legitimacy, the army is most likely to return to the barracks when its own legitimacy declines. This happens most dramatically when the country has been defeated in war. For example, following its humiliating defeat by Britain in the Falklands (or Malvinas) war, the Argentine military regime was forced to step down. Similarly, in Pakistan, the military had to transfer power to its leading civilian critic, Zulfiqar Ali Bhutto, after it lost East Pakistan (now Bangladesh) in a war with India.

Of course, there are other ways military regimes lose legitimacy. In Uruguay, economic decay and public revulsion against the political repression so weakened the military government that it unexpectedly lost a national referendum that it had been sure it could tightly control.[85] Eventually, popular discontent induced the generals to negotiate a return to civilian government. In the 1990s, in Thailand, massive student-led, pro-democracy demonstrations convinced the armed forces to withdraw (for a while).

While some combination of these factors has accounted for the departure of most military regimes, it has not guaranteed that the armed forces would stay out. Indeed, until the 1980s, the soldiers were likely to return to power. Talukder Maniruzzaman examined 71 instances of military withdrawal from office in the Third World from 1946 to 1984.[86] In 65 percent of these cases, the armed forces were back in power within five years.[87]

Since the early 1980s, however, those military regimes that have stepped down have been more likely to stay out of office. Except for Sub-Saharan Africa—where in late 2003 military regimes remained in such nations as the Republic of Congo, Ecuatorial Guinea, Central African Republic, Togo, Côte d'Ivoire, Chad, Uganda, Rwanda, and Libya—there has been a dramatic decline in Third World military rule. For example, as of 2007, the Latin American nations of Argentina, Ecuador, Brazil, Guatemala, and El Salvador, all with long histories of armed forces' intervention, had enjoyed anywhere from 18 to 29 years without military government. In South Korea, decades of military dominance came to an end in 1993.[88] Even in Africa, the last region to move away from military rule, military regimes in several countries, including Nigeria, Ghana, Benin, and Congo-Brazzaville, have given way to elected civilian governments since the early 1990s.[89]

In some cases, years of misrule undermined the military's institutional legitimacy. Thus, Argentina's elected governments since the mid-1980s have been able to reduce the country's formidable armed forces to one-third their previous size. Elsewhere, as in Mozambique, El Salvador, and Nicaragua, peace treaties ending long civil wars mandated sharp reductions in the size of the military. In other countries, however, the armed forces have maintained their share of the government budget.

Ultimately, if the armed forces are to consent to leaving the center of national politics, they will need to find new roles to justify their existence. This is particularly true in countries that face no serious foreign threats. In Latin America and much of Africa, for example, wars between nation-states, as opposed to civil conflict, have been quite rare. In assigning the military new roles, however, civilian governments must be careful not to involve it in tasks that may draw it back into politics—a danger some analysts see in the Latin American military's growing involvement in the "war on drugs."

New Roles for the Armed Forces

Many of the proposed "new roles" for the military are not really entirely new. They include combating drug trafficking (in parts of Latin America, the Caribbean, and Asia), antiterrorist activity, emergency relief efforts (following natural disasters), and construction of infrastructure such as roads. Unfortunately, in the past some of these activities have brought as many new problems as solutions.

In Mexico, Colombia, the Caribbean, and Central America, antidrug efforts have often corrupted the armed forces, as officers changed from enforcers to well-paid protectors of the drug cartels. In Mexico, for example, there have even been gun fights between antidrug units and other soldiers who were paid to protect drug bosses (though, on the whole, the armed forces have been far less corrupt than the police). Furthermore, in some countries the armed forces have often used their mandates to combat terrorism and internal subversion as carte blanche to violate human rights and crush peaceful and legitimate political opposition groups.

During the Cold War, U.S. training programs for Third World officers often stressed democratic norms. However, those missions' strong emphasis on combating guerrilla movements and other perceived subversive threats often led trainees to believe that national security objectives justified military interference in national politics, repressive tactics, and human rights violations. With the end of the Cold War, however, the United States began to deliver a more unambiguous message. During the mid-1990s, for example, a directive sent to U.S. military commanders stationed overseas called on them to encourage foreign armed forces "to consider roles . . . that are supportive of civilian control and respectful of human rights and the role of law."[90] During the Clinton administration, the International Military Education and Training program (IMET) emphasized those values.[91] If democracy is to survive and advance in the LDCs, the military must pursue its new roles in a manner that reinforces rather than subverts civilian control and that strengthens the military's respect for human rights and civil liberties. This will be no small task.

Finally, another new role for Third World militaries merits mention. In recent years countries such as Argentina, India, Pakistan, and Uruguay have supplied United Nations peacekeeping forces to world trouble spots such as Bosnia, Cambodia, the Congo, and Afghanistan. This represents a very different military role and holds great promise for supporting international peace efforts. In addition, West African regional peacekeeping forces recently have gone to Liberia and Sierra Leone. But there is some potential for mischief here as well because regional powers such as Nigeria may use such interventions as a means of extending their influence and pursuing their own foreign policy agendas.

CONCLUSION: DEMOCRACY AND THE MILITARY

By definition, the spread of democracy has reduced the number of Third World military governments. This does not mean that the specter of military takeovers has disappeared. By one count, there were 30–40 coup attempts in the 1980s and early 1990s.[92] However, by the mid-1990s, attempted military coups were largely limited to Sub-Saharan Africa.

Even in democratically elected governments, the armed forces often exercise considerable political influence in certain policy areas. Furthermore, in a number of countries, the military remains outside civilian control. For example, in Chile, where General Pinochet's outgoing dictatorship was able to dictate the terms of the 1989 transition to democracy, the new constitution afforded the armed forces considerable influence. The military was granted amnesty for most of its human rights violations, including the murder of some 2,000–3,000 civilians. The elected president lacked authority to remove the military's chief of staff, and the armed forces appointed several members of the senate. General Pinochet himself, as a former President, served as senator for life. It would take almost nine years before a Spanish judge indicted Pinochet for human rights violations, and the British authorities placed him under house arrest during a medical visit to England. Only then did the Chilean armed forces lose their aura of invincibility, and only then was Chile's civilian government able to assert its control over the military and expand trials for human rights violations.

In order to consolidate democracy, LDCs must do more than merely restore elected government. Stable and secure democracy requires a professionalized military that is committed to staying out of domestic politics. In other words, there must be both "a high level of . . . professionalism and recognition by military officers of the limits of their professional competence" and "subordination of the military to the civilian political leaders who make the basic decisions on foreign and military policy" as well as domestic policy.[93] Officers must define their professional role as defending their country from potential external threats and must recognize that their involvement in national politics will only divide the armed forces and diminish their professional capacity. But just as the generals and colonels must keep out of national politics, civilian political leaders must respect the military domain and not attempt to politicize the armed forces. All too often, aspiring political leaders who are unable to gain office through legitimate channels have approached the armed forces for support. As David Mares has noted:

> If civilians are willing to accept democracy as a value, it is hard to see how a professional military would be drawn into politics. And if civilians, especially powerful corporate groups, do not accept the rules of the democratic game, it is difficult to see how democracy could be consolidated whether or not the military intervenes.[94]

Even the most successful military governments inhibit political development. They do so because their very rationale for taking office is "the politics of antipolitics."[95] With their hierarchical perspective and their distaste for disorder, soldiers believe in a managed society. Most reject the give and take of political competition and the compromises inherent in politics. Consequently, they

> fail to see the functional aspects of the great game of politics: They severely restrict the free flow of the political process and force would-be politicians into a long period of hibernation. . . . The opportunity for gaining political skills by a people once under a military regime is continually postponed by every new military regime.[96]

DISCUSSION QUESTIONS

1. What factors influence the likelihood of military intervention in Third World politics?
2. What are the major types of military regimes, and what are their goals?

3. What are the major strengths and weaknesses of military governments?
4. How effectively have military governments been in policy areas such as national security and economic growth? Which specific military governments have been most successful?
5. What factors induce the armed forces to withdraw from politics?
6. What effect, if any, has the growth of Third World democracy had on military spending?

NOTES

1. Harold Crouch, *The Army and Politics in Indonesia* (Ithaca, NY: Cornell University Press, 1978), 345.

2. A military coup can be defined as the sudden and illegal seizure of government power (through removal of the incumbent government) by the armed forces or a faction of the military, using violence or the threat of violence. In most cases, the coup makers install themselves in power, but occasionally they install another civilian government or call new elections. Coups sometimes bring about far-reaching changes in government policies, but most do not.

3. William Thompson, "Explanations of the Military Coup," Ph.D. dissertation, University of Washington, Seattle, 1972, 11. Quoted in Amos Perlmutter, *The Military and Politics in Modern Times* (New Haven, CT: Yale University Press, 1977), 115.

4. Claude E. Welch, "Military Disengagements from Politics?: Incentives and Obstacles in Political Change," in *Military Power and Politics in Black Africa*, ed. Simon Baynham (New York: St. Martin's Press, 1986), 89–90; Steven Thomas Seitz, "The Military in Black African Politics," in *Civil-Military Interaction in Asia and Africa*, eds. Charles H. Kennedy and David J. Louscher (Leiden, The Netherlands: E. J. Brill, 1991), 65, 67.

5. Samuel Decalo, *Coups and Army Rule in Africa* (New Haven, CT: Yale University Press, 1990), 2.

6. Patrick J. McGowan, "African Military Coups D'état, 1956–2001: Frequency, Trends and Distribution," *Journal of Modern African Studies*, vol. 41, no. 3 (September, 2003), 339; for slightly different data, see George Klay Kieh, Jr., "Military Engagement in Politics in Africa," in *The Military and Politics in Africa*, eds. George Klay Kieh Jr. and Pita Ogaba Agbese (Hants, England: Ashgate, 2002), 44, Tables 3.1 and 3.2.

7. Harold A. Trinkunas, "Crafting Civilian Control in Argentina and Venezuela," in *Civil–Military Relations in Latin America*, ed. David Pion-Berlin (Chapel Hill: University of North Carolina Press, 2001), 161–193.

8. When Aquino's term ended, Ramos, running as a civilian, was democratically elected as her successor. During his term in office he increased the military's institutional influence in government. See Jeffrey Riedinger, "Caciques and Coups: The Challenge of Democratic Consolidation in the Philippines," in *Democracy and Its Limits*, eds. Howard Handelman and Mark Tessler (Notre Dame, IN: Notre Dame University Press, 1999), 176–217.

9. Morris Janowitz, *Military Institutions and Coercion in the Developing Nations:* Expanded edition of *The Military in the Political Development of New Nations* (Chicago: University of Chicago Press, 1977), 105.

10. Samuel P. Huntington, *The Soldier and the State: The Theory and Politics of Civil–Military Relations* (New York: Vintage Books, 1964).

11. Samuel P. Huntington, "Civilian Control of the Military: A Theoretical Statement," in *Political Behavior: A Reader in Theory and Research*, eds. Heinz Eulau, Samuel Eldersveld, and Morris Janowitz (New York: Free Press, 1956), 380–381.

12. Samuel P. Huntington, "Patterns of Violence in World Politics," in *Changing Patterns of Military Politics*, ed. Samuel P. Huntington (New York: Free Press, 1962), 19–22.

13. Alfred Stepan, "The New Professionalism of Internal Warfare and Military Role Expansion," in *Armies and Politics in Latin America*, rev. ed., eds. Abraham Lowenthal and J. Samuel Fitch (New York: Holmes and Meier, 1986), 134–150. See also Jose Nun, "The Middle-Class Military Coup Revisited," in *ibid.* 59–95, for similar arguments.

14. Michael C. Desch, *Civilian Control of the Military: The Changing Security Environment*, (Baltimore, MD: The Johns Hopkins Press, 1999).

15. Ruth First, *The Barrel of a Gun: Political Power in Africa and the Coup D'état* (London: Allen Lane/Penguin Press, 1970), 208, 4.

16. Michel Louis Martin, "Operational Weaknesses and Political Activism: The Military in Sub-Saharan Africa," in *To Sheathe the Sword: Civil-Military Relations in the Quest for Democracy*, eds. John P. Lovell and David E. Albright (Westport, CT: Greenwood Press, 1997), 89.

17. Samuel P. Huntington, *Political Order in Changing Societies* (New Haven, CT: Yale University Press, 1968), 194.

18. Robert Wesson, "Preface," in *New Military Politics in Latin America*, ed. Robert Wesson (New York: Praeger, 1982), v.

19. Samuel E. Finer, *The Man on Horseback: The Role of the Military in Politics*, 2d ed. (London: Penguin Books, 1976), 78–82.

20. Huntington, *Political Order in Changing Societies*.

21. Samuel P. Huntington, "Reforming Civil-Military Relations," in *Civil–Military Relations and Democracy*, eds. Larry Diamond and Marc F. Plattner (Baltimore, MD: Johns Hopkins University Press, 1996), 9. Italics added. Although this claim has generally remained true, during the 1970s countries such as Argentina, Chile, and Uruguay suffered successful coups despite having per-capita GNPs well above $1,000.

22. For a cautiously optimistic look at Venezuelan democracy and the role of the military written only a year before the leader of an earlier failed coup attempt, Lt. Colonel Hugo Chávez, was elected as president, see Gisela Gómez Sucre and María Dolores Cornett, "Civil–Military Relations in Venezuela," in *Civil-Military Relations*, ed. David R. Mares, (Boulder, CO: Westview Press, 1998), 59–75.

23. Terry Karl, "Petroleum and Political Pacts: The Transition to Democracy in Venezuela," in *Transitions from Authoritarian Rule*, eds. Guillermo O'Donnell, Philippe C. Schmitter, and Laurence Whitehead (Baltimore, MD: Johns Hopkins University Press, 1986), 196–219. See also Felipe Aguero, "The Military and Democracy in Venezuela," in *The Military and Democracy*, eds. Louis W. Goodman, Johanna S. R. Mendelson, and Juan Rial (Lexington, MA: Lexington Books, 1990), 257–276.

24. Marion J. Levy Jr., *Modernization and the Structure of Societies* (Princeton, NJ: Princeton University Press, 1966), Vol. 2, 603.

25. Lucian W. Pye, "Armies in the Process of Political Modernization," in *The Role of the Military in Underdeveloped Countries*, ed. John J. Johnson (Princeton, NJ: Princeton University Press, 1962), 69–89; for a summary of the literature depicting the armed forces as a positive, modernizing institution, see Robert Jackman, "The Predictability of Coups d'etat: A Model with African Data," *American Political Science Review*, vol. 72, no. 4 (1978), 1262–1275.

26. Manfred Halpern, *The Politics of Social Change in the Middle East and North Africa* (Princeton, NJ: Princeton University Press, 1963), 75, 253.

27. One of the most influential works was Morris Janowitz, *Military Institutions and Coercion in Developing Nations* (Chicago: University of Chicago, 1977). For a summary of those writings and further references, see Henry Bienen, "The Background to Contemporary Study of Militaries and Modernization," in *The Military and Modernization*, ed. Henry Bienen (Chicago: Atherton, 1971), 1–33; First, *The Barrel of a Gun*, 13–20.

28. Daniel Lerner and Richard D. Robinson, "Swords and Plowshares: The Turkish Army as a Modernizing Force," in *The Military and Modernization*, 117–148.

29. Eric A. Nordlinger, *Soldiers in Politics: Military Coups and Governments* (Englewood Cliffs, NJ: Prentice Hall, 1977), 32–37.

30. Karen L. Remmer, *Military Rule in Latin America* (Boston: Unwin Hyman, 1989), 3.

31. The armed forces of the least developed nations are not inevitably reform oriented. Coups in Africa and other very poor areas are often motivated solely by their leaders' self-interest or by narrow ethnic or tribal goals. Also, while the military has often been progressive in the less developed nations of South America, Africa, and the Middle East, it has been quite reactionary in Central America and the Caribbean, where it was co-opted by the upper class.

32. Nordlinger, *Soldiers in Politics*, 173; also Huntington, *Political Order*, chap. 4.

33. Huntington, *Political Order*, 221.

34. Decalo, *Coups and Army Rule in Africa*, 133.

35. John Booth, *The End and the Beginning: The Nicaraguan Revolution*, 2d ed. (Boulder, CO: Westview Press, 1985).

36. To be sure, some relatively personalistic dictators, like Argentina's Juan Perón, have introduced broader social programs. Perón sought to industrialize the country and help organized labor. Even benevolent personalistic regimes such as his, however, still have suffered from extensive corruption and overconcentration of power in the hands of one person.

37. Decalo, *Coups and Army Rule in Africa*, 139–198.

38. On personalistic dictatorships in Africa, military and civilian, see Robert Jackson and

Carl Rosberg, *Personal Rule in Africa* (Berkeley: University of California Press, 1982).

39. David J. Gould, *Bureaucratic Corruption and Underdevelopment in the Third World* (New York: Pergamon Press, 1980), xiv; Michael J. Schatzberg, *The Politics of Oppression in Zaire* (Bloomington: Indiana University Press, 1988). Mobutu changed the name of his country from the Congo to Zaire. After he was overthrown, the name changed back to the Congo.

40. Richard Millet, *Guardians of the Dynasty* (Maryknoll, NY: Orbis, 1977).

41. Decalo, *Coups and Army Rule in Africa*, 11. Decalo argues that in Africa personalities, more than broad socioeconomic or political variables, have explained military intervention. See also his *Psychoses of Power: African Personal Dictatorships* (Boulder, CO: Westview Press, 1989).

42. Edward A. Olsen and Stephen Jurika Jr., "Introduction," and Harold W. Maynard, "The Role of the Indonesian Armed Forces," in *The Armed Forces in Contemporary Asian Society*, eds. Edward A. Olsen and Stephen Jurika Jr. (Boulder, CO: Westview Press, 1986), 18, 207–208.

43. In some cases such councils have been mere facades, with one person really in power. Thus, it is not always easy to distinguish between personalistic and institutional military regimes. Ultimately, the determining factor is where real power resides rather than the formal structures.

44. Amos Perlmutter, *Political Roles and Military Rulers* (London: Frank Cass, 1981).

45. Guillermo O'Donnell, *Modernization and Bureaucratic-Authoritarianism: Studies in South American Politics* (Berkeley: University of California Press, 1973).

46. Jeffrey Lunstead, "The Armed Forces in Bangladesh Society," in *The Armed Forces in Contemporary Asian Society*, 316.

47. Ruth First, *Power in Africa* (New York: Pantheon Books, 1970), 20.

48. First, *The Barrel of a Gun*, 429.

49. Craig Baxter and Syedur Rahman, "Bangladesh's Military: Political Institutionalization and Economic Development," in *Civil-Military Interaction*, 43–60.

50. Harold Crouch, "The Military and Politics in South-East Asia," in *Military-Civilian Relations in South-East Asia*, eds. Zakaria Haji Ahmad and Harold Crouch (New York: Oxford University Press), 291. Italics added.

51. Crouch, *The Army and Politics in Indonesia*. Both Suharto and Sukarno, like many natives of the island of Java, had only one name. With more than 120 million people, Java contains over half of Indonesia's population and contributes a large share of the country's political leaders.

52. Remmer, *Military Rule in Latin America*, 3–31.

53. Seitz, "The Military in Black African Politics," in *Civil-Military Interaction*, 61–75.

54. John J. Johnson, *The Military and Society in Latin America* (Stanford, CA: Stanford University Press, 1964); O'Donnell, *Modernization and Bureaucratic-Authoritarianism*.

55. Argentina's two military regimes lasted seven years each (1966–1973 and 1976–1983), with a three-year hiatus of unstable civilian government. The Pinochet government in Chile lasted from 1973 to 1990. While the Chilean dictatorship was not as long-lived as Brazil's, General Pinochet personally ruled far longer than any of the military presidents in those four countries.

56. Guillermo O'Donnell, "Corporatism and the Question of the State," in *Authoritarianism and Corporatism in Latin America*, ed. James Malloy (Pittsburgh, PA: University of Pittsburgh Press, 1977). The most complete analysis of O'Donnell's rather complex theory is contained in David Collier, ed. *The New Authoritarianism in Latin America* (Princeton, NJ: Princeton University Press, 1979); and an excellent critique is found in Karen L. Remmer and Gilbert W. Merkx, "Bureaucratic-Authoritarianism Revisited," *Latin American Research Review*, vol. 17, no. 2 (1982), 3–40.

57. For a discussion of the difference between inclusionary and exclusionary regimes and their relationship to democracy and authoritarianism, see Remmer, *Military Rule in Latin America*, 6–17.

58. "The Political Orientation Speech Delivered by Captain Thomas Sankara in Ouagadougou, Upper Volta on October 2, 1983," in *Military Marxist Regimes in Africa*, eds. John Markakis and Michael Waller (London: Frank Cass, 1986), 145–153 (selected portions).

59. Samuel Decalo, "The Morphology of Radical Military Rule in Africa," in *Military Marxist Regimes in Africa*, 123.

60. Thomas S. Cox, *Civil-Military Relations in Sierra Leone* (Cambridge, MA: Harvard University Press, 1976), 14.

61. Kevin Middlebrook and David Scott Palmer, *Military Governments and Political Development: Lessons from Peru* (Beverly Hills, CA: Sage Publications, 1975).

62. Samuel Decalo, "Military Rule in Africa: Etiology and Morphology," in *Military Power and Politics in Black Africa*, 56, 58.

63. J. Bayo Adekanye, "The Post-Military State in Africa," in *The Political Dilemma of Military Regimes*, eds. Christopher Clapham and George Philip (London: Croom Helm, 1985), 87.

64. Crouch, "The Military and Politics in South-East Asia," in *Military-Civilian Relations*, 292–293.

65. Charles H. Kennedy and David J. Louscher, "Civil-Military Interaction: Data in Search of a Theory," in *Civil-Military Interaction*, 5.

66. Howard Handelman, "Uruguay," in *Military Government and the Movement towards Democracy in South America*, eds. Howard Handelman and Thomas Sanders (Bloomington: Indiana University Press, 1981), 218.

67. Decalo, *Coups and Army Rule in Africa*, 20.

68. Harold Crouch, "The Military in Malaysia," in *The Military, the State, and Development in Asia and the Pacific*, ed. Viberto Selochan (Boulder, CO: Westview Press), 130–131.

69. McGowan, "African Military Coups D'état, 1956–2001," 347.

70. Claude E. Welch Jr., "From 'Armies of Africans' to 'African Armies': The Evolution of Military Forces in Africa," in *African Armies: Evolution and Capabilities*, eds. Bruce E. Arlinghaus and Pauline H. Baker (Boulder, CO: Westview Press, 1986), 25.

71. Elisabeth Sköns et al., "Military Expenditures," in *The Stockholm International Peace Research Institute (SIPRI) Yearbook 2000: Armaments, Disarmament and International Security* (Oxford: Oxford University Press, 2000). Summarized on the SIPRI website (http://www.sipri.se/).

72. J. Samuel Fitch, *The Armed Forces and Democracy in Latin America* (Baltimore, MD: The Johns Hopkins University Press, 1998), 77–78.

73. Juan Rial, "Armies and Civil Society in Latin America," in *Civil-Military Relations and Democracy*, 57.

74. Michel Louis Martin, "Operational Weaknesses and Political Activism," in *To Sheathe the Sword*, 89.

75. Pamela Constable and Arturo Valenzuela, *A Nation of Enemies: Chile under Pinochet* (New York: W. W. Norton, 1991).

76. Of course, many military regimes are not very repressive. However, it is precisely those that seize power to restore order in highly polarized societies that normally are the most brutal.

77. Nordlinger, *Soldiers in Politics*, 139.

78. Remmer, *Military Rule*, 40.

79. Jueng-en Woo, *Race to the Swift* (New York: Columbia University Press, 1991).

80. For a somewhat more critical view, particularly of income distribution and welfare in Indonesia, see "Military Regimes and Social Justice in Indonesia and Thailand," in *Civil-Military Interaction*, 96–113; see also the chapters on South Korea, Indonesia, and Thailand in James W. Morely, eds., *Driven by Growth* (New York: M. E. Sharpe, 1992).

81. For a discussion of the problems involved in evaluating the economic performance of Latin America's military governments, see Karen L. Remmer, "Evaluating the Policy Impact of Military Regimes in Latin America," in *Armies and Politics*, 367–385; Remmer, *Military Rule*, chap. 4.

82. Remmer, *Military Rule*, 197–200; see also, Robert W. Jackman, "Politicians in Uniform: Military Governments and Social Change in the Third World," *American Political Science Review*, vol. 72, no. 4 (1978), 1262–1275; Seitz, "The Military in Black African Politics," in *Civil-Military Interaction*.

83. Edward A. Olsen, "The Societal Role of the ROK Armed Forces," in *The Armed Forces in Contemporary Asian Society*, 95–96.

84. Issaka K. Souaré, *Civil Wars and Coups d'Etat in West Africa* (Lanham, MD: University Press of America, 2006), 101

85. Howard Handelman, "Prelude to the 1984 Uruguayan Election: The Military Regime's Legitimacy Crisis and the 1980 Constitutional Plebiscite," in *Critical Elections in the Americas*, eds. Paul Drake and Eduardo Silva (San Diego: University of California Press, 1986), 201–214.

86. In all of these cases civilians succeeded military rulers. As we have noted, there are also many instances of military governments giving way to another military government as the result of internal coups or other intramilitary conflict.

87. Talukder Maniruzzaman, *Military Withdrawal from Politics: A Comparative Study* (Cambridge, MA: Ballinger Publishing, 1987), 21, 24–25.

88. South Korea's first democratic presidential election took place in 1987, but the victor, Roe Tae Woo, was a former military strongman. Thus, full civilian government did not come until Kim Young Sam assumed the presidency in 1993. On Korea's transition, see Byung-Kook Kim, "Korea's Crisis of Success," in *Democracy in East Asia*, eds. Larry Diamond and Marc F. Plattner (Baltimore, MD: Johns Hopkins University Press, 1998), 113–132.

89. Michael Bratton and Nicolas van de Walle, *Democratic Experiments in Africa* (New York: Cambridge University Press, 1997), 197–203.

90. Quoted in Louis W. Goodman, "Military Roles Past and Present," in *Civil-Military Relations and Democracy*, 32. The discussion that follows of "new roles" for the military draws on Goodman's chapter.

91. Joseph S. Nye Jr., "Epilogue: The Liberal Tradition," in *Civil-Military Relations and Democracy*, 153–154.

92. Samuel P. Huntington, "Reforming Civil-Military Relations," 8.

93. Ibid. 3–4.

94. David R. Mares, "Civil-Military Relations, Democracy, and the Regional Neighbors," in *Civil-Military Relations*, 18.

95. Brian Loveman and Thomas M. Davies Jr., eds. *The Politics of Antipolitics: The Military in Latin America*, 2d ed. (Lincoln: University of Nebraska Press, 1989).

96. Ibid., 6.

CHAPTER 10

THE POLITICAL ECONOMY OF THIRD WORLD DEVELOPMENT

V irtually every Third World government, except the most corrupt and incompetent, wishes to promote economic development. Economic growth coupled with a reasonably equitable income distribution offers the promise of improved living standards and, presumably, increased popular support for the ruling regime.[1] It also provides added tax revenues, thereby enhancing government capacity. And economic development can augment a nation's military strength, diplomatic influence, and international prestige. But the obvious benefits of growth should not obscure the many difficult questions that economic development policy entails. For example: How can a nation achieve growth, and how can the sometimes conflicting goals of economic development be reconciled? How should countries share the inevitable sacrifices required for generating early economic development? How can a country achieve economic development without doing irreparable harm to the environment?

The optimism expressed by early modernization theorists regarding Third World economic development looked ill-founded during the 1980s in the face of sharp economic declines in Africa and Latin America.[2] In South Asia, Sub-Saharan Africa, and other developing regions, the war on poverty often has seemed unwinnable. On the other hand, East Asia's spectacular growth since the 1960s and India's economic take-off since 1994 appear to belie dependency theory's pervasive pessimism about the limits of development in the periphery.

In recent decades, a substantial amount of the scholarship on the Third World has focused on the LDCs' *political economy*. Martin Staniland defines this field as the study of "how politics determines aspects of the economy, and how economic institutions determine the political process," as well as "the dynamic interaction between the two forces."[3] This chapter focuses on several important issues in that realm: What are the major strategies for development? What should be the role of the state in stimulating and regulating economic growth and industrialization? How should countries deal with the deep economic inequalities that persist, or even increase, during the modernization process?

THE ROLE OF THE STATE

The question of the state's proper economic role has been at the center of political and economic debates for hundreds of years, first in Western industrial economies, and more recently in the Third World. During the sixteenth and seventeenth centuries, major European powers were guided by the philosophy of *mercantilism*, which looked at a nation's economic activity as a means of enhancing the political power of the state and its monarch. Consequently, mercantilists saw government as "both source and beneficiary of economic growth."[4] That perspective, however, drew the fire of the eighteenth-century, Scottish political economist Adam Smith, who advocated a very limited state that allowed market forces a free hand. The following century, Karl Marx, reacting to the exploitative nature of early capitalism, proposed initially assigning the state a dominant economic role through ownership of the means of production and centralized control of the economy. Finally, in the twentieth century, Sir John Maynard Keynes, responding to the Great Depression, advocated a substantial degree of government economic intervention, but rejected Marxist prescriptions for state ownership and centralized planning.

Today, the collapse of the Soviet bloc's centrally controlled "command economies" and the poor economic performance of the world's remaining communist nations (except China and Vietnam, which have largely abandoned Marxist economics) have discredited the advocates of state-dominated economies. At the same time, however, no government embraces full laissez faire (i.e., allowing market forces complete free reign, with no government intervention). All countries, for example, no matter how capitalistic, have laws regulating banking, domestic commerce, and international trade. Most have introduced some environmental regulations. In the real world, then, governments must decide where to position themselves between the extreme poles of an unregulated economy and a command economy.

For a number of reasons, that choice is particularly contentious in the LDCs. The fragile nature of many Third World economies, their high levels of poverty, their poor distribution of wealth and income, their extreme dependence on international market forces, and their endangered environments all have encouraged many governments to assume an active economic role. Moreover, many developing nations also lack a strong entrepreneurial class and sufficient private capital for investment. As a consequence, their governments have often built the steel mills, railroads, or sugar refineries that the private sector could not or would not provide. More recently, governments have been asked to protect the environment against the ravages of economic development. Not surprisingly, then, state economic intervention traditionally has been more pronounced in the developing world than in the West. In recent decades, however, the spread of *"neoliberal"* economic policies—characterized by free trade, free markets, and relatively unrestrained capitalism—has sharply reduced government economic intervention in both the developing and the developed worlds.[5]

This chapter discusses a number of alternative models prescribing the role of the state in Third World economies, ranging from command economies, such as North Korea's, to very limited state intervention, as in Hong Kong. In considering these alternatives, the reader should keep in mind that these are ideal types. Few countries fit any of these models perfectly. Cuba's Marxist government, for example, permits private farming and various small businesses. Also, many nations have introduced some mix of these approaches. While the options discussed below are not exhaustive, they cover the models most widely used in the LDCs.

The Command Economy

Marxism began as a critique of capitalism in the Western world during the early stages of industrial development. Inherently, argued Marx, capitalism produced an inequitable distribution of wealth and income, with those who control the means of production (industrialists, landlords) exploiting those who worked in them (the working class, peasants). One of Marxism's appeals to its supporters, then, was its promise of great equality and social justice. In modern times, economic inequality has usually intensified as countries have moved from the lower to the middle levels of development.[6] Consequently, it is not surprising that Marxist ideology initially appealed to many Third World leaders who were troubled by the deep injustices in their own economic systems. It was particularly attractive in Latin America and parts of Africa, which had the greatest disparities between rich and poor.

A second assertion made by Marxist leaders was that only a revolutionary political-economic system could free Third World countries from the yoke of dependency. Because most dependency theorists believed that capitalist trade and investment in the developing world created an exploitative relationship between core industrial nations and the periphery, they argued that only "socialist" Third World economies could achieve economic independence and development.[7]

Finally, another of communism's appeals was its centralized state control of the economy. A *command economy*, first established in the Soviet Union, has two central features. First, the state largely owns and manages the means of production. That includes factories, banks, major trade and commercial institutions, retail establishments, and, frequently, farms. While all communist nations have allowed some private economic activity, the private sector has been quite limited, aside from nations such as China, which have largely abandoned Marxist economics in recent years. Second, in a command economy, state planners, rather than market forces, shape basic decisions regarding production (including the quantity and price of goods produced).

Interestingly, Marxism viewed market (capitalist) economies as anarchistic because they leave the most fundamental decisions over the allocation of resources and the determination of prices to the "whims" of supply and demand. Thus, Adam Przeworski has satirized the orthodox Marxists' attitude toward capitalism's "invisible [guiding] hand": People in Britain and the United States get up each morning and find their newspapers or milk cartons already sitting outside their doors without even knowing who delivered them. Yet, Przeworski noted wryly, orthodox Marxist theory insisted that the paper or milk carton could not possibly have arrived without a central planner guaranteeing its delivery.[8] In fact, he observes, under a centrally planned economy not only was home delivery not reliable, but there were recurrent shortages of paper, cartons, and milk. Indeed, the collapse of Soviet and Eastern European communism revealed the organizational failures of centralized command economies.

In fact, the flaws of command economies are now so obvious that most people are unaware of their earlier accomplishments. By dictating the movement of people and resources from one sector of the economy to another, communist countries such as the Soviet Union and China were able to jump-start their industrial takeoffs. During the 1920s and 1930s, "entire industries were created [in the USSR], along with millions of jobs that drew peasants away from the countryside and into higher-paying jobs and higher living standards."[9] Western estimates of Soviet economic performance during its industrialization phase indicate that between 1928 and 1955, GNP grew at a robust average annual rate of some 5 percent.[10] During the early decades of its revolution, China also moved quickly from a backward agrarian economy to a far more industrialized society. According to one leading authority, between 1952 and 1975, China's economy grew at an average annual rate of 8.2 percent, while industrial output surged ahead at 11.5 percent annually.[11] These rates far exceeded the norms in either capitalist developing nations or industrialized democracies.[12] Other analysts believe that China's growth rates could not have been that high because of the setbacks of the Great Leap Forward and the Cultural Revolution. Still, all agree that compared to India, Pakistan, and most LDCs, China's growth during that period, like the Soviet Union's decades earlier, was extremely impressive. Small wonder that, at one time, many Third World leaders were attracted to the Soviet and Chinese development models.

Finally, command economies have frequently made great strides toward reducing income inequalities. Indeed, it is here that communist LDCs most clearly outperformed their capitalist counterparts. In Cuba, for example, the revolution brought a substantial transfer of income from the richest 20 percent of the population to the poorest 40 percent.[13] The poor also benefited from land reform, subsidized rents, and free health care, though some of those gains were undermined in the 1990s, following the loss of Soviet economic assistance. An extensive adult literacy program and greater educational opportunities further advanced social equality. Nor was Cuba unique in this respect. Cross-national statistical comparisons indicate that communist countries as a whole have more equal income distribution than do capitalist nations at similar levels of development.[14]

Eventually, however, the weaknesses of command economies overshadow their accomplishments.[15] Lacking indicators of consumer demand, state planners have little basis for deciding what to produce and how much. Moreover, centrally controlled economies typically reward producers for meeting their output quotas, with little concern for product quality. Furthermore, even in the best of circumstances, to be at all efficient, a centralized command economy would need a highly skilled and honest bureaucracy equipped with sophisticated and accurate consumer surveys. These qualities are rare to nonexistent in Third World bureaucracies. Moreover, command economies handed inordinate power to state planners. And as Lord Acton once warned, "Power tends to corrupt, and absolute power tends to corrupt absolutely."

Thus, for example, for China's business entrepreneurs the price of doing business is bribing government officials (cadres) or their adult children.[16] Elsewhere as well, command economies have featured a large privileged class of state and party bureaucrats (*apparatchiks*), who have enjoyed perquisites unavailable to the rest of the population. Furthermore, while the Soviet Union and China enjoyed rapid growth in the early decades of their revolutions, both economies eventually lost momentum as they became more complex and, hence, harder to control centrally. Finally, command economies are more adept at building heavy industries such as steel mills or constructing basic public works projects—endeavors more typical of early industrialization—than they are at developing sophisticated high-tech production techniques or at producing quality consumer goods. The Soviet Union, for example, turned out impressive military hardware and powerful space rockets, but was unable to produce a decent automobile or home washing machine.

By the late 1970s in China and the 1980s in the USSR, with both economies deteriorating, their leaders (Deng Xiaoping and Mikhail Gorbachev) recognized the need for economic decentralization and reduced state economic control. China's subsequent transition to *market socialism* (a mixture of free market and socialist economics) has produced one of the world's fastest growing economies. However, in the Soviet Union and its major successor state, Russia, reforms resulted in an economic collapse that lasted for nearly a decade. The fall of Soviet bloc communism and China's remarkable economic transformation have inspired market-oriented reforms in other command economies. Vietnam, for example, has transferred state farmland to the peasantry, attracted billions of dollars in foreign investment, and transferred a substantial portion of its industrial production from the state to the private sector. Elsewhere in Asia and Africa, governments such as Myanmar and the Congolese Republic have privatized much of the state sector (sold it to private-sector owners) and reduced government economic controls. The end of Soviet aid has undercut some of Cuba's earlier gains in health care, nutrition, and education. Stripped of its primary benefactor, it too has been forced to accept limited free-market innovations.

In many former communist nations in Eastern and Central Europe, the demise of their command economies initially failed to improve living standards and often sharply lowered them. In Mikhail Gorbachev's Russia (1985–1991), for example, economic reforms removed many of the controls held by the state bureaucracy without replacing them with adequate free-market incentives. In other words, reformers removed the "stick" (government directives) that had previously driven the economy forward before they had introduced sufficient "carrots" (economic incentives) to replace it. Workers who had accepted Spartan living conditions and limited consumer goods in return for guaranteed employment, controlled consumer prices, and free or cheap social services (what the Chinese call the "iron rice bowl") found themselves stripped of these guarantees with no compensatory gains. Only in China and Vietnam, where many state controls remain in place, did the transition toward free-market economics rapidly raise standards of living. In Eastern and Central Europe, especially Russia, it took a decade or more for living standards to equal or surpass their communist levels.

Latin American Statism

Even in capitalist Third World countries, the state has often played a major economic role, trying to be an engine of economic growth. In the period between the two World Wars, many Latin American nations first pursued state-led industrialization. That process accelerated during the Great Depression of the 1920s and 1930s, when countries in the region had difficulty finding markets for their food and raw material exports and, consequently, lacked foreign exchange for industrial imports. Argentina, Brazil, Chile, Uruguay, and Mexico were among the early leaders in the push toward industrialization.

Unlike communist countries, Latin American nations left most economic activity in the hands of the private sector and did not centralize control over the economy. But their governments often owned strategically important enterprises and invested in industries that failed to attract sufficient domestic private capital. Consequently, prior to the recent privatization of state enterprises, many of the region's railroads, airlines, petroleum companies, mines, steel mills, electric power plants, telephone companies, and armaments factories were state owned.

Two aspects of state ownership in the region contradict popular stereotypes. First, many government takeovers were accepted or even endorsed by their country's private sectors. One reason was that the most important nationalizations— including the petroleum industries in Mexico and Venezuela, mining in Chile and Peru, and railroads in Argentina—affected companies that were owned by foreign corporations rather than local capitalists. Second, after taking control of the petroleum industry, railroads, and utilities, the state often provided private-sector industries with cheaper subsidized transportation, power, and other needed resources. In fact, until the 1980s, conservative governments in the region were as likely to expand government ownership as were left-leaning or populist regimes. For example, during the 1960s and 1970s, Brazil's right-wing military regime substantially increased the size of the state sector.

Along with its ownership of a number of essential enterprises, the state also played a pivotal role in fomenting private-sector industrial growth. In Latin America's largest economies, the government initiated import-substituting industrialization (ISI) programs in the early to mid-twentieth century. ISI (discussed more extensively later in this chapter) sought to replace imported consumer goods with domestically manufactured products.[17] Although import-substituting firms were overwhelmingly owned by the private sector, industrial growth would have been impossible without government support. This included protective import tariffs and quotas, favorable exchange rates, subsidized energy and transport costs, and low-interest loans.

In countries such as Argentina, Brazil, Chile, Colombia, and Mexico, these government-supported development policies were initially quite successful. From 1945 to 1970, rates of investment in Latin America were higher than those in the Western industrial powers, and from 1960 to 1980, the region's manufacturing output grew faster as well.[18] Virtually every Latin American country began manufacturing basic consumer goods such as textiles, clothing, packaged food, and furniture. Larger nations such as Argentina, Brazil, and Mexico established automotive industries, steel mills, and other heavy industries. Although the largest manufacturing plants were generally foreign owned, local entrepreneurs also played an important role in the region's industrial expansion. In time, industrialization altered the region's demographic and class structures. Massive rural migration to the cities transformed Latin America into the Third World's most urbanized region (see Chapter 7). In all, ISI created many blue-collar jobs and expanded the size of the middle class substantially.

But hidden beneath these accomplishments, state-sponsored ISI also promoted economic inefficiencies and income inequalities. While the nurturing of industrialization was helpful, and probably necessary, in the early stages of economic development, Latin American governments maintained protectionist measures and subsidies too broadly and too long. Rather than serving as a finely calibrated tool for getting industrialization off the ground, ISI became a politically motivated juggernaut. With industrialists, the middle class, and organized labor all united behind these policies, elected officials were unwilling to wean established industries from government support and protection long after they should have become more self-sufficient. Inefficient domestic industries received excessive protection; trade and fiscal policies designed to promote industrialization often harmed agricultural exports; and the income gap widened both between the urban and rural populations and between skilled and unskilled workers.

Mexico illustrates both the initial accomplishments and the subsequent weaknesses of statism in the region. From the mid-1930s to 1970, the national government supplied 35–40 percent of the country's total capital investment.[19] At the same time, the state-owned petroleum and railroad enterprises offered private industry subsidized energy and transportation (i.e., they sold both below their free-market values).[20] Government trade and labor policies protected Mexican companies from foreign competition and held down wages as a means of stimulating domestic investment. As a consequence, between 1935 and 1970, industrial output grew at an average annual rate of nearly 10 percent, and GNP rose 6 percent annually, making Mexico one of the world's fastest growing economies at that time.[21] During the 1970s and early 1980s, however, the state's role in the economy spiraled out of control.[22] By 1985, the government operated nearly 1,200 state enterprises (*parastatals*) involved in everything from petroleum drilling to food sales. At the same time, however, even during this era of enormous economic growth. Mexico's "economic miracle" left the rural population and the urban poor behind, creating a highly unequal distribution of income and substantial pockets of poverty.

Thus, when PEMEX, the state petroleum monopoly, discovered vast new oil reserves in the 1970s just when the world price of petroleum was tripling, the government saw an opportunity to use its oil bonanza to help the poor. At the same time, however, more powerful groups also lobbied for greater consumer subsidies, increased state support for private industry, and new jobs in the parastatals. Quite quickly, spiraling government expenditures exceeded new oil revenues, thereby contributing to huge budget deficits and enormous foreign indebtedness.

In general, Latin America's development model introduced two important areas of inefficiency, both of which typify state-led industrial growth elsewhere in the developing world. First, a large number of state-owned enterprises were overstaffed and poorly run. Contrary to the common stereotype, state enterprises are not inherently inefficient. In advanced industrialized nations such as France and Norway, governments have operated some enterprises quite effectively. But few Third World governments have the skilled and disciplined personnel needed to perform at that level. Furthermore, given the high rate of unemployment in almost all LDCs, their governments are under great political pressure to hire more employees whether the state enterprises need them or not. Consequently, parastatals are typically substantially overstaffed, with many employees who do little or nothing.[23] At the same time, labor unions and middle-class groups also lobby state enterprises to sell the public consumer goods and services at highly discounted prices. For example, in the past Argentineans rode the state railroads for a nominal fee and received highly subsidized electricity in their homes.

Elsewhere in the region, governments have subsidized or controlled prices for items such as gasoline, urban bus fares, and food.[24] Ultimately, the combination of money-losing parastatals, consumer subsidies, and subsidies to private-sector producers helped bankrupt many Latin American governments. By 1982 virtually every government in the region was deeply in debt and experiencing severe fiscal problems.

A second important weakness of Latin America's development model was the inefficiency ISI encouraged in the private sector. To be sure, governments throughout the world have effectively used protectionist measures to help infant industries get started during the early stages of development. Typically, in the ISI model, the state creates a wall of high import tariffs and quotas to protect emerging local manufacturers from foreign competition. But over time, the government needs to scale back the level of protection or else domestic firms will have little incentive to become more efficient and internationally competitive. Instead, Latin American protectionism, rather than serving as a temporary stimulus, became embedded in the economy.

Starting in the 1980s, the region's severe debt crisis and economic depression compelled almost all Latin American nations to reverse their statist economic policies. In Mexico, the de la Madrid and Salinas administrations (1982–1994) closed or privatized more than 80 percent of the country's 1,155 state enterprises, including the national airline, telephone companies, and banks.[25] In Chile, the transition to a slimmed-down state began during the dictatorship of General Augusto Pinochet (1973–1990). But when democracy was finally restored, the new governing coalition (led first by a Christian Democratic president and then by Socialists) continued many of Pinochet's economic policies, which they had once denounced.

While these reductions in public-sector activity were generally necessary, they also carried a great human cost. Throughout Latin America, millions of workers lost their jobs, as the new owners of privatized parastatals laid off "excess workers." Many other money-losing plants simply shut down. In Mexico, for example, the government's economic restructuring program eliminated an estimated 400,000 jobs. More than half the workers formerly employed in state steel mills were laid off when their companies were privatized.[26] Argentina, Chile, Peru, and Venezuela experienced similar layoffs. At the same time, reduced protectionism in much of the region opened the door to a surge of imported consumer goods, further slashing sales and jobs in domestic firms that were unable to compete. Finally, the reduction or elimination of government consumer subsidies sharply increased the cost of basic necessities.

In Mexico and Argentina, just as in Chile, populist and leftist parties that had once been the leading advocates of government economic intervention reluctantly conceded that the state sector had grown too unwieldy and needed to be cut back.[27] Excessive government spending coupled with the middle and upper classes' refusal to pay their fair share of taxes resulted in massive fiscal deficits and runaway inflation. Only by substantially cutting budgetary deficits in the past two to three decades have Latin America's governments been able to control inflation that had reached annual rates of 1,000–10,000 percent in Argentina, Brazil, Nicaragua, and Peru. The debt crisis and the related economic recession contributed to a sharp decline in Latin American living standards from the early 1980s to the early 1990s (the "lost decade"). In Peru and

Venezuela, for example, real incomes fell by nearly 40 percent.[28] Since the start of the 1990s, the region has experienced an irregular recovery. High inflation rates, which had frequently reached 100 percent annually or higher, have been brought under control, and some countries have enjoyed bursts of economic growth. But living standards have only recovered slowly, economic growth has generally been modest, and several countries have suffered severe economic crises in the past 15 years. Thus, while most analysts agree that Latin America's level of state economic interventionism and protectionism had been excessive, neoliberal reforms designed to scale down government have generally failed to improve living standards, other than in Chile.

East Asia's Developmental State

While Latin American economies have generally been struggling since the early 1980s, a number of East and Southeast Asian economies have grown at a phenomenal rate for most of the past 30 years. South Korea, Taiwan, Hong Kong, Singapore, and China (now the world's second largest economy) have received the most attention.[29] More recently, India, in South Asia, has made tremendous strides. For one thing, their impact on world trade has been enormous. China is one of the United States' leading trading partners and the world's greatest exporter of manufactured goods. But other Southeast Asian economies—Thailand, Malaysia, and Indonesia—have also grown dramatically. From the mid-1960s until the 1990s financial crisis (discussed below), Taiwan, South Korea, Singapore, Hong Kong, Thailand, Malaysia, Indonesia, and China all grew at annual rates ranging from 4 to 10 percent, and China and South Korea sometimes exceeded 10 percent.[30] In fact, from 1960 to the late 1990s, these economies grew almost three times as fast as Latin America's and five times as fast as Sub-Saharan Africa's.[31] While a number of East and Southeast Asian economies suffered serious setbacks during the region's financial crisis, they have since resumed healthy development. Moreover, the benefits of East and Southeast Asia's rapid growth have been distributed relatively equitably, with a far narrower gap between the rich and poor than in Latin America or Africa.

With the partial exception of Communist China and Vietnam (which have developed mixed socialist and free-market economies), most East and Southeast Asian countries have tied their growth to the free market. More than in other Third World regions, the private sector owned the lion's share of the economy, with a relatively small state sector.[32] Not surprisingly, this has led conservative economists to hail the East Asian economic miracle as a triumph of unfettered capitalism, a testimony to keeping government out of the economy.[33]

But many East Asian specialists argue that, to the contrary, governments in that region were key players in stimulating economic growth.[34] Examining the causes of Japan's spectacular postwar economic resurgence, Chalmers Johnson first formulated the notion of the *developmental state*.[35] We can best understand the meaning of that term by comparing the role of government in East Asia's high-growth capitalist nations (Japan, South Korea, Singapore, and Taiwan) to its function in Western nations during their initial industrial expansions some 150 years earlier. At that time, developing Western nations established *regulatory states* in which "government refrained from interfering in the marketplace, except to insure certain limited goals" (e.g., banking regulation). In contrast, the East

Asian developmental states "intervene actively in the economy in order to guide or promote particular substantive goals" (e.g., full employment, export competitiveness, energy self-sufficiency).[36]

Japan's powerful Ministry of International Trade and Industry (MITI), Johnson notes, directed that country's postwar industrial resurgence. Subsequently, South Korea, Taiwan, Singapore, Indonesia, and other industrializing nations in East and Southeast Asia adopted many aspects of Japan's state-guided capitalist development model.[37] Typically, each country had a powerful government ministry or agency "charged with the task of planning, guiding, and coordinating industrial policies."[38] They included South Korea's Economic Planning Board, Taiwan's Council for Economic Planning and Development, and Singapore's Economic Development Board, all modeled after MITI. Under the developmental state, their government economic intervention was far more extensive and direct than in the West, targeting either entire economic sectors (such as agriculture or industry), whole industries (such as computers, automobiles, or electronics), or particular companies (such as South Korea's Hyundai).[39]

Developmental states did not always implement identical policies. For example, the bonds between government and big business have been tighter in South Korea than in Taiwan, while state enterprises were more important in Taiwan than in Korea. In Singapore, government control over labor has been more comprehensive than in the other two countries.[40] But in all of them, the state played an important role, guiding the private sector toward targeted economic activities, and stimulating growth in areas that the government wished to expand. Sometimes, government planners have even pressured particular industries or companies to specialize in certain products and abandon others.

For the most part, East Asian state intervention was more indirect than it had been in Latin America, but, at least until recently, it was significant nonetheless. Among the tools East Asian governments have used to sway private-sector activity have been tax policy, control over credit, and influencing the price of raw materials. For example, when the South Korean and Taiwanese governments wished to develop the electronics, computer software, and automobile industries, they intervened aggressively, rather than leaving it to the marketplace. They established relevant research institutes; granted firms in targeted industries preferential access to credit; temporarily required companies that had been importing those targeted products to switch to domestic manufacturers; and offered trade protection to new industries for limited periods of time. South Korea temporarily banned all imports of computers when it promoted that industry, and Taiwan did the same for textiles.[41]

While the East Asian development model's tremendous success has earned it widespread admiration, some observers have remained skeptical about its applicability elsewhere. One concern is the model's apparent political requirements. Chalmers Johnson notes that most developmental states have been authoritarian—or what he calls "soft authoritarian"—during their major industrialization push.[42] Other analysts have felt that authoritarian or semi-authoritarian rule (including the ability to repress or control labor unions and to direct management) was an essential component of the region's early economic growth. Taiwan and South Korea industrialized under authoritarian governments, though both have subsequently democratized. The governments of Malaysia, Singapore, and Indonesia have all repressed democratic expression in varying degrees. Since its return to Chinese rule, Hong Kong, a former British colony, has curbed its brief experiment with democracy. Of course, Japan, the original developmental state, is a democracy, but a democracy that has been dominated for over 50 years by one party. Since its formation in 1955, the Liberal Democratic Party has governed the country for all but a few years. Thus, there is some doubt about how the developmental state would perform under the democratic pressures now spreading across the Third World.

Another important question is the transferability of East Asian political and economic practices to other parts of the Third World.[43] The developmental state seems to require qualities that are in short supply in other developing areas: a highly skilled government bureaucracy and close cooperation between business, labor, and agriculture. In Indonesia, for example, a team of government economists known as "the Berkeley Boys" (most of them holding doctoral degrees from the University of California at Berkeley) oversaw that country's economic development. South Korea's highly trained state technocrats worked closely with the country's dominant business conglomerates (*chaebols*), such as Hyundai and Samsung.[44] Similar cooperation between sophisticated government planners and big business, unchallenged by a relatively docile working class, contributed to economic surges elsewhere in East and Southeast Asia. Outside of Asia, however, only Chile's "Chicago Boys" (economists trained at the University of Chicago) brought a comparable set of skills and enjoyed similar cooperation with the business community.

Some have argued that East Asia's Confucian culture—featuring nationalism, close cooperation between different sectors of society, and a strong work ethic—has been a critical ingredient in the region's rapid economic growth.[45] If that is true, then a development model that has worked in that part of the world may not transfer well to other cultures. Of course, similar cultural explanations have been put forth to explain the West's economic takeoff. Long ago, Max Weber credited the birth of capitalism to the Protestant work ethic. But such cultural theories have always aroused considerable controversy. Critics point out, for example, that not all of Asia's star economic performers have Confucian cultures. Rapidly growing Malaysia and Indonesia, for example, are predominantly Muslim. A more telling criticism of the cultural thesis points out that Confucian culture has been around for centuries, while the East Asian economic "miracle" is only a few decades old.[46] Ironically, before the region's takeoff, some Western scholars attributed East Asia's poverty, in part, to Confucian culture.

In fact, it is implausible that there is something so uniquely East Asian about the developmental state that it cannot be reproduced elsewhere. But few African, Latin American, or Middle Eastern nations currently offer promising conditions for its use. Most still lack both the highly professional, merit-based bureaucracy and the spirit of cooperation between key economic actors that would allow them to replicate the East Asian model. And even in Asia, the economic crisis of the late 1990s revealed serious weaknesses in the developmental state model. In countries such as Indonesia, intense government involvement in the economy helped create "crony capitalism" in which the government provided well-connected investors with insider opportunities. Elsewhere, excessive government regulation stifled competition within the private sector. The developmental state has been fine-tuned since East Asia's financial crisis. Indeed, current free-trade regulations and neoliberal prescriptions from the World Trade Organization (WTO) mean that future Third World industrial development will probably involve less state intervention than in the initial Japanese model.

The Neoclassical Ideal

Quite unlike the preceding models, the neoclassical (or neoliberal) ideal assigns government a very limited economic role.[47] The state, it argues, should provide certain fundamental "public goods" such as national defense, police protection, a judicial system, and an educational system. It may also supply a physical infrastructure, including sewers and harbors, when it is not feasible for private capital to do so. And perhaps it should allocate some resources to meet the most basic needs of the very poor.[48] But, say neoclassical analysts, most Third World governments have injured their economies by moving far beyond that limited role. These critics attribute Africa's and Latin America's economic development problems to excessive state intervention in the recent past, while they credit East Asia's success to its governments' allegedly limited role.

Neoclassical economists insist that free-market forces should determine production decisions and set prices without government interference. Consequently, they have criticized government policies designed to stimulate industrial growth in the LDCs: protective tariffs and import quotas that restrict free trade and thereby drive up prices to the consumer; artificial currency exchange rates that distort the prices of exports and imports; state subsidies to producers and consumers; and government controls on prices and interest rates. All of these policies, argue the neoclassicists, distort the choices made by producers, consumers, and governments. Only when these artificial constraints are removed will the economy "get prices right" (i.e., let free-market forces determine them).

During the past two decades, the neoclassicists (also known as neoliberals) have largely won the debate against advocates of extensive state intervention. As we have observed, governments throughout Africa and Latin America have liberalized their economies in recent years, deregulating the private sector, privatizing state enterprises, removing trade barriers, and freeing prices. They have reduced subsidies for industry and for consumers, often out of financial necessity. In part, these changes resulted from pressures on the LDCs exerted by international lending agencies such as the World Bank and the International Monetary Fund (IMF). But they have also sprung from the growing conviction among Third World governments that earlier statist models have failed. Still, the growing consensus that government intervention had gotten out of hand does not mean that the neoclassical model has unequivocally triumphed. While conservative economists and politicians often depicted the East Asian economic miracle as proof positive of what free enterprise can do if government does not intervene in the economy, we have seen that leading specialists on the region such as Stephan Haggard and Alice H. Amsden disagree. They maintain that government intervention has been a fundamental ingredient of industrial growth in that region.[49] Far from "following the market," Robert Wade maintains, the East Asian developmental state has actively "governed the market."[50] So, while the neoclassicist's criticisms of statist policies often ring true, they seem to take their case too far when claiming that East Asia has had a passive state.

In fact, the only East Asian economy that has almost fully conformed to the neoclassical model has been Hong Kong's. As the least regulated economy in the region, many free-market advocates cite it as a success story for unrestricted capitalism. But Hong Kong is such a unique case that it may not be a model that can be emulated in other countries. For one thing, it is largely a city state with virtually no rural population. Like Singapore, and unlike most LDCs, it has not needed to deal with significant rural poverty and daunting associated problems. Initially, Hong Kong's wealth derived from its location as a major port for Asian trade and an outpost of the British Empire (until 1997). Other developing nations obviously do not enjoy those benefits.

While economists and other analysts continue to disagree on the broader economic effects of neoliberalism, the evidence seems to indicate that reduced government intervention has usually stimulated economic growth, particularly in economies that had earlier imposed extensive state intervention. For example, when India and Chile substantially reduced the economic role of the state, both countries embarked on a period of rapid growth. At the same time, however, such growth often has benefited only a portion of the population, leaving the poor behind. India illustrates this point well. The changeover to a predominantly free-market economy turned that nation into the world's second fastest growing major economy (after China), averaging about 8 percent annually in recent years. Yet, so far, less than one-third of the population has benefited from that growth—essentially city dwellers employed in the modern economy, especially the expanding middle class. To be sure, those beneficiaries constitute some 350 million people, no small accomplishment. But, nearly two-thirds of the country's population—the barely educated rural poor—has gained little or nothing from the boom. Many of India's most rapidly expanding industries are in the high-tech or tech-support sectors, which primarily hire people with more advanced educations. Moreover, many of the new industries are capital-intensive and generate comparatively few jobs. Thus, despite India's rapid economic growth, a 2006 government health survey revealed that 46 percent of the country's children were malnourished, essentially unchanged from the proportion in 1999 (47 percent). That level of childhood malnutrition placed India at about the same level as impoverished Bangladesh and Burkina Faso and was over five times as high as in China. Indeed, some 2.5 million Indian children die of disease or malnutrition each year.[51]

Argentina has had a more irregular pattern of economic growth since it began instituting neoliberal reforms in the late 1980s. At first these changes ushered in a period of strong economic growth. However, the economy veered downward in the late 1990s and the country suffered a severe economic and political crisis in the last days of 2001. Yet, after just a few years of decline, the economy rebounded strongly in 2003–2006, with the highest growth rate in Latin America (about 8 percent annually). Still, as in India, the benefits of that growth have not reached a large portion of the population, and neoliberal reforms dismantled many of the country's extensive welfare programs. Argentina had long enjoyed one of the most equitable income distributions in Latin America. In the mid-1970s, the most prosperous 10 percent of the population had incomes that were, on average, 12 times higher than the poorest 10 percent. By the mid-1990s, following neoliberal restructuring, that ratio had risen to 18 to 1, and by 2002, the richest portion of the population earned 43 times as much as the poorest 10 percent.[52]

In addition to its uneven benefits, some of the strongest criticisms of neo-classical economics have come from environmentalists. From their perspective, even a modified policy of laissez faire, acknowledging some state responsibility for the environment, is very inadequate. As Richard Albin notes,

> The idea that private interest, operating within unfettered markets, will tend to produce a close approximation of the socially optimal allocation of resources, was close to the truth when output (population, too) was so much smaller.[53]

But, he argues, as the world's population and associated pollution reach dangerous levels, society can no longer afford to let free-market mechanisms allocate penalties for pollution. Such remedies would come far too late. Further discussion of economic growth and its impact on the environment follows later in this chapter.

Finding a Proper Role for the State

Political scientists and economists will continue to debate the state's proper role in Third World economies. As time goes on, new models will undoubtedly emerge. Still, some areas of agreement have emerged in recent decades. On the one hand, the level of government intervention in both command economies and Latin American statism was surely excessive. At the same time, the extremely limited government role advocated by the neoclassicists is unrealistic and inadequate in most countries. East Asia's developmental state model has been the most successful. But, it is unclear whether it can be replicated elsewhere. Indeed, a model that succeeds in one country or region will not necessarily work in another. Countries vary greatly in size, human capital, natural resources, and the like. Thus, cookbook formulas will probably be inadequate. As we have noted, the strong hand of the stereotypical developmentalist state—in Japan, South Korea, Singapore, and Taiwan—would have to be modified to meet current trade regulations under the WTO. Finally, new crises—such as the oil shocks of the 1970s and 2000s, the Latin American and African debt crises in the 1980s, the 1997–1998 Asian financial crisis, and international terrorism in the first decade of the twenty-first century—force planners to alter and adapt development models.

INDUSTRIALIZATION STRATEGIES

Since the time of Britain's industrial revolution, governments have equated industrialization with economic development, national sovereignty, and military strength. Latin America's largest countries launched their major industrialization drives in the 1930s. Following World War II, a number of newly independent Asian and African countries also developed their industrial capacities. Steel mills and auto plants became symbols of national prestige.

Neoclassical economists frequently criticized industrialization programs in many LDCs, arguing that each country should specialize in economic activities for which it has a "comparative advantage." That is, it should produce and export those goods it can provide most efficiently and cheaply relative to other nations. Based on that argument, neoclassicists maintained that most Third

World nations should abandon plans for industrialization and concentrate, instead, on the production and export of raw materials or agricultural products.[54] Rather than manufacture goods such as cars, washing machines, or fertilizers, they insisted, countries such as Sri Lanka or Kenya would be better off increasing tea or coffee exports, products for which they have a comparative advantage, so that they could use those earnings to import manufactured products. Similarly, they contended that it made little sense for Nigeria to build steel mills or for Uruguay to produce refrigerators. Still, many LDCs have been reluctant to depend fully on revenues from the export of "primary goods," in part because agricultural and raw-material prices are so volatile. One possible solution (easier said than done) is to pursue balanced growth, including some industrial development (presumably manufacturing products such as Indonesian wicker furniture, which draw on local natural resources and can be exported), while still stressing primary goods production and export.

Until now, industrializing nations have generally pursued one of two alternative strategies: import-substituting industrialization (ISI) and export-oriented industrialization (EOI). In the first case, as we have seen, LDCs try to reduce their dependency on manufactured imports by producing more goods, especially consumer goods, at home. Like Latin America, Asian nations began industrialization by producing for their own consumption. But, unlike Latin American ISI, which focused on consumer goods for the home market, East Asian nations soon turned to EOI, linking their industrial development to manufactured exports. Although EOI has been most closely associated with East and Southeast Asia, it is a strategy now widely embraced in Latin America and other parts of the Third World as well. Having started that strategy later, Latin America and other developing areas have yet to catch up with Asia's export capabilities. Consequently, shirts, blouses, electronics, and running shoes sold in Western department stores are more likely to be manufactured in Singapore, Sri Lanka, Indonesia, or Thailand than in Honduras, Brazil, or Colombia.

Import-Substituting Industrialization

National economic policies are partly the product of deliberate choice, and partly the result of political and socioeconomic opportunities and constraints. As we have seen, ISI emerged as a development strategy in Latin America during the 1930s as the worldwide depression sharply reduced international trade.[55] Because the industrialized nations of North America and Europe reduced their purchases of Third-World primary goods (Uruguayan wool, Argentine beef, and Brazilian coffee, for example), Latin America nations no longer were able to earn enough foreign exchange to import the manufactured products that they needed. So, the region's early industrialization was designed, in part, to produce consumer goods that Latin American countries could no longer afford to import. But although ISI began as a response to an international economic crisis, economic planners subsequently transformed it into a long-term strategy for industrial development. With substantial unemployment at home and an urban population pressing for economic growth, government leaders faced a political imperative to industrialize. Nationalist presidents such as Argentina's Juan Perón and Brazil's Getúlio Vargas forged populist political coalitions of industrialists, blue-collar workers, and the urban middle class, all committed to industrialization.

At the same time, as we have seen, Latin American governments imposed quotas and tariffs on foreign *consumer* goods in order to protect embryonic domestic industries from international competition. But, planners also wanted to facilitate other types of imports, namely capital equipment (primarily machinery) and raw materials that domestic manufacturers needed. To reduce the cost of those imports, governments often overvalued their own currencies.[56] Eventually, most Latin American countries established multiple currency exchange rates, with differing rates for transactions tied to imports, exports, and other financial activities. To further encourage industrial development, governments also offered domestic industrialists tax incentives, low-interest loans, and direct subsidies.[57]

Because of ISI's impressive record in Latin America from the 1940s into the 1970s, the strategy was emulated in many parts of Africa and Asia, sometimes with comparable success. Turkey, for example, enjoyed strong ISI growth before shifting to EOI during the 1980s.[58] Even East Asia began its industrial development using ISI. By the 1970s, however, the ISI strategy was undermining Latin America's economies. As John Sheahan notes, "It fostered production methods adverse for employment, hurt the poor, blocked the possible growth of industrial exports, [and] encouraged high-cost consumer goods industries."[59]

To understand how poorly Latin America's *newly industrialized countries* (NICs) fared in international trade compared to East Asian NICs, it is useful to compare Mexico (one of Latin America's major industrial powers) with East Asia's "four little tigers" (South Korea, Taiwan, Hong Kong, and Singapore).[60] Mexico has a larger population than the four Asian countries combined. It also has a considerable geographic advantage over them in the export market, being located thousands of miles closer to the United States, the world's largest importer. Yet, as of the mid-1980s [prior to the North American Free Trade Agreement (NAFTA)], the combined value of manufactured exports of the four little tigers was 20 times higher than Mexico's.[61]

In many Latin American counties, export taxes and overvalued currencies put traditional primary goods exporters (agricultural products and minerals) at a competitive disadvantage, thereby depriving the country of needed foreign exchange revenues. At the same time, because local consumer-goods industries could import their needed capital goods (machinery and other manufactured products used to produce other goods) cheaply, the region never developed its own capital-goods industry and, instead, imported manufacturing technologies that were inappropriate to local needs. Subsidized imports of machinery and heavy equipment encouraged capital-intensive production (i.e., using relatively advanced technologies and machinery while employing fewer workers) rather than the labor-intensive production that predominated in Asia. The ISI model of industrialization benefited a small, relatively well-paid "labor elite" (i.e., skilled, unionized workers employed in highly mechanized factories). But it failed to provide enough jobs for the region's work force, leaving too many Latin Americans unemployed and underemployed.

Ironically, although ISI was originally designed to make Latin America more economically independent, in the end it merely replaced dependence on consumer-goods imports with dependence on imported capital goods, foreign technologies, and credit. Traditional primary exports languished, while the government did little to develop new manufactured exports. Increased balance of trade deficits contributed to Latin America's spiraling foreign debt, leading eventually to a major debt crisis and an economic depression in the 1980s.[62] That crisis, in stark contrast to East Asia's prosperity at that time, induced Latin American governments to abandon their inwardly oriented economic policies as they tried to emulate East Asia's export-driven model. The NAFTA treaty between Mexico, Canada, and the United States is the most dramatic manifestation of that region's move toward EOI.[63] Similarly, Chile, once among the most inward-looking economies in the hemisphere, has been at the forefront of export production and free trade.[64]

Export-Oriented Industrialization

East Asia's NICs began their industrialization drive through import substitution, just as their Latin American counterparts had done years earlier. Soon, however, they diversified into manufacturing for export. As governments phased out their early protectionist measures, they forced local companies to become more competitive. State planners shaped the market, both pressuring industries and offering them incentives to export. By 1980, manufactured goods constituted more than 90 percent of all South Korean and Taiwanese exports but represented only 15 percent of Mexico's and 39 percent of Brazil's.[65] Fueled by their dynamic industrial export sectors, East Asia's booming economies became the envy of the developing world. More recently, India has enjoyed impressive growth based on the export of services as well as manufactured goods.

There are a number of reasons why East Asia decided to stress manufactured exports while Latin America initially failed to do the same. For one thing, East Asia's industrialization drive began in the 1960s, a period of unprecedented expansion in world trade, inspired by the General Agreement on Trade and Tariffs (GATT, subsequently replaced by the WTO) and the West's economic boom. The opportunities offered by outwardly oriented growth were obvious to government policy makers at that time. Conversely, the expansion of Latin American industrialization began during the Great Depression of the 1930s, a period of greatly restricted world trade. Indeed, it was their very inability to export traditional products at that time that inspired Latin American nations to turn initially to ISI. In retrospect, Latin America should have moved to EOI after World War II, but ISI seemed to be working so well until the mid-1970s that there was little incentive to change. Ironically, another reason why East and Southeast Asian countries chose EOI was that their economic opportunities seemed more limited than Latin America's. Because of their smaller populations, Hong Kong, Singapore, and Taiwan (though not South Korea) did not believe that ISI, which relied upon the domestic market, was a feasible strategy for them as it had been for larger countries such as Mexico, Argentina, Brazil, and Colombia.[66] Furthermore, with fewer agricultural goods or raw materials to export, East Asians turned a weakness into a strength by emphasizing manufactured exports.

Finally East Asian industrialization policies differed from Latin America's in part because they were more influenced by U.S. economic advisers and because East Asia's government planners were more likely to have received their economic training at American universities. In contrast, during the decades after World War II, many Latin-American government economic planners were strongly influenced by the United Nations Economic Commission for Latin America (ECLA), a vigorous advocate of ISI. Until the 1980s, Latin American intellectuals remained very committed to economic nationalism and the need to limit U.S. influence. On the other hand, Taiwanese and South Korean military and political dependence on the United States during the postwar decades made their governments more receptive to American policy advisers advocating EOI. Since that time, many East Asian economic planners have received their graduate training at American universities, where they were taught the values of free trade. It was not until the 1970s and 1980s that American-trained economists favoring free trade began to direct economic policy in Latin America.[67]

GROWTH WITH EQUITY

Until this point, our discussion of economic development has focused on the quantity of national production. Indeed, production is the primary measure of economic development used in popular and scholarly analysis. Typically, a country is thought to be performing well economically when its gross national product (GNP) or gross domestic product (GDP) is growing rapidly. Economists have focused less frequently on how equitably that growth is distributed. It is to that important dimension that we now turn.

Early debate on Third World development often pitted mainstream social scientists against left-of-center scholars, with the first group primarily interested in the prerequisites of growth and the second more concerned with the fairness of economic distribution. For example, while many mainstream economists were impressed with Brazil's rapid economic expansion in the late 1960s and early 1970s, critics pointed out that the country's extremely unequal income distribution meant that few benefits of rapid growth managed to reach the poorest half of the population. On the other hand, although Cuba's income redistribution policies and social welfare programs favorably impressed left-leaning economists, conservative critics pointed to that country's weak economic growth since the late 1960s.

Some market-oriented economists insisted that increased inequality was unavoidable, indeed desirable, in the early stages of economic development in order to concentrate capital in the hands of entrepreneurs so they could invest in the economy. Their critics countered that development of that sort did little to help the majority of the people. In many developing nations, they maintained, the bottom half of the population would benefit more from meaningful redistribution of wealth and income, even with little growth, than from strong economic growth without redistribution.[68]

In time, however, analysts of varying ideological persuasions have concluded that there is no intrinsic contradiction between these two goals. In fact, a proper development strategy entails "growth with equity."[69] One study indicates that since the 1960s, countries with higher levels of income equality have developed faster than those with highly concentrated patterns. East Asia's economic takeoff since the 1970s and 1980s demonstrates that point. For example, Taiwan and South Korea have coupled spectacular economic growth rates with relatively equitable income distributions.[70] Indeed, broadly based purchasing power in both those countries has helped stimulate their economic growth. In South Korea, almost all peasant families own television sets, a feat hardly conceivable in Africa or Latin America. During the Korean television industry's takeoff, these domestic purchases supplemented exports in stimulating that product's growth.

What accounts for the higher level of economic equality in East Asia as compared to Africa or Latin America? One important factor is the pattern of land distribution in the countryside. For various reasons, farmland is generally far more equitably distributed in Asia (especially East Asia) than in Latin America.[71] While the size of Latin America's largest land holdings has declined in recent decades, estates of several thousand acres were common in the recent past, and today large landowners still dominate the countryside in nations such as Brazil and Colombia (see Chapter 6). On the other hand, the largest holdings in Asia, where there is much heavier population pressure, are rarely more than one or two hundred acres, and they are far smaller in countries like South Korea.

Landholding patterns reflect both historical legacies and contemporary government policies. Spanish colonialism established an agrarian structure in Latin America and the Philippines dominated by large *latifundia* (large estates). In contrast, Japanese colonial authorities in Korea and Taiwan encouraged smallholder farming. Although European colonial regimes established large export-oriented plantations in Southeast Asia, land ownership there was still never as concentrated as in Latin America. It is surely not coincidental that the Philippines, the only country in East Asia to share Latin America's Spanish colonial heritage, also has the region's most concentrated land and income distribution. In the postcolonial period, South Korean and Taiwanese agrarian reform programs led to even more egalitarian land distribution in those countries, just as the American-imposed reform had done in Japan after the war. By reducing rural poverty, land reform contributed to greater income equality.

Another major element of national income distribution is the relationship between rural and urban living standards. Although city dwellers enjoy higher incomes and greater social services throughout the Third World, the urban–rural gap is particularly marked in Africa and Latin America. Residents of Mexico City, for example, have incomes averaging four to five times higher than those in the countryside. There are many reasons for such discrepancies, but government policy often plays an important role. In Chapter 6 we noted that, until recently, governments in both regions generally kept the prices of basic crops below their market value in order to provide their urban political constituencies with cheap food.[72] By contrast, East Asian farmers generally have received the free-market price for their crops or even subsidized prices above market value.

Industrial policy also affects income distribution. Latin America's ISI strategy encouraged the importation of capital equipment for domestic industries. Such capital-intensive development created many relatively skilled and well-paid industrial jobs, but left behind a far larger number of poorly paid, "unskilled" urban workers and rural peasants. Conversely, East Asia's EOI strategy took advantage of that region's large labor force, thereby producing a large number of low-wage jobs.

By initially using labor-intensive methods that utilized their pools of cheap labor, Hong Kong, Taiwan, and South Korea successfully exported cheap low-tech goods such as textiles, toys, and footwear. Over time, as these industries needed more and more workers, two changes took place. First, greater demand for labor in these low-end export industries caused factory wages to rise; second, rural-to-urban migration, caused by the lure of factory jobs, reduced the supply of rural labor, thereby driving up income levels in the countryside. What had begun as a policy exploiting cheap labor eventually promoted economic growth, higher wages, and greater income equality.[73] As wage levels rose substantially in the four little tigers, those countries shifted from low-tech products to more sophisticated exports such as electronics, commercial services (most notably Singapore), computer software, computers, and automobiles (South Korea). Production of apparel and other low-wage items passed on to lower-income Asian nations such as China, Malaysia, Thailand, Indonesia, Bangladesh, and Sri Lanka. China, which first became an industrial giant by manufacturing lower-priced consumer goods and parts for foreign brands, is now also producing higher-end products, including some under Chinese brand names.

Finally, a factor that distinguishes all NICs (but especially those in East Asia) from less-developed regions is their relatively high educational level. Table 10.1 offers education data for the United States, four East Asian NICs, four Latin American NICS, and India. The first data column presents literacy rates for all adults over the age of 15. The next column indicates the percentage of school-aged youth enrolled in secondary school (high school and junior high school). Finally, the last column (Educational Index) is a composite index of the country's literacy and educational levels. The highest, or best, score that a country can achieve for this index is 1.0, while 0.0 is the lowest possible score.

TABLE 10.1 Comparative National Educational Levels

Country	Adult Literacy	Secondary School Enrollment Ratios	Educational Index
United States	99.9%	90%	.97
Hong Kong	93.3[a]	78	.88
Singapore	92.5	97[a]	.91
South Korea	97.6[a]	88	.98
Thailand	92.6	60	.86
Argentina	97.2	79	.95
Chile	95.7	NA	.91
Colombia	92.8	55	.86
Mexico	91.0	64	.86
India	61.0	NA	.61

[a]Data were unavailable in the 2006 *Human Development Report* and were drawn, instead, from the 2002 report.

NA — Data unavailable.

Source: United Nations Development Programme, *Human Development Report, 2006,* http://hdr.undp.org/hdr2006/statistics/.

All of the East Asian and the Latin American NICs listed in this table have literacy rates that are slightly below those in the United States, but considerably higher than India's (or in most African, Middle Eastern, and South Asian nations not shown in the table). As expected the countries in the table that have higher rates of poverty (Colombia, Mexico, Thailand, and, especially, India) also have the lowest school enrollment, literacy rates, and educational indices. Only Singapore, an extremely prosperous country with a very low rate of poverty, fails to perform as well in adult literacy (ranking 8th out of the 10 nations in Table 10.1). But its extremely high current school enrollment ratio (97 percent compared to 95 percent in the United States and 71 percent in Mexico) and its fairly strong educational index suggest that future generations will be more literate.

ECONOMIC DEVELOPMENT AND THE ENVIRONMENT

Throughout the world, economic development has inevitably caused environmental degradation. For example, prior to European settlement, the East Coast of the United States was covered with thick forest. Since then, population growth, urban sprawl, and farming have destroyed almost all of that growth. Today, industrial and auto pollution in the United States and Europe contaminate the surrounding air and water, sometimes affecting areas thousands of miles away. In the LDCs, rapid population growth combined with economic modernization and industrialization also has brought substantial environmental decay. In Indonesia, for example, foreign-owned mines and logging firms have dumped health-threatening waste into nearby water systems and harvested vast tracks of jungle timber, bringing birth defects (in mining areas) and flooding (in timber regions) in their wake.[74] Massive dams in China flood archeological treasures, farmland, and vacated villages. Since the 1970s, environmental groups in advanced industrialized nations have begun to question the tradeoffs between growth and the conservation of our natural-resource heritage. The prospect of global warming threatens our very existence. Some of the more radical environmentalists in the United States and Europe have proposed zero-growth strategies for highly industrialized nations. They suggest limiting population growth and creating a less consumer-oriented society.

But the option of zero growth, or even of reduced economic growth, which has never attracted significant support in the First World, is unacceptable in the Third World. In countries such as India, Indonesia, Egypt, Nigeria, and Brazil, where a substantial portion of the population lives in poverty, it would be politically suicidal and ethically questionable for government leaders to propose limiting economic growth. Environmental regulations and controls are generally far weaker in the LDCs, because of their urgent need for economic growth and because their "green" (ecology) movements developed much later and lack the political influence of their American and Western European counterparts. Moreover, LDCs often lack the government infrastructure to enforce environmental controls. Finally, extensive corruption allows polluting industries to bribe relevant public officials in many LDCs.

The Costs of Growth

The world's industrialized nations continue to be the major consumers of natural resources, the leading polluters of air and water, and the major contributors to global warming, ozone-layer depletion, and other looming environmental disasters. For example, in recent years, developed nations consumed some 80 percent of the world's paper, 80 percent of its iron and steel, and more than 85 percent of its chemicals. Per-capita use of cars in the developed world is more than 25 times greater than in the LDCs, while cement consumption is 3.5 times as high, and iron and steel consumption 13 times higher. [75]

Yet, ironically, it is those same developed countries that now insist that the LDCs become better environmental citizens. In response, Third World leaders point out that the United States, with only 4 percent of the world's population, consumes more than 25 percent of the planet's resources.[76] Hence, many of them bristle at the suggestion that developing nations make special efforts to protect the environment.[77] Still, because of their more fragile economic and ecological conditions, a number of LDCs face some of the world's most pressing environmental challenges. Peasants hungry for firewood in Rwanda, Nepal, and India deplete nearby forests. In African countries such as Sudan, Nigeria, and Burkina Faso, wood fires produce 75 percent or more of all energy. Rich cattle ranchers and poor peasants in Brazil burn vast areas of the Amazonian jungle (equal to the size of New Jersey) each year to clear the land for agricultural production. In Malaysia and Indonesia, Japanese-owned logging firms cut down large tracts of rain forest. Since 1950 alone, more than 25 percent of the earth's tropical rain forests has been destroyed. As a consequence, in places such as Central America, Indonesia, and Sub-Saharan Africa, rains and waterways wash off topsoil, rainfall patterns shift, and both droughts and floods occur more frequently. Thus, in many parts of the Third World, the arable land area is declining and deserts are growing.

Third World cities such as Shanghai, Cairo, New Delhi, Nairobi, and Sao Paulo have grown tremendously in recent decades (Chapter 7), producing enormous quantities of raw sewage, auto emissions, and industrial waste. As cars and buses (most without proper emission controls) choke the streets, air quality rapidly deteriorates. Elsewhere, mines, oil fields, chemical plants, and factories, operating with few environmental safeguards, pollute their surroundings. The consequences for local populations are often tragic —including infections, respiratory illnesses, birth defects, and loss of farmland. Other environmental costs—such as destruction of rain forests, which also contributes to global warming—have consequences that extend far beyond the developing world.

Environmental Decay as a Third World Problem

Nowhere is the difficult tradeoff between economic growth and environmental conservation more starkly illustrated than in China, home to more than one-fifth of the world's population. Since the government introduced free-market economic reforms in the 1980s, the country has enjoyed the world's highest rate of economic growth, averaging about 8 percent annually. Living standards have tripled, and millions of Chinese citizens have moved out of poverty. The number of people spared from hunger, disease, and early death is staggering. Balanced against those gains, however, are enormous increases in air and water pollution and extensive destruction of the country's farm land, raising the prospect of future famine just when China has finally managed to feed its population adequately. By 1990, China consumed 10 percent of global energy and was responsible for 11 percent of carbon dioxide emissions, a figure that continues to rise as the economy leaps forward.[78] By 2004 it had become the second largest emitter of greenhouse gases (carbon dioxide and other fossil-fuel emissions that trap the earth's heat and cause global warming).

Attracted by higher urban living standards, over 100 million Chinese peasants have migrated to the cities, often abandoning farms in productive agricultural regions. In addition, substantial quantities of farmland have been paved over for highways, factories, and urban sprawl. Since the late 1950s, China's total arable land has decreased by somewhere between 15 and 55 percent (depending on what estimate one accepts), while the nation's population has grown by some 80 percent. Though China's rate of population growth is currently relatively low (1 percent annually), loss of farmland because of economic development continues to accelerate at an alarming rate. So far, China has averted hunger by farming the remaining land more intensively, and some recent grain harvests have reached record or near-record levels. But this intensive use of fertilizers and pesticides eventually depletes the soil, and a food crunch likely looms in the coming decades. As this enormous country needs to import increasing amounts of food, prices of grains and other foods are likely to rise on the world market, with serious consequences for the poor throughout the developing countries.

Environmental Decay in the LDCs as a Global Problem

Debate over Third World environmental policy is further complicated by the fact that many LDCs are stewards of natural resources that are critical to the entire world. For example, the massive, purposeful burning of the Amazonian rain forest contributes significantly to global warming. Destruction of rain forests there, as well as in Africa and Asia, deprives the world of many plant forms that are potentially ingredients in hundreds of lifesaving medicines.[79]

Unfortunately, the economic development to which Third World people rightfully aspire poses potentially disastrous threats to the environment. It would be unconscionable to tell poor Brazilians or Egyptians that they should not hope for a higher standard of living. But barring major technological and political breakthroughs, achieving an acceptable standard of living for all Third World people could easily overtax the planet's resources. Invariably, economic development greatly increases consumption of fossil fuels (coal, petroleum, and natural gas) and brings a corresponding increase in pollution. Brazil, China, and India already rank right behind the United States in greenhouse gas emissions. As China's and India's economies continue their rapid growth, these two Asian giants will surely burn more fossil fuels for their factories and vehicles, thereby accelerating the greenhouse effect.

THE SEARCH FOR SUSTAINABLE DEVELOPMENT

Discussion of the environmental consequences of economic growth often turns to the objective of *sustainable development*, defined as economic development that "consumes resources to meet [this generation's] needs and aspirations in a way that does not compromise the ability of future generations to meet their needs."[80] Whenever feasible, it involves the use of *renewable resources* (such as wind and water power for generating electricity) in place of resources that cannot be replaced (e.g., coal and petroleum) or that are being consumed at a faster rate than they can be replaced (such as tropical rain forests and many ocean fish). It also embraces consumption of resources in ways that least pollutes the environment: limiting auto and industrial emissions, finding sustainable substitutes for pesticides and other agricultural chemicals that pollute the soil and water system, and reducing the use of products that destroy the world's ozone layer.[81]

In theory these are goals to which all nations, rich and poor alike, can aspire. Even so, developed and developing nations debate about which of them should take the lead and which should bear the greatest economic costs. At the groundbreaking 1992 United Nations Conference on Environment and Development (UNCED) in Rio de Janeiro—often called the first Earth Summit—signatories made a nonbinding commitment to reduce greenhouse emissions by the year 2000 and developed an action plan for sustainable development into the twenty-first century. The Rio Declaration listed 27 guiding principles on the environment and development, including the LDCs' right to economic development and the alleviation of poverty. Still, as one analyst observed:

> At the Rio Summit, the conflicts between the rich and poor became evident. The Northern [industrialized] countries, which felt vulnerable to global environment problems such as climate change and biodiversity loss, attempted to extract commitments on environmental conservation from the South [LDCs]. However, the South, which felt more vulnerable to perceived underdevelopment, was concerned with extracting [economic] transfers from the North.[82]

The difficult tradeoff between growth and environmental protection was vividly brought home to this author at a meeting in Jamaica with local social scientists. After one U.S. scholar spoke of the importance of preserving the island's ecology, a Jamaican economist sarcastically replied, "You Americans raped your environment in order to develop your country and raise your standard of living. Now we Jamaicans reserve the right to do the same."[83] While such feelings are counterproductive, they are understandable. Third World leaders note that the already industrialized countries ask NICs such as China and Mexico to reduce smokestack emissions and beseech Thailand and Brazil to sustain their rain forests. But it is the First World nations that have wreaked the greatest havoc on the environment and they have offered the developing nations little help to defray the costs of environmental controls.

The United States in particular has done little to allay Third World doubts. In 1997, worldwide negotiations produced the Kyoto Protocol, which envisioned a global contract binding signatories to reduce their emissions of six greenhouse gases by 2010 to 5.2 percent below their 1990 level, an estimated

29 percent below what they would have reached without an accord. Four years later (2001), 178 nations agreed in Bonn, Germany to meet objections from Japan and other nations by modifying the Kyoto Protocol so as to lower the targeted 5 percent reduction to only 2 percent. Still, the new U.S. president, George Bush, outraged the European Union and much of the world community by announcing that the United States would not ratify the Kyoto agreement. From the Bush administration's perspective—supported by a number of American business organizations and many Congressional Republicans—the dangers of global warming had been overstated and the U.S. government is unwilling to undermine its own economic growth by accepting Kyoto's environmental targets.

By breaking its previous pledge to honor Kyoto (though the protocol had never been ratified by the U.S. Senate), the administration reinforced the Third World's belief that it was being held to a double standard when it came to making economic sacrifices for the environment. Most of the international community has been determined to continue pursuing Kyoto's goals. However, because the United States accounts for 25 percent of all greenhouse emissions (the world's largest share), its decision to pull out makes it harder to reduce overall levels. In early 2005, following Russian ratification, the Kyoto accord went into effect without U.S. participation. Since that time, in the face of mounting evidence of global warming, the Bush administration has recognized warming as a problem and accepted its origins in man-made pollution. However, it has only committed itself to voluntary limitations on greenhouse emissions, an approach that few experts believe can work.

Some Signs of Progress

Despite these obstacles, there are some hopeful signs of progress. At the very least, the governments of developing countries and international development agencies have become more conscious of the growth-environmental tradeoff. Together many of them have begun looking for ways to achieve sustainable development that reduces damage to the environment. Many LDCs that previously saw the green movement as a Western conspiracy to keep them underdeveloped have come to realize that sustainable growth is in their own interest.

One of the most important means of improving living standards and preserving the environment is population control. Other policies can also help: the use of renewable fuels such as solar energy and water power (nuclear energy remains far more controversial); organic farming that replenishes, rather than depletes, the soil; government regulations that discourage, rather than encourage, irrational use of rain forest lands; and stricter antipollution controls. For example, Brazil has revised tax laws (so far with little effect) that had previously encouraged ranchers to clear the Amazonian forest. Also, Mexico City has improved its air quality by relocating cement plants and oil refineries out of the city, replacing city taxis and buses with newer vehicles with better emission controls, and requiring private cars to stay off the road one day per week.

Ultimately, however, even if the LDCs applied strict environmental measures, they still would not fully reconcile the tension between economic growth and environmental protection. Furthermore, environmental controls are generally expensive and often reduce productivity. If the world's industrial powers want the LDCs to make such sacrifices, they will probably have to underwrite much of the cost. This might involve debt forgiveness, subsidized technology transfers, and direct grants.[84]

Which of the economic models discussed earlier in this chapter is best equipped to handle the environmental challenge? The answer is not clear. It seems certain that preserving the environment requires significant state intervention. Since, for example, it is unrealistic to expect industrialists to monitor and control their own pollution or to hope that all drivers will voluntarily purchase fuel-efficient cars, most analysts feel that some government regulation is needed. Consequently, the neoclassical model, which severely limits government economic intervention and depends heavily on free-market mechanisms, seems ill-suited to protect the environment (though market mechanisms can be very helpful, such as a trading market that allows companies to sell unused portions of their legal emissions limits).

In theory, command economies seem particularly well suited to defend the environment because the state controls the means of production and can self-regulate. In fact, however, communist governments from the Soviet Union and Poland to China and North Korea have had very poor environmental records. For one thing, directives to managers of state enterprises usually demand that they maximize production, with little thought given to environmental consequences. At the same time, absent a free society and a free mass media, citizens are unable to organize environmental pressure groups or even to know the extent of ecological destruction. Thus, it appears that if developing nations are to have any chance at sustainable development, they must combine an honest, effective, and responsible state with a free democratic society where green activists can mobilize popular support.

FINDING THE RIGHT MIX

Often it has been easier to recognize what has not worked in developing countries than to identify what has. The dependency theorists' assumption that economic development was only possible if LDCs reduced their ties to the capitalist core has been shattered by the success of East Asia's export-oriented growth and the failures of protectionism in Latin America. Similarly, command economies, while often able to reduce economic inequalities, generally have had poor records of economic growth and modernization. The abject failure of North Korea's communist economy, in stark contrast to South Korea's prosperity, demonstrates that model's failures. On the other hand, the neoclassical minimal state can hardly address the deep inequities, societal cleavages, and looming ecological nightmares plaguing so many LDCs. The challenge for Third World economies is to establish a strong and effective, but not overbearing, state—one that can promote growth, equitable income distribution, and a healthy environment, while avoiding unwarranted interference in the market, crony capitalism, and authoritarianism.

Many Third World countries have now embraced East Asia's export-oriented industrial model. Beyond the previously mentioned problem of transferability, however, there are at least two other fundamental concerns about universalizing the East Asian experience. The first concerns the extent to which the world economy can continue to absorb mounting industrial exports. East Asia launched its EOI strategy during a period of unparalleled economic expansion in the First World. International trade was expanding rapidly, and developed countries could absorb a rising tide of industrial exports. Since the 1970s, however, First World economic growth has slowed down due, in part, to factors such as spikes in energy costs (most notably in the 1970s and the past few years), the transfer of industrial jobs to the NICs and, perhaps, the psychological and economic effects of terrorism since 9/11. Even should the Japanese and Western European economies recover their former dynamism, some analysts question whether the international market can absorb an ever-enlarging flow of industrial exports, most notably from China, the world's emerging industrial giant, or whether a protectionist backlash from the First World might place a cap on imports.[85] Supporters of EOI counter that there is no sign of a looming cap on industrial imports, particularly since the larger NICs have become major importers themselves.[86] However, the Asian financial crisis of 1997–1998 demonstrates that even the most sophisticated and successful development models can run into serious difficulties as new challenges develop and hidden weaknesses surface.

The Effects of Globalization on Developing Nations

Perhaps the most important and hotly debated recent economic development affecting the entire Third World is known as "globalization." Both the mass media and social scientists define globalization in related, but somewhat distinct ways. In its most fundamental sense the term refers to the increasing interdependence of national economies throughout the world. It is characterized by rising world trade in goods and services, increasing flows of cross-national finance (including banking, stock market transactions, and corporate takeovers), greater legal and illegal labor migration across national borders, accelerated international transfers of advanced technologies, expansion of multinational corporations (MNCs), and the mounting influence of world economic institutions such as the IMF, the World Bank, and the WTO. All of these changes enhance the interdependence of national economies. In short, globalization encompasses the free flow of information, goods, services, and capital across national borders. Beyond that, the term is often also understood to describe the spread of culture, consumer tastes, and technology from the West (particularly the United States) to the rest of the world.

Scholarly debate over globalization has centered on several questions: Is globalization really a new development or merely a continuation of economic trends that have existed for centuries? If it is new, when did it begin? And, most importantly for our purposes, has globalization improved or harmed Third World economies? Some scholars who claim that globalization is not a particularly new or dramatic development date it to the rise and spread of Western (European) capitalism in the sixteenth century, while others trace it to the last decades of the nineteenth century.[87] Others question whether there is anything uniquely global about the present era, arguing that the current level of global economic interdependence was matched or exceeded in earlier times. Thus, for example, the level of world trade as a percentage of the world economy is no higher today than it was in the early years of the twentieth century.

Still, the speed and breadth of today's IT revolution has greatly accelerated the interconnectedness of national economies. The effects of debt default in Russia very quickly spill over to Argentina and Brazil. A sharp drop in China's stock market or a French investment bank's problems with U.S. subprime mortgages brings down prices on the New York Stock Exchange later in the day. To be sure, skeptics point out that the volume of world trade grew only modestly from 1980 to 2000. However, as we have seen, certain regions of the developing world—Asia (especially China) and, to a lesser extent, Latin America—increased their manufactured exports substantially. Furthermore, *financial* globalization escalated dramatically during that same period. For example, in the last two decades of the twentieth century, direct foreign investment rose by 250 percent worldwide and by 400 percent in the LDCs.[88] The daily turnover of currency exchanges (from one nation's currency to another's) increased more than tenfold during that 20-year period. Moreover, other indicators of globalization—such as the volume of foreign travel, international phone calls, and cross-border use of the Internet—have exploded. As one analyst has put it, globalization is fundamentally different from earlier forms of international trade and commerce because this time "national markets are *fused* transnationally rather than [merely] linked across borders."[89]

If we accept that globalization is an important and somewhat recent development, particularly as it affects LDCs, when did this process begin? Some analysts trace it to the resurgence of world trade after World War II. In the 1960s, the term "globalization" acquired its current meaning. But, it was in the 1970s and 1980s, aided by the IT revolution, that the process took off and it is since then that the phenomenon has become the focus of intense scrutiny among scholars, journalists, and political leaders.

Perhaps the most contentious debate regarding globalization deals with its economic consequences, particularly its effect on the Third World. Neoliberals and other supporters of free trade often see globalization as a panacea, able to stimulate the economies of developed and developing nations alike. They point to the benefits that export-led growth has brought to East Asia and, now, India. By allowing for the most rational allocations of investments, labor, and natural resources across borders, they argue, globalization creates the most efficient and productive economic outcome. The IT revolution, for example, has permitted India's educated and technologically proficient middle class to provide tech support to the world. In books such as journalist Thomas Friedman's best-seller *The World Is Flat*, the optimists see globalization as a win-win situation for the developed and the developing worlds.[90]

Critics of globalization, especially on the left, see its impact completely differently. They see it as a force that has imposed greater Western economic control and cultural dominance on the Third World. Moreover, they insist, it has widened income gaps between the First and Third Worlds, as well as *within* the LDCs, caused environmental degradation, and extended poverty. One of the most influential assessments of this kind is Joseph Stiglitz's *Globalization and Its Discontents*.[91] Unlike many critics, Stiglitz—a Nobel-Prize-winning economist, former Chair of President Bill Clinton's Council of Economic Advisers, and former chief economist for the World Bank—is the most respectable of establishment figures. Yet, his book severely criticizes the United States government, the World Bank, and, especially, the IMF for pressuring Third World governments to adopt free-trade and privatization policies that have inflicted substantial pain on their populations and made their economies more vulnerable to shifts in the global economy.

While we cannot explore all aspects of this debate, we will focus on what may be the most important question: Has recent globalization deepened or alleviated Third World poverty? Much of that discussion, in turn, has centered on the issue of economic equality and inequality: Has globalization intensified or reduced the economic gaps within individual LDCs and those between LDCs and the world's wealthier nations? There seems to be general agreement that between 1945 (when the latest wave of economic integration began) and 1980, the gap between rich and poor nations widened. Evidence since the 1980s, when globalization accelerated, suggests that this economic gap may have begun to narrow.

Supporters of globalization contend that rapid industrialization in countries such as China, South Korea, and Brazil, and the expansion of international services by countries such as India have allowed the LDCs, or at least some of them, to begin catching up with the industrialized world. Further examination, however, suggests a more complex picture. The narrowing of national income gaps worldwide reflects the economic surge in East Asia, especially China, since the 1970s. On the other hand, African and Latin American incomes have fallen further behind the developed world. Advocates of globalization point out that the countries in which living standards have most improved or where poverty has most sharply declined in the past two to three decades—including China, Chile, Indonesia, and South Korea—are precisely the nations that are most intensely integrated into the global economy.[92] At the same time, the poorest nations in the world and those falling furthest behind are the countries of Sub-Saharan Africa, which have the least globalized economies.

If we turn to the issue of inequality *within* developing nations, the evidence is somewhat clearer. It appears that as countries such as Chile and China have entered the global economy more intensely, the gap between their poor and the middle and upper classes has widened. Looking more systematically at data from 65 countries from 1995–2001, economist Almas Heshmati found that income inequality was somewhat greater in more globalized economies but that globalization was but one of many factors contributing to inequality, explaining only about 10 percent of the difference between nations.[93] Depending on how they analyze the data, some economists have argued that income inequality has intensified as a result of globalization in recent decades, while others ague that it has diminished.[94] But, even if there were a consensus that inequality has increased, would that mean that standards of living for the poor are declining on an absolute basis or might the poor be advancing, but at a slower rate than the groups above them?

The most serious charge leveled against globalization is that it has intensified Third World poverty. Case studies describe Nike factories that pay their workers shockingly low wages (at least by Western standards) and peasants who were pushed off their land by foreign-owned plantations and logging operations. But, while case studies often provide useful insights, we cannot know how representative they are of the general population. That is, while a careful case study may demonstrate how MNCs reduced economic opportunities in Nuevo Laredo, Mexico or how free trade impoverished sugar plantation workers in Malaysia, we do not know whether these situations are typical of Mexico or Malaysia, much less the entire developing world, as a whole.

If, however, we examine more systematic statistics from the United Nations or the World Bank, we find that, contrary to globalization's critics, Third World poverty has actually *declined* significantly since globalization accelerated in the early 1980s. For example, according to World Bank statistics, the percentage of the developing nations' population living in "extreme poverty" [defined as those living on less than $1 per day (PPP)] fell from 40 percent in 1980 to 19 percent in 2002 (controlling for inflation). Between 2000 and 2005 alone, the number of East Asians living in extreme poverty fell by some 100 million. Between 1980 and 2002, life expectancy in the LDCs rose from 60 to 65 years (despite the horrendous effect of AIDS on Sub-Saharan Africa).

A host of factors undoubtedly helped reduce extreme poverty and increase life expectancy, and it would be oversimplified to attribute all of that improvement to globalization. But, at the very least, the progress in recent decades does challenge allegations that rapid globalization has further impoverished the LDCs. Furthermore, the most dramatic declines in extreme poverty have occurred in China and other parts of East Asia (with the rate falling from about 60 percent in 1981 to some 13 percent in 2002), the region most intensely linked to the global economy. During that same time period, absolute poverty in Sub-Saharan Africa—the least globalized region—rose slightly from under 42 to 44 percent.[95] In Latin America, a region whose level of economic globalization falls in between East Asia's and Africa's, the rate of extreme poverty has remained static since 1981.

At the same time, while *extreme* poverty fell sharply during this period, *total* poverty (which includes both those living in extreme poverty—below $1 daily—and those living on $1–2 per day) declined far more gradually, from 67 to 50 percent, with most of that decline taking place in China and East Asia. Indeed, it appears that many of those who escaped extreme poverty have only advanced to a milder form of poverty (i.e., many of those who had been living on less than $1 per day now earned $1–2 per day). Furthermore, even if the effect of globalization has generally been benign, it has also produced its share of losers. Even in a wealthy nation such as the United States, many textile mill employees and other workers in manufacturing have seen their jobs disappear when their employer moved operations to Asia or Mexico. In the Third World, where workers and peasants are not protected by Western-style unemployment compensation or other safety nets, the consequences of economic dislocations are far more severe. During last decade's Asian financial crisis, an unintended consequence of globalization, millions lost their jobs, at least for a period of time. At the same time, cheap foreign imports have destroyed local industries in much of Latin America. This has led analysts such as Joseph Stiglitz to argue that, since continued globalization seems inevitable, governments must take steps to mitigate its negative consequences on the biggest losers.[96]

CONCLUSION: DEMOCRACY AND ECONOMIC DEVELOPMENT

Earlier in this chapter, we observed that in the second half of the twentieth century, the most dynamic Third World economies were often governed by authoritarian regimes, at least at the start of their economic booms. Almost all of Asia's most impressive economic performances—in China, Taiwan, South Korea, Singapore, Thailand, Malaysia, and Indonesia—were guided by authoritarian or semi-authoritarian developmental states or (in the case of China) a modified command economy. Chile initiated Latin America's most successful transition from ISI to export-led growth under General Pinochet's military dictatorship. Based on such evidence, some have argued that authoritarian governments are better equipped to start economic development because they can control workers' wage demands and can impose long-term development plans on business.

But, for every authoritarian success story, there have been several economic disasters. Corrupt dictatorships throughout Africa, the Middle East, and Latin America have plundered their country's limited wealth, created inefficient private or state monopolies, and used the economy to reward their political allies. That is, for every South Korea, Chile or Singapore, there has been a Congo, Tajikistan, and Iran, all authoritarian regimes that experienced *negative* average annual growth rates from 1975 to 2004 (i.e., their economies lost ground). Thus, Chile's bureaucratic authoritarian regime did well economically, but its counterparts in Argentina, Uruguay, and even Brazil were considerably less successful. Overall, statistical analyses of Third World economic growth rates in recent decades reveal that authoritarian governments do not perform any better than democratic ones do. And one recent study indicated that dictatorships perform more poorly. Bruce Bueno de Mesquita et al. ranked hundreds of governments worldwide (counting each government separately for every nation) for the second half of the twentieth century and compared the 179 most autocratic governments with the 176 most democratic ones.[97] During that period, democratic administrations achieved an average real annual growth rate (adjusted for inflation) of 3.04 percent, while autocratic governments had only 1.78 percent, a substantial gap. Moreover, the authors argue convincingly that the difference in performance has a logical explanation. Governments that need to appeal to a broad coalition of voters (democracies) are more likely to pursue policies that promote broadly based economic development. On the other hand, governments that owe their incumbency to a small coalition of strategic allies (dictatorships) are more likely to be corrupt and to pursue policies designed to keep themselves in power no matter what the cost to the national economy. In recent years, the world's most populous democracy, India, has enjoyed an impressive period of sustained economic growth. Of course, the list of democratic governments includes both strong economic performers and weak ones, as does the list of authoritarian governments. But these findings, along with many others, offer hope that democratic governments and the worldwide movement toward democracy may produce faster economic growth along with greater political justice.

DISCUSSION QUESTIONS

1. What have been the major accomplishments and failures of command economies?
2. Compare the nature of state economic intervention in Latin America to East Asia's developmental state.
3. What are the major arguments presented in support of the neoclassical development model?
4. What are neoliberal economic reforms? How widely have they been used? What have been the major accomplishments and weaknesses of neoliberal reform?
5. In what ways does economic growth in the Third World contribute to environmental degradation?
6. What evidence is there that authoritarian Third World governments can promote early economic growth better than democracies can? What counterevidence do scholars offer to suggest that democracies have better economic records?

NOTES

1. Of course, we have seen that in the short to intermediate term, economic growth can be politically destabilizing. However, if growth is coupled with equitable income distribution, the chances of unrest are greatly diminished. In any event, all other factors being equal, in the end rising living standards should rebound to the regime's political advantage. Previous chapters covered the potentially destabilizing effects of unequal economic growth. Consequently, I will not discuss them in this chapter.

2. Joan M. Nelson, ed., *Economic Crisis and Policy Choice: The Politics of Adjustment in the Third World* (Princeton, NJ: Princeton University Press, 1990); Dharam Ghai, ed. *The IMF and the South: The Social Impact of Crisis and Adjustment* (London: Zed Books, 1991).

3. Martin Staniland, *What Is Political Economy?* (New Haven, CT: Yale University Press, 1985), 6.

4. Ibid. 12.

5. As originally articulated in the eighteenth century, liberalism called for limited government. Today, outside of the United States, the terms "neoliberal policies" or "liberalization" refer to policies that reduce the role of government in the economy, contrary to the way the term "liberal" is used in the United States.

6. Simon Kuznets, *Modern Economic Growth: Rate, Structure and Spread*, 7th ed. (New Haven, CT: Yale University Press, 1976); Hollis Chenery and Moises Syrquin, *Patterns of Development, 1950–1970* (London: Oxford University Press, 1975). Of course, these are general tendencies or trends, not inviolable rules. Thus, as we have seen, East and Southeast Asian countries such as Taiwan, South Korea, Indonesia, and Malaysia have entered or passed through the intermediate stage of development without an appreciable worsening of income distribution.

7. The term "socialist" may describe two very different political and economic models, causing many readers some confusion. In Western Europe, socialist parties and governments in nations such as Sweden, France, Germany, and Spain have supported liberal democracy and a high level of civil liberties (sometimes even more than their conservative opponents have). While they advocate a significant degree of government involvement in the economy—including extensive welfare programs and a limited amount of state ownership—they also favor a major role for private enterprise. On the other hand, the term "socialist" is also applied, as it is here, to countries that are in the allegedly early stages of communism, such as the USSR (Union of Soviet Socialist Republics). Thus, "socialist" nations, such as Cuba, the USSR, and China, have concentrated political power in a single political party (normally the only party permitted) and economic power in the hands of the state.

8. Adapted from Adam Przeworski, *Democracy and the Market* (New York: Cambridge University Press, 1991), 105, fn. 10.

9. Ed A. Hewett, *Reforming the Soviet Economy: Equality versus Efficiency* (Washington, DC: Brookings Institution, 1988), 38.

10. Abraham Bergson, *The Real National Income of Soviet Russia Since 1928* (Cambridge, MA: Harvard University Press, 1961), 261.

11. Harry Harding, *China's Second Revolution* (Washington, DC: Brookings Institution, 1987), 30–31.

12. Stephen White, John Gardener, and George Schopflin, *Communist and Postcommunist Political*

Systems (New York: St. Martin's Press, 1990), 322; Harding, *China's Second Revolution*, 30.

13. Claes Brundenius, *Revolutionary Cuba: The Challenge of Economic Growth with Equity* (Boulder, CO: Westview Press, 1984); Carmelo Mesa-Lago, *The Economy of Socialist Cuba: A Two-Decade Appraisal* (Albuquerque: University of New Mexico Press, 1981).

14. Erich Wede and Horst Tiefenbach, "Some Recent Explanations of Income Inequality," *International Studies Quarterly*, vol. 25 (June 1981), 255–282.

15. In practice, command economies have all been dominated by politically repressive governments. In this chapter, I take this very serious moral and political flaw as a given and, instead, focus on the system's *economic* strengths and weaknesses.

16. Liang Heng and Judith Shapiro, *After the Nightmare* (New York: Collier, 1986).

17. John Sheahan, *Patterns of Development in Latin America* (Princeton, NJ: Princeton University Press, 1987).

18. Ibid. 85.

19. Dale Story, *Industry, the State, and Public Policy in Mexico* (Austin: University of Texas Press, 1986), 68.

20. Both those industries were nationalized in the 1930s. Subsequently, the state also took over the electric power and telecommunications industries.

21. Story, *Industry, the State, and Public Policy*, 21. These statistics are extrapolated from Story's data.

22. Samuel Schmidt, *The Deterioration of the Mexican Presidency: The Years of Luis Echeverría* (Tucson: University of Arizona Press, 1991), 162–164; Elia Marún Espinosa, "Intervencionismo estatal y transformaciones del sector empresa pública en México," in *El Nuevo Estado Mexicano: Estado y Economía*, ed. Jorge Alonso et al. (Mexico City: Nueva Imagen, 1992), 193–240.

23. For startling data on overstaffing and "ghost workers" in Africa, see Richard Sandbrook, *The Politics of Africa's Economic Recovery* (New York: Cambridge University Press, 1993), 43, 61.

24. *New York Times* (December 7, 1993).

25. *New York Times* (November 2, 1993).

26. Ibid.

27. During Mexico's 1994 presidential campaign, I interviewed a leading spokesperson for the PRD, the country's principal leftist opposition party. Though he had once been a Marxist congressman, he readily conceded that President Salinas's economic liberalization program, including massive layoffs of state workers, had been necessary. That interview took place a week after the peasant uprising in Chiapas that many analysts believed shifted the Mexican political spectrum to the left.

28. Howard Handelman and Werner Baer, eds. *Paying the Costs of Austerity in Latin America* (Boulder, CO: Westview Press, 1989); Stephan Haggard and Robert R. Kaufman, eds., *The Politics of Economic Adjustment* (Princeton, NJ: Princeton University Press, 1992).

29. Many mass media outlets use GDP data based on currency exchange rates, which place China's GDP below Japan's. However, measuring GDP by purchasing power parity (PPP), the more meaningful statistic used by the UNDP and most economists, puts China in second place, behind only the U.S. and considerably ahead of Japan. http://hdr.undp.org/hdr2006/statistics/indicators/131.html.

30. Extrapolated from Sinichi Ichimura and James W. Morley, "The Varieties of Asia-Pacific Experience," in *Driven by Growth*, ed. James W. Morley (Armonk, NY: M. E. Sharpe, 1992), 6; Steven Chan, *East Asian Dynamism* (Boulder, CO: Westview Press, 1990), 8; UNDP, *Human Development Report, 1997* (New York: Oxford University Press, 1997), 21–22.

31. The World Bank, *Engendering Development* (New York and London: Oxford University Press, 2001), 207.

32. Again, China does not fit that model. A large, though rapidly falling, share of its economy is still state owned, while worker cooperatives own another substantial portion. State regulation, though greatly reduced, continues to be formidable. Thus, despite its many changes since the early 1980s, China's economic model remains distinct from the other Asian economies described in this section. Therefore, I exclude it from the discussion that follows.

33. Milton and Rose Friedman, *Freedom to Choose* (New York: Harcourt Brace Jovanovich, 1980), 57; David Felix, "Review of Economic Structure and Performance: Essays in Honor of Hollis B. Chenery," *Economic Development and Cultural Change*, vol. 36, no. 1 (1987), 188–194; Ian Little, "An Economic Reconnaissance," in *Economic Growth and Structural Change in Taiwan*, ed. Walter Galenson (Ithaca, NY: Cornell University Press, 1979).

34. Robert Wade, *Governing the Market: Economic Theory and the Role of Government in East Asian Industrialization* (Princeton, NJ: Princeton University Press, 1990); Gary Gereffi and Donald L. Wyman, eds. *Manufacturing Miracles* (Princeton, NJ: Princeton University Press,

1990); Stephan Haggard, *Pathways from the Periphery* (Ithaca, NY: Cornell University Press, 1990); Chalmers Johnson, "Political Institutions and Economic Performance: The Government–Business Relationship in Japan, South Korea, and Taiwan," in *The Political Economy of the New Asian Industrialism*, ed. Frederic C. Deyo (Ithaca, NY: Cornell University Press, 1987).

35. Chalmers Johnson, *MITI and the Japanese Miracle* (Stanford, CA: Stanford University Press, 1982).

36. Chan, *East Asian Dynamism*, 47–48.

37. Johnson, "Political Institutions and Economic Performance."

38. Chan, *East Asian Dynamism*, 49.

39. Johnson, "Political Institutions," 159.

40. Haggard, *Pathways from the Periphery*.

41. Robert Wade, "Industrial Policy in Asia: Does It Lead or Follow the Market?" in *Manufacturing Miracles*, 231–266; Wade, *Governing the Market*.

42. Johnson, "Political Institutions."

43. For a criticism of the developmental state model and its alleged benefits, see Cheng-tian Kuo, *Global Competitiveness and Industrial Growth in Taiwan and the Philippines* (Pittsburgh, PA: University of Pittsburgh Press, 1995).

44. These conglomerates dominate the economy. By the mid-1980s, Korea's 10 largest chaebols produced two-thirds of the nation's GNP. See Wade, *Governing the Market*, 309.

45. Herman Kahn, "The Confucian Ethic and Economic Growth," in *The Gap between Rich and Poor*, ed. Mitchell A. Seligson (Boulder, CO: Westview Press, 1984).

46. Christopher Ellison and Gary Gereffi, "Explaining Strategies and Patterns of Industrial Development," in *Manufacturing Miracles*, 395–396.

47. Neoclassical economics (or the neoclassical approach) is a revised formulation of Adam Smith's classical economic approach.

48. Wade, *Governing the Market*, 11.

49. Alice H. Amsden, *Asia's Next Giant: South Korea and Late Industrialization* (New York: Oxford University Press, 1989); see also the works by Haggard, Wade, and Johnson cited earlier in this chapter.

50. Wade, *Governing the Market*.

51. *New York Times*: "Even Amid Its Wealth, India Finds, Half Its Small Children are Malnourished" (February 10, 2007); "The Myth of the New India," (July 6, 2006); "Low-Tech or High, Jobs are Scare in India's Boom," (May 6, 2004).

52. *New York Times*, "A Widening Gap Erodes Argentina's Egalitarian Image" (December 25, 2006).

53. Richard Albin, "Saving the Environment: The Shrinking Realm of Laissez-Faire," in *International Political Economy*, 2d ed., eds. Jeffrey A. Frieden and David A. Lake (New York: St. Martin's, 1991), 454.

54. Bela Balassa, *The Newly Industrializing Countries in the World Economy* (New York: Pergamon Press, 1981).

55. This section draws heavily on Sheahan, *Patterns of Development in Latin America*, 82–98.

56. For example, if a nation's currency is worth 10 pesos to the dollar in the free market, governments may impose official rates of, say, 5 pesos to the dollar for trade purposes. This artificially doubles the value of the peso, thereby halving the number of dollars needed by domestic manufacturers to import a forklift or machine lathe. At the same time, consumer goods produced domestically with that imported machinery would still be protected against import competition by tariffs and quotas.

57. Ibid. 84; Werner Baer, "Import Substitution and Industrialization in Latin America: Experiences and Interpretations," *Latin American Research Review*, vol. 7, no. 1 (1972), 95–122.

58. Helen Shapiro and Lance Taylor, "The State and Industrial Strategy," in *The Political Economy of Development and Underdevelopment*, 5th ed., eds. Charles K. Wilber and Kenneth P. Jameson (New York: McGraw-Hill, 1992).

59. Sheahan, *Patterns of Development*, 86–87.

60. The name "little tigers" was meant to differentiate these early economic stars from Asia's big tigers, Japan and China.

61. Wade, *Governing the Market*, 34, 36.

62. Barbara Stallings and Robert Kaufman, eds., *Debt and Democracy in Latin America* (Boulder, CO: Westview Press, 1989); Handelman and Baer, *Paying the Costs of Austerity*; Haggard and Kaufman, *The Politics of Economic Adjustment*.

63. Haggard, *Pathways from the Periphery*.

64. Chile has had the most success of any Latin American country in pursuing an EOI strategy since the 1970s. Argentina's efforts, however, were sabotaged by the country pegging its peso to the dollar (one peso was always worth one dollar). Consequently, after a boom in the 1990s, Argentina's economy collapsed in the early years of the twenty-first century as its overvalued peso destroyed its export capability. Since that time, the Argentine economy has made a surprising recovery.

65. Gary Gereffi, "Paths of Industrialization: An Overview," in *Manufacturing Miracles*, 15. Brazil's

proportion grew steadily from 8 percent in 1965 to 45 percent in 1987. Mexico's manufacturing ratio, on the other hand, was quite volatile, falling from 31 percent of exports in 1975 to 15 percent in 1980, only to jump back to 47 percent in 1987. In large part this reflected the shifting price and significance of petroleum exports.

66. Gary Gereffi and Donald Wyman, "Determinants of Development Strategies in Latin America and Asia," in *Pacific Dynamics*, eds. Stephan Haggard and Ching-in Moon (Boulder, CO: Westview Press, 1989), 37. Gereffi and Wyman, however, cite Bela Balassa's research warning against overstating the importance of size.

67. Robert Dore, "Reflections on Culture and Social Change," in *Manufacturing Miracles*, 353–367.

68. Irma Adelman and Cynthia Taft Morris, *Economic Growth and Social Equity in Developing Countries* (Stanford, CA: Stanford University Press, 1973). Keith Griffin's research has made a similar argument.

69. Perhaps the seminal work in this area was Hollis Chenery et al., *Redistribution with Growth* (London: Oxford University Press, with World Bank and University of Sussex, 1974). Since that time, there have been many World Bank studies supporting this strategy.

70. Richard E. Barrett and Soomi Chin, "Export-Oriented Industrializing States in the Capitalist World System: Similarities and Differences," in *The Political Economy of the New Asian Industrialism*, 28–31; Ward, *Governing the Market*, 38.

71. Howard Handelman, ed. *The Politics of Rural Change in Asia and Latin America* (Bloomington: Indiana University Press, 1981).

72. Robert H. Bates, "Governments and Agricultural Markets in Africa," in *Toward a Political Economy of Development*, ed. Robert H. Bates (Berkeley: University of California Press, 1988); see also Michael J. Lofchie, *The Policy Factor: Agricultural Performance in Kenya and Tanzania* (Boulder, CO: Lynne Rienner Publishers, 1989), 57–59; Charles Harvey, ed., *Agricultural Pricing Policy in Africa* (London: Macmillan, 1988), 2.

73. Sheahan, *Patterns of Development*; Haggard, *Pathways from the Periphery*, chap. 1.

74. The *New York Times* (September 8, 2004).

75. Gareth Porter and Janet Welsh Brown, *Global Environmental Politics* (Boulder, CO: Westview Press, 1996), 113.

76. Bhaskar Nath and Ilkden Talay, "Man, Science, Technology and Sustainable Development," in *Sustainable Development*, eds.

Bhaskar Nath, Luc Hens, Dimitri Devuyst (Brussels, Belgium: VUB University Press, 1996), 37.

77. For a review of these environmental debates, see Jacqueline Vaughn Switzer and Gary Bryner, *Environmental Politics: Domestic and Global Dimensions* (New York: St. Martin's Press, 1998), 200–234.

78. Marian A. L. Miller, *The Third World in Global Environmental Politics* (Boulder, CO: Lynne Rienner Publishers, 1995), 43–44.

79. According to one expert, "the World Health Organization estimates that 80 percent of the world's population relies on plants and the traditional or herbal medicines derived from them," in "Rx makers study potential rainforest plant medical disaster." http://findarticles.com/p/articles/mi_m3374/is_n9_v13/ai_10701204.

80. Nath and Talay, "Man, Science," 36.

81. For information on the debate over sustainable development, see Ken Conca, Michael Alberty, and Geoffrey D. Dabelko, eds. *Green Planet Blues: Environmental Politics from Stockholm to Rio* (Boulder, CO: Westview Press, 1995), 205–238.

82. Andrew Blowers and Pieter Leroy, "Environment and Society: Shaping the Future," in *Environmental Policy in an International Context: Prospects*, eds. Andrew Blowers and Pieter Glasbergen (New York: John Wiley & Sons, 1996), 262.

83. Meeting of Oxfam Study-Tour participants with an economist at the University of the West Indies, Kingston, Jamaica.

84. Some environmental experts believe that it will be impossible to maintain sustainable development and that the world faces certain ecological disaster. See Joseph Wayne Smith, Graham Lyons, and Gary Sauer-Thompson, *Healing a Wounded World* (Westport, CT: Praeger Publishers, 1997).

85. Robin Broad and John Cavanaugh, "No More NICs," *Foreign Policy*, vol. 72 (Fall 1988), 81–103.

86. Communication with Stephan Haggard, April 6, 1994.

87. Malcolm Waters, *Globalization* (New York: Routledge, 1995).

88. Mauro F. Guillén, "Is Globalization Civilizing, Destructive or Feeble?" *Annual Review of Sociology*, vol. 27 (August, 2001), 235–260.

89. S. J. Kobrin, "The Architecture of Globalization," in *Governments, Globalization, and International Business*, ed. J. H. Dunning (New York: Oxford University Press, 1997), p. 148. Cited in Guillén, "Is Globalization Civilizing?"

90. Thomas Friedman, *The Earth is Flat*, updated ed. (New York: Farrar, Straus, and Giroux, 2006).

91. Joseph E. Stiglitz, *Globalization and Its Discontents* (New York: W. W. Norton, 2002).

92. There are various ways of measuring globalization. When I claim that China ranks high on globalization indices I am referring to the major indicators of *economic* globalization, most notably trade and investment. On the other hand, one widely cited globalization ranking—*Foreign Policy* magazine's "Globalization Index"—combines economic measures with indicators such as international political links, internet usage, and the extent of foreign travel. On that multidimensional index, China and India have rather low rankings. One problem with the *Foreign Policy* index is that its authors only have sufficient data on 62 countries out of some 200 worldwide. Only a few of the world's poorer nations were included.

93. Almas Heshmati, "The Relationship Between Income Inequality and Globalization" (Helsinki, Finland: The United Nations University, 2003).

94. G. Firebaugh and B. Goesling, in their article "Accounting for the Recent Decline in Global Income Inequality." *American Journal of Sociology*, vol. 110, no. 2 (September 2004), 283–312, argue that inequality decreased from 1980–2000. Robert Wade, "Is Globalization Reducing Poverty and Inequality?" *World Development*, vol. 32 no.4, (January 2004), 567–589 challenges those findings.

95. Unless noted otherwise, all of the statistics in this section come from the "World Bank Poverty Net," http://www.worldbank.org/.

96. Joseph E. Stiglitz, *Making Globalization Work* (New York: W. W. Norton, 2006).

97. Bruce Buena de Mesquita et al., "Political Competition and Economic Growth," *Journal of Democracy*, vol. 12, no. 1 (2001), 58–72. Note that they were analyzing the performances of individual governments, not of countries. Hence, over a period of nearly 50 years, during which most countries had multiple governments, there were many hundreds of cases from which they selected their sample of 355.

GLOSSARY

Afghan Arabs A term used to refer to Arabs who fought as volunteers with the fundamentalist Taliban forces in Afghanistan.

Agrarian reform Distribution of farmland to needy peasants along with the government support programs such as roads, technical assistance, and lines of credit needed to make beneficiaries economically viable.

Ancien régime The old political order. The term is often used to describe a decaying regime threatened or ousted by a revolutionary movement.

Apparatchik A career bureaucrat in the Soviet government. Often used more broadly to refer to a bureaucrat whose primary interest is in protecting his or her authority and perquisites.

Associated-dependent development A type of Third World industrialization based on an alliance of the local, political, economic, and military elites with multinational corporations and Western governments.

Authoritarian system A political system that limits or prohibits opposition groups and otherwise restricts political activity and expression.

Autonomy A substantial amount of self-rule for an ethnic group or region that falls short of full independence.

BA regimes See **Bureaucratic-Authoritarian Regimes.**

Baht The Thai national currency.

Barrio A poor urban neighborhood in Latin America or the Philippines.

Bourgeoisie A Marxist term (also used by non-Marxist scholars) for those who own society's productive resources, most notably businesspeople.

Bureaucratic-authoritarian regimes Military dictatorships, found most often in Latin America's more developed countries, that were based on an alliance between the military, government bureaucrats, local business elites, and multinational corporations.

Capital goods (or equipment) Goods such as machinery that are used for production of other goods rather than for consumption.

Capital-intensive production Industrial or agricultural production that relies more heavily on machinery and technology than on human labor.

Caretaker government An interim government (often military) that steps in to restore order but plans to step down relatively quickly.

Caste system A rigid social hierarchy in which each person is born with a status that he or she retains regardless of their education or achievement.

Chaebols Powerful industrial conglomerates that dominate the South Korean economy.

Christian (or Ecclesial) Base Communities (CEBs) Small Catholic neighborhood groups in Latin America that discuss religious questions and community problems. Commonly located in poor neighborhoods, many CEBs were politicized or radicalized in the 1960s and 1970s.

Civic action programs Development programs such as road or school construction carried out by the military.

Civil society The network of politically relevant groups that are relatively independent of state control.

Class consciousness A measure of how much a social class (workers, peasants, or the middle class) view themselves as having common goals that are distinct from, and often opposed to, the interests of other classes.

Clientelism The dispensing of public resources by political power holders or seekers who offer them as favors in exchange for votes or other forms of public support.

Collective farming Joint farming activity involving a peasant community, state farm, or cooperative of some sort. Collective farms are created (usually by the state) by merging formerly private farms into larger units.

Collectivization The act of merging individual farms into a collective unit. Collectivization may be undertaken voluntarily (as in the Israeli Kibbutz) or may be forced by the state against the will of the affected peasant smallholders. Forced collectivization led to considerable bloodshed in countries such as the Soviet Union.

Colonization Asserting control over a previously independent region. Also used to describe the settlement of tropical forests or other previously uninhabited areas by migrating farmers or large agricultural operations.

Coloreds A South African term coined during the period of White rule to describe people of mixed racial background.

Command economy An economy in which most of the means of production are owned and managed by the state and in which prices and production decisions are determined by state planners.

Commercialization of agriculture The process whereby subsistence farmers (i.e., those raising crops largely for their own family consumption) convert, sometimes unwillingly, to farming for the commercial market.

Communal politics (communalism) Politics that have a strong ethnic base and often involve conflict between ethnicities.

Comparative advantage A country's capacity to engage in a particular economic activity efficiently and cheaply relative to other nations.

Consociationalism A division of political power between formerly antagonistic groups (such as ethnicities) based on power sharing, limited autonomy, and mutual vetoes.

Consolidated democracy Democratic government that is broadly supported by all major political participants and is therefore likely to endure for the foreseeable future.

Consumer subsidies Payments made by the state that allow consumers to purchase goods at prices below their free-market value.

Core nations The richer, industrial nations of the world.

Correlation A tendency of two or more factors (variables) to change in the same direction (e.g., higher income correlates with greater education). Negative correlations move in opposite directions (e.g., alcoholism and education).

Coup d'état (coup) A seizure of political power by the military.

Crony capitalism A corrupt form of capitalist development in which powerful, well-connected businessmen use their government ties to accumulate vast wealth.

Cultural pluralism A diversity of ethnic groups.

Culture of poverty A sense of powerlessness and fatalism allegedly commonly found among the urban poor.

Currency exchange rates The value of a nation's currency relative to major currencies such as the dollar or euro.

Democratic consolidation The process through which democratic norms (democratic "rules of the game") become accepted by all powerful groups in society, including labor, business, rural landlords, the church, and the military.

Democratic transition The process of moving from an authoritarian regime to a democratic one.

Dependency Theory (or Approach) A theory that attributes Third World ("the periphery") underdevelopment to its economic and political dependence on the advanced industrial nations ("the core").

Dependentista An advocate of dependency theory.

Devaluation (of a nation's currency) Allowing a currency that was previously overvalued relative to the dollar and other "hard" (stable) currencies to decline in value. Devaluation is accomplished by switching from a government-imposed, artificial (currency) exchange rate to one determined by the free market. Thus, for example, whereas the government may have previously imposed an overvalued exchange rate of, say, ten pesos per dollar, the value of the peso is allowed to drop to its free-market value of 20 pesos per dollar. This is normally done to correct a negative trade balance in which the value of imports exceeds exports.

Developmental state A state that intervenes actively in the capitalist economy in order to guide or promote particular economic development goals.

Dirty war The military's mass violation of human rights during its fight against subversive groups in countries such as Argentina and Peru.

Double day The burden facing working women, who continue to perform most of the family's domestic responsibilities (such as cooking and child care) while also working outside the home.

Economic disincentives Economic policies or practices that discourage desired outcomes, such as government-enforced low food prices that discourage agricultural production.

Economies of scale Economic efficiencies achieved through large-scale operations.

Ejido Communal farm in Mexico that was given special status under the country's agrarian reform programs.

Employer of last resort An employer (often the state) that hires people who can find no other employment.

Encyclical A letter, normally from the Pope, to all churches or all churches in some area, expressing the Church's position on matters that affect its welfare.

EOI See **Export-Oriented Industrialization**.

Ethnicity or ethnic group A group that feels it has common traditions, beliefs, values, and history that unite it and distinguish it from other cultures.

Export-Oriented Industrialization (EOI) An industrialization model heavily tied to exporting manufactured goods.

Federalism A government form that divides power between the national government and smaller governing units such as states.

Formal Sector The more modern sector of the economy, encompassing businesses that are registered and operate within the legal system. Typically, companies in this sector pay taxes and frequently contribute to their workers' health and retirement systems.

Four Little Tigers The so-called "four little tigers" (also known as the "four little dragons") are South Korea, Taiwan, Singapore, and Hong Kong—the first Asian nations, after Japan, to develop rapidly growing, export-oriented economies.

Fundamentalism A theological doctrine that seeks to preserve a religion's traditional worldview and to resist any efforts by religious liberals to reform it. It also frequently seeks to revive the role of religion in private and public life, including dress, lifestyle, and politics. Used interchangeably with "revivalism."

GDP See **Gross Domestic Product**.

Gender Development Index (GDI) An index measuring a country's key social indicators (literacy, income, life expectancy) for women as compared to men.

Gender Empowerment Measure (GEM) An index of women's political and economic empowerment based on the proportion of major business positions and national political offices held by women.

Gender gap A systematic difference in social status or achievement between men and women (e.g., a difference in income levels).

Gender quotas A percentage of seats in an elected legislature reserved for women.

Ghost workers Employees of state enterprises and bureaucracies who were hired for political reasons. Their labor is not needed and many of them collect paychecks while rarely, if ever, showing up for work.

Globalization The tendency of today's national economies to become increasingly intertwined and interdependent.

Green movement The political movement seeking to preserve the environment.

Green revolution Dramatic increases in grain production due to improved seeds and other technological breakthroughs in the Third World (most notably in Asia).

Greenhouse effect (greenhouse gases) Carbon gases produced by burning fossil fuels that threaten to warm the world's climate dangerously by limiting the dispersion of heat from the atmosphere.

Gross Domestic Product (GDP) A measure of a nation's production that excludes certain financial transfers normally included in GNP.

Gross National Product (GNP) A measure of a nation's total production (see **Gross Domestic Product**).

Gross Real Domestic Product Gross Domestic Product as measured by purchasing power rather than currency exchange.

Gulags Internment camps for political prisoners. Originating in the Soviet Union, the term is also used to describe other repressive systems.

Hacienda A Latin American agricultural estate that, until recently, often included precapitalist labor relations.

Hectare Hectares, rather than acres, are the standard measurement of farmland area in most of the world. One hectare is equivalent to 2.47 acres.

HDI See **Human Development Index**.

Historical dialectic A Marxist term used to describe the ongoing tension between particular forces in history.

Honor killings Murders of women who have allegedly "dishonored" their families by engaging in sexual activity or some related lesser "offense." Honor killings are commonly committed by close male relatives of the victim.

Human Development Index (HDI) A composite measure of educational level, life expectancy, and per-capita GDP.

Import-Substituting Industrialization (ISI) A policy of industrial development based on manufacturing goods domestically that were previously imported.

Indigenous population The Native-American (Indian) population.

Infidel One who does not believe in religion. Often used by Islamic fundamentalists to mean one who does not believe in the Islamic religion.

Informal sector The part of the economy that is unregulated by the government while similar activities are regulated and taxed. Also, defined as "all unregistered (or unincorporated) enterprises below a certain size."

Infrastructure The underlying structures (including transportation, communication, agricultural irrigation) that are needed for effective production.

Internal warfare Military action aimed at controlling guerrilla unrest or other domestic civil insurrection.

Invisible hand The capitalist notion that the good of society is advanced most effectively when individual actors (businesspeople, workers) seek to maximize their own economic advantage.

Iron rice bowl The Chinese government's policy, now largely disregarded, of guaranteeing employment and a basic living standard to its population.

ISI See **Import-Substituting Industrialization**.

Islamism Islamic fundamentalism or revivalism. A movement designed to bring the Islamic faith to its fundamental strictly interpreted beliefs and traditions. An Islamist is a believer in Islamism.

Jihad An Islamic holy war.

Jihadist A participant in a Muslim holy war.

Khmer Rouge The communist revolutionary movement in Cambodia (Kampuchea).

Koran Divinely revealed law according to the Muslim religion.

Kulaks Wealthier peasants. Originally a term used in Russia but later applied more broadly.

Kurdistan The contiguous regions within Iran, Iraq, Turkey, and Syria that many Kurdish people believe should be their independent national homeland.

Labor-intensive industry Industries that make more extensive use of human labor, as opposed to machinery and technology. The term "labor-intensive" can be applied in other contexts, as in "labor-intensive crops" (crops, like vegetables, that require more human labor and are less easily mechanized).

Laissez faire A policy of minimal state intervention in the economy.

Latifundia Large agricultural estates.

LDCs (Less Developed Countries) The term is used synonymously with the terms "Third World" and "developing countries."

Liberal democracy A democracy that not only has free and fair elections, but also respects civil liberties and upholds basic freedoms.

Liberalization of the economy Reducing the degree of state intervention in the economy (referring to the eighteenth-century classical liberalism of Adam Smith).

Liberated zones Areas (most notably in the countryside) controlled by the revolutionary army. Used in China and Vietnam.

Liberation theology A reformist interpretation of Catholic doctrine that stresses the emancipation of the poor.

Little Tigers See **Four Little Tigers**.

Lost decade The decade of the 1980s during which Africa and Latin America suffered severe economic declines.

Machismo Male chauvinism (used particularly in Latin America).

Macro-economic policy Economic policies that affect society as a whole.

Maquiladoras Assembly plants, most notably in Mexico, that import parts from the United States and re-export assembled goods.

Marginal population People excluded from the mainstream of the nation's political and economic life.

Market socialism A hybrid of Marxist economics and free enterprise that has been adopted by countries such as China.

Mass mobilization The process whereby large segments of the population are activated politically. Governments or revolutionary movements may choose to mobilize the population.

Mestizos Persons of mixed Indian and European cultural heritage (Latin America).

MNC See **Multinational Corporations**.

Moral economy The web of economic and moral obligations that binds a social unit together. Often used in reference to peasant—landlord relations in the countryside.

Mujahideen Islamic "freedom fighters" or guerrillas in a holy war.

Mulatto A person of mixed Black and White heritage.

Mullah A Muslim cleric.

Multinational corporations Corporations with holdings and operations in a number of countries. Overwhelmingly based in the developed world, many of them exercise considerable economic power in the Third World.

Nationality A population with its own language, cultural traditions, and historical aspirations that frequently claims sovereignty over a particular territory.

Neoclassical economics Economic theory that supports a free market and little state economic intervention.

Neocolonialism Economic or cultural dominance of one sovereign nation over another.

Neoliberal reforms Economic policies, now widely in favor, based on an adaptation of Adam Smith's "classical liberalism." These reforms reduce the role of the state in the economy, enhance the role of the private sector, and allow free-market forces to operate without government interference. Specific reforms have included balancing the budget, letting the market (not government regulations) determine the value of the national currency, removing barriers to free trade, and privatizing state enterprises.

New social movements Grass-roots reformist movements that are free of traditional political party ties or class-based ideologies.

New world order A vision of a more peaceful world order under U.S. leadership that many had expected to follow the collapse of the Soviet bloc and the end of the Cold War.

NGO (Nongovernmental Organization) An organization at the local, national, or international level that is privately funded and had no connection with the government. Most NGOs stress grass-roots organization. Commonly, the support goals such as democratization, human rights, women's rights, environmental protection, housing, health care, and education.

NIC (Newly Industrialized Country) Countries in East Asia and Latin America (such as Taiwan and Mexico) that have developed a substantial industrial base in recent decades.

Nongovernmental Organization See **NGO**.

Nurturing professions Occupations such as teaching and nursing that are commonly filled by women and that involve roles commonly associated with motherhood.

Ottoman Empire Based in what is now Turkey, the empire dated to the start of the fourteenth century. At its height (the sixteenth century) it extended to much of the Middle East (including Iraq), North Africa (Egypt and parts of Libya, Morocco, Tunisia, and Algeria), and Southeastern Europe (including much of

Bulgaria, Yugoslavia, Hungary, and Romania). Its governing capacity declined sharply in the nineteenth century and it was dissolved in 1922 following its defeat in World War I.

Parastatals Semi-autonomous, state-run business enterprises, such as government-owned power plants, petroleum firms, or food processing plants.

Partial democracies Governments that have some of the elements of liberal democracy, such as competitive elections, but are not totally free.

Patron–client relations Relations between more powerful figures (patrons) and less powerful ones (clients) involving a series of reciprocal obligations that benefit both sides but are more advantageous to the patron.

People's war The term used by Chinese leader Mao Zedong and others to describe mass-based guerrilla struggles.

Perestroika The restructuring of Soviet society (most notably its economy) by President Mikhail Gorbachev.

Periphery Third World countries, commonly seen by dependency theorists as occupying a lesser rank in the international economy.

Personalistic military regime A form of military government in which a single officer dominates. Often that regime's legitimacy is based on his charisma or his web of contacts with powerful groups.

Pirate settlement Low-income urban settlements whose members have purchased their lots but lack legal title.

Pluralist democracy A form of government that allows a wide variety of groups and viewpoints to flourish and to engage in political activity independent of government control.

Political culture The set of political beliefs and values that underlie a society's political system.

Populism A multiclass, reformist political movement that promises increased welfare programs for the poor and middle class but rejects a basic restructuring of the economic order. Third World populist movements are often led by a charismatic (and sometimes demagogic) political leader.

Praetorian politics Politics lacking in legitimate authority, leaving competing groups in society to use whatever resources they have at their disposal (including violence and bribery).

Private sector The sector of the economy that is owned by individuals or private companies.

Privatization The process of transferring to the private sector portions of the economy formerly owned by the state.

Procedural democracy Standards of democracy based on political procedures (such as free elections) rather than outcomes (such as social justice).

Professionalized military A military whose officers receive a great degree of professional training.

Progressive church The reformist and radical wings of the Catholic Church (primarily in Latin America).

Proletariat The working class (blue-collar workers).

Proportional representation A method of electing legislatures in which voters select from party lists in multimember districts and seats are allocated in proportion to the percentage of votes each party receives.

Pseudo-Democracies Governments that have apparently competitive elections and other trappings of democracy but in reality are only partially free and whose elections are not fully free and fair.

Public sector The sector of the economy belonging to the state.

Real wages (income) The true purchasing power of one's wage or income when the effects of inflation are factored in.

Reconciliation approach A more contemporary perspective of modernization theory that holds that it is possible for LDCs to simultaneously attain some development goals that were previously considered contradictory, at least in the short run (such as early economic growth and equitable income distribution).

Relative deprivation The gap between an individual's or group's expectations or desires and their actual achievement.

Reserved seats Seats in a government body such as the national parliament that are specifically set aside for an underrepresented group such as women.

Responsibility system China's policy of transferring collective farmland to peasant owners.

Reverse wave The return to authoritarianism among some of the countries that had previously democratized. To date, the reverse wave following the Third [democratic] Wave has been more limited than the reversals that occurred after the first two democratic waves.

Revivalism Attempts to revive traditional religious practices and, sometimes, to revive the role of religion in politics. See also **Fundamentalism**.

Rupiah The Indonesian national currency.

SCIRI See **Supreme Council for the Islamic Revolution in Iraq**.

Secularization The separation of church and state and, more generally, the removal of religion from politics.

Shantytown A community of poor homes or shacks built by the inhabitants. Unlike slums, they are generally in outlying urban areas rather than the central city.

SIIC Supreme Islamic Iraqi Council. See **Supreme Council for the Revolution in Iraq**.

Single-Member Districts (SMD) A congressional or parliamentary electoral arrangement whereby the country is divided into a relatively large number of comparable populations and only one representative (member) is elected to the legislature in each district. SMD is largely confined to English-speaking countries such as Britain, Canada, and the United States. Other democracies generally use proportional representation.

Sites and services Housing arrangements in which the state sells or gives each inhabitant a legal title to a plot with basic services such as electricity and water, leaving the recipient to build his or her own home.

Smallholders Peasants owning small plots of land.

SMD See **Single-Member Districts**.

Social mobility The ability to move from one rank or social class in society to another.

Spontaneous shelter Urban housing built independently, and without government permission, by the occupants.

Squatter settlement Communities built by the poor who illegally or semilegally occupy unused land.

Stabilization programs Government programs, often imposed by the International Monetary Fund (IMF), to cut budget and trade deficits. The purpose is to reduce inflation and stabilize the currency.

Sub-Saharan Africa Countries in Africa below the northern tier of Arab nations. Also called Black Africa.

Subsidized housing Housing provided by the state at prices below their market value.

Substantive democracy Standards of democracy that measure government policy outcomes, such as literacy and health levels or socioeconomic equality, not just democratic procedures (as distinguished from procedural democracy).

Supreme Council for the Islamic Revolution in Iraq (SCIRI) Currently the force behind the most powerful Shi'a political party and armed militia in Iraq. It was a leader of the Shi'a resistance to Saddam Hussein and has close ties to Iran. In 2007, it changed its name to the Supreme Islamic Iraqi Council (SIIC).

Supreme Islamic Iraqi Council (SIIC) See **Supreme Council for the Islamic Revolution in Iraq (SCIRI)**.

Sustainable development Economic development that "consumes resources to meet [this generation's] needs and aspirations in a way that does not compromise the ability of future generations to meet their needs."

Technocrat A government bureaucrat with a substantial degree of technical training.

Theocracy (theocratic state) Literally defined as "the rule of God." A government ruled by or subject to religious authority and in which Church and state are closely linked.

Third Wave The widespread transition from authoritarian to democratic government that has taken place in the Third World and Eastern Europe since the mid-1970s.

Third World countries Less developed countries in Africa, Asia, Latin America, and the Middle East.

Traditional society Societies that adhere to long-standing values and customs that have not been extensively transformed by modernization.

Tribe Subnational groups who share a collective identity and language and who believe themselves to hold a common lineage.

Wars of national liberation Wars of independence fought against colonial powers.

Zipper-style quotas A type of quota system for electoral lists of candidates for parliament or other government bodies in which the candidates are ranked and the group that is assigned a quota of candidates (such as women) must be given rankings comparable to the majority group on the candidate list (in this case men).

INDEX